FINANCIAL ACCOUNTING

FINANCIAL ACCOUNTING
Concepts and Principles

David F. Fetyko
Central Michigan University

Kent Publishing Company
Boston, Massachusetts
A Division of Wadsworth, Inc.

Accounting Editor: Jon Thompson
Production Editor: Anne Kelly Draus
Managing Designer: Detta Penna
Text Designer: Marjorie Spiegelman
Copy Editor: Carol Dondrea
Cover Photography: Jon Thompson

Printed in the United States of America

1 2 3 4 5 6 7 8 9 10—84 83 82 81 80

Library of Congress Catalog Card Number: 80-65045

ISBN: 0-534-00753-8

Brief Contents

Contents

Chapter 6   Inventories   329

III   Equities   434

Chapter 8   Liabilities   436

IV   Additional Financial Reporting Problems   612

Chapter 11   Statement of Changes in Financial Position   614

Preface

The first college-level course in financial accounting poses some unique and challenging problems for instructors and students alike. Financial accounting is not just a new subject to students, but a new language as well. As a result it is frequently approached with apprehension and mastered with difficulty. Moreover, some students (particularly accounting majors) need a substantial grounding in accounting practice to prepare them for later coursework, while others (non-accounting majors) require a broader understanding of the uses and role of accounting in the business environment. This textbook was written from a very real appreciation of these problems, and the attempt to solve them has led to several specific departures from the standard presentation of other texts:

1. **Unitized approach.** Each of the thirteen chapters is divided into two, three, or four units to permit students to concentrate on mastering a limited number of concepts at one time. The text's assignment material follows each unit, so student learning is more frequently reinforced, causing better motivation if the material has been learned and giving earlier warning if further review is required. (Some problems, which are clearly identified, integrate concepts from preceding units, so students can see the interplay of related concepts.) Additionally, the unitized format provides more flexibility for the instructor in course scheduling.

2. **Performance objectives based.** Each unit begins with performance objectives. These objectives not only provide a preview of the material to come, but more importantly function as the mastery base for the unit: the text material, subsequent assignment material, and instructor's testing materials are all tied to these specific objectives.

3. **Balanced coverage of concepts and procedures.** The approach of this textbook is to treat accounting concepts and procedures in an interdependent fashion. The conceptual background supports and motivates a foundation in procedures sufficient for later accounting coursework, while the procedures themselves verify and reinforce the thorough coverage of concepts. In this way, the text fulfills the broadest possible mix of student needs.

4. **Increased use of visual aids.** The descriptive text is frequently reinforced by numerous diagrams, figures, tables, and exhibits. These elements provide additional means to learn the material and also a convenient context for later review.

5. **Use of actual corporate data.** To add the reality of the business world to the course and thereby increase student motivation, the text includes several financial statements and excerpts from financial statements of large and well-known corporations.

6. **Unique approach to supplementary materials.** Each element of the supporting package has been carefully designed to reflect the text's strong emphasis on sound pedagogy and ease of teaching and learning financial accounting. Complete descriptions follow.

SUPPLEMENTARY MATERIALS FOR THE STUDENT

Study Guide   The study guide contains review outlines, multiple choice questions, and exercises for each unit in the text. Complete solutions to all questions and exercises are given at the back of the guide.

Working Papers   A sufficient quantity of forms is included to do all the text exercises and problems. A number of the forms have been partially filled in to guide students in solving certain exercises and problems and to reduce pencil-pushing time. A chart identifies the type of form(s) needed for each exercise and problem.

Practice Set   In addition to the mini-practice-set in the text (which uses only a general journal to record transactions), this separate practice set consists of a fictitious company, transaction descriptions, and all forms necessary to record the company's financial activity for one month and to complete the accounting cycle. In addition to the general journal and general ledger, it uses subsidiary ledgers and certain special journals—the sales and cash receipts journals and the voucher and check registers. The practice set also contains a complete instructional unit on special journals, including review questions, exercises, and problems.

Check Figures   This list provides key check figures for the exercises and problems, so students can verify the general accuracy of their solutions. They are available in quantity to adopting instructors for distribution to students.

SUPPLEMENTARY MATERIALS FOR THE INSTRUCTOR

Instructor's Manual   This manual contains general information and an outline of the key concepts to be covered for each unit, descriptions and suggested solution times for exercises and problems, suggested syllabi for courses of different lengths under both the semester and quarter systems, answers to all review questions, and complete solutions to all exercises and problems.

Solution to Practice Set   This booklet contains answers to review questions and solutions to exercises and problems for the special journals unit as well as the solution to the practice set.

Transparencies   A set of professionally prepared transparencies containing solutions to selected problems is available, conveniently boxed.

Test Bank   This volume is an extensive resource of thoroughly class-tested examination materials. It includes over 1,500 multiple choice questions and problems and over 160 problems requiring complete answers, thus providing more than enough items for several terms and/or concurrent sections of courses. The volume also contains correct responses and complete solutions to all items, *and a chart cross-referencing each item to the performance objectives of each unit.*

Unit Quizzes   In addition to the test bank, two sets of unit quizzes, ready for reproduction by instructors, are available. These quizzes can be used to test students' knowledge for the instructor's purposes, or they can be used by the students for self-diagnostic feedback on their mastery of the subject matter. One set is presented in an objective format, while the other is in a subjective format. Included at the back of the volume are blank accounting forms and present value and amount tables which are ready for reproduction and use with the quizzes or with tests developed from the test bank.

ACKNOWLEDGEMENTS

Many faculty members, editors, staff personnel, and organizations deserve acknowledgement for their contributions in the development and production of this text and all the supplementary materials. Without my colleagues, Richard B. Hanna, Thomas R. Weirich, and George M. Pintar, who coauthored some of the supplementary materials, the whole package would never have been possible. A number of student workers provided essential typing services. Graduate students Steve Caldwell, Cliff Morse, Chuck Hill, and Kathy Brown helped write and proofread answers to questions, exercises, and problems. Several instructors helped at various stages: Mark Salamasick in writing test questions, Steve Jakubowski and Gary Schroen in writing and proofing answers to questions, exercises, and problems, Dave Karmon in proofing most of the instructor's manual, and Vern Kwiatkowski in proofing part of the test bank.

I especially appreciate the constructive reviews and recommended revisions provided by the following professors: Elwyn L. Christensen, California State University at Fresno; G. Michael Crooch, Arthur Anderson & Co.; Patricia L. Duckworth, Metropolitan State College; David R. L. Gabhart, Michigan State University; Martin L. Gosmán, Boston University; S. Michael Groomer, Indiana University; Hugh D. Grove, University of Denver; Wayne Higley, University of Nebraska at Omaha; Robert W. Ingram, University of South Carolina; Joseph P. Matoney, University of Rhode Island; William J. Morris, Jr., North Texas State University; Ronald B. Pawliczek, Boston College; Bill N. Schwartz, Arizona State University; John R. Simon, Northern Illinois University; and William A. Stahlin, Trenton State College.

My thanks also go to the following organizations and corporations for permission to quote and/or reproduce material from their publications and reports: The American Institute of Certified Public Accountants, the National Association of Accountants, the Financial Accounting Standards Board, the Institute for Personal and Career Development at Central Michigan University, Coachmen Industries. Inc., the Proctor & Gamble Company, Michigan Sugar Company, The Dow Chemical Company, Total Petroleum (North America) Ltd., Bliss & Laughlin Industries, Hershey Foods Corporation, Revlon, Inc., The Goodyear Tire and Rubber Company, and Ralston Purina Company.

Sincere appreciation is owed to Jon Thompson, accounting editor at Wadsworth Publishing Company, and all other editors and staff at Wadsworth, especially Jeanne Heise and Anne Kelly Draus, who worked so hard to publish this text and its supplements. Finally, I want to express my appreciation to all students at Central Michigan University who used the preliminary edition of this book. Their comments and reactions were especially useful in making the book more pedagogically sound.

Your comments and suggestions, as students and instructors using this book and the supplementary materials, are solicited for consideration in making any future improvements.

David F. Fetyko
Mt. Pleasant, Michigan
December, 1979

FINANCIAL ACCOUNTING

Introduction
to Accounting

Chapter 1

Introduction to Accounting

To begin to get an adequate understanding of accounting, one should learn something about its historical roots; the economic, political, and social environment in which it functions; its social contributions; and the current demand for accountability. The primary goal of this chapter is to provide you with this foundation. The chapter defines accounting, describes its environment and history, and discusses its social contributions and accountability. It also identifies accounting objectives, and distinguishes among accounting assumptions, principles, and practices, procedures, and methods.

Unit 1
What Is Accounting?

All of us today, as consumers and taxpayers, as owners of insurance policies and savings deposits, or as businessmen and investors—we are all affected by the art and science of accountancy. Yet few of us have more than a vague understanding of the subject.

American Institute of Certified Public Accountants,
Designers of Order *(New York: AICPA, 1970), p. 1.*

In this unit accounting is first defined and distinguished from one of its branches, bookkeeping. Then the importance of the study of accounting from both individual and societal viewpoints is explained, and the demand for accountability is discussed. Finally, the accounting profession and the roles of accountants in society are described.

Performance Objectives

Upon completing this unit you should be able to:

1. define and use the accounting terms introduced in this unit (these terms are printed in boldface type).
2. a. explain what is meant by the "discipline of accounting."
   b. explain the general distinction between "accounting" and "bookkeeping."
3. explain the importance of the study of accounting from both an individual and a societal viewpoint.
4. explain what is meant by "the accounting profession."
5. explain the major roles of accountants in society.

"Frankly, this book contains everything you've always wanted to know about accounting but were afraid to ask."

Reprinted with permission of the National Association of Accountants from Management Accounting, October 1971, p. 45.

Definition of Accounting

The definition of accounting has changed over the years. In the 1940s accounting was described as "the art of recording, classifying, and summarizing in a significant manner and in terms of money, transactions and events which are, in part at least, of a financial character, and interpreting the results thereof.[1] This definition emphasizes the routine, clerical aspects of accounting. It reflects what was considered the primary mission of accounting at that time—presenting financial data to management, owners, and creditors—and it indicates the basic data accumulation process, which was manual. But the definition also tends to be misleading, since the interpretation of data is considered primarily a responsibility of the data users rather than of the accountants who gather and report the data.

Since the early forties, the basic data accumulation process has become largely mechanized, while the accounting system as a whole has become part of the information system that serves all business functions and collects both financial and nonfinan-

---

[1]American Institute of Certified Public Accountants, *Accounting Terminology Bulletin No. 1* (New York: AICPA, 1941).

cial data. The expansion of accountability into new areas and the increased demand for accountability in all areas have broadened the mission of accounting. *Accountability* refers to being held liable or responsible for actions and/or money. Accounting is now recognized as a social force—a discipline that can help assess the human, monetary, and physical resources necessary to develop and implement business, government, or social programs.

Reflecting these changes, **accounting** can be defined as "the discipline responsible for providing the information needed to evaluate the present and planned activities of all organizations in society."[2] Besides taking into account all the activities of all the organizations in society, this definition encompasses the three key activities performed by accountants: (1) identifying the information to be gathered and reported, (2) determining the dollar amount to be recorded and reported, and (3) deciding how to communicate the information, as well as ensuring that it is communicated.

Distinction Between Accounting and Bookkeeping

To many people outside the accounting profession, as well as to students taking an introductory course, accounting seems to be a highly procedural discipline that involves routine tasks and requires low-level skills. In reality, however, accounting is a complex discipline with varied tasks that are interesting and challenging.

Accounting is basically conceptual in nature; it is concerned with the following:

1. *designing* information processing and reporting systems
2. *measuring* information
3. preparing *special* reports
4. *evaluating* internal controls
5. occasionally *interpreting* information
6. preparing and recording *unusual* or *special* entries
7. *occasionally* preparing routine reports

Bookkeeping is a branch of accounting. It involves the routine, clerical tasks necessary to prepare, record, and process data to the point where financial statements are prepared. However, bookkeeping is a basic part of accounting, and an understanding of it is required before higher level tasks can be performed.

Bookkeeping is procedural in nature and involves the following:

1. recording and processing *routine* information
2. preparing *routine* reports

---

[2]Based on descriptions of accounting in *Accounting for Your Future* (New York: AICPA, 1976), p. 1, and *A Statement of Basic Accounting Theory* (Chicago: American Accounting Association, 1966), p. 1.

An accountant is often viewed as a Bob Cratchit-type wearing a green eyeshade and sitting on a high stool, hunched over an open ledger, quill in hand. But this is a picture of a bygone era. Today's accountant is an achiever, a college-educated person with good skills in mathematics and in written and verbal communications. This man or woman is self-disciplined and motivated, has an inquisitive mind, and can identify as well as solve problems. He or she should be viewed as analyzing data or information generated by a computer, discussing a report with a supervisor or manager, reviewing accounting records, or advising managers or clients on accounting, financial, or tax problems.

Also different from our old-fashioned view are the methods that are used by modern accountants. Today, although bookkeepers in small businesses often keep handwritten records, much bookkeeping is done using mechanical bookkeeping machines, punched card equipment, and computers. Clerks, trained in high school or vocational school, prepare the data for processing and operate the equipment on which the data are recorded.

Why Study Accounting?

Many students taking this first course in accounting have either already decided to major in accounting or are thinking of doing so. Other students are taking this course because understanding how accounting data are collected, processed, reported, and used in decision making is important for individuals in many fields, including financial management, production management, sales, law, administration in nonprofit organizations such as hospitals and educational institutions, banking, investment counseling, management consulting, and self-employment.

In addition, as the opening quotation indicates, each of us has or will have insurance policies, savings accounts, and checking accounts, and do or will pay taxes. Many of us will have investments and will be covered by pension or profit-sharing plans. All of us, therefore, should be concerned with the social responsibility of business organizations and the efficient use of our tax dollars by public officials. An adequate knowledge of accounting can help us in our personal affairs and enable us to become informed and effective members of society.

The objective of this text is twofold. First, students should understand the principles and concepts underlying the financial statements typically issued to investors, creditors, and the general public. Second, students should understand the financial accounting principles and concepts essential for further study in accounting. The first part of the objective is oriented toward the student who will be an eventual user of financial statements for decision making and the exercise of accountability. The second part of the objective is oriented toward the student who will go on to study managerial accounting—a course in the concepts and techniques of using accounting data to plan and control operations in both business and nonprofit organizations. Like this course, it is essential for further study.

Social Contributions of Accounting

The social contributions of accounting and accountants are numerous. Professionally, accountants who do good work render an important service to society. The basic role of accounting is to provide information on the activities of all organizations in society, and to the extent that this information helps the decision-making process, accounting makes a significant contribution to society. Without relevant and reliable information, effective, efficient decisions allocating scarce economic resources among all elements of society cannot be made, and everyone's standard of living suffers.

Outside the profession, accountants are involved in community affairs and perform voluntary services for charitable organizations—responsibilities accepted by good citizens with needed skills.

Accounting, then, facilitates economic growth and makes significant contributions to society. It provides information to investors, creditors, and others. These people rely on accounting information before providing the capital to finance the large-scale production of the goods and services needed in an economically advanced society. It provides information to the tax system so wealth can be effectively distributed among all members of society; and to government agencies seeking to protect laborers, consumers, investors, creditors, and others from exploitation. Accounting also provides information that can be used to evaluate the effectiveness of management, organizations, and programs. Through such evaluations, scarce economic resources can be channeled where they will provide the greatest benefits to society. Individuals will find that accounting information can help them handle their financial and business affairs and understand the financial affairs of organizations that affect their lives.

Demand for Accountability

We live in an "age of **accountability**." Although individuals and organizations have always been held accountable for their actions, this generally meant financial accountability, and it was to owners and creditors for resources invested or loaned. In the past two or three decades, however, there has been a rapid increase in the demand for operational and social, as well as financial, accountability. Figure 1.1 portrays this rapid growth in accountability.[3]

Today, government and nonprofit organizations are being asked to account for their actions in obtaining and expending resources. Managers and administrators are being asked to account for the effectiveness of their organizations, and for their own effectiveness in managing and administering them. And the social responsibility of all organizations, but especially business organizations, is a topic of widespread interest and a new area in which accountability is demanded.

In order to hold individuals or organizations accountable for their actions, infor-

---

[3]Permission to reprint granted by Leo Herbert.

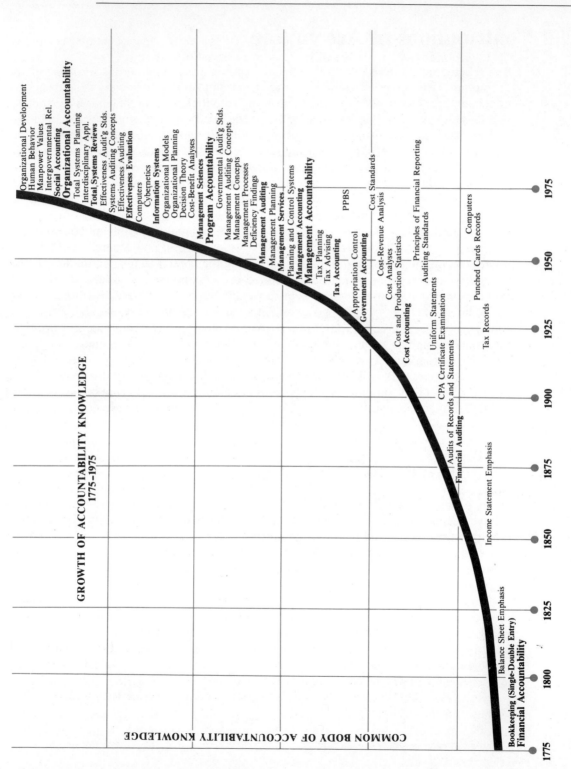

Figure 1.1   *Growth of accountability knowledge 1775–1975 (from Leo Herbert, March 1974)*

mation regarding these actions is required. And accounting and accountants can play an important role in providing the necessary information.

The Accounting Profession

There are four major areas of accounting within the **accounting profession**—*public accounting, management accounting, government* (and nonprofit organization) *accounting,* and *accounting education*—and thus four general types of accountants. Following are brief descriptions of these four areas of accounting and the roles accountants play in each. These will give you an idea of the career opportunities possible and indicate the importance of accounting in individual organizations and in society.

Public Accounting   Accountants known as **independent public accountants** or **CPAs** (certified public accountants) provide accounting services to the general public. CPAs are licensed by their states after meeting certain educational (usually a college degree with a major in accounting), experience, and moral character requirements, and after passing a 2½-day examination on accounting theory, accounting practice, auditing, and business law prepared and graded by the AICPA (American Institute of Certified Public Accountants).

CPAs provide three types of services to the general public: auditing services, tax services, and management advisory services. Auditing services are considered by many to be the most important. In auditing, CPAs *examine an organization's financial statements* and *render their professional opinion on the fairness* of the presentation. This service is called the **attest function,** and only licensed CPAs are permitted by state law to provide it. Investors, consumers, creditors, and other users rely on the CPA's opinion on the audited financial statements to make decisions, since the opinion is made independently of both clients and users of the information. A quotation from Stuart Chase, an American writer on economics, indicates the importance of the attest function as a service in the public interest: "The auditor's certificate, signed by a CPA, is something like the sterling mark on silver."

Tax services came naturally for CPAs involved with client audits. As income taxation became an important means of raising government revenue, CPAs began helping their clients prepare their tax returns. Gradually they expanded this service to others. Some CPA firms derive a significant portion of revenues from tax business: from preparing tax returns, giving tax advice, assisting in tax planning, representing clients before tax agencies, and helping clients comply with various tax laws.

Management consulting or advisory services also came naturally from audit work. Auditing requires CPAs to become familiar with the operations of their clients. As they do so, they are put into a position where they can offer various management advisory services. These services include: (1) accounting and financial services, (2) personnel recruitment for accounting and nonaccounting positions, (3) accounting and information systems design, and (4) production and marketing services. Management advisory services are important to many CPA firms, but the revenues derived from them are still relatively small compared to total revenues.

Over the past 50 years public accounting has become a well-established profession. In reaching this position it has attained the characteristics common to most well-established professions:[4]

1. It renders essential services to society.
2. It is governed by a code of ethics that is enforced through disciplinary procedures.
3. Admission to the profession is regulated by law.
4. It has an identifying designation (CPA) recognized by law.
5. Its members possess a specialized body of knowledge acquired through formal education.
6. It has a language that is fully understandable only by its members.

Management Accounting   **Management accountants** are employed by, and provide accounting services for, business organizations. These services include internal auditing, which determines if a company's records and controls are reliable; cost accounting; financial reporting and analysis; budgeting; data processing; tax accounting; and systems design. Management accountants cannot attest to the fairness of presentation of their employer's financial statements even if they are CPAs—as employees, they help accumulate the data and prepare the statements and thus are not independent. They hold such positions as vice-president of finance, controller or chief accounting officer, treasurer, and head of various accounting service departments. They also hold staff positions within the accounting service departments. In general, management accountants are responsible for satisfying the information needs of management, of outsiders such as creditors, owners, and the government, who have a particular interest in the business, and of the public, who have a general interest in the organization.

Large organizations can usually provide all accounting services required, except the attest function, with their own personnel. Occasionally, of course, a specialized problem may require the services of independent CPAs or other outside consultants, or these outside consultants may be sought in order to gain a fresh, independent viewpoint. Small organizations, however, usually do not have the in-house expertise available, and must rely more heavily on the services of independent CPAs and other outside consultants.

Management accounting does not have all the characteristics of a well-established profession, but it can be generally considered as a profession. Webster defines *profession* as "a calling requiring specialized knowledge and often long and intensive academic preparation."[5] In order to establish professional status and designation for management accountants and internal auditors, two programs were established in the early 1970s. One is the CMA (Certificate in Management Accounting) program estab-

---

[4]John L. Carey and K. Fred Skousen, *Getting Acquainted with Accounting*, 2d ed. (Boston: Houghton Mifflin, 1977), p. 101.

[5]*Webster's New Collegiate Dictionary* (Springfield, Mass.: G. & C. Merriam, 1975).

lished by the NAA (National Association of Accountants). The other is the CIA (Certified Internal Auditor) program established by the Institute of Internal Auditors.

Neither the CMA nor the CIA designation is recognized by law, but both of these emerging professions may yet achieve public recognition comparable to that of the CPA. Note that the objectives of the CMA program, which follow, are aimed at recognition as a profession:[6]

1. to foster higher educational standards in the field of management accounting
2. to establish management accounting as a recognized profession by identifying the role of the management accountant and the underlying body of knowledge, and by outlining a course of study by which such knowledge can be acquired
3. to assist employers, educators, and students by establishing an objective measure of an individual's knowledge and competence in the profession of management accounting

Government Accounting   **Government** and **nonprofit organization accountants** provide accounting services for the government and for such nonprofit organizations as hospitals, educational institutions, religious organizations, and charitable agencies. These accountants cannot, however, perform the attest function for the financial statements of their employers even if they are CPAs, because they are not independent.

All levels of government also have special audit agencies to enforce laws, evaluate the effectiveness of government agencies and programs, and determine compliance with government policy and contracts. For example, the IRS (Internal Revenue Service) audits tax returns to check compliance with tax laws, the GAO (General Accounting Office) evaluates the effectiveness of government agencies and programs and checks their compliance with government policy, and the Defense Contract Audit Agency determines contractor compliance with government policy and contracts. Similar agencies are found at the state level and, sometimes, the local level.

Government accounting can be considered a profession if the broader definition of the term is used.

Accounting Education   **Accounting educators** are responsible for training all accountants, including other accounting educators. In addition, they contribute heavily to accounting research (that is, the investigation and analysis of accounting issues) and are actively involved in many professional accounting organizations and consulting activities.

Recently a movement has started to establish professional schools of accountancy patterned after professional schools of law, medicine, dentistry, and engineering. Also being advocated is a five-year professional program in accountancy. At present, how-

---

[6]"Certificate in Management Accounting Established by NAA," *Management Accounting,* March 1972, p. 13.

ever, only a few such schools or programs have been established. Along with these movements, an accounting accreditation agency has been created. This agency is currently developing standards for curriculum, student admissions, and faculty qualifications.

SUMMARY

In this unit accounting was defined and distinguished from bookkeeping, and the importance of studying accounting was discussed. Also, the four major areas of accounting and the roles of accountants in each were briefly described. The information in this unit is essential background for studying and understanding accounting. The next unit provides additional background information by examining the history and environment of accounting.

REVIEW QUESTIONS

1-1   Give a modern definition of accounting. What three key activities performed by accountants are included in this definition?

1-2   Distinguish between bookkeeping and accounting.

1-3   Indicate whether each of the following activities is *A* (accounting function) or *B* (bookkeeping function):

    a.   recording business transactions
    b.   analyzing the cash receipts system for adoption of computerized procedures
    c.   preparing a budget for operating expenses
    d.   preparing a monthly financial report
    e.   preparing federal and state income tax returns
    f.   computing account balances on the company's records

1-4   What is meant by the term *accountability*? In what areas is there a growing demand for accountability today?

1-5   It has been said that accounting makes a significant contribution to society by providing information for the efficient and effective allocation of scarce economic resources. Explain by citing several ways accounting does this.

1-6   Explain how you expect the study of financial accounting to benefit you personally, given your career objectives.

1-7   What characteristics does a well-developed profession usually possess? Is accounting a profession? Explain.

1-8   Identify four major areas of accounting. Briefly describe the types of services provided by accountants in each area.

1-9   Following is a list of accounting roles and a list of job tasks. Match each job task with the appropriate accountant's role and write the applicable code letter (a,b,c,d); if the job task is not one normally performed by accountants, write e for your answer. More than one code letter may be used for an answer.

Roles of Accountants
a.   independent public accountants
b.   management accountants
c.   government accountants
d.   accounting educators
e.   not a normal or appropriate job task performed by accountants

Job Tasks
_____   **(1)**   rendering an opinion on an entity's financial statement, based on the results of an independent audit
_____   **(2)**   preparing an entity's income tax returns
_____   **(3)**   installing an entity's computerized payroll accounting system
_____   **(4)**   auditing tax returns
_____   **(5)**   deciding on the type of computer equipment to purchase for (3) above
_____   **(6)**   checking the effectiveness of an entity's internal controls
_____   **(7)**   helping prepare an entity's annual operating budget
_____   **(8)**   preparing and interpreting a cost reduction study
_____   **(9)**   implementing the recommendations of the study in (8) above
_____   **(10)**   recording an entity's transactions
_____   **(11)**   teaching and conducting research as a member of a university faculty
_____   **(12)**   consulting with business and nonprofit organizations on accounting problems

Unit 2
Accounting: Its History and Environment

You should know that an inspector of temple finances has arrived in these parts and intends to review your accounts also. Do not be unduly disturbed, however, for I will get you off. As quickly as you can, write up your books and bring them here to me, for he is a very strict fellow. If you cannot bring the books yourself, at any rate send them to me and I will see you through, for I have become friendly with him. . . .

Letter from one Egyptian priest to another, second century B.C.

In this unit, additional necessary background is provided. Major stages in the historical development of accounting are summarized, and the environment in which accounting functions is described. Also discussed are the contributions of various organizations that have influenced accounting development in the United States.

Performance Objectives

Upon completing this unit you should be able to:

1. a. identify the major eras in the development of accounting.
   b. identify major influences that both affect accounting and are affected by it.
2. a. identify the accounting organizations responsible for issuing and/or enforcing authoritative pronouncements on accounting practice.
   b. identify which accounting organizations are responsible for issuing and/or enforcing which official pronouncements.

A Brief History of Accounting

Since the beginning of civilization humanity has tried to keep account of economic activity. Eric Hoffer believes this account-keeping is actually the foundation of written language:[1]

> We are often told that the invention of writing in the Middle East about 3000 B.C. marked an epoch in man's career because it revolutionized the transmission of knowledge and ideas. Actually, for many centuries after its invention writing was used solely to keep track of the intake and outgo of treasuries and warehouses. Writing was invented not to write books but to keep books.

There are six major eras in the history of accounting: (1) the primitive accounting era (3000 B.C.–A.D. 1300); (2) the double-entry accounting era (1200–1600); (3) the industrial and corporate business growth era (1500–1900); (4) the early twentieth-century era (1900–1930); (5) the middle twentieth-century era (1930–1970); and (6) the late twentieth-century era (1970–present). There has been significant interaction between the development of accounting and economic development.

Accounting records have changed greatly through the years. Coordinated financial statements presenting operating results and financial position, for example, were not prepared until after the development of the double-entry bookkeeping system. Also, until the development and growth of the corporation, the major objective of accounting was to provide information to the owner of a business. For this reason, personal and business records were often kept together, and profit or loss was determined only at irregular intervals instead of at specific times. When business ownership became widely dispersed among stockholders not actively engaged in management, however, the need arose for reliable information and for independent audits to attest to its reliability. These needs led to the birth of the public accounting profession. The stock market crash of 1929 led to more government regulation and the development of generally accepted accounting principles and auditing standards aimed at the protection of investors and creditors. Today the economy has developed still further and business activities have become even more complex. These changes have created a demand for greater accountability, improved accounting principles, more accounting services, and quality accounting education.

Environment of Accounting

All forces that affect accounting or influence the operation of business and nonprofit organizations constitute the environment of accounting. These are the forces that af-

---

[1]Eric Hoffer, *The Temper of Our Times* (New York: Harper & Row, 1966).

fect the development of the principles, practices, procedures, and methods used to account for organization activities. If, in turn, accounting principles, practices, procedures, and methods are adapted to meet changing political, economic, social, legal, and other environmental conditions, the information needs of society are more likely to be met. The better accounting does its job of providing information necessary to allocate scarce resources and evaluate organization activities, the more society benefits and advances. Thus, accounting affects the very forces by which it is affected. Figure 2.1 depicts the interaction between accounting and its environment.

As organizations and their activities have become more complex, the number and complexity of accounting problems have also grown. New accounting principles and practices, procedures, and methods are constantly being developed to meet current

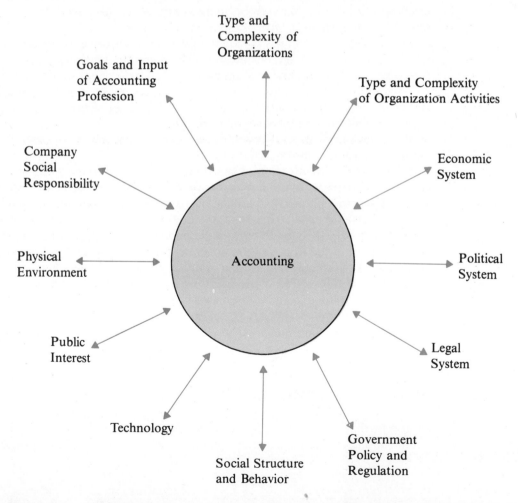

Figure 2.1   Significant forces that both affect accounting and are affected by it

financial information needs. These needs reflect, in a broader way, a country's economic system and its stage of development. In the United States the free enterprise system allows for a wide variety of information users, including owners, creditors, employees, the government, and the general public, as well as those who help users make investment decisions or evaluate the effective use of resources. Thus a broad range of information is required. In addition, the United States is more economically advanced than most other countries and requires more sophisticated information.

The political and legal systems, as well as government policy and regulations, affect accounting by helping set accounting principles, practices, procedures, and methods. They are, in turn, affected by the financial information they need to keep functioning. In the same way, the government, individuals, and the general public affect and are affected by accounting through their right to intervene in the allocation and use of resources. Social structure and customs also affect the way business organizations, the economic, legal, and political systems, accounting in general, and the accounting profession in particular are accepted and respected. Thus, social structure and behavior affect the development of accounting.

Technology is another force involved with accounting. Technological advances have required the development of mass production techniques. These techniques require large sums of capital investment, and investors depend on reliable financial information before providing it. Technological advances have also led to creation of the computer, which has vastly changed both the method of processing information and the type of information that can be provided.

Accounting is expected to serve the public interest. However, the term *public interest* is not easily defined. One growing belief is that *public interest* means the diverse interests of many groups. With this definition, the needs of each group must be determined. Once determined, these needs too help shape the accounting principles, practices, procedures, and methods used to satisfy the information needs of the public.

Today there is great concern about the physical environment and a growing interest in the environmental impact of business operations and government projects. There is also considerable concern about company social responsibility and a growing demand for information regarding its fulfillment. Accounting and accountants are actively involved in providing information on environmental impact and social responsibility.

By reason of their training and experience, accountants themselves can influence the development of accounting. As members of the accounting profession, they can exercise their responsibility and self-interest to resolve information gathering and reporting problems, to satisfy the needs of information users, and to establish accounting principles, practices, procedures, and methods. The accounting profession, therefore, is affected to a great extent by the goals and input of its members.

Organizations Affecting Accounting

Many organizations helped develop the accounting principles and practices used today. Figure 2.2 provides an overview of these organizations. The earliest attempts at

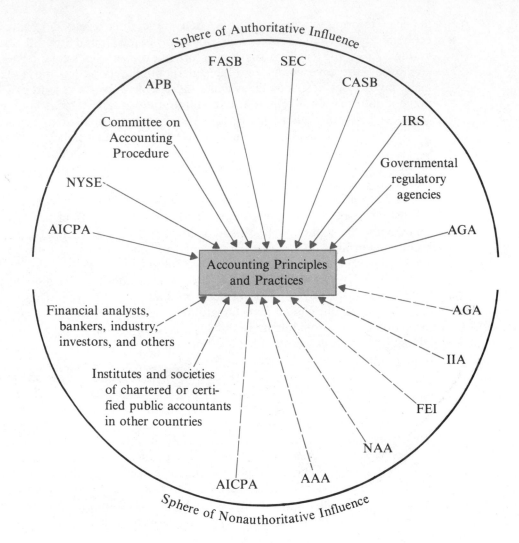

Figure 2.2   Influences on development of accounting principles and practices

establishing accounting principles were made by the *AICPA* (American Institute of Certified Public Accountants). Guidelines for preparing financial statements were issued by the institute as early as 1894. In 1917 the institute issued a statement on "uniform accounting" at the request of the Federal Trade Commission. (Revised editions were released in 1918 and 1929.) In 1930 a special committee was established by the institute to cooperate with the *NYSE* (New York Stock Exchange) on accounting matters of concern to both organizations. An outgrowth of this committee was the AICPA *Committee on Accounting Procedure,* which was established in 1939.

Between 1939 and 1959 the Committee on Accounting Procedure issued a series of official pronouncements called the *Accounting Research Bulletins,* which dealt with then-current accounting problems. This committee derived its authority from its general acceptance by the accounting profession. Since its work (decisions spelled out in the bulletins) did not result in a well-structured body of accounting theory, the AICPA in 1959 dissolved the committee and organized the *APB (Accounting Principles Board)* to succeed it.

During its existence from 1959 to 1973 the APB issued official pronouncements called the *APB Opinions*. Like its predecessor, the objective of the APB was to establish basic accounting principles. The AICPA also established an Accounting Research Division, which issued a series of *Accounting Research Studies*. Many of the APB Opinions were based on these research studies. In 1964 the governing body of the AICPA adopted a resolution stating that the APB Opinions and the Accounting Research Bulletins still in force constituted "substantial authoritative support" for "generally accepted accounting principles." Thus, CPAs became bound by their code of professional ethics to ensure that their clients followed these pronouncements in preparing their financial statements. Departures from the code might be justified under certain circumstances, but the burden of proof rests with the CPA. The APB also issued four unofficial, informative statements (*APB Statements* No. 1–4). In addition, the AICPA research staff issued interpretations of several controversial points of practice. These interpretations were considered authoritative when no APB Opinion or Accounting Research Bulletin existed on the matter.

Throughout its existence the APB was criticized for its slow response to accounting problems and abuses. In addition, its opinions on thorny issues were frequently opposed by CPAs, their clients, and government regulatory agencies. Finally, in 1973 an AICPA study group recommended disbanding the APB and creating a new, independent organization.

As a result of the AICPA study the *FASB (Financial Accounting Standards Board)* was established and began operating on July 1, 1973. The FASB has seven full-time members, only four of whom must be CPAs. Members of the old APB were all required to be CPAs. In addition, APB members could retain their positions with public accounting firms, industry, government, or institutions since their services as APB members were voluntary and part-time. The FASB has greater independence and broader representation, and it was hoped that these would lead to wider acceptance of its pronouncements. Its members not only must terminate their previous affiliations with CPA firms and the firms' clients, but they are fully paid for their services. Another advantage is that FASB pronouncements are based on a variety of inputs (see Figure 2.3).

Two sets of official pronouncements are issued by the FASB: the *Statements of Financial Accounting Standards* and the *FASB Interpretations*. Both offer substantial authoritative support for generally accepted accounting principles. The interpretations are necessary to resolve problems that arise in applying official pronouncements in practical situations.

A number of government organizations have also had a significant influence on the development of accounting principles. The *SEC (Securities and Exchange Commission)* was set up by the Securities and Exchange Act of 1934 and was given the authority to prescribe the accounting procedures and form that organizations must use when filing financial statements with it. Although SEC policy has been to let the

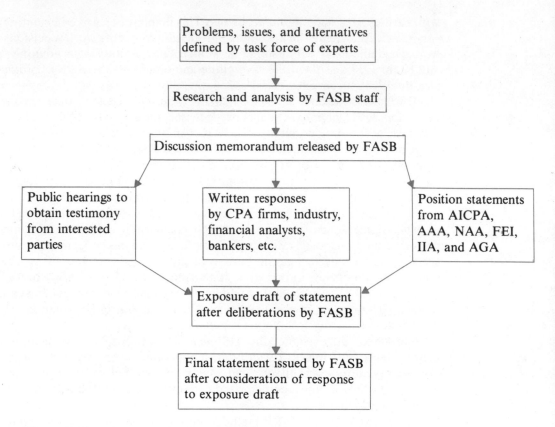

Figure 2.3   Inputs and process leading to issuance of an FASB Statement

accounting profession prescribe accounting procedures, the commission nevertheless exerts continual pressure on the accounting profession to narrow accounting alternatives and to move more swiftly in resolving accounting issues. The official pronouncements issued and enforced by the SEC include (1) *Regulation S-X,* (2) the *Accounting Series Releases,* and (3) the *Staff Accounting Bulletins.* Regulation S-X contains instructions and forms for filing financial statements with the SEC. The Accounting Series Releases contain the official accounting opinions of the chief accountant for the SEC. And the Staff Accounting Bulletins provide answers and interpretations the SEC staff has given for specific situations. In addition, decisions on cases brought before the SEC are relevant to accountants and auditors involved with the commission.

The *CASB (Cost Accounting Standards Board)* was organized by Congress in 1970 to develop and promulgate uniform cost accounting standards for certain contractors and subcontractors doing business with the Department of Defense, the Atomic Energy Commission, NASA, and the General Services Administration. The official pronouncements of the CASB, known as *Cost Accounting Standards,* deal with costs that must be reflected on financial statements.

The *IRS (Internal Revenue Service)* is responsible for enforcing the *Internal Revenue Code* adopted by Congress, all *Regulations, Revenue Rulings,* and *Revenue Procedures* adopted by the IRS, and any *tax decisions resulting from court cases.* Accountants preparing tax returns or giving tax advice must comply with tax law. Tax accounting differs from financial accounting on some revenues and expenses that determine income, because each has different objectives. Government regulation of business has grown significantly in this century. In order to protect the public interest, state regulatory commissions and federal regulatory agencies like the Interstate Commerce Commission (ICC), Federal Power Commission (FPC), Federal Trade Commission (FTC), and Federal Communications Commission (FCC) have been given powers such as specifying accounting practices and uniform accounting systems, requiring financial disclosure, and setting rates. Accountants and auditors for regulated industries must be aware of the rules set by these agencies. Of course, regulation does not always lead to improved accounting and reporting—sometimes agencies cling to outmoded methods that retard the development of sound accounting and reporting or that are in conflict with generally accepted accounting principles.

The *Federal Financial Management Standards Board,* established by the *AGA (Association of Government Accountants),* initiates standards and opinions for the association, thus providing generally accepted accounting principles for government units.

The *NYSE (New York Stock Exchange)* also influences the development of accounting principles. The exchange prescribes standards, which are periodically revised, for statements issued by listed companies. The most important of these is perhaps a 1934 statement, issued in cooperation with the Controllers' Institute, now the Financial Executives Institute (FEI), and the AICPA, of five broad accounting principles and several basic concepts underlying the preparation of financial statements.

Several professional accounting organizations have also contributed to the development of accounting principles and practices, even though their contributions are not authoritative in themselves. These organizations include: the *AICPA, American Accounting Association (AAA), National Association of Accountants (NAA), Financial Executives Institute (FEI), Institute of Internal Auditors (IIA), and the Association of Government Accountants (AGA).* Most of them sponsor research, publish professional journals, and provide input to the FASB, SEC, and CASB—activities that help support authoritative accounting principles and practices.

Finally, the official pronouncements and research of institutes or societies of chartered or certified public accountants in other countries have some influence on the accounting principles and practices adopted in the United States.

SUMMARY

In this unit, the history and environment of accounting and the organizations influencing the development of accounting were described. This information should help the student understand and appreciate the place of accounting in society. It is necessary background for a better understanding of the objectives, principles, and practices of accounting.

REVIEW QUESTIONS

2-1   Identify six major eras in the development of accounting.

✗**2-2**   Briefly describe the impact of the double-entry system of bookkeeping on the development of accounting. What impact did the growth of industry and the corporate form of business have on the development of accounting?

✗**2-3**   How is accounting affected by its environment and how does it, in turn, affect its environment?

2-4   List the organizations that have had a direct, authoritative influence on accounting in the United States.

2-5   What organization is primarily responsible for setting accounting principles today? What were its predecessors?

2-6   The Statements of Financial Accounting Standards issued by the FASB are considered substantial authoritative support for generally accepted accounting principles. What is the current status of the APB Opinions and Accounting Research Bulletins as sources of authoritative support?

2-7   What role has the SEC had in the development of accounting principles, practices, procedures, and methods?

2-8   List the professional accounting organizations that have indirectly influenced the development of accounting in the United States.

2-9   Identify the organization that issues and/or enforces (or used to do so) each of the following authoritative pronouncements:

a.   APB Opinions
b.   Internal Revenue Code and Regulations
c.   Regulation S-X
d.   Statements of Financial Accounting Standards
e.   Accounting Research Bulletins
f.   Accounting Series Releases
g.   Cost Accounting Standards

Unit 3
Communicating Information

Important principles may and must be flexible.

Abraham Lincoln

Accounting is an information system that accumulates both financial and nonfinancial data about an enterprise, processes the data into information useful to decision makers, and then communicates this information to them. Decision makers receive the information in the form of financial statements and reports prepared according to accepted accounting guidelines.

If useful information is to be communicated, the needs of potential users must first be understood. Then sound guidelines and rules for preparing financial statements can be developed. The goal of this unit is to identify the users of accounting information, introduce the student to the objectives of financial accounting, and explain the assumptions and principles underlying the practices and procedures used to prepare financial statements.

Performance Objectives

Upon completing this unit you should be able to:

1. define and use the accounting terms introduced in this unit (these terms are printed in boldface type).
2. identify potential users of financial reports and distinguish between internal and external users.
3. identify the primary objective of financial accounting.
4. a. distinguish among accounting assumptions, accounting principles, and accounting practices, procedures, and methods.
   b. explain the meaning of the accounting assumptions and principles given.

25

Users of Financial Information

Many different users of financial reports can be identified, but little is known about their needs. Accountants, therefore, usually assume what these needs are and prepare financial statements in a form they assume will meet the needs of all users. Accountants must also anticipate all the potential uses of financial statement information. If they anticipate incorrectly all necessary information may not be disclosed and the information will be of limited use. In the same way, the reports may be limited by irrelevant or redundant information.

Users of financial information can be classified as external or internal. **External users** use the information to make decisions for their own benefit or for the benefit of other external individuals or organizations. Their decisions may have a direct, indirect, or no effect on the reporting organization. **Internal users** use the information to make decisions that will directly affect the reporting organization.

Typical external users include creditors, stockholders or owners, financial analysts, trade associations, labor unions and employees, stock exchanges, customers, the financial press, government agencies, and the general public. Typical internal users include managers, administrators, directors, and trustees. Differences in the decision-making process reflect the different information needs of these two groups of users. External users need information so they can make personal decisions or decisions for other noninvolved entities. Financial accounting is primarily concerned with getting information to external users. External users also generally know less of accounting and financial statements and need less detail in the statements than internal users. Thus, information presented to them is generally condensed and reported in a format understandable to them. Internal users, however, need not only the basic financial statements but also additional information in order to be effective in management decision making. Since most financial accounting and management accounting information come from the same information system data base, the data can be reclassified, reported in greater detail, or rearranged in different formats to satisfy the needs of internal users. Table 3.1 indicates how financial information is used by a variety of users.

Objectives of Financial Accounting

The information in financial reports should reflect the needs of its primary users. Failure to do so can result in the presentation of irrelevant information. Despite this possibility, the **objectives of financial accounting** have not been definitively identified. Recently, the APB, the AICPA, and the FASB conducted studies of the fundamental concepts underlying financial statements and tried to specify these objectives.[1] All

---

[1]"Basic Concepts and Accounting Principles Underlying Financial Statements of Business Enterprises," APB Statement No. 4 (AICPA, October 1970), pp. 9–10; *Objectives of Financial Statements* (AICPA, 1973), pp. 61–66; "Statement of Financial Accounting Concepts No. 1: Objectives of Financial Reporting by Business Enterprises" (FASB, 1978).

Table 3.1

Uses of Financial Information

Users	*Types of Decisions Involved*
Creditors	Will the company be able to repay its debts? Does management run the business effectively? Is the company profitable?
Stockholders, owners, financial analysts, investors	Is the company profitable? What is the return on owners' investment? Is the investment attractive compared to other similar investments? What is the company's dividend policy?
Trade associations	What data for various companies in the association are accumulated and disseminated to members and/or the public?
Labor unions and employees	What share of the profits are employees entitled to for salaries, benefits, and profit-sharing agreements? What were the company's profits? What is the company's potential for continued success (relates to job security)?
Stock exchanges	Do the statements meet the exchange's disclosure and reporting requirements, which are meant to protect the interests of investors?
Customers	Does management run the business effectively? Is the company stable and potentially successful enough to ensure a reliable supply of quality goods or services?
Financial press	What data are used to report on the success of various businesses and on economic trends?
Government agencies	What is the company's taxable income? Does the company meet specific disclosure and reporting requirements that are meant to protect the interests of investors and creditors? Is the company following other government rules and regulations? Does the company adhere to government social policies, e.g., minority employment? What data regarding various industries are accumulated for use by the government and/or the public?
General public	Which companies are successful? Which companies contribute to their communities and society as a whole?
Managers, administrators, trustees, directors	Is the company profitable? Is the organization effectively and efficiently run? Is the company meeting government rules and regulations? What contributions are being made to society? Should the company pay dividends, and if so, how much?

three studies agreed that the primary objective is to provide financial information about the economic activities of business enterprises that is useful in making rational investment and credit decisions. The studies also agreed that, to be useful, financial statement information should have certain **qualities** or **characteristics,** including: relevance, verifiability, freedom from bias (neutrality), comparability, understandability, timeliness, and completeness. However, these terms are highly abstract, and there is often disagreement as to what they really mean. In addition, characteristics can sometimes conflict, and trade-offs may be necessary when deciding what to present, how to measure it, and how to present it.

Each study also enumerated more specific objectives, including the following:

1. to serve primarily investors and creditors who have limited authority, ability, or resources to obtain information regarding an enterprise's economic activities

2. to provide users with information that is useful in predicting, comparing, and evaluating an enterprise's earning power; such information includes:

   a. a statement of financial position, that is, a statement indicating the enterprise's resources and obligations at the end of specific time periods

   b. a statement of enterprise income or earnings for specific time periods

   c. a statement of changes in financial position, that is, a statement describing the enterprise's financial activities and their effect on resources and obligations for specific time periods

3. to provide information that is useful in predicting, comparing, and evaluating potential cash flows to investors and creditors through interest or dividend payments and from the sale, redemption, or maturity of securities or loans

4. to report on enterprise activities that affect society and are important to the role of the enterprise in its social environment

Currently these objectives are at least partially achieved. Financial statements, for example, are designed to provide information to investors and creditors. However, little is now known about the needs of these users and about the role this information plays in the decision-making process. As a consequence, it has been assumed that one set of general purpose statements meets the multiple needs of different users. The alternative assumption is that statements should be designed to meet the specific needs of each category of users. Neither assumption is altogether satisfactory. General purpose statements may not meet the specific needs of users; also, information needed by one user group may be buried in information needed by others. Specific purpose statements, on the other hand, may be too costly to prepare; also, all potential user groups may not be anticipated. As more becomes known of user needs and the role of financial information in the decision-making process, these assumptions can be weighed, and the underlying accounting objectives and statement structure and content can be altered.

Today, financial statements describe current financial position, periodic earnings, and changes in financial position. They do not, however, necessarily provide users with sufficient information to help them predict, compare, and evaluate the cash flows they might expect from their investments or loans. Some business organizations are beginning to provide information on activities that affect society, but it will be some time before this practice becomes widespread.

Accounting Assumptions and Principles

Financial statements are not currently built on a standardized set of assumptions, principles, practices, and procedures. However, the need for a conceptual framework for financial accounting theory and practice seems generally accepted. The structure and components of the framework seem generally agreed upon also. The FASB answers the question "Why is a conceptual framework needed?" as follows:[2]

> Perhaps because accounting in general and financial statements in particular exude an aura of precision and exactitude, many persons are astonished to learn that a conceptual framework for financial accounting and reporting has not been articulated authoritatively. Though many organizations, committees, and individuals have published their own constructs of a conceptual framework, none by itself has come to be universally accepted and relied on in practice. Notable among those efforts is Accounting Principles Board Statement No. 4, "Basic Concepts and Accounting Principles Underlying Financial Statements of Business Enterprises" (1970), but it purports primarily to describe the way things are and not to prescribe how they ought to be.

The FASB describes the **conceptual framework for financial accounting** as a constitution, a coherent system of interrelated objectives and fundamentals that can lead to consistent standards and that prescribes the nature, function, and limits of financial accounting and financial statements. The objectives identify the goals and purposes of accounting. The **fundamentals underlying financial accounting** are the concepts that guide the selection of events to be accounted for, the measurement of those events, and the means of summarizing and communicating them to interested parties. Such concepts are fundamental in that other concepts flow from them and repeated reference to them is necessary in establishing, interpreting, and applying accounting and reporting standards.[3]

Note that the conceptual framework is hierarchical. Accounting and reporting standards must be consistent with underlying accounting concepts, which must in

[2]"An Analysis of Issues Related to Conceptual Framework for Financial Accounting and Reporting: Elements of Financial Statements and Their Measurement," FASB Discussion Memorandum, (FASB, 1976), p. 2.

[3]FASB, "Analysis of Issues," p. 2.

turn be consistent with accounting objectives. In the accounting literature terms such as assumption, postulate, standard, concept, principle, practice, method, and procedure are often used interchangeably. However, as our discussion will show, each has its own specific meaning. A suggested hierarchical framework for accounting theory and practice is presented in Figure 3.1. This framework is consistent with the ideas of both the APB and the FASB.

If a sound, consistent framework is to be established, the objectives of accounting should be determined first. Then basic assumptions that describe the accounting environment—**accounting assumptions** or underlying accounting assumptions—must be identified. Next, broad operating rules or guides to accounting action should be developed. These are few in number and are referred to as **accounting principles,** underlying accounting principles, or generally accepted accounting principles. Following from these should come the specific and detailed measurement and reporting practices and methods accountants apply in their daily work. These are called **accounting practices, procedures, and methods.**

Although there is no consensus as to how many accounting assumptions and principles there are, there is some agreement that certain ones are fundamental. These assumptions and principles are described in the following sections.

Separate-Entity Assumption   The **accounting entity** concept is one of the most elementary and important concepts in accounting. Information is irrelevant unless the entity can be identified. At the same time, users are concerned with the activities of specific entities. Accounting, therefore, must distinguish among entities so accumulated data pertain to each entity as distinct from all others.

The accounting entity in any situation is the economic unit—the individual, business enterprise, nonprofit organization, or group of these—for which the financial statements are being prepared or for which the accounting services are being performed. In a broad sense an accounting entity can be any object, event, or attribute of an object or event for which there is an input-output relationship.[4] Common ownership and overlapping activities or interests, however, may make it difficult to identify the accounting entity or entities in specific situations. For example, assume that Jacob Smith obtains a charter to incorporate his real estate business, which he has operated as an unincorporated business for several years. In order to close the books of the unincorporated business and open the books of the incorporated business, he hires a certified public accounting firm. In this situation who or what is the accounting entity (or entities)?

The question can be answered by asking: For whom are the accounting services being provided? The answer is *not* Jacob Smith, because the services are not being provided personally for Jacob Smith. The accounting services are being provided for two different accounting entities, the unincorporated business and the incorporated business. The change in organization form creates a new accounting entity, the incorporated business.

---

[4]*Uniform CPA Examination Questions and Unofficial Answers,* (AICPA, May 1972), p. 81.

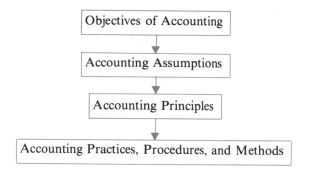

Figure 3.1   Hierarchical conceptual framework for accounting

An accounting entity can also be defined as an area of economic interest to a particular individual or group. The particular individual or group and the nature of the interest have to be identified before the economic entity can be identified.

To identify the accounting entity in a specific situation, the question to be asked is: Whose activities are the focal point of the financial statements or the accounting services being provided? In the situation described, the personal activities of Jacob Smith are not the focal point of the accounting services being provided. The focal point is the activities of the unincorporated and incorporated businesses. In this situation, then, there are two accounting entities, the unincorporated business and the incorporated business.

Business entities may be organized as a sole proprietorship, a partnership, or a corporation. A **sole proprietorship** is a business owned by one person. The business and the owner are not separate **legal entities,** but they are separate accounting entities. The activities of the business are accounted for separately from the personal activities of the owner. In many sole proprietorships the owner is also the manager of the business. This form of business organization is commonly found among small, independent businesses, such as farms, grocery stores, drug stores, gas stations, and soft ice cream stores, and among professionals such as lawyers, doctors, and CPAs.

A partnership is ''an association of two or more persons to carry on, as co-owners, a business for profit.''[5] The rights of the partners are usually covered in a wirtten agreement called the *partnership contract* or *articles of copartnership*. The business is not a separate legal entity from the partners (owners), but they are all separate accounting entities. The activities of the business must be accounted for separately from the personal activities of the partners, and the personal activities of each partner must be accounted for separately from the others'. The same types of businesses operated as sole proprietorships are frequently operated as partnerships because partners can provide more capital and a wider range of skills, and a partnership enables a larger scale of operations.

---

[5]From the Uniform Partnership Act adopted by most states.

A **corporation** is a business that has a charter to incorporate according to the laws of a particular state. The owners of the business are known as shareholders or stockholders. When the business is incorporated, the laws of the state recognize the corporation as a legal entity separate from the owners. The owners are liable for the debts of the corporation only to the extent of their investment; this is called *limited liability*. In sole proprietorships and partnerships the owners have unlimited liability, that is, the creditors can hold the owners responsible for the debts of the business beyond the amount of their investments. In small corporations owners are often managers or at least a part of management. In large corporations members of management usually have only a small ownership interest; the majority ownership interest is usually held by a number of shareholders who have no part in managing the corporation. A corporation, then, is both a legal entity and an accounting entity separate from the owners.

Although unincorporated businesses outnumber incorporated businesses, the corporate form of business is by far the more dominant economic force in the United States. The corporation can raise larger sums of capital through the wide distribution of ownership interests in the form of readily transferable shares of stock and through borrowing as a separate legal entity. Unincorporated businesses are limited to raising capital through investments and through personal borrowing by the owner(s). The largest businesses in the United States are all corporations. See, for example, *Fortune* magazine's lists of the 500 largest industrial organizations and the 50 largest merchandising firms. Individuals starting a business, however, should consider the advantages and disadvantages of both forms of business organization before deciding on the form for theirs. Generally, the accounting principles, practices, procedures, and methods of both forms are the same.

Continuity or Going-Concern Assumption   The life of an entity is usually uncertain at any given time. A high percentage of businesses fail within a few years, but some have existed for more than a hundred. In order to measure any entity's financial position and operating results accurately, however, it is necessary to assume that the entity will continue to operate indefinitely. (The continuity assumption should be dropped, of course, when definite plans to terminate business operations are made and statements reflecting the amounts to be realized through liquidation are needed.)

The continuity assumption underlies the cost, revenue, and matching principles. Assume, for example, that an entity acquires a building at a cost of $375,000 that is expected to have a useful life of 30 years. Because the building will provide benefits over the 30 years, its cost should be allocated over the 30 years. This allocation, however, can be made only if it is assumed that the business will be a going concern for that long. In addition, the portion of the cost not yet allocated to expense, rather than a liquidation value, can be used if it can be assumed that the entity will exist long enough to recover the cost of the building.

Time-Period Assumption   Financial information should be timely, that is, presented often enough and soon enough to be useful. Financial reports that cover relatively short periods of time, such as a month, quarter, or year, are assumed to be essential, and most entities have adopted an annual accounting period for financial reporting.

The **accounting period** is the span of time over which accounting data are accumulated and then presented in financial statements. Although the accounting period may cover any length of time, quarterly and annual financial reports are most commonly issued to external users. The quarterly reports are referred to as *interim reports* because they cover an interim or small segment of the larger annual accounting period.

The annual accounting period may cover any 12-month period. Many companies use the calendar year because it is simpler for record-keeping and reporting. Other companies use a different 12-month period—referred to as the **fiscal year.** The fiscal year can start and end on any dates a company prefers. Some companies select a fiscal period that corresponds with their natural business year. The **natural business year** ends when the entity's normal operations reach their natural, lowest level of activity. Although an entity should find it more convenient to wrap up the accounting process when operations are at their lowest level, surprisingly few companies have adopted the natural business year as their accounting period.

Unit-of-Measure or Stable-Dollar Assumption   Money is the basic measuring unit in financial statements. The monetary unit represents a unit of value or a purchasing unit. Each dollar, for example, provides its holder with the ability to command a certain amount of goods and services. It is a basic assumption in accounting that the monetary unit has a constant or stable amount of purchasing power. In reality, however, this purchasing power changes continuously.

In the United States one general measure of price changes and, thus, of the purchasing power of the dollar is the consumer price index. Between 1967 and the end of 1978 this index doubled—that is, at the end of 1978 the purchasing power of a dollar was only half of what it was in 1967. Thus, a dollar at the end of 1978 bought only half the goods and services it bought in 1967.

One criticism of accounting is that financial statements are misleading because they still adhere to the stable-dollar assumption. Amounts reported on financial statements, for example, are the original costs; changes in purchasing power are ignored. Assume that machinery with a 20-year life is purchased at a cost of $25,000 in 1967, and that additional machinery of the same type is purchased at a cost of $50,000 in 1978. On the financial statements, machinery is reported at a combined cost of $75,000, even though the purchasing power of the 1978 dollar is about half that of the 1967 dollar. Depreciation expense too is based on original costs without any adjustments for changes in the purchasing power of the dollar.

Accounting has held steadfast to the stable-dollar assumption because it results in more objective measurements, that is, in more precise and verifiable measurements, using the number of dollars expended and received in business transactions. In recent years the APB and FASB have reconsidered their adherence to the stable-dollar assumption; however, nothing has so far changed, despite a lot of research and discussion. One reason for this was a strong push at the same time for the adoption of current value accounting. In late 1979 the FASB issued a statement that will require certain large companies to report supplementary data to reflect the effects of both general price changes and changes in current costs. Restatement of financial statements for general price level changes and changes to current values is examined in greater detail in Unit 36.

Exchanges and Exchange-Prices Assumption   Business transactions involve an exchange of economic resources and obligations between independent parties. For example, assume that ABC Corporation acquires equipment from XYZ Corporation. In this exchange, an economic resource, equipment, is received by ABC Corporation. In order to acquire the equipment, ABC Corporation must give up another economic resource, cash, or incur an obligation that will require the payment of cash at a later date. ABC Corporation must record its acquisition of the equipment, and XYZ Corporation must record its sale of the equipment. The amount to be recorded will be based on the price or value of the economic resources to be exchanged. Thus, if the negotiated price is $8,500, both companies will use that figure in recording the transaction. When there are no established prices, and cash is not exchanged, a measurement problem arises—such complex cases are discussed in later units.

Cost Principle   All goods and services acquired by an entity are recorded at their acquisition cost. **Cost** is measured by the then-current "fair market value" or cash equivalent of the economic resources given up or the economic obligations incurred to acquire them. These original costs are then used to measure the entity's financial position and operating results. However, fair market values frequently change before goods and services are used in business operations. For this reason, an increasing number of accountants advocate using current values for financial reporting and decision making, believing them to be more relevant. Accounting, however, continues to adhere to the cost principle because, for some types of goods and services, problems arise in measuring current values. Original costs, on the other hand, which are based on completed business transactions, are objectively measurable and verifiable. Problems and techniques involved in restating financial statements to current values are examined in Unit 36.

Revenue or Realization Principle   **Revenue** represents the inflow of economic resources from the sale of goods or the performance of services. There are usually several distinct steps in the process of earning revenue. For example, merchandise must be purchased, carried in stock, advertised, displayed, and sold, and the sale price of the merchandise must be collected from customers. When services are performed to earn revenue, a considerable amount of time may be required to complete the services and collect the fees earned. Under the revenue or realization principle two criteria must be met in order to establish that revenue has been earned and should be recorded: (1) the earning process must be completed or virtually completed and (2) an exchange between independent parties must have taken place. With most merchandise sales revenue recognition occurs when ownership of the goods is transferred from the seller to the buyer. With services, revenue is usually recognized when the services are completed. Under a long-term contract, however, revenue is often recognized on a percentage-of-completion basis throughout the term of the contract. Other exceptions in revenue recognition are made when warranted by circumstances to better measure an entity's operating results. Some of these exceptions are discussed in Unit 5.

Matching Principle   An **expense** is an expired cost, that is, the cost of goods or services that are consumed or used in generating an entity's revenue. Merchandise is sold, for example, and becomes an expense. Expenses are incurred, too, in selling the merchandise or services. Expenses are also incurred in administering a business. The matching principle requires that, to be treated as expenses, costs be associated with the revenue earned,

Sometimes, there is a direct association between costs and revenues. For example, sales commissions and the cost of products sold or services provided can be identified directly with the revenue received. Other costs are associated with a specific accounting period. Examples of such costs are depreciation of buildings and equipment, rent, insurance, and supplies used. Certain costs cannot be associated with either revenues or a specific accounting period. For example, costs such as officers' salaries, advertising, delivery charges, and losses from lawsuits have no future benefits and no useful purpose is served by associating them with revenues or specific time periods. These costs, therefore, are assigned to expense in the current accounting period.

Accounting Practices, Procedures, and Methods

The detailed practices, procedures, and methods used to process and report accounting data must be consistent with accounting objectives, assumptions, and principles. They are subject to change if they are found to be unacceptable, unusable, or difficult to apply, and they are affected by certain constraints, which are discussed in the following section. These practices, procedures, and methods are discussed in more detail in later units.

Constraints on Accounting

The development of accounting principles, practices, and methods is constrained by limitations on the availability of data, uncertainty regarding the continued existence of the enterprise and the purchasing power of the monetary unit, and the ability of users to assimilate large amounts of data and interpret them correctly. As a result of these constraints, accountants apply two concepts in measuring and communicating data—conservatism and materiality:

1. *Conservatism* is an approach taken toward accounting measurements that results in measurements being selected that have the least favorable effect on owners' interests; this approach avoids overstatement of net assets and net income.
2. *Materiality* is an approach taken toward the data that leads to insignificant items being ignored, while material (significant) items that might influence the decisions of users are adequately disclosed.

Qualities of Financial Information

In order to be useful, information in financial statements should have certain qualities or characteristics. These were identified in the section on the objectives of financial accounting, and are discussed briefly here.

1. *Relevance:* information must be related to or associated with the actions it is designed to facilitate or the result desired; the known or assumed information needs of users are of paramount importance in determining the presence of this quality.
2. *Verifiability:* accounting data should be verifiable by independent parties; if two or more qualified parties examine the same data, they should reach essentially similar measures and conclusions.
3. *Freedom from bias (neutrality):* accounting data should be impartially determined; the techniques used to identify what data to measure and report should also be free of bias.
4. *Comparability:* if data are to be comparable for consecutive time periods or between enterprises, they should be:
   a. *consistent:* measurement and reporting practices must be applied consistently from one period to the next.
   b. *uniform:* uniform measurement and reporting practices, to the extent practicable, should be applied within a firm, by different firms in the same industry, and by different industries.
5. *Understandability:* information should be presented in a manner and use terminology that reasonably informed users can understand.
6. *Timeliness:* information must be current and must be reported at frequent intervals to reveal significant changes.
7. *Completeness (full disclosure):* all information that might influence the decisions of users should be disclosed.

Elements of the Accounting Structure

A structure for gathering, processing, and reporting data in accordance with accounting principles is necessary. Such a structure has been developed and includes the following elements:

1. a double-entry system of bookkeeping, with debit-credit rules
2. a set of records, including journals, a general ledger, and subsidiary ledgers, to record, classify, and summarize accounting data
3. a set of accounts for classifying the economic effects of

transactions; the major classifications are assets, liabilities, owner's equity, revenues, and expenses

4. a set of basic financial reports, including an income statement, a balance sheet, a statement of changes in financial position, and a statement of changes in retained earnings (or a statement of changes in capital)

SUMMARY

The objectives of accounting and the distinctions among accounting assumptions, principles, and practices, procedures, and methods were discussed in this unit, as were specific accounting assumptions and principles. A full understanding of the conceptual framework of accounting is not possible at this point, but it was presented as background for the accounting concepts and principles discussed later. The types of users of financial information were also examined in this unit. The next chapter examines the end product of accounting—the basic financial statements presented to users of financial information.

REVIEW QUESTIONS

3-1   What is the primary objective of financial accounting and financial statements?

3-2   Are the needs of all users met with general purpose financial statements? Explain.

3-3   Distinguish between external and internal users of financial statements and financial information. Give three examples of external and three examples of internal users.

3-4   Distinguish among accounting assumptions, accounting principles, and accounting practices, procedures, and methods.

3-5   Below are the hierarchical components of a conceptual framework for accounting. Indicate the position of each in the hierarchy by numbering them from 1 to 4. (1 represents the top position in the hierarchy.)

_____   accounting principles
_____   objectives of accounting
_____   accounting practices, procedures, and methods
_____   accounting assumptions

3-6   Distinguish among the following terms: (a) accounting period, (b) fiscal period, (c) natural business year.

3-7   Give two definitions of an accounting entity. What are two questions that may be helpful in identifying the accounting entity in a specific situation?

3-8   Identify the accounting entity or entities in each situation:

    a.   A CPA was engaged to prepare the income tax returns for the Able-Baker Company, a partnership, and for the partners.

    b.   Harry Barnes owns three different incorporated businesses. Harry hired a CPA to prepare a financial report required by the bank for a personal loan Harry is seeking.

3-9   Name and describe the three basic forms of business organization.

3-10   Are sole proprietorships, partnerships, and corporations accounting entities separate from their owners? Are they legal entities separate from their owners? Explain.

EXERCISES

X **3-1**   Answer each of the following questions concerned with accounting principles or assumptions.

    _____   **a.**   Charging off a wastebasket with an estimated useful life of 20 years as an expense of the period when it is purchased is an example of applying the:
        (1)   consistency principle.
        (2)   matching principle.
        (3)   materiality principle.
        (4)   cost principle.

    _____   **b.**   Proponents of historical costs maintain that in comparison with all other valuation alternatives for general purpose financial reporting, statements prepared using historical costs are more:
        (1)   objective.
        (2)   relevant.
        (3)   indicative of the entity's purchasing power.
        (4)   conservative.

    _____   **c.**   The accounting concept of matching is best demonstrated by:
        (1)   not recognizing any expense unless some revenue is realized.
        (2)   associating effort (cost) with accomplishment (revenue).
        (3)   recognizing expenses only as cash is paid.
        (4)   recognizing all expenses in the same period that merchandise is sold or services are performed.

    _____   **d.**   The APB (Accounting Principles Board) has not functioned for several years. What is the best statement regarding its current position in relation to generally accepted accounting principles?
        (1)   APB Opinions remain in effect if not specifically modified or rescinded.
        (2)   APB Opinions are no longer in effect.
        (3)   Compliance with its pronouncements is voluntary.
        (4)   All APB Opinions have been superseded by FASB Statements.

_____ **e.** The consistency standard of reporting requires that:
   (1) expenses be reported as charges against the period in which they are incurred.
   (2) no change be made in an accounting principle after it is first adopted.
   (3) no change be made in financial statement format or terminology.
   (4) accounting procedures be adopted that give a consistent profit.

_____ **f.** Accounting requires the preparation of statements that summarize exchange transactions in terms of some unit of measurement. Revenue is expressed as the number of dollars received or the dollar equivalent of the commodities or services received; cost is expressed as the number of dollars paid out or the dollar equivalent of the items given up. Fluctuations in the value of the dollar are ignored. The above describes what accounting assumption or principle?
   (1) going-concern
   (2) unit-of-measure
   (3) historical-cost
   (4) realization

_____ **g.** When costs can be reasonably associated with specific revenues but not with specific products, the costs should be:
   (1) charged to expense in the period incurred.
   (2) allocated to specific products based on the best estimate of the production processing time.
   (3) expensed in the period in which the related revenue is recognized.
   (4) recorded as assets and charged to expense over a period not to exceed 60 months.

_____ **h.** Revenue is generally recognized when the earning process is virtually complete and an exchange has taken place. What principle is described by this statement?
   (1) consistency
   (2) matching
   (3) realization
   (4) conservatism

_____ **i.** Determining periodic earnings and financial position depends on measuring economic resources and obligations, and changes in these, as the changes occur. This explanation pertains to:
   (1) disclosure.
   (2) accrual accounting.
   (3) materiality.
   (4) the matching concept.

_____ **j.** One source delineates three levels of accounting principles: basic, broad operating, and detailed. Which level comprises "generally accepted accounting principles"?
   (1) basic only
   (2) basic and broad operating only

(3)　broad operating and detailed only

(4)　basic, broad operating, and detailed

_____ **k.** The concept of objectivity is complied with when an accounting transaction occurs that:

(1)　involves an arm's-length transaction between two independent interests.

(2)　furthers the objectives of the company.

(3)　is promptly recorded in a fixed amount of dollars.

(4)　allocates revenues or expense items in a rational and systematic manner.

_____ **l.** Generally, revenues should be recognized at a point when:

(1)　management decides it is appropriate to do so.

(2)　the product is available for sale to the ultimate consumer.

(3)　an exchange has taken place and the earnings process is virtually complete.

(4)　an order for a definite amount of merchandise has been received for shipment.

_____ **m.** Why are certain costs of doing business recorded as an asset when incurred and then charged to expense over subsequent accounting cycles?

(1)　to reduce the federal income tax liability

(2)　to aid management in the decision-making process

(3)　to match the costs of production with revenues as earned

(4)　to adhere to the accounting concept of conservatism

_____ **n.** What accounting concept justifies the usage of the accrual basis of accounting?

(1)　going-concern

(2)　materiality

(3)　consistency

(4)　stable monetary unit

_____ **o.** What is the underlying concept that supports the immediate recognition of a loss?

(1)　matching

(2)　consistency

(3)　judgment

(4)　conservatism

3-2 Identify any inaccuracies in the following statement regarding the purpose or objective of accounting.

Accounting is a service activity. Its function is to provide quantitative financial information which is intended to be useful in making economic decisions about and for economic entities. Thus the accounting function might be viewed primarily as being a tool or device for providing quantitative financial information to management to facilitate decision making.

3-3   When published financial statements of U.S. companies are prepared, dollar amounts are added together as if they represented dollars of equivalent purchasing power. In fact, however, inflation in recent years has resulted in a significant decline in the purchasing power of the dollar. Although there is considerable concern over the relevance of published financial data prepared in this manner, currently published financial statements are prepared in conformity with generally accepted accounting principles. Explain why accounting and accountants adhere to this practice.

3-4   An accountant must be familiar with the concepts involved in determining the earnings of a business entity. The amount of earnings reported for a business entity depends, in general, on the proper recognition of revenue and expense for a given time period. In some situations, costs are recognized as expenses at the time of product sale; in other situations, other criteria for recognizing costs as expenses or losses apply.

Required   **a.**   Describe the revenue or realization principle.
    b.   Describe the matching principle.
    c.   Explain the rationale for recognizing certain costs as expenses at the time of product sale.
    d.   Explain the rationale for recognizing other costs as expenses or losses of a particular accounting period.

PROBLEMS

3-1   In recent years the accounting profession has shown substantial interest in delineating the objectives and principles of accounting. APB Statement No. 4, "Basic Concepts and Accounting Principles Underlying Financial Statements of Business Enterprises," for example, (1) discusses the nature of financial accounting, the environmental forces that influence it, and the potential and limitations of financial accounting in providing useful information; (2) sets forth the objectives of financial accounting and financial statements; and (3) describes current generally accepted accounting principles.

    Another example is Statement of Financial Accounting Concepts No. 1, "Objectives of Financial Report by Business Enterprises," which (1) discusses the environmental context of objectives for financial reporting, the characteristics and limitations on information provided, potential users and their interests, and general purpose external reporting and (2) sets forth the objectives of financial reporting.

Required   Do these statements agree on the basic purpose of financial accounting and financial statements? Identify the points on which they agree and those on which they differ.

3-2   **a.**   For accounting purposes a business enterprise recognizes that revenue has been earned when the transaction is recorded. In some situations, revenue is recognized approximately as it is earned in the economic sense. In other situations, however, accountants have developed other criteria, such as at the point of sale, for recognizing revenue.

Required   **(1)**   Explain why revenue is often recognized as earned at time of sale.

            (2)   Explain in what situations it would be appropriate to recognize revenue (a) during production of products or performance of services, (b) at the completion of production of products or performance of services, and (c) only upon collection of cash from the sale of products or performance of services.

b.   Some costs are recognized as an expense when revenue is recognized. Other costs are recognized as expenses or losses according to other criteria.

Required   Describe the criteria used to recognize costs as expenses or losses.

3-3   The concept of the accounting entity is often considered the most fundamental of accounting concepts.

Required   **a.**   What is an accounting entity?

            b.   Why is the accounting entity concept considered fundamental to accounting?

            c.   For each of the following indicate whether the accounting entity concept is applicable:

                 (1)   a unit created by or under law

                 (2)   the product-line segment of an enterprise

                 (3)   a combination of legal units and/or product-line segments

                 (4)   all the activities of an owner or a group of owners

                 (5)   an industry

                 (6)   the economy of the United States

3-4   Elmo Company operates several plants at which limestone is processed into quicklime and hydrated lime. The Bland Plant, where most of the equipment was installed many years ago, continually deposits a dusty white substance over the surrounding countryside. Citing the unsanitary condition of the neighboring community of Adeltown, the pollution of the Adel River, and the high incidence of lung disease among workers at Bland, the state's Pollution Control Agency has ordered the installation of air pollution control equipment. Also, the agency has assessed the plant a substantial penalty, which will be used to clean up Adeltown. After considering the costs involved (which could not have been reasonably estimated prior to the agency's action), Elmo decides to comply with the agency's orders, the alternative being to cease operations at Bland at the end of the current fiscal year. The officers of Elmo agree that the air pollution control equipment should be capitalized and depreciated over its useful life, but they disagree about the period(s) to which the penalty should be charged.

Elmo's Davis Plant causes approximately as much pollution as Bland. Davis, however, is located in another state, where there is little likelihood of governmental regulation, and Elmo has no plans for pollution control at this plant. One of Elmo's officers, Mr. Pearce, says that uncontrolled pollution at Davis constitutes a very real cost to society, which is not recorded anywhere under current practice. He suggests that this "social cost" of the Davis Plant be included annually in Elmo's income statement. Further, he suggests that measurement of this cost is easily obtainable by reference to the depreciation on Bland's pollution control equipment.

Required **a.** Discuss whether or not it would be appropriate to recognize the penalty as an expense or loss of the current year?

b. Is Mr. Pearce correct in stating that the costs associated with Davis's pollution are entirely unrecorded? Explain.

c. Should the "social cost" of the Davis Plant be recognized in Elmo's financial statements? Explain.

Chapter 2

Basic Financial Statements

The end product of the accounting process is a set of financial statements intended to communicate information about an entity's financial position, operating results, and changes in financial position to a variety of users. This chapter examines the model, purpose, form, and content of the basic financial statements usually presented to external users.

Unit 4
The Balance Sheet

In each man's account book, Fortune makes out two pages.

Pliny the Elder (c. A.D. 23–79), Historia Naturalis

The first of the basic financial statements to be examined is the balance sheet, which reports an entity's financial position at a given time. The model, purpose, form, and content of the balance sheet are discussed in this unit.

Performance Objectives

Upon completing this unit you should be able to:

1. define and use the accounting terms introduced in this unit.
2. a. determine the amount of the missing component of the accounting (balance sheet) equation.
   b. determine depreciation expense, book value, and/or the useful life for a plant asset.
3. describe the form, content, purposes, and model of a balance sheet.
4. determine the proper classification for assets, liabilities, and owners' equity items on a classified balance sheet.
5. prepare, in good form, a classified balance sheet.

Purpose and Model

According to the objectives of financial accounting, information on an entity's resources and obligations (that is, the entity's financial position) should be provided to users who want to predict, compare, and evaluate the entity's earning power. The statement that serves this purpose is the balance sheet. It reports the resources owned or controlled, the obligations owed, and the residual interest of the owner(s) at the date indicated in the statement heading. By comparing balance sheets for successive periods, users can observe trends that will help them judge, among other things, the entity's ability to pay existing obligations on time, the likelihood of additional debts being paid when due, and the likelihood of owners receiving a return on their investment, as well as the investment itself. Such resources as inventories, property, plant, and equipment are benefits that contribute to future profits, and information on them can help users assess future profitability.

The basic model for the balance sheet is expressed by the **accounting equation:**

$$\text{assets} = \text{liabilities} + \text{owners' equity}$$
$$A = L + OE$$

Assets   **Assets** are economic resources owned or controlled by an entity that are expected to benefit future operations. They include cash and monetary claims against customers and others, investments in the stocks and bonds of other companies, inventories of goods being held for sale, and supplies, land, buildings, and equipment held for use in future business operations.

Liabilities   **Liabilities** are obligations owed to others. They are both the portion of the entity's assets provided by the creditors and the creditors' claims against the entity's assets. Liabilities include obligations for assets or services acquired on credit, for cash loans received, for expenses incurred but not paid, for deposits or advance payments from customers, for mortgages on land and buildings, and, in the case of corporations, for bonds issued.

Owners' Equity   **Owners' equity** is the portion of the entity's assets that belongs to the owners after the claims of the creditors are met—that is, the residual interest of the owners in the entity. It is money invested in and profits retained in the entity after profits are distributed to the owners. (See Table 4.1 for the kinds of assets, liabilities, and owners' equity accounts reported on a balance sheet.)

The Accounting Equation

Recall that the basic accounting equation, assets = liabilities + owners' equity, is also the model for the balance sheet. This equation may be restated to emphasize the residual interest of the owners in the entity:

$$\text{assets} - \text{liabilities} = \text{owners' equity}$$
$$A - L = OE$$

This form of the accounting equation also expresses an important concept used repeatedly in accounting, that is, the concept of net assets. **Net assets** are the excess of assets over liabilities; they equal owners' equity:

$$\text{assets} - \text{liabilities} = \text{owners' equity}$$
$$\text{assets} - \text{liabilities} = \text{net assets}$$
$$\text{net assets} = \text{owners' equity}$$

The relationships indicated by the accounting equation and the net assets concept are used in many accounting problems and should be thoroughly understood. The following cases illustrate the various relationships.

Case 1   Anchor Corp. reported liabilities of $300,000 and owners' equity of $180,000. Thus, assets are $480,000:

$$\text{assets} = \text{liabilities} + \text{owners' equity}$$
$$\text{assets} = \$300,000 + \$180,000$$
$$\text{assets} = \$480,000$$

Case 2   Belt Corp. reported assets of $400,000 and owners' equity of $240,000. Thus, liabilities are $160,000:

$$\text{assets} = \text{liabilities} + \text{owners' equity}$$
$$\text{liabilities} = \text{assets} - \text{owners' equity}$$
$$\text{liabilities} = \$400,000 - \$240,000$$
$$\text{liabilities} = \$160,000$$

Case 3   Conn, Inc., reported assets of $270,000 and liabilities of $100,000. Thus, owners' equity is $170,000; note that net assets also equal $170,000:

$$\text{assets} = \text{liabilities} + \text{owners' equity}$$
$$\text{owners' equity} = \text{assets} - \text{liabilities}$$
$$\text{owners' equity} = \$270,000 - \$100,000$$
$$\text{owners' equity} = \$170,000$$
$$\text{owners' equity} = \text{net assets}$$
$$\text{net assets} = \$170,000$$

A Simple Balance Sheet

Small businesses with only a few assets, liabilities, and owners' equity items might prepare a simple balance sheet with only these three classifications. This balance

Table 4.1

Typical Balance Sheet Accounts

Current Assets

Cash: includes cash on hand and in banks that can be used for current operations

Temporary investments: stocks, bonds, certificates of deposits, and other securities held for conversion into cash when needed in the near future

Accounts receivable: amounts due from customers who have purchased goods or services on regular credit terms (usually less than one year)

Allowance for uncollectible accounts: an estimate of the amount of accounts receivable that will be uncollectible

Notes receivable, short-term: written promises by customers and other parties to pay a definite sum of money at a future date (one year or less); may be accepted when merchandise is sold, services are performed, various noncurrent assets are sold, or money is loaned

Interest receivable: a claim for interest earned, but not received by the end of the accounting period (interest is usually received when the related receivable is collected or at other specific dates)

Inventory or merchandise inventory: the cost of goods being held for sale in the regular course of business

Prepaid expenses: the cost of services acquired, but not to be used in business operations until later in the current period or in the next period, e.g., supplies and insurance

Supplies on hand: see Prepaid expenses

Unexpired or prepaid insurance: see Prepaid expenses

Long-term Investments and Funds

Investment in stock or bonds: stocks or bonds of other entities held for some long-term purpose

Bond sinking fund: cash and investments held to retire a bond obligation; when the obligation matures, the investments are converted into cash and the bonds redeemed

Notes receivable, long-term: similar to notes receivable, short-term, except that these notes are due more than one year after balance sheet date

Plant (or Fixed) Assets

Land: the cost of land owned and used in business operations; land not being used in business operations is classified under other assets

Buildings: the cost of all buildings owned and used in business operations, e.g., office buildings, stores, warehouses, manufacturing plants, garages

Equipment: the cost of all equipment owned and used in business operations, e.g., office furniture, office equipment, store fixtures, store equipment, delivery trucks, company autos, manufacturing equipment

Machinery: see Equipment

Accumulated depreciation: an account used to indicate the portion of the cost of a plant asset that has been assigned to expense up to the current date; a separate account is used for each type of plant asset except land, which is not depreciated

Intangible Assets

Goodwill: an amount paid when a business is acquired, because the value of the business as a whole exceeds the value of its individual assets; goodwill arises from such intangible factors as customer service, employee morale, quality products, and business location

Patents: the cost of patents acquired from others and certain costs for patents developed by the entity; patents are obtained from the government and give the entity exclusive rights to use and control an invention

Organization costs: costs incurred in organizing and incorporating a business, including legal and accounting fees, fees paid to the state, promotion costs, costs of initial directors' and stockholders' meetings

Copyright: costs incurred for the exclusive right to publish, sell, or use a work of art, music, or literature

Franchise or license: costs incurred for the exclusive right to market a particular product and/or use a certain tradename in a specified territory

Leasehold: advance payments for the use of property according to terms contained in a lease contract

Trademark or tradename: costs incurred for the permanent, exclusive right to use and control a particular identifying mark or name

(continued)

Table 4.1 (continued)

Other Assets

Plant assets held for future use: the cost of plant assets acquired and being held for use in future business operations (can be classified as a long-term investment)

Plant assets held for sale: the remaining cost of plant assets no longer used in business operations and being sold or planning to be sold (can be classified as a long-term investment)

Current Liabilities

Accounts payable: obligations to suppliers for goods and services purchased on regular credit terms (usually less than one year)

Notes payable, short-term: written promises by an entity to pay a definite sum of money at a future date (one year or less); notes are usually for a longer period than usual credit terms; may be issued when merchandise, services, or various noncurrent assets are acquired or when money is borrowed

Interest payable: an obligation for interest expense incurred but not paid by the end of the accounting period; interest is usually paid when the related debt is due or at other specific dates

Income taxes payable: obligation for taxes owed on income for the accounting period

Salaries or wages payable: an obligation for salaries or wages earned by employees but not paid by the end of the accounting period

Liability for income taxes withheld: amount owed to the government for income taxes withheld from employees' wages

Liability for payroll taxes: amount owed by an entity for payroll taxes assessed against it

Unearned service revenue: an obligation to provide services in the future that arises when customers pay in advance for the services

Unearned fees: see Unearned service revenue

Advances from customers: an obligation to provide goods in the future that arises when customers pay in advance for the goods

Long-term Liabilities

Bonds payable: an obligation incurred when certain debt instruments, called *bonds,* are issued by a corporation to borrow money

Lease liability: an obligation incurred to acquire assets or services under a lease contract

Mortgage payable: an obligation for money borrowed to finance the purchase of land or buildings; the assets purchased are pledged as security for repayment of the loan

Notes payable, long-term: similar to notes payable, short-term, except these notes are due more than one year after the balance sheet date

Stockholders' Equity (Corporate Businesses)

Common or capital stock: an account used to indicate part of the amount (equal to the par or stated value of the stock) invested in a corporation by its owners

Contributed capital in excess of par or stated value: an account used to indicate amounts invested in a corporation by its owners in excess of the par or stated value of the stock issued

Retained earnings: an account used to indicate the amount of profits retained in a corporation after net losses incurred and profit distributions (dividends) to the stockholders are deducted

Dividends paid or declared: an account that can be used to indicate the amount of the corporation's retained profits that the board of directors decided to distribute to stockholders during the period

Reserve for _____: an account that can be used to indicate the portion of retained earnings restricted (i.e., appropriated) by a corporation's board of directors for a specific purpose; the purpose of the restriction is reflected in the account title, e.g., "Reserve for Bonds" indicates a restriction on retained earnings available for dividends as a result of an agreement with bondholders (this type of account is explained more fully in Unit 6)

Capital or Owners' Equity (Noncorporate Businesses)

John (or Jane) Doe, capital: an account used to indicate the amounts invested by a proprietor or partner and his (or her) share of profits retained in the business

John (or Jane) Doe, drawing: an account used to indicate amounts drawn out of the business on a regular basis by a proprietor or partner in lieu of a salary

Exhibit 4.1

Rein Company
Balance Sheet
As of December 31, 19x8

Assets:		Liabilities:	
Cash	$ 30,000	Accounts Payable	$ 48,000
Accounts Receivable (net of allowance for		Salaries Payable	2,000
uncollectible accounts of $2,000)	43,000	Income Taxes Payable	7,500
Inventory	36,000	Mortgage Payable	50,000
Prepaid Expenses	3,000	Total Liabilities	$107,500
Land	20,000	Stockholders' Equity:	
Buildings (net of accumulated depreciation		Common Stock, $10 par value, 10,000 shares	
of $25,000)	75,000	authorized, issued, and outstanding	$100,000
Equipment (net of accumulated depreciation		Retained Earnings	57,500
of $18,000)	58,000	Total Stockholders' Equity	$157,500
Total Assets	$265,000	Total Liabilities and Stockholders' Equity	$265,000

sheet format is called an *unclassified balance sheet* because no subclassifications of assets, liabilities, or owners' equity are given. Exhibit 4.1 illustrates a simple balance sheet for the Rein Company as of December 31, 19x8. Note that total liabilities plus total stockholders' equity ($107,500 + $157,500) equals total assets ($265,000). This equality should have been expected based on a knowledge of the accounting equation. The heading for the balance sheet consists of three lines, one each for the company name, the statement title, and the date of the statement. Since the composition and balances of assets, liabilities, and owners' equity change daily, the date line must give the date on which the reported balances actually existed. The date line may read *As of (month, day, year)* or *At (month, day, year),* or merely indicate the exact date *(day, month, year).* A record called an *account* or *ledger account* is maintained for each item on an entity's financial statements. The many accounts used by large companies are classified to help users analyze the entity's financial condition.

Classification of Accounts

Over the years the presentation of accounts on the balance sheet has become, to a large degree, standardized. The classifications and subclassifications used by most corporations include the following:

Assets:
  Current assets
  Long-term investments and funds
  Plant (or fixed) assets
  Intangible assets
  Other assets

Liabilities:
  Current liabilities
  Long-term liabilities
Stockholders' (owners') equity:
  Contributed capital
  Retained earnings

Exhibit 4.2 illustrates a classified balance sheet for the Shein Company as of December 31, 19x8. Table 4.1 provides explanations of typical balance sheet accounts.

Exhibit 4.2

Shein Company
Balance Sheet
December 31, 19x8

Assets

Current Assets:		
Cash	$ 35,000	
Temporary Investments (market value, $22,000)	18,000	
Accounts Receivable (less allowance for uncollectible accounts of		
$9,000)	101,000	
Notes Receivable, Short-term	15,000	
Interest Receivable	300	
Inventory	105,100	
Supplies on Hand	800	
Unexpired Insurance	1,200	
Total Current Assets		$276,400
Long-term Investments and Funds:		
Investment in Rein Company Common Stock	$ 55,000	
Bond Sinking Fund	17,600	
Total Long-term Investments and Funds		72,600
Plant Assets:		
Land	$ 28,000	
Building (less accumulated depreciation of $80,000)	70,000	
Equipment (less accumulated depreciation of $25,000)	35,000	
Total Plant Assets		133,000
Intangible Assets:		
Goodwill	$ 30,000	
Organization Costs	10,000	
Total Intangible Assets		40,000
Other Assets:		
Used Equipment Held for Sale		8,000
Total Assets		$530,000

Liabilities

Current Liabilities:		
Accounts Payable	$ 65,300	
Notes Payable, Short-term	20,000	
Interest Payable	2,600	
Income Taxes Payable	8,700	
Salaries Payable	3,400	
Total Current Liabilities		$100,000
Long-term Liabilities		
8% Bonds Payable (maturity 10 years after balance sheet date)		100,000
Total Liabilities		$200,000

Stockholders' Equity

Contributed Capital:		
Common Stock, $10 par, 20,000 shares authorized, issued, and		
outstanding	$200,000	
Contributed Capital in Excess of Par Value	40,000	
Total Contributed Capital		$240,000
Retained Earnings		90,000
Total Stockholders' Equity		$330,000
Total Liabilities and Stockholders' Equity		$530,000

Current Assets   **Current assets** consist of cash and other assets that can be converted into cash or consumed within 12 months after the balance sheet date or within the normal operating cycle of the entity, whichever is longer. Assets classified as current assets include, in addition to cash, temporary or short-term investments, accounts receivable, short-term notes receivable, interest receivable, inventories, supplies, and various types of prepaid expenses. Temporary investments can be sold to satisfy cash needs on very short notice. Accounts receivable, short-term notes receivable, and interest receivable are expected to result in the receipt of cash within the period required for classification as current assets. Inventories of merchandise will be sold for cash or on credit. When merchandise is sold on credit, cash payment is usually expected to occur within a short period of time, such as 30 days or 60 days. Supplies and prepaid expenses are advance payments for services or benefits to be consumed in the current and the following accounting period(s). (See Exhibit 4.2.)

Current assets are usually presented in the order of their decreasing liquidity. That is, current assets that are more readily convertible into cash or that are expected to be realized in the form of cash are listed before less liquid current assets. (See the current assets in Exhibit 4.2.)

The **normal operating cycle** of an entity is the average length of time that elapses between the use of cash to purchase merchandise (or provide services) and the subsequent realization of cash from the sale of that merchandise (or the performance of those services). The following diagram illustrates the various stages within the normal operating cycle:

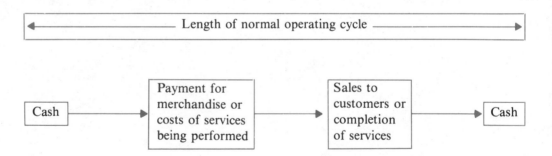

During the normal operating cycle of a merchandising company, goods are purchased, inventoried, and sold; also, customers are billed and collections made from customers for credit sales. The normal operating cycle varies from one type of business to another. Supermarkets have a relatively short operating cycle because goods turn over frequently and sales are usually on a cash basis. However, a machine manufacturer may have an operating cycle of more than one year because of the time that it takes to produce the equipment. Businesses that sell goods on an installment basis, like appliance dealers, may also have an operating cycle of more than one year because of the time required to complete collection of the installments. When the operating cycle exceeds one year, inventories and receivables related to the entity's ordinary business activities are classified as current assets even though cash will not be realized from them during the 12 months after the balance sheet date.

To provide additional information that is useful to users, parenthetical expressions and special accounts are often used. For example, the market value of temporary investments is disclosed parenthetically in the Shein Company balance sheet to indicate the amount of cash that could have been realized from the sale of the investments on December 31, 19x8. The maturity date of the bond liability and the number of shares of stock authorized, issued, and outstanding, and the par value of the stock are also presented parenthetically.

In Exhibit 4.1 the provision for customer account balances estimated to be uncollectible ($2,000) was disclosed parenthetically, and this amount was deducted before including accounts receivable in total assets. Thus, only the amount expected to be collected ($43,000) is reported as the balance of accounts receivable.

Long-term Investments and Funds   Some entities invest in the stocks or bonds of other entities in order to control them or to establish good business relationships with customers or suppliers. The reasons for long-term investments will be explained further in Units 29 and 30. Such **investments and funds** are committed for **long-term** or indefinite periods. Because the company does not intend to liquidate these investments to provide cash for current operations, a separate, noncurrent classification is used to report these investment balances.

When bonds are issued, an agreement to accumulate funds to pay the debt at maturity may be included in the contract with the bondholders. The long-term, restricted nature of these funds requires the use of a separate, noncurrent classification to report the amount of funds accumulated. Other funds of this nature may be maintained by the entity and reported in this classification.

The balance sheet in Exhibit 4.2 includes in the long-term investments and funds account: investment in Rein Company common stock and bond sinking fund. The long-term investments and funds classification may also include the balances of noncurrent receivables not related to the entity's ordinary business activities, assets held for speculative purposes, and cash balances that are restricted and cannot be used to carry out current operations or to meet current obligations.

Plant (or Fixed) Assets   Assets of a tangible or physical nature that will provide benefits to an entity over several accounting periods are called **plant assets** or *fixed* assets. Plant assets include land, buildings, and various types of equipment used in carrying out business operations. The matching principle requires that a portion of the cost of plant assets, other than land, be assigned to expense during each period in which these assets are used. This process is called **depreciation.** Depreciation is a process that allocates the cost of plant assets to expense over the periods that will benefit from their use. It does *not* provide replacement funds or reflect the current value of plant assets on the balance sheet.

Depreciation expense may be calculated by several methods (see Unit 21). For now we will use only the *straight-line depreciation method,* which assigns the same amount of cost to expense during each period. Estimates of the asset's expected useful life to the entity and its residual or salvage value at the end of its useful life must be made in order to calculate depreciation expense.

Assume, for example, that an asset with a cost of $20,000 and an expected residual value of $2,000 is to be depreciated over its expected useful life of ten years. Depreciation expense for each year, using the straight-line method, is calculated as follows:

$$\frac{\text{depreciation}}{\text{expense}} = \frac{\text{cost} - \text{residual value}}{\text{expected useful life}} = \frac{\$20,000 - 2,000}{10} = \$1,800 \text{ per year}$$

Plant assets are reported on the balance sheet at their book value, that is, their value as recorded on the entity's accounting records. The **book value** of plant assets is their cost less accumulated depreciation to date. The plant asset accounts, however, are not directly reduced as depreciation is recorded. At the same time that depreciation is recorded as an expense, the same amount is recorded in a contra or offset account called accumulated depreciation.

Contra or **offset accounts** are used in determining the value of certain asset, liability, owners' equity, revenue, and expense accounts. Their balance is always deducted from the balance of the account to which they are related. In this unit accumulated depreciation, allowance for uncollectible accounts, dividends paid, and an owner's drawing account are examples of contra accounts used in valuing certain balance sheet accounts. Additional contra accounts will be introduced in Unit 5.

In the example, depreciation expense was $1,800 each year. This amount is also added to the accumulated depreciation account each year. Thus, the asset's book value is $18,200 at the end of one year ($20,000 − 1,800), $16,400 at the end of two years [$20,000 − (2 × $1,800)], and so on, until, at the end of its ten-year useful life, the book value is $2,000 [$20,000 − (10 × $1,800)]. Note that the asset's book value is equal to its residual or salvage value after it is depreciated for its full useful life. Book value can also be referred to as the undepreciated cost of an asset because it represents the portion of the cost not yet assigned to expense.

Depreciation is not recorded on land because land tends to have an indefinite life and often increases in value. The book value of land, then, is its recorded cost. Land improvements, such as shrubbery, fences, parking lots, sidewalks, and so on, are subject to depreciation because of their limited life and the need for their replacement. In Exhibit 4.2 land is reported at its book value, which is equal to its cost of $28,000; buildings and equipment are reported at their book value of $70,000 and $35,000 respectively. The accumulated depreciation for each asset is indicated parenthetically.

Intangible Assets   Assets that usually do not have a tangible or physical nature are called **intangible assets.** Examples include patents, copyrights, franchises, trademarks and tradenames, organization costs, leaseholds, and goodwill. They represent some right that is acquired by the entity and will provide benefits for several accounting periods.

The cost of an intangible asset is assigned to expense over its expected useful life or legal life, whichever is shorter. This process, called **amortization,** is similar to depreciation. Normally intangible assets are amortized by the same amount over each period expected to benefit. Unlike depreciation, however, the annual charge for amortization expense is usually deducted directly from the intangible asset account. A contra or offset account for accumulated amortization is not used very often. Thus, the balance of an intangible asset is likely to be its unamortized cost.

Some entities add another classification for assets like organization costs and other prepayments expected to benefit several accounting periods. This classification is called **deferred charges.** Items recorded in this classification are similar to the prepaid expenses recorded as current assets. The primary difference is that deferred charges benefit several accounting periods while prepaid expenses benefit primarily the current period. In Exhibit 4.2 organization costs and goodwill are reported as intangible assets.

Other Assets   This classification is used to report any assets that cannot be properly classified elsewhere. Examples of items in this classification are land held for future use and plant assets held for sale because they are no longer being used. In Exhibit 4.2 equipment no longer being used is reported under other assets.

Current Liabilities   Obligations that require the use of current assets or that result in other current obligations are classified as **current liabilities.** As with current assets, a period of 12 months, or the normal operating cycle if longer, is used to determine which liabilities will be classified as current. Current liabilities include accounts payable, short-term notes payable, obligations for expenses incurred but not paid at the end of the accounting period, obligations for money withheld or collected on behalf of the government or other third parties, and obligations related to revenues collected in advance. Although current liabilities are not reported on the balance sheet in any definite order, the sequence just given is traditional. Business entities often incur expenses, such as salaries, interest, income taxes, and property taxes, which are not paid at the end of the accounting period. Under the matching principle, these expenses must be assigned to the current period, and a related liability must be recorded at the same time. Exhibit 4.2 shows accounts payable, short-term notes payable, and obligations for expenses incurred but not paid at the end of the accounting period as current liabilities.

Employers are required to withhold income and social security taxes and deduct union dues and certain fringe benefit contributions from employees' wages, and collect sales and excise taxes from customers. Liabilities for the amounts withheld, deducted, or collected are recorded since the entity must remit these amounts to the appropriate government agency or other third party.

Another type of current liability is the obligation related to revenues collected in advance. The customer is entitled to goods classified as current assets or to goods or services that will require the use of current assets. The obligation arising from revenues collected in advance is classified as a current liability if the revenue will be earned within 12 months, or during the normal operating cycle if longer. Various titles are used for this account, including rent collected in advance, unearned subscription revenue, advances from customers, unearned fees, and fees received in advance. The term **deferred revenue** is frequently used to refer to revenues that are collected in advance but are earned in a subsequent accounting period.

Long-term Liabilities   Obligations that are due more than 12 months after the balance sheet date, and consequently require resources that become available in those later accounting periods are classified as **long-term liabilities.** Examples of long-term liabilities include long-term notes payable, bonds payable, mortgages payable, and long-term lease obligations. In Exhibit 4.2 the long-term liability is an obligation for bonds that are due ten years after the balance sheet date.

Stockholders' Equity   The two major subclassifications for stockholders' equity in a corporation are contributed capital and retained earnings. The **contributed capital** subclassification is used to report the amounts invested by the owners (stockholders). When a single class of stock is issued by the corporation, the title of the account used for the par or stated value of the stock will be common stock or capital stock. The par or stated value must be specified for each share of stock according to state incorporation laws; it does not indicate the actual value of the stock or the amount at which the stock will necessarily be sold (this concept is discussed further in Unit 26). The par or stated value per share, the number of shares authorized in the company's charter from the state, and the number of shares issued and outstanding are disclosed parenthetically or in notes to the statements.

Contributed capital also includes accounts for other contributions made to the corporation and for any amounts received in excess of the par or stated value for the stock issued. In Exhibit 4.2 Shein Company reported that it was authorized to issue and had issued all 20,000 shares of its $10 par value common stock. Also, as the exhibit shows, the company received $40,000 in excess of the par value on the stock issued.

The second major subclassification for stockholders' equity is **retained earnings.** State laws require that profits retained in a corporation be reported separately from contributions made to the company. The account in which retained profits are recorded can be titled retained earnings, retained income, or profits reinvested in the business. In Exhibit 4.2 the balance in this account is $90,000.

Profit distributions to stockholders, called **dividends,** are generally limited to the amount of profits earned by the company. Some companies use only the retained earnings account, reducing it when dividends are declared. Other companies use a special account when dividends are declared. The balance of this account, titled dividends, dividends declared, or dividends paid, is then transferred to and reduces retained earnings at the end of the accounting period. This special account is not reported on the balance sheet.

Owners' Equity in Noncorporate Businesses   In sole proprietorships the owners' investments and profits retained in the business are reported in a single account called a *capital account*. During the accounting period another account, called a *drawing account,* is used to record amounts drawn from the business for personal use by the owners. Since an owner does not actually earn and receive a salary, regular drawings in anticipation of profits may be made. These drawings are similar to dividends. The balance in the drawing account is transferred to and reduces the capital account at the end of the accounting period. Thus, the drawing account does not appear on the balance sheet.

The capital and drawing accounts are usually prefixed by the owner's name, for example, John Smith, capital and John Smith, drawing. In a partnership, there is a capital account and a drawing account for each partner. The owners' equity section on the balance sheet for these forms of businesses will be titled capital, proprietor's equity, or perhaps partners' equity.

Alternate Formats

The balance sheet is usually presented in one of two formats—the account form and the report form—although other formats are acceptable. Exhibit 4.1 illustrates the **account form,** in which assets are reported on the left and liabilities and owners' equity on the right. The account form is normally used in published annual reports, with assets presented on the left-hand page and liabilities and owners' equity on the right-hand page of two facing pages. This arrangement is more suitable for comparative data, that is, data for two or more years, and enhances the readability of the statement. The accounts follow the usual classifications.

Exhibit 4.2 illustrates the **report form.** The accounts are properly classified, and the classifications are usually presented in the traditional sequence.

Valuation of Assets and Liabilities

Different valuation bases or approaches are used in accounting practice to measure and valuate assets reported on the balance sheet. Although the principal valuation basis is cost, alternative bases are sometimes used in order to better measure net income and to present more relevant information regarding financial condition. Accounts receivable, for example, are reported at their **net realizable value,** that is, the amount of cash expected to be collected from customers. A provision for uncollectible accounts is deducted from the amount due from customers. Damaged or obsolete merchandise is also reported at net realizable value, that is, the expected selling price less expected reconditioning and disposal costs. Short-term and long-term investments in common stock are reported at the **lower-of-cost-or-market value** to indicate the amount that would be realized if the securities were liquidated. Inventories are often reported at lower-of-cost-or-market to indicate the expected contribution to future revenues represented by the ending inventory. These alternative valuation bases also result in charges against current revenues for costs that have expired or from which future benefits will not be derived. When the provision for uncollectible accounts is established, a charge is recorded for uncollectible accounts expense. When the market value of temporary investments or inventory is lower than cost, a loss is recorded to show the decline in value.

Accounting has been criticized for not reporting assets at **current values.** Current values could be determined by current market (selling) prices, current replacement costs (cost of replacing with a similar asset), or other measures that reflect current value. In recent years rapid inflation rates have renewed interest in the effects of inflation on financial position and operating results and in the relevance of current values to decision making. The SEC has decided that information on the current replacement costs of inventories, cost of goods sold, plant assets, and depreciation must be made available to users of financial statements.[1] Late in 1979 the FASB issued a statement that requires certain large corporations to disclose similar information on current values and the effects of changes in general purchasing power. Current value accounting and restatement of financial statements to reflect changes in the purchasing power of the dollar are considered in Chapter 13.

Receivables and liabilities are measured and reported at their **present value,** that is, their current cash equivalent. Measurement and valuation at present value exclude future interest from the account balances. Thus, the accounts are reported at the amount of cash required to settle the obligation at the current date. Receivables and payables related to normal business activities and due in customary trade terms not exceeding one year are recorded and reported at the amount of the transaction. It is customary not to charge interest on amounts due in these transactions; also, the amount of interest involved would be considered insignificant.

The appropriate methods of measuring and valuing specific assets and liabilities are discussed in later chapters.

REVIEW PROBLEM

The following information is taken from the records of Flint Company for 19x4.

Office equipment	$180,000	Accounts receivable	$150,000
Accumulated depre-		Accounts payable	116,200
ciation—office		Notes payable,	
equipment	72,000	long-term	60,000
Store equipment	200,000	Common stock	250,000
Accumulated depre-		Notes receivable,	
ciation—store		short-term	15,000
equipment	80,000	Prepaid expenses	8,000
Cash	31,000	Contributed capital in	
Inventory	125,000	excess of par value	40,000
Organization costs	12,000	Investment in Saginaw	
Salaries payable	6,000	Corp. common	
Land held for future		stock	80,000
building site	24,000	Income taxes payable	21,300
		Allowance for uncol-	
		lectible accounts	18,000
		Retained earnings	?

The company was authorized to issue 30,000 shares of $10 par value common stock; 25,000 shares of common stock were outstanding throughout 19x4.

Required   Prepare a classified balance sheet for Flint Company as of December 31, 19x4, in good form.

---

[1]Accounting Series Release No. 190 (SEC, March 23, 1976).

Solution to review problem

Flint Company
Balance Sheet
December 31, 19x4

Assets

Current assets:		
Cash	$ 31,000	
Accounts receivable (less allowance for uncollectible accounts of $18,000)	132,000	
Notes receivable, short-term	15,000	
Inventory	125,000	
Prepaid expenses	8,000	
Total current assets		$311,000
Long-term investments and funds:		
Investment in Saginaw Corp. common stock		80,000
Plant assets:		
Store equipment (less accumulated depreciation of $80,000)	$120,000	
Office equipment (less accumulated depreciation of $72,000)	108,000	
Total plant assets		228,000
Intangible assets:		
Organization costs		12,000
Other assets:		
Land held for future building site		24,000
Total assets		$655,000

Liabilities

Current liabilities:		
Accounts payable	$116,200	
Income taxes payable	21,300	
Salaries payable	6,000	
Total current liabilities		$143,500
Long-term liabilities:		
Notes payable, long-term		60,000
Total liabilities		$203,500

Stockholders' Equity

Contributed capital:		
Common stock, $10 par, 30,000 shares authorized, 25,000 shares issued and outstanding	$250,000	
Contributed capital in excess of par	40,000	
Total contributed capital	$290,000	
Retained earnings	161,500*	
Total stockholders' equity		451,500
Total liabilities and stockholders' equity		$655,000

Computation of retained earnings. Total assets must equal total liabilities plus stockholders' equity; this equality is expressed by the accounting equation, $A = L + OE$. Also, owners' equity in a corporation consists of contributed capital and retained earnings. Therefore, retained earnings can be calculated as follows:

assets = liabilities + owners' equity
assets = liabilities + contributed capital + retained earnings
retained earnings = assets − liabilities − contributed capital
retained earnings = $655,000 − 203,500 − 290,000
retained earnings = $161,500

SUMMARY

The form, content, purpose, and model of the balance sheet were discussed in this unit. Each classification within the assets, liabilities, and owners' equity accounts was examined. Table 4.1 explained the various accounts frequently found on balance sheets. Exhibits 4.1 and 4.2 provided examples of the two most commonly used balance sheet formats. Finally, the basis of valuing assets and liabilities was explained briefly.

REVIEW QUESTIONS

4-1   What is the purpose of a balance sheet? Is this purpose consistent with the objectives of financial accounting? Explain.

4-2   Describe the basic model for a balance sheet. Define the major components of the balance sheet model.

4-3   Define current assets and the normal operating cycle. How does the normal operating cycle affect the classification of assets?

4-4   What is a contra or offset account? Give two examples of contra or offset accounts related to assets. How are the contra or offset accounts reported on the balance sheet?

4-5   What types of accounts are classified as long-term investments and funds?

4-6   Define plant (or fixed) assets and intangible assets. How are the two similar? How are they different?

4-7   Explain the concept of depreciation as it is traditionally used in accounting.

4-8   Define current liabilities. How are current liabilities linked to current assets?

4-9   What are the two subclassifications for owners' equity in a corporation? What, in general, is included under each subclassification?

4-10   How is owners' equity reported in a noncorporate business entity?

4-11   Describe two alternate formats for a balance sheet. When can each of the two forms be used?

4-12   The valuation of assets on the balance sheet is a mixture of cost and various other values, such as market value, net realizable value, etc. Explain.

4-13   Liabilities are measured and reported at their present value or current cash equivalent. Explain.

EXERCISES

4-1 Each of the following cases involves the basic accounting equation: $A = L + OE$. Determine the missing element for each case.

Case A Total assets = $180,000; current liabilities = $40,000; stockholders' equity = $110,000; long-term liabilities = $_____

Case B Current assets = $60,000; current liabilities = $45,000; long-term liabilities = $50,000; contributed capital = $100,000; retained earnings = $25,000; all other assets = $_____

Case C Total assets = $30,000; total liabilities = $120,000; contributed capital = $145,000; retained earnings = $_____

4-2 Rearrange the following current assets in order of decreasing liquidity:

Supplies inventory	Prepaid insurance
Accounts receivable	Cash
Inventory	Temporary investments
Notes receivable, short-term	Interest receivable

4-3 Using the following information, prepare an unclassified balance sheet for the Clements Company at the close of its fiscal period, January 31.

Richard Clements, capital	$?
Land	3,000
Accounts payable	8,000
Equipment	10,000
Cash	6,000
Notes payable	5,000
Building	25,000
Accounts receivable	12,000

4-4 The following selected account balances were taken from the ledger for Madison Corp. at the end of its accounting period, December 31, 19x6:

Temporary investments	$15,000	Organization cost	$ 5,000
Equipment	30,000	Cash	24,000
Accounts payable	14,000	Inventory	21,000
Capital stock, $10 par		Notes payable,	
10,000 shares authorized		long-term	10,000
4,000 shares issued at par	?	8% bonds payable,	
Accounts receivable	18,000	issued at par	30,000
Salaries payable	1,000	Income taxes payable	3,000
Accumulated depreciation	9,000	Retained earnings	?

Required Prepare a classified balance sheet as of December 31, 19x6.

4-5   Peninsula Company uses the following balance sheet classifications:

a.	Current assets		e.	Other assets
b.	Long-term investments and funds		f.	Current liabilities
			g.	Long-term liabilities
c.	Plant assets		h.	Contributed capital
d.	Intangible assets		i.	Retained earnings

For each of the following accounts, write the letter of the correct account classification in the space provided. If the account should be reported on another statement, use a zero for your answer.

_____   **(1)**   allowance for uncollectible accounts
_____   **(2)**   contributed capital in excess of par
_____   **(3)**   patents
_____   **(4)**   cash
_____   **(5)**   investment in Isle Corp. stock
_____   **(6)**   accounts payable
_____   **(7)**   land
_____   **(8)**   accounts receivable
_____   **(9)**   interest payable
_____   **(10)**   common stock
_____   **(11)**   inventory (ending)
_____   **(12)**   land held for sale
_____   **(13)**   temporary investments
_____   **(14)**   salaries payable
_____   **(15)**   mortgage payable
_____   **(16)**   retained earnings
_____   **(17)**   building
_____   **(18)**   accumulated depreciation—building
_____   **(19)**   notes receivable, long-term
_____   **(20)**   goodwill
_____   **(21)**   prepaid expenses
_____   **(22)**   bonds payable
_____   **(23)**   depreciation expense—building
_____   **(24)**   supplies on hand

PROBLEMS

4-1   Following are the balance sheet accounts and their balances for Hoagie Corp at the end of 19x8:

Accounts payable	$17,100	Cash	$18,000
Temporary investments	6,500	Equipment	16,800
Land	10,000	Accumulated depreciation,	
Buildings	87,500	equipment	6,400
Accumulated depreciation,		Accounts receivable	26,800
buildings	8,000	Allowance for uncollectible	
Inventory	18,600	accounts	1,400

Salaries payable	800	Retained earnings	39,000
Common stock, $10 par	50,000	Mortgage payable	45,000
Contributed capital in		Prepaid expenses	900
excess of par	15,000	Income taxes payable	7,500
Notes receivable, short-		Interest receivable	100
term	5,000		

Required   Prepare a classified balance sheet at the end of 19x8.

4-2   The following data were taken from the records of Borgia Company at the end of 19x4:

Accounts receivable	$ 51,000	Patents	$ 14,000
Bonds payable	100,000	Accounts payable	44,000
Machinery	48,000	Common stock, $5 par	100,000
Accumulated depreciation,		Supplies on hand	1,500
machinery	15,000	Interest payable	200
Land	24,000	Buildings	185,000
Notes payable, short-term	10,000	Accumulated depreciation,	
Cash	36,000	buildings	22,500
Inventories	63,000	Long-term investment in	
Allowance for uncollectible		Medici Co. stock	18,000
accounts	2,500	Retained earnings	?
Unexpired insurance	2,000	Contributed capital in	
Salaries payable	1,800	excess of par	35,000
		Advances from customers	3,500

Required   Prepare a classified balance sheet at the end of 19x4.

4-3   The bookkeeper for Fanning Company prepared the following balance sheet:

Fanning Company Balance Sheet For the Year Ended December 31, 19x4		
Assets		
Current Assets:		
Cash	$ 25,000	
Inventories	40,000	
Receivables	35,000	
Total Current Assets		$100,000
Long-term Investments and Funds:		
Temporary Investments	$ 30,000	
Investment in Hamm Corp. Common Stock	15,000	
Total Long-term Investments and Funds		45,000
Fixed Assets:		
Land	$ 20,000	
Building	150,000	
Equipment	90,000	
Total	$260,000	
Less: Accumulated Depreciation	28,000	
Total Fixed Assets		232,000

Intangible Assets and Deferred Charges:		
Organization Costs	$ 4,000	
Patents	8,000	
Prepaid Insurance	600	
Office Supplies	400	
Total Intangible Assets and Deferred Charges		13,000
Total Assets		$390,000

Liabilities and Stockholders' Equity

Current Liabilities:		
Accounts Payable	$ 32,000	
Long-term Notes, due July 1, 19x5	5,000	
Accrued Expenses	3,000	
Total Current Liabilities		$ 40,000
Long-term Liabilities:		
Long-term Notes, due in equal installments on July 1, 19x6 and 19x7		10,000
Deferred Revenues:		
Advances from Customers		2,000
Contributed Capital:		
Common Stock, $10 par	$200,000	
Contributed Capital in Excess of Par	60,000	
Total Contributed Capital		260,000
Earned Surplus		78,000
Total Liabilities and Stockholders' Equity		$390,000

Required   List the weaknesses and errors in the balance sheet presented.

4-4   During the accounting period Kain Company keeps its records on a cash basis. The following balances were on the books at the end of 19x3:

Cash	$22,500
Equipment (ten-year life)	10,000
Accumulated depreciation (for 19x1 and 19x2)	2,000
Kain, capital (as of Jan. 1, 19x3)	48,000
Kain, drawing	12,000

The CPA hired by the company determined that the additional information needed to prepare a balance sheet as of December 31, 19x3 included:

Outstanding bills for operating expenses	$ 6,500
Balances due from customers (net of a provision for uncollectible accounts of $1,400)	19,600
Prepaid expenses	800
Accrued salaries	600
Unsold merchandise on hand at December 31, 19x3	16,200

Required   Prepare an unclassified balance sheet for Kain Company as of December 31, 19x3.

4-5 Refer to the balance sheet for Procter & Gamble presented in the appendix to Unit 6 to answer the following questions:

a. What is the end of the company's accounting period?
b. What asset classifications are used by the company?
c. What liability classifications are used by the company?
d. How are the following items disclosed on the balance sheet?
   (1) provision for uncollectible accounts
   (2) accumulated depreciation
e. Did the following items increase or decrease during the fiscal year ended June 30, 1978?
   (1) current assets
   (2) plant assets
   (3) total assets
   (4) current liabilities
   (5) stockholders' equity
   (6) net assets

Unit 5
The Income Statement

I am indeed rich, since my income is superior to my expense. . . .
Edward Gibbon (1737–1794), Autobiography

The second basic financial statement to be discussed is the income statement. It reports the results of an entity's operations during a specified period of time. The model, purpose, form, and content of the income statement are examined in this unit.

Performance Objectives

Upon completing this unit you should be able to:

1. define and use the accounting terms introduced in this unit.
2. determine each of the following:
   a. net income using the accrual or cash basis of accounting
   b. earnings per share
   c. gross margin
   d. gross margin percentage
   e. markup on cost
   f. return on total investment
   g. return on owners' investment
3. describe the form, content, purpose, and model of an income statement.
4. determine the proper classification for revenues and expenses on a classified income statement.
5. prepare, in good form, a classified income statement.

Purpose and Model

The income statement reports the results of business operations, net income or net loss, for an entity for a specified period of time. Users of financial statements are interested in an indicator of profitability, because profits enable a company to pay dividends, expand operations, pay debts, meet interest requirements on debts, and so forth. Profits also tend to increase the value of the owners' investment, and profitability over a series of years tends to predict future profitability. Thus, the income statement is of primary interest to many users. In addition to reporting net income, the income statement lists the major types of revenues and expenses, indicates earnings per share of common stock, and provides other descriptive information that has a bearing on the entity's profit performance.

Income Statement Model   The basic model for the income statement is expressed by the equation:

$$\text{revenues} - \text{expenses} = \text{net income}$$
$$R \quad - \quad E \quad = \quad NI$$

Revenues are the inflow of resources from the performance of services or the sale of goods. The resources received may be cash, particularly in such firms as grocery stores, department stores, and gas stations. Often, however, there are claims to cash that arise from sales made or services performed on credit; these claims are recorded and reported as accounts receivables.

Expenses are incurred to generate revenue. They are actually costs that have been consumed in business operations or that expire during the accounting period. Expenses may be recorded when cash is paid or an obligation to pay cash at a future date results from a credit transaction.

Net income is the excess of revenues over expenses for the period covered by the income statement. If expenses exceed revenues, a *net loss* is incurred for the period. For corporations net income is translated into **earnings per share** (EPS) of common stock. The basic formula for a simple earnings per share computation is:

$$\text{earnings per share (EPS)} = \frac{\text{net income}}{\substack{\text{weighted average number of} \\ \text{shares of common stock outstanding}}}$$

An example of a simple income statement is presented in Exhibit 5.1. It has a three-line heading, and the body of the statement reports the major sources of revenue and expense. The heading consists of the company name, statement title, and a date line that describes the period covered by the income statement—that is, the period during which the reported revenue was earned and the expenses incurred. Since the Rein Company had 10,000 shares of common stock outstanding, earnings per share was computed as follows:

$$\text{EPS} = \frac{\$31,950}{10,000} = \$3.20$$

Exhibit 5.1

Rein Company Income Statement For the Year Ended December 31, 19x8	
Revenues:	
Sales	$200,000
Interest Revenue	1,000
Total Revenues	$201,000
Expenses:	
Cost of Goods Sold	$100,000
Salaries	42,000
Utilities	3,200
Depreciation	11,600
Income Taxes	7,050
Interest Expense	800
Miscellaneous Expenses	4,400
Total Expenses	$169,050
Net Income	$ 31,950
Earnings per Share of Common Stock	$3.20

Because EPS is of particular interest to investors and creditors, its appearance on corporation income statements is mandatory. The EPS figure is reported immediately below net income (see Exhibit 5.1). Sole proprietorships and partnerships do not present an EPS figure because they do not issue common stock.

Extension of Accounting Equation   Net income earned by an entity accrues to its owner(s), that is, net income increases the ownership interest in the entity. Similarly, a net loss decreases owners' equity. Thus, the accounting equation can be extended by adding net income to (or deducting net loss from) the right side of the equation:

Accounting equation:

$$\text{assets} = \text{liabilities} + \text{owners' equity}$$
$$A = L + OE$$

Extension of accounting equation to include net income (that is, revenues minus expenses):

$$\text{assets} = \text{liabilities} + \text{owners' equity} + \text{net income}$$
$$A = L + OE + NI$$
$$\text{assets} = \text{liabilities} + \text{owners' equity} + (\text{revenues} - \text{expenses})$$
$$A = L + OE + (R - E)$$

The extended accounting equation reflects one type of link between the balance sheet and income statement. When revenues exceed expenses, net income has been earned and owners' equity increases. For example, assume a company reports the following figures, including a net income of $60,000. In this case, owners' equity also increases by $60,000:

$$A = L + OE + (R - E)$$
$$\$550,000 = \$220,000 + \$270,000 + (\$480,000 - \$420,000)$$
$$\$550,000 = \$220,000 + \$270,000 + (\$60,000)$$
$$\$550,000 = \$220,000 + \$330,000$$

Other links between the balance sheet and income statement relate to revenue realization and expense recognition. Assets are received when revenue is recorded. Also, assets such as supplies, prepaid insurance, buildings, and equipment are charged to expense as they are consumed or used in generating revenues.

Revenue Realization

The revenues reported on the income statement for an accounting period are determined by the revenue or realization principle. This principle states that revenue should be recognized when it is realized (in other words, when it is earned). Realization occurs when both the earning process is fully or substantially completed and an exchange has taken place.

For most merchandise sales, these two conditions are met at the point of sale (that is, when an exchange occurs) whether or not cash is received by the seller. The point of sale is fixed by the terms of the sales agreement between the seller and the buyer. For example, an exchange occurs when a customer purchases merchandise for cash or credit from a department store. The customer receives the merchandise, and the department store receives cash or a claim to cash within specified credit terms. The earning process for the department store is substantially completed because it has acquired the merchandise from its suppliers or manufacturers, has displayed and advertised it, and has completed the sales agreement with the customer. Although cash may not be received immediately, most customers will pay their bills or, in case they don't, a reasonable estimate of uncollectible accounts can be made and provided for in the period in which the sale occurs.

For services, these two conditions are usually met when the services are completed. An exchange has taken place because the client has received the services, and the provider of the services has received cash or a claim to cash within specified credit terms. The earning process has been substantially completed at this point because the service company has secured the clients and performed the required services. Again, if cash is not received immediately, collection is reasonably assured or a provision for uncollectible accounts can be made.

When services are performed or goods produced over more than one accounting period, revenue is often recognized in each period in order to provide a more accurate report of business profitability. An exchange has taken place because the client has received services or the customer owns goods he or she contracted to have produced; the provider of the services or the producer of the goods has received partial payment or has a claim against the client or customer. The earning process, therefore, is considered substantially completed for the portion of the contract already completed. Revenue may be recognized throughout the production cycle for long-term construction projects (such as bridges, dams, and large building projects) and for the production of manufacturing equipment.

If collection of the full sales price is highly uncertain, revenue is realized only when cash is actually received. Although an exchange has taken place, the earning process is not considered substantially completed until then. For example, assume that shares of stock are received in exchange for land that was offered for sale at $36,000, but that the stock has no established market value. In this case, the revenue from the sale of the land cannot be accurately determined—that is, the revenue cannot be recognized—until the stock is sold for cash.

Expense Recognition

Two accounting principles are applied in determining which expenses to include in the periodic income statement. These are the cost and the matching principles. The cost principle states that the cost of any assets or benefits acquired should be measured by the amount of resources given up or the obligations incurred in an exchange transaction. The exchange price is fixed by the monetary unit, for example, the U.S. dollar.

In a noncash exchange cost is stated at the current cash equivalent. For example, equipment to be used in business operations is purchased for $6,300 cash. The cost of the equipment, then, is the $6,300 cash purchase price. If the equipment had been purchased on credit instead, its cost would be the current cash equivalent price of the obligations—that is, the amount that would be paid in a cash purchase or $6,300.

The distinction between cost and expense is important in determining the expenses assigned to different accounting periods. A **cost** is a measure of the resources expended to acquire assets or services that will be used to generate revenue. If the assets or services are used or consumed in business operations during the current accounting period, the cost becomes an expense. Thus, a simple definition of an **expense** is an expired or consumed cost. For example, the cost of supplies that will be used in business operations is the amount of resources expended to acquire them. At the end of the accounting period the cost of the supplies consumed during the period will be included in operating expenses; the cost of the unused supplies will be reported as an asset on the balance sheet. Assume a company purchases supplies at a cost of $2,600. At the end of the accounting period, supplies with a cost of $700 are unused. This $700 is reported as an asset. The remaining $1,900 ($2,600 − 700) of supplies, used or consumed during the period, is reported as operating expenses.

To summarize, when the expenditure of resources will benefit future periods, the cost is reported as an asset. When the benefits are used or expire, the cost becomes an expense. Although these terms are sometimes used interchangeably, there is a distinction between them that should be kept in mind. The context in which they are used usually indicates the meaning intended.

The matching principle is applied in order to assign costs as expenses during the appropriate accounting period. Some costs are assigned on the basis of their direct association with specific revenues. The cost of products sold and salesmen's commissions, for example, are directly related to the revenue from the sale of the products. These costs are reported as expenses in the same period as the related revenue.

Other costs are associated with the time period in which their benefits are consumed and are reported as expenses in that time period. Depreciation, rent, insurance, supplies used, and property taxes are examples.

Still other costs are assigned to expense in the period when their benefits expire because no future benefits are expected. These costs cannot be deferred (that is, carried forward) to be charged to expense in a future period. Most selling expenses, for example, benefit the current period and not future periods. Likewise, losses from lawsuits, fires, storm damage, and worthless investments do not provide future benefits. Attempts to associate office and officer salaries with revenue over several accounting periods also serve no useful purpose. Costs like these are immediately recognized as expenses when the expenditures or losses occur.

Accounting Concept of Income

The current accounting income concept stresses determining and reporting a single income figure, net income, to provide information that will be useful in decision making. (The question of whether a single income concept satisfies the needs of most users, however, is still to be resolved.) Net income is the excess of revenues over expenses for a specific time period. Revenues and expenses are measured according to accounting principles—in particular, the realization, cost, and matching principles.

Accounting principles are based primarily on completed business transactions and data that can be objectively determined and verified. For example, revenues are not recognized until the earning process is substantially completed and an exchange has taken place. Most expenses are based on historical costs rather than current values because historical costs are more objectively determinable. Some expenses are associated with specific time periods because it would be difficult to match these expenses with the revenues they produce. Other expenses are simply ignored because objective measurement techniques are lacking. Examples of this include costs related to environmental damage caused by a company and costs related to human resources used by the company. Because of the stress on completed transactions and objectively determined data, the accounting concept of income has been criticized by economists, accounting theorists, and financial information users. The concept is also criticized because it accepts alternative accounting practices and it fails to recognize changes in both the purchasing power of the monetary unit and the current value of assets and obligations.

Alternative income concepts proposed by accounting theorists and others also have faults. Nevertheless, they all lead to the apparently sound conclusion that more than one concept of income may be appropriate for user needs. And the first step in selecting the appropriate income concept is determining these user needs.

In this text the measurement and reporting techniques stressed are those that conform to present-day accounting principles. This approach is necessary if the student of accounting is to understand financial statements as they are currently prepared. Where appropriate, however, deficiencies in the current state of the art of accounting and possible remedies are pointed out.

Accrual vs. Cash Basis of Accounting

When the revenue principle and the matching principle are used to record revenues and expenses, respectively, the accrual basis of accounting is applied. The **accrual basis of accounting** is the accounting approach in which revenues are recognized as they are realized and expenses as they are incurred. Under a **cash basis of accounting** revenue is recognized only when cash is collected and expenses only when cash is paid.

There are often lags between the time revenue is realized (earned) and the cash is received. For most merchandise the criteria for revenue realization are usually met at the time of sale. However, cash from credit sales will be received at a later date. When credit sales occur near the end of the accounting period, cash may not be received until the following period. Sometimes cash is received in advance, and the revenue is earned later in the same accounting period or in a later period when the goods are delivered or the services performed.

There are also lags between the time an expense is incurred and the cash is paid. Services may be acquired on credit, in which case the cash is paid later in the same period or in a different one. In other situations, cash may be paid for services to be used in generating revenue later in the same period or in a different one.

To determine an entity's net income properly and report its financial position according to accounting principles, the accrual basis should be used. Some entities, however, use a **modified accrual basis of accounting.** With this approach, revenues and expenses related to normal business activities are recorded on the accrual basis, while other revenues and expenses are recorded on the cash basis. The modified accrual basis may be convenient for record-keeping purposes in some businesses, but any method other than the accrual basis may result in distortions of operating results and financial position. A strict cash basis of accounting, for example, is unlikely, under generally accepted accounting principles, to reflect net income and financial position adequately. However, cash flow information, in addition to accrual basis financial statement data, may be necessary to meet the needs of users. Reporting cash flow information is discussed briefly in Unit 6 and more fully in Unit 32.

Statement Formats

Two general forms of the income statement are commonly used to present operating results: the single-step form and the multiple-step form. Exhibit 5.1 illustrates the **single-step form.** One step is used to determine net income: total expenses are deducted from total revenues. The main exception to this is for extraordinary items, which must be reported in a separate section just before net income (see page 77).

The single-step form is widely used in published financial statements because it is easy to understand. Major types of revenue and expense are reported separately, while miscellaneous, insignificant amounts are aggregated. Net income and the major sources of revenue and expense, which are found on this form, are of primary interest to external users.

The **multiple-step form** is also called a *classified income statement*. Revenues and expenses are classified into two or more categories each, and, as a result, net income is determined in several steps. After each step, the income resulting from the operation is given an appropriate label. The final operation results in net income (or net loss). The basic outline for the multiple-step income statement is as follows:

> Operating revenue
> − *Cost of goods sold*
> Gross margin
> − *Operating expenses*
> Income from operations
> ± *Incidental revenue and expense*
> Income from income taxes and extraordinary items
> − *Income taxes*
> Income before extraordinary items
> ± *Extraordinary items*
> Net income

Exhibit 5.2 illustrates the multiple-step income statement. This form presents more detail regarding revenues and expenses and various income figures that are useful to some users, especially management. However, it requires a greater understanding of financial reporting and accounting and is likely to be useful only to more sophisticated users of financial statements.

Table 5.1 has explanations of typical income statement accounts.

Operating Revenue   This classification is used to report the revenue gained from the entity's primary business activities. For example, an entity engaged only in buying and selling merchandise reports sales revenue in this classification. Related accounts for sales discounts and sales returns and allowances would also appear here. Discounts granted to customers for early payment, the sales price of goods returned, and adjustments in sales price allowed to customers are deducted from gross sales revenue to determine net sales for the period. In Exhibit 5.2 gross sales are $850,000; sales returns and allowances of $4,500 are deducted to determine net sales of $845,500 for 19x8.

For an entity engaged only in providing services, the appropriate revenue account, such as fees earned, service revenues, and so on, is reported in this section. If an entity is engaged in more than one primary business activity, two or more revenue accounts may appear here. For example, a heating and air conditioning contractor may use separate sales revenue accounts for heating equipment and air conditioning

Exhibit 5.2

Shein Company
Income Statement
For the Year Ended December 31, 19x8

Gross sales			$850,000
Less: Sales returns and allowances			4,500
Net sales			$845,500
Cost of goods sold			507,300
Gross margin			$338,200
Operating expenses:			
Selling expenses:			
Sales salaries and commissions	$88,900		
Advertising	14,700		
Delivery expense	12,200		
Depreciation of store equipment	6,600		
Store supplies used	2,100		
Miscellaneous selling expenses	3,400		
Total selling expenses		$127,900	
General and administrative expenses:			
Officers' salaries	$60,000		
Office salaries	36,800		
Depreciation of office equipment	4,400		
Office supplies used	3,200		
Uncollectible accounts expense	8,500		
Miscellaneous general and			
administrative expenses	4,300		
Total general and administrative			
expenses		117,200	
Total operating expenses			245,100
Income from operations			$ 93,100
Incidental revenue and expense			
Interest revenue		$ 4,400	
Gain on sale of investments		7,800	
Total		$ 12,200	
Interest expense		8,900	
Net incidental revenue			3,300
Income before income taxes and extraordinary			
items			$ 96,400
Income taxes			25,310
Income before extraordinary items			$ 71,090
Extraordinary items:			
Storm damage loss (net of tax effect of			
$10,090)			16,410
Net income			$ 54,680
Earnings per share of common stock:			
Income before extraordinary items			$ 3.55
Extraordinary items: Storm damage loss			.82
Net income			$ 2.73

Table 5.1

Typical Income Statement Accounts

Operating Revenues

Sales: the total revenue (cash sales and credit sales) received from the sale of goods to customers; entered on the income statement as gross sales

Sales returns and allowances: the sales price of goods sold to customers but returned for a refund; also includes the amount of any reduction allowed for unsatisfactory or damaged goods received by customers

Sales discounts: reductions in the amount due for goods purchased on credit, given to customers for early payment

Fees earned: the total revenue received from the performance of services for clients or customers

Cost of Goods Sold

Cost of goods sold: the cost of merchandise sold to customers

Operating Expenses

Selling Expenses: all expenses that can be directly identified with the marketing function of a business; these expenses include the costs of purchasing, storing, displaying, advertising, selling, and delivering merchandise; examples include:

   Sales commissions: the portion of the sales price of merchandise sold that is paid to salespeople as compensation for their efforts in making the sales

   Advertising: the cost of promoting and publicizing products or services offered by an entity

   Delivery expense: the cost of shipping goods to customers (when borne by the seller)

General and Administrative Expenses: all expenses, other than those directly related to the marketing function, that are incurred to administer a business and carry out its general office activities; examples include:

   Uncollectible accounts expense: the amount of revenue, previously recorded, that must be written off as uncollectible

   Officers salaries: salaries paid to company executives

Expenses That Vary According to Function: account title indicates the function, e.g., sales salaries, office supplies used, store rent; these include:

   Salaries and wages: compensation paid to employees for services provided to an entity

   Utilities expense: the cost of gas, electricity, water, and phone services used in operating an entity

   Rent expense: the cost of using assets (e.g., buildings and equipment), which are owned by other parties, in operating an entity

   Supplies used: the cost of various supplies used in operating an entity

   Depreciation expense: the cost of plant assets assigned to expense because the assets were used during the period

   Miscellaneous or other expenses: an account used for a variety of relatively minor expenses

Incidental Revenue and Expenses

Interest revenue: revenue earned from charges to customers and others for the use of money owed to the entity and from investments in bonds issued by other entities

Dividend revenue: revenue earned from dividends received on investments in stocks of other companies

Gains from sales of plant assets or investments: profits made when an entity disposes of its plant assets or investments at a price greater than the recorded cost

Interest expense: the cost of using borrowed money or of acquiring assets or services with payment to be made over an extended period of time

Losses from sales of plant assets or investments: losses incurred when an entity disposes of its plant assets or investments at a price below their recorded cost

equipment, as well as separate service revenue accounts for the installation and repair of each type of equipment.

Cost of Goods Sold   The cost of products to entities that sell them is a major expense. Information on the **cost of goods sold** is important in running a business effectively. How to compute this cost is explained in Unit 9. In Exhibit 5.2 the Shein Company reported the cost of goods sold in 19x8 as $507,300.

Gross Margin   The difference between net sales and cost of goods sold is called the **gross margin** or *gross profit*. It indicates the dollar amount by which the cost of the products sold were marked up to cover operating and other expenses and losses, and to earn a profit for the entity. Gross margin in Exhibit 5.2 is $338,200 ($845,500 − 507,300).

Two ratios of interest to some users of financial statements are the **gross margin percentage** (or markup on net sales) and the **markup on cost.** Both ratios indicate the amount that merchandise was marked up in setting selling prices to cover operating expenses and earn a profit. The gross margin percentage expresses this markup as a percentage of selling price, whereas markup on cost expresses it as a percentage of the cost of the merchandise sold. These ratios are determined as follows (the data are from Exhibit 5.2):

$$\frac{\text{gross margin}}{\text{percentage}} = \frac{\text{gross margin}}{\text{net sales}} = \frac{\$338,200}{\$845,500} = 40\%$$

$$\frac{\text{markup on}}{\text{cost}} = \frac{\text{gross margin}}{\text{cost of goods sold}} = \frac{\$338,200}{\$507,300} = 66^2/_3\%$$

Operating Expenses   The expenses necessary to sell products or services and to administer and operate the business on a day-to-day basis are reported as **operating expenses** on the income statement. **Selling expenses** are all expenses related to the sales activities for the period. **General and administrative expenses** are all expenses related to administering and operating the business for the period. Note the types of expenses included in each classification in Exhibit 5.2.

Income from Operations   The difference between net sales and total operating expenses is called **income from operations.** This figure indicates the pretax income from operations, that is, pretax income earned from the primary business activities. Income from operations for the Shein Company for 19x8 is $93,100 ($338,200 − 245,100). Some users feel this is a more relevant income figure than net income because it represents the normal pretax profit to be expected; incidental revenue and expense and extraordinary items, both of which may fluctuate radically from one period to the next, are excluded from income from operations.

Incidental Revenue and Expenses   The net **incidental revenue or expense** for the period is considered outside the scope of primary business activities. Thus, incidental revenues and expenses are reported separately after income from operations. Incidental revenues include interest and dividend revenue, rent revenues (if not a primary business activity), and gains on the sale of investments (if they do not qualify for treatment as an extraordinary item). Incidental expenses include interest expense and losses on the sale of investments (if they do not qualify for treatment as an extraordinary item). Other gains and losses that are not treated as extraordinary items, but that must be disclosed, are also included here. The Shein Company reported incidental revenues totaling $12,200 and incidental expenses of $8,900. The net incidental revenue of $3,300 was then added to income from operations of $93,100 to determine the next income figure of $96,400, *income before income taxes and extraordinary items.*

Income Before Income Taxes and Extraordinary Items   Income taxes are deducted from income before income taxes and extraordinary items to determine the next income figure, which is called **income before extraordinary items.** The income taxes of $25,310 for Shein Company were computed using current income tax rates for corporations.[1] This amount was then deducted from income before income taxes and extraordinary items of $96,400 to determine income before extraordinary items of $71,090.

Sole proprietorships and partnerships are not taxed directly on net income as corporations are. Instead, income from these businesses is included in the individual proprietor's or partners' gross income and is subject to the income tax rates for individuals. Partners' shares of net income are divided according to their profit-loss sharing agreement.

If Shein Company had had no extraordinary items for 19*x8,* net income of $71,090 would have been reported, and the income statement would have appeared as follows:

Income before income taxes	$96,400
Less: Income taxes	25,310
Net income	$71,090
Earnings per share of common stock	$ 3.55

Extraordinary Items   The APB established two criteria for treatment as an **extraordinary item:** (1) The underlying event or transaction must possess a high degree of abnormality and be clearly unrelated or only incidentally related to ordinary and typical business activities and (2) there should be a reasonable expectation that the underlying event or transaction is not likely to recur in the foreseeable future. In determining whether these criteria are met, the political, economic, and geographical environment in which the entity operates must be considered.

The effect of these criteria is to eliminate most items of the type that had been reported as extraordinary items before APB Opinion No. 30 was issued in 1973. In any event, few transactions are treated as extraordinary items by all companies. One that

---

[1]Federal income tax rates for corporations effective at the time the text was written were: 17% on taxable income of $0 to $25,000, 20% of $25,000 to $50,000, 30% of $50,000 to $75,000, 40% of $75,000 to $100,000, and 46% over $100,000.

would be is the gain or loss on early retirement of debt. In most cases, however, the circumstances must be evaluated for each transaction or·event after it has occurred. Examples of transactions or events that may qualify as extraordinary items if material in amount are losses from a major disaster, such as an earthquake; gains or losses from an expropriation of assets by a government; and gains or losses based on a new, pro-hibiting law or regulation.

If only one criterion is met, but the amount is material, separate disclosure of the gain or loss on the income statement or in the notes to the financial statements is re-quired. These unusual or infrequent items would be disclosed in the incidental revenue or expenses section of a classified income statement.

Extraordinary items are reported **net of taxes,** that is, net of their income tax ef-fect, if any. Some extraordinary gains are subject to income taxation, while some ex-traordinary losses are deductible. In calculating the amount of the extraordinary gain to be included in net income, taxes payable on the gain are deducted. Savings in in-come taxes resulting from an extraordinary loss are also deducted in calculating the amount of the loss included in net income. The amount of taxes payable on the gain or saved on the loss is disclosed parenthetically or in the notes. In Exhibit 5.2 Shein Company reported an extraordinary loss, net of taxes, of $16,410. Tax savings of $10,090 were disclosed parenthetically; thus, the loss before tax effects was $26,500 ($16,410 + 10,090). The tax savings related to the loss were calculated using current tax rates.[2]

Net Income   Net income is the final income figure on the income statement. It reflects the entity's profit performance for the accounting period, and therefore is of primary interest to users of financial statements. It is double underlined to emphasize its importance as the final result. Many users calculate the ratio of net income to net sales to determine what portion of each sales dollar ends up as profit. For the Shein Company this ratio is calculated as:

$$\text{ratio of net income to net sales} = \frac{\text{net income}}{\text{net sales}} = \frac{\$ \ 54{,}680}{\$845{,}500} = 6.47\%$$

Earnings per Share   When extraordinary items are reported on the income state-ment, earnings per share should be presented for (1) income before extraordinary items, (2) net extraordinary gain or loss, and (3) net income. The Shein Company had 20,000 shares of common stock outstanding during 19*x8.* Thus, earnings per share of common stock was calculated as follows:

$$\text{Income before extraordinary items: } \frac{\$71{,}090}{20{,}000} = \$3.55$$

---

[2]With income before taxes and extraordinary items of $96,400, $21,400 of the loss is covered by income in the 40% bracket ($96,400 − 75,000 = $21,400). The balance of the loss, $5,100 ($26,500 − 21,400), is covered by income in the 30% bracket. Thus, the tax savings are calculated as follows: ($21,400 × 40%) + ($5,100 × 30%) = $8,560 + $1,530 = $10,090.

$$\text{Extraordinary item, storm damage loss: } \frac{\$16,410}{20,000} = \$.82$$

$$\text{Net income: } \frac{\$54,680}{20,000} = \$2.73$$

If no extraordinary items are reported, a single earnings per share figure for net income is presented. See Exhibit 5.1 for an example.

Return on Investment

In addition to earnings per share, the ratio of net income to net sales, gross margin percentage, and markup on cost percentage, another important ratio for users of financial statements who want to evaluate a business's operating results is **return on investment** (ROI). In calculating this ratio, investment may be defined as either **return on total investment** (total assets or total liabilities and owners' equity) or **return on owners'** (stockholders') **investment.** The ratio expresses the relationship between profit and investment.

Formulas for return on total investment and return on owners' investment follow (calculations are based on data from the financial statements of the Shein Company; see Exhibits 4.2 and 5.2):

$$\frac{\text{return on total}}{\text{investment}^3} = \frac{\text{net income}}{\text{total assets}}$$

$$= \frac{\$54,680}{\$530,000} = 10.32\%$$

$$\frac{\text{return on owners'}}{\text{investment}} = \frac{\text{net income}}{\text{total stockholders' equity}}$$

$$= \frac{\$54,680}{\$330,000} = 16.57\%$$

Return on total investment is a measure of how effectively management used all resources available, including those provided by both creditors and stockholders. Return on owners' investment, however, is a basic measure of an entity's profitability. Stockholders invest in an entity to obtain some return on their investment. This return may occur through the periodic receipt of dividends and/or the disposal of their investment after it has appreciated in value. Return on owners' investment, therefore, is

---

[3]In practice several different approaches are used to calculate return on total investment. For simplicity, we use net income here as the numerator of the ratio. These ratios are explained further in Unit 34.

an indicator of potential return to the stockholders. If a business is profitable, it should be able to pay dividends, and/or the value of its stock should increase.

REVIEW PROBLEM

The following information is taken from the records of the Flint Company for 19x4.

Cost of goods sold	$1,000,000	Sales returns	$ 10,000
Interest revenue	5,000	Sales salaries	231,000
Store rent	48,000	Office salaries	173,000
Depreciation of store		Bad debts expense	18,000
equipment	20,000	Miscellaneous office	
Depreciation of		expenses	3,000
office equipment	18,000	Miscellaneous selling	
Gross sales	1,810,000	expenses	4,000
Income taxes	87,300	Extraordinary item:	
Advertising	32,000	Earthquake loss	
Office rent	36,000	(net of taxes of	
Interest expense	12,000	$14,400)	15,600

During 19x4 there were 25,000 shares of common stock outstanding.

Required   1. Prepare in good form a classified income statement for Flint Company for 19x4.
2. Calculate the gross margin percentage, the markup on cost, and the ratio of net income to net sales.
3. Calculate the return on total investment and the return on owners' investment. See the review problem for Unit 4 for the relevant investment figures.

Solution to review problem

1. See Exhibit 5.3.
2. gross margin percentage $= \dfrac{\text{gross margin}}{\text{net sales}} = \dfrac{\$\ 800,000}{\$1,800,000} = 44.4\%$

   markup on cost $= \dfrac{\text{gross margin}}{\text{cost of goods sold}} = \dfrac{\$\ 800,000}{\$1,000,000} = 80\%$

   $\dfrac{\text{ratio of net income}}{\text{to net sales}} = \dfrac{\text{net income}}{\text{net sales}} = \dfrac{\$\ 107,100}{\$1,800,000} = 5.9\%$

3. $\dfrac{\text{return on total}}{\text{investment}} = \dfrac{\text{net income}}{\text{total assets}} = \dfrac{\$107,100}{\$655,000} = 16.35\%$

$$\text{return on owners'} \atop \text{investment} = \frac{\text{net income}}{\text{total stockholders' equity}}$$

$$= \frac{\$107,100}{\$451,500} = 23.72\%$$

Exhibit 5.3

Flint Company
Income Statement
For the Year Ended December 31, 19x4

Gross sales			$1,810,000
Less: Sales returns			10,000
Net sales			1,800,000
Cost of goods sold			1,000,000
Gross margin			$ 800,000
Operating expenses:			
Selling expenses:			
Sales salaries	$231,000		
Store rent	48,000		
Advertising	32,000		
Depreciation of store equipment	20,000		
Miscellaneous selling expense	4,000		
Total selling expenses		$335,000	
General and administrative expenses:			
Office salaries	$173,000		
Office rent	36,000		
Bad debts expense	18,000		
Depreciation of office equipment	18,000		
Miscellaneous office expenses	3,000		
Total general and administrative expenses		248,000	
Total operating expenses			583,000
Income from operations			$ 217,000
Incidental revenue and expense:			
Interest expense		$ 12,000	
Interest revenue		5,000	
Net incidental expense			$7,000
Income before income taxes and extraordinary items:			$ 210,000
Less: Income taxes			87,300
Income before extraordinary items			$ 122,700
Extraordinary items:			
Earthquake loss (net of taxes of $14,400)			15,600
Net income			$ 107,100
Earnings per share of common stock:			
Income before extraordinary items			$ 4.90
Extraordinary item: Earthquake loss			.62
Net income			$ 4.28

SUMMARY

The form, purpose, content, and model of the income statement were discussed in this unit. The two basic forms, the single-step and multiple-step (or classified) income statement forms, were illustrated (see Exhibits 5.1 and 5.2). All major classifications for revenue and expense and all income figures reported on a classified income statement were explained. A few key financial ratios or statistics were discussed, including earnings per share, the ratio of net income to net sales, gross margin percentage, markup on cost, return on total investment, and return on owners' investment. Typical accounts that appear on the income statement were explained in Table 5.1.

REVIEW QUESTIONS

5-1 What is the purpose of an income statement? Is this purpose consistent with the objectives of financial accounting? Explain.

5-2 Describe the basic model for an income statement. Define the major components of the income statement model. Show how the accounting equation $(A = L + OE)$ can be extended to include revenues and expenses.

5-3 What two conditions are necessary to recognize revenue during the accounting period? How are these conditions related to the revenue or realization principle?

5-4 Define and distinguish between cost and expense.

5-5 How are the cost and matching principles related to the measurement and recognition of expenses during the accounting period?

5-6 Distinguish between the cash and accrual bases of accounting. Which of these two bases is normally in accord with accounting principles?

5-7 Describe two commonly used formats for the income statement. When is each format normally used?

5-8 Define gross margin, gross margin percentage, and markup on cost, and the ratio of net income to net sales.

5-9 Distinguish among income from operations, income before extraordinary items, and net income. Which of these three income figures do you feel is most relevant to financial statement users?

5-10 Describe the two criteria for treating a gain or loss as an extraordinary item. Give three examples of gains or losses that would qualify as extraordinary items if the two criteria are met.

5-11   Define earnings per share (EPS). Why must EPS be presented on the income statement?

5-12   How are extraordinary items reported on the income statement? How are earnings per share presented on the income statement if (a) there are no extraordinary items and (b) there are extraordinary items?

5-13   Define return on investment where investment means (a) total investment and (b) owners' investment. Why are return on investment ratios significant to users of financial statements?

EXERCISES

5-1   Using the following data, prepare an income statement for Randolph Corp. for 19x2, in the single-step format:

Rent expense	$ 12,000
Utilities expense	8,500
Service revenue	140,000
Depreciation expense	6,400
Interest revenue	800
Extraordinary item: Earthquake loss (net of taxes of $9,600)	10,400
Interest expense	900
Salaries expense	62,000
Income taxes	11,000

Assume that 20,000 shares of common stock were outstanding during the year.

5-2   Using the following data, prepare an income statement for Pepp Company for 19x2, in the multiple-step format:

Sales	$352,000
Selling expenses	46,000
Interest expense	2,400
Extraordinary item: Gain on sale of land held for plant site (net of taxes of $7,200)	7,800
General and administrative expenses	38,000
Cost of goods sold	210,000
Sales returns and allowances	2,000
Income taxes	12,100

Assume that 50,000 shares of common stock were outstanding during the year.

5-3   The records for Mandrake, Inc., showed the following information for 19x1, its first year of operation:

Cash receipts:	
Collections from customers	$ 85,600
Bank loan	10,000
Sale of stock	25,000
Interest collected	600
Total	$121,200
Cash disbursements:	
Operating expenses paid	$ 41,000
Interest paid	400
Equipment purchased	4,200
Total	$ 45,600

The company hired a CPA to prepare financial statements at the end of the year. The CPA determined the following:

Outstanding bills for expenses at the end of 19x1	$ 3,600
Amounts due from customers at the end of 19x1	11,100
Depreciation for 19x1	2,500
Unpaid interest at the end of 19x1	200
Income taxes owed for 19x1	10,400

Required   Prepare a single-step income statement for 19x1 using the accrual basis of accounting.

5-4   Meggs Company reported the following figures on its financial statements for 19x2:

Net sales	$630,000
Cost of goods sold	$420,000
Depreciation expense—equipment	$ 8,000
Net income	$ 48,000
Shares of stock outstanding during 19x2	12,000
Total stockholders' equity	$240,000
Total liabilities	$160,000
Equipment	$ 80,000

Required   Calculate the following:

a.   earnings per share
b.   ratio of net income to net sales
c.   gross margin
d.   gross margin percentage
e.   markup on cost
f.   return on total investment
g.   return on owners' investment
h.   expected useful life of equipment

5-5   Dandy Company uses the following classifications of accounts on its income statement:

a.   Operating revenue
b.   Cost of goods sold
c.   Selling expenses
d.   General and administrative expenses
e.   Incidental revenue and expense
f.   Income taxes
g.   Extraordinary items

For each of the following accounts, write the letter of the correct account classification in the space provided.

_____	**(1)**	depreciation of store equipment
_____	**(2)**	interest revenue
_____	**(3)**	cost of goods sold
_____	**(4)**	sales
_____	**(5)**	uncollectible accounts expense
_____	**(6)**	income taxes on operating income
_____	**(7)**	salespeople's commissions
_____	**(8)**	office salaries
_____	**(9)**	sales returns and allowances
_____	**(10)**	storm loss (considered to be unusual and not likely to recur)
_____	**(11)**	interest expense
_____	**(12)**	store supplies used
_____	**(13)**	dividend revenue
_____	**(14)**	miscellaneous office expenses
_____	**(15)**	advertising expense
_____	**(16)**	income tax reduction due to storm loss

5-6   Spencer Corp. had 10,000 shares of common stock outstanding during 19*x3*. The company accountant calculated the following ratios:

> earnings per share: $3.00
> ratio of net income to net sales: 10%
> gross margin percentage: 40%
> markup on cost: 66²/₃%

Assuming an income tax rate of 50%, calculate the figures to complete the following income statement:

Net sales	$_____
Cost of goods sold	_____
Gross margin	_____
Operating expenses	_____
Income from operations	_____
Income taxes	_____
Net income	_____
Earnings per share of common stock	$3.00

PROBLEMS

5-1   The following are data taken from the records of Jeremy Corp. for 19*x7:*

Utilities expense	$ 8,500	Depreciation expense	$ 7,500
Salaries expense	64,000	Miscellaneous expense	3,500

Service revenue	140,000	Earthquake loss	
Interest expense	1,200	(considered to be	
Uncollectible accounts		unusual and not	
expense	3,800	likely to recur), net	
Supplies used	2,500	of taxes of $5,000	15,000
Income taxes	10,300		

Required   Prepare an income statement using the single-step format, assuming 20,000 shares of common stock were outstanding during 19x7.

5-2   The records of Kagle Company indicate the following accounts and balances at the end of 19x7:

Selling expenses	$ 65,000	General and adminis-	
Sales discounts	3,000	trative expenses	$ 54,000
Income taxes	8,600	Cost of goods sold	240,000
Interest expense	2,000	Flood loss (considered	
Sales returns	7,000	to be unusual and	
Interest revenue	1,000	unlikely to recur)	10,000
Cash sales	60,000	Income tax savings	
Credit sales	350,000	due to flood loss	2,200

During 19x7 there were 15,000 shares of common stock outstanding. Assume that total assets and total liabilities at the end of the year were $320,000 and $110,000, respectively.

Required   **a.**   Prepare an income statement for 19x7 using the multiple-step form.
   b.   Calculate the following for 19x7:
   (1)   gross margin percentage
   (2)   markup on cost
   (3)   ratio of net income to net sales
   (4)   return on total investment
   (5)   return on owners' investment

5-3   (This problem covers Units 4 and 5.) The following are account balances from the records of Winmore Company at the end of 19x5:

Cash	$ 28,000	Accumulated depreci-	
Accounts receivable	56,000	ation—buildings	$36,000
Merchandise inventory	70,000	Accumulated depreci-	
Prepaid expenses	3,000	ation—equipment	48,000
Land	17,000	Accounts payable	45,200
Buildings	180,000	Salaries payable	800
Equipment	75,000	Mortgage payable	120,000
Patents	8,000	Cash sales	40,000
Sales returns	2,000	Credit sales	280,000
Cost of goods sold	159,000	Interest revenue	500
Selling expenses	66,000	Income tax savings on	
General expenses	34,000	storm loss	4,000

Interest expense	9,000	Common stock, $10	
Income tax expense		par, 10,000 shares	
(on operating in-		authorized, issued,	
come)	20,200	and outstanding	100,000
Storm loss	10,000	Contributed capital in	
Dividends paid	20,000	excess of par	25,000
Allowance for uncol-		Retained earnings,	
lectible accounts	2,500	January 1, 19x5	55,200

Required   Prepare a classified income statement and a classified balance sheet for the year ended December 31, 19x5, for Winmore Company.

5-4   (This problem covers Units 4 and 5.) The following are account balances for Winsom Corporation at December 31, 19x7:

Cash	$ 42,000
Temporary investments	26,000
Accounts receivable	77,000
Allowance for uncollectible accounts	2,000
Merchandise inventory	84,000
Prepaid insurance	1,800
Bond sinking fund	52,200
Machinery	180,000
Accumulated depreciation	45,000
Land held for future plant site	18,000
Accounts payable	60,000
Notes payable	20,000
Wages payable	1,000
Bonds payable	100,000
Common stock, $20 par, 10,000 shares authorized, 8,000	
shares issued and outstanding	160,000
Contributed capital in excess of par	40,000
Retained earnings, January 1, 19x7	26,000
Cash dividends paid	12,000
Credit sales	330,000
Cash sales	65,000
Sales returns and allowances	3,000
Cost of goods sold	235,000
Selling expenses	57,000
General and administrative expenses	74,000
Interest revenue	2,500
Interest expense	8,500
Income tax expense (excluding taxes on gain from sale of land	
and building)	8,000
Gain from sale of land and building	36,000
Tax on gain from sale of land and building	9,000

Required   **a.**   Using the data listed, prepare in good form a classified income statement and a classified balance sheet for the year ended December 31, 19x7, for Winsom Corporation.

    b.   Calculate the following ratios:
       (1)   ratio of net income to net sales
       (2)   gross margin percentage
       (3)   markup on cost
       (4)   return on total investment
       (5)   return on owners' investment

5-5   Melodie Corp. uses the following account classifications on its income statement and balance sheet:

Income Statement		*Balance Sheet*	
a.	Operating revenue	**h.**	Current assets
b.	Cost of goods sold	**i.**	Long-term investments and funds
c.	Selling expenses	**j.**	Plant assets
d.	General and administrative expenses	**k.**	Intangible assets
e.	Incidental revenue and expenses	**l.**	Other assets
f.	Income taxes	**m.**	Current liabilities
g.	Extraordinary items	**n.**	Long-term liabilities
		o.	Contributed capital
		p.	Retained earnings

For each of the following accounts, write the letter of the correct account classification in the space provided.

_____	**(1)**	prepaid insurance	_____	**(15)**	mortgage payable
_____	**(2)**	sales commissions	_____	**(16)**	capital stock
_____	**(3)**	accounts payable	_____	**(17)**	notes payable, short-term
_____	**(4)**	uncollectible accounts expense	_____	**(18)**	sales
			_____	**(19)**	allowance for uncollectible accounts
_____	**(5)**	contributed capital in excess of par			
			_____	**(20)**	equipment
_____	**(6)**	temporary investments	_____	**(21)**	depreciation expense, equipment
_____	**(7)**	office supplies used	_____	**(22)**	accumulated depreciation, equipment
_____	**(8)**	sales returns			
_____	**(9)**	interest expense	_____	**(23)**	interest revenue
_____	**(10)**	goodwill	_____	**(24)**	organization costs
_____	**(11)**	cost of goods sold	_____	**(25)**	inventory
_____	**(12)**	salaries payable	_____	**(26)**	storm loss (considered unusual and unlikely to recur)
_____	**(13)**	store rent			
_____	**(14)**	accounts receivable			

5-6   Damore Corp. reported the following figures on its financial statements for 19x6, 19x7, and 19x8:

	19x6	19x7	19x8
Net sales	$300,000	$360,000	$400,000
Cost of goods sold	165,000	216,000	232,000
Operating expenses	90,000	102,600	108,000
Income taxes	9,400	8,600	15,300
Current assets	120,000	135,000	145,000
All other assets	80,000	85,000	90,000
Long-term liabilities	40,000	35,000	30,000
Total liabilities	90,000	105,000	110,000

Assume 20,000 shares of common stock were outstanding each year. Assume too that there were no incidental revenues and expenses or extraordinary items in any of the years.

Required **a.** Calculate the following figures for each year:
    (1) gross margin
    (2) net income
    (3) total assets
    (4) current liabilities
    (5) total stockholders' equity

   b. Calculate the following ratios or figures for each year:
    (1) earnings per share
    (2) ratio of net income to net sales
    (3) gross margin percentage
    (4) return on total investment
    (5) return on owners' investment

   c. Comment on the operating results over the 3-year period based on the trends indicated in part b.

5-7 Refer to the income statement for Procter & Gamble presented in the appendix to Unit 6 to answer the following questions:

a. Is the single-step or multiple-step form used?
b. What is the company's fiscal year?
c. Did the company report any extraordinary items?
d. Did earnings per share and net income increase or decrease during the year ended June 30, 1978?
e. Calculate the following:
  (1) gross margin percentage
  (2) markup on cost
  (3) ratio of net income to sales
  (4) return on total investment
  (5) return on owners' investment
f. Did the following items increase or decrease during the year ended June 30, 1978?
  (1) net sales
  (2) cost of goods sold
  (3) operating expenses

Unit 6
Other Financial Statements and Information

Auditors are like St. Thomas; they require to see before they believe.

Bruce Marshall, The Divided Lady, *1960*

In addition to an income statement and a balance sheet, two other statements are usually included in a corporation's annual report. One of these, the statement of changes in financial position, must always be included. The other will be a retained earnings statement or a statement of changes in stockholders' equity.

The form, content, purpose, and model for a retained earnings statement, a statement of changes in stockholders' equity, and a statement of changes in financial position are examined briefly in this unit. (A more in-depth examination of these statements is made in Chapters 9 and 11.) This examination completes the summary of the end product of accounting, the financial statements, and of the environment in which they are prepared.

Performance Objectives

Upon completing this unit you should be able to:

1. define and use the accounting terms introduced in this unit.
2. a. determine each of the following:
     (1) working capital
     (2) the ending retained earnings balance
   b. explain the significance of each of the following to users of financial statements:
     (1) notes to the financial statements
     (2) summary of significant accounting policies
     (3) the CPA's (auditor's) opinion
     (4) comparative financial statements
3. describe the form, content, purpose, and model of a retained earnings statement, a statement of changes in stockholders' equity, and a statement of changes in financial position.
4. prepare in good form a retained earnings statement, a statement of changes in stockholders' equity, and a statement of changes in financial position.

Retained Earnings Statement

The *retained earnings statement* shows the changes in retained earnings that occurred during a corporation's accounting period. Information on these changes may help users evaluate the potential uses of the retained profits. Resources provided by profits may, for example, be used to pay dividends, to absorb losses in future periods, and to expand business operations without seeking additional resources from creditors and stockholders.

The format for a retained earnings statement is:

Beginning retained earnings
±Prior period adjustments
──────────────────────────
Corrected beginning retained earnings
+Net income (from income statement)
──────────────────────────
Total
−Net loss (from income statement)
−Dividends
──────────────────────────
Ending retained earnings

Exhibit 6.1 illustrates the retained earnings statement for the Shein Company for the year ended December 31, 19x8. The heading for the statement consists of the company name, the statement title, and the date line. The date line should be the same as that for the income statement because the changes occur throughout the accounting period.

When there are only a few changes, as in Exhibit 6.1, the information can be presented in a combined statement of income and retained earnings. Under this method, the retained earnings information is reported after net income is determined. The retained earnings statement is, in effect, added to the bottom of the income statement. Recall that the Shein Company reported net income of $54,680 for 19x8 (see Exhibit 5.2). Starting with net income, the bottom portion of a combined statement of income and retained earnings for the Shein Company would appear as follows:

Net income		$ 54,680
Retained earnings, January 1, 19x8	$71,600	
Prior period adjustments:		
Reduction for correction of error related to prior year	8,500	
Corrected retained earnings, January 1, 19x8		63,100
Total		$117,780
Less: Dividends		20,000
Retained earnings, December 31, 19x8		$ 97,780

Prior Period Adjustments   Certain material adjustments related to the business operations of prior periods **(prior period adjustments)** are reported as corrections to the retained earnings balance in the period in which the adjustments are deemed necessary. Under FASB Statement No. 16 only two types of items can be treated as prior period adjustments. One consists of corrections of errors in previously issued finan-

Exhibit 6.1

Shein Company Retained Earnings Statement For the Year Ended December 31, 19x8	
Retained earnings, January 1, 19x8	$ 71,600
Prior period adjustments:	
Reduction for correction of error related to prior year	8,500
Corrected retained earnings, January 1, 19x8	$ 63,100
Add: Net income	54,680
Total	$117,780
Less: Dividends	20,000
Retained earnings, December 31, 19x8	$ 97,780

cial statements; the other is beyond the scope of this text.[1] These errors should be rare, especially for companies regularly audited by CPAs. To be treated as a prior period adjustment, an error must have a material effect on the financial statements and result from a mathematical mistake, a mistake in applying accounting principles, an oversight, or a misuse of the facts that existed at that time.

The effect of this FASB pronouncement is to require that virtually every item of revenue or expense and gain or loss be included when determining net income for the current period. The FASB and many other accounting authorities believe that limiting discretion, whenever possible, in the preparation of financial statements will allow more useful information to be presented to decision makers. However, this viewpoint is not held universally. Some accounting authorities feel that such limitations can straitjacket accounting by hindering its adaptability to changing times and varying circumstances.

Restrictions on Retained Earnings   There are many restrictions on retained earnings. State laws, for example, may restrict a corporation's ability to declare dividends from the retained earnings balance. Also, a board of directors may voluntarily restrict retained earnings or enter into a contractual agreement that does so. The modern practice is to report these restrictions in the *notes to the financial statements* (see Exhibit 6.2). Examples of these restrictions are (1) resolving to not pay dividends, so retained earnings will be available to absorb unusual or infrequent losses, such as lawsuit losses, fire losses, and earthquake losses, (2) agreeing with bondholders to limit payment of dividends from available retained earnings, and (3) limiting the retained earnings available for dividends to an amount equal to the cost of an entity's own stock, which has been issued and then reacquired, but not retired. Restrictions on retained earnings are often referred to as **appropriations of retained earnings;** the amount of retained earnings restricted is often called **appropriated retained earnings.** In the past special accounts were used to report appropriations of retained earnings. These accounts, which are still used by some companies, are called **reserves**—for example, reserve for bonded indebtedness and reserve for contingent losses (see Exhibit 6.3).

---

[1]The second type of prior period adjustment under FASB Statement No. 16 is for adjustments resulting from realization of income tax benefits of preacquisition operating loss carryforwards of purchased subsidiaries.

Exhibit 6.2

Shareholders' equity:	1977	1976
Common Stock	2,515	2,506
Paid-in capital	102,275	101,883
Net unrealized loss on investment in preferred stocks (note 2)	(10,652)	(10,182)
Retained earnings (note 4)	44,952	32,521
	139,090	126,728
	$496,815	$509,583

Note 4: Long-Term Debt
The Company has complied with restrictions and limitations required under the revolving credit agreement and the convertible subordinated trust indentures. Under the most restrictive covenant, the Company is limited as to the payment of cash dividends at December 31, 1977 to $17,477,000.

Source: *The 1977 annual report of Ramada Inns, Inc.; only the portion of note 4 that describes the restriction on retained earnings available for cash dividends has been reproduced here.*

Exhibit 6.3

	1976	1975
Shareholders' Investment		
Common shares, $0.25 par value	$ 9.8	$ 4.4
Capital in excess of par value	347.6	207.7
Reserve for foreign business risks (created out of retained earnings)	5.0	5.0
Retained earnings	558.4	429.2
Total Shareholders' Investment	$920.8	$646.3

Source: *The 1976 annual report of Dresser Industries, Inc., as reproduced in* Accounting Trends and Techniques, *1977 edition (New York: AICPA, 1977).*

Reporting Changes in Stockholders' Equity

Changes in retained earnings have been reported in published financial statements for a long time. However, disclosure of changes in other components of stockholders' equity was not widespread. Then in 1965 the APB concluded that changes in the number of shares of each class of stock authorized, issued, and outstanding, the balance of each stock account, and the balance of any other contributed capital accounts should be disclosed. The best method for disclosing this information was left to the judgment of accountants.

In some situations this information can be adequately disclosed in the notes to the financial statements (see Exhibit 6.4). In other situations a supplementary schedule or a separate statement may be best (see Exhibit 6.5). Also, changes in retained earnings can be reported in the same statement as changes in contributed capital (see Exhibit 6.6). This topic is examined in greater depth in Chapter 9.

Exhibit 6.4

Common Stock

In January 1977, the Company effected a three-for-one split-up of its common stock, increasing its authorized common stock from 60,000,000 shares of $1.25 par value to 180,000,000 shares of $.41²/₃ par value. All references in the consolidated financial statements to the number of common shares, price per share, and other per share amounts have been adjusted to reflect this common stock split-up.

Common stock outstanding at September 30, 1977 comprised 107,446,938 shares, an increase of 404,592 shares during the year. The prior year's increase was 87,936 shares. These increases were primarily the result of shares issued on exercise of employees' stock options.

At September 30, 1977 there were 6,508,335 shares of common stock reserved for conversion of the 5³/₄% convertible subordinated debentures and 2,522,878 shares reserved under various employee benefit plans.

Source: *Footnotes to the financial statements in the 1977 annual report of Ralston Purina Company.*

Exhibit 6.5

Consolidated Statement of Capital Surplus

| | Year Ended December 31 | |
	1977	1976
Balance at Beginning of the Year	$428,790,235	$384,959,169
Add:		
Excess of selling or market price over par value of common stock issued to employees	6,307,377	36,905,674
Income tax benefit realized from sale of common stock to employees	292,093	6,626,133
Excess of face value of debentures over par value of common stock issued on conversion	26,200	11,463
Retirement and reissuance of treasury shares	260,922	287,796
Balance at End of the Year	$435,676,827	$428,790,235

Source: *The 1977 annual report of The Dow Chemical Company.*

Exhibit 6.6

Revlon, Inc. and Subsidiaries
Consolidated Statements of Stockholders' Equity
Years Ended December 31, 1977 and 1976

| | Common Stock Issued | | Additional | Retained | Treasury Stock, |
	Shares	Amount	Paid-In Capital	Earnings	At Cost
1977					
Balance—January 1	30,154,169	$30,154,000	$72,301,000	$355,776,000	$2,012,000
Net earnings				97,794,000	
Dividends on common stock				(30,222,000)	
Common stock issued:					
Executive Stock					
Option Plan	165,644	166,000	6,086,000		

(continued)

Exhibit 6.6 (continued)

Employees' Stock Purchase Plan ...	97,131	97,000	3,496,000		
Conversion of debentures	2,410	2,000	80,000		
Retirement of treasury stock	(19,861)	(19,000)	(13,000)	(302,000)	(334,000)
Pooled company	19,861	19,000	14,000	267,000	
Balance—December 31	30,419,354	$30,419,000	$81,964,000	$423,313,000	$1,678,000
1976					
Balance—January 1	14,959,980	$14,960,000	$77,729,000	$301,704,000	$2,611,000
Two-for-one stock split	14,959,980	14,960,000	(14,960,000)		
Net earnings				81,473,000	
Dividends on common stock				(23,757,000)	
Common stock issued:					
Executive Stock Option Plan	207,616	208,000	6,581,000		
Employees' Stock Purchase Plan ...	64,134	64,000	2,343,000		
Conversion of debentures	1,821	2,000	60,000		
Retirement of treasury stock	(39,362)	(40,000)	(7,000)	(552,000)	(599,000)
Capital transactions of pooled companies prior to acquisition				555,000	(3,092,000)
Balance—December 31	30,154,169	$30,154,000	$72,301,000	$355,776,000	$2,012,000

Source: *The 1977 annual report of Revlon, Inc.*

Statement of Changes in Financial Position

The objectives of financial accounting, which were examined in Unit 3, indicated that changes in an entity's resources and obligations should be disclosed. The purpose of the *statement of changes in financial position* is to explain all changes in financial position and to disclose the sources and uses of an entity's **financial resources.** Other financial statements do not present all this information. A comparison of the balance sheets for two consecutive periods, for example, will indicate only the net changes in each resource and obligation. New equipment may be purchased and old equipment sold during the period, but, by comparing the balances at the end of the two periods, only the net change will be indicated. However, both the purchase and the sale may be significant enough to require disclosure. The income statement indicates only the changes in financial resources resulting from business operations. A retained earnings statement and a statement of changes in stockholders' equity indicate only selected changes affecting retained earnings and/or contributed capital.

A high degree of flexibility in preparing the statement of changes in financial position is allowed as long as certain requirements are met and all significant **financial ac-**

Exhibit 6.7

Shein Company
Statement of Changes in Financial Position
For the Year Ended December 31, 19x8

Resources provided by:		
Operations:		
Revenue collected	$814,700	
Payments for expenses	750,900	
Cash provided by operations		$ 63,800
Other sources:		
Sale of investments		22,800
Short-term loan		20,000
Total resources provided		$106,600
Resources applied to:		
Payment of cash dividends	$ 20,000	
Contribution to bond sinking fund	6,000	
Investment in Rein Company stock	55,000	
Total resources applied		$ 81,000
Increase in cash resources		$ 25,600

tivities are disclosed. Two general approaches are widely used: the working capital and the cash approaches. **Working capital** is the excess of current assets over current liabilities. It represents the amount of financial resources available to carry out business activities other than the payment of current obligations. The model for both approaches to the statement of changes in financial position is:

$$\text{resource inflows} - \text{resource outflows} = \text{change in resources}$$

Exhibit 6.7 is an illustration of the statement of changes in financial position using the cash approach. The heading for the statement is the same type as that used for the income statement and retained earnings statement because the financial activities reported occurred throughout the accounting period. Both the working capital and cash approaches will be examined more fully in Chapter 11.

Resource Inflows   The balance sheet and income statement are analyzed to determine how the entity obtained financial resources during the accounting period. The primary **resource inflows** result from (1) business operations (resources provided by revenues minus resources used by expenses), (2) the issuance of the entity's stock, (3) loans, and (4) the sale of investments and fixed assets. For the Shein Company in Exhibit 6.7, the primary cash resource inflows were business operations ($63,800), proceeds from the sale of investments ($22,800), and a short-term loan ($20,000).

Resource Outflows   The balance sheet and income statement are analyzed also to determine how the entity used financial resources during the accounting period. Primary **resource outflows** result from (1) payment of dividends, (2) purchase of investments and fixed assets, (3) retirement of debts, and (4) acquisition of the entity's own stock. For the Shein Company in Exhibit 6.7 the primary cash resource outflows were for the payment of dividends ($20,000), payment to a bond sinking fund ($6,000), and the purchase of stock in another company ($55,000). Because cash resource inflows ($106,600) exceeded cash resource outflows ($81,000), cash resources for the Shein Company increased $25,600 during 19x8.

For an example of a statement of changes in financial position prepared using the working capital approach, see the appendix to this unit for the financial statements for Coachmen Industries.

Notes to Financial Statements

One qualitative characteristic that makes financial information useful is completeness or full disclosure. All significant information that will be helpful to decision makers should be included with financial statements. Too much detail or explanation in the body of the financial statements, however, can interfere with the user's ability to understand and interpret the information. Therefore, details and verbal explanations are often included in a section called **"notes to the financial statements."**

These notes, which are keyed to figures on the basic financial statements, are considered an integral part of the statements. Failure to read them might lead to incorrect decisions on the part of users. For an example see the notes to the financial statements of Coachmen Industries in the appendix to this unit.

Summary of Significant Accounting Policies

APB Opinion No. 22 requires the inclusion of a **summary of significant accounting policies** in a section preceding the notes to the financial statements or as the first note. This summary is considered an integral part of the financial statements. See note 1 to the statements for Coachmen Industries in the appendix to this unit for an example of such a summary.

The accounting policies adopted by an entity can significantly affect its operating results, financial position, and changes in financial position. Statement users can better understand and interpret the information if they know the significant accounting policies of the entity. The policies that should be included are those that involve selecting from (1) acceptable alternatives, (2) principles and methods peculiar to the industry, and (3) unusual or innovative applications of accounting principles.

Auditor's Opinion

Publicly owned companies must be audited annually by a CPA; other companies may also be audited by a CPA. The CPA's opinion or report, prepared when the audit is complete, is included with published financial statements. The **auditor's opinion** must also accompany financial statements submitted to stock exchanges, banks, the SEC, and various government regulatory agencies. The opinion of a CPA increases the reliability of financial statements which are the responsibility of the company's management and accountants. However, it is the CPA's opinion that is often the focal point of litigation when future developments indicate that the statements were not reliable.

The audit report expresses the CPA's opinion as to whether or not the financial statements fairly present the entity's financial position, operating results, and changes in financial position, in conformity with generally accepted accounting principles. There are two paragraphs to the standard, unqualified audit report: a scope paragraph and an opinion paragraph. The *scope paragraph* indicates the scope of the audit conducted by the CPA. The *opinion paragraph* expresses the CPA's opinion based on the results of the audit. An example of a standard, favorable audit report accompanies the Coachmen Industries financial statements in the appendix to this unit.

Comparative Financial Statements

Although financial information for the current accounting is very important and useful by itself, the information is more useful when data for a prior period or several prior periods are also presented, so comparisons can be made and trends can be analyzed and interpreted. Published financial statements, therefore, are usually presented in comparative form, with data for the different periods set side by side. See the Coachmen Industries financial statements in the appendix to this unit for examples of comparative financial statements.

Additional Information Presented in Annual Reports

Corporate annual reports frequently provide other information besides that found in the financial statements, footnotes, and summary of significant accounting policies. Most annual reports contain a letter from the chairman of the board of directors and/or the president of the company to the stockholders. This letter usually presents the chairman's or president's comments on the past year's operating results and expectations and plans for the future.

Most annual reports also include a 5- or 10-year statistical summary indicating such information as sales, costs of production, operating expenses, net income, earnings per share, ratio of net income to net sales, return on investment, dividends per share, working capital, total assets, total stockholders' equity, and other selected financial ratios. A summary of the financial highlights for the current and past years, which includes some of the same information as the 5- or 10-year statistical summary, is often included at the beginning of the annual report.

Many companies also review product activities and organization changes. Charts, graphs, and tables often are used to convey information that management believes will be relevant to stockholders.

REVIEW PROBLEMS

1. The following information is taken from the records of the Flint Company for 19x4:

Retained earnings, January 1, 19x4	$ 90,000
Correction of error understating revenues in prior year	14,400
Cash dividends	50,000
Net income	107,100

Required   Prepare a retained earnings statement in good form for 19x4.

2. An analysis of the cash records for the Flint Company for 19x4 indicated the following information:

Cash receipts:	
Revenues collected	$1,740,000
Sale of common stock	60,000
Total	$1,800,000
Cash payments:	
Cash dividends	$ 50,000
Expenses	1,714,000
Land for future building site	24,000
Total	$1,788,000
Excess of cash receipts over cash payments	$ 12,000

Required   Prepare a statement of changes in financial position in good form for 19x4.

Solution to review problems

1.

Flint Company
Retained Earnings Statement
For the Year Ended December 31, 19x4

Retained earnings, January 1, 19x4	$ 90,000
Prior period adjustments: Correction of error understating revenues in prior year	14,400
Corrected retained earnings, January 1, 19x4	$104,400
Add: Net income (per income statement)	107,100
Total	$211,500
Less: Cash dividends	50,000
Retained earnings, December 31, 19x4	$161,500

2.

Flint Company
Statement of Changes in Financial Position
For the Year Ended December 31, 19x4

Resources provided by:		
Operations:		
Revenues collected	$1,740,000	
Payment of expenses	1,714,000	
Cash provided by operations		$26,000
Other sources:		
Sale of common stock		60,000
Total resources provided		$86,000
Resources applied to:		
Payment of cash dividends	$ 50,000	
Purchase of land for future building site	24,000	
Total resources applied		74,000
Increase in cash resources		$12,000

SUMMARY

The form, content, purpose, and model for a retained earnings statement, a statement of changes in stockholders' equity, and a statement of changes in financial position were discussed in this unit. One or more of these statements is usually prepared to complete the set of basic financial statements distributed to users. The notes to the financial statements were also discussed, as well as the summary of significant accounting policies. Finally, the usefulness of comparative financial statements and the significance of the CPA's audit opinion were explained.

REVIEW QUESTIONS

6-1 What is the purpose of: (1) a retained earnings statement, (2) a statement of changes in stockholders' equity, and (3) a statement of changes in financial position?

6-2 List the primary components of a retained earnings statement.

6-3 What types of items can be treated as prior period adjustments?

6-4 How are prior period adjustments reported on the retained earnings statement?

6-5 What is a reserve account? How is it reported on the balance sheet?

6-6 What is the preferred method for reporting restrictions on retained earnings today?

6-7 Describe the model for the statement of changes in financial position. Indicate two different approaches that can be used to prepare it.

6-8 List the primary resource inflows and outflows reported on the statement of changes in financial position.

6-9   Define working capital. What is the significance of working capital?

6-10 The notes to the financial statements and the summary of significant accounting policies are considered integral parts of financial statements. Explain.

6-11 What is the auditor's opinion paragraph in the standard, favorable audit report?

6-12 What are comparative financial statements? How are they useful?

EXERCISES

6-1   From the following information, prepare a retained earnings statement for Crystal Corp. for the year ended December 31, 19*x2*:

Dividends	$ 8,000
Net income	32,000
Retained earnings, January 1, 19*x2*	66,000
Correction of error made in prior period (revenues for prior period were greater than reported)	5,000

6-2   Several business activities for Zane Corp. follow; indicate whether each activity results in a resource inflow or a resource outflow during the period:

a.   sale of fixed assets
b.   bank loan obtained
c.   purchase of land
d.   payment of dividends
e.   sales to customers
f.   payment of operating expenses
g.   retirement of long-term debt
h.   sale of Zane Corp. stock

6-3   From the following data for Hammer Corp., prepare a statement of changes in financial position for 19*x4* using the cash approach:

Cash collected from customers	$175,000
Sale of Hammer Corp. stock	40,000
Long-term note issued for cash	15,000
Dividends paid	12,000
Purchase of equipment	18,000
Payment of operating expenses	158,000

6-4   Gaddey Corp. reported the following balances at the end of 19*x2*:

Current assets	$160,000
Plant assets	240,000
Current liabilities	100,000
Long-term liabilities	100,000

Contributed capital	140,000
Retained earnings	60,000

Net income was reported as $50,000 for 19x2.

Required **a.** Calculate working capital at December 31, 19x2.
b. Calculate return on owners' investment and return on total investment.

PROBLEMS

6-1 Lynwood Corp. reported the following balances on its balance sheet at the end of 19x6:

Total assets	$720,000
Current assets	320,000
Long-term liabilities	180,000
Total liabilities	280,000
Contributed capital	300,000

The following additional information was obtained from company records:

Dividends paid	$ 20,000
Net income for 19x6	48,000
Correction of error made in	
prior period (expenses were	
greater than reported)	12,000

Required **a.** Prepare a retained earnings statement for 19x6.
b. Calculate return on owners' investment and return on total investment.
c. Calculate working capital.

6-2 The accountant for Finney, Inc., obtained the following information regarding cash receipts and cash payments for 19x4:

Cash receipts:	
Collected from customers	$485,000
Miscellaneous revenues collected	4,000
Sale of plant assets	12,000
Issuance of bonds	100,000
Total	$601,000
Cash payments:	
Dividends paid	$ 25,000
Investment in Berger Corp. stock	120,000
Merchandise purchased	310,000
Operating expenses paid	146,000
Future plant site acquired	22,000
Total	$623,000

Required   Prepare a statement of changes in financial position for 19*x4* using the cash approach.

6-3   (This problem covers Units 4, 5, and 6.) Dearborn Corp. uses the calendar year as its accounting period. The accountant for the company derived the following account balances from the company records for 19*x7:*

Depreciation expense	$ 7,000	Allowance for uncol-	
Fees earned	250,000	lectible accounts	$ 2,000
Cash	85,000	Retained earnings,	
Common stock, $10		January 1, 19*x7*	40,000
par, 20,000 shares		Accounts receivable	35,000
authorized	80,000	Notes payable,	
Utilities expense	10,000	long-term	20,000
Dividends paid	12,000	Supplies expense	5,000
Accounts payable	36,000	Equipment	105,000
Prepaid expenses	1,000	Rent expense	30,000
Salaries expense	120,000	Correction of error	
Accumulated		made in prior	
depreciation	14,000	year (expenses	
Salaries payable	2,000	were greater than	
Income tax expense	37,000	reported)	3,000
Miscellaneous		Contributed capital in	
expenses	4,000	excess of par value	10,000

The accountant also obtained the following summary of cash receipts and cash payments:

Cash receipts:		Cash payments:	
Collections from		Operating	
customers	$240,000	expenses	
Long-term notes		paid	$164,000
issued	20,000	Purchase of	
		equipment	20,000
		Income taxes paid	37,000
		Dividends paid	12,000

Required   **a.**   Prepare an income statement for 19*x7* using the single-step format.
   b.   Prepare a retained earnings statement for 19*x7*.
   c.   Prepare a classified balance sheet as of December 31, 19*x7*.
   d.   Prepare a statement of changes in financial position for 19*x7* using the cash approach.

6-4   Refer to the statements for Procter & Gamble presented in the appendix to this unit to answer the following questions:

   a.   How did the company disclose changes in retained earnings?
   b.   How did the company disclose changes in contributed capital?
   c.   Did retained earnings increase or decrease during the fiscal year ended June 30, 1978?
   d.   Did the company report any prior period adjustments?

e. What type of resource inflows and outflows (cash or working capital) are reported in the statement of changes in financial position?

f. Identify the amount reported for the fiscal year ended June 30, 1978, for each of the following items:
    (1) dividends
    (2) net income
    (3) increase (or decrease) in working capital

6-5 Refer to the statements for Coachmen Industries in the appendix to this unit and complete the following:

a. Determine the amount and percentage of increase (or decrease) in each of the following items; state whether the amount is an increase or decrease:
    (1) net sales
    (2) cost of goods sold
    (3) net income
    (4) earnings per share
    (5) current assets
    (6) plant assets
    (7) total assets
    (8) stockholders' equity

b. Calculate the following for 1977:
    (1) gross margin percentage
    (2) ratio of net income to sales
    (3) return on total investment
    (4) return on owners' investment
    (5) working capital

c. Determine the amount reported for 1977, if any, for each of the following items; indicate where you obtained the information for each item:
    (1) extraordinary items
    (2) number of shares of common stock outstanding at year-end
    (3) dividends on common stock
    (4) number of shares of common stock sold
    (5) number of shares of common stock issued upon exercise of stock options
    (6) contingent liabilities
    (7) increase in working capital
    (8) working capital provided by operations

d. Identify the two largest resource inflows (other than operations) and the two largest resource outflows during 1977.

e. What is the company's policy on depreciating property and equipment?

f. Did the company disclose any changes in accounting methods during 1977? Explain.

g. Did the company report any information on quarterly sales, net income, and EPS? How was this information disclosed in the annual financial statements?

h. (1) Who were the company's independent auditors?
    (2) What statements were covered by the auditors' report?
    (3) What was the auditors' conclusion regarding the company's financial statements?

i. Based on the answers to questions a–d and other information disclosed in the company's financial statements, comment on the company's financial position and operating results for 1977.

j. What factors may help account for the significant increase in almost all account balances for 1977 compared to 1976? Consider economic conditions, market factors, and management policy decisions in answering this question.

APPENDIX 6 EXAMPLES OF FINANCIAL STATEMENTS FROM PUBLISHED ANNUAL REPORTS

Coachmen Industries, Inc.
- Balance Sheets—account form
- Income Statements—multiple-step form
- Statements of Stockholders' Equity
- Statements of Changes in Financial Position—working capital basis
- Notes to Financial Statements
- Auditor's Report

Procter & Gamble Company
- Income Statements—single-step form
- Balance Sheets—account form
- Retained Earnings Statements
- Statements of Changes in Financial Position—cash basis (modified to include marketable securities as well as cash)

Michigan Sugar Company
- Combined Statements of Income and Retained Earnings
- Balance Sheets—report form
- Statements of Changes in Financial Position—working capital basis

Consolidated Balance Sheets

COACHMEN INDUSTRIES, INC.
December 31, 1977 and 1976

ASSETS	1977	1976
CURRENT ASSETS		
Cash	$ 3,034,470	$ 5,672,895
Trade receivables, less allowance for doubtful accounts 1977 $199,000; 1976 $109,100	22,171,136	15,712,136
Inventories (Note 2)	30,671,665	24,245,572
Prepaid expenses	1,257,169	255,577
Deferred income tax charges, net	541,877	424,817
Total current assets	$57,676,317	$46,310,997
INVESTMENTS		
Land, at cost (Note 3)	$ 182,860	$ 224,569
Rental properties, at cost, less accumulated straight-line depreciation 1977 $133,408; 1976 $103,030 (Note 3)	650,199	806,964
Other, principally long-term advances to dealers	609,821	583,771
	$ 1,442,880	$ 1,615,304
PROPERTY AND EQUIPMENT, at cost (Note 3)		
Land and land improvements	$ 2,827,890	$ 2,100,302
Buildings	11,095,190	9,102,196
Machinery and equipment	3,754,639	3,135,370
Transportation equipment	3,363,668	2,786,431
Office furniture and fixtures	677,838	563,237
	$21,719,225	$17,687,536
Less accumulated depreciation	5,068,090	3,689,903
	$16,651,135	$13,997,633
INTANGIBLES	$ 480,921	$ 484,621
	$76,251,253	$62,408,555

The Notes to Financial Statements are an integral part of these statements.

LIABILITIES AND STOCKHOLDERS' EQUITY	1977	1976
CURRENT LIABILITIES		
Notes payable (Note 3)	$10,000,000	$ 138,941
Current maturities of long-term debt (Note 3)	993,010	997,040
Accounts payable, trade	9,526,398	13,742,824
Accrued expenses	6,182,264	5,530,218
Income taxes payable	2,653,208	4,580,393
Total current liabilities	$29,354,880	$24,989,416
LONG-TERM DEBT, net of current maturities (Note 3)	$ 3,346,414	$ 4,063,489
DEFERRED INCOME TAX CREDITS	$ 479,863	$ 305,653
CONTINGENT LIABILITIES (Note 6)		
STOCKHOLDERS' EQUITY		
Common stock, no par value; authorized 10,000,000 shares; issued and outstanding 1977 3,513,833 shares; 1976 3,485,008 shares (Note 4)	$15,262,957	$15,122,170
Additional paid-in capital	151,300	98,500
Retained earnings	27,655,839	17,829,327
	$43,070,096	$33,049,997
	$76,251,253	$62,408,555

Consolidated Statements of Income

COACHMEN INDUSTRIES, INC.
Years Ended December 31, 1977 and 1976

	1977	1976
Net sales	$288,006,411	$224,617,513
Cost of goods sold	240,922,341	188,410,833
Gross profit	$ 47,084,070	$ 36,206,680
Other operating revenue, delivery charges	4,655,354	3,688,130
	$ 51,739,424	$ 39,894,810
Delivery expenses	$ 8,106,762	$ 6,260,490
Selling expenses	12,408,057	9,149,976
General and administrative expenses	8,666,716	7,188,586
	$ 29,181,535	$ 22,599,052
Operating income	$ 22,557,889	$ 17,295,758
Financial expense, net	447,939	97,059
Income before taxes on income	$ 22,109,950	$ 17,198,699
Federal and state income taxes, including increase (decrease) due to deferred income taxes 1977 $57,150; 1976 $(34,323)	$ 10,970,000	8,371,000
Net income	$ 11,139,950	$ 8,827,699
Weighted average number of shares of common stock outstanding (Note 4)	3,499,846	3,321,920
Earnings per common share (Note 4)	$ 3.18	$ 2.66

Consolidated Statements of Stockholders' Equity

COACHMEN INDUSTRIES, INC.
Years Ended December 31, 1977 and 1976

	Common Stock	Additional Paid-In Capital	Retained Earnings
Balance, December 31, 1975	$ 5,870,013	$67,600	$ 9,492,117
Net income	—	—	8,827,699
Sale of 600,000 shares of common stock (Note 4)	9,095,528	—	—
Issuance of 30,050 shares of common stock upon the exercise of options	156,629	—	—
Tax benefit arising from employee sales of common stock acquired pursuant to employee stock option plan	—	30,900	—
Dividends on common stock	—	—	(490,489)
Balance, December 31, 1976	$15,122,170	$98,500	$17,829,327
Net income			11,139,950
Issuance of 28,825 shares of common stock upon the exercise of options	140,787	—	—
Tax benefit arising from employee sales of common stock acquired pursuant to employee stock option plan	—	52,800	—
Dividends on common stock	—	—	(1,313,438)
Balance, December 31, 1977	$15,262,957	$151,300	$27,655,839

The Notes to Financial Statements are an integral part of these statements.

Consolidated Statements of Changes in Financial Position

COACHMEN INDUSTRIES, INC.
Years Ended December 31, 1977 and 1976

	1977	1976
FINANCIAL RESOURCES PROVIDED BY		
Operations:		
Net income	$11,139,950	$ 8,827,699
Items which did not require outlay of working capital during the year:		
Depreciation	1,774,570	1,303,234
Deferred liability under incentive bonus plans	205,326	164,984
Deferred income taxes	174,210	153,353
Other	56,500	34,600
Total working capital provided by operations	$13,350,556	$10,483,870
Proceeds from disposition of investments and property and equipment, net of gain	558,867	377,556
Proceeds from long-term mortgages and loans	147,989	1,764,058
Equity financing, net proceeds from the sale of common stock	140,787	9,252,157
	$14,198,199	$21,877,641
FINANCIAL RESOURCES APPLIED TO		
Acquisition of long-term assets:		
Purchase of property and equipment	$ 4,611,376	$ 5,943,980
Additions to investments	203,139	753,426
Long-term debt transferred to current liabilities	1,070,390	1,243,915
Cash dividends paid	1,313,438	490,489
	$ 7,198,343	$ 8,431,810
Increase in working capital, as below	$ 6,999,856	$ 13,445,831
SUMMARY OF CHANGES IN WORKING CAPITAL COMPONENTS		
Increase (decrease) in:		
Cash	$ (2,638,425)	$ 3,482,935
Trade receivables	6,459,000	9,542,777
Inventories	6,426,093	10,629,000
Prepaid and deferred expenses	1,118,652	270,191
Decrease (increase) in:		
Current portion of notes and contracts payable	(9,857,029)	(279,427)
Accounts payable and accrued expenses	3,564,380	(9,032,888)
Income taxes payable	1,927,185	(1,166,757)
Increase in working capital	$ 6,999,856	$13,445,831

The Notes to Financial Statements are an integral part of these statements.

Notes to Financial Statements

Note 1. Nature of Business and Significant Accounting Policies

The Company's operations consist primarily of the manufacture and sale of recreational vehicles and related parts and accessories. Accordingly the sales and other revenue, operating income and identifiable assets all primarily relate to this single business activity.

The accounting policies related to the carrying value of investments and property and equipment are indicated in the captions on the consolidated balance sheets. Information as to accounting for inventories and the method of computing earnings per common share is included in the other Notes to Financial Statements. Other significant accounting policies are as follows:

Principles of consolidation:
The accompanying consolidated financial statements include the accounts of the Company and its subsidiaries, all of which are wholly-owned. All material intercompany accounts and transactions have been eliminated in consolidation.

Property and equipment accounting policies:
Depreciation is computed on the straight-line method on the costs of the assets, at rates based on their estimated service lives. A summary of estimated service lives in use is as follows:

Rental properties	15-20 years
Land improvements	3-15 years
Buildings	10-30 years
Machinery and equipment	3-10 years
Transportation equipment	2-7 years
Office furniture and fixtures	2-10 years

Maintenance and repairs expenditures are charged to operations, and renewals and betterments are capitalized. Items of property which are sold, retired or otherwise disposed of are removed from the asset and accumulated depreciation accounts, and any gains or losses thereon are reflected in operations.

Intangibles:
The intangibles represent the excess of cost over identifiable net assets of subsidiaries acquired. The Company is amortizing intangibles with an unamortized balance at December 31, 1977 of $136,808, arising through acquisitions after September 30, 1970, over a 40-year period by the straight-line method. Intangibles of $344,113 are not being amortized since, in the opinion of management, there has been no diminution in value and there is no apparent limitation on their useful lives.

Deferred income taxes:
Deferred income taxes have been recognized on timing differences relating to DISC income, depreciation, certain warranty and compensation expenses and plant start-up costs. These items are reported for income tax purposes in different years than they are recognized for financial reporting purposes.

Deferred income taxes have not been recognized on the undistributed net income of the wholly-owned subsidiaries because those companies file consolidated income tax returns with the parent company; and therefore, any dividends paid to the parent company would be nontaxable.

Investment credit accounting policy:
The Company follows the policy of treating the investment tax credit as a reduction of the federal income tax expense in the year in which the credit is realized.

Accounting for warranties:
The Company follows the policy of accruing an estimated liability for warranties at the time the warranted products are sold.

Note 2. Inventories

Inventories, priced at the lower of cost (first-in, first-out method) or market, at December 31, 1977 and 1976 consisted of the following:

	1977	1976
Raw materials	$10,146,501	$ 7,533,245
Work in process	2,056,611	1,893,597
Finished goods	18,468,553	14,818,730
	$30,671,665	$24,245,572

Note 3. Pledged Assets, Notes Payable and Long-Term Debt

Notes payable and long-term debt, and the related collateral, at December 31, 1977 consisted of the following:
Notes payable:
The Company has available a $15,000,000 unsecured line of credit bearing interest at the prime rate for bank borrowings. The Company had borrowings under this agreement of $10,000,000 at December 31, 1977. There were no borrowings under this agreement at December 31, 1976.

Long-term debt:

	Current Maturities	Long-Term Maturities
First mortgage notes, 5-7%, payable in varying installments, collateralized by real estate with a depreciated cost of approximately $2,029,000, maturing 1980-1998	$142,620	$1,268,629
Installment purchase contracts on real estate and equipment with a depreciated cost of approximately $1,782,000 bearing interest at 5-8¼%, payable in varying installments, maturing 1981-1987	193,264	1,614,948
Notes, 6½%, payable in semiannual installments of $46,263 plus interest, collateralized by the capital stock of a subsidiary, Flannigan Industries, Inc., maturing 1979	92,527	92,527
Notes, 6-8%, unsecured, payable in annual installments of $564,599 plus interest, maturing 1978	564,599	–
Deferred liability under incentive bonus plans, bearing interest at 4%	–	370,310
	$993,010	$3,346,414

Note 4. Common Stock and Earnings Per Common Share

Stock issuance:
On March 31, 1976, the Company sold 300,000 shares (600,000 shares after the two-for-one stock split) of its previously unissued common stock to a group of underwriters for public distribution pursuant to a registration statement filed with the Securities and Exchange Commission. The proceeds from the sale totaled $9,095,528, net of related expenses of $84,472.

Recapitalization:
On May 10, 1976, the Company's Articles of Incorporation were amended to authorize the increase in the authorized number of shares of no par value common stock from 3,000,000 shares to 10,000,000 shares. Subsequently, a two-for-one split was effected for stockholders of record at August 16, 1976.

All references to common shares and earnings per common share in the accompanying consolidated financial statements are stated as if the two-for-one split occurred on January 1, 1976.

Stock options:
The Company has a key employee qualified stock option plan whereby 289,575 authorized but unissued shares of common stock of the Company are reserved at December 31, 1977 for issuance upon exercise of options granted, or to be granted, to executives and key employees of the Company. Options granted under the plan are for a period of five years at a price not less than the fair market value of the stock on the date of grant. No such options may be exercised during the first year after grant, and they may be exercised to the extent of 25% per year during the second, third, fourth and fifth years thereafter on a cumulative basis. No option may be granted to any person who would then hold more than 5% of the common stock of the Company.

At December 31, 1977, the following options covering 148,525 shares were outstanding to officers and employees of the Company, under the terms set forth in the preceding paragraph:

Year of Grant	Balance Dec. 31, 1976	Granted	Exercised	Canceled	Balance Dec. 31, 1977	Option Price
1972	7,000	–	2,600	4,400	–	$ 9.94-$14.75
1973	24,200	–	9,125	800	14,275	2.13- 8.50
1974	24,250	–	10,850	2,000	11,400	1.69- 2.43
1975	40,800	–	6,200	4,400	30,200	2.56- 10.00
1976	82,500	–	50	18,500	63,950	12.38- 15.00
1977	–	35,500	–	6,800	28,700	13.00- 18.50
	178,750	35,500	28,825	36,900	148,525	

At December 31, 1977, options for the purchase of 45,325 shares of common stock were exercisable. Authorized options for the purchase of 141,050 shares and 139,650 shares were available for granting at December 31, 1977 and 1976, respectively. Proceeds from the exercise of stock options are credited to the common stock account.

Earnings per common share:
Earnings per common share are based on the weighted average number of shares of common stock outstanding.

The common stock equivalents (employee stock options) have not entered into the computation of earnings per common share because their inclusion would not have a material dilutive effect.

Fully diluted earnings per common share do not differ materially from primary earnings per common share.

(Continued)

Notes to Financial Statements
(Continued)

Note 5. Incentive Bonus Plans

The Company has incentive bonus plans for certain officers and key management personnel. The amounts charged to expense for the years ended December 31, 1977 and 1976 aggregated $702,483 and $563,537 respectively. Such amounts are determined in accordance with the provisions of the bonus plan.

Note 6. Contingent Liabilities

The Company was contingently liable at December 31, 1977 to banks and other financial institutions on repurchase agreements in connection with financing provided by such institutions to customers for the purchase of the Company's products. Losses under these agreements have been insignificant in past years and the Company's exposure to such losses is limited by the resale value of the products required to be repurchased. Management expects that no material losses will be incurred as a result of the repurchase agreements.

Note 7. Unaudited Interim Financial Information

Presented below is certain selected unaudited quarterly financial information for the years ended December 31, 1977 and 1976:

| | 1977 Quarter Ended | | | |
	March 31	June 30	Sept. 30	Dec. 31
Net sales	$79,407,750	$91,868,235	$66,844,545	$49,885,881
Gross profit	12,884,721	15,836,081	12,201,181	6,162,087
Net income	3,157,890	4,422,465	3,087,445	472,150
Earnings per common share	$.91	$1.27	$.88	$.13

| | 1976 Quarter Ended | | | |
	March 31	June 30	Sept. 30	Dec. 31
Net sales	$45,565,774	$68,003,569	$60,691,480	$50,356,690
Gross profit	7,732,883	11,577,768	10,425,078	6,470,951
Net income	1,636,246	3,341,434	2,705,633	1,144,386
Earnings per common share	$.55	$.94	$.76	$.33

The common stock equivalents described in Note 4 have entered into the computation of earnings per common share for the 1976 quarters ended March 31, June 30 and September 30. However, the common stock equivalents have not entered into the computation of earnings per common share for the quarter ended December 31 and for the year ended December 31, 1976 because their inclusion would not have a material dilutive effect for these periods.

Because of these differences in computation, the total of the reported quarterly earnings per common share is $.08 less than the amount reported for the year ended December 31, 1976. The common stock equivalents did not enter into the computations of earnings per common share for any of the quarters during 1977 because their inclusion would not have had a material dilutive effect.

Auditor's Report

To the Board of Directors
Coachmen Industries, Inc.
Middlebury, Indiana

We have examined the accompanying consolidated balance sheets of Coachmen Industries, Inc. and its subsidiaries as of December 31, 1977 and 1976 and the related consolidated statements of income, stockholders' equity and changes in financial position for the years then ended. Our examinations were made in accordance with generally accepted auditing standards and, accordingly, included such tests of the accounting records and such other auditing procedures as we considered necessary in the circumstances.

In our opinion, the consolidated financial statements mentioned above present fairly the consolidated financial position of Coachmen Industries, Inc. and its subsidiaries at December 31, 1977 and 1976, and the consolidated results of their operations and changes in their financial position for the years then ended, in conformity with generally accepted accounting principles applied on a consistent basis.

McGladrey, Hansen, Dunn & Company

McGLADREY, HANSEN, DUNN & COMPANY
Certified Public Accountants

Elkhart, Indiana
February 13, 1978

Consolidated Statement Of Earnings
The Procter & Gamble Company And Subsidiaries
Years Ended June 30, 1978 and 1977

	1978	1977
INCOME		
Net sales	**$8,099,687,000**	$7,284,255,000
Interest and other income	**63,329,000**	65,119,000
	8,163,016,000	7,349,374,000
COSTS AND EXPENSES		
Cost of products sold	**5,539,940,000**	5,039,687,000
Marketing, administrative, and other expenses	**1,615,084,000**	1,397,104,000
Interest expense	**54,623,000**	53,042,000
Federal and foreign income taxes	**441,701,000**	398,078,000
	7,651,348,000	6,887,911,000
NET EARNINGS	**$ 511,668,000**	$ 461,463,000
Per Common Share		
Net earnings	**$6.19**	$5.59
Average shares outstanding: 1978 — 82,624,361 1977 — 82,586,031		
Dividends	**$2.70**	$2.40

Consolidated Balance Sheet
The Procter & Gamble Company And Subsidiaries
June 30, 1978 and 1977

ASSETS	1978	1977
CURRENT ASSETS		
Cash and marketable securities	$ **722,994,000**	$ 744,683,000
Accounts receivable, less allowance for doubtful accounts of $4,774,000 for 1978 and $3,186,000 for 1977	**606,355,000**	536,042,000
Inventories	**1,046,610,000**	968,480,000
Prepaid expenses and other current assets	**99,346,000**	92,520,000
	2,475,305,000	2,341,725,000
PROPERTY, PLANT, AND EQUIPMENT, at cost		
Buildings	**617,129,000**	556,125,000
Machinery and equipment	**2,632,171,000**	2,274,149,000
	3,249,300,000	2,830,274,000
Less accumulated depreciation	**978,763,000**	880,077,000
	2,270,537,000	1,950,197,000
Land	**59,315,000**	52,178,000
Timberlands, less depletion	**58,824,000**	55,450,000
	2,388,676,000	2,057,825,000
OTHER ASSETS, INCLUDING GOODWILL	**119,836,000**	87,636,000
TOTAL	**$4,983,817,000**	$4,487,186,000

LIABILITIES	1978	1977
CURRENT LIABILITIES		
Accounts payable	$ 707,829,000	$ 573,955,000
Accrued liabilities	188,277,000	161,484,000
Taxes payable	171,766,000	187,557,000
Debt due within one year	99,798,000	125,455,000
	1,167,670,000	1,048,451,000
LONG-TERM DEBT	573,823,000	533,338,000
DEFERRED INCOME TAXES	327,003,000	281,158,000
SHAREHOLDERS' EQUITY		
Preferred shares	467,000	477,000
Common shares	82,645,000	82,605,000
Additional paid-in capital	187,032,000	184,520,000
Earnings retained in the business	2,645,177,000	2,356,637,000
	2,915,321,000	2,624,239,000
TOTAL	$4,983,817,000	$4,487,186,000

Consolidated Statement Of Earnings Retained In The Business

The Procter & Gamble Company And Subsidiaries
Years Ended June 30, 1978 and 1977

	1978	1977
Balance at beginning of year	$2,356,637,000	$2,093,483,000
Net earnings	511,668,000	461,463,000
Dividends to shareholders		
Common	(223,083,000)	(198,208,000)
Preferred	(38,000)	(40,000)
Excess of cost over stated value of common shares and 8% preferred shares purchased for treasury	(7,000)	(61,000)
Balance at end of year	$2,645,177,000	$2,356,637,000

Consolidated Statement of Changes In Financial Position

The Procter & Gamble Company And Subsidiaries
Years Ended June 30, 1978 and 1977

SOURCE OF FUNDS	1978	1977
Net earnings	$ 511,668,000	$ 461,463,000
Depreciation and depletion	139,444,000	124,987,000
Deferred income taxes	41,639,000	34,201,000
Total from operations	692,751,000	620,651,000
Increase in long-term debt	57,249,000	7,815,000
Increase in current liabilities	144,876,000	85,008,000
	894,876,000	713,474,000
USE OF FUNDS		
Capital expenditures	476,446,000	294,475,000
Dividends to shareholders	223,121,000	198,248,000
Reduction of long-term debt	16,764,000	40,440,000
Decrease in debt due within one year	25,657,000	(49,490,000)
Increase in inventories	78,130,000	167,530,000
Increase in accounts receivable	70,313,000	100,325,000
Other items, net	26,134,000	12,563,000
	916,565,000	764,091,000
INCREASE (DECREASE) IN CASH AND MARKETABLE SECURITIES	$ (21,689,000)	$ (50,617,000)

MICHIGAN SUGAR COMPANY

STATEMENTS OF INCOME AND INCOME RETAINED

	Year Ended September 30	
	1977	**1976**
REVENUE:		
Proceeds from sales of products less discounts, returns and allowances......	$52,854,486	$61,643,168
Interest and other income (net)..	347,860	356,346
	53,202,346	61,999,514
COST AND EXPENSES:		
Cost of production...	45,628,519	49,898,245
General, administrative, selling and delivery expenses.....................	5,814,824	5,767,143
Interest expense—		
Long-term debt...	263,772	276,997
Seasonal borrowings...	367,782	273,175
	52,074,897	56,215,560
INCOME BEFORE INCOME TAXES.................................	1,127,449	5,783,954
ESTIMATED INCOME TAXES (Note 6):		
Currently payable...	263,000	2,482,000
Deferred...	214,000	186,000
	477,000	2,668,000
NET INCOME FOR THE YEAR..	650,449	3,115,954
INCOME RETAINED AT BEGINNING OF YEAR......................	20,550,696	18,562,184
Cash dividends:		
Preferred 6% non-voting cumulative stock—$.24 a share..............	(38,088)	(38,088)
Common stock—$.85 and $.90 a share, respectively..................	(1,028,676)	(1,089,354)
INCOME RETAINED AT END OF YEAR.............................	$20,134,381	$20,550,696
Net income per share of common stock after deduction of preferred dividends of $38,088 in each year...	$ .51	$2.54

BALANCE SHEETS

| | September 30 | |
	1977	1976
CURRENT ASSETS:		
Cash.	$ 776,595	$ 755,835
Short-term investments, at cost (approximating market)	4,467,479	4,774,120
Accounts receivable.	2,443,030	2,927,664
Growing crop expenses—current season (Note 1).	253,691	240,534
Inventories (Notes 1 and 2).	10,662,360	11,201,374
Prepaid expenses.	296,684	376,851
Total current assets.	18,899,839	20,276,378
PROPERTY, PLANT AND EQUIPMENT (Note 1):		
Land and buildings.	4,980,767	4,293,125
Machinery and equipment.	21,932,619	21,438,218
	26,913,386	25,731,343
Less—Accumulated depreciation.	12,478,108	11,589,161
	14,435,278	14,142,182
OTHER ASSETS AND DEFERRED CHARGES.	48,324	56,237
	$33,383,441	$34,474,797
CURRENT LIABILITIES:		
Long-term debt due within one year.	$ 230,000	$ 230,000
Accounts payable.	1,348,774	1,179,059
Owing to beet growers.	1,645,000	1,737,767
Income taxes.	62,730	690,256
Accrued taxes, payrolls and other liabilities.	712,032	790,870
Accrued interest.	134,082	135,070
Total current liabilities.	4,132,618	4,763,022
FEDERAL INCOME TAXES DEFERRED TO FUTURE YEARS (Note 1). .	1,596,833	1,411,470
LONG-TERM DEBT, less portion due within one year (Note 3)	3,520,050	3,750,050
STOCKHOLDERS' EQUITY (Note 4):		
Preferred 6% non-voting cumulative stock—$4 par value		
Authorized 500,000 shares, outstanding 158,699 shares.	634,796	634,796
Common stock—$1 par value		
Authorized 2,000,000 shares, outstanding 1,210,208 shares	1,210,208	1,210,208
Capital surplus.	2,154,555	2,154,555
Income retained.	20,134,381	20,550,696
	24,133,940	24,550,255
	$33,383,441	$34,474,797

STATEMENTS OF CHANGES IN FINANCIAL POSITION

	Year Ended September 30	
	1977	1976
FINANCIAL RESOURCES WERE PROVIDED BY:		
Net income for the year	$ 650,449	$ 3,115,954
Items not affecting working capital—		
Depreciation	967,259	901,613
Deferred federal income taxes	214,000	186,000
Working capital provided by operations	1,831,708	4,203,567
Other	15,426	28,331
Total resources provided	1,847,134	4,231,898
FINANCIAL RESOURCES WERE USED FOR:		
Acquisition of property, plant and equipment	1,253,723	2,030,043
Reduction of long-term debt	230,000	230,000
Dividends paid—		
Preferred stock	38,088	38,088
Common stock	1,028,676	1,089,354
Other	42,782	6,254
Total resources used	2,593,269	3,393,739
Increase (Decrease) in Working Capital	$ (746,135)	$ 838,159
INCREASE (DECREASE) IN COMPONENTS OF WORKING CAPITAL:		
Current Assets—		
Cash	$ 20,760	$ (100,101)
Short-term investments	(306,641)	(5,170,701)
Accounts receivable	(484,634)	(650,979)
Inventories	(539,014)	(2,526,920)
Prepaid expenses	(67,010)	171,774
	(1,376,539)	(8,276,927)
Current Liabilities—		
Accounts payable	169,715	69,135
Owing to beet growers	(92,767)	(3,970,472)
Income taxes	(627,526)	(5,097,180)
Other liabilities and accrued expenses	(79,826)	(116,569)
	(630,404)	(9,115,086)
Increase (Decrease) in Working Capital	$ (746,135)	$ 838,159

Chapter 3

Processing Business Transactions

Before financial statements can be prepared, information must be gathered and processed into a workable form. The economic effects of business activities must be analyzed, recorded, summarized, and classified continuously throughout the accounting period. This chapter examines these steps in the accounting process, beginning with the analysis of business transactions. The basic accounting records and the rules for recording business transactions are presented. Transactions for both service-type businesses (that is, businesses that perform services as their primary operating activity) and merchandising-type businesses (that is, businesses that sell merchandise as their primary operating activity) are discussed and illustrated.

Unit 7
Analysis of Business Transactions

When the book lies open in front of you and you look at the book (not the book at you) then the side where you have your heart is the left or Debit side. The side away from your heart is the right side and is called Credit.

Matthäus Schwartz, Model of Accounting

Performance Objectives

Upon completing this unit you should be able to:
1. define and use the accounting terms introduced in this unit.
2. a. indicate the correct debit-credit rule for increasing and decreasing any account.
   b. indicate the normal balance for any account.
3. analyze the economic effects of business transactions on the assets, liabilities, owners' equity, revenue, and expense accounts for a service-type business organization.

The Nature of Business Transactions

Everyday a business may be involved in hundreds or thousands of events or activities that can be called *transactions*. However, not all transactions have an economic effect on the business. Those events or activities that cause changes in the assets and equities of a business are called **business transactions.** These involve the exchange of goods and services between the business and other businesses, government units, individuals, and other groups in society. Business transactions provide the raw data that are input into the accounting process. These raw data are analyzed to determine the economic effects of the transactions on the entity's accounts. The economic effects, in turn, are recorded and then classified to produce the output or end product of the process, which is the financial statements. Thus, the **accounting process** may be pictured as an information system consisting of input, internal processing, and output. The following diagram illustrates these aspects of the accounting process:

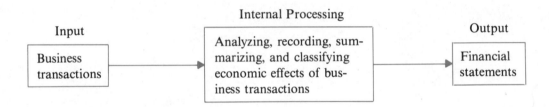

Input

Business transactions

Internal Processing

Analyzing, recording, summarizing, and classifying economic effects of business transactions

Output

Financial statements

Source documents provide supporting or underlying evidence for most business transactions. Sales invoices provide evidence for credit sales; purchase invoices provide evidence for purchases of merchandise, supplies, fixed assets, and expenses on credit. Cash sales slips and cash register tapes provide evidence for cash sales. Checks provide evidence for payments to creditors. Remittance advices and customers' checks provide evidence for collections from customers on their accounts. Special documents provide evidence for accounts written off as uncollectible.

Source documents provide the raw data that must be analyzed and recorded. Since a key concept of control is to record business transactions as soon as possible after they occur, the accounting system must first provide for the systematic accumulation of source documents. The raw data obtained from the documents are then analyzed to determine the economic effects of the transactions. Every transaction has a *dual economic effect* because it results in, as well as results from some exchange, transfer, or reclassification. In an exchange something is acquired or received and something is given up, incurred, issued, earned, or consumed. For example, in purchasing a plant asset, the plant asset is received and cash is given up immediately or an obligation to pay cash later is incurred. In a transfer or reclassification, at least two accounts are affected. When supplies are used in generating revenue, for example, expenses increase and assets decrease.

Economic Effects of Business Transactions

In each account affected by a business transaction, there is an increase or decrease. That is, the transaction has an **economic effect** on the accounts. These effects can be analyzed by asking and answering two main questions and a number of secondary questions.

Question	Economic Effect
What was acquired, or received, or reduced?	
An asset was acquired?	Assets increase.
A debt was reduced?	Liabilities decrease.
Owners' investment was reduced?	Owners' equity decreases.
Profits retained in the business were reduced?	Owners' equity decreases.
Claims were received against others for sales or services?	Assets increase.
Services or benefits were acquired to generate revenue?	Expenses increase.
What was given up, incurred, increased, earned, or consumed?	
An asset was given up?	Assets decrease.
A liability was incurred?	Liabilities increase.
Stock was issued or owners' interest increased?	Owners' equity increases.
Profits retained in the business were increased?	Owners' equity increases.
Revenue was earned from sales or services?	Revenues increase.
Merchandise was sold or assets consumed to generate revenue?	Assets decrease.

Exhibit 7.1 analyzes the economic effects of several transactions for I. C. Weather, CPA, a sole proprietor. Note the equality of the extended accounting equation after each transaction is analyzed, as well as the equality of the increases and decreases for each transaction. Review the process of analyzing business transactions to determine their economic effect. Follow the process step by step at first. Later, familiarity with commonly encountered transactions will eliminate the need for such an approach.

The Ledger Account

Recording a large number of transactions and classifying the needed information are impossible unless a standardized accounting record is used. Accounting uses such a record, an account or **ledger account.** With a ledger account information regarding each asset, liability, owners' equity item, revenue, and expense can be accumulated. The account must have designated spaces to record both increases and decreases.

Exhibit 7.1

I. C. Weather:
Analysis of Economic Effect of Business Transactions

Description of Transaction	Assets	=	Liabilities	+	Owners' Equity	+	(Revenues	−	Expenses)
1. I. C. Weather invests $20,000 in the business.	+$20,000 (cash)	=		+	+$20,000 (capital)				
	$20,000	=		+	$20,000				
2. Office supplies costing $350 are purchased on credit.	+ 350 (supplies)		+350 (accounts payable)						
	$20,350	=	$350	+	$20,000				
3. Clients are billed $4,000 for services rendered.	+ 4,000 (accounts receivable)						+$4,000 (fees earned)		
	$24,350	=	$350	+	$20,000	+	($4,000		)
4. The supplier is paid $150 for supplies purchased on credit in (2) above.	− 150 (cash)		−150 (accounts payable)						
	$24,200	=	$200	+	$20,000	+	($4,000		)
5. Employee salaries totaling $2,100 are paid.	− 2,100 (cash)								+$2,100 (salaries)
	$22,100	=	$200	+	$20,000	+	($4,000	−	2,100)
6. $2,500 is collected from clients billed for services in (3) above.	+ 2,500 (cash) − 2,500 (accounts receivable)								
	$22,100	=	$200	+	$20,000	+	($4,000	−	$2,100)
7. Amount of supplies consumed, $300, is recorded.	− 300 (supplies)								+300 (supplies used)
	$21,800	=	$200	+	$20,000	+	($4,000	−	2,400)
8. I. C. Weather withdraws $800 for personal use.	− 800 (cash)				−800 (drawings)				
	$21,000	=	$200	+	$19,200	+	($4,000	−	2,400)

	Description of Transaction	Question	Answer	Economic Effect
1.	I. C. Weather invests $20,000 in the business.	What was received?	An asset (cash)	Assets increase	$20,000
		What was issued?	An ownership interest in the business	Owners' equity (capital) increases	$20,000
2.	Office supplies costing $350 are purchased on credit.	What was acquired?	An asset (supplies)	Assets increase	$ 350
		What was incurred?	A liability (accounts payable)	Liabilities increase	$ 350
3.	Clients are billed $4,000 for services rendered.	What was received?	An asset (accounts receivable) for claims against clients	Assets increase	$ 4,000
		What was earned?	Revenue realized (fees earned) by performing services	Revenues increase	$ 4,000
4.	The supplier is paid $150 for supplies purchased on credit in (2) above.	What was reduced?	A debt (accounts payable)	Liabilities decrease	$ 150
		What was given up?	An asset (cash)	Assets decrease	$ 150
5.	Employee salaries totaling $2,100 are paid.	What was acquired?	Employee services (salaries expense) to generate revenue	Expenses increase	$ 2,100
		What was given up?	An asset (cash)	Assets decrease	$ 2,100
6.	$2,500 is collected from clients billed for services in (3) above.	What was received?	An asset (cash)	Assets increase	$ 2,500
		What was given up?	An asset (accounts receivable) for claims against clients	Assets decrease	$ 2,500
7.	Amount of supplies consumed, $300, is recorded.	What was received?	Benefits from supplies used to generate revenues	Expenses increase	$ 300
		What was consumed?	An asset (supplies)	Assets decrease	$ 300
8.	I. C. Weather withdraws $800 for personal use.	What was reduced?	Owners's equity as a result of withdrawal of money by owner	Owners' equity decreases	$ 800
		What was given up?	An asset (cash)	Assets decrease	$ 800

The form of the account resembles the letter T; thus, this form is called a **T-account:**

Ledger account (T-account form)	
Left or debit side	Right or credit side

The T-account has two sides. The left side is called the *debit side;* the right side is called the *credit side*. An entry made on the left side is called a **debit,** and the account is said to be debited; an entry made on the right side is called a **credit,** and the account is said to be credited. It is important to understand that the use of these two terms as described is completely arbitrary. The inventor of the ledger account concept could have reversed these names or called the two sides anything else that he desired.

A *double-entry bookkeeping system* was created to provide a means of checking the accuracy of recording business transactions. In the double-entry system, the sum of the debits must equal the sum of the credits for each individual transaction and for the sum of the balances for all accounts. This is accomplished by designating certain accounts to be increased by debits and other accounts to be increased by credits.

Note that the extended accounting equation is a mathematical equation and can be rearranged algebraicly:[1]

$$\text{assets} = \text{liabilities} + \text{owners' equity} + \text{revenues} - \text{expenses}$$
$$A = L + OE + R - E$$

$$\text{assets} + \text{expenses} = \text{liabilities} + \text{owners' equity} + \text{revenues}$$
$$A + E = L + OE + R$$

This rearrangement results in two different groups of accounts: (1) assets and expenses, and (2) liabilities, owners' equity, and revenues. The rules for increasing and decreasing accounts were then established (summarized in Table 7.1):

1. Asset and expense accounts increase by debits and decrease by credits.
2. Liability, owners' equity, and revenue accounts increase by credits and decrease by debits.
3. The **normal balance** of any account will correspond with the manner in which the account increases.
4. The total of assets and expenses (the debit balance accounts) is equal to the total of liabilities, owners' equity, and revenues (the credit balance accounts).
5. The amount of the accounts debited is equal to the amount of the accounts credited for each business transaction recorded.

---

[1]When the same amount is added to both sides of an equation, the equality is maintained. For example, by adding expenses *(E)* to both sides of the extended accounting equation, we end up with expenses *(E)* added to the left side but cancelled out on the right.

Table 7.1

Rules for Account Changes			
Type of Account	*Increases by*	*Decreases by*	*Normal Balance*
Assets	Debit	Credit	Debit
Expenses	Debit	Credit	Debit
Liabilities	Credit	Debit	Credit
Owners' equity	Credit	Debit	Credit
Revenues	Credit	Debit	Credit

Analysis of Economic Effects Using T-Accounts

It is possible to record the economic effects of business transactions directly in the ledger accounts. As an example, the eight transactions presented in Exhibit 7.1 are analyzed and recorded in T-accounts using the debit-credit rules for increasing and decreasing accounts. Carefully study the analysis of each transaction before proceeding.

1. Transaction: I. C. Weather invests $20,000 in the business.

Cash	
(1) 20,000	

Question: What was received?
Answer: An asset, cash
Economic effect: $20,000 increase in asset
Rule to increase asset: Debit the assct cash $20,000.

I. C. Weather, Capital	
	(1) 20,000

Question: What was issued?
Answer: Ownership interest (capital) in business
Economic effect: $20,000 increase in owner's equity
Rule to increase owner's equity: Credit the owner's equity account, I. C. Weather, capital, $20,000.

2. Transaction: Office supplies costing $350 are purchased on credit.

Supplies	
(2) 350	

Question: What was acquired?
Answer: An asset, supplies
Economic effect: $350 increase in asset
Rule to increase assets: Debit the asset supplies $350.

Accounts Payable	
	(2) 350

Question: What was incurred?
Answer: A liability, accounts payable
Economic effect: $350 increase in liability
Rule to increase liability: Credit the liability accounts payable $350.

3. Transaction: Clients are billed $4,000 for services rendered.

Accounts Receivable	
(3) 4,000	

Question: What was received?
Answer: An asset, accounts receivable, for claims against clients
Economic effect: $4,000 increase in asset
Rule to increase asset: Debit the asset accounts receivable $4,000.

Fees Earned	
	(3) 4,000

Question: What was earned?
Answer: Revenue realized, fees earned, by performing services
Economic effect: $4,000 increase in revenue
Rule to increase revenue: Credit the revenue account fees earned $4,000.

4. Transaction: The supplier is paid $150 for supplies purchased on credit in (2) above.

Accounts Payable	
(4) 150	(2) 350

Question: What was reduced?
Answer: A debt, accounts payable
Economic effect: $150 decrease in liability
Rule to decrease liability: Debit the liability accounts payable $150.

Cash	
(1) 20,000	(4) 150

Question: What was given up?
Answer: An asset, cash
Economic effect: $150 decrease in asset
Rule to decrease asset: Credit the asset cash $150.

5. Transaction: Employee salaries totaling $2,100 are paid.

Salaries Expense	
(5) 2,100	

Question: What was acquired?
Answer: Employee services, salaries expense, to generate revenues
Economic effect: $2,100 increase in expense
Rule to increase expense: Debit the expense salaries expense $2,100.

Cash	
(1) 20,000	(4) 150
	(5) 2,100

Question: What was given up?
Answer: An asset, cash
Economic effect: $2,100 decrease in asset
Rule to decrease asset: Credit the asset cash $2,100.

6. Transaction: $2,500 is collected from clients billed for services in (3) above.

Cash	
(1) 20,000	(4) 150
(6) 2,500	(5) 2,100

Question: What was received?
Answer: An asset, cash
Economic effect: $2,500 increase in asset
Rule to increase asset: Debit the asset cash $2,500.

Accounts Receivable	
(3) 4,000	(6) 2,500

Question: What was given up?
Answer: An asset, accounts receivable, for claims against clients
Economic effect: $2,500 decrease in asset
Rule to decrease asset: Credit the asset accounts receivable $2,500.

7. Transaction: Amount of supplies consumed, $300, is recorded.

Supplies Used	
(7) 300	

Question: What was received?
Answer: Benefits from supplies used to generate revenue
Economic effect: $300 increase in expense
Rule to increase expense: Debit the expense supplies used $300.

Supplies	
(2) 350	(7) 300

Question: What was consumed?
Answer: An asset, supplies
Economic effect: $300 decrease in asset
Rule to decrease asset: Credit the asset supplies $300.

8. Transaction: I. C. Weather withdraws $800 for personal use.

I. C. Weather, Drawing	
(8) 800	

Question: What was reduced?
Answer: Owners' equity, as a result of withdrawal of money by owner
Economic effect: $800 decrease in owners' equity (recorded in owner's drawing account)
Rule to decrease owners' equity: Debit the owner's drawing account $800.

Cash	
(1) 20,000	(4) 150
(6) 2,500	(5) 2,100
	(8) 800

Question: What was given up?
Answer: An asset, cash
Economic effect: $800 decrease in asset
Rule to decrease asset: Credit the asset cash $800.

The balance of an account is determined by adding separately the debit entries and the credit entries recorded in the account; then the smaller sum is deducted from the larger to compute the balance. Following are the accounts affected by the eight transactions, along with their debit and credit entries.

Cash	
(1) 20,000	(4) 150
(6) 2,500	(5) 2,100
22,500	(8) 800
	3,050

Accounts Receivable	
(3) 4,000	(6) 2,500

Supplies	
(2) 350	(7) 300

Accounts Payable	
(4) 150	(2) 350

I. C. Weather, Capital	
	(1) 20,000

I. C. Weather, Drawing	
(8) 800	

Fees Earned	Salaries Expense	Supplies Used
(3) 4,000	(5) 2,100	(7) 300

Exhibit 7.2 shows how the balance of each account is computed.

Exhibit 7.2

Account	Sum of Debits	Sum of Credits	Difference (Balance)	Type of Balance
Cash	$22,500	$ 3,050	$19,450	Debit
Accounts receivable	4,000	2,500	1,500	Debit
Supplies	350	300	50	Debit
Accounts payable	150	350	200	Credit
I. C. Weather, capital	—	20,000	20,000	Credit
I. C. Weather, drawing	800	—	800	Debit
Fees earned	—	4,000	4,000	Credit
Salaries expense	2,100	—	2,100	Debit
Supplies used	300	—	300	Debit

Note that the balances of the assets (cash, accounts receivable, and supplies) and of the expenses (salaries expense and supplies used) correspond with the normal balance expected for assets and expenses, a debit balance. Similarly, the balances for liabilities (accounts payable), owner's equity (I. C. Weather, capital), and revenue (fees earned) correspond with the normal balance expected for these accounts, a credit balance. The account, I. C. Weather, drawing, is an offset or contra account used to accumulate amounts of owners' equity withdrawn by the owner during the accounting period; because it represents a decrease in owners' equity, it has a debit balance. Contra or offset accounts always have a balance opposite that of the account to which they are related.

Although recording all business transactions directly in the ledger accounts is feasible, it is not the best method. A more efficient and more accurate method of initially recording all business transactions, using an accounting record called a *journal,* is discussed in Unit 8.

The Accounting Cycle

Following is a summary of all the steps in the accounting cycle. This summary will help you understand the detailed discussions of these steps as each was presented throughout the chapter.

1. Analyze business transactions for their economic effects.
2. Journalize the business transactions in a book of original entry in chronological order. Transactions are recorded in a journal as soon as possible after they occur.
3. Post the journal entries to the ledger accounts. The data are transferred from the journal to the ledger in order to classify them according to type of asset, liability, owners' equity, revenue, and expense account maintained by the entity.
4. Prepare a trial balance. A list of all accounts and their balances is prepared to prove the equality of debits and credits before the remaining steps in the accounting cycle are completed.
5. Prepare a worksheet. This multi-column form allows the accountant to gather in one place all the data needed to prepare the financial statements, adjusting entries, and closing entries.
   a. Enter the trial balance on the worksheet.
   b. Enter the adjustments on the worksheet. These adjustments are necessary to update the assets, liabilities, revenues, and expenses so they properly reflect financial position and operating results.
   c. Prepare an adjusted trial balance. The trial balance figures, plus or minus the adjustments, are entered on the worksheet. (Optional step.)
   d. Complete the worksheet. The adjusted trial balance figures (or the trial balance figures plus or minus the adjustments) are extended to columns for income statement, balance sheet, and possibly the retained earnings statement.
6. Prepare the income statement, balance sheet, and retained earnings statement using information from the worksheet.
7. Journalize and post the adjustments using information from the worksheet.
8. Journalize and post the closing entries using information from the worksheet. These entries prepare the revenue and expense accounts for the next period by reducing their balances to zero.
9. Prepare a post-closing trial balance. This is a list of the accounts that still have a balance after the closing entries and their balances are prepared (only the balance sheet accounts should still have balances).
10. Journalize and post the reversing entries. These optional entries reverse certain adjustments to facilitate bookkeeping during the next accounting period. (This step is not covered in this text.)

REVIEW PROBLEM

The following are transactions involving Akin Corp. in January:

Jan. 2	Sold 1,000 shares of $20 par value stock for $20 per share.
Jan. 5	Purchased office equipment, $1,200, and office supplies, $200, on credit.
Jan. 9	Billed clients $6,000 for services rendered.
Jan. 18	Paid the bill for office equipment and office supplies; see Jan. 5 transaction.
Jan. 24	Collected $3,600 from clients billed on Jan. 9.
Jan. 31	Paid operating expenses for January, $2,400.

Required   **1.**   **a.**   Using the following format, analyze the economic effects of each transaction:

		What was acquired or received or reduced?			What was given up, incurred, issued, earned, or consumed?		
Date	Description of transaction	Answer to question	Economic effect	Rule to increase or decrease	Answer to question	Economic effect	Rule to increase or decrease

b.   Indicate the normal balance for each account:

Account	Normal Balance

2.   Record each transaction in T-accounts.

Solution to review problem

1.   **a.**   See Exhibit 7.3.

b.

Account	Normal Balance
Cash	Debit
Common stock	Credit
Office equipment	Debit
Office supplies	Debit
Accounts payable	Credit
Accounts receivable	Debit
Service revenues	Credit
Operating expenses	Debit

Exhibit 7.3

Date	Description of transaction	What was acquired or received or reduced?			What was given up, incurred, issued, earned, or consumed?		
		Answer to question	Economic effect	Rule to increase or decrease	Answer to question	Economic effect	Rule to increase or decrease
Jan. 2	Sold 1,000 shares of $20 par value stock for $20 per share	An asset, cash, received	Assets increase	Debit the asset, cash.	Stock issued to investor (owner)	Owners' equity increases	Credit the owners' equity account, common stock.
Jan. 5	Purchased office equipment, $1,200, and office supplies, $200, on credit	Assets, office equipment and office supplies, acquired	Assets increase	Debit the assets, office equipment and office supplies.	A liability, accounts payable, incurred	Liabilities increase	Credit the liability, accounts payable.
Jan. 9	Billed clients $6,000 for services rendered	An asset, accounts receivable, received	Assets increase	Debit the asset, accounts receivable.	Revenue earned by performing services	Revenues increase	Credit the revenue account, service revenues.
Jan. 18	Paid the bill for office equipment and office supplies; see Jan. 5 transaction	A liability, accounts payable, reduced	Liabilities decrease	Debit the liability, accounts payable.	An asset, cash, given up	Assets decrease	Credit the asset, cash.
Jan. 24	Collected $3,600 from clients billed on Jan. 9	An asset, cash, received	Assets increase	Debit the asset, cash.	An asset, accounts receivable, given up	Assets decrease	Credit the asset, accounts receivable.
Jan. 31	Paid operating expenses for January, $2,400	Benefits acquired to generate revenues	Expenses increase	Debit the expense account, operating expenses.	An asset, cash, given up	Assets decrease	Credit the asset, cash.

2.

Cash	
1/2 20,000	1/18 1,400
1/24 3,600	1/31 2,400

Accounts Receivable	
1/9 6,000	1/24 3,600

Office Supplies	
1/5 200	

Office Equipment	
1/5 1,200	

Accounts Payable	
1/18 1,400	1/5 1,400

Common Stock	
	1/2 20,000

Service Revenues	
	1/9 6,000

Operating Expenses	
1/31 2,400	

SUMMARY

The procedure required to analyze the dual economic effects of business transactions was explained in this unit. The ledger account concept was introduced, and the rules for expressing economic effects in terms of debits and credits were explained and illustrated. This ability to analyze the economic effects of business transactions and express them in terms of debits and credits is essential to an understanding of Unit 8.

REVIEW QUESTIONS

7-1 What are business transactions?

7-2 Explain how the accounting process can be compared to an information system consisting of input, internal processing, and output.

7-3 What are source documents? What role do source documents play in the accounting process?

7-4   Explain how each business transaction has a dual economic effect on an entity.

7-5   How can the basic accounting equation, i.e., the model for the balance sheet, be extended to reflect revenues and expenses?

7-6   Following are the questions used to analyze the dual economic effects of business transactions. For each subquestion, assuming the response is positive, indicate the economic effect of such a transaction. The first item has been completed as an example.

    a.   What was received, acquired, or reduced?

(1)	An asset was received or acquired?	**(1)**	Assets increase.
(2)	A debt was reduced?	**(2)**	
(3)	Owners' investment was reduced?	**(3)**	
(4)	Profits retained in the business were reduced?	**(4)**	
(5)	Claims were received against customers for sales or services performed?	**(5)**	
(6)	Services or benefits to generate revenue were received or acquired?	**(6)**	

    b.   What was given up, incurred, issued, earned, or consumed?

(1)	An asset was given up?	**(1)**	Assets decrease.
(2)	A liability was incurred?	**(2)**	
(3)	Stock was issued or the owners' interest increases?	**(3)**	
(4)	Profits retained in the business increased?	**(4)**	
(5)	Revenue was earned from sales or services?	**(5)**	
(6)	Merchandise was sold or assets were consumed to generate revenue?	**(6)**	

7-7   Define the following terms:

    a.   ledger account   **c.**   debit
    b.   T-account   **d.**   credit

7-8   Complete the following table to indicate the rules for increasing and decreasing each type of account and to indicate the normal balance for each type of account.

Type of Account	Rule to Increase the Account	Rule to Decrease the Account	Normal Balance
Assets Liabilities Owners' equity Revenues Expenses			

7-9   What is meant by the accounting process or cycle?

7-10   Listed below are the steps in the accounting cycle as presented in this unit. Indicate the correct sequence for the steps by numbering them from 1 to 10.

_____   Prepare a worksheet.
_____   Post the journal entries to the ledger.
_____   Journalize and post the reversing entries.
_____   Prepare a trial balance.
_____   Analyze the business transactions for their economic effects.
_____   Prepare the financial statements.
_____   Prepare a post-closing trial balance.
_____   Journalize the business transactions in a book of original entry.
_____   Journalize and post the adjusting entries.
_____   Journalize and post the closing entries.

EXERCISES

7-1   Show the economic effect of each of the following business transactions on the extended accounting equation using the following format (see Exhibit 7.1 for an example of this format).

Description of Transaction	Assets = Liabilities + Equity + Revenues − Expenses

Transactions

May 1   Henry Smythe invested $5,000 cash, and office furniture valued at $570, in a travel business he started, Tours Unlimited.

May 5   Additional office furniture was purchased on credit at a cost of $250.

May 8	Office supplies costing $35 were purchased for cash.
May 12	The office furniture bill from May 5 was paid.
May 18	Advertising space in a local newspaper was purchased for $60 cash.
May 29	Henry Smythe withdrew $1,000 of his original investment since the money was not needed for business operations.
May 31	Payment was received from customers for services performed, $800.

7-2   Refer to the data in exercise 7-1. Analyze the economic effects of each transaction and indicate the debit-credit rule to increase or decrease each account affected by the transaction. Use the following format for your answer (see Exhibit 7.3 for use of this format).

		What was acquired, received, or reduced?			What was given up, incurred, issued, earned, or consumed?		
Date	Description of transaction	Answer to question	Economic effect	Rule to increase or decrease	Answer to question	Economic effect	Rule to increase or decrease

7-3   Refer to the data in exercise 7-1. Enter each transaction directly into T-accounts.

7-4   For each of the following accounts, place an X on the correct side of each column to indicate how that account is increased and decreased and to indicate its normal balance.

	Increased by		Decreased by		Normal Balance	
Accounts	Debits	Credits	Debits	Credits	Debit	Credit
Example: Cash	X			X	X	
a. Land						
b. Accounts payable						
c. Retained earnings						
d. Sales						
e. Depreciation expense						
f. Allowance for uncollectible accounts						
g. Inventory						
h. Mortgage payable						

7-5   The following are descriptions of the economic effects of business transactions:

    a.   Increase in one asset, decrease in another.
    b.   Increase in an asset, increase in a liability.
    c.   Increase in an asset, increase in proprietorship.
    d.   Decrease in an asset, decrease in proprietorship.
    e.   Increase in an asset, increase in a revenue.

f. Decrease in an asset, increase in an expense.

g. Increase in a liability, increase in an expense.

h. Decrease in a liability, decrease in an asset.

For each of the following transactions, write in the space provided the letter of the description that explains its economic effects.

_____ **(1)** Nelson invests $2,000 cash in the business.

_____ **(2)** Check no. 100 for $575 is issued to Oliver Co. for the purchase of an electric calculator.

_____ **(3)** Supplies costing $290 are purchased from the Locust Co.; terms, 30 days.

_____ **(4)** A bill for $300 covering research investigations completed for clients is sent to the Sunlight Co.; terms, 10 days.

_____ **(5)** Salaries are paid to tabulating clerks by check, $210.

_____ **(6)** Supplies that cost $30, purchased previously from the Locust Co., are used on current research projects.

_____ **(7)** Fees totaling $400 are received in cash.

_____ **(8)** A bill for $25 covering telephone services for the past month is received from the Bell Telephone Co. Payment will be made later.

_____ **(9)** Nelson withdraws $360 for personal use.

_____ **(10)** Postage stamps used to mail reports to clients today are purchased for cash, $7.

PROBLEMS

7-1 The following transactions were completed by the U-Freeze Locker Service Co. during August:

Aug. 1	Mr. Thaw invested $4,000 cash and a cash register valued at $500 in the business.
Aug. 3	Paid the rent for August, $175.
Aug. 5	Purchased supplies on account, $150.
Aug. 8	Received $550 from cash customers for lockers rented to them.
Aug. 12	Paid creditors on account, $125.
Aug. 18	Charged customers $350 for lockers rented to them during the first half of August.
Aug. 24	Collected $275 from customers in payment on their accounts.
Aug. 27	Purchased equipment, paying cash $500 and giving a note for the balance of $2,000.
Aug. 31	Paid the monthly salary to the sole employee, $400.
Aug. 31	Mr. Thaw withdrew $300 for personal use.

Analyze the economic effects of each transaction and indicate the debit-credit rule to increase or decrease each account affected by them. Use the following format for your answer (see Exhibit 7.3 for the use of this format).

Date	Description of transaction	What was acquired, received, or reduced?			What was given up, incurred, issued, earned, or consumed?		
		Answer to question	Economic effect	Rule to increase or decrease	Answer to question	Economic effect	Rule to increase or decrease

7-2   Refer to the data in problem 7–1. Enter each transaction directly into T-accounts.

7-3   This problem reviews the types of accounts, the rules for increasing and decreasing accounts, and the normal balance of accounts. Fill in each column. For the first column indicate the type of accounts using these symbols:

> A: assets   R: revenues
> L: liabilities   E: expenses
> OE: owners' equity

If the account is a contra or offset account, place a C before the account letter (e.g., a contra-asset account should be marked C-A and a contra-revenue account should be marked C-R). For the second and third columns, place an X on the correct side to indicate how each account is increased or decreased. For the fourth column, indicate the normal balance by writing Dr for debit or Cr for credit.

	Type of Account	Increased by		Decreased by		Normal Balance
		Debits	Credits	Debits	Credits	
Example: Supplies expense	E	X			X	Dr

a.	Jack Beatle, capital	**k.**	Accounts receivable
b.	Store equipment	**l.**	Building
c.	Cost of goods sold	**m.**	Notes payable
d.	Sales	**n.**	Prepaid insurance
e.	Accounts payable	**o.**	Advertising
f.	Sales returns and allowance	**p.**	Supplies on hand
g.	Office salaries	**q.**	Service fees earned
h.	Allowance for uncollectible accounts	**r.**	Temporary investments
		s.	Bonds payable
i.	Interest revenue	**t.**	Accumulated depreciation — store equipment
j.	Jack Beatle, drawing		

7-4   The following are descriptions of the economic effects of business transactions:

> **a.**   Increase in one asset, decrease in another.
> **b.**   Increase in an asset, increase in a liability.
> **c.**   Increase in an asset, increase in owners' equity.
> **d.**   Decrease in an asset, decrease in owners' equity.

e. Increase in an asset, increase in a revenue.
f. Decrease in an asset, increase in an expense.
g. Increase in a liability, increase in an expense.
h. Decrease in a liability, decrease in an asset.

For each of the following transactions, write in the space provided the letter of the description that explains its economic effects.

Sept. 1	Received $10,000 cash invested by the owner.
Sept. 2	Paid the monthly premium on an insurance policy, $50.
Sept. 9	Purchased office equipment, $450, on credit.
Sept. 11	Completed legal work for a customer and collected $200 cash for the work completed.
Sept. 13	Completed legal work for another customer and billed him $400 for the work completed.
Sept. 18	Paid for the equipment purchased on Sept. 9.
Sept. 21	Received a bill for $40 from the Public Service Company for electricity used during the past month; this bill will be paid next month.
Sept. 26	Paid the employees their weekly salaries totaling $375.
Sept. 29	Collected the $400 billed to a customer on Sept. 13.
Sept. 30	Paid $850 to the owner for his personal use.

7-5 Several business transactions are described below:

a. Services were performed and customers were billed.
b. The owner invested additional cash in the business.
c. Salaries were paid to employees.
d. Office supplies were purchased on credit.
e. Office equipment was purchased for cash.
f. Payment was received on the amounts billed to customers in (a).
g. A loan was obtained from the local bank.
h. Payment was made for the supplies purchased in (d).
i. The owner withdrew cash from the business for personal use.
j. Services were performed for customers; cash payment was received immediately.
k. Office equipment was purchased and one-third of the cost was paid immediately; the balance is due in two equal installments at the end of the next two months.
l. The bank loan in (g) was repaid; the amount borrowed plus interest was paid to the bank.
m. A utility bill was received and the liability for the amount due was recorded.

Required Indicate the economic effects of these transactions. For example, for transaction a: Assets increase and revenues increase.

Unit 8
Processing Business Transactions

Some merchants are lazy and negligent, want to keep everything in their heads and trust themselves too much. They make a note of their transactions on writing pads and scraps of paper, stick them on the wall and keep their accounts by writing on the window-sill. Rather than use a little diligence and effort they let their business go to ruin and cannot understand why in the end they are forced to abscond. . . .

Matthäus Schwartz, Model of Accounting

The economic effects of business transactions should be recorded in one place in chronological order as soon as possible after they occur. Later these data can be transferred to ledger accounts, where the data needed to prepare financial statements can accumulate. This unit examines the processing of business transactions in steps 2, 3, and 4 of the accounting cycle: journalizing the transactions, posting the journal entries, and preparing a trial balance.

Performance Objectives

Upon completing this unit you should be able to:

1. define and use the accounting terms introduced in this unit.
2. record typical business transactions for a service organization in a general journal.
3. post general journal entries for typical business transactions for a service organization to the general ledger.
4. prepare a trial balance for a service organization.
5. prepare financial statements for a service-type organization.

The General Journal

The **general journal** is an accounting record designed for recording, in chronological sequence, the economic effects of business transactions. It is referred to as a **book of original entry** because it is here that business transactions are initially recorded. All business transactions can be recorded in the general journal. Frequently, it is referred to simply as the journal.

Recording business transactions initially in a journal makes it easy to trace them later. In a journal the dual economic effects of the transactions are recorded in one place, based on the transaction date. If transactions were recorded directly in ledger accounts, the economic effects would be recorded in separate accounts, and it would be difficult for accountants to trace errors or for auditors to verify the accuracy of the recording process. An **audit trail** is needed—thus, transactions are first recorded entirely in one place in a journal; then, the effects on each account are posted to the ledger accounts in another step. This system makes it possible to trace the postings from the journal to the ledger accounts or from the postings in the ledger accounts to the journal. The efficiency and accuracy of the initial recording process are improved by entering the transaction in one place.

Figure 8.1 illustrates the general journal form. The main features of the general journal are:

1. title of record and page number—a **posting reference** in each ledger account uses this information to indicate the location of the relevant journal entry.
2. date column—the date of each transaction is recorded here.
3. column for account titles and explanation—the name of the accounts debited and credited and a brief, written description of each transaction are entered here.
4. PR (posting reference) column—the number of the account to which each debit and credit entry has been posted is entered here.
5. debit amount column—the amount of each debit entry is entered here.
6. credit amount column—the amount of each credit entry is entered here.

Journalizing Business Transactions

As soon as business transactions are identified, their economic effects should be analyzed and then **journalized** or recorded in a book of original entry. Exhibit 8.1 illustrates how a business transaction is recorded in one book of original entry, the general journal. The two transactions illustrated are:

General Journal

Date	Accounts and Explanation	PR	Debit	Credit

Page

Figure 8.1   General journal form

Exhibit 8.1

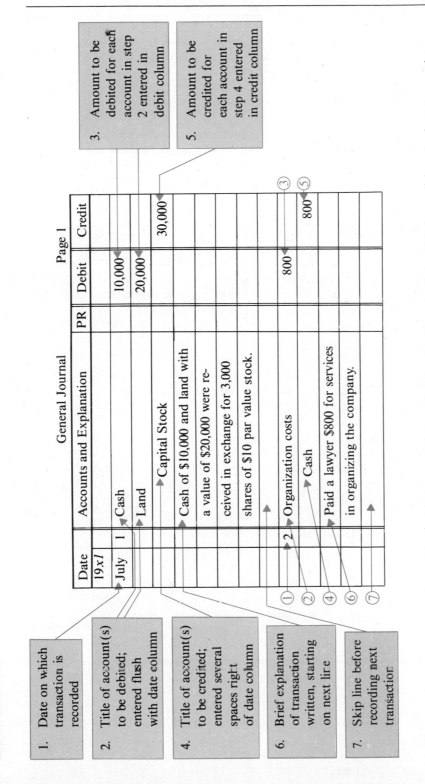

Note: Circled numbers for the second entry represent steps 1 through 7 (as given for transaction 1) in journalizing a business transaction.

July 1, 19*x1*   The company issued 3,000 shares of $10 par value stock in exchange for $10,000 cash and land valued at $20,000.

July 2, 19*x1*   The company paid a lawyer $800 for services in organizing the company.

The sum of the debits is equal to the sum of the credits in each journal entry in the exhibit. This equality of debits and credits is the basis of the double-entry system of bookkeeping. It allows a check on the accuracy of the bookkeeping process. The procedures for locating errors are discussed on pages 149–151.

The General Ledger

The ledger accounts are maintained in a book called the **general ledger** or the ledger. The ledger is also referred to as a **book of final entry** because business transactions are initially recorded in a journal and then finally in the ledger before the financial statements are prepared. Each account maintained by the company has its own page or pages in the ledger. Several sheets may be used for a single account as time goes by and the number of transactions recorded increases.

To locate the accounts and provide a convenient posting reference, a page or account number is assigned to each account. When an accounting system for an entity is first designed, a list of all accounts to be used is drawn up. The accounts are then assigned code (account) numbers. Any logical numbering system can be used as long as gaps are left to add new accounts as the need arises. A list of all accounts currently used by an entity, along with their account numbers, is called a **chart of accounts.** Exhibit 8.2 illustrates a chart of accounts for the Mackinaw Company.

Different forms of ledger accounts are used. One standard form, shown in Figure 8.2, has two sides: one for debit entries and the other for credit entries. The key features of this form are:

1. account name and number space
2. date column on each side of the account page to enter the date the transaction was recorded in the journal
3. explanation column on each side of the account page for special notations and for calculating the account balance
4. PR or posting reference column on each side of the account page to indicate the journal page from which the information was obtained
5. amount column on each side of the account page for the amount debited or credited in the journal

Another commonly used form of the ledger account is illustrated in Figure 8.3. This form is useful where a running balance for an account is desirable. Its features are single columns for (1) the date of the transaction, (2) explanation, and (3) posting reference (PR), and three amount columns, one each for (4) debits, (5) credits, and (6) the account balance.

Exhibit 8.2

Mackinaw Company
Chart of Accounts

Account Number	Account Title
101	Cash
103	Accounts receivable
105	Supplies inventory
112	Prepaid insurance
121	Land
122	Buildings
123	Accumulated depreciation on building
125	Furniture and fixtures
126	Accumulated depreciation on furniture and fixtures
131	Land for future plant site
151	Accounts payable
152	Property taxes payable
153	Income taxes payable
161	Mortgage payable
162	Note payable, long-term
201	Capital stock
202	Contributed capital in excess of par
203	Retained earnings
211	Service revenue
221	Utilities expense
222	Salary and wage expense
223	Insurance expense
224	Property tax expense
225	Depreciation expense
226	Miscellaneous expenses
231	Interest revenue
241	Interest expense
251	Income tax expense

When transactions are posted from the journal to the ledger, posting references are entered in the PR columns in both the journal and the ledger accounts. An audit trail consisting of the journal page number of an entry and the ledger account number is necessary to trace errors and audit a company's records. The process of recording the journal page number in the PR column of the ledger account and the ledger account number in the PR column of the journal is called **cross-referencing.** Cross-referencing enables entries to be traced from the journal to the ledger or from the ledger to the journal.

Posting Journal Entries

After business transactions are journalized, their economic effects must be transferred, that is, **posted,** to the appropriate ledger accounts. The posting process summarizes the economic effects of all transactions on each account maintained by an entity. The balance of each account can then be determined and reported on the appro-

Account Title Account Number ______

Date	Explanation	PR	Amount	Date	Explanation	PR	Amount

Figure 8.2 *Standard ledger account form*

Account Title Account Number______

Date	Explanation	PR	Debit	Credit	Balance

Figure 8.3 *Three-column ledger account form*

priate financial statement. Because transactions are recorded in chronological order in the general journal, it would be difficult to determine account balances if the posting step were omitted.

Exhibit 8.3 illustrates the steps in posting a journal entry. The appropriate sections of the journal and the ledger accounts to be posted are shown. Assume that the June 1 entry has already been posted. The next account to be posted is accounts receivable from the June 2 transaction. Steps 1 through 4 are completed by entering the date and the amount in the appropriate columns, the page number and symbol for the journal (J6) in the PR column of the ledger account, and the ledger account number of the account posted (No. 111) in the PR column in the journal. These four steps are repeated to post the next account, fees earned (No. 401).

The journal page number entered in the PR column of the ledger and the ledger account number entered in the PR column in the general journal establish a cross-referencing between the journal and ledger. This cross-referencing represents an audit trail that can be used to verify the accuracy of the posting activity. An entry in the ledger can be traced back to the journal to verify that it is posted to the correct account and that the correct amount has been posted. Also, an entry in the journal can be traced to the ledger to verify the accuracy of the posting.

The Trial Balance

A **trial balance** is a list of all ledger accounts and their balances at a specific date. Usually the accounts contain the normal balance for their type of account, that is, debit balances for assets and expenses and credit balances for liability, owners' equity, and revenue accounts. The trial balance has the same type of heading as a balance sheet. It consists of three columns: a list of account titles, a debit balance column, and a credit balance column.

A trial balance is prepared at the end of the accounting period to verify the accuracy of the recording and posting processes. If total debits equal total credits, the accountant may assume that equal amounts for debits and credits have been recorded and posted. However, certain errors are not uncovered by the trial balance because the total debits and total credits will still be equal even though the errors have been made. Errors not uncovered by preparing a trial balance include:

1. Failure to record or post an entire transaction—for example, failure to record the purchase of supplies on credit for $50 results in understating both the asset (supplies inventory) and the liability (accounts payable) by $50.
2. Recording the wrong amount for a transaction—for example, recording the payment of rent expense as $560 instead of the correct amount of $650 results in understating both the debit entry (rent expense) and the credit entry (cash) by $90 ($650 − 560 = $90).
3. Posting a debit or credit to the wrong account—for example, if an expenditure of $3,000 for equipment components is

Exhibit 8.3

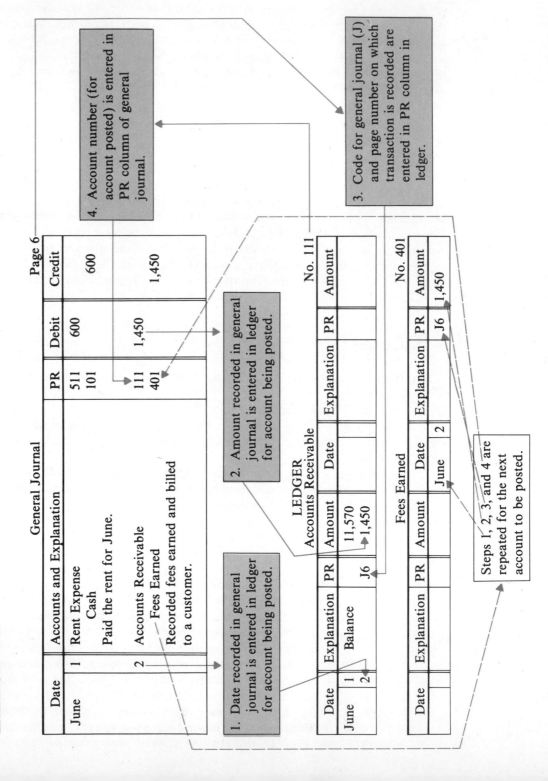

erroneously charged (that is, debited) to repair expense rather than to the asset, equipment, total debits will still equal total credits, but the wrong account will have been debited.

If the trial balance does not balance, that is, if debits do not equal credits, there are procedures you can follow to discover the error. These are:

1. Readd the columns of the trial balance.
2. Divide the difference between the total debits and total credits by 2; then look for an account balance equal to this quotient that has been entered in the wrong column (for example, if the difference is $2,700, look for an account balance of $1,350 ($2,700/2) entered in the wrong column).
3. Double-check the balances in the trial balance by comparing them with the balances in the ledger.
4. Recompute the balances in the ledger.
5. Double-check the postings in the ledger account by tracing them back to the journal and comparing the amounts posted with the amounts recorded in the journal.

The trial balance is illustrated in the review problem. Using a trial balance as the starting point in the preparation of financial statements is discussed in Unit 12.

REVIEW PROBLEM—A COMPLETE ILLUSTRATION

The eight transactions analyzed in Exhibit 7.1 are repeated here. Dates have been added so the transactions can be used to illustrate the journalizing and posting of business transactions for a service organization:

June 1, 19*x1*	I. C. Weather invests $20,000 in the business.
June 2, 19*x1*	Office supplies costing $350 are purchased on credit.
June 6, 19*x1*	Clients are billed $4,000 for services rendered.
June 8, 19*x1*	The supplier is paid $150 for supplies purchased on credit on June 2.
June 10, 19*x1*	Employee salaries totaling $2,100 are paid.
June 12, 19*x1*	$2,500 is collected from clients billed for services on June 6.
June 15, 19*x1*	Amount of supplies consumed, $300, is recorded.
June 15, 19*x1*	I. C. Weather withdraws $800 for personal use.

The following illustrates the journal entries for these eight transactions, the relevant ledger accounts after posting the journal entries, and a trial balance as of June 15, 19*x1*. Explanations of these entries are also given. If necessary, refer back to Exhibit

7.1 and pages 127–130 for the more detailed analysis of the economic effects of these transactions.

Date 19x1	Accounts and Explanation	PR	Debit	Credit
	General Journal	**Page 1**		
June 1	Cash	101	20,000	
	I. C. Weather, Capital	301		20,000
	Owner invests $20,000 in the business.			
2	Supplies	131	350	
	Accounts Payable	201		350
	Purchased office supplies on credit.			
6	Accounts Receivable	111	4,000	
	Fees Earned	401		4,000
	Billed clients for services rendered.			
8	Accounts Payable	201	150	
	Cash	101		150
	Paid supplier part of balance owed from June 2.			
10	Salaries Expense	501	2,100	
	Cash	101		2,100
	Paid employee salaries.			
12	Cash	101	2,500	
	Accounts Receivable	111		2,500
	Collected from customers billed on June 6.			
15	Supplies Used	502	300	
	Supplies	131		300
	Recorded supplies used.			
15	I. C. Weather, Drawing	302	800	
	Cash	101		800
	Owner withdraws cash for personal use.			

Explanations of journal entries

June 1   When the owner invests $20,000 in the business, assets and owner's equity increase. Thus, the asset cash is debited for $20,000 and the owner's capital account is credited for $20,000.

June 2   The purchase of supplies on credit increases assets and liabilities. Thus, the asset supplies is debited $350 and the liability accounts payable is credited $350.

June 6   When clients are billed for services rendered, assets and revenues increase. Thus, the asset accounts receivable is debited for $4,000 and the revenue account fees earned is credited for $4,000.

June 8   The payment of part of the balance owed to the

supplier decreases liabilities and assets. Thus, the liability accounts payable is debited for $150 and the asset cash is credited for $150.

June 10   When salaries are paid to employees, expenses increase and assets decrease. Thus, the expense account salaries expense is debited for $2,100 and the asset cash is credited for $2,100.

June 12   The collection of amounts previously billed to clients increases one asset and decreases another asset. Thus, the asset cash is debited for $2,500 and the asset accounts receivable is credited for $2,500.

June 15   After supplies are used to carry out operations to generate revenue, an entry to increase expenses and decrease assets is needed. Thus, the expense account supplies used is debited for $300 and the asset supplies is credited $300.

June 15   When the owner draws cash for personal use, an entry to decrease owner's equity and assets is made. Thus, the owner's drawing account is debited $800 to reduce owner's equity and the asset cash is credited $800.

Ledger

Cash			101
6/1 J1	20,000	6/8 J1	150
6/12 J1	2,500	6/10 J1	2,100
		6/15 J1	800

Accounts Receivable			111
6/6 J1	4,000	6/12 J1	2,500

Supplies			131
6/2 J1	350	6/15 J1	300

Accounts Payable			201
6/8 J1	150	6/2 J1	350

I. C. Weather, Capital			301
		6/1 J1	20,000

I. C. Weather, Drawing			302
6/15 J1	800		

Fees Earned			401
		6/6 J1	4,000

Salaries Expense			501
6/10 J1	2,100		

Supplies Used		502
6/15 J1	300	

I. C. Weather, CPA
Trial Balance
As of June 15, 19x1

Cash	$19,450	$
Accounts Receivable	1,500	
Supplies	50	
Accounts Payable		200
I. C. Weather, Capital		20,000
I. C. Weather, Drawing	800	
Fees Earned		4,000
Salaries Expense	2,100	
Supplies Used	300	
	$24,200	$24,200

SUMMARY

This unit described how business transactions are recorded initially in chronological sequence in a general journal and then transferred to a general ledger to summarize the economic effects on each asset, liability, owners' equity, revenue, and expense account. The use of a trial balance to partially prove the accuracy of recording the economic effects of business transactions in the general journal and general ledger was also described. Only business transactions for service-type organizations were used in this unit; business transactions for merchandise-type organizations will be discussed in the next unit.

REVIEW QUESTIONS

8-1   What is a book of original entry? Is the general journal a book of original entry? Explain.

8-2   Describe the steps in journalizing a business transaction.

8-3   What is the general ledger? Why is it called a book of final entry?

8-4   What is a chart of accounts?

8-5   Cross-referencing provides an audit trail to trace entries from the ledger to the journal. Explain.

8-6   Describe the steps in posting journal entries to the general ledger.

8-7   What is a trial balance? What is the purpose of a trial balance?

EXERCISES

8-1   The following are the October transactions for the Olde Timer Fixit Shoppe:

Oct.   1   Purchased new equipment for $200, paying $50 down, with the balance due in three equal installments starting Oct. 31.

1   Paid the rent for October, $150.

4   Received $50 for repair services from customers who picked up their repaired items.

10   Billed customers $460 for repair services performed during the first part of October.

22   Collected $380 from charge customers on account.

25   Received a bill from the Public Service Corp. for utility services provided. The bill was for $15 and is to be paid next month.

28   Perry Wilkes, the owner, withdrew $400, for personal use.

31   Paid the first installment on the new equipment purchased on October 1.

Required   Record each transaction in a general journal. It is not necessary to write explanations for the transactions. Refer to the chart of accounts in exercise 8-2 for the account titles to use.

8-2   On September 30 the balance sheet for the Olde Timer Fixit Shoppe appeared as follows:

Olde Timer Fixit Shoppe
Balance Sheet
September 30, 19x9

Cash	$ 650	Accounts payable	$ —0—
Accounts receivable	75	Wilkes, capital	1,125
Equipment	400		
	$1,125		$1,125

The chart of accounts for the company is presented below:

Olde Timer Fixit Shoppe
Chart of Accounts

101 Cash	401 Fees earned
111 Accounts receivable	501 Rent expense
121 Supplies on hand	502 Supplies used
141 Equipment	503 Utilities expense
142 Accumulated depreciation	504 Depreciation expense
201 Accounts payable	505 Miscellaneous expense
301 Wilkes, capital	801 Income summary
302 Wilkes, drawing	

Required   **a.**   Open T-accounts for the accounts that appear in the September 30, 19x9, balance sheet and enter their balances. Use the account numbers presented in the chart of accounts.

b.   Post the journal entries you made in completing exercise 8–1. Open T-accounts as needed; refer to the chart of accounts for account titles and numbers.

8-3   Refer to your solution to exercise 8-2. Calculate the account balances and prepare a trial balance as of October 31, 19x9.

8-4   The following are the accounts used by Harrigan Corp.

1. Cash
2. Accounts receivable
3. Supplies inventory
4. Equipment
5. Accumulated depreciation
6. Accounts payable
7. Notes payable, short-term
8. Notes payable, long-term
9. Capital stock
10. Retained earnings

11. Service revenue
12. Salaries expense
13. Rent expense
14. Utilities expense
15. Supplies used
16. Depreciation expense
17. Miscellaneous expense
18. Interest revenue
19. Interest expense
20. Income tax expense

Several transactions that occurred during the current accounting period are described below. For each transaction write the number of the account(s) debited and credited.

Transactions	Account(s) Debited	Account(s) Credited
Example: Sold common stock.	1	9
1. Purchased electric calculator on credit		
2. Purchased supplies for cash		
3. Billed a customer for services performed		
4. Paid salaries to clerks		
5. Collected balance owed by a customer		
6. Paid for the electric calculator purchased in (1) above		
7. Received a bill for utilities; payment due in 10 days		
8. Purchased postage stamps		

8-5   Refer back to the transactions in exercise 7-1. Prepare all necessary journal entries and post the journal entries to the general ledger (set up all necessary T-accounts to complete the posting process).

8-6   Refer back to the transactions in exercise 7-5. Prepare all necessary journal entries.

PROBLEMS

8-1   The following are a list of account names and numbers and a list of transactions completed by Charles Dana, CPA. For each transaction write in the columns at the right the number(s) of the accounts debited and credited.

1. Cash
2. Accounts receivable
3. Office supplies on hand
4. Prepaid insurance
5. Office equipment
6. Accumulated depreciation—office equipment
7. Accounting library
8. Accounts payable
9. C. Dana, capital
10. C. Dana, drawing
11. Fees earned
12. Salaries expense
13. Office supplies used
14. Insurance expense
15. Rent expense
16. Utilities expense
17. Depreciation expense—office equipment
18. Miscellaneous expense

	Debit	Credit
Example: Charles Dana began the practice of public accounting by investing cash and an accounting library.	1, 7	9

a. Paid the rent for one month on the office space.
b. Paid the premium on an insurance policy.
c. Purchased office equipment and office supplies on credit.
d. Completed accounting services for a client and collected cash for the work completed.
e. Returned a portion of the office equipment purchased on credit in (c).
f. Completed accounting work on credit for a client and billed her for the work completed.
g. Paid the balance due on the equipment and supplies purchased in (c).
h. Collected in full from the client billed for the work in (f).
i. Paid Public Service Company for the electricity consumed during the month just ended.
j. Charles Dana withdrew cash for his personal living expenses.
k. Paid salaries to the secretary and junior accountant.
l. Paid for stamps and a lockbox at the local post office.

8-2   Gillespie Corp. completed the following transactions during its first month of business operations:

July	1	Issued 20,000 shares of $10 par value stock at $10 per share.
	2	Purchased office equipment, $3,600, and supplies, $150, on credit.

3	Paid the rent for July, $500.
5	Received a bill from the local newspaper for advertising; the bill for $120 is due within 10 days.
8	Paid an attorney $2,000 for services performed in organizing the company.
9	Paid $600 for an insurance policy.
10	Billed customers $3,200 for services performed.
12	Returned $600 worth of equipment that had been acquired on July 2.
15	Collected $2,200 of the amount billed to customers on July 10.
17	Paid employee salaries for the first half of the month, $2,400.
18	Paid the balance of the amount due for equipment and supplies acquired on July 2 (also, refer back to the July 12 transaction to return part of the equipment).
21	Borrowed $10,000 from the bank by issuing an 8%, 6-month note.

Required   Record each of the transactions in a general journal.

8-3   The following are the chart of accounts, the balance sheet at March 31, 19*x8,* and the transactions for April for Daly, Inc.

Chart of Accounts

101 Cash	241 Notes payable, long-term
111 Temporary investments	251 Mortgage payable
121 Accounts receivable	301 Common stock
122 Allowable for uncollectible accounts	302 Contributed capital in excess of par
131 Supplies on hand	351 Retained earnings
132 Prepaid insurance	401 Fees earned
151 Land	501 Salaries expense
161 Building	502 Depreciation expense—building
162 Accumulated depreciation	503 Depreciation expense—office equipment
171 Office equipment	504 Utilities expense
172 Accumulated depreciation	505 Insurance expense
201 Accounts payable	506 Supplies used
211 Notes payable, short-term	701 Interest expense

Daly, Inc.
Balance Sheet
March 31, 19*x8*

Assets

Current assets:	
Cash	$ 95,000
Accounts receivable (less allowance for uncollectible accounts of $4,000)	76,000

Supplies on hand	800
Prepaid insurance	1,200
Total current assets	$173,000
Plant assets:	
Land	$ 30,000
Building (less accumulated depreciation of $10,000)	90,000
Office equipment (less accumulated depreciation of $10,000)	15,000
Total plant assets	$135,000
Total assets	$308,000

Liabilities

Current liabilities	
Accounts payable	$ 22,000
Notes payable, short-term	20,000
Total current liabilities	$ 42,000
Long-term liabilities:	
Mortgage payable	60,000
Total liabilities	$102,000

Stockholders' Equity

Contributed capital:	
Common stock, $10 par, 12,000 shares issued	$120,000
Contributed capital in excess of par	24,000
Total contributed capital	$144,000
Retained earnings	62,000
Total stockholders' equity	$206,000
Total liabilities and stockholders equity	$308,000

Transactions

April	1	Purchased supplies for cash, $35.
	1	Purchased office equipment with a cost of $1,500; paid $300 cash down payment; issued a note for the balance (note is due in three equal monthly payments, plus 8% interest on the outstanding balance, starting April 30).
	4	Purchased temporary investments with a cost of $10,500.
	5	Billed customers $15,400 for services rendered.
	8	Purchased supplies on credit, $150.
	11	Paid outstanding bills from March 31, $13,500.
	14	Converted short-term notes payable to long-term notes due in two years.
	17	Billed customers $22,600 for services rendered.
	20	Received the bills for utilities, $4,800.
	23	Received payments from customers with outstanding balances on March 31, $28,400.
	26	Sold 1,000 shares of $10 par value common stock for $12 per share.
	29	Received payments from customers billed on April 5 and 17, $18,500.
	30	Made the payment due on the short-term note issued April 1.
	30	Paid employee salaries for the month, $9,300.
	30	Made the monthly mortgage payment of $800, which included interest of $525.

Required a. Prepare general journal entries for the transactions described. Use the account titles presented in the chart of accounts.

b. Enter the balances from the March 31 balance sheet in T-accounts. Post the entries recorded in part a. Open additional T-accounts as needed.

c. Prepare a trial balance as of April 30, 19x8.

8-4   The following are excerpts from the records of Goliath Company:

	General Journal				Page 12
Date	**Accounts**	**PR**	**Debit**	**Credit**	
Mar. 3	Fees Earned	401	3,600		
	Accounts Receivable	111		3,600	
	To record amounts billed to customers for services performed.				
5	Office Expenses	501	850		
	Cash	101		850	
	To record purchase of office furniture.				
7	Salaries Expense	511	1,400		
	Cash	101		1,400	
	To record payment of weekly payroll.				
15	Cash	101	3,600		
	Fees Earned	401		3,600	
	To record collection of amounts billed to customers on March 3.				
21	Supplies Inventory	521	325		
	Accounts Payable	201		325	
	To record purchase of supplies on credit.				
31	Accounts Payable	201	325		
	Cash	101		325	
	To record payment for supplies purchased on March 21.				

General Ledger

	Cash		101
3/15 J12	3,600	3/5 J12	850
		3/7 J12	1,400

	Accounts Receivable		111
		3/3 J12	3,600

Supplies Inventory	121

Office Furniture	151

Accounts Payable		201
3/31 J12	325	3/21 J12	325

Fees Earned		401
3/3 J12	3,600	3/15 J12	3,600

Office Expenses		501
3/5 J12	850		

Salaries Expense		511
		3/7 J12	1,400

Supplies Expense		521
3/21 J12	325		

Required **a.** Identify and list each of the errors made by the bookkeeper for Goliath Company in (1) journalizing the business transactions and (2) posting the journal entries.

b. Reconstruct the general journal and general ledger for Goliath Company so the journal entries are correctly prepared and posted.

8-5 Refer back to the transactions in problem 7–1. Prepare all necessary journal entries, post the journal entries to the general ledger, and prepare a trial balance at August 31. Set up T-accounts to complete the posting process.

8-6 Refer back to the transactions in problem 7–4. Prepare all necessary journal entries.

Unit 9
Accounting for Basic Merchandise Purchase and Sales Transactions

The craft of the merchant is this bringing a thing from where it abounds to where it is costly.

Ralph Waldo Emerson, Wealth

In Unit 8 we discussed the process of recording business transactions and concentrated on business activities for a service-type organization. In this unit we discuss the accounting for basic purchase and sales transactions that result from the primary business activities of a merchandising-type organization, such as a retail store and wholesaler. These organizations buy goods that are ready for sale and resell them to either consumers or retailers.

Performance Objectives

Upon completing this unit you should be able to:

1. define and use the accounting terms introduced in this unit.
2. determine any of the following:
   a. the discount and/or credit period for an invoice
   b. cost of goods sold for a period
   c. the amount of one or more components in the calculation of cost of goods sold and gross margin
   d. the amount due for an invoice subject to a trade discount and/or a cash discount
3. prepare general journal entries for the basic purchase and sales transactions for a merchandising-type organization; these entries include transactions involving:
   a. sales, sales discounts, sales returns and allowances, and delivery expense
   b. purchases, purchase returns and allowances, and freight-in
4. prepare financial statements for a merchandising-type organization.

162

Sales Transactions

Revenue is realized when the earning process is substantially completed and an economic exchange has occurred (see Unit 3). For companies that sell merchandise, the earning process is substantially completed when title to the merchandise passes from the seller to the buyer. The seller has purchased, stored, displayed, and advertised the goods before contracting to sell them to customers. It is not necessary to collect cash before revenue is realized because the expense of uncollectible accounts can be estimated based on past experience. Thus, revenue from both cash and credit sales of merchandise should be recognized on the books of the seller when the sales transaction is completed.

Cash sales are usually recorded daily on the basis of cash register totals and/or cash sales slips filled out by sales clerks. The journal entry form for cash sales is:

Apr. 5	Cash	4,870	
	Sales		4,870
	To record cash sales for the day.		

Credit sales are recorded by totaling sales invoices or charge sales slips prepared by company personnel. The entry form for credit sales is:

Apr. 5	Accounts Receivable	11,740	
	Sales		11,740
	To record credit sales for the day.		

A method is necessary to maintain a record of the amount owed by each charge customer. Some companies file copies of sales invoices by customer name in a file of unpaid invoices. When the customer pays an invoice, the invoice is removed from that file, marked "Paid," and placed in a file of paid invoices. Another method, which involves a separate ledger, called a *subsidiary ledger,* provides better control and will be described in Unit 15. In many businesses records of sales, collections, and customer balances are maintained by computer because these transactions are numerous and similar in nature and thus suited for computerized record-keeping.

Trade Discounts   Some wholesalers and manufacturers offer **trade discounts.** They quote prices in catalogs or price lists and describe discount percentages that can be taken by customers with orders of a specific size. The list prices or discount percentages can be changed whenever the seller determines that selling prices should be changed.

Sales are always recorded net of applicable trade discounts because these discounts establish the sales price of the merchandise. For example, assume that merchandise with a list price of $10,000 is sold subject to a 10 percent trade discount. The sale is recorded at $9,000 (list price of $10,000 minus the trade discount of $1,000 [$10,000 × 10% = $1,000]):

Apr. 10	Accounts Receivable	9,000	
	Sales		9,000
	To record credit sale net of trade discount.		

Cash Discounts and Credit Terms   Companies often offer credit customers a **cash discount** for prompt payment of invoices. The purpose of these discounts is to lessen the risk of nonpayment by customers and to accelerate the vendor's cash inflow. The risk of nonpayment tends to increase the longer the account balance is outstanding. The vendor expects to offset the cost of the cash discounts by reducing his losses from uncollectible accounts and using the cash to pay his own bills promptly or investing the cash until needed.

The cash discount is usually large enough to make it financially worthwhile for the customer to pay promptly. For example, a 1 percent discount if the invoice is paid within 10 days instead of 30 days comes to an annual savings of approximately 18 percent. (The extra 20 days that elapse if payment is made in 30 days is approximately 1/18 of a year, and 18 × 1% = 18%). This extra 18 percent that would have to be paid without the discount exceeds the interest rate most businesses have to pay to borrow cash, and thus it is advisable to pay all invoices within the **discount period** even if cash must be borrowed.

The vendor will specify the terms under which he grants credit to customers. Examples of **credit terms** without any cash discounts are: n/10, n/30, and n/10 EOM. The terms *n/10* and *n/30* mean that the invoice amount is due within 10 days and 30 days, respectively, after the date of the invoice. The term *n/10 EOM* means that the invoice amount is due within 10 days after the end of the month indicated in the invoice date. The **credit period** is the length of time the customer has to pay without his or her account becoming overdue. It extends from the date of the invoice to the last day indicated by the credit terms.

Assume that a company sells merchandise subject to credit terms of n/30. For an invoice dated January 12, the credit period starts on January 12 and extends through the next 30 days, not including the date of the invoice. In this example the 30 days includes the 19 remaining days in January and the first 11 days in February. Thus, the credit period for this invoice is January 12 through February 11. The account is overdue if the customer does not remit the payment by February 11. Payment should be considered on time if postmarked on the last day permitted by the credit or discount terms.

An example of credit terms with a cash discount is 2/10, n/30. If the invoice is paid within 10 days, a 2 percent discount on the sales price of the merchandise can be taken; otherwise, the invoice amount is due within 30 days after its date. When the sale is recorded, the full sales price is recorded as sales revenue. If payment is made within the discount period, the customer remits the invoice amount less the discount. The seller records the discount when the remittance is received. Technically, the customer is not permitted to take the cash discount if payment is made after the discount period. However, companies do not always hold rigidly to the limit of the discount period, especially for big customers. They tend to view the discount as an inducement to these customers to continue doing business with them.

Assume that a company sells merchandise for $3,500 subject to credit terms of 2/10, n/30. If the invoice is dated January 12 and the customer mails his check on January 22, the last day of the discount period, the entries that record the sale and receipt of the remittance from the customer would be:

Jan. 12	Accounts Receivable	3,500	
	Sales		3,500
	To record a credit sale.		

Jan. 22	Cash	3,430	
	Sales Discounts	70	
	Accounts Receivable		3,500
	To record payment of Jan. 12 invoice within discount period.		

The discount period in the example extended from January 12 through January 22 because January 22 is the tenth day after the date of the invoice. Mailing payment on January 22 is accepted as payment on that date. The cash discount of $70 ($3,500 × 2%) is recorded as a **sales discount** in an account of the same name. Presentation of this contra or offset account on the income statement is discussed later in this unit. If payment was mailed after January 22, the cash discount would not be allowed, and the remittance would then be for $3,500. The entry for the remittance would be:

Jan. 23 (or later)	Cash	3,500	
	Accounts Receivable		3,500
	To record payment of Jan. 12 invoice after expiration of the discount period.		

Sales Returns and Allowances   Sometimes goods are returned by a customer because they were unsatisfactory or damaged. In other situations an allowance, that is, a reduction in the sales price, may be granted to a customer to convince the customer to keep goods that were incorrectly shipped or that arrived in a damaged condition. A contra or offset account, **sales returns and allowances,** is normally used to record the amount of the sales returns and allowances. This account provides information needed for management control purposes. Assume that goods with a sales price of $250 are returned for credit against the customer's account. The entry would be:

Sales Returns and Allowances	250	
Accounts Receivable		250
To record sales return and credit to customer's account.		

If the sales return or allowance is for goods sold for cash, the entry for a cash refund would be:

Sales Returns and Allowances	250	
Cash		250
To record cash refund for goods returned by customer.		

Merchandise Purchases and Cost of Goods Sold

A major expense for merchandise-type organizations is the cost of the merchandise they sell. This expense can be associated directly with the revenue generated from the sale of the merchandise. Thus, the expense for the **cost of goods sold** should be reported in the same period the revenue is realized.

Companies that sell merchandise usually must maintain a stock of the various types of merchandise they sell in order to satisfy normal customer demands. Throughout the accounting period additional purchases are made to replenish the stock of merchandise available for sale. At the end of the period the stock of unsold merchandise must be reported as an asset, while the cost of the merchandise sold is reported as an expense. The flow of merchandise costs is depicted in Figure 9.1.

Two different inventory systems may be used to account for merchandise purchases, inventory balances, and cost of goods sold: the periodic system and the perpetual system. Under the **periodic inventory system** merchandise purchases are recorded in an expense-type account, **purchases,** and the inventory balance and cost of goods sold are determined only at the end of the accounting period. Under the **per-**

Figure 9.1   Flow of merchandise costs

petual inventory system a running or continuous balance for inventory is maintained; also, a separate record is maintained for each inventory item stocked by the company. The perpetual system, which provides better control over inventory, is discussed further in Unit 17.

Merchandise Purchases   The entry for the purchase of merchandise is normally made when the invoice from the supplier is received, although the purchase is actually completed when title to the goods passes from the supplier (seller) to the buyer. Discrepancies between the purchases recorded and the goods to which title has been acquired are reconciled and adjusted at the end of the accounting period.

Companies that take advantage of all cash (purchase) discounts usually record purchases net of the discount. In this text we assume that all purchases should be recorded net of available cash discounts. If merchandise with a cost of $6,500 is purchased subject to credit terms of 2/10, n/30, the entry to record the purchase net of the cash discount would be:

May 1	Purchases	6,370	
	Accounts Payable		6,370
	To record purchase of merchandise net of cash discount of $130 (2% × $6,500 = $130).		

If the invoice is paid on May 11, the last day of the discount period, the entry would be:

May 11	Accounts Payable	6,370	
	Cash		6,370
	To pay May 1 invoice for purchase of merchandise within the discount period.		

If the invoice is paid after the discount period expires, the company has incurred a financial expense for the discount lost. An expense account, **discounts lost,** would be debited as follows, assuming payment on the last day of the credit period:

May 31	Accounts Payable	6,370	
	Discounts Lost	130	
	Cash		6,500
	To record payment of May 1 invoice for purchase of merchandise after the discount period.		

Companies that are uncertain whether they will be taking advantage of cash discounts or that rarely take advantage of cash discounts usually record the purchase of merchandise at the invoice amount. If payment is then made within the discount period, the cash discounts are recorded by crediting a contra account, purchase discounts. This account is deducted from the purchases account on the income statement. The entries to record the purchase of merchandise at the invoice amount and to record payment within the discount period would be:

May 1	Purchases	6,500	
	Accounts Payable		6,500
	To record purchase of merchandise at invoice amount of $6,500; not, credit terms are 2/10, net 30.		

May 11	Accounts Payable	6,500	
	Purchase Discounts		130
	Cash		6,370
	To record payment of invoice within discount period; discount of $130 (2% × $6,500) is recorded.		

Purchase Returns and Allowances   Sometimes goods are returned to the supplier, and credit is received against the amount owed to the supplier or against future purchases. Also, credit might be received for a price reduction on unsatisfactory or damaged goods. Under the periodic system the credit received is recorded in a separate account, **purchase returns and allowances,** to provide information for management control. Purchase returns and allowances is a contra or offset account deducted from purchases on the income statement. Assume that merchandise with an invoice price of $200 is returned to the supplier for credit. If the purchase was recorded net of a cash discount, the entry for the credit must be recorded net of the cash discount. The entry for the credit would be:

May 14	Accounts Payable	196	
	Purchase Returns and Allowances		196
	To record credit for merchandise returned to supplier net of 2% cash discount [$200 − 2% ($200) = $196].		

Freight-in   The cost of merchandise purchased should include sales and other taxes, if any, and freight charges, but exclude trade discounts and cash discounts. However, in the periodic system freight charges paid separately by the buyer are usually recorded in an expense-type account, freight-in or transportation-in, as follows:

May 8	Freight-in	120	
	Cash		120
	To record payment of freight paid on		
	May 1 purchase of merchandise.		

Determining Cost of Goods Sold   At the end of the accounting period, the cost of all goods available for sale can be determined. The cost of the **net purchases** (purchases plus freight-in minus purchase returns and allowances) is added to beginning inventory. Thus, in Exhibit 9.1 net purchases of $508,000 are added to beginning inventory of $80,000 to yield **cost of goods available for sale** of $588,000. The value of the ending inventory is then deducted from the cost of the goods available for sale to determine **cost of goods sold.** In Exhibit 9.1 ending inventory is $90,000; thus, cost of goods sold is $498,000 ($588,000 − 90,000).

Reporting Sales and Cost of Goods Sold

In reporting sales on an income statement, some companies present only **net sales,** that is, the net revenue from sales after sales discounts and sales returns and allowances are deducted. Others disclose the **gross sales** figure and determine net sales by deducting sales discounts and sales returns and allowances on the face of the income statement. This second method is presented as follows:

Gross sales		$850,000
Less: Sales discounts	$ 7,000	
Sales returns and allowances	13,000	20,000
Net sales		$830,000

Cost of goods sold can be presented on the income statement as illustrated in Exhibit 9.2 or in a separate schedule for management information only. In the latter case, the amount for cost of goods sold is reported and deducted from net sales on the income statement as illustrated in Exhibit 9.3. Recall that net sales minus cost of goods sold equals gross margin. Thus, in Exhibits 9.2 and 9.3 gross margin of $332,000 ($830,000 − $498,000) is reported.

Exhibit 9.1

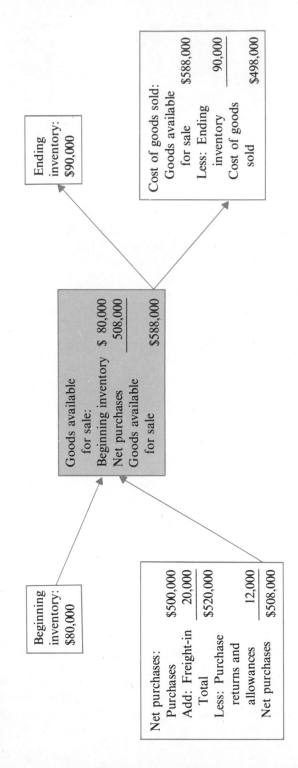

Beginning
inventory:
$80,000

Net purchases:
Purchases $500,000
Add: Freight-in   20,000
Total $520,000
Less: Purchase
returns and
allowances   12,000
Net purchases $508,000

Goods available
for sale:
Beginning inventory $ 80,000
Net purchases   508,000
Goods available
for sale $588,000

Ending
inventory:
$90,000

Cost of goods sold:
Goods available
for sale $588,000
Less: Ending
inventory   90,000
Cost of goods
sold $498,000

Exhibit 9.2

Gross sales		$850,000
Less: Sales discounts	$ 7,000	
Sales returns and allowances	13,000	20,000
Net sales		$830,000
Cost of goods sold:		
Beginning inventory	$ 80,000	
Purchases	$500,000	
Freight-in	20,000	
Total cost of purchases	$520,000	
Less: Purchase returns and allowances	12,000	
Net purchases	508,000	
Goods available for sale	$588,000	
Less: Ending inventory	90,000	
Cost of goods sold		498,000
Gross margin		$332,000

Exhibit 9.3

Income Statement

Net sales		$830,000
Cost of goods sold (see schedule A)		498,000
Gross margin		$332,000

Schedule A
Schedule of Cost of Goods Sold

Beginning inventory		$ 80,000
Purchases	$500,000	
Freight-in	20,000	
Total cost of purchases	$520,000	
Less: Purchase returns and allowances	12,000	
Net purchases		508,000
Goods available for sale		$588,000
Less: Ending inventory		90,000
Cost of goods sold		$498,000

REVIEW PROBLEMS

1. Longshott Company completed the following transactions during March;

    Mar. 1   Purchased merchandise from Irwin, Inc., at a cost of $10,000 subject to credit terms of 2/10, n/30.

    4   Sold merchandise on credit to Wilson Corp. with a sales price of $8,000 and a cost of $4,800, subject to credit terms of 2/10, n/30.

	5	Paid freight charges of $450 on goods purchased from Irwin, Inc., on March 1.	
	8	Returned merchandise with a cost of $500 to Irwin, Inc. for credit.	
	10	Gave credit to Wilson Corp. for merchandise returned with a sales price of $500 and a cost of $300.	
	11	Paid delivery charges of $360 on the goods sold to Wilson Corp. on March. 4.	
	12	Purchased merchandise from Jenner Co. at a cost of $7,500 subject to credit terms of 2/10, n/30.	
	16	Sold merchandise on credit to Zenn Company with a sales price of $3,000 and a cost of $1,800, subject to credit terms of 2/10, n/30.	
	22	Paid the amount due to Jenner Co. for the March 12 purchase.	
	26	Received payment from Zenn Company for the amount due on the March 16 sale.	
	30	Paid amount due to Irwin, Inc. for March 1 purchase less the credit for goods returned on March 8.	
	31	Collected amount due from Wilson Corp. for March 4 sale less the credit for goods returned on March 10.	

Required   Prepare the entries to record the March transactions for Longshott Company using the periodic system.

2.   At the end of the accounting period the records of Slippshodd Company showed the following:

Purchases	$420,000
Sales	650,000
Beginning Inventory	75,000
Sales Discounts	5,000
Purchase Returns and Allowances	9,000
Sales Returns and Allowances	10,000
Freight-in	17,000
Delivery Expense	14,000
Ending Inventory	68,000

Required   Prepare a partial income statement.

Solution to the review problems

1.	3/1	Purchases	9,800	
		Accounts Payable		9,800
		To record purchase net of cash discount.		

3/4	Accounts Receivable	8,000	
	Sales		8,000
	To record sale on credit.		

| 3/4 | No entry for cost of goods sold in periodic system. | | |

3/5	Freight-in	450	
	Cash		450
	Paid freight on goods purchased on March 1.		

3/8	Accounts Payable	490	
	Purchase Returns		490
	Returned goods to supplier; record net of discount [$500 − 2% ($500) = $490].		

3/10	Sales Returns	500	
	Accounts Receivable		500
	Goods returned by customer.		

| 3/10 | No entry for cost of goods returned in periodic system. | | |

3/11	Delivery Expense	360	
	Cash		360
	Paid delivery charges on goods sold on March 4.		

3/12	Purchases	7,350	
	Accounts Payable		7,350
	To record purchase net of cash discount.		

3/16	Accounts Receivable	3,000	
	Sales		3,000
	To record sale on credit.		

| 3/16 | No entry for cost of goods sold in periodic system. | | |

3/22	Accounts Payable	7,350	
	Cash		7,350
	Paid bill for March 12 purchase within discount period.		

3/26	Cash	2,940	
	Sales Discounts	60	
	Accounts Receivable		3,000
	Received payment for March 16 sale within discount period.		

3/30	Accounts Payable	9,310	
	Discounts Lost	190	
	Cash		9,500
	Paid bill for March 1 purchase less goods returned March 8 ($10,000 − 500 = $9,500); also, record discount lost ($9,500 × 2% = $190).		

3/31	Cash	7,500	
	Accounts Receivable		7,500
	Received payment for March 4 sale after discount period.		

2.

Gross Sales			$650,000
Less: Sales discounts		$ 5,000	
Sales returns and allowances		10,000	15,000
Net sales			$635,000
Cost of goods sold:			
Beginning inventory			$ 75,000
Purchases		$420,000	
Freight-in		17,000	
Total cost of purchases		$437,000	
Less: Purchase returns and allowances		9,000	
Net purchases			428,000
Goods available for sale			$503,000
Less: Ending inventory			68,000
Cost of goods sold			$435,000
Gross margin			$200,000

Note   Delivery expense would be reported as one of the selling expenses under operating expenses. Delivery expense is incurred to ship merchandise from the company to its customers; freight-in is incurred to have merchandise shipped to the company from its suppliers.

SUMMARY

The accounting procedures for merchandise sales and purchases were discussed in this unit. Also, methods of reporting sales revenue and the cost of goods sold were described and illustrated. Refer particularly to Exhibits 9.1 and 9.2 and Figure 9.1 when you review this unit.

REVIEW QUESTIONS

9-1 Distinguish between a trade discount and a cash discount. What is the effect of each type of discount on the amount recorded as sales revenue?

9-2 Distinguish between the credit period and discount period.

9-3 What is meant by the term *sales returns and allowances*?

9-4 How are sales returns and allowances and sales discounts reported on the income statement?

9-5 If purchases are recorded net of cash discounts, how should the amount of the discount be accounted for if payment is made after the expiration of the discount period?

9-6 When would the accounts freight-in and purchase returns and allowances be used and how would they be reported on the income statement?

9-7 Distinguish between freight-in and delivery expense.

9-8 Describe the accounting for the following transactions by the buyer and the seller:

    a. Merchandise with a list price of $3,500 is sold subject to a trade discount of 10 percent and credit terms of 2/10, n/30.
    b. Merchandise with a list price of $500 is returned by the customer for credit because the goods were damaged. The goods were returned five days after they were sold.
    c. The customer pays the amount due within the 10-day discount period.

9-9 When should revenue from the sale of merchandise generally be recognized? Why is it recognized at this point?

9-10 Describe the calculation of cost of goods sold.

EXERCISES

9-1 Winston Corp. sold merchandise with a list price of $5,000 to Salem Corp. on credit. The merchandise was subject to a trade discount of 10%; the credit terms were 2/10, n/30. The invoice was dated March 15.

    Required   **a.** At what amount should the sale be recorded by Winston Corp?
                b. What is the credit period for this sale?
                c. What is the discount period for this sale?
                d. How much should Salem Corp. remit if payment is made on March 25?
                e. How much should Salem Corp. remit if payment is made after the discount period expires?

9-2   Refer to the data in exercise 9–1. Prepare the journal entries for the following transactions on the books of Winston Corp.:

    a.   the sale on March 15
    b.   a sales return of merchandise with a list price of $600 on March 18
    c.   payment of the balance due by Salem Corp. if remitted on (1) March 25 and (2) April 14

9-3   Fill in the blanks for the following merchandise transactions.

	List Price of Mdse.	Trade Discount %	Sales Price of Mdse.	Credit Terms	Cash to Be Remitted (within discount period)
a.	$1,500	10%	$_____	n/30	$_____
b.	2,000	10%	_____	2/10, n/30	_____
c.	_____	25%	1,200	net cash	_____
d.	_____	20%	1,000	1/10 EOM	_____
e.	1,000	_%	800	_/15, n/60	784

9-4   Fill in the blanks for the missing items in the computation of cost of goods sold and gross margin.

	Net Sales	Beginning Inventory	Net Purchases	Available for Sale	Ending Inventory	Cost of Goods Sold	Gross Margin
a.	$100,000	$10,000	$ 60,000	$_____	$_____	$ 58,000	$_____
b.	_____	_____	77,000	_____	15,000	75,000	50,000
c.	200,000	25,000	_____	140,000	_____	120,000	_____
d.	_____	_____	135,000	165,000	25,000	_____	60,000
e.	300,000	25,000	_____	208,000	_____	_____	120,000

9-5   Durango Corp. completed the following merchandise transactions during February:

Feb. 1	Purchased merchandise on credit; list price was $4,000 and was subject to a 10 percent trade discount; credit terms were 1/10, n/30.
5	Returned damaged merchandise with a list price of $400; the merchandise had been purchased on February 1.
8	Purchased merchandise with a list price of $2,500; credit terms were 2/10, n/30.
13	Paid freight charges of $280 on the merchandise purchased on February 1.
18	Paid the amount due on the February 8 purchase.
20	Sold merchandise with a cost of $3,000 for $4,500 on credit.
23	Gave credit for merchandise returned by a customer; the cost was $500; the sales price was $750.
28	Paid the amount due on the February 1 purchase.

All purchases are recorded net of cash discounts.

Required   Prepare the entry for each transaction described if the periodic inventory system is used.

9-6   The following are selected accounts and balances from the trial balance of Apex Corp. at March 31, 19x3:

Inventory	$ 38,000
Sales	400,000
Sales discounts	5,000
Sales returns and allowances	10,000
Purchases	240,000
Freight-in	12,000
Purchase returns and allowances	4,000
Discounts lost	500
Delivery expense	16,000

The ending inventory was valued at a cost of $46,000.

Required   Prepare a partial income statement to determine cost of goods sold and gross margin.

PROBLEMS

9-1   During October Acorn Sales Co. completed the following sales and related transactions:

Oct. 1	Sold merchandise on credit to Filbert Company; the list price was $8,000 and was subject to a 10 percent trade discount.
3	Sold merchandise on credit to Almond Corp.; billed Almond Corp. for the list price of $2,200.
4	Gave credit to Filbert Company for merchandise returned that had a list price of $500.
5	Sold merchandise to Walnut Company on credit; the list price was $10,000 and was subject to a trade discount of 10 percent.
9	Allowed Walnut Company an additional 5% reduction in original list price because some of the merchandise had been damaged, but was being kept by Walnut Company.
11	Paid the freight charges, $1,350, to deliver the goods sold on October 1, 3, and 5.
13	Received payment from Filbert Company for the balance due; the check was dated and mailed October 11.
15	Received payment from Almond Corp. for the balance due; the check was dated and mailed October 12.
26	Recorded cash sales of $2,700.

30	Received payment from Walnut Company for the balance due; the check was dated and mailed October 28.
31	Gave a cash refund of $50 to a customer for merchandise returned.

All credit sales are made subject to credit terms of 2/10, n/30.

Required   Prepare the journal entries to record these transactions.

9-2   The following are several transactions for the North Woods Sports Store for the month of July.

July 1	Purchased merchandise on account from Sports Distributors, Inc., for $800.
3	Purchased merchandise on account from the Sportswear Corp. for $450.
5	Paid $45 to the Continental Trucking Lines for the freight charges on the July 1 purchase.
6	Sold merchandise on account to the city of Farmingham for $250.
8	Returned merchandise with a cost of $80 to the Sportswear Corp. for credit since the wrong sizes were received.
9	Paid $10 freight charges on the merchandise shipped to the city of Farmingham on July 6.
11	Paid the amount due to Sports Distributors, Inc.
15	Cash sales for the first half of the month amounted to $1,250.
18	A customer returned merchandise for a cash refund of $25.
20	Sold merchandise on account to the Wild River Baseball League, $150.
22	Paid the amount due to the Sportswear Corp.
25	Received payment from the city of Farmingham; the check was dated June 24.
27	Paid cash for merchandise purchased, $75.
31	Cash sales for the second half of the month amounted to $1,925.
31	Received payment from the Wild River Baseball League; the check was dated July 30.

The company uses the periodic inventory system. The inventory balance was $7,420 at July 1 and $6,080 at July 31.

Required   **a.**   Prepare the journal entries for the July transactions.
              b.   Calculate cost of goods sold and gross margin for July.

(Suggestion   Set up T-accounts for sales, sales returns and allowances, purchases, freight-in, and purchase returns and allowances, and post these accounts to obtain the amounts needed for part b.)

9-3   The following are the November transactions for the Thirsty Beverage Company:

Nov. 2	Purchased merchandise on account from Hi-Spot Cola Company for $2,800; terms were 2/10, n/30.
3	Sold merchandise on account to the Best Value Super Markets Corp. for $3,200; terms were 1/10, n/30. The cost of the merchandise was $2,400.
5	Paid freight charges of $85 to Fast Way Freight Company on the merchandise shipped to Best Value Super Markets Corp.
6	Best Value Super Markets Corp. returned merchandise that had been erroneously shipped to them. The cost of the merchandise returned was $225; its sales price was $300.
10	Purchased merchandise on account from Top Flavour Soft Drink Company for $3,750; terms were 2/10, n/30.
12	Paid $60 freight charges to X-Country Truck Lines on the merchandise received from Top Flavour Soft Drink Company.
14	Received a check, dated Nov. 13, from Best Value Super Markets Corp. in settlement of their account.
15	Returned $150 of damaged merchandise to the Top Flavour Soft Drink Company for credit.
16	Sold merchandise on account to Quality Food Stores, Inc., for $1,800; credit terms were 1/10, n/30. The cost of the merchandise was $1,350.
20	Paid the amount due to Top Flavour Soft Drink Company.
28	Paid the amount due to Hi-Spot Cola Company.
30	Received a check dated Nov. 29 from Quality Food Stores, Inc., in settlement of their account.

Required   Prepare the journal entries for these transactions, assuming the periodic inventory system is used.

9-4   Hannibal Corp. uses the periodic inventory system. During the current year, 19x5, some of the company records were lost. The following data were reconstructed from the company's bank records:

Cash deposits—total	$148,000
Bank loan included in cash deposits	15,000
Cash disbursements for:	
Merchandise	66,500
Operating expenses	53,000

All cash deposits, except for the bank loan, are collections from customers for sales on credit or for cash sales. The balance sheet at the end of 19x4 indicated the following:

Accounts receivable	$ 22,500
Inventory	17,000
Accounts payable	15,500

At the end of 19*x5* the company's accountant determined the following balances:

Accounts receivable	$ 20,800
Inventory	18,400
Accounts payable	16,200
Depreciation for 19*x5*	2,500

Required   Prepare an income statement for 19*x5* that shows the details for the calculation of cost of goods sold. Assume an income tax rate of 30%.

Chapter 4

Completion of the Accounting Cycle

This chapter explains the remaining steps in the accounting cycle, those occurring at the end of the accounting period.

The economic effects of some business transactions are not realized entirely within a single accounting period. Certain transactions may earn revenue over two or more accounting periods or incur costs that benefit two or more periods. However, the realization and matching principles require that revenues earned and their related expenses be measured for each accounting period. Only then can accurate reports of operating results and financial position be prepared and presented to users of financial information. Thus, adjustments to certain accounts are required to distinguish between the earned and unearned revenue and the expired and unexpired costs at the end of an accounting period. These adjustments are explained in Unit 10.

After the financial statements are prepared at the end of the accounting period, the revenue and expense accounts must be prepared for entries during the next period. The use of closing entries to accomplish this is explained in Unit 11. Unit 12 explains how a worksheet facilitates all end-of-period procedures.

Unit 10
Matching Revenues and Expenses

Accounting is the living art
Of balancing the earthly part.

Alexis Lawrence Romanoff, Encyclopedia of Thoughts *(1975)*

The adjustments required to distinguish between earned and unearned revenue and expired and unexpired costs at the end of the accounting period and to prepare accurate financial statements for the period are examined in this unit.

Performance Objectives

Upon completing this unit you should be able to:

1. define and use the accounting terms introduced in this unit.
2. prepare all necessary adjusting entries and an adjusted trial balance at the end of an entity's accounting period.

Need for Adjusting Entries

An entity's accountants and management select its accounting period. But it is impossible to select an end for an accounting period so that the economic effects of all transactions are realized by the date selected. Advance payments may have been received from customers or clients, but the revenue, for example, may not be fully realized because the merchandise has not been transferred or the services completed. Or services may have been provided, but the revenue may not yet be recorded—for example, interest on outstanding receivables; rent earned but still due from tenants; interest on bond investments.

Similar situations involve expenses that should be assigned to the accounting period. Advance payments may be made for benefits to be consumed or used in operating the business, but by the end of the period not all the services or benefits may have expired. The unexpired costs—for example, supplies on hand, unexpired insurance, plant assets, and intangible assets—should be reported as assets. Expired costs should be reported as expenses. Expenses may also have been incurred by the end of the accounting period, but not yet recorded—for example, accrued salaries, property taxes, income taxes.

Each of these situations results in revenue realization, cost expiration, or the consumption or use of services or benefits on a continuing basis. Because revenues are earned or expenses are incurred daily or over relatively short spans of time in small amounts, it is impractical to recognize the revenue or expense except at the end of the accounting period. Then they are recognized through **adjusting entries.** The diagrams in Exhibit 10.1 show the continuous realization of revenue and incurrence of expense that lead to the need for adjusting entries.

Assume in both diagrams in the figure that the accounting period is the calendar year. In the first diagram, interest revenue of $600 is recognized on a $10,000, 9%, 1-year note on December 31, 19x5. The note was dated May 1, 19x5. By the end of 19x5 two-thirds of the interest had been earned; however, because it is impractical to recognize the interest revenue daily, the $600 earned is recognized in an adjusting entry at the end of the accounting period, December 31, 19x5. The balance of the interest, $300, is recognized on May 1, 19x6, when the note and the entire interest are collected. In the second diagram, depreciation of $1,200 annually is recognized at the end of each accounting period. Since it is impractical to record depreciation daily as the benefits are received and the costs expire, an adjusting entry is made at the end of each accounting period.

Types of Adjusting Entries

All adjusting entries can be classified into four types:

1. Adjustments requiring allocations between assets and expenses—these adjustments may be grouped into two categories:

Exhibit 10.1

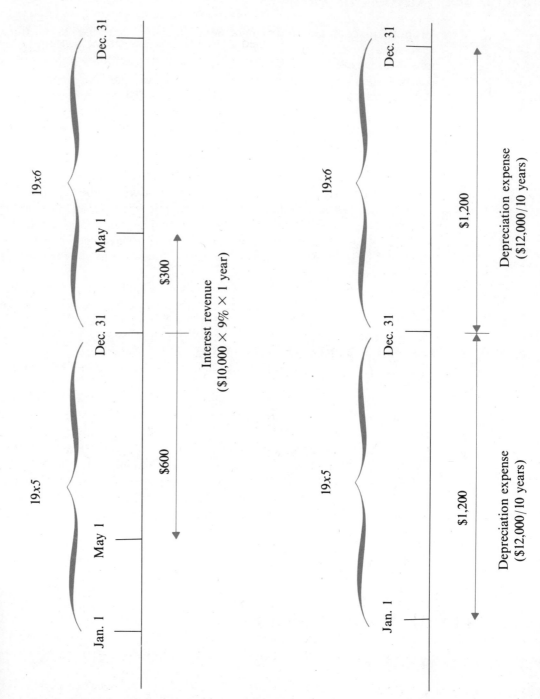

  a. Allocation of the costs for assets or services required prior to their use in carrying out business operations—unexpired costs are carried forward as assets and expired costs are assigned to expense; examples include allocating to expense the cost for merchandise available for sale, insurance, supplies, buildings, equipment, and patents.

  b. Allocation of portions of certain asset balances to expense for amounts not expected to be realized; examples include allocating portions of accounts receivable to expense for uncollectible accounts and allocating portions of temporary investments and inventory to expense when current market value is lower than original cost.

2. Adjustments requiring allocations between liabilities and revenues—advance payments received from customers for goods or services to be delivered or performed later are allocated between liabilities (for unearned revenue) and revenues (for earned revenue); examples include allocating advance payments for merchandise, service contracts, rent, and subscriptions.

3. Adjustments for unrecorded expenses—expenses incurred but not paid or recorded during the period must be recorded at the end of the period; examples include unrecorded expenses for salaries, income taxes, sales taxes, property taxes, payroll taxes, interest, and product guarantees and warranties.

4. Adjustments for unrecorded revenues—revenues earned but not received or recorded during the period must be recorded at the end of the period; examples include unrecorded interest revenue and rent revenue.

Accountants frequently refer to these four types of adjustments using their own special terminology. Adjustments requiring allocations between assets and expenses are **deferred expense** adjustments. Adjustments requiring allocations between liabilities and revenues are **deferred revenue** adjustments. Adjustments for unrecorded expenses are **accrued expense** adjustments, and adjustments for unrecorded revenues are **accrued revenue** adjustments.

Adjustments are recorded in the general journal. Since the data for them must be collected at the end of the period, adjusting entries are usually recorded early in the next period. However, the books for the period just ended are kept open, and the adjusting entries are entered and dated as of the last day of that period.

Allocations Between Assets and Expenses

When costs are incurred for services or benefits to be consumed or used in business operations of the current and future accounting periods, the preferred procedure is to record the costs initially in an asset account and then allocate them to expense in an adjusting entry at the end of each accounting period. A deferred expense type of adjusting entry is used to allocate the costs between assets and expenses because unexpired costs are deferred in an asset account until charged to expense in a future period or periods. The most common of these adjustments are allocations involving prepaid expenses, depreciation of plant assets, amortization of intangible assets, cost of goods sold, and estimation of bad debts.

Allocations Involving Prepaid Expenses   Assume that a company began the current period with a balance of $150 in supplies inventory and purchased $1,800 of supplies during the period. The purchases are charged to the supplies inventory account (an asset). If the company determines that the balance of supplies on hand at the end of the period is $200, the cost of the supplies used during the period would be $1,750 ($150 + 1,800 − 200). An adjusting entry is required to transfer $1,750 from the asset, supplies inventory, to the expense, supplies used. The adjusting entry allocates the cost of the supplies available, $1,950 ($150 + 1,800), between assets and expense: $1,750 is allocated to expense and $200 is allocated to assets. Exhibit 10.2 presents an analysis of the allocation of supplies available between assets and expense, along with T-accounts to depict the flow of costs. The entries to record the purchase of the supplies and the adjustment for supplies used are:

Jan. 1–	Supplies Inventory	1,800	
Dec. 31	Cash or Accounts Payable		1,800
	To record purchase of supplies.		
Dec. 31	Supplies Used	1,750	
	Supplies Inventory		1,750
	Adjusting entry for supplies used.		

When expenses are prepaid, the costs can be charged to an expense account instead of an asset account. For example, assume that the supplies discussed earlier are recorded in the expense account, supplies used, as they are acquired. The adjusting entry to allocate the cost of supplies between assets and expenses requires a charge to the asset account of $50 to increase the balance from $150 to $200. Exhibit 10.3 presents the analysis of this allocation between asset and expense and the flow of costs. The entries to record the purchase of the supplies and the necessary adjustment in this case are:

Jan. 1–	Supplies Used	1,800	
Dec. 31	Supplies Inventory		1,800
	To record purchase of supplies.		
Dec. 31	Supplies Inventory	50	
	Supplies Used		50
	Adjusting entry for unused supplies.		

Exhibit 10.2

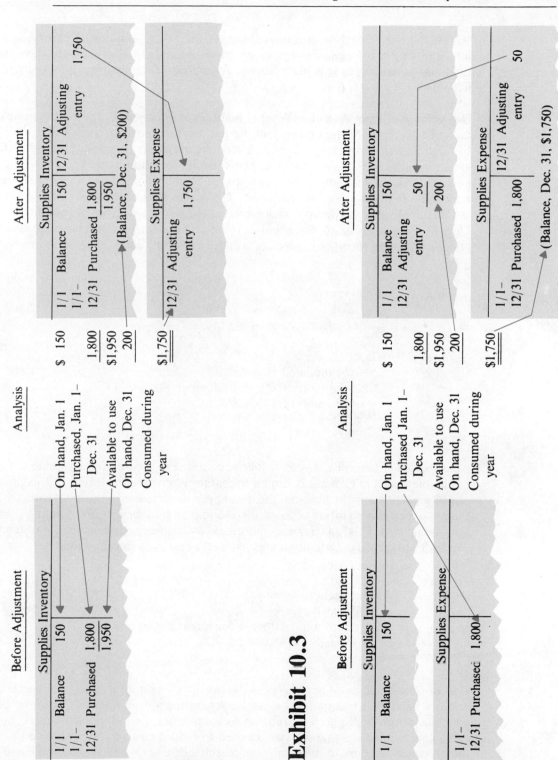

Exhibit 10.3

At the end of each period the balance of the asset, supplies inventory, would be adjusted to the balance of supplies on hand. As indicated previously, however, to facilitate bookkeeping it is preferable to record prepaid expenses initially in an asset account.

Depreciation of Plant Assets   When a plant asset is acquired, the cost is recorded in an asset account. At the end of each period, part of the cost is allocated to expense through an adjusting entry. The asset account, however, is not credited directly; instead, a contra or offset account, accumulated depreciation, is credited. Assume that a company purchased equipment with a cost of $12,800, a residual value of $800, and an expected life of ten years on January 1. The assignment of the cost of the equipment, less residual value to expense, is depicted in the second diagram of Exhibit 10.1. (See Unit 4 for a discussion of depreciation.) The original entry to purchase the equipment and the adjusting entry for depreciation at the end of the accounting period would be:

Jan. 1	Equipment	12,800	
	Cash or Accounts Payable		12,800
	To record purchase of equipment.		
Dec. 31	Depreciation Expense	1,200	
	Accumulated Depreciation		1,200
	Adjusting entry for annual depreciation expense ($12,800 − 800/10 = $1,200).		

Amortization of Intangible Assets   The accounting procedure for assigning the cost of intangible assets to expense is similar to that for plant assets. However, this process is called *amortization*. In addition, the usual practice is to credit the asset directly rather than use a contra or offset account for accumulated amortization. Assume that a patent with a cost of $45,000 is being amortized over an expected useful life of ten years. The entry to record amortization expense at the end of each year would be:

Dec. 31	Amortization Expense	4,500	
	Patents		4,500
	To record annual charge for amortization of patents ($45,000/10 = $4,500).		

Cost of Goods Sold   When the periodic inventory system is used, the beginning inventory balance is maintained on the books throughout the period. The cost of merchandise purchased, purchase returns and allowances, and freight-in are recorded in special accounts. Thus, an entry is needed to record cost of goods sold and to adjust the inventory account to the balance of merchandise actually in stock at the end of the period. Under the perpetual system this entry is not necessary because the inventory balance is adjusted and the cost of goods sold is recorded as merchandise inflows and outflows occur.

Exhibit 10.4 depicts in both diagram and T-account formats the flow of costs in determining cost of goods sold. Note that the balances of beginning inventory, purchases, freight-in, and purchase returns and allowances are transferred to a cost of goods sold account. At this point the balance of the cost of goods sold account equals the cost of the goods available for sale, $228,000 ($42,000 + 184,000 + 5,000 − 3,000). The ending inventory balance is then transferred from the cost of goods sold account to the inventory account; the balance left in the cost of goods sold account is then equal to the cost of goods sold, $183,000 ($228,000 − 45,000). The adjustment for cost of goods sold can be made in a single entry as follows:

Dec. 31	Inventory (ending balance)	45,000	
	Cost of Goods Sold	183,000	
	Purchase Returns and Allowances	3,000	
	Inventory (beginning balance)		42,000
	Purchases		184,000
	Freight-in		5,000
	To record adjusting entry for cost of goods sold.		

Uncollectible Accounts Expense   Most companies that give credit to customers to purchase merchandise or services experience losses from uncollectible accounts. Because there is a direct relationship between credit sales or unpaid customer balances and losses from uncollectible accounts, a company's prior experience can be used to estimate the expense of uncollectible accounts. Methods of estimating this expense are discussed fully in Unit 15. Until then, the amount to be recorded as uncollectible accounts expense will be given.

Assume that a company has determined that $3,650 should be recorded as uncollectible accounts expense for the current year. The adjusting entry requires a debit to an expense account and a credit to the contra-asset or offset account, allowance for uncollectible accounts:

Dec. 31	Uncollectible Accounts Expense	3,650	
	Allowance for Uncollectible Accounts		3,650
	To record provision for uncollectible accounts expense.		

A contra account is credited rather than accounts receivable because it is not known at this point which customers will not pay their account balances. Recall that

Exhibit 10.4

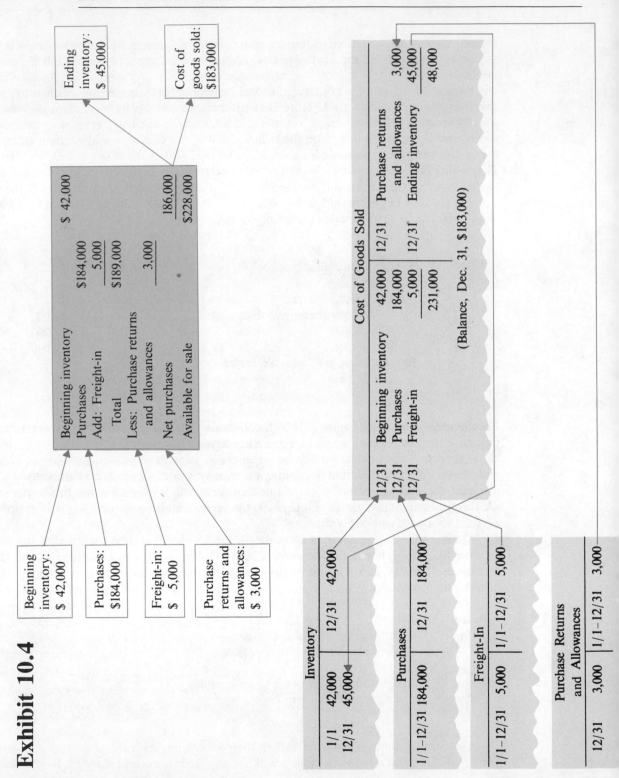

the contra account is deducted from accounts receivable on the balance sheet. In this example, the effect of the adjustment is to allocate $3,650 of the asset, accounts receivable, to expense. Assume that the balance of accounts receivable was $85,000 and the balance of allowance for uncollectible accounts was $200 before the adjusting entry. The net realizable value of accounts receivable decreases $3,650 as a result of the adjustment:

	Balance Before Adjustment	Balance After Adjustment	Increase (Decrease) in Balances
Accounts receivable	$85,000	$85,000	$ 0
Allowance for uncollectible accounts	200	3,850*	3,650
Net realizable value of accounts receivable	$84,800	$81,150	$(3,650)

*$200 + 3,650 = $3,850

Allocations Between Liabilities and Revenues

Advance payments may be received from customers or clients for goods or services to be provided later. To facilitate bookkeeping, these payments should be recorded in a liability account, and then allocated to revenue in an adjusting entry at the end of the accounting period. The entry to allocate the amount of the payments between liabilities (for unearned revenue) and revenues (for earned revenue) is a deferred revenue type of adjusting entry. Unearned revenues are deferred in a liability account until credited to revenues in a future period or periods. Examples of advance payments for services include rent, interest, subscriptions, or fees collected before services are provided. Customers may also pay for merchandise in advance or make deposits on goods ordered.

Assume that a company collected rent of $300 per month in advance for six months from a tenant on November 1, 19x4, and recorded the amount received, $1,800, in a liability account, unearned rent. At the end of the accounting period, December 31, an adjusting entry is necessary to allocate the $1,800 between the revenue account, rent revenue, and the liability account, unearned rent. By December 31 two months rent ($600) has been earned, while four months rent ($1,200) is still unearned. The analysis and T-accounts in Exhibit 10.5 depict the allocation between the liability and the revenue accounts. The original entry to collect the rent in advance and the adjusting entry are:

Nov. 1	Cash	1,800	
	Unearned Rent		1,800
	To record rent collected in advance.		

Exhibit 10.5

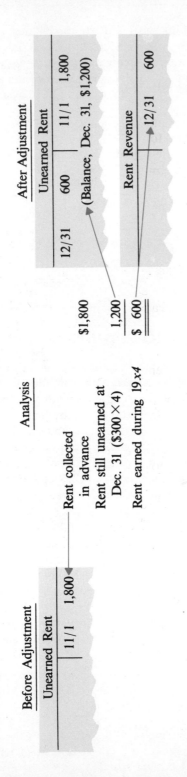

Before Adjustment

Unearned Rent

| 11/1 | 1,800 |

Analysis

Rent collected
in advance

Rent still unearned at
Dec. 31 ($300 × 4)

Rent earned during 19x4

$1,800
1,200
$ 600

After Adjustment

Unearned Rent

| 12/31 | 600 | 11/1 | 1,800 |
| | (Balance, Dec. 31, $1,200) |

Rent Revenue

| | 12/31 | 600 |

Exhibit 10.6

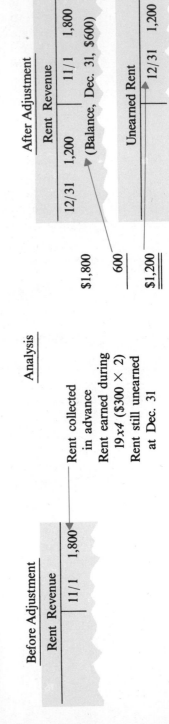

Before Adjustment

Rent Revenue

| 11/1 | 1,800 |

Analysis

Rent collected
in advance

Rent earned during
19x4 ($300 × 2)

Rent still unearned
at Dec. 31

$1,800
600
$1,200

After Adjustment

Rent Revenue

| 12/31 | 1,200 | 11/1 | 1,800 |
| | (Balance, Dec. 31, $600) |

Unearned Rent

| | 12/31 | 1,200 |

Dec. 31	Unearned Rent	600	
	Rent Revenue		600
	Adjusting entry for rent earned.		

It is preferable to record advance payments of revenue initially in a liability account to facilitate subsequent bookkeeping. However, the payments can be recorded initially in a revenue account. Assume that the rent collected in advance in the previous example was initially recorded in the revenue account on November 1. In the adjusting entry it is necessary to transfer $1,200 for unearned rent to a liability account, leaving $600 for rent earned in the revenue account. The analysis and T-accounts to depict this allocation are shown in Exhibit 10.6. The original entry and the adjusting entry are:

Nov. 1	Cash	1,800	
	Rent Revenue		1,800
	To record rent collected in advance.		
Dec. 31	Rent Revenue	1,200	
	Unearned Rent		1,200
	Adjusting entry for unearned rent.		

Unrecorded Expenses

Expenses that accrue on a continuing basis during the accounting period, but that are unpaid and unrecorded by the end of the period, must be recorded at that time if operating results and financial position are to be accurately measured in accordance with the matching principle. These expenses are recognized through an adjusting entry. As an example, the entries to issue a note, to accrue interest at year's end, and to pay the note and interest at the maturity date are presented on the following page. Exhibit 10.7 depicts the facts described in this situation.

Exhibit 10.7

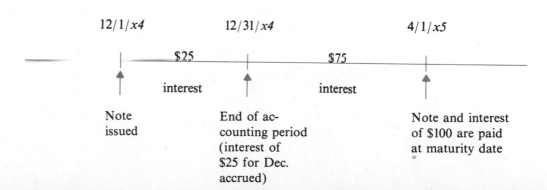

Dec. 1, 19x4	Cash	5,000	
	Notes Payable		5,000
	Note issued for cash loan.		

Dec. 31, 19x4	Interest Expense	25	
	Interest Payable		25
	Adjusting entry for accrued interest ($5,000 × 6% × 1/12 = $25).		

Apr. 1, 19x5	Notes Payable	5,000	
	Interest Payable	25	
	Interest Expense	75	
	Cash		5,100
	To record payment of note and interest.		

When the note and interest are paid on the maturity date, April 1, 19x5, both the liability for the note and the liability for accrued interest must be reduced. In addition, the interest expense that accrued for the remaining term of the note must be recognized. In the example, the liability for accrued interest of $25 is reduced and the interest expense that accrued during the remaining three months, $75 ($5,000 × 6% × 3/12), is recognized.

Another example of the accrued expense type of adjusting entry is the adjustment required for salaries accrued at the end of the accounting period. Assume that the weekly payroll of $8,000 for a company is paid on Friday. If the company has a 5-day workweek and the current accounting period ends on a Tuesday, salaries of $3,200 have accrued for the first two days of the workweek ($8,000/5 × 2 = $3,200). An adjusting entry is required to record the expense and liability for accrued salaries. When the weekly payroll is paid on Friday, the salaries for the last three days are charged to expense and the liability for accrued salaries is eliminated. Exhibit 10.8 depicts the facts in this situation. The adjusting entry and the entry to pay the weekly payroll subsequent to the adjusting entry are:

Dec. 31	Salaries Expense	3,200	
	Salaries Payable		3,200
	To accrue salaries for 2 days.		

Jan. 3	Salaries Payable	3,200	
	Salaries Expense	4,800	
	Cash		8,000
	To record weekly payroll, including payment of salaries accrued at end of previous period.		

Exhibit 10.8

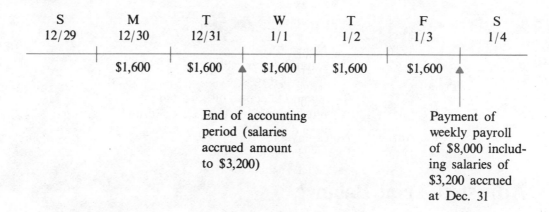

Unrecorded Revenues

Revenues that accrue on a continuing basis during the accounting period, but that have not been received or recorded by the end of the period, must be recorded then if operating results and financial position are to be accurately measured in accordance with the matching principle. These revenues are recognized through the accrued revenue type of adjusting entry. Examples of revenues that may be accrued through adjusting entries are interest on outstanding receivables, interest on bond investments, and rent due from tenants.

Assume that a company accepts a $10,000, 1-year, 9% note on May 1, 19x5 for the sale of merchandise to a customer. In this situation interest on the note is normally collected at the maturity date, May 1, 19x6. If the accounting period ends before the maturity date of the note, the accrued interest earned during the period must be recorded. The first diagram in Exhibit 10.1 shows that $600 of interest ($10,000 × 9% × 8/12 = $600) is earned between May 1, 19x5, and December 31, 19x5. Thus, the following adjusting entry is required:

Dec. 31,	Interest Receivable	600	
19x5	Interest Revenue		600
	Adjusting entry for accrued interest revenue.		

When the customer pays the note and interest at May 1, 19x6, the interest earned from January 1, 19x6, to May 1, 19x6, must be recorded and the receivable for accrued interest must be eliminated. The entry to record the collection of the note and interest on May 1, 19x6, is:

May 1, 19x6	Cash	10,900	
	Notes Receivable		10,000
	Interest Receivable		600
	Interest Revenue		300
	To record collection of note and interest, including interest accrued at end of 19x5.		

Adjusted Trial Balance

Recall that a trial balance, listing the accounts in the general ledger and their balances, is prepared at the end of the accounting period before the adjusting entries are made. After the adjusting entries are posted to the general ledger, another trial balance may be prepared to prove the equality of debits and credits for the journalizing and posting of the adjustments. This second trial balance is called an **adjusted trial balance** because a number of accounts that appeared in the trial balance have had their balances adjusted. Also, some accounts, such as depreciation expense, uncollectible accounts expense, salaries payable, interest receivable, and interest payable, will have balances after the adjustments, whereas they had none before. The heading for the adjusted trial balance is the same as that used for a trial balance. An example appears in the solution to the review problem.

Review of Accounting Cycle

In Units 7–9 the first four steps in the accounting cycle were examined. These steps were: (1) analysis of economic effects of business transactions, (2) journalizing business transactions, (3) posting journal entries, and (4) preparing a trial balance.

Accountants normally use a worksheet to complete the accounting cycle. When the worksheet is completed, the financial statements are prepared, and the adjusting and closing entries are journalized and posted. However, the accounting cycle can be completed without using a worksheet. In this case, a trial balance is prepared at the end of the period and the remaining steps in the accounting cycle are then: (5) journalizing and posting the adjustments, (6) preparing an adjusted trial balance, (7) journalizing and posting the closing entries, (8) preparing a post-closing trial balance (optional), and (9) preparing the basic financial statements. Adjusting entries and preparing an adjusted trial balance (steps 5 and 6) were discussed in this unit. The last three steps are discussed in Unit 11. When a worksheet is not prepared, the adjusted trial balance becomes important because It is then used as a basis for the information to complete steps 7 and 9. Unit 12 discusses how a worksheet is used to complete the accounting cycle.

REVIEW PROBLEM

The following is a trial balance for Spynx Company and the adjusting data at the end of the current accounting period:

Spynx Company
Trial Balance
December 31, 19x6

Cash	$ 3,900	
Notes Receivable	2,000	
Accounts Receivable	17,000	
Allowance for Uncollectible Accounts		$ 200
Merchandise Inventory	14,500	
Supplies Inventory	900	
Prepaid Insurance	1,200	
Land	8,000	
Buildings	29,000	
Accumulated Depreciation—Buildings		3,000
Equipment	5,600	
Accumulated Depreciation—Equipment		1,500
Accounts Payable		5,600
Unearned Rent		3,600
Spynx, Capital		81,000
Spynx, Drawing	12,000	
Sales		85,000
Purchases	63,000	
Sales Salaries	12,800	
Advertising Expense	900	
Office Salaries	7,700	
Utilities Expense	1,400	
	$179,900	$179,900

Adjusting data

a. The company estimated that uncollectible accounts expense is $600 for 19x6.

b. An inventory of supplies on hand at the end of 19x5 and 19x6 indicated balances of $100 and $150, respectively.

c. The building has an estimated life of 25 years and is expected to have a salvage value of $4,000.

d. The insurance records indicate that a 2-year policy for $1,200 was purchased at the beginning of 19x6.

e. A memo from the president's office states: "Storage space in the company's building was rented out for two years on Sept. 1; the rent of $3,600 was collected in advance."

f. The weekly payroll of $600 (for a 5-day workweek) is paid every Friday. December 31 is a Thursday; $400 pertains to sales salaries and $200 to office salaries.

g. Interest earned on the note receivable but not received as of Dec. 31 amounted to $50.

h. A customer paid $100 in advance for goods to be delivered in January 19x7. The amount was included in sales.

i. Equipment has an estimated life of ten years and an estimated salvage value of $600.

j. The merchandise inventory balance at December 31, 19x6, is $15,200.

Required

1. Prepare the adjusting entries required at the end of 19x6.
2. Identify each adjusting entry by type: deferred expense, deferred revenue, accrued expense, or accrued revenue.
3. Post the adjusting entries to T-accounts (enter the balances from the trial balance in each T-account used before posting the entries).
4. Prepare an adjusted trial balance as of December 31, 19x6.

Solution to review problem

1.	a.	Dec. 31	Uncollectible Accounts Expense	600	
			Allowance for Uncollectible Accounts		600
	b.	31	Supplies Expense	750	
			Supplies Inventory		750
	c.	31	Depreciation Expense— Building	1,000	
			Accumulated Depreciation— Building		1,000
	d.	31	Insurance Expense	600	
			Prepaid Insurance		600
	e.	31	Unearned Rent	600	
			Rent Revenue		600
	f.	31	Sales Salaries	320	
			Office Salaries	160	
			Salaries Payable		480

g.	Dec. 31	Interest Receivable	50	
		Interest Revenue		50
h.	31	Sales	100	
		Advances from Customers		100
i.	31	Depreciation Expense— Equipment	500	
		Accumulated Depreciation— Equipment		500
j.	31	Inventory (ending)	15,200	
		Cost of Goods Sold	62,300	
		Inventory (beginning)		14,500
		Purchases		63,000

Notes to solution

a. $600 is charged to uncollectible accounts expense, increasing the allowance for uncollectible accounts by $600.

b. Supplies were recorded initially in supplies inventory; because the supplies inventory balance is $150 at December 31, 19x6, and the total of supplies available is $900, the adjustment for supplies used is $750 ($900 − 150).

c. Depreciation on buildings: ($29,000 − 4,000)/25 yrs. − $1,000.

d. Cost of expired insurance allocated to expense: $1,200/2 yrs. = $600.

e. Advance rent payments earned and allocated to rent revenue: $3,600/24 mos. = $150/mo.; $150/mo. × 4 mo. = $600.

f. Accrued salaries for four days: sales salaries, $400 × 4/5 = $320; office salaries, $200 × 4/5 = $160.

g. Accrued interest revenue of $50 recorded.

h. Unearned sales revenue of $100 transferred from sales to a liability account, advances from customers.

i. Depreciation on equipment: ($5,600 − 600)/10 yrs. = $500.

j. The accounts and amounts used to determine cost of goods sold are included in this adjusting entry.

2. Allocations between assets and expenses (deferred expenses): a, b, c, d, i, j
Allocations between liabilities and revenues (deferred revenues): e, h
Unrecorded (accrued) expenses: f
Unrecorded (accrued) revenues: g

3.

Uncollectible Accounts Expense	
(a) 600	

Allowance for Uncollectible Accounts	
	200
	(a) 600

Supplies Inventory	
900	(b) 750

Supplies Expense	
(b) 750	

Depreciation Expense— Buildings	
(c) 1,000	

Accumulated Depreciation—Buildings	
	3,000
	(c) 1,000

Insurance Expense	
(d) 600	

Prepaid Insurance	
1,200	(d) 600

Unearned Rent	
(e) 600	3,600

Rent Revenue	
	(e) 600

Sales Salaries	
12,800	
(f) 320	

Office Salaries	
7,700	
(f) 160	

Salaries Payable	
	(f) 480

Interest Receivable	
(g) 50	

Interest Revenue	
	(g) 50

Sales	
(h) 100	85,000

Advances from Customers	
	(h) 100

Depreciation Expense— Equipment	
(i) 500	

Accumulated Depreciation— Equipment	
	1,500
	(i)　500

Cost of Goods Sold	
(j)　62,300	

Inventory	
14,500	(j)　14,500
(j)　15,200	

Purchases	
63,000	(j)　63,000

4.

Spynx Company Adjusted Trial Balance December 31, 19x6		
Cash	$ 3,900	
Notes receivable	2,000	
Accounts receivable	17,000	
Allowance for uncollectible accounts		$　800
Interest receivable	50	
Merchandise inventory	15,200	
Supplies inventory	150	
Prepaid insurance	600	
Land	8,000	
Buildings	29,000	
Accumulated depreciation—buildings		4,000
Equipment	5,600	
Accumulated depreciation—equipment		2,000
Accounts payable		5,600
Unearned rent		3,000
Advances from customers		100
Salaries payable		480
Spynx, capital		81,000
Spynx, drawing	12,000	
Sales		84,900
Cost of goods sold	62,300	
Sales salaries	13,120	
Advertising expense	900	
Office salaries	7,860	
Utilities expense	1,400	
Supplies expense	750	
Uncollectible accounts expense	600	
Depreciation expense—buildings	1,000	
Depreciation expense—equipment	500	
Insurance expense	600	
Rent revenue		600
Interest revenue		50
	$182,530	$182,530

SUMMARY

The economic effects of some business transactions are realized on a continuing basis and carry over to other accounting periods. Therefore, the balances of some assets, liabilities, revenues, and expenses must be adjusted at the end of the accounting period to measure and report operating results and financial position accurately. Four general types of adjustments were described in this unit: deferred expenses, deferred revenues, accrued expenses, and accrued revenues. In addition, the use of an adjusted trial balance to prove the equality of debits and credits after journalizing and posting the adjustments was explained.

REVIEW QUESTIONS

10-1   What are adjusting entries? Why are they needed?

10-2   Adjusting entries may be classified into four types. Name them and give two examples of each.

10-3   Complete the following chart:

Item	Also Called?	Brief Definition (in your own words)	Balance Sheet Classification
a. Deferred expense			
b. Accrued expense			
c. Deferred revenue			
d. Accrued revenue			

10-4   What is an adjusted trial balance? What is its purpose?

10-5   What accounts might appear in an adjusted trial balance but not a trial balance?

EXERCISES

10-1   For each case described, answer or complete the following:

    a.   What procedures are necessary at the end of the period to apply the matching principle?

    b.   Identify the type of adjusting entry required.

    c.   Identify the accounts to be debited and credited in preparing the adjusting entry.

Case 1   The entire rental for a computer was collected in advance and initially recorded in a liability account. The rental lasts for a period of 3 years.

Case 2   A truck is purchased; its useful life is 5 years.

Case 3   Interest has been earned on a note received from a customer, but the interest will not be received until the note is due, in the next accounting period.

Case 4   Interest is owed on a note issued to the bank for a cash loan; the interest will not be paid until the note is due, in the next accounting period.

10-2   The Hassel Company completed the transactions described below during 19x3:

   a.   Purchased office supplies totaling $1,650 during the year. The supplies are recorded in an expense account as they are purchased. The beginning and ending inventories of supplies were $200 and $350, respectively.
   b.   Equipment with a cost of $3,300, an estimated residual value of $300, and an estimated useful life of 8 years was purchased at the beginning of 19x3.
   c.   Property taxes are estimated at $150 per month. The property taxes are payable in July for the previous 12 months. The last payment for property taxes was on July 5, 19x3.
   d.   An 8%, 4-month note for $6,000 was received from a customer on December 1, 19x3. The note and interest are due on April 1, 19x4.
   e.   Fees were collected in advance from clients in the amount of $3,600 during 19x3. The fees were recorded in a liability account when received. At the end of 19x3 $800 of these fees are still unearned.
   f.   The company rents certain types of office equipment as one of its business activities. During 19x3 $4,500 of rental fees were collected in advance and recorded in a revenue account. At the end of 19x3 $400 of these rental fees were still unearned.
   g.   Merchandise purchases for the year totaled $86,000. In addition, freight charges of $2,500 were paid for shipment of the merchandise to the company, and the company returned damaged merchandise with a cost of $1,200 to suppliers. Inventory balances at the beginning and end of the year were $14,100 and $12,300, respectively.

Required   (1)   Identify the type of adjusting entry required in each situation described.
            (2)   Prepare the necessary adjusting entry for each situation.

10-3   The following are selected accounts and their balances from the trial balance of Winn Company as of December 31, 19x4:

Accounts receivable $ 26,000
Allowance for uncollectible accounts
   (credit balance)   150

Prepaid insurance	1,800
Building	60,000
Accumulated depreciation	7,000
Unearned contract revenue	165,000
Salaries expense	78,000

The following information is necessary to prepare adjusting entries at the end of 19*x4:*

a. The allowance for uncollectible accounts is to be increased to $1,300.
b. The balance in prepaid insurance represents the balance of a 2-year policy purchased on July 1, 19*x3.*
c. The building is being depreciated over a 40-year life and has an estimated residual value of $4,000.
d. The company services equipment on a contract basis; the contracts are paid in advance and recorded in a liability account. An analysis of the unexpired contracts indicates that $6,000 of the amount recorded as a liability will be earned in 19*x5.*
e. Salaries are paid weekly; at the end of 19*x4,* which ended on a Tuesday, accrued salaries amounted to $800. Assume a 5-day workweek.

Required   Prepare the necessary adjusting entries for 19*x4.*

10-4 Determine the missing amount(s) in each of the following situations and prepare the adjusting entries required in each.

a. Office supplies on hand at the beginning of the accounting period, $200; office supplies purchased during the period, $1,200; office supplies used during the period, $1,250; office supplies on hand at the end of the period, $_____.
b. Unearned fees at the beginning and end of the period, $800 and $1,200, respectively; amount of unearned fees realized during the period, $3,600; unearned fees collected during the period, $_____.
c. Salaries paid during the period, $38,000; salaries accrued at the beginning and end of the period, $400 and $600, respectively; salary expense for the period, $_____.
d. Equipment account balance at the beginning and end of the period, $18,000; accumulated depreciation at the beginning and end of the period, $3,200 and $4,800, respectively; estimated residual value of equipment, $2,000; depreciation expense for the period, $_____; estimated useful life of equipment, _____ years.
e. Inventory balances at the beginning and end of the period were $32,600 and $35,800, respectively; during the period sales were $215,000, sales returns were $1,400, purchases were $106,200, freight-in was $2,400, and purchase returns were $1,700; cost of goods sold for the period was $_____ and gross margin was $_____.

PROBLEMS

10-1   The following is the trial balance of the I. N. Clement Company as of December 31, 19x5:

Cash	$15,000	
Accounts receivable	22,000	
Notes receivable	5,000	
Office supplies	800	
Prepaid insurance	1,200	
Office equipment	8,600	
Accumulated depreciation		$ 1,600
Accounts payable		13,600
Notes payable		2,000
Unearned fees		2,400
I. N. Clement, capital		24,000
I. N. Clement, drawing	9,000	
Fees earned		54,000
Salaries expense	28,200	
Advertising expense	3,600	
Utilities expense	1,700	
Miscellaneous expense	2,500	
	$97,600	$97,600

Adjusting data

a.   An inventory of office supplies at December 31 indicated that $150 of supplies were still on hand.

b.   On April 1 of the current year a 2-year insurance policy was purchased for $1,200.

c.   Included in advertising expense are advertising brochures that cost $300 and will be used next year.

d.   Included in fees earned is $800 from a customer who paid in advance for services to be rendered next year.

e.   At December 31 the company had earned one-third of the advance fees of $2,400 paid by a customer on a long-term contract for services.

f.   On October 1 of the current year the company received a $5,000, 6%, 6-month note from a customer. Interest of $150 is to be collected at maturity.

g.   The weekly payroll is $750 for a 5-day workweek; the current year ends on a Wednesday.

h.   The company borrowed $2,000 from the bank by issuing a $2,000, 6%, 3-month note on November 30 of the current year. Interest is to be paid at maturity.

i.   The office equipment had a 10-year life with a $600 scrap value when acquired.

Required   **(1)**   Prepare all necessary adjusting entries.

   (2)   Prepare an adjusted trial balance as of December 31, 19x5.

(*Note:*   Set up T-accounts for each account affected by the adjusting entries; then post the entries to determine the account balances for the adjusted trial balance.)

10-2   The following accounts are from the trial balance of the Whispering Pines Motel at December 31, 19*x7:*

Laundry supplies	$ 5,400
Prepaid insurance	4,500
Furniture	37,400
Accumulated depreciation	7,000
Building	184,000
Accumulated depreciation	12,000
Room rental revenue	176,000
Wages expense	68,000

Adjusting data

a.   An inventory of laundry supplies at the end of 19*x7* indicates a balance of $450.

b.   The balance of prepaid insurance represents the remainder of the cost of a 3-year policy purchased on July 1, 19*x6.*

c.   Furniture has an expected salvage value of $2,400 and an expected useful life of 10 years.

d.   The building has an expected salvage value of $4,000 and an expected useful life of 30 years.

e.   Included in room rental revenue are room charges totaling $1,200 received in advance.

f.   Accrued wages at the end of 19*x7* amounted to $800.

g.   Bills for $500 for recent conferences and banquets had been prepared, but were not recorded or mailed at the end of 19*x7.*

h.   Property taxes are accrued at $250 per month; property taxes were recorded last when they were paid in July for the preceding 12 months.

Required   Prepare the necessary adjusting entries for 19*x7.*

10-3   Following are the trial balance and adjusted trial balance for Renn Company at the end of 19*x6.*

	Trial Balance		Adjusted Trial Balance	
	Debit	Credit	Debit	Credit
Cash	$ 40,000	$	$ 40,000	$
Accounts receivable	34,000		34,000	
Allowance for uncollectible accounts		200		1,700
Notes receivable	10,000		10,000	
Interest receivable			200	
Supplies inventory	1,400		300	
Equipment	26,000		26,000	
Accumulated depreciation		7,200		9,600

Accounts payable		11,000		11,000
Income taxes payable				5,500
Unearned fees		2,200		700
Capital stock		25,000		25,000
Retained earnings		7,700		7,700
Fees earned		165,000		166,500
Salaries expense	56,000		56,000	
Rent expense	24,000		24,000	
Depreciation expense			2,400	
Supplies expense			1,100	
Uncollectible accounts expense			1,500	
Utilities expense	8,500		8,500	
Miscellaneous expense	4,200		4,200	
Interest expense	800		800	
Interest revenue		400		600
Income tax expense	13,800		19,300	
	$218,700	$218,700	$228,300	$228,300

Required   Reconstruct the adjusting entries that were made to derive the figures appearing in the adjusted trial balance.

10-4   The following is the trial balance of Voyager RV Sales Company at December 31, 19x7:

Voyager RV Sales Company
Trial Balance
December 31, 19x7

Cash	$ 16,200	
Accounts Receivable	27,000	
Allowance for Uncollectible Accounts		$ 700
Inventory	84,500	
Prepaid Insurance	2,500	
Land	11,000	
Building	64,000	
Accumulated Depreciation		12,000
Furniture and Fixtures	8,500	
Accumulated Depreciation		3,000
Accounts Payable		42,700
Advances from Customers		7,200
Notes Payable, Long-Term		30,000
Common Stock, $10 par		50,000
Retained Earnings		26,900
Sales		356,000
Sales Returns and Allowances	2,900	
Purchases	242,000	
Freight-in	5,800	
Purchase Returns and Allowances		2,300
Sales Salaries	41,400	
Advertising	10,600	
Miscellaneous Selling Expenses	3,300	
Office Salaries	8,300	
Office Supplies Expense	900	
Miscellaneous Office Expense	1,900	
Totals	$530,800	$530,800

Adjusting data

a. The inventory balance at December 31, 19x7, is $88,300.

b. Uncollectible accounts expense is estimated at $3,560.

c. The balance in prepaid insurance represents a 2-year policy purchased at the beginning of 19x7.

d. The building is being depreciated over 30 years; the estimated residual value is $4,000.

e. Furniture and fixtures are being depreciated over 10 years; the estimated residual value is $500.

f. An analysis of advances from customers indicates that $3,200 is still unearned at the end of 19x7.

g. The long-term note was issued for a cash loan on May 1, 19x7; the interest rate is 8%; interest is payable annually on May 1 over the 3-year term of the note.

h. Accrued salaries at the end of 19x7 were: sales salaries, $500; office salaries, $100.

i. An inventory of office supplies indicates a balance of $200 at the end of 19x7.

j. Accrued income taxes are $15,756 for 19x7.

Required

(1) Prepare all necessary adjusting entries at the end of 19x7.

(2) Prepare an adjusted trial balance at December 31, 19x7.
    (*Note:*   Set up T-accounts for each account affected by the adjusting entries; then post the entries to determine the account balances for the adjusted trial balance.)

(3) Prepare an income statement and a balance sheet for the year ended December 31, 19x7. Allocate one-half of insurance and depreciation expenses to selling expenses and the balance to general and administrative expenses.

Unit 11
Closing Entries

Books should be closed each year, especially in partnership because frequent accounting makes for long friendship.

Fra Luca Paciolo, Summa de Arithmetica

At the end of each accounting period, entries are recorded that prepare the revenue and expense accounts for the next period. These entries separate the net income or net loss for each period from that of others. This unit examines these closing entries.

Performance Objectives

Upon completing this unit you should be able to:

1. define and use the accounting terms introduced in this unit.
2. prepare the necessary closing entries and a post-closing trial balance at the end of the accounting period for either a service-type or a merchandising-type organization.

Need for Closing Entries

To separate the revenues and expenses (and thus, net income) of one accounting period from those of another, it is necessary to close out these accounts and any contra accounts related to them. Unless the balances of the revenue and expense accounts were eliminated at the end of the accounting period, they would be carried over to the next. The entries from this next period would then be added to them, and the process would continue from period to period, with the balances growing cumulatively larger. This would make it difficult to prepare an income statement for only the most recent period.

The purpose of **closing entries**, then, is to transfer net income to retained earnings or to the owner's capital account at the end of each period so that the periodic matching process is completed for one period before the next begins. Recall that some companies use a temporary account (dividends or dividends paid for corporations, and drawing for sole proprietors and partners) to record the charge for profit distributions to owners during the period. These temporary accounts must be closed out before the correct ending balance in either retained earnings or capital is achieved. Thus, the balance of dividends or dividends paid must be transferred to retained earnings. Similarly, the balance of each drawing account must be transferred to its related capital account.

Procedures for Closing Entries

Various procedures can be used to close out revenues and expenses, related contra accounts, and dividends paid or drawing accounts. One of these involves a special clearing account called **income summary** and four separate closing entries:

1. Revenues and any related contra accounts are closed out to income summary.
2. Expenses and any related contra accounts are closed out to income summary.
3. The income summary account is closed out to retained earnings (or the capital account[s]).
4. The dividends paid account is closed out to retained earnings (or the drawing account[s] is closed out to the capital account[s]).

The information needed to prepare the closing entries may be obtained from an adjusted trial balance, the general ledger, or a worksheet (see Unit 12 for this last approach). Mynx Company's adjusted trial balance at the end of 19*x4* (see Exhibit 11.1) is used to illustrate closing entries.

The four closing entries for Mynx Company, a service-type organization, are illustrated in Exhibit 11.2. In the first entry, the revenue accounts, which have credit balances, are closed out. This is accomplished by debiting each revenue account for the amount of its balance. The income summary account is then credited for the total of all

Exhibit 11.1

Mynx Company		
Adjusted Trial Balance		
December 31, 19x4		
Cash	$ 30,000	
Receivables	20,000	
Prepaid expenses	2,000	
Equipment	25,000	
Accumulated depreciation		$ 6,000
Accounts payable		12,000
Accrued expenses		1,000
Capital stock		25,000
Retained earnings		15,000
Dividends paid	5,000	
Fees earned		90,000
Salaries expense	48,000	
Utilities expense	6,000	
Depreciation expense	3,000	
Supplies used	2,000	
Miscellaneous expenses	4,000	
Miscellaneous revenues		2,000
Income tax expense	6,000	
	$151,000	$151,000

revenues closed out. In the second entry the expense accounts are closed out. Because they have debit balances, they are credited in the closing entry, and income summary is debited for their total. These first two closing entries, then, transfer revenues and expenses to income summary (see the income summary T-account). The balance in the income summary account at this point is $23,000 ($92,000 − 69,000), which is the net income for the period because revenucs exceed expenses by this amount. The third entry closes out this income summary account and transfers net income to retained earnings. It does this by debiting income summary and crediting retained earnings for $23,000. In the last closing entry, dividends paid is credited and retained earnings is debited for $5,000, thus charging retained earnings for profits distributed to stockholders during the period.

Some accountants prefer using a different closing procedure, one in which all revenues and expenses are closed out and net income, less dividends, is transferred directly to retained earnings in a single entry. Other closing procedures can be used, but all accomplish the same purpose, that is, transferring net income to retained earnings. In this text, the closing procedure illustrated in Exhibit 11.2 will be followed.

Closing Entries for a Merchandising-Type Organization

Closing entries for a merchandising-type organization are the same as those for a service-type organization. However, a merchandiser must also close out the cost of goods sold account. Under the periodic inventory system, the purchases, freight-in,

Exhibit 11.2

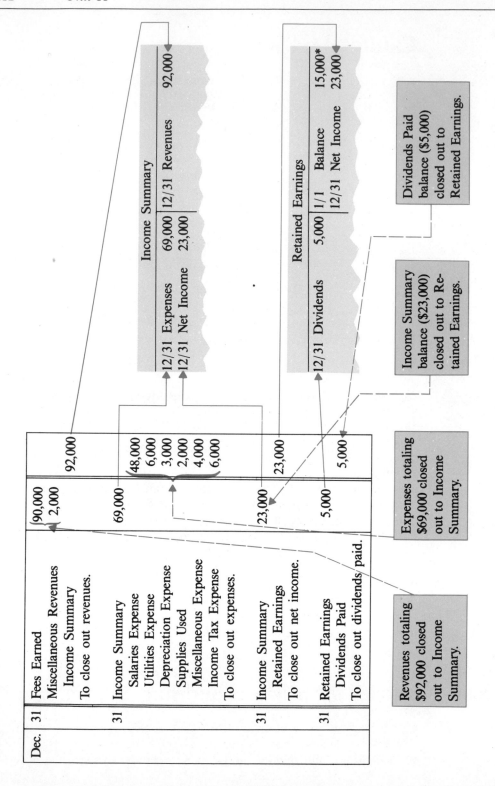

and purchase returns and allowances accounts will have been reduced to a zero balance when the adjusting entry for cost of goods sold was prepared. The contra accounts, sales discounts and sales returns and allowances, must also be closed out. When separate entries are prepared to close out revenues and expenses, these contra accounts can be included with the entry to close out revenues or with the entry to close out expenses. They can be closed out with revenues because they are related to sales. Or they can be closed out with expenses because they have debit balances as do the expense accounts. The former approach will be followed in this text.

Assume that Jynx Company determined that the balances for beginning and ending inventory, purchases, and related accounts for 19*x4* were:

Inventory, January 1, 19*x4*	$ 72,000
Inventory, December 31, 19*x4*	64,000
Purchases	244,000
Freight-in	12,000
Purchase returns and allowances	6,000

The adjusting entry for cost of goods sold and the effects of the entry on these accounts are illustrated in Exhibit 11.3. Note that the inventory account contains the ending balance of $64,000 and the purchases, freight-in, and purchase returns and allowances accounts have zero balances after the adjusting entry. The cost of goods sold account then appears in the adjusted trial balance (see Exhibit 11.4). If the perpetual inventory system is used, this adjusting entry is not necessary (see Unit 17).

Exhibit 11.5 (pages 216–217) shows the closing entries for the Jynx Company. Note that the cost of goods sold account is included in the entry to close out expenses. Also note that the contra accounts, sales discounts and sales returns and allowances, are included in the entry to close out revenues.

Post-Closing Trial Balance

After the closing entries are journalized and posted, and before entries are recorded for the next accounting period, a trial balance can be prepared to prove the equality of debits and credits. This trial balance is called a **post-closing trial balance.** Because the revenue, expense, income summary, and dividends paid (or drawing) accounts should have been reduced to a zero balance through the journalizing and posting of the closing entries, only the balance sheet accounts should appear in the post-closing trial balance. Journalizing or posting the closing entries to the wrong accounts and recording incorrect amounts are errors that may be caught by scanning the post-closing trial balance. If an account other than a balance sheet account appears in the post-closing trial balance, an error exists and should be traced and corrected. A post-closing trial balance for Jynx Company is presented in Exhibit 11.6 (page 218). Note that the ending balances for inventory ($64,000) and retained earnings ($52,000 + $20,000 net income − $12,000 dividends = $60,000) appear in the post-closing trial balance.

Exhibit 11.3

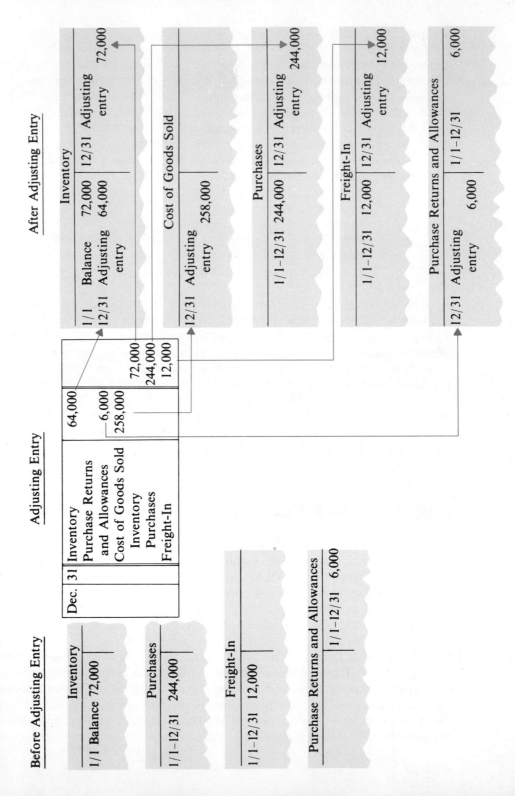

Exhibit 11.4

Jynx Company Adjusted Trial Balance December 31, 19x4		
Cash	$ 30,000	
Accounts Receivable	60,000	
Allowance for Uncollectible Accounts		$ 3,000
Inventory	64,000	
Prepaid Expenses	2,000	
Equipment	45,000	
Accumulated Depreciation		12,000
Accounts Payable		48,000
Accrued Expenses		3,000
Capital Stock		75,000
Retained Earnings		52,000
Dividends Paid	12,000	
Sales		400,000
Sales Discounts	5,000	
Sales Returns and Allowances	8,000	
Cost of Goods Sold	258,000	
Selling Expenses	68,000	
General and Administrative Expenses	35,000	
Income Tax Expense	5,000	
Interest Revenue		1,000
Interest Expense	2,000	
	$594,000	$594,000

Completion of the Accounting Cycle

Several procedures in the accounting cycle occur at the end of the accounting period. After the closing entries are journalized and posted, a post-closing trial balance can be prepared. Then, to complete the accounting cycle when a worksheet is not used, the basic financial statements are prepared. The information for the balance sheet, income statement, and retained earnings statements are obtained from the adjusted trial balance. The next unit explains how a worksheet can be used to complete the accounting cycle.

REVIEW PROBLEM

Refer to the adjusted trial balance for the Spynx Company, which was prepared in the solution to the review problem in Unit 10. Prepare the closing entries and a post-closing trial balance as of December 31, 19x6. (The solution to the review problem begins in the middle of page 218.)

Exhibit 11.5

Before Closing Entry

Sales
| | 400,000 |

Sales Discounts
| 5,000 | |

Sales Returns and Allowances
| 8,000 | |

Interest Revenue
| | 1,000 |

Cost of Goods Sold
| 258,000 | |

Closing Entry

Dec. 31	Sales	400,000	
	Interest Revenue	1,000	
	Sales Discounts		5,000
	Sales Returns and Allowances		8,000
	Income Summary		388,000
	To close out revenue and related accounts.		
31	Income Summary	368,000	
	Cost of Goods Sold		258,000
	Selling Expenses		68,000
	General and Administrative Expenses		35,000
	Income Tax Expense		5,000
	Interest Expense		2,000
	To close out expense accounts.		
31	Income Summary	20,000	
	Retained Earnings		20,000
	To close out income summary and transfer net income to retained earnings.		
31	Retained Earnings	12,000	
	Dividends Paid		12,000
	To close out dividends paid.		

After Closing Entry

Sales
| 12/31 CE 400,000 | 400,000 |

Sales Discounts
| 5,000 | 12/31 CE 5,000 |

Sales Returns and Allowances
| 8,000 | 12/31 CE 8,000 |

Interest Revenue
| 12/31 CE 1,000 | 1,000 |

Cost of Goods Sold
| 258,000 | 12/31 CE 258,000 |

Selling Expenses

68,000	12/31 CE 68,000

General and Administrative Expenses

35,000	12/31 CE 35,000

Income Tax Expense

5,000	12/31 CE 5,000

Interest Expense

2,000	12/31 CE 2,000

Income Summary

12/31 CE 368,000	12/31 CE 388,000
12/31 CE 20,000	

Retained Earnings

12/31 CE 12,000	52,000
	12/31 CE 20,000

Dividends Paid

12,000	12/31 CE 12,000

Selling Expenses

68,000	

General and Administrative Expenses

35,000	

Income Tax Expense

5,000	

Interest Expense

2,000	

Retained Earnings

	52,000

Dividends Paid

12,000	

Exhibit 11.6

Jynx Company Post-Closing Trial Balance December 31, 19x4		
Cash	$ 30,000	
Accounts Receivable	60,000	
Allowance for Uncollectible Accounts		$ 3,000
Inventory	64,000	
Prepaid Expenses	2,000	
Equipment	45,000	
Accumulated Depreciation		12,000
Accounts Payable		48,000
Accrued Expenses		3,000
Capital Stock		75,000
Retained Earnings		60,000
	$201,000	$201,000

Solution to review problem

Dec. 31	Sales	84,900	
	Rent Revenue	600	
	Interest Revenue	50	
	Income Summary		85,550
31	Income Summary	89,030	
	Cost of Goods Sold		62,300
	Sales Salaries		13,120
	Advertising Expense		900
	Office Salaries		7,860
	Utilities Expense		1,400
	Supplies Expense		750
	Bad Debt Expense		600
	Depreciation Expense—		
	Buildings		1,000
	Depreciation Expense—		
	Equipment		500
	Insurance Expense		600
31	Spynx, Capital	3,480	
	Income Summary		3,480
31	Spynx, Capital	12,000	
	Spynx, Drawing		12,000

Note on closing entries   The debits to income summary exceed the credits by $3,480 ($89,030 − 85,550); thus, a net loss of $3,480 was incurred. In the closing entry, income summary is credited and Spynx, capital is debited for the net loss.

Spynx Company **Post-Closing Trial Balance** **December 31, 19x6**		
Cash	$ 3,900	
Notes Receivable	2,000	
Accounts Receivable	17,000	
Allowance for Bad Debts		$ 800
Interest Receivable	50	
Merchandise Inventory	15,200	
Supplies Inventory	150	
Prepaid Insurance	600	
Land	8,000	
Buildings	29,000	
Accumulated Depreciation—Buildings		4,000
Equipment	5,600	
Accumulated Depreciation—Equipment		2,000
Accounts Payable		5,600
Unearned Rent		3,000
Advances from Customers		100
Salaries Payable		480
Spynx, Capital		65,520
	$81,500	$81,500

Note on post-closing trial balance   Only the balance sheet accounts have balances in the post-closing trial balance. These balances will be the same as those in the adjusted trial balance, except for the capital account. The capital account in this case has a balance of $65,520 after the net loss and drawing account are closed out:

Capital balance before closing entries		$81,000
Less: Net loss	$ 3,480	
Drawing account	12,000	15,480
Capital balance after closing entries		$65,520

SUMMARY

To separate the revenues and expenses of one period from those of others and to transfer net income (or loss) and dividends (if recorded in a separate account) to retained earnings, closing entries are necessary. In a proprietorship or partnership the net income or loss and the drawing account(s) must be transferred to the capital account(s). The procedures for preparing these closing entries and a post-closing trial balance were explained in this unit. The next unit explains how the year-end accounting procedures discussed in Units 10 and 11 can be carried out using a worksheet.

REVIEW QUESTIONS

11-1   What are closing entries? Why are they needed?

11-2   Describe the four closing entries that may be made if revenues and expenses are closed out separately to a special clearing account.

11-3   What is the purpose of the income summary account?

11-4   What is a post-closing trial balance? What is its purpose?

11-5   Distinguish among a trial balance, adjusted trial balance, and post-closing trial balance.

11-6   What accounts appear in a post-closing trial balance? How do they compare with the accounts appearing in a trial balance and adjusted trial balance?

EXERCISES

11-1   Following are the accounts from the adjusted trial balance of the Y. B. Blue Company at December 31, 19*x6:*

Cash	$ 3,800	
Accounts receivable	1,300	
Supplies	200	
Store equipment	8,400	
Accumulated depreciation		$ 2,400
Notes payable		5,000
Y. B. Blue, capital		4,200
Y. B. Blue, drawing	6,500	
Rental fees earned		13,700
Rent expense	3,000	
Supplies expense	1,200	
Depreciation expense	800	
Utilities expense	400	
Service fees earned		300
	$25,600	$25,600

Required   Prepare the closing entries required at the end of 19*x6.*

11-2   Refer to the data in exercise 11–1. Prepare a post-closing trial balance as of December 31, 19*x6.*

11-3   The adjusted trial balance of the Finn Company at December 31, 19*x8*, is presented at the top of the next page.

Required   **a.**   Prepare the necessary closing entries.
          b.   Prepare a post-closing trial balance.

Finn Company
Trial Balance
December 31, 19x8

Cash	$ 36,000	
Accounts receivable	27,000	
Allowance for uncollectible accounts		$ 1,350
Prepaid expenses	600	
Equipment	18,400	
Accumulated depreciation		5,100
Accounts payable		12,200
Unearned fees		850
Capital stock		25,000
Retained earnings		6,900
Dividends paid	2,500	
Fees earned		142,000
Salaries expense	74,200	
Rent expense	24,000	
Depreciation expense	1,700	
Utilities expense	2,800	
Miscellaneous expense	1,900	
Interest revenue		600
Income tax expense	4,900	
	$194,000	$194,000

11-4 Following is the adjusted trial balance as of Feb. 29, 19x4, for the Bestofall Clothing Store. Prepare the adjusting entry for cost of goods sold and the closing entries for this company on Feb. 29, 19x4. The inventory balance at Feb. 29, 19x4, is $5,750.

Bestofall Clothing Store
Adjusted Trial Balance
February 29, 19x4

Cash	$ 2,000	
Accounts receivable	1,100	
Allowance for uncollectible accounts		$ 50
Merchandise inventory, February 1	6,200	
Accounts payable		350
I. M. King, capital		8,450
I. M. King, drawing	800	
Sales		4,500
Purchases	2,700	
Advertising expense	150	
Rent expense	250	
Utilities expense	100	
Miscellaneous expense	50	
	$13,350	$13,350

11-5 The Wheel-n-Deal Company's trial balance on January 31, 19x3, appeared as follows:

Cash	$ 4,800	
Accounts Receivable	8,200	
Allowance for Uncollectible Accounts		$ 200
Merchandise Inventory, January 1	12,500	
Store Equipment	6,000	

Accumulated Depreciation		1,600
Accounts Payable		4,400
Tex S. Deal, Capital		28,100
Sales		17,200
Purchases	13,300	
Purchase Returns		100
Freight-in	700	
Wages	2,900	
Rent	2,400	
Utilities	800	
	$51,600	$51,600

Merchandise inventory, January 31: $14,200.

Required **a.** Prepare the adjusting entry for cost of goods sold and the closing entries at January 31, 19x3.

b. Calculate the following for January 19x3:
  (1) cost of goods sold
  (2) gross margin
  (3) net income or loss

c. Calculate the following at January 31, 19x3:
  (1) total assets
  (2) Tex S. Deal, capital

PROBLEMS

11-1 The following is the adjusted trial balance for Fulcrum Corporation at December 31, 19x4:

Fulcrum Corporation Adjusted Trial Balance December 31, 19x4		
Cash	$ 15,000	
Receivables	40,000	
Prepaid Expenses	2,000	
Equipment	52,000	
Accumulated Depreciation		$ 8,000
Accounts Payable		27,000
Advances from Customers		3,000
Salaries Payable		1,000
Common Stock		25,000
Retained Earnings		6,000
Service Revenue		175,000
Salaries Expense	89,000	
Rent Expense	24,000	
Depreciation Expense	4,000	
Other Expenses	19,000	
	$245,000	$245,000

Required **a.** Prepare the closing entries at the end of 19x4.
b. Prepare a post-closing trial balance at December 31, 19x4.

11-2 Following is the trial balance at December 31, 19x9, for Pivot Corporation:

Pivot Corporation Trial Balance December 31, 19x9		
Cash	$ 41,000	
Notes Receivable	10,000	
Accounts Receivable	35,000	
Allowance for Uncollectible Accounts		$ 250
Supplies Inventory	1,650	
Land	28,000	
Building	156,000	
Accumulated Depreciation		30,000
Equipment	27,500	
Accumulated Depreciation		5,000
Accounts Payable		13,500
Unearned Rent		3,600
Mortgage Payable		110,000
Capital Stock, $10 par value		50,000
Retained Earnings		21,800
Dividends Paid	7,500	
Fees Earned		225,000
Salaries Expense	132,000	
Utilities Expense	8,900	
Miscellaneous Expenses	4,400	
Interest Expense	7,200	
	$459,150	$459,150

Adjusting data

a. The provision for uncollectible accounts is to be increased to $1,750.
b. The note receivable is a 9%, 3-month note received on November 1, 19x9.
c. An inventory of supplies on hand at December 31, 19x9, indicates a balance of $200.
d. The building has an expected life of 30 years and an expected residual value of $6,000.
e. The equipment has an expected life of 10 years and an expected residual value of $2,500.
f. Unearned rent represents a 6-month advance payment for the rental of excess space in the company's building. The lease was signed on October 1, 19x9.
g. Accrued salaries at the end of 19x9 were $1,500.

Required
(1) Prepare the adjusting entries required at the end of 19x9.
(2) Set up T-accounts for each account included in the adjusting entries and enter its balance, if any, from the trial balance.
(3) Post the adjusting entries to the T-accounts set up in part 2.
(4) Prepare the closing entries required at the end of 19x9.
(5) Prepare a classified balance sheet and a single-step income statement. Ignore income taxes.

11-3 The following are the accounts from the trial balance for Square Deal Sales Company at the end of 19*x8:*

Cash	$ 3,956
Notes receivable	4,800
Accounts receivable	7,360
Allowance for uncollectible accounts	17
Inventory 1/1/*x8*	12,588
Prepaid insurance	2,232
Land	6,775
Building	29,000
Accumulated depreciation—building	4,000
Equipment	5,645
Accumulated depreciation—equipment	3,600
Accounts payable	5,142
Unearned rent	2,856
Capital stock, $5 par value	25,000
Retained earnings	12,807
Dividends paid	6,000
Sales	82,295
Sales discounts	800
Purchases	38,457
Freight-in	709
Purchase returns	800
Advertising expense	987
Salaries	13,504
Delivery expense	1,292
Utilities expense	2,130
Interest income	343
Interest expense	625

Adjusting data

a. Uncollectible accounts expense is estimated at $815.

b. Prepaid insurance represents the balance of a 3-year policy purchased on July 1, 19*x6.*

c. The building is being depreciated over a 25-year life with an expected residual value of $4,000.

d. The equipment is being depreciated over a 6-year life with an expected residual value of $245.

e. The balance of unearned rent represents an advance payment for 4 months, and was received on December 1, 19*x8.*

f. The note receivable is a 3-month note that was received on November 1, 19*x8,* and pays interest at 10% annually.

g. The ending merchandise inventory balance is $14,238.

Required

(1) Prepare the necessary adjusting entries for 19*x8.*

(2) Set up T-accounts for each account included in the adjusting entries and enter its balance, if any, from the trial balance.

(3) Post the adjusting entries to the T-accounts set up in part 2.

(4)   Prepare the closing entries for 19*x8*.

(5)   Prepare a post-closing trial balance at December 31, 19*x8*.

11-4   Mandrake Corporation completed the following selected transactions during December 19*x7*:

Dec.   1   Purchased merchandise on credit with a cost of $5,000, subject to credit terms of 2/10, n/30.

4   Returned damaged merchandise with a cost of $200 for credit.

8   Sold merchandise with a cost of $3,000 for $6,000 on credit, subject to credit terms of 2/10, n/30.

12   Accepted the return of merchandise sold on December 8; the merchandise had a cost of $100 and a sales price of $200.

18   Received payment for the merchandise sold on December 8 less the goods returned on December 12.

31   Paid for the merchandise purchased on December 1 less the goods returned on December 4.

After journalizing and posting these transactions, the trial balance at December 31, 19*x7* for Mandrake Corporation included the following:

Sales	$340,000
Sales discounts	6,000
Sales returns	4,000
Purchases	185,000
Freight-in	12,000
Purchase returns	3,000
Selling expenses	74,000
General and administrative expenses	40,000
Discounts lost	1,000
Income tax expense	5,000

Beginning and ending inventory balances for 19*x7* were $38,000 and $42,000, respectively.

Required   Assume the company uses the periodic inventory system; record (a) the six December transactions described, (b) the adjusting entry for cost of goods sold, and (c) the closing entries for 19*x7*.

11-5   The bookkeeper for Boggs Company prepared the following closing entries at the end of 19*x3*:

Income Summary	121,600	
Accumulated Depreciation		5,400
Accounts Payable		16,500
Salaries Payable		400
Advances from Customers		600
Sales		98,500
Interest Revenue		200

Accounts Receivable	14,700	
Inventory (January 1)	19,400	
Equipment	18,500	
Purchases	48,300	
Salaries Expense	24,000	
Depreciation Expense	1,800	
Utilities Expense	2,400	
Supplies Expense	900	
Miscellaneous Expenses	1,300	
Income Summary		131,300
Income Summary	9,700	
Boggs, Capital		9,700
Boggs, Drawing	12,000	
Boggs, Capital		12,000

The company's cash balance and ending inventory are $11,200 and $21,300, respectively. Assume that all other accounts are included in these closing entries.

Required   **a.**   Prepare the closing entries as they should have been prepared by the bookkeeper.

            b.   Prepare an income statement and a balance sheet at the end of 19x3.

Unit 12
Worksheets

I think it will very evidently appear to any considerate Person that all this [i.e., the study of accounting] can't be done in six Weeks, much less in twenty-four hours. Such hasty Performances in Book-keeping or in any other Branch of Literature, being more likely to produce a crazy and tottering Building, subject to fall at every Blast, if not wholly undermine it, rather than make it firm and lasting.

Thomas Dillworth, The Young Book-keeper's Assistant, *1785*

Worksheets facilitate the preparation of adjusting entries, closing entries, and financial statements at the end of the accounting period. This unit examines worksheets, their purpose and format and their preparation and completion. In doing so, the unit reviews the concepts explained in Chapter 2 and in Units 10 and 11.

Performance Objectives

Upon completing this unit you should be able to:

1. define and use the accounting terms introduced in this unit.
2. complete a worksheet for either a service-type or merchandising-type organization.
3. prepare financial statements, adjusting entries, and closing entries using the information on a completed worksheet.

The Purpose and Format of Worksheets

Worksheets facilitate the accounting and bookkeeping work required to complete the accounting cycle. With a worksheet all the data needed to prepare financial statements, adjusting entries, and closing entries are accumulated in one place. A worksheet is prepared on a multi-column form with space for account titles and a pair of debit-credit columns for each of the following (see Exhibit 12.1):

1. trial balance—the trial balance prepared at the end of the accounting period is entered on the worksheet in the first pair of debit-credit columns.
2. adjustments—the adjusting entries are entered in the second pair of debit-credit columns.
3. adjusted trial balance (optional)—the trial balance figures plus or minus any adjustments are entered in the next pair of columns.
4. income statement—the account balances that appear on the income statement are extended from the adjusted trial balance columns to the next pair of columns.
5. retained earnings statement (optional; not shown in Exhibit 12.1)—the account balances that appear on the retained earnings statement are extended from the adjusted trial balance columns to the columns after those for the income statement.
6. balance sheet—the account balances that appear on the balance sheet are extended from the adjusted trial balance columns to the last pair of columns.

The adjusted trial balance columns are optional because the trial balance figures, plus or minus any adjustments, can be extended directly to the income statement, retained earnings statement, and balance sheet columns. The main advantage of the adjusted trial columns is that they allow you to prove the accuracy of the trial balance and adjustments before you attempt to complete the worksheet. Errors might be located more quickly by isolating them in the trial balance or adjustments.

The retained earnings statement columns are optional because frequently there are only a few accounts to be reported on this statement. Dividends and prior period adjustments are often recorded directly in the retained earnings account, and a separate analysis of that account can be made to prepare the retained earnings statement. In this case the retained earnings account and any special account for dividends or prior period adjustments can be extended to the balance sheet columns. The retained earnings statement can then be prepared by referring to the data in the balance sheet columns.

After the worksheet is completed, the financial statements are prepared from the data in the income statement, retained earnings statement, and balance sheet columns. The adjusting entries are recorded in the general journal by referring to the adjustments columns. The closing entries are recorded in the general journal by refer-

Exhibit 12.1

Krystal Company
Worksheet
For the Year Ended December 31, 19x5

	Trial Balance Dr.	Trial Balance Cr.	Adjustments Dr.	Adjustments Cr.	Adjusted Trial Balance Dr.	Adjusted Trial Balance Cr.	Income Statement Dr.	Income Statement Cr.	Balance Sheet Dr.	Balance Sheet Cr.
Cash	10,000				10,000				10,000	
Accounts Receivable	12,000				12,000				12,000	
Allowance for Uncollectible Accounts		200		(a) 400		600				600
Office Supplies	600			(b) 500	100				100	
Equipment	4,200				4,200				4,200	
Accumulated Depreciation		800		(c) 400		1,200				1,200
Accounts Payable		2,000				2,000				2,000
Unearned Service Revenue		1,000	(d) 600			400				400
Capital Stock		10,000				10,000				10,000
Retained Earnings		2,800				2,800				2,800
Dividends Paid	1,500				1,500				1,500	
Service Revenue		32,000		(d) 600		32,600		32,600		
Salaries Expense	16,000		(e) 300		16,300		16,300			
Utilities Expense	1,200				1,200		1,200			
Rent Expense	3,000				3,000		3,000			
Miscellaneous Expense	800				800		800			
Miscellaneous Revenue		500		(f) 100		600		600		
	49,300	49,300								
Uncollectible Accounts Expense			(a) 400		400		400			
Supplies Used			(b) 500		500		500			
Depreciation Expense			(c) 400		400		400			
Salaries Payable				(e) 300		300				300
Miscellaneous Revenue Receivable			(f) 100		100				100	
			2,300	2,300	50,500	50,500	22,600	33,200	27,900	17,300
Income Tax Expense							(g) 2,120			
Income Tax Payable										(g) 2,120
Net Income							8,480			8,480
							33,200	33,200	27,900	27,900

Adjustments:

(a) Uncollectible accounts expense: $400 ($600 − 200)
(b) Supplies used: $500 ($600 − 100)
(c) Depreciation expense: $400 ($4,200 − 200/10 yrs.)
(d) Unearned service revenue earned: $600 ($1,000 − 400)
(e) Accrued salaries expense: $300
(f) Accrued miscellaneous revenue: $100
(g) Income tax expense: $2,120 [($33,200 − 22,600) × 20%]

ring to the income statement and retained earnings statement columns (or the balance sheet columns if retained earnings statement columns are not used).

Preparation and Completion of a Worksheet

The worksheet in Exhibit 12.1 was prepared using the following trial balance and adjusting data for Krystal Company at the end of 19*x5:*

Krystal Company
Trial Balance
December 31, 19*x5*

Cash	$10,000	
Accounts Receivable	12,000	
Allowance for Uncollectible Accounts		$ 200
Office Supplies	600	
Equipment	4,200	
Accumulated Depreciation		800
Accounts Payable		2,000
Unearned Service Revenue		1,000
Capital Stock		10,000
Retained Earnings		2,800
Dividends Paid	1,500	
Service Revenue		32,000
Salaries Expense	16,000	
Utilities Expense	1,200	
Rent Expense	3,000	
Miscellaneous Expense	800	
Miscellaneous Revenue		500
	$49,300	$49,300

Adjusting data

a. The allowance for uncollectible accounts is to be increased to $600.

b. An inventory of supplies at the end of 19*x5* indicated a balance of $100 worth of unused supplies.

c. Equipment has an expected salvage value of $200 and an expected useful life of ten years.

d. Service revenue still unearned at December 31, 19*x5,* is $400 of the $1,000 recorded in the unearned service revenue account.

e. Salaries owed, but not paid or recorded, at the end of 19*x5* were $300.

f. Miscellaneous revenue earned, but not received or recorded, at the end of 19*x5* was $100.

g. The income tax rate is 20%.

The steps required to prepare and complete a worksheet are:

Step 1.   The trial balance at December 31, 19x5, is entered on the worksheet; the account titles are entered at the left and the debit and credit balances are entered in the first pair of columns.

Step 2.   The adjusting entries are made in the second pair of columns in the same way they are to be recorded in the general journal. Each adjustment is coded by a letter or number so the debit(s) and credit(s) for each can be easily located to journalize and to identify errors. (The journal entries for the adjustments are presented on pages 233 and 236.) Accounts that do not appear in the trial balance, but that are included in an adjusting entry, are listed below the trial balance total. The adjustments columns are totaled to assure that they balance.

Step 3.   The balance of each account, plus or minus any adjustment, is extended to the adjusted trial balance columns. Debit balances and debit adjustments are added; and credit balances and credit adjustments are added. When a balance and an adjustment are the opposite (one is a credit and the other a debit), the adjustment is deducted from the balance and the difference is extended to the adjusted trial balance columns. If the account had no balance before the adjustment, the amount of the adjustment is extended. The columns are totaled to assure that they balance.

Step 4.   The account balances are extended from the adjusted trial balance columns to the appropriate financial statement columns. In Exhibit 12.1 the revenue and expense account balances were extended to the income statement columns and the asset, liability, owners' equity, and dividends account balances were extended to the balance sheet columns. Retained earnings statement columns were not used; the data for this statement are obtained from the balance sheet columns.

Step 5.   The income statement columns are totaled. The difference in the column totals is income (or loss) before taxes for corporations or net income (or loss) for sole proprietorships and partnerships. If the credit total exceeds the debit total, there is a profit. If the debit total exceeds the credit total, there is a loss.

    a.   For corporations: Income taxes are computed and entered on the next two lines. Income tax expense is written in the account title space and the amount is entered in the income statement debit column; income taxes payable is written in the account title space and the amount is entered in the balance sheet credit column. Net income is then written in the account title space and the amount is entered in the income statement debit column and the balance sheet credit column. Net income balances the columns. When the retained earnings statement is prepared, net income is added to retained earnings. (A net loss would be entered in the income statement credit and balance sheet debit columns. The tax effect of the net loss would also be entered in the income statement credit and balance sheet debit columns.)

    b. For sole proprietorships and partnerships: Net income or net loss is entered in the same columns used for corporations, but no income taxes are entered on the worksheet. The income of these two forms of business organizations is taxed directly to the owners.

Step 6. When retained earnings statement columns are used, net income is entered in the retained earnings statement credit column (a net loss is entered in the retained earnings statement debit column). When these columns are totaled, the difference is the ending retained earnings balance. A credit difference (balance) is entered in the debit column as a balancing figure and also in the balance sheet credit column as a component of owners' equity. A debit difference (balance) is entered in the credit column and also in the balance sheet debit column (see Exhibit 12.2).

If net income or net loss in step 5 (and the retained earnings account balance in step 6) does not balance the remaining pairs of columns, an error has been made and must be located. The steps to be followed until the error is discovered are:

1. Recalculate the differences between the totals for the income statement and retained earnings statement columns.
2. Readd the column totals.
3. **a.** Verify the extensions from the adjusted trial balance columns.
   b. If adjusted trial balance columns are not used, verify the amounts extended (trial balance plus or minus adjustments).
4. Verify the adjusting entries.

Even if worksheet columns do balance, there still may be errors. Incorrect amounts can be given for an entire adjusting entry, debits or credits can be added to the wrong account, and accounts can be extended to the wrong statement columns—

and worksheet columns may still balance. Therefore, care must be exercised in completing a worksheet.

Completion of the Accounting Cycle

When the worksheet is finished, the accounting cycle can be completed as follows:

1. Prepare the income statement, retained earnings statement, and the balance sheet from the data in the appropriate worksheet columns.
2. Journalize and post the adjusting entries from the data in the adjustments columns of the worksheet.
3. Journalize and post the closing entries from the data in the income statement and retained earnings statement (or balance sheet) columns of the worksheet.
4. Prepare a post-closing trial balance using the balances in the general ledger (optional).

The adjusting and closing entries for Krystal Company in Exhibit 12.1 are presented below:

Adjusting entries

a.	Uncollectible accounts expense	400	
	Allowance for uncollectible accounts		400
	To record uncollectible accounts expense.		
b.	Supplies used	500	
	Office supplies		500
	To record supplies use ($600 − 100 = 500).		
c.	Depreciation expense	400	
	Accumulated depreciation		400
	To record depreciation expense for 19x5.		
d.	Unearned service revenue	600	
	Service revenue		600
	To record revenue collected in advance and subsequently earned during 19x5.		
e.	Salaries expense	300	
	Salaries payable		300
	To record accrued salaries.		

Exhibit 12.2

Global Corporation
Worksheet
For the Year Ended December 31, 19x5

	Trial Balance Dr.	Trial Balance Cr.	Adjustments Dr.	Adjustments Cr.	Income Statement Dr.	Income Statement Cr.	Retained Earnings Statement Dr.	Retained Earnings Statement Cr.	Balance Sheet Dr.	Balance Sheet Cr.
Cash	5,000								5,000	
Accounts Receivable	25,000								25,000	
Allowance for Uncollectible Accounts		200		(a) 1,000						1,200
Merchandise Inventory	18,000		(f) 24,000	(f) 18,000					24,000	
Prepaid Insurance	1,200			(b) 600					600	
Equipment	31,200								31,200	
Accumulated Depreciation		9,000		(c) 3,000						12,000
Accounts Payable		20,000								20,000
Advances from Customers		3,000	(d) 2,000							1,000
Capital Stock		30,000								30,000
Retained Earnings		23,100						23,100		
Dividends Paid	7,000						7,000			
Sales		101,000		(d) 2,000		103,000				
Sales Returns	500				500					
Sales Discounts	500				500					
Purchases	52,000			(f) 52,000						
Freight-in	2,700			(f) 2,700						
Purchase Returns		1,000	(f) 1,000							
Sales Salaries	16,000		(e) 500		16,500					
Store Rent	3,000				3,000					
Advertising Expense	2,500				2,500					
Other Selling Expense	3,500				3,500					
Office Salaries	16,000		(e) 500		16,500					
Office Rent	1,200				1,200					
Other Office Expense	2,000				2,000					
	187,300	187,300								

Account	Adjustments Debit	Adjustments Credit	Income Statement Debit	Income Statement Credit	Retained Earnings Debit	Retained Earnings Credit	Balance Sheet Debit	Balance Sheet Credit
Uncollectible Accounts Expense	(a) 1,000		1,000					
Insurance Expense —Store	(b) 400		400					
Insurance Expense —Office	(b) 200		200					
Depreciation Expense —Store	(c) 2,000		2,000					
Depreciation Expense —Office	(c) 1,000		1,000					
Salaries Payable		(e) 1,000						1,000
Cost of Goods Sold	(f) 47,700		47,700					
	80,300	80,300	98,500	103,000		7,000		
Income Tax Expense			(g) 3,600					
Income Taxes Payable								(g) 900
Net Income			3,600					900
			103,000	103,000	23,100	26,700		66,100
					3,600			85,800
					26,700	7,000		
Retained Earnings, Dec. 31, 19x5						19,700		19,700
					26,700	26,700		85,800

f.	Miscellaneous revenue receivable	100	
	Miscellaneous revenue		100
	To record accrued miscellaneous revenue.		
g.	Income tax expense	2,120	
	Income taxes payable		2,120
	To record income taxes [($33,200 − 22,600) × 20% = $2,120].		

Closing entries

Service revenue	32,600	
Miscellaneous revenue	600	
Income summary		33,200
To close out revenues.		
Income summary ($22,600 + 2,120)	24,720	
Salaries expense		16,300
Utilities expense		1,200
Rent expense		3,000
Miscellaneous expense		800
Uncollectible accounts expense		400
Supplies used		500
Depreciation expense		400
Income tax expense		2,120
To close out expenses.		
Income summary	8,480	
Retained earnings		8,480
To close out income summary and transfer net income to retained earnings.		
Retained earnings	1,500	
Dividends paid		1,500
To close out dividends paid.		

Worksheet Procedures for a Merchandising-Type Organization

The same steps are performed in preparing and completing a worksheet for merchandising organizations as for service organizations. Recall from Unit 10, however, that an adjusting entry for cost of goods sold is required when the periodic inventory system is used. The cost of goods sold account is then closed out with the other expenses. The contra accounts, sales discounts and sales returns and allowances, can be closed out with either the revenue accounts or the expense accounts. To illustrate, the trial balance and adjusting data are given for Global Company (which uses the periodic system) at the end of 19x5.

Global Company
Trial Balance
December 31, 19x5

Cash	$ 5,000	
Accounts Receivable	25,000	
Allowance for Uncollectible Accounts		$ 200
Merchandise Inventory	18,000	
Prepaid Insurance	1,200	
Equipment	31,200	
Accumulated Depreciation		9,000
Accounts Payable		20,000
Advances from Customers		3,000
Capital Stock		30,000
Retained Earnings		23,100
Dividends Paid	7,000	
Sales		101,000
Sales Returns	500	
Sales Discounts	500	
Purchases	52,000	
Freight-in	2,700	
Purchase Returns		1,000
Sales Salaries	16,000	
Store Rent	3,000	
Advertising Expense	2,500	
Other Selling Expenses	3,500	
Office Salaries	16,000	
Office Rent	1,200	
Other Office Expenses	2,000	
	$187,300	$187,300

Adjusting data

a. Uncollectible accounts expense for 19x5 is $1,000.

b. A 2-year insurance policy was purchased at the beginning of 19x5; two-thirds of the cost is to be treated as a selling expense, the other third as an office expense.

c. Equipment has a residual value of $1,200 and is being depreciated over a 10-year life. Two-thirds of depreciation is to be treated as a selling expense, the other third as an office expense.

d. During 19x5 the company received $3,000 in advances on merchandise from customers; by the end of 19x5, $2,000 of these advances had been earned.

e. Accrued salaries at the end of 19x5 were: sales salaries, $500; office salaries, $500.

f.   The ending merchandise inventory balance was $24,000.
g.   The income tax rate is 20%.

The adjustments are entered in the adjustments columns of the worksheet in the same debit-credit format as they will be entered in the general journal. See the following adjusting entries and the worksheet in Exhibit 12.2. Since the worksheet has retained earnings statement columns, the retained earnings balance of $23,100 and dividends paid balance of $7,000 are extended to these columns from the trial balance. Net income of $3,600 is entered in the retained earnings statement credit column, and the ending retained earnings balance of $19,700 (the difference between debit and credit totals) is determined and entered in the retained earnings statement debit and balance sheet credit columns as balancing figures. When the worksheet is completed, the financial statements are prepared, and the adjusting and closing entries are journalized and posted. Following are the adjusting and closing entries prepared from the worksheet in Exhibit 12.2:

Adjusting entries

a.	Uncollectible Accounts Expense	1,000	
	Allowance for Uncollectible Accounts		1,000
	To record uncollectible accounts expense.		
b.	Insurance Expense—Store	400	
	Insurance Expense—Office	200	
	Prepaid Insurance		600
	To record insurance expense [($1,200/2 yrs.) = $600; $600 × 2/3 = $400; $600 × 1/3 = $200].		
c.	Depreciation Expense—Store	2,000	
	Depreciation Expense—Office	1,000	
	Accumulated Depreciation		3,000
	To record depreciation expense [($31,200 − 1,200)/10 yrs. = $3,000; $3,000 × 2/3 = $2,000; $3,000 × 1/3 = $1,000].		
d.	Advances from Customers ($3,000 − 1,000)	2,000	
	Sales		2,000
	To record $2,000 of advances earned during 19x5.		
e.	Sales Salaries	500	
	Office Salaries	500	
	Salaries Payable		1,000
	To record accrued salaries.		

f.	Merchandise Inventory (ending)	24,000	
	Purchase Returns	1,000	
	Cost of Goods Sold	47,700	
	Inventory (beginning)		18,000
	Purchases		52,000
	Freight-in		2,700
	To record cost of goods sold.		
g.	Income Tax Expense	900	
	Income Taxes Payable		900
	To record income taxes		
	[($103,000 − 98,500) × 20% =		
	$900].		

Closing entries

Sales	103,000	
Sales Discounts		500
Sales Returns		500
Income Summary		102,000
To close out sales revenue and related accounts.[1]		
Income Summary	98,400	
Cost of Goods Sold		47,700
Sales Salaries		16,500
Store Rent		3,000
Advertising Expense		2,500
Other Selling Expenses		3,500
Office Salaries		16,500
Office Rent		1,200
Other Office Expenses		2,000
Uncollectible Accounts Expense		1,000
Insurance Expense—Store		400
Insurance Expense—Office		200
Depreciation Expense—Store		2,000
Depreciation Expense—Office		1,000
Income Tax Expense		900
To close out expenses.		

---

[1]The contra-revenue accounts, sales discounts and sales returns, can be included in the entry to close out expense because they have debit balances as do the expense accounts.

Income Summary	3,600	
Retained Earnings		3,600
To close out income summary and transfer net income to retained earnings.		
Retained Earnings	7,000	
Dividends Paid		7,000
To close out dividends paid.		

On a classified income statement, operating expenses would be presented in two groups: selling expenses and general and administrative expenses. Selling expenses include sales salaries, store rent, advertising expense, other selling expenses, insurance expense—store, and depreciation expense—store. General and administrative expenses include office salaries, office rent, other office expenses, uncollectible accounts expense, insurance expense—office, and depreciation expense—office.

Cost of goods sold would be presented either on the income statement or on a supporting schedule as follows:

Beginning inventory		$18,000
Purchases	$52,000	
Add: Freight-in	2,700	
Total cost of purchases	$54,700	
Less: Purchase returns	1,000	
Net purchases		53,700
Cost of goods available for sale		$71,700
Less: Ending inventory		24,000
Cost of goods sold		$47,700

REVIEW PROBLEM

Following are the trial balance and adjusting data for Boomgunn Company as of December 31, 19x6:

Boomgunn Company
Trial Balance
December 31, 19x6

Cash	$ 13,000	
Accounts receivable	11,000	
Allowance for uncollectible accounts		$ 100
Merchandise inventory	14,000	
Prepaid insurance	1,500	
Land	2,500	
Building	33,000	
Accumulated depreciation—building		2,000
Equipment	8,200	
Accumulated depreciation—equipment		2,000
Accounts payable		16,500
Advances from customers		2,500
Mortgage payable		20,000
Kermit Boomgunn, capital		45,150

Kermit Boomgunn, drawing	10,800	
Sales		45,500
Sales discounts	750	
Purchases	26,000	
Freight-in	800	
Purchase returns		400
Sales salaries	6,500	
Advertising expense	1,200	
Delivery expense	300	
Office salaries	4,800	
Utilities expense	1,250	
Supplies expense	950	
Interest expense	1,200	
Rental revenue		3,600
	$137,750	$137,750

Adjusting data

a. An evaluation of the outstanding receivables indicates that the allowance for uncollectible accounts should be increased to $550.

b. The balance of prepaid insurance represents a 3-year policy purchased at the beginning of 19x6.

c. The building has an estimated residual value of $3,000 and an estimated useful life of 30 years.

d. The equipment has an estimated residual value of $200 and an estimated useful life of 8 years.

e. Advances from customers still unearned at December 31, 19x6, totaled $1,000.

f. Accrued salaries at December 31, 19x6, were: sales salaries, $150, and office salaries, $100.

g. The inventory of unused supplies at December 31, 19x6, totaled $150.

h. The balance of rental revenue represents an advance payment for 1 year's rent at $300 per month starting September 1, 19x6.

i. The ending inventory at December 31, 19x6, is $15,600.

In preparing the income statement, one-half of the building and equipment depreciation expense and one-half of the supplies, insurance, and utilities expenses are to be assigned to selling expenses and the other half to general and administrative expenses.

Required

1. Prepare a worksheet with columns for trial balance, adjustments, income statement, and balance sheet.

2. Prepare the following:
    a. a classified income statement
    b. a statement of changes in proprietor's capital
    c. a classified balance sheet

3. Prepare the adjusting and closing entries that would be recorded in the general journal.

Solution to review problem

1. See Exhibit 12.3.

2. a. See Exhibit 12.4.
 b. See Exhibit 12.5.
 c. See Exhibit 12.6.
3. *Adjusting entries*

a. Uncollectible accounts expense   450
    Allowance for uncollectible accounts   450
To record bad debts expense
    ($550 − 100 = $450).

b. Insurance expense   500
    Prepaid insurance   500
To record insurance expense
    ($1,500/3 yrs. = $500).

c. Depreciation expense—building   1,000
    Accumulated depreciation—building   1,000
To record building depreciation
    [($33,000 − 3,000)/30 yrs. =
    $1,000].

d. Depreciation expense—equipment   1,000
    Accumulated depreciation—equipment   1,000
To record equipment depreciation
    [($8,200 − 200)/8 yrs. = $1,000].

e. Advances from customers   1,500
    Sales   1,500
To record advances earned during
    19*x6* ($2,500 − 1,000 = $1,500).

f. Sales salaries   150
Office salaries   100
    Salaries payable   250
To record accrued salaries.

g. Supplies inventory   150
    Supplies expense   150
To record inventory of unused
    supplies.

h. Rental revenue   2,400
    Unearned rent   2,400
To record rent collected in advance
    but unearned at end of 19*x6*
    ($3,600 × 8/12 = $2,400).

i.	Merchandise inventory (ending)	15,600	
	Purchase returns	400	
	Cost of goods sold	24,800	
	Merchandise inventory (beginning)		14,000
	Purchases		26,000
	Freight-in		800
	To record cost of goods sold.		

Closing entries

Sales	47,000	
Rental revenue	1,200	
Sales discounts		750
Income summary		47,450
To close out revenues and related accounts.[2]		
Income summary	44,050	
Cost of goods sold		24,800
Sales salaries		6,650
Advertising expense		1,200
Delivery expense		300
Office salaries		4,900
Utilities expense		1,250
Supplies expense		800
Interest expense		1,200
Uncollectible accounts expense		450
Insurance expense		500
Depreciation expense—building		1,000
Depreciation expense—equipment		1,000
To close out expenses.		
Income summary	3,400	
Kermit Boomgunn, capital		3,400
To close out income summary and transfer net income to owner's capital account.		
Kermit Boomgunn, capital	10,800	
Kermit Boomgunn, drawing		10,800
To close out the owner's drawing account.		

---

[2]The contra-revenue account, sales discounts, can be included in the closing entry for expenses because it has a debit balance as do expense accounts.

Exhibit 12.3

Boomgunn Company
Worksheet
For the Year Ended December 31, 19x6

	Trial Balance Dr.	Trial Balance Cr.	Adjustments Dr.	Adjustments Cr.	Income Statement Dr.	Income Statement Cr.	Balance Sheet Dr.	Balance Sheet Cr.
Cash	13,000						13,000	
Accounts receivable	11,000						11,000	
Allowance for uncollectible accounts		100		(a) 450				550
Merchandise inventory	14,000		(i) 15,600	(i) 14,000			15,600	
Prepaid insurance	1,500			(b) 500			1,000	
Land	2,500						2,500	
Building	33,000						33,000	
Accumulated depreciation—building		2,000		(c) 1,000				3,000
Equipment	8,200						8,200	
Accumulated depreciation—equipment		2,000		(d) 1,000				3,000
Accounts payable		16,500						16,500
Advances from customers		2,500	(e) 1,500					1,000
Mortgage payable		20,000						20,000
Kermit Boomgunn, capital		45,150						45,150
Kermit Boomgunn, drawing	10,800						10,800	
Sales		45,500		(e) 1,500		47,000		
Sales discounts	750				750			
Purchases	26,000			(i) 26,000				
Freight-in	800			(i) 800				
Purchase returns		400	(i) 400					
Sales salaries	6,500		(f) 150		6,650			
Advertising expense	1,200				1,200			
Delivery expense	300				300			
Office salaries	4,800		(f) 100		4,900			
Utilities expense	1,250				1,250			
Supplies expense	950			(g) 150	800			
Interest expense	1,200				1,200			
Rental revenue		3,600	(h) 2,400			1,200		
	137,750	137,750						
Uncollectible accounts expense			(a) 450		450			
Insurance expense			(b) 500		500			
Depreciation expense—building			(c) 1,000		1,000			
Depreciation expense—equipment			(d) 1,000		1,000			
Salaries payable				(f) 250				250
Supplies inventory			(g) 150				150	
Unearned rent				(h) 2,400				2,400
Cost of goods sold			(i) 24,800		24,800			
			48,050	48,050	44,800	48,200	95,250	91,850
Net income					3,400			3,400
					48,200	48,200	95,250	95,250

Exhibit 12.4

Boomgunn Company
Income Statement
For the Year Ended December 31, 19x6

Sales			$47,000
Less: Sales discounts			750
Net sales			$46,250
Cost of goods sold:			
Beginning inventory		$14,000	
Purchases	$26,000		
Add: Freight-in	800		
Total cost of purchases	$26,800		
Less: Purchase returns	400		
Net purchases		26,400	
Cost of goods available for sale		$40,400	
Less: Ending inventory		15,600	
Cost of goods sold			24,800
Gross margin			$21,450
Operating expenses:			
Selling expenses			
Sales salaries	$ 6,650		
Advertising expense	1,200		
Delivery expense	300		
Utilities expense	625		
Supplies expense	400		
Insurance expense	250		
Depreciation expense—building	500		
Depreciation expense—equipment	500		
Total selling expenses		$10,425	
General and administrative expenses:			
Office salaries	$ 4,900		
Utilities expense	625		
Supplies expense	400		
Uncollectible accounts expense	450		
Insurance expense	250		
Depreciation expense—building	500		
Depreciation expense—equipment	500		
Total general and administrative expenses		7,625	
Total operating expenses			18,050
Income from operations			$ 3,400
Incidental revenue and expense			
Rental revenue		$ 1,200	
Interest expense		1,200	
Net incidental revenue and expense			0
Net income			$ 3,400

Exhibit 12.5

Boomgunn Company
Statement of Changes in Proprietor's Capital
For the Year Ended December 31, 19x6

Capital, January 1, 19x6	$45,150
Add: Net income (per income statement)	3,400
Total	$48,550
Deduct: Drawings	10,800
Capital, December 31, 19x6	$37,750

Exhibit 12.6

Boomgunn Company
Balance Sheet
December 31, 19x6

Assets

Current assets:		
Cash	$13,000	
Accounts receivable (net of allowance for uncollectible accounts		
of $550)	10,450	
Merchandise inventory	15,600	
Prepaid insurance	1,000	
Supplies inventory	150	
Total current assets		$40,200
Plant assets:		
Land	$ 2,500	
Building (net of accumulated depreciation of $3,000)	30,000	
Equipment (net of accumulated depreciation of $3,000)	5,200	
Total plant assets		37,700
Total assets		$77,900

Liabilities and Capital

Current liabilities:		
Accounts payable	$16,500	
Advances from customers	1,000	
Salaries payable	250	
Unearned rent	2,400	
Total current liabilities		$20,150
Long-term liabilities:		
Mortgage payable		20,000
Total liabilities		$40,150
Capital:		
Kermit Boomgunn, capital		37,750
Total liabilities and capital		$77,900

SUMMARY

Accountants use worksheets to pull together the information needed to complete the accounting cycle. In this unit worksheets were explained and illustrated. Using them as a basis, we then reviewed the steps in the accounting cycle that occur at the end of an accounting period.

REVIEW QUESTIONS

12-1   What is a worksheet? What is its purpose?

12-2   Why are the adjusted trial balance and retained earnings statement columns optional on a worksheet?

12-3   What steps in the accounting cycle are completed using the data on the worksheet?

12-4   What differences, if any, are there in completing a worksheet for (a) a corporation vs. a sole proprietorship or partnership and (b) a merchandising vs. a service organization?

EXERCISES

12-1   The following are several accounting procedures. Arrange the procedures in the sequence in which they would occur in completing the accounting cycle. The first step is given as an example.

    a.   Prepare a schedule of account balances after posting the closing entries.
    b.   Receive an invoice for merchandise purchased.
    c.   Prepare and enter a trial balance on a 10-column worksheet.
    d.   Transfer data from the journal to the ledger.
    e.   Collect data and analyze them for adjustments.
    f.   Prepare the financial statements.
    g.   Record the transaction in (b) in a book of original entry.
    h.   Transfer revenue and expense account balances to income summary; transfer income summary balance to retained earnings.
    i.   Analyze the invoice in (b) for its economic effects on the business.
    j.   Complete the 10-column worksheet in (c).
    k.   Record the adjustments in a book of original entry and post them to the ledger.

Step   **Procedures and code numbers**
  1   Receive an invoice for merchandise purchased (b).

12-2   The following are the trial balance and additional data for Boondoggle Realty Company for the fiscal year ending June 30, 19x2. Prepare a worksheet that includes columns for trial balance, adjustments, income statement, and balance sheet.

Cash	$ 2,500	
Accounts Receivable	18,400	
Notes Receivable	10,000	
Office Equipment	3,600	
Accumulated Depreciation		$ 900
Accounts Payable		4,100
Philip Boondoggle, Capital		17,700
Philip Boondoggle, Drawing	7,200	

Fees Earned		31,200
Salaries Expense	6,000	
Advertising Expense	1,200	
Rent Expense	2,800	
Utilities Expense	700	
Miscellaneous Expense	1,900	
Interest Income		400
	$54,300	$54,300

Additional Data

a. Interest on the notes receivable has been earned at a 5% rate since April 1, but will not be collected until later in the year.
b. The office equipment has a 10-year life and a $600 scrap value.
c. Included in fees earned is $800 that will not be earned until later in the year.
d. Rent, at $200 per month, has been prepaid during June for July and August.

12-3 Refer to the worksheet completed for exercise 12-2. Journalize the adjusting and closing entries for the fiscal year ending June 30, 19*x*2.

12-4 Murdock Company uses the following financial statement columns on its worksheet:

a. Income statement—debit
b. Income statement—credit
c. Retained earnings statement—debit
d. Retained earnings statement—credit
e. Balance sheet—debit
f. Balance sheet—credit

For each of the following accounts or items, write, in the space provided, the code letter of the column(s) to which its balance or amount will be extended in completing the worksheet after the adjustments are entered.

_____ (1) Fees earned
_____ (2) Accounts receivable
_____ (3) Salaries expense
_____ (4) Equipment
_____ (5) Dividends paid
_____ (6) Unearned fees
_____ (7) Capital stock
_____ (8) Depreciation expense—equipment
_____ (9) Retained earnings,
beginning balance

_____ (10) Allowance for uncollectible accounts
_____ (11) Accounts payable
_____ (12) Interest revenue
_____ (13) Accumulated depreciation—equipment
_____ (14) Net income
_____ (15) Retained earnings,
ending balance

12-5 Using the following trial balance and additional data for the Mod Shop for the month of March 19*x*2, prepare a worksheet with columns for trial balance, adjustments, income statement, and balance sheet.

The Mod Shop Trial Balance March 31, 19x2		
Cash	$ 1,500	
Accounts Receivable	3,200	
Inventory	9,100	
Prepaid Insurance	600	
Store Equipment	5,100	
Accumulated Depreciation		$ 300
Accounts Payable		2,700
Advance Deposits from Customers		800
Sara Dilley, Capital		12,400
Sara Dilley, Drawing	600	
Sales		12,600
Sales Returns and Allowances	300	
Purchases	6,700	
Freight-in	500	
Purchase Returns and Allowances		100
Salaries Expense	700	
Rent Expense	300	
Utilities Expense	100	
Miscellaneous Expense	200	
	$28,900	$28,900

Additional data

a. A 1-year insurance policy was purchased for $600 on March 1 of the current year.

b. Store equipment has an 8-year life and a $300 scrap value.

c. During March $300 of the advance deposits from customers were earned.

d. Salaries of $100 were owed to employees as of March 31 and are to be paid in April.

e. The March 31 inventory was $9,900.

12-6   Refer to the worksheet completed for exercise 12-5. Journalize the adjusting and closing entries for March 19x2.

12-7   Shamrock Company uses the following financial statement columns on its worksheet:

a. Income statement—debit   d. Balance sheet—credit
b. Income statement—credit   e. None—the account has no
c. Balance sheet—debit   balance after adjustment

For each of the following accounts or items, write, in the space provided, the code letter of the column(s) to which its balance or amount will be extended in completing the worksheet after the adjustments are entered.

_____   (1) Beginning inventory   _____   (4) Beginning retained
_____   (2) Sales discounts   earnings
_____   (3) Prepaid expenses   _____   (5) Sales

_____	(6)	Interest expense	_____	(11) Supplies used
_____	(7)	Dividends paid	_____	(12) Ending inventory
_____	(8)	Purchase returns	_____	(13) Depreciation expense—equipment
_____	(9)	Salaries payable		
_____	(10)	Accumulated depreciation—equipment	_____	(14) Freight-in
			_____	(15) Net loss

PROBLEMS

12-1 The following are the trial balance and adjusting data for Barron Company, a service organization, at the end of 19x2:

Barron Company
Trial Balance
December 31, 19x2

Cash	$ 26,500	
Accounts Receivable	30,000	
Allowance for Uncollectible Accounts		$ 200
Supplies Inventory	1,500	
Furniture and Fixtures	25,000	
Accumulated Depreciation		6,000
Franchises and Licenses	4,000	
Accounts Payable		18,500
Notes Payable, Long-term		15,000
Redd Barron, Capital		26,300
Red Barron, Drawing	18,000	
Service Revenue		200,000
Salaries Expense	96,000	
Rent Expense	39,000	
Utilities Expense	11,000	
Insurance Expense	6,000	
Miscellaneous Expense	9,000	
	$266,000	$266,000

Adjusting data

a. Uncollectible accounts expense is estimated at $2,000.

b. The supplies inventory balance at the end of 19x2 was $300.

c. The residual value and expected useful life of furniture and fixtures were $1,000 and 10 years, respectively.

d. The balance of franchises and licenses is to be amortized over 5 years.

e. The long-term note was issued on July 1, 19x2; interest is payable annually on July 1 at 8%.

f. The rent for January 19x3 ($3,000) was paid in advance and charged to rent expense.

g. A 3-year insurance policy was purchased at a cost of $6,000 at the beginning of 19x2.

Required Prepare and complete a worksheet for Barron Company at the end of 19x2. The worksheet should have columns for trial balance, adjustments, income statement, and balance sheet.

12-2 Following are the trial balance and adjusting data for Serge Company at December 31, 19x8.

Serge Company
Trial Balance
December 31, 19x8

Cash	$ 36,900	
Notes Receivable	2,000	
Accounts Receivable	24,500	
Allowance for Uncollectible Accounts		$ 100
Supplies Inventory	250	
Prepaid Insurance	1,800	
Office Equipment	11,600	
Accumulated Depreciation		1,800
Notes Payable		4,000
Accounts Payable		12,800
Capital Stock, $10 par		30,000
Retained Earnings		6,250
Dividends Paid	4,500	
Fees Earned		140,000
Salaries Expense	82,000	
Advertising Expense	9,700	
Rent Expense	12,000	
Utilities Expense	4,100	
Supplies Expense	1,850	
Miscellaneous Expenses	3,100	
Interest Expense	650	
	$194,950	$194,950

Adjusting data

a. The balance of prepaid insurance represents the remainder of a 2-year policy purchased on July 1, 19x7.

b. Office equipment includes (i) furniture (purchased January 2, 19x6, at a cost of $6,300; salvage value is $300; expected life is 10 years) and (ii) machines (purchased May 1, 19x7, at a cost of $5,300; salvage value is $800; expected life is 5 years).

c. Notes payable consists of a 6%, 2-month note issued on December 1, 19x8.

d. The inventory of supplies as of December 31, 19x8 is $150.

e. Notes receivable consists of a 6%, 4-month note received on November 1, 19x8.

f. A client paid a $750 fee in advance when she contracted with the company to perform certain work. As of December 31, 19x8, the work has not been completed. The fee is included in the fees earned balance.

g. The weekly payroll (for a 5-day workweek) is $1,625. The salaries are paid every Wednesday for the preceding week; 19x8 ends on a Monday.

h. An examination of the payroll records indicates that certain employees received advances against their 19x8 salaries in the amount of $225. The advances were charged to expense.

i. In December 19x8, the company contracted for spot TV commercials to be run in January and February 19x9. The agreement called for an advance payment of $1,250, which the company has paid and charged to expense.

j. Uncollectible accounts expense is estimated at $1,400.

k. The income tax rate is 40%.

Required

(1) Prepare and complete a worksheet with columns for trial balance, adjustments, income statement, and balance sheet.

(2) Prepare a single-step income statement, a retained earnings statement, and a classified balance sheet.

(3) Prepare the adjusting and closing entries.

(4) Prepare a post-closing trial balance.

12-3 The trial balance and adjusting data for Ming Company at the end of 19x4 are:

Ming Company Trial Balance December 31, 19x4		
Cash	$ 42,000	
Accounts Receivable	54,000	
Allowance for Uncollectible Accounts		$ 500
Inventory	47,000	
Supplies Inventory	3,200	
Prepaid Insurance	4,800	
Land	20,000	
Building	210,000	
Accumulated Depreciation		60,000
Equipment	84,000	
Accumulated Depreciation		24,000
Accounts Payable		45,000
Advances from Customers		8,000
Mortgage Payable		120,000
Ming, Capital		216,000
Ming, Drawing	24,000	
Sales		347,000
Sales Discounts	2,000	
Purchases	185,000	
Freight-in	12,000	
Purchase Returns		1,500
Selling Expenses	72,000	
General and Administrative Expenses	48,000	
Interest Expense	14,000	
	$822,000	$822,000

Adjusting data

a. The merchandise inventory balance at December 31, 19x4, is $53,000.

b. The supplies inventory balance at the end of 19x4 is $700.

c. A 2-year insurance policy with a cost of $4,800 was purchased at the beginning of 19x4.

d. The building is being depreciated over 40 years and has an expected residual value of $10,000.

e. Equipment has an expected residual value of $4,000 and an expected useful life of 10 years.

f. An analysis of the balance in advances from customers indicates that $3,000 is still unearned at the end of 19x4.

g. Uncollectible accounts expense is estimated at $3,500.

h. Interest has accrued on the mortgage for one month; the interest rate is 8% annually.

Required   Prepare and complete a worksheet for Ming Company at the end of 19x4. The worksheet has columns for trial balance, adjustments, income statement, and balance sheet.

12-4   The trial balance and adjusting data for Como Corporation at December 31, 19x9, are:

Como Corporation
Trial Balance
December 31, 19x9

Cash	$ 32,400	
Accounts Receivable	27,500	
Allowance for Uncollectible Accounts		$ 200
Notes Receivable	6,000	
Inventory	10,600	
Supplies on Hand	900	
Unexpired Insurance	800	
Prepaid Rent	2,400	
Store Fixtures	4,500	
Accumulated Depreciation		1,000
Delivery Equipment	3,900	
Accumulated Depreciation		1,500
Accounts Payable		2,400
Notes Payable		3,800
Capital Stock, $10 par		50,000
Retained Earnings		16,800
Dividends Paid	5,000	
Sales		137,200
Sales Returns	1,300	
Sales Discounts	900	
Purchases	62,600	
Purchase Returns		200
Freight-in	1,200	
Sales Salaries	21,400	
Advertising Expense	4,600	
Delivery Expense	3,300	
Office Salaries	13,000	
Office Expense	11,000	
Interest Income		1,300
Interest Expense	1,100	
	$214,400	$214,400

Adjusting data

a. The prepaid rent was paid on May 1, 19x9, for a 2-year period.

b. An inventory of the supplies on hand at December 31 revealed that $300 was unused.

c. The stores fixtures are expected to have a salvage value of $500 and depreciation is taken at the rate of 10% annually.

d. The delivery equipment is expected to have a life of 3 years and a salvage value of $900.

e. Uncollectible accounts expense is estimated at $1,350.

f. A contract for advertising was signed on April 1, 19x9, for a 1-year period; the cost of $1,600 was paid on the same day.

g. At December 31, 19x9, all interest income had been received, but only $1,000 had been earned during the year.

h. An examination of sales salaries revealed the following:

Balance in ledger account	$21,400
Less: Salaries paid in advance	1,500
	$19,900
Add: Accrued salaries at December 31, 19x9	500
Expense for 19x9	$20,400

i. Interest owed but not paid by December 31 was $200.

j. Unexpired insurance represents the balance of a 2-year policy that was acquired and paid for on October 1, 19x8.

k. The ending inventory balance is $12,400.

l. The income tax rate is 40%.

Required   **(1)** Prepare a worksheet including columns for trial balance, adjustments, income statement, retained earnings, and balance sheet.

           (2) Prepare a classified income statement, a retained earnings statement, and a classified balance sheet.

           (3) Prepare the adjusting and closing entries.

           (4) Prepare a post-closing trial balance.

Mini-Practice Set

The trial balance for Hooligan Company at December 1, 19x4, is:

Hooligan Company
Trial Balance
December 1, 19x4

Cash	$ 42,000	
Accounts receivable	38,000	
Allowance for uncollectible accounts		$ 1,200
Inventory	32,000	
Prepaid insurance	2,400	
Land	24,000	
Building	156,000	
Accumulated depreciation—building		20,000
Equipment	48,000	
Accumulated depreciation—equipment		18,000
Accounts payable		29,700
Notes payable, short-term		10,000
Mortgage payable		120,000
Capital stock ($10 par value)		100,000
Retained earnings		46,600

Dividends paid	10,000	
Sales		258,000
Sales returns	5,000	
Sales discounts	3,000	
Purchases	142,600	
Freight-in	13,200	
Purchase returns		1,800
Sales salaries	33,000	
Advertising expense	11,000	
Store supplies expense	3,200	
Other selling expenses	2,800	
Office salaries	22,000	
Office supplies expense	2,100	
Other office expenses	1,500	
Interest expense	13,500	
	$605,300	$605,300

Balances due from customers and due to creditors at December 1, 19x4, are:

Accounts Receivable	
Janes Company	$ 6,000
Mayes, Inc.	18,000
Baye Corp.	14,000
	$38,000

Accounts Payable	
Hayes Corp.	$ 9,900
Banes, Inc.	8,910
Crane Company	10,890
	$29,700

The following transactions were completed during December:

Dec.	1	Received a 3-month, 8% note for $6,000 from Janes Company in settlement of their past due account.
	2	Purchased merchandise on account from the Dent Company ($6,000) and the Hayes Corp. ($8,000), subject to credit terms of 1/10, n/30.
	4	Purchased supplies on credit from Donn Supply Co., subject to terms of n/15: store supplies, $500; office supplies, $300 (record in the expense accounts).
	5	Paid the following invoices outstanding at December 1:

Creditor	Invoice Date	Invoice Amount	Credit Terms
Hayes Corp.	Nov. 28, 19x4	$10,000	1/10, n/30
Banes, Inc.	Nov. 5, 19x4	9,000	1/10, n/30

	8	Returned merchandise with an invoice price of $500 on December 2 to Dent Company for credit.
	9	Received payment from customers for the following invoices:

Customer	Invoice Date	Invoice Amount	Credit Terms
Mayes, Inc.	Nov. 10, 19x4	$18,000	2/10, n/30
Baye Corp.	Nov. 30, 19x4	14,000	2/10, n/30

10	Sold merchandise to Janes Company ($5,000); Mayes, Inc. ($10,000); and Clint Corp. ($15,000) on credit, subject to credit terms of 2/10, n/30.
12	Paid the following invoices:

Creditor	Invoice Date	Invoice Amount	Credit Terms
Crane Company	Nov. 20, 19x4	$11,000	1/10, n/30
Donn Supply Co.	Dec. 4, 19x4	800	n/15

15	Recorded cash sales of $4,500.
16	Paid the note payable to the City Bank for $10,000 plus interest at 8% for 6 months.
17	Accepted a return of merchandise with a sales price of $1,000 from Mayes, Inc. (see the December 10 sale).
18	Received an advance of $8,000 from Pane Company for merchandise; the advance was recorded in a liability account.
20	Purchased merchandise with an invoice price of $7,000 from Crane Company; terms were 1/10, n/30.
22	Sold merchandise for $8,000 to Baye Corp.; terms were 2/10, n/30.
24	Received a bill from Addes Corp. in the amount of $3,500 for advertising for December.
26	Paid freight charges of $1,500 to Thru-Way Lines Inc. for merchandise received during December.
30	Sold 1,000 shares of capital stock at $12 per share.
31	Paid salaries for December: sales salaries, $3,000; office salaries, $2,000.
31	Recorded cash sales of $7,500.
31	Made the monthly mortgage payment of $1,500, which included $1,000 for interest.

Adjusting data

a. Uncollectible accounts expense is estimated at $3,000.
b. The balance of prepaid insurance represents the remainder of a 3-year policy purchased at the beginning of 19x3.
c. An inventory of supplies indicated the following balances at the end of 19x4: store supplies, $600; office supplies, $300.

    d.   The building has a useful life of 30 years and an expected residual value of $6,000; equipment has a useful life of 10 years and an expected residual value of 3,000.

    e.   Merchandise with an invoice price of $5,000 was shipped to Pane Company by the end of December in partial fulfillment of their advance (see the December 18 transaction).

    f.   Interest is accrued on the Janes Company note, which was received on December 1.

    g.   The ending inventory balance is $36,000.

    h.   The income tax rate is 40%.

Required

    (1)   Record the December transactions in the general journal.

    (2)   Post from the general journal to the general ledger.

    (3)   Prepare a trial balance, entering it directly on a worksheet with columns for trial balance, adjustments, income statement, and balance sheet.

    (4)   Complete the worksheet.

    (5)   Prepare a classified income statement, a retained earnings statement, and a classified balance sheet.

    (6)   Journalize and post the adjusting and closing entries.

    (7)   Prepare a post-closing trial balance.

Assets

Chapter 5

Cash, Temporary Investments, and Receivables

Chapters 5 through 10 examine the problems encountered in identifying, measuring, and reporting the balance sheet accounts and the related income statement accounts. In this chapter the problems that arise in accounting for the monetary assets (cash, temporary investments, and accounts and notes receivable) and related revenues and expenses are examined.

Unit 13
Cash

The good merchant usually divides his assets into three parts: one-third ready money, one-third accounts receivable, and one-third goods. For when his creditor comes he can pay him in cash without having to sell his goods at a loss, so that even when his debtors do not hold to their terms he can still keep faith and goodwill.

Matthäus Schwartz, Model of Accounting, *1518*

Cash and assets that are claims to cash are called *monetary assets*. Cash is the most liquid of these, and is received and paid out daily in most businesses. Because of this frequency and high volume of cash transactions and the ease of transmitting cash from one person or account to another, procedures for controlling them are essential. This unit discusses procedures for controlling cash and for measuring and reporting the cash balance, and examines the composition of the cash balances.

Performance Objectives

Upon completing this unit you should be able to:

1. define and use the accounting terms introduced in this unit.
2. describe:
   a. what constitutes the cash balance to be reported as a current asset.
   b. appropriate internal control features for cash.
   c. how cash balance is measured and reported.
3. determine the cash balance to be reported as a current asset.
4. a. identify how certain bank statement and cash transaction items should be treated in preparing a bank reconciliation.
   b. prepare a bank reconciliation.

Components of Cash

Cash includes any medium of exchange that a bank will accept for immediate addition to an entity's bank account without putting restrictions against drawing on the amount deposited. Thus, cash includes coin, currency, checks, money orders, and bank drafts. Frequently an entity retains some cash on hand—to pay small bills or make change, for example—and doesn't always deposit checks, money orders, and bank drafts the same day they are received. Nevertheless, because these media of exchange would be accepted for immediate addition to a bank account, they are still considered part of the cash balance.

Cash excludes such items as postage stamps, IOUs, and notes receivable. Postage stamps should be included in the supplies account. IOUs and notes receivable are not considered cash even if they are transferrable to other parties (that is, negotiable) or if the maturity date has arrived. They should be carried on the books as receivables until payment is received.

Postdated checks and insufficient funds checks are also not included in cash. A **postdated check** is a check that has been dated later than the day on which the payee receives it. They are normally not accepted for deposit to a bank account until the date on the check. **Insufficient funds (NSF) checks** are checks that have "bounced," that is, been returned by the bank, because the check writer did not have enough funds in his bank account to cover the amount of the check. A postdated check should be carried on the books as a receivable until the date of the check. An insufficient funds check should be returned to the issuer or held until the issuer indicates that his account now has sufficient funds. A receivable balance should be carried on the books until payment is received or until the check can be redeposited.

Internal Control of Cash

A satisfactory **internal control** system is essential in any organization. The objectives of such a system are:

1. To safeguard the organization's assets
2. To check the reliability of the organization's financial records
3. To provide reasonable assurance that transactions are executed in accordance with established policies and are properly recorded
4. To provide reasonable assurance that access to assets is permitted only in accordance with established policies
5. To provide reasonable assurance that actual assets are compared to recorded assets at reasonable intervals and that any differences are properly resolved

Internal control includes the plan of organization—the organizational structure—and all procedures and records established to achieve the objectives described. Although the plan and objectives differ among organizations, several key elements should always be present if an internal control system is to be considered satisfactory. These key elements are:

1. clearly fixed responsibilities for each function
2. adequate policies to handle all transactions
3. adequate division of duties within each function and between functions, including:
   a. separating custody of assets from responsibility for recording transactions involving those assets
   b. separating authority to execute transactions from the handling of related assets
   c. separating recording of transactions from authority to execute transactions

The following quotation from *Model of Accounting* (Matthäus Schwartz, 1518) points out that people have been aware of the advantages of a division of duties for a long time:

> Internal control in a business employing three clerks: If the three of them wanted to be rogues and thieves they could cause much loss and damage to a merchant with a substantial trade. But the reason why three clerks are employed is that rarely will three people reveal to each other their evil intentions. So none of them knows the mind of the other two and they all stay with their job. If one of them falls down on his duties, the others will find him out. In this way the principal is not cheated and the servants remain faithful against their own will.

If the key elements of internal control are incorporated in the design of a satisfactory system of control for cash and cash transactions, these procedures will normally be followed:

1. Responsibility for the custody of cash, the processing of cash, and the accounting for cash transactions is assigned to different individuals.
2. An adequate system is established to handle cash receipts and payments and to record all cash transactions.
3. The custody and handling of cash are separated from recording cash transactions.
4. The handling of cash receipts is separated from the handling of cash payments.
5. All cash receipts are deposited intact daily.
6. All cash payments, except small amounts from cash on hand, are made by check; an adequate approval system authorizes the payments.

7. Cash on hand is adequately controlled.
8. All documents for cash receipts and payments—for example, checks, remittance advices, sales slips—are properly designed and prenumbered.
9. Employees have abilities commensurate with their responsibilities.
10. Protective measures and devices, such as bonding of employees handling cash, safes, cash registers, burglar alarms, and so on, are used.

Bank Reconciliation

The accounting department compares the monthly bank statement with the accounting records to determine if errors occurred in recording cash transactions and to identify any unrecorded transactions. This procedure is referred to as reconciling the bank statement with the company's records. In this reconciliation process, a statement called a **bank reconciliation** is prepared by the accountant for each checking account the company maintains. It is necessary to reconcile the bank statement and the company records because: (1) time lags occur between the company's recording of cash receipts (deposits) and cash payments (checks) and the bank's recording of these as credits and charges to the company's account; (2) errors can be made by either the company or the bank in recording transactions; and (3) the company doesn't know of some credits and charges to its account until the bank statement is received.

Exhibit 13.1 represents a typical bank statement. A **bank statement** is a report on the cash transaction activity for a bank account for a specific period of time, usually a month. A bank statement shows the opening balance, charges (company checks presented for payment, various service fees, and customers' bad checks), credits (deposits and other additions), and the ending balance of the account for the period. Bank statement dates are usually staggered throughout the month to help ease the bank's workload.

One form of bank reconciliation statement, known as the **true or correct balance form,** is widely used because the reconciled balance indicates the true or correct amount of cash the company has at the bank statement date. If a balance sheet is prepared at the bank statement date, this is the cash balance reported. The true or correct balance format starts with two figures: the ending cash balance per bank statement and the cash balance on the same date according to company records. The two figures are adjusted for errors, unrecorded transactions, and deposits and checks that have not yet cleared the bank. These adjusted or reconciled amounts should agree and are the true or correct cash balance at bank statement date.

Typical adjustments to the bank statement and company ledger balances are:

1. Additions to bank statement balance
    a. *cash on hand*—undeposited cash and checks, and any balance of cash normally kept on hand; if included in the

Exhibit 13.1

Statement of Account

THE BIGG CITY BANK

Bigg City, Michigan

Little Corp.

1234 Industrial Dr.

Bigg City, MI 48899

Statement Date:
October 31, 19x6
Account Number:
98-76-5432

Opening Balance	Credits		Charges		Service Charge	Ending Balance
	Amount	No.	Amount	No.		
$14,700	$13,640	5	$12,800	14	$ 20	$15,520

Checks and Charges			Credits	Date	Balance
					$14,700
			1,200	10-2	15,900
2,700	500	10 PC		10-4	12,690
			4,150	10-7	16,840
250	1,800			10-7	14,790
1,100		90 EC		10-10	13,600
		240 DM		10-11	13,360
			3,400	10-14	16,760
400	3,100			10-18	13,260
			2,850	10-21	16,110
150	800	1,000		10-24	14,160
		10 CC	2,040 CM	10-27	15,190
650				10-28	15,540
		20 SC		10-31	15,520

PC—printing charge; EC—error correction; DM—debit memo;
CM—credit memo; CC—collection charge; SC—service charge.

same cash account in the company ledger as the checking account balance, this amount must be added; if recorded in a separate account, adjustment is not necessary

b. *deposits in transit* — deposits made to the company's bank account, and properly recorded as cash receipts by the company, but not yet credited by the bank.

c. *bank errors that understate the cash balance* — may be errors in recording deposits, checks, or other credits and charges

2. Deductions from bank statement balance

   a. *outstanding checks* — checks written and sent to payees, and properly recorded as cash payments by the company, but not yet charged against the company's account by bank statement date

   b. *bank errors that overstate the cash balance* — may be errors in recording deposits, checks, or other credits and charges

3. Additions to company ledger balance

   a. *credits to the bank account not recorded by the company* — may arise from collections of notes made by the bank, bank loans, discounted notes, etc., added directly to the company's bank account, but not recorded by the company as cash receipts by bank statement date

   b. *company errors that understate the cash balance* — may be errors in recording or posting cash receipts or cash payments or in preparing bank deposits or checks

   c. *cash overage* — occurs when the adjusted balance per bank statement exceeds the balance per company ledger after all adjustments have been identified and made

4. Deductions from the company ledger balance

   a. *charges to the bank account not recorded by the company* — may arise from bank service charges for maintaining the account, printing checks, collecting notes, returned checks, etc., and from NSF (insufficient funds) checks included in deposits made by the company, but not recorded as reductions in the ledger account balance for cash by the company by bank statement date

   b. *company errors that overstate the cash balance* — may be errors in recording or posting cash receipts or cash payments or in preparing bank deposits or checks

   c. *cash shortage* — occurs when the adjusted balance per bank statement is less than the balance per company ledger after all adjustments have been identified and made

Exhibit 13.2 illustrates a bank reconciliation statement using the true or correct balance format. The bank statement in Exhibit 13.1, the following T-account for the

Exhibit 13.2

Little Corp.			
Bank Reconciliation			
October 31, 19x6			
Bank statement balance at October 31			$15,520
Add: Deposit in transit			1,870
Total			$17,390
Deduct: Outstanding checks: No. 1091		$100	
No. 1101		840	
No. 1102		620	1,560
Adjusted bank statement balance at October 31			$15,830
Company ledger balance at October 31			$13,710
Add: Note and interest collected by bank			2,040
Error on check no. 1097			360
Total			$16,110
Deduct: Check printing charge		$ 10	
Customer's NSF check		240	
Collection charge on note		10	
October service charge		20	280
Adjusted ledger balance at October 31			$15,830

company's cash account, and information from the September bank reconciliation give the information needed to prepare the bank reconciliation at the end of October.

Cash in Bank					
Oct. 1	Balance	14,975	Oct. 3	September	
31	Cash receipts			service charge	15
	(deposits only)	12,270	31	Cash payments	
				(checks only)	13,520

Note Company ledger balance at October 31 is computed as follows: $14,975 + 12,270 − 15 − 13,520 = $13,710.

The bank reconciliation statement at September 30, 19x6, indicated:

Deposits in transit		$1,200
Outstanding checks: No. 1089	$500	
No. 1090	250	
No. 1091	100	850
Bank service charge		15

The accountant for Little Corp. compared October cash receipts deposited with credits to the bank account and investigated the differences:

Credits to Bank Account	October Cash Receipts Deposited	Notes on Differences
$1,200	$ —	Deposit in transit at Sept. 30
4,150	4,150	
3,400	3,400	
2,850	2,850	
2,040	—	Note and interest collected
—	1,870	Deposit in transit at Oct. 31

The accountant also compared October cash payments recorded and charges to the bank account and investigated the differences:

Charges to Bank Account	October Cash Payments Recorded	Notes on Differences
$ —	$ 15	September service charge
2,700	2,700	
500	—	Outstanding check at Sept. 30
10 PC	—	Checking printing charge
250	—	Outstanding check at Sept. 30
1,800	1,800	
1,100	1,100	
90 EC	—	Correction of bank error
240 DM		Customer's NSF check
400	400	
3,100	3,100	
150	510	Error on check no. 1097; correct amount is $150
800	800	
1,000	1,000	
650	650	
10	—	Collection charge on note
20	—	October service charge
—	840	Check no. 1101 outstanding at Oct. 31
—	620	Check no. 1102 outstanding at Oct. 31

In addition, the accountant noted that check no. 1091, which was outstanding at September 30, was still outstanding at October 31. Using the information provided by this analysis, the bank reconciliation in Exhibit 13.2 was prepared.

Every adjustment to the company ledger balance on the bank reconciliation represents an unrecorded cash receipt or cash payment or an error correction that must be recorded. Thus, the accountant prepared the following journal entries:

Nov. 1	Cash	2,040	
	Notes receivable		2,000
	Interest revenue		40
	To record note and interest collected		
	by bank in October and added to		
	bank account.		
1	Cash	360	
	Accounts payable		360
	To correct error in preparing check no.		
	1097 to pay an invoice ($510 − 150		
	= $360).		
1	Miscellaneous expenses	40	
	Cash		40
	To record bank check printing, service,		
	and collection charges for October		
	($10 + 10 + 20 = $40).		
1	Accounts receivable	240	
	Cash		240
	To restore customer's balance because		
	his checked "bounced."		

After these four entries are posted to the ledger account, the true or correct balance at October 31 (and at the beginning of November) is reflected in the cash account. The debits and credits to the cash account are summarized in the following T-account. Note that the difference equals the adjusted or true cash balance of $15,830 indicated by the bank reconciliation ($29,645 − 13,815 = $15,830):

		Cash			
Oct. 1	Balance	14,975	Oct. 3	September service charge	15
31	Cash receipts (deposits only)	12,270	31	Cash payments (checks only)	13,520
Nov. 1	Note and interest collected by bank	2,040	Nov. 1	Check printing, service, and collection charges for October	40
1	Correct error on check no. 1097	360	1	Customer's NSF check charge	240
		29,645			13,815

Cash on Hand or Petty Cash

To control cash payments most bills are paid by check. However, small amounts of cash may be needed occasionally to pay postage due or taxi fares or buy small quantities of supplies, for example. Since preparing checks for these small amounts would be inconvenient and expensive, a special cash fund is often established. A separate ledger account, called ''cash on hand'' or ''petty cash,'' may be set up. The title ''petty cash'' normally is used when an imprest petty cash fund is established.

An **imprest petty cash fund** is one established for a fixed dollar amount and reimbursed when the fund is nearly depleted. The expenditures may be recorded in a petty cash record, but no entries are made in the journals or ledgers until the fund is replenished. At any date the sum of the cash on hand and the petty cash vouchers signed for expenditures should be equal to the fixed amount of the fund. This feature provides good control over custody of the fund. At periodic intervals surprise audits of the fund are conducted to prevent mishandling of cash and to verify the accuracy of the records.

When the fund is established, a check made out to ''petty cash'' is prepared. The amount of the fund should cover the small cash payment needs expected monthly. The person in charge of the fund cashes the check and keeps it in a safe place, such as a locked cash box or drawer. Assume a petty cash fund for $200 is established. The journal entry would be:

Petty cash	200	
Cash		200
To establish petty cash fund.		

As disbursements are made, petty cash vouchers are signed and the purpose of the expenditure noted. The fund should be replenished when it is nearly or completely depleted. It is also desirable to replenish it at the end of the accounting period, although not doing so has little effect on the financial statements. Expenditures are recorded only when the fund is replenished. When it is replenished, if the sum of the expenditures and cash on hand is less than the fixed amount of the fund, there is a shortage, which must be recorded. Assume that the $200 fund is replenished when cash on hand is $30.40 and expenditures total $168.55. The entry to record the replenishment would be:

Supplies inventory	41.50	
Postage expense	36.35	
Freight-in	83.20	
Miscellaneous expenses	7.50	
Cash shortage	1.05	
Cash		169.60
To replenish petty cash fund.		

There is a shortage of $1.05 because the expenditures total only $168.55 whereas the balance indicates that $169.60 has been spent ($200.000 − 30.40 = $169.60). This shortage may result from errors in disbursing the cash or in record-keeping. Note that the petty cash account is debited only when the fund is established or increased and credited only when the fund is decreased or abolished. A flexible or fluctuating balance petty cash fund can be used, but the imprest petty cash fund provides better control because of its fixed balance.

Reporting Cash Balances

One or more accounts can be maintained in the ledger for cash balances used to meet current operating needs. Many companies establish separate ledger accounts for their checking accounts and each special fund (such as petty cash, change, and payroll) that is maintained. Cash balances can be reported under current assets by listing each account and its balance or by reporting a single amount labeled "cash" or "cash on hand and in bank."

Only cash that can be used for current operating needs can be reported as a current asset. Cash set aside for specific, noncurrent purposes, such as bond retirement, pension payments, and plant expansion, must be reported under long-term investments and funds on the balance sheet. Cash in foreign banks should be reported separately as a current asset if the company is free to spend or transfer it, or under long-term investments and funds if the company is restricted from transferring it to the United States. Savings accounts are usually classified as cash under current assets because the company ordinarily can withdraw the cash as needed. **Certificates of deposit** (CDs) are classified as short-term or long-term investments, depending on their maturity date, because of restrictions and penalties on withdrawal of the balance before maturity. A CD is an investment contract (similar to a savings account) between a depositor and a bank or savings and loan association; terms include a specific maturity date, a guaranteed interest rate (greater than the rate for passbook savings accounts), and restrictions and penalties for withdrawal before maturity. Management is likely to purchase CDs with maturities that match current investment aims, either short term or long term.

A **bank overdraft,** that is, an overdrawn bank account, should be reported as a current liability unless the *right of offset* exists. This right allows the bank to offset an overdraft in a depositor's account with balances in other accounts the depositor maintains. If the right of offset exists, the overdraft amount is deducted from the balances of the other accounts when determining the net cash balance to be reported on the balance sheet.

REVIEW PROBLEM

The bank reconciliation statement at the end of May for Hood Company indicated the following:

Deposits in transit	$ 1,500	Service charges	$ 50
Outstanding checks	1,750	Customer NSF checks	600
Unadjusted bank balance	11,700	Unadjusted ledger balance	12,100

The bank statement for June showed the following:

Beginning balance		$11,700
Credits: Deposits	$26,400	
Bank loan	10,000	36,400
Charges: Service charges	$ 30	
Customer NSF checks	220	
Checks	32,100	32,350
Ending balance		15,750

An analysis of the company's cash records for June revealed:

Deposits of cash receipts (excluding loans)	$26,000
Service charges for May	50
Customer NSF checks from May	600
Checks written	33,100
Ending balance (including $250 of cash on hand)	4,610

An analysis of checks returned with the bank statement showed that all outstanding checks at May 31 cleared the bank during June.

Required   1. Prepare a bank reconciliation statement at June 30.
          2. Prepare all journal entries necessary to adjust the cash account to its true or correct balance at June 30.

Solution to review problem
1.

	Hood Company **Bank Reconciliation** **June 30, 19xx**		
Balance per bank statement			$15,750
Add: Cash on hand		$ 250	
Deposit in transit		1,100	1,350
Total			$17,100
Deduct: Outstanding checks			2,750
Adjusted balance per bank statement			$14,350
Balance per company ledger			$ 4,610
Add: Bank loan added to bank account			10,000
Total			$14,610
Deduct: Service charges		$ 30	
Customer NSF checks		220	250
Total			$14,360
Deduct: Cash shortage			10
Adjusted balance per company ledger			$14,350

Computations of deposit in transit:		$26,000
Deposits made by company during June	$26,400	
Deposits recorded by bank during June	1,500	24,900
Less: Deposit in transit at May 31		$ 1,100
Deposits in transit at June 30		
Computation of outstanding checks:		$33,100
Checks written by company during June	$32,100	
Checks charged against account by bank during June	1,750	30,350
Less: Outstanding checks at May 31		$ 2,750
Outstanding checks at June 30		
Computation of cash shortage:		
Balance per company ledger after all identifiable adjustments		$14,360
Balance per bank statement after all identifiable adjustments		14,350
Cash shortage		$ 10

2.

Cash	10,000	
Bank loan payable		10,000
To record bank loan previously unrecorded.		
Miscellaneous expenses	30	
Accounts receivable	220	
Cash		250
To record bank service charges and customer NSF checks returned by bank for June.		

SUMMARY

Internal control procedures for cash and cash transactions were discussed in this unit. One of these procedures, proving the cash balance with a bank reconciliation, was examined in detail. The composition of the cash balance and how to report cash balances were also discussed.

REVIEW QUESTIONS

13-1   What are the components of the cash balance reported as a current asset on the balance sheet?

13-2   How are each of the following items reported on the balance sheet?

    a.   checks and money orders received from customers, but not deposited
    b.   postage stamps
    c.   IOUs
    d.   postdated checks received from customers
    e.   customers' insufficient funds checks returned by the bank

13-3   What is meant by internal control? What are the key objectives of an internal control system?

13-4   Name three key elements that should be present in any internal control system. What duties or functions should be separated if adequate internal control is to be provided?

13-5   What is a bank reconciliation? Why is a bank reconciliation necessary?

13-6   **a.**   Identify the typical adjustments to the bank statement balance necessary to determine the true cash balance at the bank statement date.
    b.   Identify the typical adjustments to the company ledger balance necessary to determine the true cash balance at the bank statement date.

13-7   Are any entries necessary after the bank reconciliation is prepared? Explain.

13-8   What is an imprest petty cash fund? When are entries made to the petty cash account?

13-9   What is a bank overdraft? How is it reported on the balance sheet?

13-10   What is a CD? How are CDs reported on the balance sheet?

EXERCISES

13-1   Indicate whether each of the following items should be included or excluded from the cash balance that will be reported as a current asset.

		Include	Exclude
a.	checking account balance	_____	_____
b.	customers' insufficient funds check	_____	_____
c.	employee IOUs	_____	_____
d.	CDs	_____	_____
e.	bank passbook savings account	_____	_____
f.	petty cash fund balance	_____	_____
g.	postage stamps	_____	_____

13-2 The accountant for the Jeoparde Company gathered the following data necessary for the reconciliation of the company's checking account:

Balance, cash account, October 31	$2,317
Balance, bank statement, October 31	2,875
Deposit made on October 31—not shown on bank statement	300
Note ($100) & interest ($10) collected by bank—not recorded in cash account	110
Check no. 429, for $218, was listed on the bank statement incorrectly as $213	5
Outstanding checks:	

#417	$120
#440	400
#441	225

	745
Bank service charge for October	2

Required **a.** Prepare the bank reconciliation statement.

b. Prepare the entries necessary to correct the cash account balance as of October 31.

13-3 From the following information, prepare the journal entries that must be made on the books of Bay Sales Company.

Nov. 1	Establish a petty cash fund for $100.
Nov. 10	Paid postage expense, $15—petty cash voucher no. 1.
Nov. 15	Paid Green Bay Western Railroad $35 for freight on merchandise purchased—petty cash voucher no. 2.
Nov. 20	Purchased office supplies, $25—petty cash voucher no. 3.
Nov. 25	Reimbursed the petty cash fund $75.

13-4 The accountant for Kwest Company prepared the following bank reconciliation at the end of June 19*x3*:

Kwest Company
Bank Reconciliation
June 30, 19*x3*

Bank statement balance at June 30		$3,450
Add: Deposit in transit	$420	
Correction of error by bank in recording deposit	90	
Collection fees and service charges for June	25	
Customer's NSF check	165	700
Total		$4,150
Deduct: Outstanding checks	$740	
Note and interest collected by bank, but not recorded by company	820	1,560
Checking account balance per company books at June 30		$2,590
Cash on hand at June 30		150
Cash balance per company books at June 30		$2,740

The company treasurer believes the company has a larger cash balance than $2,740 and has asked you to prepare a new bank reconcilitation to indicate the company's true cash balance at June 30, 19*x3*.

PROBLEMS

13-1   The following are several items included in the cash balance of Hiram Company by the company cashier:

Petty cash fund (vouchers for $165; currency and coin, $35)	$ 200
Checking account balance	10,850
Regular bank savings account	2,500
CDs	5,000
Undeposited customers' checks	1,720
Customer's postdated check	540
Postage stamps	39
Employee IOU	300

Required   Determine the correct cash balance to be reported as a current asset. Explain how each item not included in the cash balance should be reported on the balance sheet.

13-2   The Caribou Company is setting up an imprest petty cash fund. The following are the November and December petty cash transactions.

Nov. 15   Established a petty cash fund of $50.
Dec. 5   Replenished the petty cash fund. The cash on hand in the fund amounted to $8. A summary of the petty cash vouchers showed the following expenditures:

Office supplies	$ 6
Cab fares	8
Postage stamps	10
Freight-in	17

Dec. 15   Increased the petty cash fund balance by $25.
Dec. 31   Replenished the petty cash fund at the end of the accounting period. Cash on hand amounted to $31; petty cash vouchers showed the following:

Office supplies	$11
Postage stamps	15
Freight-in	18

Required   Record the petty cash transactions for November and December in the general journal.

13-3   On January 31 the cash account of the Kleen-Kare Laundry Company showed a balance of $3,625 in the general ledger. The bank statement reported a cash balance of $3,846 as of January 31. In analyzing the bank statement items and the cash transactions per books, the company accountant discovered the following items:

a.   A deposit of $743 was made on January 31, but not indicated on the bank statement.
b.   The following checks were written but not indicated on the bank statement: no. 414 ($75), no. 418 ($110), no. 421 ($211), and no. 422 ($178).

   c.   A note of $500 and interest of $10 were collected by the bank for the company but not recorded by the company.

   d.   A service charge of $3 was indicated on the bank statement for collecting the note in c.

   e.   Check no. 416 for $218 was erroneously recorded by the bookkeeper as $281; the check was for payment of utilities.

   f.   A bank deposit for $649 was erroneously recorded by the bank as $469.

Required   **(1)**   Prepare a bank reconciliation as of January 31.

               (2)   Prepare any necessary entries on the books of Kleen-Kare Laundry Company as indicated by the bank reconciliation.

13-4   Following are data from the August 31, 19x5, bank reconciliation of Thurston Corp.

Deposit in transit		$1,800
Outstanding checks at August 31:		
No. 1058	$175	
No. 1064	325	
No. 1065	850	1,300
Bank service charge		25
Customer's NSF check		480

The September 30, 19x5 bank statement showed the following:

Date	Deposits and Credits		Charges		Balance
Aug. 31					$10,800
Sept. 1	$1,800		$ 175		12,425
4		$ 325		$2,000	10,100
7	5,650	600		750	14,400
9		1,100		400	12,900
15	3,000		800		15,100
17		1,700		250	13,150
20	480		1,210		12,420
23	3,800		540		15,680
24			480 NSF		15,200
29		2,100		350	12,750
30	1,020 NC		30 SC		13,740

NSF—Non-Sufficient-Funds check charge; NC—note collected; SC—service charge

The company records showed the following cash balance at September 30:

Cash on hand	$ 300
Checking account	14,380

An analysis of the company's records showed the following deposits and checks written:

Date	Deposits	Check No.	Amount
		Checks Written	
Sept. 1		1066	$ 2,000
4		1067	600
5		1068	750
7	$ 5,650	1069	1,100
		1070	400
10		1071	800
12		1072	1,700
13		1073	550
15	3,000	1074	250
17		1075	1,210
20	480	1076	540
23	3,800	1077	350
26		1078	650
28		1079	1,300
30	2,400		
Totals	$15,330		$12,200

Assume that the bank statement is correct except for the $2,100 charge on September 29, which is a check written by the Thurgood Corp. but charged by the bank to Thurston Corp. The customer's NSF check at August 21 was redeposited on September 20.

Required   **a.**   Prepare a bank reconciliation at September 30, 19x5.

b.   Prepare all necessary entries on the books of Thurston Corp. that are indicated by the bank reconciliation prepared in part a.

13-5   The chief accountant for Eron Corp. has asked you to help collect the data needed to prepare the company's balance sheet at the end of 19x5. Your analysis of company records and documents indicates the following:

a.   The petty cash fund account shows a balance of $250. The petty cashier actually has $55 in cash, and petty cash vouchers for: various expenses, $101; supplies, $38; transportation costs on merchandise purchases, $54.

b.   The bank reconciliation for November 30, 19x5, showed: deposits in transit, $375; outstanding checks, $680; bank service charges, $20.

c.   The bank statement dated December 31, 19x5, showed: check charges, $8,880; bank service charges, $25; deposits, $7,950; ending balance, $3,010.

d.   The company cash account showed the following December transactions: cash receipts, $8,550; cash payments by check, $8,870; November service charges, $20; ending balance, $3,100.

e.   Customer checks received December 31 (and included in cash receipts in d.) but not deposited amounted to $490.

f.   Other items held at December 31; postage stamps, $40; employee IOUs, $350; customer's postdated check, $240 (included in cash receipts in d.).

Required   **(1)**   Prepare a bank reconciliation at December 31, 19x5. (Note: adjust the cash balance per books to include replenishment of the petty cash fund.)

(2)   Prepare all entries indicated by the bank reconciliation including the replenishment of the petty cash fund.

(3)   Prepare a partial balance sheet at December 31, 19x5, showing the cash balance only.

Unit 14
Temporary Investments

Ready money is the best ware.

Richard L. Greene, The Early English Carols

Many companies invest cash in a variety of securities that they keep until they need cash. This unit examines the nature of temporary investments and the procedures used to measure and report them.

Performance Objectives

Upon completing this unit you should be able to:

1. define and use the accounting terms introduced in this unit.
2. describe:
   a. the criteria for reporting securities and cash deposits as temporary investments
   b. what constitutes the balance to be reported under current assets for temporary investments
   c. how to measure and report the balance for temporary investments
3. determine:
   a. the balance to be reported under current assets for temporary investments
   b. the gain or loss realized on the sale or valuation of temporary investments
4. identify or prepare the journal entries for temporary investment transactions.

Nature of Temporary Investments

Temporary investments include cash deposits and securities that can be readily converted into cash. Management should be able to obtain the cash on deposit or convert the securities into cash whenever a need arises to pay current obligations or to meet current operating needs. Also, management should intend to hold these deposits and/or securities only for a short period until a need arises. Usually this short period will be 12 months after balance sheet date, or the normal operating cycle if longer. Thus, there are two criteria for classification of cash deposits and securities as temporary investments: (1) their marketability, that is, the ability to obtain cash on short notice without a risk of losses from quick conversion and (2) management intention to hold them for a short period.

Temporary investments include the following, if these two criteria are met: certificates of deposit; corporate, government, and nonprofit organization bonds; common stocks; commercial paper; and treasury bills. **Commercial paper** is a series of short-term, unsecured, promissory notes sold by large companies with top credit ratings to financial institutions that then distribute the notes to banks and investors. **Treasury bills** are short-term securities with maturities ranging from 91 days to one year that are issued weekly by the U.S. Treasury. Both commercial paper and treasury bills are sold at a discount, that is, below their par or face value, and redeemed at maturity at par.

The degree of risk and the rate of return influence management's decision regarding the type of securities or CDs to purchase. CDs, commercial paper, government bonds, and treasury bills involve relatively small risks from default or marketability on short notice, but they usually carry lower interest rates. Corporate bonds that have been issued by companies with high credit ratings and that are near maturity also offer relatively low risk. Common stocks and bonds that are not close to maturity have greater risk of unfavorable price fluctuations.

Companies make temporary investments to obtain a return on seasonally idle cash or excess cash and also to hold as a secondary cash reserve. Some businesses have seasonal peaks and wind up with cash that is not needed until they start building up inventories for the next peak season. Or, occasionally, a company may have an excess of cash in the bank because of increased or decreased business volume. And some companies prefer having a secondary cash reserve to avoid the necessity of relying on bank loans when cash needs arise. In any of these situations, it is desirable to obtain even a minimal return on the assets through temporary investments.

Control of Temporary Investments

Control over all assets is desirable, but control over the more liquid assets is essential. Investments in CDs and securities can be diverted to personal use if controls are weak. Purchases and sales of temporary investments should have the written authorization of specified company officials. The certificates received when the investments are made should be kept in a bank safety deposit box, and there should be two company officials present when the safety deposit box is opened. Records of purchases and sale dates, types of securities, quantities, serial numbers, and cost and sales prices and interest or dividend rates and dates should be maintained. The need for cash in normal operations should be coordinated with the purchases and sales of temporary investments.

Accounting for Temporary Investment Transactions

The cost of temporary investments includes the purchase price and any brokerage fees and transfer taxes that must be paid to acquire them. Stock prices are stated in terms of dollars per share—for example, a stock quotation of 38¼ means $38.25 per share. Bond prices are stated as a percentage of their par or face value. Typical par or face values are $100, $500, $1,000, and $10,000. A bond with a par value of $1,000 and a quoted price of 102½ sells for $1,025 ($1,000 × 102½%). The cost of the investments should be charged to a temporary investments or marketable securities account.

The entry to record the purchase of 200 shares of Amos Corp. common stock at $26 per share plus brokerage fees of $356 on April 1, 19x5, would be:

April 1	Temporary Investments	5,556	
	Cash		5,556
	To record purchase of Amos Corp.		
	stock as temporary investments		
	[(200 × $26) + $356 = $5,556].		

The entry to record the purchase of ten U.S. government 6% bonds with a face value of $1,000 each at 98 plus brokerage fees of $450 on May 1, 19x5, would be:

May 1	Temporary Investments	10,250	
	Cash		10,250
	To record purchase of U.S. government		
	bonds as temporary investments [($1,000		
	× 10 × 98%) + $450 = $10,250].		

In this bond purchase entry it is assumed that the bonds were bought on an interest payment date. All bond purchases and sales will take place on an interest payment date in this unit. The problem of accounting for the purchase or sale of bonds between interest dates is discussed in Unit 30. Interest on bonds is normally paid semiannually on specified interest payment dates, one-half being paid at each date. For the bonds in the example, assume that the interest payment dates are May 1 and November 1.

One-half the interest, $300 ($10,000 × 6% × ½), is received on November 1. Note that interest is always computed on the face value of the bonds at the rate stated in the bond contract.

Interest revenue is recognized when the interest check is received. The entry for the receipt of interest on November 1 would be:

Nov. 1	Cash	300	
	Interest Revenue		300
	To recognize interest revenue received		
	on temporary investments		
	($10,000 × 6% × 1/2 = $300).		

If the company's accounting period ends during an interest period, an adjusting entry for accrued revenue is necessary (see Unit 10). Assume that the accounting period ends on December 31; the entry to accrue interest revenue since the last interest payment date of November 1 would be:

Dec. 31	Interest Receivable	100	
	Interest Revenue		100
	To accrue interest revenue for two		
	months on temporary investments		
	($10,000 × 6% × 2/12 = $100).		

The subsequent entry to record the receipt of interest for six months on May 1, 19x6, would require the elimination of the receivable set up on December 31, 19x5, and the recognition of interest revenue for four months (January 1 to May 1, 19x6):

May 1	Cash	300	
	Interest Receivable		100
	Interest Revenue		200
	To record receipt of interest for six		
	months on temporary investments		
	($10,000 × 6% × 1/2 = $300).		

Dividends on common stock are usually recognized as revenue when they are received by the investor. They are not accrued at the end of the accounting period like interest because dividends are payable only if declared by the issuing company's board of directors. The entry to record a $1 per share dividend received from Amos Corp. on December 15, 19x5, would be:

Dec. 15	Cash	200	
	Dividend Revenue		200
	To recognize dividends received on temporary investments (200 × $1 = $200).		

When temporary investments in securities are sold, a gain or loss may be realized—a gain if the cash proceeds from the sale exceed the cost; a loss if the cash proceeds are less than the cost. Assume that 50 shares of Amos Corp. stock are sold at $30 per share less brokerage fees of $100 on February 1, 19x6, and that half of the government bonds are sold at 99 less brokerage fees of $250 on May 1, 19x6. The entries to record these sales would be:

Feb. 1	Cash	1,400	
	Temporary Investments		1,389
	Gain on Sale of Temporary Investments		11
	To record sale of temporary investments.		

Computation of gain:
Proceeds from sale [(50 × $30) − $100]	$1,400
Cost of shares sold ($5,556 × 50/200)	1,389
Gain realized	$ 11

May 1	Cash	4,700	
	Loss on Sale of Temporary Investments	425	
	Temporary Investments		5,125
	To record sale of temporary investments.		

Computation of loss:
Proceeds from sale [($5,000 × 99%) − 250]	$4,700
Cost of bonds sold ($10,250 × 1/2)	5,125
Loss realized	$ 425

Valuation of Temporary Investments

Two methods of valuing temporary investments have been generally accepted in accounting practice: the cost and the lower-of-cost-or-market methods. When the cost method is used, the only entries necessary are those already illustrated. When the **lower-of-cost-or-market method** is used, an entry to adjust the balance of temporary investments is needed if (1) market value is lower than cost or (2) there are changes in the provision for losses from one period to the next. The lower-of-cost-or-market method is an example of applying conservatism in accounting: the unfavorable effects on financial position (a reduction in recoverable value of assets) and on operating results (a loss or reduction in the value of assets) are recorded as soon as the loss is reasonably assured; however, increases in value are ignored, except to the extent that previous losses were recorded (that is, gains can be recognized only up to the amount of losses previously recorded). The advantage of this method is that the portion of the cost of temporary investments a company does not expect to recover when the investments are sold is recognized in the accounts and disclosed in the financial statements for the period in which the decline in their value occurred.

In December 1975, the FASB issued Statement of Financial Accounting Standards (SFAS) No. 12, which requires the use of the lower-of-cost-or-market method for investments in marketable equity securities. **Marketable equity securities** were defined by the FASB as stock and rights to purchase or sell stock at fixed or determinable prices, for which prices are currently available in a national securities market. SFAS No. 12 includes the following requirements for temporary investments in marketable equity securities:

1. Marketable equity securities shall be valued at the lower of aggregate cost or aggregate market value at balance sheet date.
2. The excess of aggregate cost over aggregate market shall be accounted for in a **valuation allowance** (that is, a contra or offset) account.
3. Changes in the valuation allowance shall be included in the determination of net income as unrealized gains or losses, along with gains or losses realized on the sale of securities.

The lower-of-cost-or-market method is applied to *all* types of temporary investments in this text although SFAS No. 12 applies only to marketable equity securities. This latter practice is receiving wider acceptance; however, marketable equity securities should be considered as a separate group or portfolio from other temporary investments when applying the lower-of-cost-or-market method. Assume that Amos Company owns the following portfolios of short-term investments:

Marketable Equity Securities

	Cost	Market Value 12/31/x5	Market Value 12/31/x6
AA stock	$5,600	$5,300	$5,450
BB stock	3,200	3,350	3,300
Total	$8,800	$8,650	$8,750

Bonds

	Cost	Market Value 12/31/x5	Market Value 12/31/x6
XX Corp.	$5,050	$5,020	$4,980
YY Corp.	4,850	4,740	4,700
Total	$9,900	$9,760	$9,680

At the end of 19x5 aggregate market value is less than aggregate cost by $150 ($8,800 − 8,650) for marketable equity securities and $140 ($9,900 − 9,760) for bonds. These amounts should be recorded as unrealized losses and included in the determination of net income for 19x5. Also, valuation allowances for these amounts should be established. The required entries would be:

Dec. 31, 19x5	Unrealized loss on valuation of short-term marketable equity securities	150	
	Allowance for valuation of short-term marketable equity securities		150
	To apply lower-of-cost-or-market method to short-term marketable equity securities.		

Dec. 31, 19x5	Unrealized loss on valuation of short-term bond investments	140	
	Allowance for valuation of short-term bond investments		140
	To apply lower-of-cost-or-market method to short-term bond investments.		

At the end of each subsequent year the valuation allowance is adjusted to the balance required to reflect the difference between cost and market value. If a larger balance is required, an additional loss is recorded. For example, an unrealized loss of $80 ($220 − 140) is recorded for the bonds in 19x6 because their year-end market value is now $220 ($9,900 − 9,680) lower than cost compared to $140 at the end of the prior year. On the other hand, if a smaller balance is required, an unrealized gain is recorded. For the marketable equity securities in the example, an unrealized gain of $100 ($150 − 50) is recorded in 19x6 because their year-end market value is now only $50 ($8,800 − 8,750) lower than cost, whereas it was $150 lower a year earlier. However, the amount of unrealized gain is limited to the amount of unrealized loss recorded in prior years. In this example, that limit was not reached. Also, note that the valuation allowance is adjusted only at year-end, even if there are disposals of securities during the year. The entries required at the end of 19x6 to apply the lower-of-cost-or-market method, then, are:

Dec. 31, 19x6	Unrealized loss on valuation of short-term bond investments	80	
	Allowance for valuation of short-term bond investments		80
	To increase valuation allowance on short-term bond investments to $220 ($220 − 140).		
Dec. 31, 19x6	Allowance for valuation of short-term marketable equity securities	100	
	Unrealized gains on valuation of short-term marketable equity securities		100
	To decrease valuation allowance for short-term marketable equity securities $100 ($150 − 50).		

Reporting Temporary Investments

Temporary investments are reported on the balance sheet as a current asset. They are listed immediately after cash because they are the most liquid of the noncash assets; they can be converted into cash on very short notice. If temporary investments are valued at cost, the market value should be disclosed parenthetically (or in a footnote) as follows:

Current assets:		
Cash		xxxx
Temporary investments, at cost (market value, $27,200)		26,500

When temporary investments are valued at market value under the lower-of-cost-or-market method, they are reported net of the valuation allowance under current assets. Any **unrealized gain or loss** recognized from applying the lower-of-cost-or-market method is reported as incidental revenue or expense on a classified income statement. Any **gain or loss realized on the sale of temporary investments** also is reported as incidental revenue or expense. Neither type of gain or loss qualifies as an extraordinary item. SFAS No. 12 requires that the following information be disclosed in footnotes:

Exhibit 14.1

Partial Balance Sheet

Current assets:
Cash $ xxx
Short-term marketable equity securities, at market value (see note 1)   8,750
Short-term bond investments, at market value (see note 1)   9,680

Partial Income Statement

Incidental revenue and expense:
Unrealized loss on valuation of short-term marketable equity securities (see note 1) $ 80
Unrealized gain on valuation of short-term bond investments (see note 1)   100

Notes

1.   *At December 31, 19x6, the company's short-term investment portfolios were valued at lower-of-cost-or-market. Marketable equity securities had a cost of $8,800; the cost of bonds was $9,900. As a result of changes in the valuation allowances for these investments, unrealized gains of $100 on bonds and unrealized losses of $80 on marketable equity securities were included in net income in 19x6. There were no disposals of short-term investments during the year.*

1.   the aggregate cost and aggregate market value for marketable equity securities that are classified as temporary investments
2.   the net realized gain or loss that is included in net income for the period
3.   the amount of unrealized gain or loss included in net income for the period

Exhibit 14.1 illustrates the method of reporting all necessary information on temporary investments. It is based on Amos Company's portfolios of short-term investments at the end of 19x6.

REVIEW PROBLEM

Klammer Company owned the following temporary investments at the end of 19x5; they were valued using the lower-of-cost-or-market method:

Security	Quantity	Total Cost	Total Market Value
ABC Company common stock	300 shares	$10,800	$10,500
XYZ Company 8% bonds ($10,000 par value)	10 bonds	10,300	10,225

During 19*x6* the following temporary investment transactions occurred:

Feb. 1	Purchased 400 shares of DEF Company common stock at $28 per share plus brokerage fees of $280.
Mar. 1	Sold the 300 shares of ABC Company common stock at $34 per share less brokerage fees of $270.
Apr. 1	Received the semiannual interest payment on the XYZ Company 8% bonds. Interest had been accrued for 3 months on December 31, 19*x5;* the adjusting entry was not reversed.
Oct. 1	Received the semiannual interest payment on the XYZ Company 8% bonds.
Dec. 1	Received a $1.50 dividend per share on the DEF Company common stock.
Dec. 31	Accrued interest on the XYZ Company 8% bonds.
Dec. 31	The values of the temporary investments at the end of 19*x6* were: DEF Company common stock, $27 per share; XYZ Company 8% bonds, 100¾.

Required   Prepare all necessary entries for 19*x6*.

Solution to review problem

Feb. 1	Temporary Investments	11,480	
	Cash		11,480
	To record purchase of DEF Company stock as temporary investments [(400 × $28) + $280 = $11,480].		
Mar. 1	Cash	9,930	
	Loss on Sale of Temporary		
	Investments	870	
	Temporary Investments		10,800
	To record sale of ABC Company stock.		
	Computation of loss:		
	Cost of ABC Company stock		$10,800
	Proceeds from sale of stock [(300 × $34) − $270]		9,930
	Loss realized		$ 870

Apr. 1	Cash	400	
	Interest Receivable		200
	Interest Revenue		200
	To record collection of semiannual interest on XYZ Company 8% bonds: accrued at 12/31/x5, $200 ($10,000 × 8% × 3/12); interest revenue for 1/1–4/1, $200 ($10,000 × 8% × 3/12).		
Oct. 1	Cash	400	
	Interest Revenue		400
	To record collection of semiannual interest on XYZ Company 8% bonds ($10,000 × 8% × 6/12 = $400).		
Dec. 1	Cash	600	
	Dividend Revenue		600
	To record dividends received on DEF Company stock (400 × $1.50 = $600).		
Dec. 31	Interest Receivable	200	
	Interest Revenue		200
	To accrue interest for three months on XYZ Company 8% bonds ($10,000 × 8% × 3/12 = $200).		
Dec. 31	Unrealized Loss on Valuation of Short-term Marketable Equity Securities	380	
	Allowance for Valuation of Short-term Marketable Equity Securities		380
	To increase valuation allowance; $680 ($11,480 − 10,800) now needed compared to $300 ($10,800 − 10,500) one year earlier.		
Dec. 31	Unrealized Loss on Short-term Bond Investment	150	
	Allowance for Valuation of Short-term Bond Investment		150
	To increase valuation allowance; $225 ($10,300 − 10,075) now needed compared to $75 ($10,300 − 10,225) one year earlier.		

Security	Quantity	Total Cost	Total Market Value*
DEF Company common stock	400 shares	$11,480	$10,800
XYZ Company 8% bonds	10 bonds	10,300	10,075

*400 × $27 = $10,800; $10,000 × 100¾% = $10,075.

SUMMARY

All aspects of accounting for temporary investments were examined in this unit. First, the two criteria for classifying cash deposits and securities as temporary investments were explained. Next, the accounting for transactions to purchase and sell these investments and to recognize revenue from them was discussed and illustrated. Finally, problems in measuring the balance to be reported were discussed.

REVIEW QUESTIONS

14-1   What are temporary investments? What two criteria are used to determine whether or not a cash deposit or security should be classified as a temporary investment?

14-2   What types of cash deposits and securities typically are included in temporary investments? What factors are considered in choosing the type of cash deposits or securities to be held as temporary investments?

14-3   Why do companies acquire temporary investments?

14-4   Identify several key internal control procedures for temporary investments.

14-5   How is the cost of a temporary investment determined?

14-6   a.   When are interest and dividend revenue recognized?
       b.   How is a gain or loss on the sale of temporary investments determined?

14-7   Identify two methods of valuing temporary investments. When should each method be used?

14-8   When the lower-of-cost-or-market method is used, how should the excess of aggregate cost over aggregate market of temporary investments be accounted for at the end of each accounting period?

14-9 How are the following reported on the financial statements?
a. temporary investments
b. allowance for valuation of temporary investments
c. gain or loss on sale of temporary investments
d. unrealized loss or gain from valuation of temporary investments

14-10 What type of information should be disclosed in the footnotes regarding temporary investments?

EXERCISES

14-1 Clancey Corp. purchased 8% government bonds with a par value of $15,000 for 101½ plus brokerage fees of $225 on April 1, 19*x4*. The bonds pay interest semiannually on April 1 and October 1 and mature on October 1, 19*x5*. The company's accounting period ends on December 31.

Required Prepare the following entries for 19*x4*:
a. April 1 for the purchase of the bonds
b. October 1 for the collection of interest
c. December 31 for the accrual of interest

14-2 Haney Corp. purchased 200 shares each of Rollem Corp. and Klippen Corp. stock at $26 and $35, respectively, on February 15, 19*x4*. The company paid brokerage fees of $150 and $200, respectively, on these purchases. On June 10, 19*x4*, Haney sold one-half of the Klippen Corp. stock at $38 per share less brokerage fees of $100. Dividends of $1 per share were received on the Rollem Corp. stock on November 30, 19*x4*. On December 31, 19*x4*, the end of the accounting period, the market value of the Rollem Corp. stock was $5,000; and of the Klippen Corp. stock, $3,850.

Required Prepare the following entries for 19*x4*:
a. the purchase of the stock on February 15
b. the sale of stock on June 10
c. the receipt of dividends on November 20
d. the application of the lower-of-cost-or-market method on December 31

14-3 Raye Corp. owned the following investments at the end of 19*x5* and 19*x6*:

	19*x5*		19*x6*	
	Cost	Market Value	Cost	Market Value
U.S. government bonds	$ 9,600	$ 9,500	$15,000	$14,700
Maye common stock	18,000	17,600	9,000	8,200
Daye common stock			12,000	12,400
Total	$27,600	$27,100	$36,000	$35,300

During 19x6 Raye Corp. sold half of its investment in Maye common stock for $8,550. Raye Corp. uses the lower-of-cost-or-market method in valuing its investments. The investments are being held as a secondary cash reserve for current operations.

Required   **a.**   Prepare the entries to apply the lower-of-cost-or-market method at the end of 19x5 and 19x6 and to record the sale of Maye stock during 19x6.

              b.   Prepare a partial balance sheet and a partial income statement at the end of 19x6.

14-4   Following is information obtained from the records of Kildare Company at the end of 19x2:

     a.   Cash on hand is $1,250, including undeposited customer checks of $900.

     b.   Checking account balance according to ledger is $3,450, and according to bank statement, $3,650.

     c.   Deposits in transit and outstanding checks at December 31, were $320 and $540, respectively.

     d.   Balance in allowance for valuation of marketable equity securities from December 31, 19x1, is $450.

     e.   Summary of securities held as temporary investments at December 31, 19x2:

Security	Cost	Market Value at December 31, 19x2
Bonds	$12,100	$12,250
Stocks	16,800	16,450
	$28,900	$28,700

     f.   The company held a 3-month, $5,000 CD with a 6% annual interest rate and a maturity date of February 1, 19x3.

     g.   The bonds have a $12,000 par value, and pay interest semiannually on April 1 and October 1. The annual interest rate is 8%. The bonds were purchased on April 1, 19x2.

Required   Prepare a partial balance sheet and a partial income statement at the end of 19x2.

PROBLEMS

14-1   The temporary investment portfolio of Sampson Corp. included the following at December 31, 19x2:

	Cost	Market Value
AB Corp. 5% bonds ($9,000 par value)	$ 9,300	$ 9,200
BC Corp. stock (100 shares, $20 par value)	3,200	3,350
CD Corp. 6% bonds ($8,000 par value)	8,000	7,850
	$20,500	$20,400

Selected transactions relating to temporary investments during 19x3 were:

Feb. 1	Received semiannual interest on the CD Corp. bonds. Sampson Corp. does not prepare reversing entries.
July 1	Received the semiannual interest on the AB Corp. bonds and sold the bonds for $9,150.
Aug. 1	Purchased 300 shares of DE Corp. stock for $31 per share plus brokerage fees of $200.

At December 31, 19x3, the portfolio of temporary investments consisted of:

	Cost	Market Value
BC Corp. stock (100 shares, $20 par value)	$3,200	$ 3,450
CD Corp. 6% bonds ($8,000 par value)	8,000	7,800
DE Corp. stock (300 shares, $10 par value)	?	9,100
	$?	$20,350

Required

a. Prepare the entries for the February 1, July 1, and August 1, 19x3, transactions.

b. Prepare the adjusting entries on December 31, 19x3, for:
  (1) accrued interest on the CD Corp. bonds (interest payable semiannually on February 1 and August 1)
  (2) applying the lower-of-cost-or-market method for valuing temporary investments; this method also was applied at December 31, 19x2

c. Prepare a partial balance sheet and a partial income statement at the end of 19x3.

14-2 Clarion Corp. completed the following temporary investment transactions during 19x7:

Feb. 1	Purchased ten U.S. government bonds at 98 plus brokerage fees of $120; each bond has a par value of $1,000; interest is

payable semiannually on February 1 and August 1; the annual interest rate is 6%.

Apr. 10   Purchased 1,000 shares of Sonn Corp. stock at $14 per share plus brokerage fees of $150.

June 21   Sold 400 shares of Sonn Corp. stock at $17 per share less brokerage fees of $80.

Aug. 1   Received the semiannual interest payment on the government bonds.

Dec. 1   Purchased a $5,000, 90-day certificate of deposit; the annual interest rate is 6%.

Dec. 15   Received dividends of $.50 per share on the remaining 600 shares of Sonn Corp. stock.

Dec. 31   The market value of the securities at the end of 19x7 were: U.S. government bonds, 97; Sonn Corp. stock, 15½.

Required   a.   Prepare all entries for 19x7, including the accrual of interest revenue at December 31, 19x7.

b.   Prepare a partial balance sheet and a partial income statement at the end of 19x7.

14-3   The following information was obtained from the records and documents of Roberts Company at the end of 19x1:

a.   Balances in ledger: petty cash, $200; cash, $4,160; temporary investments in marketable equity securities, $24,450; allowance for valuation of marketable equity securities, $150.

b.   Cash and vouchers in petty cash drawer: cash, $35; vouchers, $165.

c.   Data from bank reconciliation at December 31, 19x1: deposits in transit, $520; outstanding checks, $860; bank statement balance, $4,200; service charges for December, $30; customer's NSF check, $270.

d.   The temporary investments held at the end of 19x1 included the following securities:

Security	Cost	Market Value at December 31, 19x1
Karr Corp. bonds	$ 8,050	$ 7,920
Harte, Inc., stock	11,400	11,180

e.   The company also held a 6-month, 6% CD for $5,000; the CD was dated November 1, 19x1.

f.   Other items included the following: travel advances to employees, $600; IOUs from company officers, $800; cash deposits with utilities, $300.

g.   Marketable equity securities with a cost of $13,050 were sold for $12,800.

h.   The Karr Corp. bonds were purchased on July 1, 19x1. They have a par value of $8,000; interest of 8% is payable semiannually on January 1 and July 1.

Required   Prepare a partial balance sheet and a partial income statement at the end
of 19*x1*.

14-4   The following is the asset section of the balance sheet included in the 1977 annual report
of Total Petroleum (North America) Ltd.

Assets

	December 31	
	1977	1976
Current Assets:		
Cash	$ 5,311,000	$ 5,624,000
Short-term investments	11,247,000	3,711,000
Accounts and notes receivable, less allowance for doubtful accounts of $492,000 (1976— $443,000)	28,080,000	23,250,000
Inventories of purchased crude oil and products	18,351,000	15,835,000
Inventories of merchandise, materials, and supplies	3,786,000	3,469,000
Prepaid expenses and other	6,464,000	5,963,000
	$ 73,239,000	$ 57,582,000
Short-Term Investments Held for Refinery Acquisition	40,000,000	—
Long-Term Receivables and Other Assets	3,337,000	3,045,000
Property, Plant, and Equipment, Net	234,614,000	203,974,000
	$351,190,000	$264,871,000

Required   **a.**   What activity in short-term investments can be assumed from the
balance sheet data?

b.   What are the likely reasons for Total's management acquiring the
short-term investments reported as a current asset?

c.   Why is $40,000,000 of short-term investments reported as a
noncurrent asset at the end of 1977? Is this classification
appropriate?

d.   Evaluate the presentation of short-term investments under current
assets. Total did not present any footnotes on short-term
investments in the annual report.

Unit 15
Accounts Receivable

A false balance is abomination to the Lord . . .

Proverbs 11:1

For many businesses accounts receivable is one of the most significant assets to be accounted for and controlled. This unit examines the distinction between trade and nontrade receivables and discusses the procedures used to account for and report accounts receivable, related revenues, and losses from uncollectible accounts.

Performance Objectives

Upon completing this unit you should be able to:

1. define and use the accounting terms introduced in this unit.
2. describe:
   a. the distinction between trade and nontrade receivables
   b. how accounts receivable balances can be controlled using a subsidiary ledger
   c. how the balances of accounts receivable, the allowance for uncollectible accounts, and uncollectible accounts expense are measured and reported
3. determine:
   a. the net realizable value of accounts receivable
   b. the balance for the allowance for uncollectible accounts
   c. uncollectible accounts expense
4. identify or prepare the journal entries for transactions involving accounts receivable and uncollectible accounts.

Exhibit 15.1

Current assets:	
Cash	$ 40,000
Temporary investments, carried at market value (cost, $38,000)	35,000
Notes and accounts receivable (net of allowance for uncollectible accounts of $7,500)	157,500
Nontrade notes receivable	10,000
Receivables from officers and employees	4,000
Accrued interest receivable	500
Merchandise inventory	165,000
Prepaid expenses	8,000
Total current assets	$420,000

Classification of Receivables

Receivables are monetary claims a company has against others. They can be classified as trade and nontrade receivables. **Trade receivables** arise when goods are sold or services are performed on credit. They include the accounts receivable and notes receivable accounts. **Nontrade receivables** arise from transactions that are not considered part of the primary or regular trade activities of the business. They include receivables that arise from such activities as the sale of plant assets, loans to employees, and accruals of interest, rent, or other incidental revenues earned but not yet received. To distinguish between trade and nontrade receivables the word *trade* is sometimes included and the word *nontrade* should always be included in the account titles.

Receivables that are due within one year after balance sheet date are classified as current assets. Trade receivables that are due within a normal operating cycle longer than one year are also classified as current assets. An example of this type of trade receivable is accounts receivable for appliances and furniture that can be paid for in installments over a period greater than one year. Nontrade receivables due more than one year after balance sheet date should be classified in a noncurrent asset account, such as other assets. When both are due within a year, they are classified as current assets, with trade receivables generally listed before nontrade receivables. Both are listed after temporary investments, because they tend to be less liquid than temporary investments, and before merchandise inventory, because they tend to be more liquid than inventories and prepaid expenses. Trade receivables are reported net of the allowance for uncollectible accounts. A typical current asset section of a balance sheet for a merchandising-type organization is illustrated in Exhibit 15.1.

Control of Accounts Receivables and Sales Transactions

To control accounts receivable, detailed information concerning the balance owed by each credit customer or client is required. This information can be maintained in a ledger that has an account for each customer or client. Such a ledger is called a **subsidiary ledger** because it supports the totals posted to the accounts receivable account in the general ledger. The accounts receivable account in this case is referred to as a **control account,** and its balance should equal the sum of the balances in the subsidiary ledger if the same data have been posted to both.

Assume that summaries of customers' balances at the beginning of a month, credit sales for the month, and collections of accounts receivable for the month showed the following:

Customer balances (beginning of month):	
Dack Corp.	$ 6,000
Hack Corp.	4,200
Tack Corp.	1,600
Zack Corp.	5,500
Total	$17,300

Credit Sales		Collections of Accounts Receivable	
Mack Corp.	$ 8,400	Dack Corp.	$ 6,000
Dack Corp.	3,600	Hack Corp.	4,200
Rack Corp.	2,800	Tack Corp.	1,600
Zack Corp.	4,500	Total	$11,800
Total	$19,300		

Exhibit 15.2 shows the entries for credit sales and collection of accounts receivable and illustrates the relevant general and subsidiary ledger accounts after these transactions are posted. The summaries of credit sales and collections of accounts receivable were used to prepare the general journal entries and to post to the subsidiary ledger accounts. The control account, accounts receivable, was posted from the general journal. The exhibit also shows a schedule of accounts receivable balances, which was prepared from the information in the subsidiary ledger after the posting was completed for the month. Note that the balance ($24,800) in the control account agrees with the sum of the customers' balances in the schedule. This indicates that the company most likely has correctly recorded and posted sales and collection transactions for that month.

Exhibit 15.2

General Journal

Accounts Receivable	19,300	
Sales		19,300
To record sales on account based on daily summary of sales.		
Cash	11,800	
Accounts Receivable		11,800
To record collections on account based on daily summary of collections.		

General Ledger

	Accounts Receivable		
Balance	17,300	Collections	11,800
Sales	19,300		

(New balance: $24,800)

Subsidiary Ledger of Accounts Receivable

Dack Corp.

Date	Explanation	Dr.	Cr.	Bal.
	Balance			6,000
	Sale	3,600		9,600
	Collection		6,000	3,600

Hack Corp.

Date	Explanation	Dr.	Cr.	Bal.
	Balance			4,200
	Collection		4,200	—0—

Mack Corp.

	Sale	8,400		8,400

Rack Corp.

	Sale	2,800		2,800

Tack Corp.

	Balance			1,600
	Collection		1,600	—0—

Zack Corp.

	Balance			5,500
	Sale	4,500		10,000

Schedule of Accounts Receivable
End of Month

Dack Corp.	$ 3,600
Mack Corp.	8,400
Rack Corp.	2,800
Zack Corp.	10,000
	$24,800

Valuation of Receivables

All receivables should be valued at the **present value** (that is, the current cash equivalent) of the payments required to settle the debtor's obligation in full. The present
value of trade receivables due within customary credit terms is their face amount
because interest normally is not charged. The present value of nontrade receivables
will be the face amount if an interest rate is stated. If an interest rate is not stated,
however, the implied interest must be calculated and deducted from the face amount
to determine the present value. (The problem of accounting for interest-bearing and
non-interest-bearing receivables is discussed in Unit 16.)

   Trade receivables are reported on the balance sheet at their **net realizable value,**
that is, at their face amount less a provision for uncollectible accounts. Even though
the credit worthiness of prospective customers may be checked carefully before sales
are made, and sound collection policies used, some accounts and notes eventually will
prove uncollectible. The amount likely to be realized in cash is the relevant figure for
users of financial statements. In Exhibit 15.1 the face amount of the trade notes and
accounts receivables was $165,000, and the provision for uncollectible accounts was
$7,500. Thus, the net realizable value of trade receivables included in current assets
was $157,500.

Losses from Uncollectible Accounts

Companies that regularly sell merchandise on credit expect to have some losses from
uncollectible customers' accounts. Under the matching principle, losses from uncollectible accounts should be assigned to expense in the same accounting period the
sales revenue is realized. However, the determination that an account is uncollectible
is often not made until a later period. Thus, in order to apply the matching principle,
the expense for uncollectible accounts is normally estimated at the end of the accounting period.

Percentage of Sales Method   With the **percentage of sales method** of estimating uncollectible accounts expense, a specific percentage is applied to the appropriate sales
figure. The percentage to be applied is determined from the company's past experience with losses from uncollectible accounts. To match the loss against appropriate
revenue more precisely, the percentage should be applied only to net credit sales,
because only credit sales can prove uncollectible. In practice, however, the percentage is sometimes applied to gross sales (cash and credit) or net sales (gross sales less
sales discounts, returns, and allowances). If there are only a few cash sales or discounts, returns, and allowances, or if there is a relatively constant relationship between credit sales and cash sales, these alternative practices are acceptable; and only
minor, if any, distortions in net income will result. Note that the percentage of sales
method emphasizes the measurement of net income because an estimate of the portion
of the current period's sales expected to be uncollectible is made and charged to
expense.

The entry to record uncollectible accounts expense requires a charge to an expense account and a credit to a contra or offset account titled "allowance for uncollectible accounts." At the time the estimate is made, the specific accounts that will prove uncollectible are not known. Thus, the accounts receivable account should not be credited directly. Only after a particular account is determined to be uncollectible is accounts receivable credited; in addition, the contra account is debited. Expenses cannot be charged to write off the uncollectible account because the expense was recorded earlier when uncollectible accounts expense for the period was estimated.

Assume that a company reported gross sales of $800,000; sales discounts of $10,000; and sales returns and allowances of $5,000. Also assume that the expense for uncollectible accounts is estimated at 1 percent of net sales. The amount recorded as uncollectible accounts expense at the end of the accounting period will be $7,850 [($800,000 − 10,000 − 5,000) × 1%]. The entry required will be:

Uncollectible Accounts Expense	7,850	
Allowance for Uncollectible Accounts		7,850
To record estimate of uncollectible accounts		
expense for the period.		

Percentage of Receivables Method   The **percentage of receivables method** emphasizes the measurement of the net realizable value of accounts receivable. First, an uncollectible account rate based on past experience is applied to the ending balance of trade receivables. The result is an estimate of the total amount of trade receivables expected to be uncollectible. Then, this amount is adjusted for any balance in the allowance account at the time of the estimate. A credit balance in the allowance account is deducted from the estimated amount of uncollectible accounts; a debit balance is added. (A debit balance can arise as write-offs of uncollectible accounts occur during the period and before the adjustment for uncollectible accounts expense is recorded at the end of the period.) After the adjusting entry for uncollectible accounts is recorded, the balance in the allowance account will be equal to the total amount of the trade receivables expected to be uncollectible.

Assume that a company estimates uncollectible accounts at 5 percent of ending trade receivables. If ending trade receivables for the current period are $160,000, the balance desired in the allowance for uncollectible accounts will be $8,000 ($160,000 × 5%). If the allowance account has a credit balance of $600 before adjustment, the amount of the adjusting entry will be $7,400 ($8,000 − 600):

Uncollectible Accounts Expense	7,400	
Allowance for Uncollectible Accounts		7,400
To record provision for uncollectible accounts.		

Aging Trade Receivables   Applying a flat rate to the total ending trade receivables does not take into account that customer account balances may vary widely in amount and in length of time outstanding. The longer a customer's account or note balance is outstanding, the greater becomes the possibility of noncollection. A more accurate estimate of the net realizable value of trade receivables, then, is obtained by *aging the receivables* and applying a different uncollectible accounts rate to each age group. With this **aging the receivables method,** customers' balances are analyzed to determine the dollar amount of each outstanding invoice that falls into various age groups established by the company. Lower rates are applied to the receivables outstanding for shorter periods of time, and higher rates to receivables outstanding for longer periods of time. All rates and age groups are based on the company's past experience.

The following is an example of an aging schedule for trade receivables. After determining that a balance of $7,600 is desired in the allowance for uncollectible accounts, a credit balance of $600 in the allowance account is deducted to determine the amount of the adjusting entry, $7,000 ($7,600 − 600).

Trade Receivables Aging Schedule

Length of Time Balance Is Outstanding	Amount of Receivables	Uncollectible Accounts Rate	Balance Needed in Allowance Account
0–30 days	$ 80,000	1%	$ 800
31–60 days	40,000	2%	800
61–120 days	30,000	10%	3,000
Over 120 days	10,000	30%	3,000
Totals	$160,000		$7,600

Uncollectible Accounts Expense	7,000	
Allowance for Uncollectible Accounts		7,000
To record provision for uncollectible accounts.		

Comparing Methods   A company must choose which of these three methods of estimating uncollectible accounts it will apply. Assume the company has net sales of $785,000; ending trade receivables of $160,000; and a credit balance of $600 in the allowance account before adjustment. The charges to uncollectible accounts expense and the net realizable value of trade receivables (after the adjusting entry) are summarized in the following chart. Note that the figures in the uncollectible accounts expense column and those in the net realizable value of trade receivables column vary according to which method is used. The accountant must judge which method most accurately measures net income and financial position for the company.

Method of Estimating Uncollectible Accounts	Balance in Trade Receivables	Balance in Allowance Account*	Net Realizable Value of Trade Receivables	Uncollectible Accounts Expense
Percentage of sales	$160,000	$8,450	$151,550	$7,850
Percentage of receivables	160,000	8,000	152,000	7,400
Aging of receivables	160,000	7,600	152,400	7,000

*$7,850 + 600 = $8,450; $7,400 + 600 = $8,000; $7,000 + 600 = $7,600

Accounting for Uncollectible Accounts

When uncollectible accounts expense is estimated at the end of the accounting period, a contra or offset account (allowance for uncollectible accounts) is credited. The credit to the allowance account decreases the net realizable value of trade receivables. Assume that a company has balances of $125,000 and $300 in accounts receivable and the allowance account, respectively, before an adjusting entry of $4,700 for uncollectible accounts. Note that the net realizable value of accounts receivable decreases $4,700 as a result of the $4,700 increase in the allowance account balance:

	Before Adjusting Entry	After Adjusting Entry
Accounts Receivable	$125,000	$125,000
Less: Allowance for Uncollectible Accounts	300	5,000
Net realizable value of Accounts Receivable	$124,700	$120,000

A contra account is used when the uncollectible accounts adjusting entry is recorded because the specific accounts or notes that will prove uncollectible are not yet known. When the company decides that an account is uncollectible, an authorization to write off the account is prepared. The entry for the write-off includes a charge to the allowance account and credits to the accounts receivable control account and the customer's account in the subsidiary ledger. Assume a company writes off the uncollectible account of Kann Corp. of $850. The entry for the write-off would be:

Allowance for Uncollectible Accounts	850	
Accounts Receivable—Kann Corp.		850

To write off a customer's uncollectible account.

Note that the net realizable value of trade receivables is not affected by the write-off entry. Both accounts receivable and the allowance account are decreased by the same amount:

	Before Write-off	After Write-off
Accounts Receivable	$125,000	$124,150
Less: Allowance for Uncollectible Accounts	5,000	4,150
Net realizable value of Accounts Receivable	$120,000	$120,000

Sometimes accounts that have been written off as uncollectible are collected at a later date. When this occurs, an entry is made to reverse the original write-off of the account, thus correcting the books. Then a regular entry is made recording the collection of a payment on a customer's account. Assume that the Kann Corp. account, previously written off, is collected. The entries to reverse the write-off and to record the cash receipt would be:

Accounts Receivable—Kann Corp.	850	
Allowance for Uncollectible Accounts		850

To reverse entry writing off customer's account.

Cash	850	
Accounts Receivable—Kann Corp.		850

To record payment on customer's account.

Reporting Trade Receivables and Uncollectible Accounts Expense

Losses from uncollectible accounts are normally classified as a general and administrative expense because they are viewed as an expense of selling on credit. The re-

sponsibility for authorizing write-offs is usually given to a company officer not connected with the sales function. Better internal control is achieved by fixing such
responsibility outside the sales function. Instead of reporting losses from uncollectible
accounts as an operating expense, some companies deduct them from gross sales
revenue. This procedure is based on the premise that revenue is not realized unless
the sales price of the merchandise is eventually collected.

Accounts receivable are reported on the balance sheet at their net realizable
value, that is, net of the allowance for uncollectible accounts. The net realizable value
is the amount of cash the company expects to eventually collect from balances owed
by customers.

Assume a company reported the following balances before estimating uncollectible accounts for the current period:

Accounts Receivable	$150,000
Allowance for Uncollectible Accounts (credit balance)	800
Sales	850,000
Sales Discounts	7,000
Sales Returns and Allowances	13,000

If the company estimates uncollectible accounts at 1 percent of net sales, the
adjusted balance of the allowance account is determined as follows:

Uncollectible Accounts Expense [1% × $850,000 − 7,000 − 13,000]	$8,300
Add: credit balance in allowance account	800
Adjusted balance of allowance account	$9,100

The net realizable value of accounts receivable of $140,900 ($150,000 − 9,100) can
be reported on the balance sheet by either of the two methods illustrated in Exhibit
15.3.

Exhibit 15.3

Method 1		
Current Assets:		
Cash		$ xxxx
Accounts receivable	$150,000	
Less: Allowance for uncollectible accounts	9,100	140,900

Method 2		
Current Assets:		
Cash		$ xxxx
Accounts receivable (net of provision for uncollectible accounts of $9,100)		140,900

REVIEW PROBLEM

The Ranke Corporation trial balance at December 31, 19x7, included the following balances:

Accounts Receivable	$ 240,000
Allowance for Uncollectible Accounts (debit balance)	1,100
Sales	1,300,000
Sales Discounts	10,000
Sales Returns and Allowances	15,000

Required   1. Calculate uncollectible accounts expense for 19x7 and the net realizable value of accounts receivable at December 31, 19x7, if the company estimates uncollectible accounts at:
    a.   1% of net sales
    b.   5% of ending accounts receivable
  2. Assume an aging schedule indicates that a balance of $13,500 is needed in the allowance for uncollectible accounts at December 31, 19x7, and prepare the necessary adjusting entry.
  3. Prepare the entry to write off $3,800 of uncollectible accounts on March 31, 19x8.
  4. Prepare the entries on June 1, 19x8, to record the collection of a $600 account written off on March 31, 19x8.

Solution to review problem

1.

	Percentage of Sales Method*	Percentage of Receivables Method**
Accounts receivable	$240,000	$240,000
Allowance for uncollectible accounts after adjustment	11,650	12,000
Net realizable value of accounts receivable	$228,350	$228,000
Uncollectible accounts expense	$ 12,750	$ 13,100

*($1,300,000 − 10,000 − 15,000) × 1% = $12,750; $12,750 credit − $1,100 debit = $11,650 credit balance in allowance account.
**$240,000 × 5% = $12,000 credit balance needed in allowance account; $12,000 + 1,100 = $13,100 added to allowance account and charged to expense to yield $12,000 credit balance.

2.	Dec. 31, 19x7	Uncollectible Accounts Expense	14,600	
		Allowance for Uncollectible		
		Accounts		14,600
		To record addition to allowance for uncollectible accounts to yield $13,500 balance ($13,500 + 1,100 = $14,600).		

3.	Mar. 31, 19x8	Allowance for Uncollectible Accounts	3,800	
		Accounts Receivable		3,800
		To record write-off of uncollectible accounts.		

4.	June 1, 19x8	Accounts Receivable	600	
		Allowance for Uncollectible		
		Accounts		600
		To reverse entry writing off customer accounts.		
		Cash	600	
		Accounts Receivable		600
		To record collection of amount previously written off.		

SUMMARY

The distinction between trade and nontrade receivables and the use of a subsidiary ledger to control accounts receivable balances were discussed in this unit. The main emphasis of the unit, however, was on the measurement of the net realizable value of trade receivables and of losses from uncollectible accounts and on the accounting for uncollectible accounts.

REVIEW QUESTIONS

15-1 Distinguish between trade and nontrade receivables, and identify the major types of each.

15-2 How are trade and nontrade receivables classified on the balance sheet?

15-3 Explain how a subsidiary ledger can be used to control accounts receivable and provide useful information to management.

15-4   How are trade and nontrade receivables valued on the balance sheet?

15-5   What is meant by the term *losses from uncollectible accounts?* Why are these losses normally estimated and recorded as an expense at the end of the accounting period? How is uncollectible accounts expense classified on an income statement?

15-6   Indicate three methods of estimating uncollectible accounts and uncollectible accounts expense. Which method emphasizes the determination of net income, and which methods emphasize the valuation of accounts receivable?

15-7   How is uncollectible accounts expense estimated if (a) the percentage of sales method is used and (b) the percentage of receivables method is used?

15-8   Describe the aging of receivables method of estimating uncollectible accounts and uncollectible accounts expense.

15-9   **a.**   What entry is required when an account is determined to be uncollectible?
         b.   How would a company account for the subsequent recovery of an account that was written off earlier?

EXERCISES

15-1   Clayburne, Inc., reported customers' balances of $140,000 and a credit balance of $7,500 in the allowance for uncollectible accounts at the beginning of 19x6. During 19x6 credit sales totaled $800,000; collections on customers' accounts totaled $780,000; and accounts with balances totaling $7,300 were written off as uncollectible. At the end of 19x6 uncollectible accounts expense was estimated at 1% of credit sales.

Required   **a.**   Determine the ending balances in the accounts receivable control account and the allowance for uncollectible accounts.
         b.   Calculate the net realizable value of accounts receivable at December 31, 19x6.
         c.   Prepare a partial balance sheet at December 31, 19x6.
         d.   How can the company prove the accuracy of the recording and posting of transactions affecting accounts receivable?
         e.   Prepare the entries to write off the uncollectible accounts and to record the adjusting entry for them.

15-2   Selected accounts from the trial balance of the Flim-Flam Company as of December 31 are as follows:

Accounts Receivable	$ 65,000
Allowance for Uncollectible Accounts (credit balance)	200
Sales	256,000
Sales Returns and Allowances	4,000
Sales Discounts	2,000

Required   Calculate the charge to uncollectible accounts expense if the company uses the following methods to estimate uncollectible accounts: (a) 1% of gross sales, (b) 1% of net sales, (c) 4% of accounts receivable.

15-3   On April 30 the Shadey Sales Company aged its accounts receivable. The results and the uncollectible percentage (based on past experience) for each grouping are:

Not yet due	$42,500	1%
0–30 days past due	14,800	2
31–60 days past due	8,200	5
61–90 days past due	5,400	10
Over 90 days past due	3,600	50

Required   Assume a debit balance of $150 is shown in the allowance for uncollectible accounts on April 30, and prepare the necessary adjusting entry for uncollectible accounts.

15-4   The Tourine Corp. estimates uncollectible accounts at 4% of outstanding trade receivables at the end of the accounting period. During 19x6 accounts totaling $5,850 were written off as uncollectible; but written-off accounts totaling $700 were subsequently collected. The balance of the allowance for uncollectible accounts at the beginning of 19x6 was $5,900. The balances of the receivables at the end of 19x6 were:

Notes Receivable	$ 20,000
Accounts Receivable	130,000
Nontrade Notes Receivable	10,000

Required   **a.**   Prepare all entries for 19x6 to account for the uncollectible accounts.
           b.   Prepare a partial balance sheet at December 31, 19x6.

PROBLEMS

15-1   The following data were taken from the general ledger of Shifty Sales Company at December 31, 19x8:

Accounts receivable	$ 45,000
Allowance for uncollectible accounts (credit balance)	350
Sales	180,000
Sales returns and allowances	1,200
Sales discounts	1,500

On July 16, 19x9, the account balance of U.S. Gyp Co. for $420 was determined to be uncollectible. On December 18, 19x9, in the spirit of Christmas, U.S. Gyp Co. paid the $420 balance.

Required   **a.**   Prepare the adjusting entry for uncollectible accounts if the company estimates them at (1) 1% of net sales and (2) 4% of accounts receivable.

b. Prepare the entry to write off the U.S. Gyp Co. account.

c. Prepare the entries to record the recovery of the U.S. Gyp Co. account.

15-2 The records of Disco Corp. at December 31, 19x6, showed the following information:

Accounts receivable, January 1, 19x6	$125,000
Allowance for uncollectible accounts, January 1, 19x6 (credit balance)	5,400
Credit sales	600,000
Cash sales	240,000
Collections of amounts owed by customers	585,000
Accounts written off as uncollectible	5,800
Merchandise returned by customers who purchased the merchandise on credit	5,000

Required **a.** Calculate the following:
   (1) accounts receivable at December 31, 19x6
   (2) uncollectible accounts expense for 19x6 if estimated at 1% of credit sales
   (3) allowance for uncollectible accounts at December 31, 19x6, after the write-off of uncollectible accounts and the adjusting entry for part (2)

b. Prepare the following:
   (1) a partial balance sheet at December 31, 19x6
   (2) a partial income statement for 19x6

15-3 The records and documents of Steifel Company showed the following at the end of 19x3:

a. The petty cash fund balance was $300; the fund was replenished on December 31.

b. The bank statement showed a checking account balance of $3,150 at December 31.

c. A comparison of the bank statement and the company cash records showed deposits in transit and outstanding checks of $400 and $720, respectively, at December 31.

d. Temporary investments held at December 31 had a cost of $10,740 and a market value of $10,400.

e. Trade notes and accounts receivable balances were $20,000 and $160,000, respectively, at the end of 19x3.

f. The allowance accounts for the valuation of temporary investments and for uncollectible accounts had a balance of $200 each before adjustment.

Steifel Company estimates uncollectible accounts expense at 5% of the outstanding trade receivables balance and uses the lower-of-cost-or-market method to value temporary investments. Interest at 8% has accrued for two months on the $20,000 trade note receivable.

Required Prepare a partial balance sheet and a partial income statement at the end of 19x3.

15-4   The records of Wingate, Inc., showed the following balances at the end of 19x2:

Accounts receivable	$120,000
Allowance for uncollectible accounts (before the write-off of uncollectible accounts for 19x2)	5,500
Sales (90% on credit)	650,000
Sales discounts (on credit sales only)	10,000
Sales returns and allowances (90% on credit sales)	15,000

The company treasurer recently completed an analysis of the outstanding accounts and determined that accounts totaling $7,000 are uncollectible and should be written off. On December 31 the company had received a check for $1,200 from a customer whose account had been written off as uncollectible in 19x1; however, this check has not yet been recorded and is not included in the balances given for the end of 19x2. Uncollectible accounts expense is estimated at 1% of net credit sales.

Required   **a.**   Prepare the entries to record the following transactions:
   (1)   the collection of the account previously written off
   (2)   the write-off of the uncollectible accounts
   (3)   the uncollectible accounts expense for 19x2
   b.   Prepare a partial income statement to reflect net sales for 19x2.
   c.   Prepare a partial balance sheet to reflect the realizable value of accounts receivable at December 31, 19x2.
   d.   If an aging schedule indicates that $6,000 of the accounts receivable are likely to be uncollectible, what action should be taken in view of your answers to parts a, b, and c?

Unit 16
Notes Receivable

Worry: the interest paid by those who borrow trouble.

Judge George W. Lyon,
The New York Times Book Review, *October 23, 1932*

Companies receive promissory notes as a result of trade and nontrade transactions. This unit examines the procedures for accounting for these notes and the related interest revenue, for reporting notes on the financial statements, and for discounting notes receivable.

Performance Objectives

Upon completing this unit you should be able to:

1. define and use the accounting terms introduced in this unit.
2. describe:
   a. what constitutes the balance to be reported for notes receivable
   b. how the balance of notes receivable is measured and reported
3. determine:
   a. the present value of interest-bearing or non-interest-bearing notes receivable
   b. the maturity value for interest-bearing or non-interest-bearing notes receivable
   c. the cash proceeds from a discounted note receivable
   d. the amount due for a dishonored note receivable
4. identify or prepare the journal entries for notes receivable and related interest revenue transactions.

Calculation of Interest

Interest is the amount charged for the use of money. The basic formula for the calculation of interest is:

$$I \quad = \quad P \quad \times R \times T$$
$$\text{interest} = \text{principal} \times \text{rate} \times \text{time}$$

The interest rate stated is an annual rate, so if the time period is more or less than one year, the rate must be adjusted. If the term of the note is stated in years, the factor for time in the interest formula will be a whole number. For example, a $10,000, 8%, 2-year note dated April 10, 19x2, has an annual interest charge of $800 ($10,000 × 8% × 1) or $1,600 for the 2-year term ($10,000 × 8% × 2). The note will mature, that is, be due, on the same day two years later; thus, the **maturity date** is April 10, 19x4. The interest will be payable annually or at the maturity date, as stipulated in the terms of the note. Most short-term notes require payment of interest at the maturity date.

If the term of the note is stated in months, the time factor in the interest formula will be a fraction with a denominator of 12. The maturity date will be determined by counting forward the exact number of months to the same day as that in the date of the note. For example, a $10,000, 8%, 3-month note dated April 10, 19x3, has an interest charge of $200 ($10,000 × 8% × 3/12) and matures on July 10, 19x2.

When the term of the note is stated in days, a common business practice is to use a 360-day year. This practice simplifies the computation of interest. Thus, the denominator for the time factor in the interest formula is 360. Government securities, however, use a 365-day year. To determine the maturity date of a note with a term stated in days, the exact number of days must be counted. For example, a $10,000, 8%, 90-day note dated April 10, 19x2, has a maturity date of July 9, 19x2, because July 9 is the nintieth day after the date of the note. The date of the note is not included in the 90 days. The interest charge for the note is $200 ($10,000 × 8% × 90/360).

Using a 360-day year causes interest to be the same for both 90-day and 3-month, 8%, $10,000 notes. However, the 90-day note was due one day earlier than the 3-month note because the exact number of days was counted to determine the maturity date of the 90-day note. Using the 360-day year also makes the effective interest rate slightly higher than the stated rate of interest.

Accounting for Interest-Bearing Notes

A **promissory note** is an unconditional promise in writing to pay a definite sum of money on demand or at a definite future date. If an interest rate is specified, the note is said to be **interest-bearing;** if it is not specified, the note is said to be **non-interest-bearing.** The person who signs the note is called the **maker** of the note; the person to whom payment is to be made is called the **payee.** Promissory notes usually are **negotiable,** that is, they can be transferred by endorsement from the payee to another party.

Promissory notes are occasionally received from customers or clients when merchandise is sold or services performed. However, most sale or service transactions initially result in charges to customers' open accounts (accounts receivable). Only later, if a customer is unable to pay within the regular credit terms, is a promissory note issued in exchange for the open account charge. A note tells the seller when he can collect the amount due; it also establishes an interest charge and gives the seller an instrument that can be converted into cash before the note matures.

Exhibit 16.1 illustrates a promissory note. The maker of the note is Romeo Corp. and the payee is Juliet Company. The note is interest-bearing, and the **face value,** or principal, of the note is $3,000. (For non-interest-bearing notes, the face value is the same as the maturity value.) Assume that Juliet Company sold merchandise with a sales price of $3,000 to Romeo Corp. and accepted an 8%, 3-month note dated November 1, 19x4, the date of the sale. The entry to record the sale on the books of Juliet Company would be:

Nov. 1	Notes receivable	3,000	
	Sales		3,000
	To record note received on sale of merchandise.		

Exhibit 16.1

$3,000.00   Detroit, Michigan   November 1, 19x4

_____ 90 days _____ after date <u>we</u> promise to pay to

The order of ___Juliet Company_____

_____ Three Thousand and no/100 - Dollars

Payable at ___Detroit City Bank_____

With interest at ___8%_____

Romeo Corp.

No. ___41___   Due ___January 30, 19x5___   ___H. Romeo_____, Treasurer

If the accounting period ends before a note matures, an adjusting entry for accrued interest revenue is necessary. Assume that the accounting period for the payee, Juliet Company, ends on December 31. The adjusting entry to accrue interest for 60 days (November 1–December 31) would be:

Dec. 31	Interest receivable	40	
	Interest revenue		40
	To accrue interest on the Romeo Corp.		
	note for 60 days ($3,000 × 8%		
	× 60/360 = $40).		

When the note matures on January 30, 19x5, the entry to record the collection of the note and the interest requires that interest revenue for the balance of the term of the note be recognized and the receivable for the accrued interest at the end of the previous accounting period be eliminated.

Jan. 30	Cash	3,060	
	Notes receivable		3,000
	Interest receivable		40
	Interest revenue		20
	To record collection of note and		
	interest: $40 accrued on 12/31/x4		
	and $20 for Jan. 1–30, 19x5		
	($3,000 × 8% × 30/360 = $20).		

The following diagram depicts the face value, maturity value, and the recognition of interest revenue for the interest-bearing note in Exhibit 16.1.

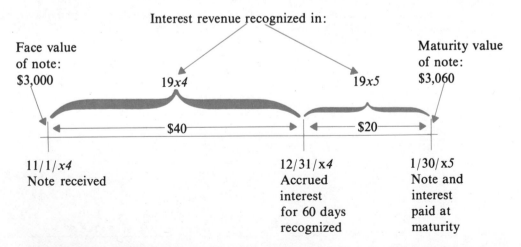

If the maker of the note does not pay at the maturity date, the note is said to be **defaulted** or **dishonored**. When the default occurs, an entry should be made transferring the face amount of the note and the interest due (that is, the *maturity value* of the note) to accounts receivable for *trade notes* (those arising from primary business activities) or to a special account, defaulted (or dishonored) notes receivable, for either *trade* or *nontrade notes*. Assume that the note in the previous example was defaulted at maturity; the entry to record the default would be:

Jan. 30	Accounts receivable (or defaulted notes receivable)	3,060	
	Notes receivable		3,000
	Interest receivable		40
	Interest revenue		20
	To record default on customer's note.		

Additional interest at either the rate specified by the original note or the legal rate allowed can be charged to the maker for the period between the original maturity date and the eventual date of collection. If the defaulted note is not collected, it must be written off as an uncollectible account.

Accounting for Non-Interest-Bearing Notes

When notes are issued without interest being stated in their terms, the implied interest must be determined in accord with APB Opinion No. 21. The implied interest is recorded in a contra or offset account, **discount on notes receivable.** This practice is required so that non-interest-bearing notes are recorded at their present value (that is, their current cash equivalent, which excludes interest). When a non-interest-bearing note is issued by a customer to acquire merchandise, services, other assets or benefits, or to settle an outstanding obligation, the interest is added to the purchase price or the amount of the obligation in order to determine the face amount (or principal) of the note. Exhibit 16.2 is an example of a non-interest-bearing note. The note was issued by Romeo Corp. to settle an outstanding account for $3,000; 8% interest for three months is included in the face amount of the note. Thus, the face amount of the note is $3,060 [$3,000 + ($3,000 × 8% × 3/12) = $3,060].

The entry on the books of Juliet Company for the acceptance of the note would be:

Nov. 1	Notes receivable	3,060	
	Discount on notes receivable		60
	Accounts receivable		3,000
	To record acceptance of non-interest-bearing note to apply to customer's account.		

Exhibit 16.2

$3,060.00   Detroit, Michigan   Nov. 1, 19x4

_____ 90 days _____ after date we promise to pay to

The order of _____ Juliet Corp. _____

_____ Three Thousand Sixty and no/100 - Dollars

Payable at _____ Detroit City Bank _____

Without interest

                                            Romeo Corp.

                                            H. Romeo

No.   42   Due   Jan. 30, 19x5   ,   Treasurer

The account, discount on notes receivable, represents unearned interest revenue. As the note is held, the interest revenue is earned. Unearned interest revenue must be transferred to interest revenue when the note is collected or at the end of the accounting period if that occurs before the note matures. Assume that the accounting period for Juliet Company ends on December 31. The entries to recognize interest revenue on December 31, 19x4, and to record the collection of the note and the recognition of the remaining interest revenue on January 30, 19x5, would be:

Dec. 31	Discount on notes receivable	40	
	Interest revenue		40
	To recognize interest earned by end of period ($60 × 60/90 = $40).		
Jan. 30	Cash	3,060	
	Discount on notes receivable	20	
	Cash		3,060
	Interest revenue		20
	To record collection of note and recognize balance of unearned interest ($60 − 40 = $20).		

The following diagram depicts the face value, maturity value, and the recognition of interest revenue for the non-interest-bearing note in Exhibit 16.2.

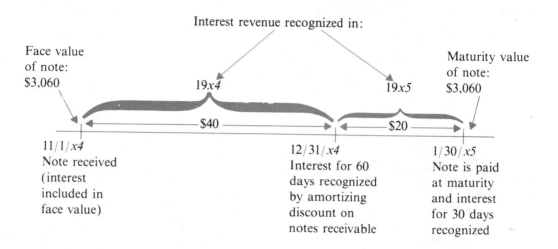

Discounting Notes Receivable

If a note is negotiable, it can be transferred or sold to another party. When notes are sold to banks or others before maturity to obtain cash, a **discount charge** (that is, interest) is deducted from the maturity value of the note by the banks or others to determine the cash proceeds from the sale. Thus, the sale of the note is referred to as **discounting notes receivable.** Usually notes will be discounted "with recourse," that is, the endorser is liable for payment of the note if the maker of the note defaults at maturity. This type of obligation is called a **contingent liability** and requires footnote disclosure. (Accounting for contingencies is discussed further in Unit 24.)

The discount charge is calculated on the maturity value of the note. The maturity value of an interest-bearing note is its face value plus interest due at maturity. The maturity value of a non-interest-bearing note is the same as the face value because interest has been included in the face value. Assume that a $4,000, 8%, 90-day note dated June 1, 19*x4,* is discounted at a bank at 9% on July 1, 19*x4.* The holding period for the payee of the note starts the day after the date of the note, in this case, June 2. The note is discounted on the thirtieth day (29 days in June and 1 day in July), and thus, the holding period for the payee is 30 days. The holding period for the party accepting the note when it is discounted begins the date after it is discounted. In this example, the holding period for the bank is 60 days (July 2 until the maturity date, August 30); the discount charge will be for this 60-day holding period. The cash proceeds from discounting the note are determined as follows:

Face value of note	$4,000.00
Interest due at maturity ($4,000 × 8% × 90/360)	80.00
Maturity value of note	$4,080.00
Discount charge ($4,080 × 9% × 60/360)	61.20
Cash proceeds	$4,018.80

The following diagram depicts the allocation of interest between the designated payee on the note and the bank that discounts it:

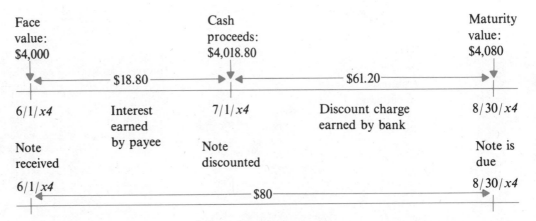

Interest for 90 days to be
paid by maker of note

The difference between the face value of the note and the cash proceeds is recorded as interest revenue (or expense). Interest revenue represents the excess of the interest due at maturity over the discount charge; interest expense represents the excess of the discount charge over the interest due at maturity. The entry to record the discounting of the note in the example would be:

July 1	Cash	4,018.80	
	Notes receivable		4,000.00
	Interest revenue		18.80
	To record discounting of note.		

If the note is paid to the bank at maturity, no further entry is required. However, if the maker of the note defaults, the bank will seek payment from the payee. Because it must make extra collection efforts, the bank usually charges the payee a protest or collection fee. When the payee records his payment to the bank, he adds this protest fee to the amount the maker was supposed to pay. Assume the maker of the note in the previous example defaults, and the bank collects the amount due plus a $10 protest fee from the payee. The entry for the payment to the bank would be:

Aug. 30	Accounts receivable (or defaulted notes receivable)	4,090	
	Cash		4,090
	To record payment to bank of maturity value ($4,080) plus protest fee ($10) on defaulted customer's note which has been discounted.		

Interest on the face amount of the note at the stated rate of interest or at the rate permitted by state law from the date of default to the date of collection can also be charged. If the amount becomes uncollectible, the account is written off.

Reporting Notes Receivable

Trade notes are classified as current assets because they are due within one year after balance sheet date or within the normal operating cycle if longer. Nontrade notes are classified as current assets if they mature within one year after balance sheet date, or as noncurrent assets (that is, long-term investments or other assets) if they mature more than one year after. Any accrued interest on interest-bearing notes will be included in the same classification as the related notes.

The appropriate procedures for reporting notes receivable balances are illustrated in Exhibit 16.3. The assumptions made in preparing this exhibit are:

		Face Value of Note	Date of Note	Interest Rate	Terms of Note
1.	Notes receivable	$10,000	Oct. 1, 19x4	8%	6 months
2.	Nontrade notes receivable	5,150	Nov. 1, 19x4	*	3 months
3.	Defaulted notes receivable	1,000	Nov. 1, 19x4	8%	60 days
4.	Discounted note	10,000	Dec. 1, 19x4	9%	90 days

*Non-interest-bearing; balance of discount on notes receivable is $100 at December 31, 19x4.

All notes should be reported at their present value on the balance sheet. Interest-bearing notes are often reported at their face value, with any accrued interest reported separately. This procedure is illustrated for the first note receivable in Exhibit 16.3. The alternative approach is to report the notes and accrued interest as a single figure in order to indicate the present value of the notes at balance sheet date. To report non-interest-bearing notes at their present value, the balance of discount on notes receivable is deducted from the face value of the notes (see the second note receivable

Exhibit 16.3

Partial Balance Sheet
December 31, 19x4

Current Assets:
Notes receivable (see note 1)		$10,000
Nontrade notes receivable	$5,150	
Less: Discount on notes receivable	100	5,050
Interest receivable		200
Defaulted notes receivable		1,013

Notes

1. The company is contingently liable at December 31, 19x4, in the amount of $10,225 for a customer's note discounted at the bank.

Computations

Discount on notes receivable: see note (*) for the data given.
Interest receivable: $10,000 × 8% × 3/12 = $200.
Defaulted notes receivable: $1,000 + ($1,000 × 8% × 60/360) = $1,013.
Contingent liability for discounted note: $10,000 + ($10,000 × 9% × 90/360) = $10,225.

in Exhibit 16.3). The balance of discount on notes receivable represents interest still unearned at balance sheet date.

Defaulted notes receivable will be reported as a current or noncurrent asset depending on their probable date of collection (see the third note receivable in Exhibit 16.3). Notes that have been discounted, but have not yet matured, create a contingent liability to the endorser. This liability should be disclosed in the footnotes to the financial statements (see the footnote in Exhibit 16.3).

REVIEW PROBLEM

Gusto Corporation accepted the following notes during 19x7:

Mar. 1	Received an 8%, 60-day note for $3,000 from Havoc Company to apply to their overdue account.
June 1	Sold merchandise for $2,500 to Collosus Corp. in exchange for a 120-day, non-interest-bearing note for $2,575.
Oct. 1	Received a 4-month, non-interest-bearing note for $1,540 to apply to the overdue account for $1,500 of Magnus Company.
Nov. 1	Sold merchandise for $4,000 to Salisbury Corp. in exchange for a 9%, 3-month note.

The Havoc Company note was discounted at the bank on March 21 at 10%.

Required Prepare the entries necessary to:

1. accept the four notes.
2. discount the Havoc Company note on March 21 at 10%.
3. record the payment of the amount due on the Havoc Company note plus a protest fee of $15 if the note is defaulted by the maker.
4. collect the Collosus Corp. note.
5. recognize interest revenue at the end of the accounting period, December 31, 19x7.

Solution to review problem

1.	Mar. 1	Notes Receivable	3,000	
		Accounts Receivable		3,000
		To record note applied to customer's account.		
	June 1	Notes Receivable	2,575	
		Sales		2,500
		Discount on Notes Receivable		75
		To record note received for sale of merchandise.		
	Oct. 1	Notes Receivable	1,540	
		Accounts Receivable		1,500
		Discount on Notes Receivable		40
		To record note applied to customer's account.		
	Nov. 1	Notes Receivable	4,000	
		Sales		4,000
		To record note received for sale of merchandise.		
2.	Mar. 21	Cash	3,006.22	
		Notes Receivable		3,000.00
		Interest Revenue		6.22
		To record discounting of customer's note.		

Computation of cash proceeds:

Face value of note	$3,000.00
Interest at maturity ($3,000 × 8% × 60/360)	40.00
Maturity value of note	$3,040.00
Discount charge ($3,040 × 10% × 40/360)	33.78
Cash proceeds	$3,006.22

3.	Apr. 30	Accounts Receivable (or Defaulted Notes Receivable)	3,055	
		Cash		3,055
		To pay bank amount due ($3,040) plus protest fee ($15) on defaulted note that had been discounted.		

4.	Sept. 29	Cash	2,575	
		Discount on Notes Receivable	75	
		Notes Receivable		2,575
		Interest Revenue		75
		To record collection of note and recognize interest earned.		

5.	Dec. 31	Discount on Notes Receivable	30	
		Interest Revenue		30
		To recognize interest earned on Oct. 1 note ($40 × 3/4 = $30).		

	Dec. 31	Interest Receivable	60	
		Interest Revenue		60
		To recognize interest earned on Nov. 1 note ($4000 × 9% × 2/12 = $60).		

SUMMARY

This unit concentrated on the accounting, measurement, and financial reporting problems and practices of the payee for both interest-bearing and non-interest-bearing notes receivable. In Unit 24 the problems and practices for both types of notes from the viewpoint of the maker of the notes are examined.

REVIEW QUESTIONS

16-1 How is interest calculated on notes in business practice if the term of the note is stated in days?

16-2 How is the maturity date of a note determined if the term of the note is stated in (a) months and (b) days?

16-3   What is a promissory note? What does it mean if a note is "negotiable"?

16-4   Distinguish between an interest-bearing note and a non-interest-bearing note. How is implied interest on a non-interest-bearing note accounted for by the payee?

16-5   If the maker of a note defaults (dishonors the note), how does the payee account for the defaulted (dishonored) note?

16-6   When is interest usually recognized on short-term notes?

16-7   How can the payee of a note obtain cash immediately instead of waiting for payment at maturity?

16-8   Describe how the cash proceeds from a discounted note receivable are determined.

16-9   How are the following accounts reported on the balance sheet?

    a.   trade notes receivable
    b.   nontrade notes receivable
    c.   discount on notes receivable
    d.   defaulted notes receivable

16-10   Discounting a note receivable results in contingent liability for the payee. Explain why a contingent liability arises in this situation and how the contingent liability should be reported.

EXERCISES

16-1   Determine the maturity date and maturity value of the following notes:

    a.   6%, 1-year note for $2,500 dated August 5, 19x4
    b.   7%, 3-month note for $3,000 dated February 16, 19x4
    c.   8%, 60-day note for $1,500 dated March 11, 19x4

16-2   Record the following transactions on the books of the seller, Sword Corp.

July 1	Sold merchandise to Sabre Co.; accepted a 6%, 90-day note for the sales price of $800.
Sept. 29	Received payment from Sabre Co. in settlement of its note.

Prepare the entry on the books of Sword Corp. on Sept. 29 if Sabre Co. dishonors its note.

16-3   Crane Corporation accepted a 90-day, non-interest-bearing note for $8,160 on May 5, 19x3, for the sale of merchandise with a sales price of $8,000.

    Required   Prepare the entries to accept the note on May 5, 19x3, and to collect the note at maturity.

16-4 Farmer Company accepted the following notes during 19x2:

Oct. 2   Received a 4-month, non-interest-bearing note dated October 1, 19x2, for $5,100 to apply to the overdue account balance of $5,000 for Derry Company.

Nov. 2   Received a 90-day, 8% note dated November 1, 19x2, to apply to the overdue account balance of $4,000 for Crane Company.

Required   Prepare the entries to:

a. accept the notes on October 2 and November 1, 19x2.
b. recognize interest revenue at the end of the accounting period on December 31, 19x2.
c. collect the notes at maturity in 19x3.

16-5 Ponderosa Company received a 7%, 90-day note dated May 1, 19x3, for $4,000 for the sale of merchandise to J. D. Clyde Company on May 1, 19x3. The note was discounted at 8% at the Frontier Bank on May 31, 19x3.

Required   Determine the cash proceeds from discounting the note.

16-6 Record the following transactions on the books of the seller, Grady Company.

Aug. 15   Sold merchandise for $1,200 on open account to Flaherty, Inc.; credit terms are 2/10, n/30.

Sept. 15   Flaherty is unable to pay on time and issues a 6%, 60-day note for the balance due.

Sept. 25   Grady Company discounts the Flaherty note at the bank at 7%.

Oct. 25   Flaherty pays his note at the bank on time.

Prepare the entry on the books of the Grady Company if Flaherty, Inc., dishonors its note at maturity, and the bank collects the amount due plus a protest fee of $6 from the Grady Company.

PROBLEMS

16-1 Hamady, Inc., completed the following transactions during 19x6 and 19x7:

19x6

Mar. 2   Accepted a 60-day, 6%, $5,000 note dated March 1 from a customer in settlement of his past due account in the amount of $5,000.

Mar. 31   Discounted the note received on March 1 at 8% at the bank.

Apr. 30   The maker of the March 1 note defaulted on the note. Hamady paid the bank amount due plus a $10 protest fee.

May 3   Accepted a one-year, $20,000 non-interest-bearing note dated May 1 on the sale of excess land that had cost

	$11,500. Normally interest at 10% would be charged on this type of transaction.
Nov. 18	Received a 90-day, 7% note dated November 16 from a customer on the sale of merchandise for $8,000.
Dec. 1	Wrote off as uncollectible the amount due on the March 1 note. (Refer to the April 30 transaction for necessary information.)
Dec. 31	Recorded interest revenue on the May 1 and November 16 notes.
19x7	
May 1	Collected the amount due on the May 1 and November 16 notes. No reversing entries were made on January 1.

Required **a.** Prepare all entries required for these transactions.

  b. Prepare a partial balance sheet at December 31, 19x6.

16-2 In settlement of its account the Knight Company gave the Armor Corporation a 150-day, 6% note for $1,400 on October 16, 19x1. On December 16 the Armor Corporation discounted the note at 7% at the Medieval Bank.

On March 9, 19x2, when the note was due, the Knight Company dishonored its note. The Medieval Bank collected the amount due, plus a protest fee of $10, from the Armor Corporation.

On June 15, 19x2, the Armor Corporation determined that the amount due from the Knight Company was uncollectible. The Armor Corporation uses an estimated method for determining uncollectible accounts expense.

On September 5, 19x2, the Armor Corporation received a check for $1,487, which included additional interest of $42, from the Knight Company.

Required Make all the entries on the books of the payee, including any adjusting entries necessary, on December 31, 19x1.

16-3 Karlton Corp. accepted the following notes near the end of 19x6:

Note 1—an 8%, 90-day note for $6,500, dated November 1, 19x6, for the sale of merchandise.

Note 2—a 3-month note for $4,590, dated December 1, 19x6, for a past-due account balance of $4,500.

Required **a.** Prepare all entries necessary to account for the acceptance of the notes and the recognition of interest revenue for 19x6.

  b. Prepare a partial balance sheet and a partial income statement at the end of 19x6.

  c. Prepare the entries necessary to account for the collection of the notes at maturity.

  d. Prepare the entries necessary if both notes are dishonored at maturity. Also prepare the entries necessary if (1) note 1 is subsequently collected on March 1, 19x7, plus interest on the face value of the note since maturity and (2) note 2 is subsequently written off as uncollectible on August 20, 19x7.

16-4   The trial balance of Whiss Company at December 31, 19*x4*, included the following:

Notes Receivable	$ 8,000
Accounts Receivable	73,800
Allowance for Uncollectible Accounts (credit balance)	2,150
Nontrade Notes Receivable	13,200
Discount on Notes Receivable	1,200
Long-term Notes Receivable	20,000

The following information was obtained by the accountant regarding the notes and accounts receivable:

a.   The $8,000 note carries a 9% interest rate, is dated October 2, 19*x4*, and matures on January 30, 19*x5*.

b.   Accounts receivable includes an $1,800 account balance that is now considered to be uncollectible.

c.   Uncollectible accounts are estimated at 5 percent of the trade receivables outstanding at year-end.

d.   The $13,200 note is a non-interest-bearing, 1-year note dated April 1, 19*x4*.

e.   The $20,000 note is a 2-year note dated September 1, 19*x4;* the note is due in two equal installments of $10,000 each plus interest at 9% on the balance outstanding at September 1, 19*x5* and 19*x6*.

Required   (1)   Prepare all entries necessary at December 31, 19*x4*, as indicated by the information in a to e.

(2)   Prepare a partial balance sheet and a partial income statement at the end of 19*x4*.

Chapter 6

Inventories

Some problems of accounting for merchandise were discussed in earlier units. In this chapter we examine problems involving: accounting for merchandise purchases and sales under the perpetual inventory system, determining what should be included in inventory, assigning costs to inventory and cost of goods sold, valuing inventory, disclosing all relevant information regarding inventory, and estimating inventory balances.

Unit 17
Determining and Controlling Inventory Balances

A small error in the beginning is a great one in the end.

St. Thomas Aquinas, Concerning Being and Essence

Accounting for merchandise purchases under the periodic inventory system was examined in Unit 9. The perpetual inventory system, which provides better internal control, is examined in this unit. An entity's inventory balance should include all merchandise it has title to at balance sheet date. In this unit problems involved with identifying all the merchandise owned and the effects of errors in determining the inventory balance are discussed.

Performance Objectives

Upon completing this unit you should be able to:

1. define and use the accounting terms introduced in this unit.
2. describe:
    a. the distinctions between the periodic and perpetual inventory systems
    b. the advantages and disadvantages of the periodic and perpetual inventory systems
    c. what constitutes the ending inventory balance
    d. how errors in overstating and understating ending inventory affect cost of goods sold and income before taxes
3. prepare the journal entries to record merchandise purchase and sale transactions under both the periodic and perpetual inventory systems.
4. determine the correct ending inventory balance given data for merchandise balances and shipments.

The Perpetual Inventory System

The distinction between the periodic and perpetual inventory systems was explained briefly in Unit 9. Recall that under the **periodic system** the ending inventory is determined by a **physical** (that is, actual) **inventory** count at the end of the accounting period. Then, the cost of goods sold is determined using information on beginning inventory, purchases for the period, and the ending inventory balance. Under the **perpetual inventory system** a continuous record of the inventory balance is maintained. As purchases and sales occur, the inventory balance is updated on a perpetual inventory record card (see Figure 17.1). Also, entries to update the inventory account in the general ledger are made as each merchandise inflow and outflow occurs. A separate record card is maintained for each item carried in inventory by a company that uses the perpetual system.

Code No.: BP 01036							Item Name: Black pipe—1″ × 36″		
Location: Row A Rack 6		Order Point: 1,500					Order Size: 8,000		
Trans-action Date	Purchases			Sales			Balance		
	Quantity	Unit Cost	Total Cost	Quantity	Unit Cost	Total Cost	Quantity	Unit Cost	Total Cost
June 1							2,500	$1.50	$ 3,750
6				1,500	$1.50	$2,250	1,000	1.50	1,500
10	8,000	$1.50	$12,000				9,000	1.50	13,500
17				3,000	1.50	4,500	6,000	1.50	9,000

Figure 17.1   Perpetual inventory record card

Both inventory systems have some advantages. The periodic system is simple and easy to use and requires minimal record-keeping costs. However, information on inventory balances and the cost of goods sold is not available during the accounting period for purposes of cost control and interim financial reporting, except by estimation. The perpetual system, on the other hand, provides the information needed during the accounting period, but is more complex and requires significant record-keeping costs. The perpetual system also provides better control over the quantities of each inventory item. The quantity actually in stock can be compared to the perpetual record card to identify discrepancies due to record-keeping errors, theft, and other shortages. Businesses, such as manufacturing companies, large department stores, and automobile dealers, normally use the perpetual system. Other businesses, such as drug stores, clothing stores, gift shops, and grocery stores, normally use the periodic system. However, the state of computer technology today makes the use of a perpetual system available at reasonable cost to even small businesses. Thus, each business must weigh the costs and benefits of each system and decide which is best for it.

Merchandise Purchase Transactions— The Perpetual System

When the perpetual system is used, a continuous record of the inventory balance is maintained. Thus, every merchandise transaction affects the inventory account. The cost of the merchandise purchased and any freight charges are charged to the inventory account. Assume that merchandise with a sales price of $6,500 is purchased subject to credit terms of 2/10, n/30, the invoice is dated May 1, and freight charges of $120 related to the purchase are paid on May 8. The entries to record the purchase net of the cash discount and the freight charges would be:

May 1	Inventory	6,370	
	Accounts Payable		6,370
	To record merchandise purchased net of cash discount of $130 ($6,500 × 2%).		
May 8	Inventory	120	
	Cash		120
	To record freight charges on May 1 purchase of merchandise.		

The entries to pay the bill for the merchandise either within or after the discount period are the same under the perpetual system as they are under the periodic system.

Purchase Returns and Allowances   Recall that a separate account, purchase returns and allowances, was used under the periodic system to record the credit received for unsatisfactory or damaged goods. Under the perpetual system, the inventory balance is affected by purchase return and allowance transactions and must be credited. (The purchase returns and allowances account is not used.) The entry for the credit must be recorded net of a cash discount if the purchase was recorded that way. Assume that goods with an invoice price of $200, subject to a 2% cash discount, are returned to the supplier for credit. The entry under the perpetual system would be:

May 14	Accounts Payable	196	
	Inventory		196
	To record credit for merchandise returned to supplier net of cash discount [$200 − 2% ($200) = $196].		

Cost of Goods Sold In the perpetual system cost of goods sold is recorded and inventory is reduced in an entry that is made at the same time the sale is recorded. The entries to record a sale for $6,000 and the cost of the sale for $4,000 would be:

May 18	Accounts Receivable	6,000	
	Sales		6,000
	To record sale on credit.		

May 18	Cost of Goods Sold	4,000	
	Inventory		4,000
	To record cost of goods sold.		

Sales Returns If goods are returned by a customer, the inventory balance is again affected. Under the perpetual system, in addition to the entry giving credit to the customer, an entry must be made returning the goods to inventory and reducing the previously recorded cost of goods sold. The entries to record a customer's return of goods with a cost of $200 and a sales price of $300 would be:

May 23	Sales Returns and Allowances	300	
	Accounts Receivable		300
	To record credit given to customer for goods returned.		

May 23	Inventory	200	
	Cost of Goods Sold		200
	To put goods back into inventory and reduce cost of goods sold for goods returned by customer.		

Comparison of Periodic and Perpetual Systems

Exhibit 17.1 compares the periodic and perpetual systems. Note that the inventory account is affected by every merchandise inflow and outflow under the perpetual system. Under the periodic system, separate accounts are used for purchases, purchase returns and allowances, and freight-in. Note too that even though the merchandise was paid for on May 11, credit rather than a cash refund was received for the merchandise returned on May 14. This procedure is commonly followed when future merchandise orders are expected to be made with the same supplier.

Exhibit 17.1

Date	Transaction	Periodic System		Perpetual System	
May 1	Purchased merchandise: cost, $6,500; credit terms, 2/10, n/30; $6,500 − 2% ($6,500) = $6,370.	Purchases Accounts Payable To record merchandise purchased on credit.	6,370 6,370	Inventory Accounts Payable To record merchandise purchased on credit.	6,370 6,370
8	Paid freight charges of $120 on merchandise purchased on May 1.	Freight-in Cash To record freight charge on merchandise purchased.	120 120	Inventory Cash To record freight charge on merchandise purchased.	120 120
11	Paid the invoice for the May 1 purchase on last day of discount period.	Accounts Payable Cash To pay invoice for merchandise.	6,370 6,370	Accounts Payable Cash To pay invoice for merchandise.	6,370 6,370
14	Returned merchandise: invoice price, $200; credit terms, 2/10, n/30; $200 − 2% ($200) = $196.	Accounts Payable Purchase Returns and Allowances To record merchandise returned to supplier.	196 196	Accounts Payable Inventory To record merchandise returned to supplier.	196 196
18	Sold merchandise on credit: cost, $4,000; sales price, $6,000.	Accounts Receivable Sales To record sale on credit. No entry for cost of sale under periodic system.	6,000 6,000	Accounts Receivable Sales To record sale on credit. Cost of Goods Sold Inventory To record cost of sale.	6,000 6,000 4,000 4,000
23	Merchandise returned by customer: cost, $200; sales price, $300.	Sales Returns and Allowances Accounts Receivable To record credit for goods returned by customer. No entry to return goods to inventory under periodic system.	300 300	Sales Returns and Allowances Accounts Receivable To record credit for goods returned by customer. Inventory Cost of Goods Sold To return goods to inventory.	300 300 200 200

Items Included in Inventory

In general, inventory includes all merchandise to which an entity holds legal title at any specific date. However, determining all the merchandise legally owned by a company is often difficult. Some goods may be located on premises owned by others; and some goods owned by others may be located on company premises. In addition, goods may be in transit between the buyer and seller. The accountant, then, is confronted with a problem in determining the inventory balance. The accountant also needs to know when title to goods is transferred so that purchases and sales are reported in the correct accounting period.

The point at which legal title to merchandise is transferred depends on the intent of the parties involved. Usually the intent is to transfer title when merchandise is delivered by the seller to the buyer or, if merchandise is delivered by **common carrier** (a transportation agent), when the shipping terms specified in the sales/purchase agreement are met. Common shipping terms are *FOB destination* and *FOB shipping point*. FOB means "free on board" and is used to indicate who pays the freight charges as well as when title is transferred. **FOB destination** means that the seller pays the freight and title passes when the goods arrive at their destination. Thus, title to goods in transit belongs to the seller. **FOB shipping point** means that the buyer pays the freight and title passes when the goods are given to the common carrier for shipment. Thus, title to goods in transit belongs to the buyer. Title transfer is not affected by the date the invoice is mailed or received.

If, according to the terms of a sales/purchase agreement, goods are to be held by the seller until shipping instructions are received from the buyer, the goods should be segregated and held for the buyer; title passes when the goods are segregated. Also, goods that are custom-made normally belong to the buyer when completed. For **goods on consignment,** title belongs to the company that places the goods (the **consignor),** not to the company holding the goods (the **consignee**). Title is retained by the consignor until sold to a third party; the consignee merely acts as an agent for the consignor in trying to sell the goods for a commission. The consignee never acquires title to the goods. Goods held for sale by a sales agent are similar to goods held on consignment.

Merchandise on display, merchandise awaiting shipment, and merchandise received but not yet put in stock are included in inventory, as well as goods in the stockroom. Damaged, repossessed, and deteriorated goods should be removed from the merchandise inventory account and carried in a separate account. Also, a loss should be recognized for the decline in utility in selling these goods in the ordinary course of business (see Unit 19).

When the periodic inventory system is used, a physical inventory must be made at the end of the accounting period. When the perpetual inventory system is used, a physical inventory is usually made at regular intervals to check the accuracy of the inventory records. The procedures for taking the physical inventory must be designed to ensure that all goods owned by the company, and only those owned, are included in the inventory count, and to ensure that all purchases and sales are properly recorded.

Exhibit 17.2

Income Statement (with error overstating inventory)

	19x5	19x6
Sales	$200,000	$250,000
Cost of goods sold:		
Beginning inventory	$ 30,000	$ 36,500
Purchases	125,000	155,000
Available for sale	$155,000	$191,500
Less: Ending inventory	36,500	40,000
Cost of goods sold	$118,500	$151,500
Gross margin	$ 81,500	$ 98,500
Operating expenses	60,000	70,000
Operating income	$ 21,500	$ 28,500

Income Statement (recast to correct error)

	19x5	19x6
Sales	$200,000	$250,000
Cost of goods sold:		
Beginning inventory	$ 30,000	$ 35,000
Purchases	125,000	155,000
Available for sale	$155,000	$190,000
Less: Ending inventory	35,000	40,000
Cost of goods sold	$120,000	$150,000
Gross margin	$ 80,000	$100,000
Operating expenses	60,000	70,000
Operating income	$ 20,000	$ 30,000

Effects of Inventory Errors

Errors in determining the inventory balance affect both the balance sheet and the income statement. Assume that a company incorrectly included $1,500 in the ending inventory balance for 19x5. Exhibit 17.2 illustrates the income statements for 19x5 and 19x6, both with the error and then recast to correct the error made in 19x5. The error results in an overstatement of ending inventory for 19x5 and beginning inventory for 19x6. In addition, income for 19x5 is overstated and income for 19x6 is understated by $1,500. A general rule about the effect of an error in overstating or understating ending inventory is: If ending inventory is overstated (or understated) for a period, income for the period is overstated (or understated); if the error is not detected, income for the next period will be understated (overstated).

Assigning Costs to Inventories and Cost of Goods Sold

Ideally, the costs of merchandise purchased should be associated with the units of merchandise sold or remaining in inventory. However, many companies handle large quantities of merchandise and are frequently buying and selling. Also, purchase prices often change throughout an accounting period. Identifying and keeping track of the cost of each unit of product as goods flow in and out of the business can be very difficult and expensive. When the periodic system is used, unit costs must be assigned to the quantities determined by the physical inventory to compute the total cost of the inventory. When the cost of ending inventory is determined, the cost of goods sold is determined by deducting ending inventory from the cost of goods available for sale. When the perpetual system is used, however, unit costs can be assigned to inventory as merchandise is purchased; also, unit costs can be assigned as merchandise is sold to determine cost of goods sold. The methods of assigning unit costs to determine the cost of the inventory balance and the cost of goods sold will be covered in the next unit.

REVIEW PROBLEMS

1. Geri Corp. completed the following transactions during December 19x4:

Dec. 11   Purchased merchandise with a price of $4,000 from Mander Corp.; terms were 2/10, n/30.
14   Returned merchandise with a price of $500 to Mander Corp. for credit.
16   Sold merchandise with a cost of $2,000 to Boundrie Corp. for $3,500; terms were 2/10, n/30.
20   Received merchandise returned by Boundrie Corp. for credit; the cost of the goods was $200; their sales price was $350.

Required   Prepare all necessary entries on the books of Geri Corp. if the perpetual inventory system is used.

2. At the end of 19x4 Geri Corp. prepared a preliminary income statement that showed:

Net sales	$365,000
Cost of goods sold	215,000
Operating expenses	110,000
Inventory shortage	1,200

The ending inventory balance according to the inventory records was $36,500. A physical inventory showed a balance of only $35,300. During early 19x5 the auditors uncovered the following situations:

a. A mathematical mistake resulted in a $500 understatement of the physical inventory.
b. Merchandise with a cost of $1,500 was shipped by a

supplier FOB shipping point; it was not recorded in 19*x4* as a purchase and was not included in the physical inventory.

  c. Merchandise shipped to a customer FOB destination was in transit on December 31; the sale and cost of goods sold were recorded in 19*x4;* the goods were excluded from the physical inventory; their cost was $3,000 and sales price was $5,000.

Required Prepare a corrected income statement for 19*x4*. Also, determine the correct ending inventory balance to be reported on the balance sheet.

Solution to review problems

1.	Dec. 11	Inventory	3,920	
		Accounts payable		3,920
		To record purchase of merchandise [$4,000 − 2% ($4,000) = $3,920].		
	14	Accounts payable	490	
		Inventory		490
		To return merchandise to supplier for credit [$500 − 2% ($500) = $490].		
	16	Accounts receivable	3,500	
		Sales		3,500
		To record sale on credit.		
	16	Cost of goods sold	2,000	
		Inventory		2,000
		To record cost of sales under perpetual system.		
	20	Sales returns	350	
		Accounts receivable		350
		To give customer credit for returned merchandise.		
	20	Inventory	200	
		Cost of goods sold		200
		To record cost of merchandise returned by customer.		

2.

Geri Corp.
Income Statement
For the Year Ended December 31, 19x4

Net sales*	$360,000
Cost of goods sold*	212,000
Gross margin	$148,000
Operating expenses	110,000
Operating income	$ 38,000
Other expenses:	
Inventory shortage**	700
Income before taxes	$ 37,300

Computation of corrected ending inventory balance:

Ending inventory (according to original physical inventory)	$35,300
Add: Understatement due to mathematical mistake**	500
Understatement for merchandise in transit from supplier***	1,500
Understatement for merchandise in transit to customer*	3,000
Corrected ending inventory balance	$40,300

*The sale of goods with a cost of $3,000 and a sales price of $5,000 should not have been recorded in 19x4; because the goods were still in transit, title had not passed. Title passes when the goods are received in 19x5 by the customer. Thus, net sales and cost of goods sold are reduced $5,000 and $3,000, respectively, for 19x4.

**Because the physical inventory was understated by $500 due to a mathematical mistake, the inventory shortage is only $700 [$36,500 − ($35,300 + 500)].

***The merchandise in transit from the supplier should have been recorded as an addition to inventory and included in the physical inventory for 19x4.

SUMMARY

In this unit the accounting for merchandise purchases and sales under the perpetual system was explained and illustrated, and the system was compared with the periodic system. What constitutes the inventory balance, and the effects of inventory errors on cost of goods sold and income also were discussed. In the next unit the assignment of costs to inventory and cost of goods under both the periodic and perpetual systems is examined.

REVIEW QUESTIONS

17-1   In general, what should a company include in inventory?

17-2   What are the effects on cost of goods sold and income before taxes if a company (a) understates or (b) overstates its ending inventory?

17-3   Identify the party who pays the freight charges and the party who owns merchandise in transit if the shipping terms are (a) FOB destination and (b) FOB shipping point.

17-4   Who owns merchandise being held by an entity on consignment?

17-5   Distinguish between the periodic and perpetual inventory systems.

17-6   Explain how the perpetual inventory system and a physical inventory help control inventory balances.

EXERCISES

17-1   Refer to the data in exercise 9-5. Prepare all entries required if the company uses the perpetual inventory system instead of the periodic inventory system.

17-2   Simeon Corp. completed the following selected transactions during September:

Sept.	1	Purchased merchandise on account from Damean Company for $6,500; terms were 2/10, n/30.
	4	Returned damaged merchandise with an invoice price of $500 to Damean Company for credit against the amount owed.
	8	Paid freight charges of $850 on the merchandise purchased on September 1.
	10	Sold merchandise with a cost of $3,000 to Leon Corp. for $5,000; terms were 2/10, n/30.
	13	Leon Corp. returned merchandise with a cost of $500 and a sales price of $800 for credit.

Required   Prepare the entries for these transactions if Simeon Corp. uses (a) the periodic inventory system and (b) the perpetual inventory system.

17-3   At the end of the current year, the accountant for Konn Company analyzed several purchase and sale transactions that occurred near the end of the period. The results of his analysis indicated the following:

a.   Goods ordered from a supplier that were in transit were shipped FOB destination and are included in the inventory balance.

b.   Goods sold to a customer that were in transit were shipped FOB shipping point and are included in inventory.

c.   Goods on display in the store were excluded from inventory.

d.   Goods held on consignment from other companies were included in inventory.

e.   Goods sold to a customer, but being held for shipment at a later date at the customer's request, were excluded from inventory.

Required   Indicate whether ending inventory, cost of goods sold, and income before taxes are overstated, understated, or not affected by the manner in which the goods were handled in each of these cases.

17-4   Indicate whether each of the following should be included or excluded in the inventory of Mogg Corp. at the end of 19*x2*:

		Include	Exclude
a.	goods in transit to a customer shipped FOB destination		
b.	goods in transit from a supplier shipped FOB shipping point		
c.	goods shipped to consignees, which are unsold		
d.	goods in the shipping room awaiting shipment		
e.	goods in the receiving room awaiting return to suppliers		
f.	goods custom-made for customers; goods are finished, but not shipped		

17-5   Determine the correct inventory balance for Shamus Company based on the following information:

a.	Inventory balance according to perpetual records		$65,450
b.	Goods included in inventory balance:		
	(1)	goods in shipping room	3,600
	(2)	goods shipped to customer, but still in transit	1,850
	(3)	damaged goods being held for sale to customers	900
	(4)	goods on display in showroom	2,750
c.	Goods not included in inventory balance:		
	(1)	goods in transit from supplier	4,200
	(2)	goods in receiving room; to be inspected before being put in stock	750
	(3)	goods held on consignment by Shamus	1,200

All goods are shipped to customers FOB destination; shipments from suppliers are sent FOB shipping point.

Required   Determine the correct inventory balance. State the reason for adjusting or not adjusting the inventory balance according to the perpetual records for each item in parts b and c.

PROBLEMS

17-1   Refer to the data in problem 9–3. Prepare all entries required if the company uses the perpetual inventory system instead of the periodic inventory system.

17-2   The following are selected transactions for Colonial Corp.:

April	1	Purchased merchandise on credit from Fife Company for $8,000; terms were 2/10, n/30.
	3	Paid freight charges of $640 to Ponie Express Lines for the merchandise purchased on April 1.
	5	Returned merchandise with an invoice price of $500 to Fife Company.
	8	Sold merchandise with a cost of $4,800 for $7,200 to Drumm Company; terms were 2/10, n/30.
	10	Gave credit to Drumm Company for merchandise returned: cost, $200; sales price, $300.
	18	Received payment for the amount due from Drumm Company; the check was dated April 17.
	30	Paid the amount due to Fife Company.

Required   **a.**   Prepare the journal entry for each of these transactions if the company uses (1) the periodic inventory system and (2) the perpetual inventory system.

b.   Discuss the advantages and/or disadvantages of the perpetual inventory system as compared to the periodic inventory system.

17-3   The accountant for Randell Clothing Store prepared the following income statement for the last quarter of 19x1:

Sales		$40,000
Cost of Goods Sold		
	Beginning Inventory	$ 8,500
	Purchases	21,700
	Available for Sale	$29,200
	Ending Inventory	7,200
	Cost of Goods Sold	$22,000
Gross Margin		$18,000
Operating Expenses		14,400
Operating Income		$ 3,600

The auditors discovered several errors in the determination of the ending inventory:

a.   In computing the ending inventory, an item was extended as $50; the correct amount was $500.

b.   Merchandise with a cost of $50 and a sales price of $100 was included in the ending inventory even though it had been sold and recorded as a sale for May.

c.   Merchandise with a cost of $600 was recorded as a June purchase. On May 31 it was in transit with shipping terms of FOB destination.

d.   Merchandise received on consignment was included in the ending inventory, $700 cost.

e.   Merchandise with a cost of $800 was charged to promotion expense since it was on display in the store windows.

Required   **(1)**   Determine the correct ending inventory balance.

(2)   Prepare a corrected income statement for the first quarter of 19x1.

17-4   The merchandise inventory for Blobb Company at the end of 19*x2* includes the following:

a.	goods in stockroom	$ 85,400
b.	goods on display in store	1,100
c.	goods in transit to customer FOB shipping point	1,800
d.	goods in transit from supplier FOB destination	3,600
e.	goods held on consignment from consignors	1,450
f.	goods in shipping room awaiting shipment	750
g.	goods received from supplier, but awaiting inspection in receiving department	2,700
h.	damaged goods being held for resale	850
i.	goods purchased and held in public warehouses	10,500
j.	goods purchased but held by supplier at the request of Blobb Company for shipment at later dates	4,850
	Total	$113,000

Required   Determine the amount of the correct inventory balance at December 31, 19*x2*. Explain the reason for including or excluding each item in the corrected inventory balance.

17-5   The auditor for Jarrod Corp. analyzed purchase and sales transactions that occurred shortly before and after the end of the accounting period. The following items appeared on his workpapers:

a.   goods excluded from inventory; shipped to customers FOB destination but still in transit at year-end
b.   goods included in inventory, but still on order from suppliers
c.   goods included in inventory, but held on consignment by Jarrod
d.   goods excluded from inventory because they are used for displays in the company's stores
e.   goods excluded from inventory, but held in public warehouses
f.   goods excluded from inventory; awaiting shipment in the company's shipping room
g.   goods included in inventory; awaiting return to suppliers because they arrived in damaged condition

Required   Indicate whether inventory, cost of goods sold, and income before taxes are overstated, understated, or not affected in each of these cases.

Unit 18
Inventory Pricing Methods

First FIFO, Then LIFO, Now FISH
LIFO (Last In-First Out) is getting its share of attention now because of its advantage in a period of high inflation. FIFO (First In-First Out) for the moment is out of favor. But accountants already are talking about a new inventory accounting method for the stagflation era: FISH—First In-Still Here.

Management Accounting, *March 1975, p. 63*

Several commonly used methods of assigning unit costs to inventory and cost of goods sold under both the periodic and perpetual inventory systems are discussed and illustrated in this unit. These methods are known as **inventory pricing methods** because they are used to assign cost prices and must be distinguished from methods used to value inventories.

Performance Objectives

Upon completing this unit you should be able to:

1. define and use the accounting terms introduced in this unit.
2. describe:
   a. the advantages or disadvantages of the fifo, lifo, average cost, and specific-identification inventory pricing methods
   b. the effects on inventory balance, cost of goods sold, and net income of using one of the following inventory pricing methods as opposed to the others: fifo, lifo, average cost
   c. the effects on inventory balance, cost of goods sold, and net income of using the periodic inventory system instead of the perpetual inventory system to price inventory and cost of goods sold under the fifo, lifo, and average cost methods
3. determine ending inventory, cost of goods sold, or cost of goods available for sale under either the periodic or perpetual inventory system using the fifo, lifo, average cost, and specific-identification methods.

Inventory Pricing Methods

Four methods of assigning unit costs to inventory and cost of goods sold have become generally accepted: the specific-identification, average cost, fifo (first-in, first-out), and lifo (last-in, first-out) methods. Each of these four can be used with either the periodic or perpetual inventory system. Each method is a systematic, rational approach to matching unit costs with revenues. Thus, the flow of unit costs does not have to follow the physical flow of merchandise.

The following data will be used to illustrate the inventory pricing methods:

Date	Description	Quantity	Unit Cost	Total Cost
June 1	Balance	2,000	$3.00	$ 6,000
6	Purchase	3,000	3.10	9,300
11	Sale	4,000		
18	Purchase	5,000	3.18	15,900
25	Sale	3,000		
30	Balance	3,000		

The total costs to be assigned will be the **cost of the goods available for sale** (beginning inventory plus purchase). In this case, the cost of goods available for sale is $31,200 ($6,000 + $9,300 + $15,900).

Specific-Identification   Under the **specific-identification method** the cost of each unit of product must be directly identified with the unit. This can be achieved by affixing a tag or label to the unit with a code for the unit cost, or by recording the serial number and unit cost of each unit. When the physical inventory is taken, the price codes on the tags or labels or the serial numbers of the units in stock are identified and related back to actual unit costs to determine the cost of the ending inventory. To determine **cost of goods sold** under the periodic inventory system, the cost of the ending inventory is then deducted from the cost of goods available for sale. If the perpetual inventory system is used, the cost of each unit sold is identified from the price tag or label or the serial number so that the entry for cost of goods sold can be prepared.

The specific-identification method is best used where there are relatively small quantities of a few items with relatively large unit costs. It is suitable for items like automobiles, for example, where each unit is likely to be different from other units. When there are identical units in stock, this method allows manipulation of the units picked to be sold or left in stock. Higher price or lower price units can be chosen to have a particular effect on income. For example, if a company is selecting an appliance to be sold to a customer and there are several identical units in stock with unit costs of either $340 or $370, selection of a lower cost unit will result in the assignment of $30 less to cost of goods sold and the reporting of $30 more of income before taxes.

Based on the data for this section, assume that the sale on June 11 consists of all 2,000 units on hand at June 1 and 2,000 units from the purchase on June 6. Assume too that the sale on June 25 consists of units purchased on June 18. The cost of goods sold for June and the cost of the ending inventory of 3,000 units on June 30 are determined as follows:

Cost of Goods Sold for June		
Sale on June 11:		
2,000 units at $3.00 each	$6,000	
2,000 units at $3.10 each	6,200	$12,200
Sale on June 25:		
3,000 units at $3.18 each		9,540
Total		$21,740

Cost of Ending Inventory at June 30	
From purchase on June 6	
1,000 units at $3.10 each	$ 3,100
From purchase on June 18	
2,000 units at $3.18 each	6,360
Total	$ 9,460

The results can be verified by adding the costs assigned to cost of goods sold ($21,740) and ending inventory ($9,460). This sum, $31,200, should equal the cost of goods available for sale ($6,000 + 9,300 + 15,900 = $31,200). When the specific-identification method is used, the results will be the same under both the periodic and perpetual inventory systems.

Average Cost   The **average cost method** is based on the premise that each unit has the same utility to the company whether it is sold or left in stock. Under this method the total cost of the units available for sale is averaged and the same unit cost assigned to all units, both those sold and those still in stock. When the periodic inventory method is used, a single average cost is determined for the accounting period. When the perpetual inventory system is used, a new average cost is determined after each purchase and unit cost information is maintained. The average cost method is best suited to situations where there is little price fluctuation during the period and the quantities of each item in stock tend to be mingled. It is a systematic, rational method that is relatively easy to apply and is generally free from any manipulation. When the perpetual system is used, the results of the average cost method tend to approximate the results yielded by the fifo method.

Weighted average cost method   The average cost method, when used under the periodic system, is known as the **weighted average method.** The average unit cost is determined by dividing the total cost of goods available for sale by the total number of units available for sale, for example:

$$\frac{\text{cost of goods available for sale}}{\text{units available for sale}} = \frac{\$31,200}{10,000} = \$3.12 \text{ average unit cost}$$

The number of units available for sale is determined by adding the units on hand at the beginning of the period to the units purchased during the period (2,000 + 3,000 + 5,000 = 10,000). The cost of the goods available for sale is determined by adding the cost of the units on hand at the beginning of the period and the cost of the units purchased during the period ($6,000 + 9,300 + 15,900 = $31,200). To determine the cost of ending inventory the quantity of units on hand is multiplied by the average unit cost.

Cost of Ending Inventory at June 30

3,000 units at $3.12 each	$9,360

In computing the average unit cost, figures may have to be rounded. In this text all unit costs are rounded to the nearest tenth of one cent, that is, to the third place to the right of the decimal point. The cost of goods sold is determined by deducting the cost of the ending inventory from the cost of goods available for sale.

Cost of Goods Sold for June

Cost of goods available for sale	$31,200
Less: Cost of ending inventory	9,360
Cost of goods sold	$21,840

Moving average cost method   When the perpetual system is used, the average cost method is called the **moving average method** because a new average cost is computed after each purchase. If the unit cost of the purchases changes, the moving average changes. Exhibit 18.1 illustrates the computation of inventory costs and cost of goods sold for the moving average method using a perpetual inventory record card.

The unit costs after the June 6 and 18 purchases are determined as follows:

$$\frac{\text{cost of units available for sale}}{\text{number of units available for sale}} = \text{average cost}$$

$$\frac{\$15,300}{5,000} = \$3.06 \text{ at June 6}$$

$$\frac{\$18,960}{6,000} = \$3.16 \text{ at June 18}$$

Exhibit 18.1

Date	Purchases			Sales			Balance		
	Q	UC	TC	Q	UC	TC	Q	UC	TC
June 1							2,000	$3.00	$ 6,000
6	3,000	$3.10	$ 9,300				5,000	3.06	15,300
11				4,000	$3.06	$12,240			
18	5,000	3.18	15,900				6,000	3.16	18,960
25				3,000	3.16	9,480	3,000	3.16	9,480

Q—quantity; UC—unit cost; TC—total cost

Because purchase prices changed during June, the results for the weighted average and moving average methods differ:

	Weighted Average	Moving Average
Average unit cost for ending inventory	$ 3.12	$ 3.16
Ending inventory	$ 9,360	$ 9,480
Cost of goods sold	$21,840	$21,720

The cost of goods sold is the sum of the total cost (TC) column for sales in Exhibit 18.1 ($12,240 + 9,480 = $21,720). It can also be determined by deducting ending inventory from cost of goods available for sale ($31,200 − 9,480 = $21,720).

First-In, First-Out   Under the **fifo (first-in, first-out) method** the costs of the first units purchased are assigned to the first units sold. The costs of the units purchased most recently during the period are assigned to ending inventory. The fact that the fifo cost flow assumption is realistic compared to the merchandise flow in many businesses is used as an argument to support the fifo method. Fifo is also a systematic, rational approach that is relatively easy to apply and is free from manipulation. It seems best suited for situations where inventory turnover is fairly rapid and prices do not change frequently. In fact, the greatest criticism is that, unless turnover is rapid, the fifo method poorly matches revenue and expense. If it is assumed that sales prices fluctuate with changes in unit costs, then revenue and expense are poorly matched because earlier unit costs are matched with current sales prices (the first units in are assumed to be the first ones sold). However, because the last units purchased are assumed to be left in stock, the fifo method reflects relatively current values on the balance sheet. Fifo, therefore, is considered relatively good for measuring financial position, but relatively poor for measuring net income.

Fifo yields the same results under both the periodic and perpetual inventory systems. Using the data on page 345 and applying the periodic system, the cost of the ending inventory and cost of goods sold for June are determined as follows (the cost of the 3,000 units left in stock is assumed to come entirely from the last purchase, on June 18):

Cost of Ending Inventory at June 30	
3,000 units at $3.18 each	$ 9,540

Cost of Goods Sold for June	
Cost of goods available for sale	$31,200
Less: Cost of ending inventory	9,540
Cost of goods sold	$21,660

Students should verify on their own that the results under the perpetual system are the same as those under the periodic system illustrated above.

Last-In, First-Out   Under the **lifo (last-in, first-out) method** it is assumed that the last units purchased are the first units sold. Thus, the ending inventory consists of the earliest units acquired, that is, any units in stock at the beginning of the period plus, as necessary, units from the earliest purchase(s) for the period. Lifo is a systematic, rational approach that is relatively easy to apply. However, it is not consistent with the usual physical flow of merchandise in most situations and is subject to manipulation. Because the units purchased most recently are assumed to be sold, management can either make or refrain from making acquisitions near the end of the period to control the unit costs assigned to cost of goods sold and, thus, to manipulate income (see pages 350–352).

The chief argument for lifo is that it matches revenue and expense better than other methods. Assuming that sales prices fluctuate as unit costs change, then revenue and expense are well matched because the most recent unit costs are assigned to expense (cost of goods sold) and matched with the current sales prices. However, this situation results in the ending inventory balance reflecting older, rather than current, unit costs—thus lifo is a poor measure of current financial position. This problem becomes more critical as prices change significantly over the years, and the layers of unit costs built up in earlier years are carried forward in the inventory balance.

Lifo—Periodic system   Using the data on page 345 and applying periodic inventory procedures, the cost of the ending inventory and the cost of goods sold are determined for the lifo method. Under the lifo concept the ending inventory consists of the costs of the earliest acquisitions—in this case, 2,000 units from the beginning inventory and 1,000 units from the earliest purchase in June.

Cost of Ending Inventory at June 30	
From beginning inventory:	
2,000 units at $3.00 each	$ 6,000
From the purchase on June 6	
1,000 units at $3.10 each	3,100
Total	$ 9,100

Cost of Goods Sold for June	
Cost of goods available for sale	$31,200
Less: Cost of ending inventory	9,100
Cost of goods sold	$22,100

Lifo—Perpetual system   Exhibit 18.2 illustrates the lifo method using the perpetual system. After each purchase or sale is entered on the perpetual record card, all layers making up the balance are listed in the sequence in which they were acquired. This procedure makes it easier to identify the unit costs for units sold. For example, after the purchase on June 6 the balance consists of 2,000 units at $3.00 each and 3,000

Exhibit 18.2

Date	Purchases			Sales			Balance		
	Q	UC	TC	Q	UC	TC	Q	UC	TC
June 1							2,000	$3.00	$ 6,000
6	3,000	$3.10	$ 9,300				2,000	3.00	6,000
							3,000	3.10	9,300
11				3,000	$3.10	$9,300	1,000	3.00	3,000
				1,000	3.00	3,000			
18	5,000	3.18	15,900				1,000	3.00	3,000
							5,000	3.18	15,900
25				3,000	3.18	9,540	1,000	3.00	3,000
							2,000	3.18	6,360

Q—quantity; UC—unit cost; TC—total cost

units at $3.10 each. When 4,000 units are sold on June 11, the cost of the first 3,000 units comes from the most recent purchase (June 6) and the cost of the other 1,000 units comes from beginning inventory. After the purchase on June 18 the balance includes the cost of the remaining 1,000 units from beginning inventory and the cost of the 5,000 units just purchased. The cost of the units sold on June 25 comes entirely from the latest purchase (5,000 units on June 18). Thus, the ending inventory consists of the cost of the 1,000 units from beginning inventory and the cost of the 2,000 units from the June 18 purchase.

Note that lifo yields different results under the periodic and perpetual systems when there is a temporary decrease in the number of units that were carried forward from the previous period. That is, results vary under each system if, at some point, the number of units sold exceeds the number of units that have been purchased during the period, and if the number of units on hand at the end of the period equals or is greater than the number on hand at the beginning. Under the perpetual system the unit costs from the beginning inventory must be assigned to cost of goods sold. In Exhibit 18.2 there was a temporary decrease of 1,000 units when 4,000 units were sold on June 11 because only 3,000 units had been purchased by that date. By the end of June, though, enough additional units had been purchased so that the ending inventory (3,000 units) exceeded the beginning inventory (2,000 units). The effect of these transactions was to assign the cost of 1,000 units from beginning inventory to cost of goods sold. Under the periodic system, however, the costs of all units in the beginning inventory are assumed to remain and are assigned to the ending inventory. Therefore, the costs of all 2,000 units in beginning inventory are left to be assigned to ending inventory.

Manipulation of income is thus possible. This potential manipulation is demonstrated in Exhibit 18.3 based on the following data:

Sales (17,000 units)	$144,500
Available for sale during the period:	
12,000 units at $5.30	$ 63,600
8,000 units at $4.80	$ 38,400
Inventory balance near end of period	3,000 units
Purchase made near end of period to	
reduce income for the period:	
5,000 units at $4.00	$ 20,000
Operating expenses	$ 48,000

As the exhibit shows, the purchase of 5,000 units near the end of the period increases operating income by $6,500. Under the lifo method the ending inventory consists of units carried over from the previous period and units acquired early in the current period, cost of goods sold consists of units acquired later in the period. Thus, the cost of the 5,000 units purchased near the end of the period, $20,000 or $4.00 each, is charged to cost of goods sold; but 5,000 units are now added to ending inventory at $5.30 each. The difference in cost of goods sold of $6,500 results from shifting 5,000 units at $5.30 each to inventory and charging 5,000 units at $4.00 each to cost of goods

Exhibit 18.3

	Without Purchase of 5,000 Units	With Purchase of 5,000 Units
Sales	$144,500	$144,500
Available for sale:		
12,000 units at $5.30	$ 63,600	$ 63,600
8,000 units at $4.80	38,400	38,400
5,000 units at $4.00		20,000
Total available for sale	$102,000	$122,000
Ending inventory (lifo)		
3,000 units at $5.30	15,900	
8,000 units at $5.30		42,400
Cost of goods sold	$ 86,100	$ 79,600
Gross margin	$ 58,400	$ 64,900
Operating expenses	48,000	48,000
Operating income	$ 10,400	$ 16,900

sold [($5.30 − 4.00) × 5,000 = $6,500]. Because cost of goods sold decreases $6,500, gross margin and operating income increase $6,500.

Comparing Inventory Pricing Methods

The four inventory pricing methods yield different results. In addition, two of these methods may yield different results under the periodic and perpetual inventory systems. Faced with generally accepted alternative methods with different effects on financial position and operating results, an entity may well ask which method is best. Each method tends to be rational and systematic, and each is relatively easy to apply. Thus, several criteria should be considered in selecting an appropriate inventory pricing method:

1. Does the method provide a good measure of net income for the current and future periods?
2. Does the method provide a good measure of financial position at the end of each period?
3. Is the method rational and systematic in its approach so that it is objective and free from bias or manipulation?
4. Is the method relatively easy to apply?

No one method meets all four criteria. For example, fifo meets all the criteria except the first; lifo meets the first and fourth criteria and, in part, the third.

Frequently, the final decision in selecting an inventory method rests on the income and income tax effects of each. The larger the ending inventory balance, given a certain amount of revenue and the cost of goods available for sale, the smaller the cost of goods sold and the larger the income before taxes. Assume a company earned revenue of $200,000 during the current period and had $160,000 of merchandise available for sale. If two alternative inventory pricing methods yield ending inventory balances of $40,000 and $37,000, the method yielding the larger balance will yield the smaller cost of goods sold and the larger income before taxes. The difference will be $3,000, as the following illustrates:

Sales	$200,000	$200,000
Cost of goods sold:		
Cost of goods available for sale	$160,000	$160,000
Less: Ending inventory	40,000	37,000
Cost of goods sold	$120,000	$123,000
Gross margin	$ 80,000	$ 77,000
Operating expenses	60,000	60,000
Operating income	$ 20,000	$ 17,000

The income effects of using a particular inventory pricing method can be carried forward indefinitely if the general price trend for purchases is consistent. Companies may prefer a method that gives consistently lower income results, so they will pay lower income taxes. They may feel that, even if they have to pay taxes eventually, they will benefit from deferring the payments because of the time value of money. Each dollar retained in the business can be invested and provide a return, and borrowing might be avoided.

The only restriction on selecting a pricing method is that income tax law requires lifo to be used for financial reporting if it is used for income tax purposes.

The following, based on the data on page 345, summarizes the results of the four methods discussed:

	Periodic System		Perpetual System	
Inventory Pricing Methods	Ending Inventory	Cost of Goods Sold	Ending Inventory	Cost of Goods Sold
Specific-Identification	$9,460	$21,740	$9,460	$21,740
Average Cost	9,360	21,840	9,480	21,720
Fifo	9,540	21,660	9,540	21,660
Lifo	9,100	22,100	9,360	21,840

When financial position and income effects are compared, the specific-identification method should be ignored because there is no consistent pattern; the cost of ending inventory and cost of goods sold depend on the units selected when they are sold. Note that the price trend for the data used was upward during June. In a period of generally rising prices, lifo yields the lowest asset balance, the highest cost of goods sold, and the lowest net income; fifo yields the highest asset balance, lowest cost of goods sold, and highest net income; the average cost method yields results between those for fifo and lifo. In a period of generally falling prices, the effects for fifo and lifo reverse, and the effects for the average cost method again fall between.

After its initial acceptance for income tax purposes in 1939, lifo became a popular inventory pricing method. During the 1960s, however, its popularity dwindled considerably as prices stabilized or fluctuated moderately. Then, in the mid-1970s, when inflationary pressures became more severe, many companies started switching to the lifo method to match current revenue and current costs and to defer income taxes. The AICPA annual publication *Accounting Trends and Techniques,* which surveys the annual reports of 600 companies, indicates the following trends in use of the inventory pricing methods:[1]

| | Percentage of Total Disclosures | | | |
	1955	1965	1970	1975
Average cost	25.3%	26.0%	26.5%	22.5%
Fifo	23.9	31.5	38.2	36.1
Lifo	35.0	28.3	19.1	30.2
Other methods	15.8	14.2	16.2	13.2
	100.0%	100.0%	100.0%	100.0%

REVIEW PROBLEM

The records of Masters, Inc., indicated the following activity for one product for January:

Date	Description	Quantity	Unit Cost
Jan. 1	Balance	3,000	$2.00
8	Purchase	5,000	1.96
14	Sale	6,000	
20	Purchase	4,000	1.90
27	Sale	3,000	

(Data for specific-identification method: Jan. 14 sale—2,000 units from Jan. 1 and 4,000 units from Jan. 8; Jan. 27 sale—3,000 units from Jan. 20.)

Required   Determine the ending inventory and cost of goods sold under the periodic and perpetual systems for the four main inventory pricing methods.

---

[1]AICPA, *Accounting Trends and Techniques,* 1970 (p. 53), 1973 (p. 98), 1976 (p. 89).

Solution to review problem

Specific-identification (periodic and perpetual systems)
Cost of ending inventory:
From Jan. 1 balance:
 1,000 units at $2.00 each $ 2,000
From Jan. 8 purchase:
 1,000 units at $1.96 each   1,960
From Jan. 20 purchase:
 1,000 units at $1.90 each   <u>1,900</u>
 Total   <u>$ 5,860</u>

Cost of goods sold:
Jan. 14 sale
 2,000 units at $2.00 each $4,000
 4,000 units at $1.96 each   <u>7,840</u> $11,840
Jan. 27 sale:
 3,000 units at $1.90 each   <u>5,700</u>
 Total   <u>$17,540</u>

Weighted average cost (periodic system)
Cost of ending inventory:*
 3,000 units at $1.95 each   <u>$ 5,850</u>

Cost of goods sold
Cost of goods available for sale
 3,000 × $2.00 $6,000
 5,000 × $1.96   9,800
 4,000 × $1.90   <u>7,600</u> $23,400
 Less: Ending inventory   <u>5,850</u>
 Cost of goods sold   <u>$17,550</u>

*3,000 + 5,000 − 6,000 + 4,000 − 3,000 = 3,000 units in stock on January 31; $23,400/12,000 = $1.95 average unit cost.

Moving Average Cost (perpetual system)

	Purchases			Sales			Balance		
Date	Q	UC	TC	Q	UC	TC	Q	UC	TC
Jan. 1							3,000	$2.00	$ 6,000
8	5,000	$1.96	$9,800				8,000	1.975	15,800
14				6,000	$1.975	$11,850	2,000	1.975	3,950
20	4,000	1.90	7,600				6,000	1.925	11,550
27				3,000	1.925	5,775	3,000	1.925	5,775

Cost of goods sold: $11,850 + $5,775 = <u>$17,625</u> or $23,400 − $5,775 = <u>$17,625</u>

Fifo (periodic and perpetual system)
Cost of ending inventory:
    3,000 units at $1.90 each $ 5,700

Cost of goods sold:
    Cost of goods available for sale $23,400
    Less: Ending inventory   5,700
    Cost of goods sold $17,700

Lifo (periodic system)
Cost of ending inventory:
    3,000 units at $2.00 each $ 6,000

Cost of goods sold:
    Cost of goods available for sale $23,400
    Less: Ending inventory   6,000
    Cost of goods sold $17,400

Lifo (perpetual system)

Date	Purchases			Sales			Balance		
	Q	UC	TC	Q	UC	TC	Q	UC	TC
Jan. 1							3,000	$2.00	$6,000
8	5,000	$1.96	$9,800				3,000	2.00	6,000
							5,000	1.96	9,800
14				5,000	$1.96	$9,800	2,000	2.00	4,000
				1,000	2.00	2,000			
20	4,000	1.90	7,600				2,000	2.00	4,000
							4,000	1.90	7,600
27				3,000	1.90	5,700	2,000	2.00	4,000
							1,000	1.90	1,900

Ending inventory: $4,000 + 1,900 = $5,900

Cost of goods sold: $9,800 + 2,000 + 5,700 = $17,500

SUMMARY

The four commonly used inventory pricing methods—specific-identification, average cost, fifo, and lifo—were discussed and illustrated in this unit. Because these methods yield different income and asset balance results, the method a company selects should suit the circumstances under which it operates. These pricing methods are used to determine the cost value of the ending inventory. In the next unit alternate inventory valuation methods are examined.

REVIEW QUESTIONS

18-1 Identify and briefly describe the four commonly used inventory pricing methods.

18-2 Under what circumstances would each of the following inventory pricing methods be most appropriate?

    a. specific-identification   **c.** fifo
    b. average cost   **d.** lifo

18-3 Distinguish between the weighted average and moving average inventory pricing methods.

18-4 Sometimes different results are obtained if inventory is priced using the lifo method under the periodic inventory system in contrast to the perpetual inventory system. Explain.

18-5 Indicate the chief arguments for and against the (a) fifo and (b) lifo inventory pricing methods.

18-6 **a.** What criteria *should* be applied in selecting the appropriate inventory pricing method given a specific set of circumstances?
    b. What factors often influence the *actual* selection of an inventory pricing method?

18-7 What are the effects on the inventory balance, cost of goods sold, and income before taxes of selecting lifo over fifo during a period of (a) rising prices and (b) falling prices?

18-8 Under which inventory pricing method(s) will the results always be the same for both the periodic and perpetual inventory systems?

EXERCISES

18-1 Complete the following crossword puzzle by filling in the names of the appropriate inventory systems and pricing methods. When more than one word is to be filled in, leave a blank space between words.

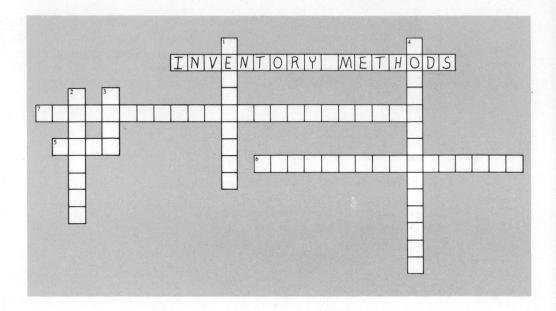

Down

1   An inventory system in which a continuous record of the balance is maintained.
2   An inventory system in which the inventory balance is determined only at the end of the period.
3   The pricing method in which the cost of the most recent purchases are assigned to inventory.
4   The pricing method in which a new unit cost is determined for all goods available for sale after each purchase.

Across

5   The pricing method in which the cost of the most recent purchases is assigned to cost of goods sold.
6   The pricing method in which the same unit cost is assigned to ending inventory and all units sold during the period.
7   The pricing method in which price code tags or serial numbers are used to identify the unit cost of units left in stock or sold.

18-2   The Grabbow Sales Company completed the following transactions during August for one of its products:

Date	Transaction	Quantity	Unit Cost	Total Cost
Aug. 1	Balance	200	$3.00	$ 600
8	Purchase	300	3.10	930
15	Sale	400		
23	Purchase	400	3.16	1,264
29	Sale	200		
31	Balance	300		

(Data for specific-identification: August 15 sale—200 units each from August 1 and 8; August 29 sale—200 units from August 23.)

Required   If the *periodic inventory system* is used, determine the ending inventory and cost of goods sold using the specific-identification, weighted average, fifo, and lifo inventory pricing methods.

18-3   Refer to the data in exercise 18–2. If the *perpetual inventory system* is used, determine the ending inventory and cost of goods sold using the moving average, fifo, and lifo inventory pricing methods.

18-4   Following are three alternative sets of financial information for Damask Company:

| | Alternatives | | |
	1	2	3
Ending inventory	$ 30,000	$ 28,000	$ 25,000
Cost of goods sold	170,000	172,000	175,000
Income before taxes	25,000	23,000	20,000

Required   Identify whether each alternative would result from using the fifo, lifo, or average cost inventory pricing method if prices during the period were (a) rising and (b) falling.

18-5   Mickie Sales Company completed the following transactions during March for one of its products:

Date	Transaction	Quantity	Unit Cost
March 1	Balance	6,000	$2.50
7	Purchase	10,000	2.60
14	Sale	12,000	
17	Purchase	20,000	2.75
21	Sale	8,000	
27	Sale	7,000	

Required   Assuming periodic inventory procedures, compute the inventory balance at March 31 and cost of goods sold for March by applying the pricing method that will yield the lowest amount of taxable income for the current period.

18-6   Refer to the data in exercise 18–5. Determine the difference in the reported inventory balance and income before taxes if the company uses the lifo method as contrasted to the fifo method. Assume perpetual inventory procedures.

PROBLEMS

18-1   During August the Rankel Corporation completed the following transactions for one of its products:

Date	Transaction	Units	Unit Cost
Aug. 1	On Hand	400	$2.20
3	Purchase	500	2.30
8	Sale	600	
11	Purchase	800	2.35
14	Sale	400	
20	Purchase	300	2.40
27	Sale	500	
31	On Hand	500	

Required   Determine the ending inventory and cost of goods sold if the following inventory pricing methods are used:

    a. specific-identification (August 8 sale: 200 units from August 1 and 400 units from August 3; August 14 sale: 400 units from August 11; August 27 sale: 200 units from August 20 and 300 units from August 11)
    b. weighted average
    c. moving average
    d. fifo
    e. lifo (periodic inventory system)
    f. lifo (perpetual inventory system)

18-2   Following are four alternative income statements for the first quarter of 19*x1*:

	Alternatives			
	1	2	3	4
Sales	$136,000	$136,000	$136,000	$136,000
Cost of Goods Sold	92,500	92,670	92,790	93,100
Gross Margin	$ 43,500	$ 43,330	$ 43,210	$ 42,900
Operating Expense	32,000	32,000	32,000	32,000
Operating Income	$ 11,500	$ 11,330	$ 11,210	$ 10,900

The company sells a single product for which the following information on purchases and sales was gathered:

Date	Transaction	Quantity	Unit Cost	Total Cost
Jan. 1	Balance	4,000	$5.00	$20,000
10	Purchase	6,000	5.10	30,600
20	Sale	5,000		
Feb. 5	Purchase	5,000	5.20	26,000
15	Sale	5,000		
Mar. 1	Purchase	5,000	5.30	26,500
16	Sale	8,000		
31	Balance	2,000		

Required   Identify the inventory pricing method used for each alternative quarterly income statement.

18-3   Dann Corp. completed the following transactions for one of its major products during April:

Date	Transaction	Units	Unit Cost	Total Cost
April 1	Balance	5,000	$4.50	$22,500
6	Purchase	8,000	4.40	35,200
11	Sale	10,000		
16	Purchase	12,000	4.45	53,400
24	Sale	4,000		
30	Sale	3,000		

Required   **a.**   Determine the cost of goods available for sale.
           b.   Calculate cost of goods sold for April if the weighted average inventory method is used.

c. Calculate the inventory balance at April 30 if the fifo inventory method is used.

d. Determine the composition of the inventory balance at April 30 if the lifo inventory method is used with (1) periodic inventory procedures and (2) perpetual inventory procedures.

e. Calculate the unit cost for the inventory balance at April 30 if the moving average inventory method is used.

18-4   Figg Company uses the perpetual inventory system. During December 19x4, the company recorded purchases and sales for one of its products as follows:

Purchases		Sales	
Dec. 5	6,000 units at $3.40	Dec. 3	3,000 units
12	4,000 units at $3.45	10	4,000 units
19	5,000 units at $3.50	17	5,000 units
26	3,000 units at $3.45	24	4,000 units
		30	6,000 units

The balance of this product on December 1, 19x4, was 8,000 units at $3.45 each. On January 3, 19x5, the company received 7,000 units, which were shipped FOB shipping point by the supplier on December 29, 19x4. Their cost was $3.50 per unit. The December 30 sale was shipped FOB destination and was still in transit on December 31, 19x4.

Required   a. Determine the number of units to be included in the December 31, 19x4, inventory balance.

b. Calculate the inventory balance at December 31, 19x4, and cost of goods sold under the fifo, lifo, and average cost methods. (Carry unit costs to four decimal places.)

Unit 19
Inventory Valuation and Estimation Methods

It is usual with Merchants, when they make a general Balance of their Books, to value the Goods that they have by them at the Market Price they then go at, at the time of their balancing, but some do not so.

R. Hayes, The Gentleman's Complete Book-keeper, *1741*

Under certain circumstances inventory should be valued at an amount other than original cost in order to reflect the expected utility of the merchandise in generating revenue in the ordinary course of business. And in some situations it may be desirable or necessary to estimate the cost of the inventory balance at the end of the period rather than assign unit costs to the merchandise in stock. Several commonly used methods of valuing and estimating inventory balances are examined in this unit.

Performance Objectives

Upon completing this unit you should be able to:

1. define and use the accounting terms introduced in this unit.
2. a. identify the inventory valuation or estimation method that should be used in specific situations.
    b. describe how inventory should be valued, estimated, or reported on the balance sheet.
3. determine the amount to be reported as ending inventory under any of the following valuation or estimation methods:
    a. lower-of-cost-or-market
    b. net realizable value
    c. gross margin
    d. retail

Inventory Valuation and Estimation Methods

There are several **inventory valuation methods.** Under the cost principle, inventories are valued at cost, using one of the inventory pricing methods discussed in Unit 18. Recall that the purpose of inventory pricing methods is to assign unit costs to inventory and cost of goods sold. Under certain circumstances, however, some other value may be appropriate to ensure that an entity's financial position and operating results are accurately reported. The following figures from *Accounting Trends and Techniques* show the results of the AICPA's annual survey of accounting practices as disclosed in the annual reports of 600 companies:[1]

| | Percentage of Total Disclosures | | | |
	1955	1965	1970	1974
Cost	21.7%	12.2%	10.2%	12.3%
Lower-of-cost-or-market	58.0	67.4	72.9	75.6
Other valuation methods	20.3	20.4	16.9	12.1
	100.0%	100.0%	100.0%	100.0%

As indicated, the most commonly used inventory valuation method is the *lower-of-cost-or-market method*. But other valuation methods are used in specialized situations. Agricultural products, by-products, damaged goods, and repossessed merchandise are often valued at their *net realizable value*. Rare minerals and certain commodities for which there is a controlled market price and immaterial disposal costs can be valued at their *selling price* because the criteria for revenue realization (which were discussed in Units 3 and 5) are met when production occurs. A few manufacturing companies value inventories at *direct costs,* that is, the variable costs of production, exluding fixed factory overhead. Other manufacturing companies value inventories at *standard costs,* that is, costs as measured using predetermined standards for prices and quantities of materials, labor, and other manufacturing costs incurred to produce goods still in inventory. Neither the direct cost nor the standard cost methods normally yield inventory values acceptable for external financial reporting. They are, however, useful for management planning and control.

In some situations it is difficult or impossible to determine the cost of the inventory, and a method of estimating cost is appropriate or necessary. One **inventory estimation method,** the *gross margin method* may be used to estimate the cost of goods that have been destroyed, or it may be used when a physical inventory is impractical. Another estimation method, the *retail method* may be used by retail sales businesses to avoid the detailed assignment of unit costs to inventory.

---

[1]*Accounting Trends and Techniques* (New York: AICPA, 1970, 1973, and 1975). This type of information was discontinued in 1975.

Lower-of-Cost-or-Market Method   The **lower-of-cost-or-market method** is an exception to the cost principle. Inventory is valued at the lower of acquisition cost or current market value. Current **market value** is usually considered to be the current replacement cost at balance sheet date.[2] Cost can be determined by any of the inventory pricing methods discussed in the previous unit except lifo; income tax law does not permit lifo to be used with the lower-of-cost-or-market method. Also, income tax law does not permit lifo to be used for tax purposes if another cost method is used for financial reporting. The lower-of-cost-or-market method is appropriate when the utility of selling inventory items in the normal course of business operations has been impaired. This may occur when current replacement cost (market value) declines and (1) sales price must be reduced to the point where normal profit cannot be earned and/or (2) the selling costs cannot be recovered in future periods when the inventory is sold.

The lower-of-cost-or-market method is usually applied on an item-by-item basis. The cost and market value of each item are compared to determine which is lower; a decrease in value in one item is not offset by an increase in value of another item. Occasionally, however, inventory items are grouped into categories such as product lines or departments. The total market value and total cost of each category are compared to determine which is lower; within a category an increase in value of one item may offset a decrease in value of another item. The total cost and total market value of the entire inventory also can be compared, under certain circumstances, to determine which is lower. Applying the lower-of-cost-or-market method to categories or to the entire inventory is acceptable when the overall utility of each category or the entire inventory is more relevant than the utility of each inventory item. The lowest inventory value, however, is always obtained by the item-by-item approach. Exhibit 19.1 illustrates the three approaches.

Exhibit 19.1

	Quantity	Unit Cost	Unit Market Value	Total Cost	Total Market Value	Lower-of-Cost-or-Market By Item	Lower-of-Cost-or-Market By Category	Lower-of-Cost-or-Market For Total
Category I								
Item A	1,000	$2.00	$2.05	$ 2,000	$ 2,050	$ 2,000		
Item B	500	4.00	3.85	2,000	1,925	1,925		
Category I Totals				$ 4,000	$ 3,925		$ 3,925	
Category II								
Item C	800	5.00	5.10	$ 4,000	$ 4,080	4,000		
Item D	300	8.00	7.90	2,400	2,370	2,370		
Category II Totals				$ 6,400	$ 6,450		6,400	
Overall Totals				$10,400	$10,375	$10,295	$10,325	$10,375

---

[2]*Accounting Research Bulletin No. 43* (New York: AICPA, 1961), chapter 4, p. 31.

On an item-by-item approach, cost is lower for items A and C while market value (usually replacement cost) is lower for items B and D; the inventory value for financial reporting would be $10,295. For category I market value ($3,925) is lower than cost, but for category II cost ($6,400) is lower than market value; the sum of these lower amounts, $10,325, would be used for financial reporting in the second approach. If the total cost and total market value for the entire inventory are compared, the inventory balance would be reported as $10,375. In this illustration, market value is lower than cost for all three approaches; this is not always true.

The difference between the total cost and a lower market value for inventory can be accounted for in different ways. In this text cost will be recorded in the inventory account and the difference between cost and a lower market value in a contra or offset account. At the end of each period the contra account balance is adjusted to the new balance necessary after cost and market value are determined and compared.

Use the data in the exhibit and assume that the contra account has no balance from the previous year. The adjusting entry required to apply the lower-of-cost-or-market method for the item-by-item approach, then, would be:

Loss from reduction of inventory to market value	105	
Allowance for reduction of inventory to		
market value		105
To apply lower-of-cost-or-market method ($10,400		
$- 10,295 = \$105$).		

At the end of the next period an additional loss would be recorded if the balance needed in the allowance account was greater than $105; a gain would be recorded if the balance needed was less than $105. The amount of gain recognized, however, cannot exceed the balance of the allowance account; if a larger amount were recognized, an inventory balance in excess of cost would be reported in violation of the cost principle. The loss or gain would be reported as incidental revenue or expense on a classified (multiple-step) income statement. Assume that the cost and market value of the inventory at the end of the next period are $11,200 and $11,150, respectively. The adjusting entry to apply the lower-of-cost-or-market method would be:

Allowance for reduction of inventory to market		
value	55	
Gain on recovery of reduction of inventory to		
market value		55
To apply lower-of-cost-or-market method ($11,200		
$- 11,150 = \$50; \$105 - 50 = \$55$).		

On the balance sheet the inventory value is included in current assets, and the method of valuation is disclosed parenthetically (or in the footnotes) as follows:

Current assets:	
Cash	$ xxxx
Accounts receivable	xxxx
Inventory, at lower-of-cost-or-market	11,150

Net Realizable Value   **Net realizable value** is the expected sales price less the expected costs of completion and disposal of the goods. It is the amount that should allow the company to break even on the sale of the goods if the expected revenue and costs directly traceable to the goods are realized. The **net realizable value method** of valuation is appropriate for damaged, obsolete, or deteriorated merchandise, **repossessed merchandise** (that is, goods sold on the installment basis that are repossessed by the seller because the buyer defaults on payments), and **by-products** (that is, residual products that result from the production of a company's main products).

Assume that a company identifies damaged merchandise with a cost of $1,500 and a normal sales price of $2,400 when it takes its physical inventory. If the merchandise can be sold for $1,600 in its damaged condition and costs directly traceable to the sale are $200, the goods should be transferred to a separate account and recorded at a net realizable value of $1,400 ($1,600 − 200). A loss of $100 ($1,500 − 1,400) is recognized because net realizable value is less than cost. If the perpetual inventory system is used, the entry to record the transfer would be:

Inventory of Damaged Merchandise	1,400	
Loss on Damaged Inventory Items	100	
Inventory		1,500
To transfer damaged goods to separate account at		
net realizable value.		

Gross Margin Method   The **gross margin method** can be used to estimate the cost of inventory only if net sales and the cost of goods available for sale can be determined from an entity's records. First, the average **gross margin percentage** for the past few years is determined by dividing the average gross margin by the average net sales for those years. This percentage is then applied to net sales for the current period to estimate the dollar amount for gross margin. Next, the estimate of gross margin is deducted from net sales to estimate cost of goods sold. Cost of goods sold, in turn, is deducted from cost of goods available for sale to estimate the cost of the inventory. The following illustrates the gross margin method:

$$\frac{\text{average gross margin for past 3 years}}{\text{average net sales for past 3 years}} = \frac{\$120,000}{\$300,000} = \frac{40\% \text{ gross margin}}{\text{percentage}}$$

Net sales for current year	$320,000
Gross margin percentage	40%
Estimated gross margin for current year	$128,000

Net sales for current year	$320,000
Less: Estimated gross margin for year	128,000
Estimated cost of goods sold for year	$192,000
Inventory at beginning of year	$ 40,000
Net purchases for year	195,000
Cost of goods available for sale	$235,000
Less: Estimated cost of goods sold	192,000
Estimated cost of inventory	$ 43,000

An alternate approach is to apply the cost of goods sold rate to net sales to estimate directly cost of goods sold. The past **cost of goods sold rate** is determined by dividing cost of goods sold by net sales or by deducting the gross margin percentage from 100 percent. For the previous illustration, cost of goods sold could have been estimated as follows:

Net sales for current year	$320,000
Cost of goods sold rate (100% − 40%)	60%
Estimated cost of goods sold for year	$192,000

The gross margin method is used when inventory cannot be counted, when it would be impractical to count it, or when the reasonableness of the inventory balance is being tested. For example, the gross margin method is appropriate if inventory has been destroyed or it is otherwise impossible to count the items; if auditors are testing the reasonableness of recorded inventory balances or the physical inventory value; if interim reports are being prepared, and the periodic inventory system is used; or if budgets are being developed.

If the gross margin on items included in inventory varies significantly, the goods should be classified into groups of items with similar gross margin percentages and a separate estimate of the cost of inventory made for each group. Failure to follow this procedure could lead to misleading estimates of inventory and cost of goods sold, especially if the mix of products sold varies from period to period. Sometimes the average gross margin percentage for the past years is not representative of the current percentage relationship between gross margin and net sales. When this is true, an estimate of the current gross margin percentage is substituted for the historical average to estimate accurately inventory cost and cost of goods sold.

Retail Method   The **retail method** is a method by which inventory cost is estimated from the retail sales value of ending inventory. It is often used in retail-type businesses like clothing and department stores. Although the method avoids the detailed tracing of cost prices to specific items or groups of items still in stock, additional data regarding the retail value of purchases, beginning inventory, and purchase returns, and net markups and net markdowns in selling prices must be collected. **Net markups** are increases in the original retail prices of merchandise less cancellations of such increases. **Net markdowns** are decreases in the original retail prices of merchandise less cancellations of such decreases.

In applying the retail method, a **cost-to-retail percentage** is calculated by dividing the cost of goods available for sale by the retail value of goods available for sale. Usually the cost-to-retail percentage is calculated after adding in net markups, but before deducting the net markdowns. This approach yields the lowest possible cost-to-retail percentage and is said to approximate the lower-of-cost-or-market method. The cost-to-retail percentage is applied to the retail value of the physical inventory to determine the estimated lower-of-cost-or-market value of the ending inventory. The following is an illustration of the retail method:

	Cost	Retail
Inventory, January 1, 19x4	$ 45,000	$ 68,000
Purchases	200,000	300,000
Freight-in	10,000	
Purchase returns	(5,000)	(8,000)
Net markups		15,000
Available for sale	$250,000	$375,000
Cost-to-retail percentage		
$\dfrac{\$250,000}{\$375,000}$	66⅔%	
Physical inventory at retail		$ 72,000
Ending inventory at cost ($72,000 × 66⅔%)	$ 48,000	

To identify a possible shortage or any errors in the record-keeping or physical inventory, an estimated retail value for the ending inventory can be calculated by deducting net markdowns and sales (less sales returns) from the retail value of goods available for sale. The estimated retail value of the ending inventory is then compared to the retail value of the physical inventory to identify the amount of any shortage or error at retail values. The cost of the shortage or error is determined by applying the cost-to-retail percentage to the retail value of the shortage as follows:

Available for sale at retail		$375,000
Less: Net markdowns	$ 25,000	
Sales less sales returns	275,000	300,000
Estimated ending inventory at retail		$ 75,000
Physical inventory at retail		72,000
Inventory shortage at retail		$ 3,000
Inventory shortage at cost ($3,000 × 66⅔%)		$ 2,000

When the retail method is used, the inventory items are usually classified into groups with similar gross margin percentages. A separate cost-to-retail percentage is then determined for each group and used to estimate the inventory value of each group. This is done for the same reason it is when the gross margin method is used. The retail method is used to: (1) determine the inventory value to be reported on the balance sheet; (2) control inventory by providing an estimate of the inventory balance which can be compared to the actual balance as a means of identifying errors and shortages; and (3) estimate the inventory balance for interim financial statements and budgets.

REVIEW PROBLEM

Determine the inventory balance to be reported on the financial statements in each of the following independent cases.

Case A   A company sells three products, X, Y, and Z. The quantity on hand at the end of the current period and unit costs and current replacement costs are:

Product	Quantity	Unit Cost	Unit Replacement Cost
X	200	$4.00	$4.20
Y	1,000	3.50	3.40
Z	700	5.00	4.90

Case B   The physical inventory identifies obsolete merchandise with a cost of $1,200; a normal selling price of $1,800; an expected selling price of $900; and expected disposal costs of $100.

Case C   A company's records indicate the following:

Beginning inventory	$ 20,000
Net purchases	$180,000
Net sales	$279,000
Gross margin percentage	33⅓%

Case D   A company's records indicate the following:

	Cost	Retail
Beginning inventory	$ 30,000	$ 50,000
Net purchases	170,000	245,000
Net markups		5,000
Net markdowns		10,000
Physical inventory		60,000

Solution to review problem

Case A

Product	Quantity	Unit Cost	Unit Market Value	Unit Lower-of-Cost-or-Market	Total Lower-of-Cost-or-Market
X	200	$4.00	$4.20	$4.00	$ 800
Y	1,000	3.50	3.40	3.40	3,400
Z	700	5.00	4.90	4.90	3,430
					$7,630

Case B

Expected sales price	$900
Less: Expected disposal costs	100
Net realizable value	$800

Case C

Net sales	$279,000
Cost of goods sold rate (100% − 33⅓%)	66⅔%
Estimated cost of goods sold	$186,000
Beginning inventory	$ 20,000
Net purchases	180,000
Cost of goods available for sale	$200,000
Less: Estimated cost of goods sold	186,000
Estimated cost of inventory	$ 14,000

Case D

	Cost	Retail
Beginning inventory	$ 30,000	$ 50,000
Net purchases	170,000	245,000
Net markups		5,000
Available for sale	$200,000	$300,000
Cost-to-retail percentage ($200,000/$300,000)	66⅔%	
Physical inventory at retail		$ 60,000
Ending inventory at lower-of-cost-or-market ($60,000 × 66⅔%)	$ 40,000	

SUMMARY

Cost is the basis of inventory valuation that is in accord with generally accepted accounting principles. Under certain circumstances, however, an exception is necessary if financial position and operating results are to be presented fairly. Two commonly used alternate valuation methods, lower-of-cost-or-market and net realizable value, were discussed in this unit. Two methods of estimating inventory value when actual valuation is difficult or impossible—the gross margin and retail methods—were also explained. Whatever valuation method is used should be properly disclosed parenthetically or in the notes to the financial statements.

REVIEW QUESTIONS

19-1   How should inventory be valued for financial reporting?

19-2   Describe how inventory should be valued under the lower-of-cost-or-market method.

19-3   The lower-of-cost-or-market method is a conservative accounting procedure. Explain.

19-4   When should the lower-of-cost-or-market method be used?

19-5   How is the difference between cost and a lower market value accounted for at the end of each accounting period?

19-6   **a.**   Define "net realizable value."
  b.   When should the net realizable value method of valuation be used for inventory?

19-7   Describe the gross margin method of estimating inventory cost.

19-8   When can the gross margin method be used?

19-9   Describe the retail method of estimating inventory cost.

19-10   When can the retail method be used?

19-11   Why is the cost-to-retail percentage in the retail method usually determined with net markups included in, but net markdowns excluded from, the retail value of goods available for sale?

19-12   Why should inventory items be classified into groups with similar gross margin percentages when the gross margin or retail methods are used?

EXERCISES

19-1   Zachary Company values inventory at the lower-of-cost-or-market. At the end of the current period the data for inventory included the following:

	Quantity	Unit Cost	Unit Replacement Cost
Category I:			
Item A	2,000	$2.80	$2.70
Item B	800	1.50	1.60
Category II:			
Item X	3,000	3.40	3.50
Item Y	500	2.25	2.10
Item Z	1,200	1.25	1.20

Required   Determine the inventory value for financial reporting if the lower-of-cost-or-market method is applied (a) item-by-item, (b) by categories, and (c) for the entire inventory.

19-2   Melodie Corp. determined the following values for inventory at the end of three consecutive years:

Year	Cost	Market Value
19x1	$32,000	$32,000
19x2	35,000	33,500
19x3	30,000	29,600

Required   Prepare any necessary adjusting entry at the end of each year to apply the lower-of-cost-or-market method.

19-3   Clemetine Company completed its physical inventory at the end of the current period, and the following information on damaged and obsolete merchandise was obtained.

	Original Cost	Original Sales Price	Expected Sales Price	Expected Selling Costs
Damaged goods	$2,400	$4,000	$2,500	$300
Obsolete goods	1,200	2,000	800	100

Required   Determine the value of the damaged goods and the obsolete goods for financial reporting.

19-4   The accountant for the Petrie Company is preparing interim financial statements for the second quarter of the current year. Rather than taking a physical inventory, she uses the gross margin method to estimate the ending inventory. Using the following data, estimate the ending inventory as of June 30.

Inventory, March 31	$ 5,800
Sales	92,400
Purchases	56,750
Purchase discounts	1,200
Freight-in	2,700
Average gross margin percentage for the second quarter of the last three years	40%

19-5 Dudley Drummer operates a retail store and has asked you to compute the ending inventory at cost as of December 31, 19x4. His sales for 19x4 amounted to $150,000. An actual count of the merchandise on hand on December 31 totaled $45,000 at retail prices. The records show the following information:

	Cost	Retail
Beginning inventory, January 1	$ 35,600	$ 44,200
Purchases (net)	101,950	152,300

Required   **a.** Determine the estimated lower-of-cost-or-market value for inventory at December 31, 19x4.

 b. Determine the cost of any inventory shortage.

PROBLEMS

19-1 The Riskie Sales Company uses the lower-of-cost-or-market method to value its inventory. The company sells five different products, which can be classified into two separate categories. The following are the items, their unit costs and market prices, and the quantities on hand at December 31, 19x1:

	Quantity	Unit Cost	Unit Current Replacement Cost
Category I:			
Product A	1,200	$1.50	$1.60
Product B	8,500	.60	.58
Category II:			
Product X	450	2.20	2.20
Product Y	2,400	.80	.82
Product Z	4,100	1.10	1.05

At December 31, 19x2, the cost and market value of the ending inventory are $15,100 and $14,450, respectively.

Required a. Determine the value of the ending inventory at December 31, 19x1, if the lower-of-cost-or-market method is applied (1) item-by-item, (2) by categories, and (3) for the entire inventory.

b. Prepare the necessary adjusting entries at December 31, 19x1 and 19x2, to apply the lower-of-cost-or-market method on an item-by-item basis.

c. Prepare partial financial statements at the end of 19x2.

19-2 The Blek Company has had an average gross profit on sales of 40 percent for several years. The company suspects unexplained losses of merchandise from its warehouse during the current year. The following information is taken from the records:

Beginning inventory	$ 4,200
Purchases	26,000
Transportation-in	400
Cost of delivering sales	800
Net sales	40,000
Physical ending inventory (at average cost)	3,200

Required a. Determine a reasonable estimate of inventory cost at the end of the period.

b. Determine the apparent stock shortage at the end of the period.

19-3 The Bilgewater Department Store uses the retail inventory method to estimate its ending inventory. On January 31 of the current year a physical inventory showed that the company had $32,000 of merchandise on hand at retail prices. The accounting department accumulated the following data:

	Cost	Retail
Beginning Inventory	$ 15,000	$ 25,000
Purchases	150,000	235,000
Purchase Returns	6,000	9,000
Purchase Discounts	1,000	
Freight-in	2,000	
Sales		214,000
Sales Returns		4,000
Net Markups		5,000
Net Markdowns		10,000

Required a. Determine the cost of the January 31 inventory to be reported on the company's financial statements.

b. Determine the amount of any inventory shortage.

19-4 Plumm Corp., which sells a single product, has completed its first year of operations. Company officers would like to use the inventory method that will consistently yield the lowest income before taxes and thus the lowest income tax payment. The following is a summary of business operations for 19x1:

Month	Purchases		Sales	
	Units	Unit Cost	Units	Unit Price
January	10,000	$2.40	4,000	$4.00
February	8,000	2.40	9,000	4.00
March	6,000	2.45	5,000	4.00
April	10,000	2.45	8,000	4.00
May	12,000	2.50	10,000	4.25
June	15,000	2.55	16,000	4.25
July	12,000	2.60	14,000	4.25
August	10,000	2.60	12,000	4.25
September	8,000	2.55	7,000	4.25
October	12,000	2.50	9,000	4.25
November	15,000	2.50	10,000	4.00
December	12,000	2.45	15,000	4.00

At the end of the year the current replacement cost of the product was $2.40. The company uses periodic inventory procedures.

Required **a.** Which of the following inventory methods yields the lowest income before taxes for 19x1?

   (1) lifo
   (2) lower-of-fifo-cost-or-market
   (3) lower-of-average-cost-or-market
   (4) fifo
   (5) average cost

b. What inventory method will consistently yield the lowest income before taxes? Explain.

Chapter 7

Plant, Intangible, and Other Assets

Business entities own noncurrent assets, such as land, buildings, machinery, equipment, patents, and other rights and costs, that will be used in generating revenue over more than one accounting period. This chapter explains and illustrates the measurement and reporting problems for these noncurrent assets.

Unit 20
Acquisition and Disposal of Plant Assets

It's going to be a tough decision when the purchasing agent starts negotiating to buy the machine that's to replace him.

Dave Murray, as quoted in Reader's Digest, *November 1962*

The problems of measuring and recording acquisition costs and costs incurred subsequent to acquisition for plant assets, and of accounting for the disposal of plant assets are discussed in this unit.

Performance Objectives

Upon completion of this unit you should be able to:

1. define and use the accounting terms introduced in this unit.
2. describe or explain:
   a. the distinction between capital and revenue expenditures
   b. the costs to be included as part of the cost of specific plant assets
   c. how to measure the cost of a plant asset acquired in a noncash exchange
   d. how to report plant assets on the balance sheet
   e. how to account for the disposition or write-off of plant assets
3. determine:
   a. the costs to be charged to a plant asset account as a capital expenditure
   b. the costs to be charged to expense as a revenue expenditure
   c. the cost of a plant asset acquired in a noncash exchange
   d. the gain or loss to be recognized on the disposition of a plant asset

Nature and Control of Plant Assets

Plant assets are tangible, long-lived assets intended for use in business operations and *not* intended for resale. That is, they are to be used in regular business activities; they may be sold when no longer useful for this purpose—but they are not intended to be sold as trade products. Plant assets are of three types:

1. those *not* subject to depreciation, such as land.
2. those subject to depreciation, such as buildings, equipment, furniture, vehicles, and tools.
3. those subject to depletion, such as natural resources (see Unit 22).

Measuring and Recording Acquisition Costs

The acquisition cost of plant assets should be determined according to the cost principle. Thus, the cost of plant assets, as well as other noncurrent assets, should be measured by one of the following:

1. amount of cash paid
2. present value of liabilities incurred
3. market value of stock issued, or the fair value of the assets acquired if the latter is more clearly determinable
4. a. the fair value of noncash assets or services exchanged, or the fair value of the assets acquired if the latter is more clearly determinable
   b. the book value of noncash assets given up in an exchange, but not exceeding the fair value of the assets received

Fair value may be interpreted to mean the current cash equivalent price of the noncash assets received or given up in an exchange. **Present value** means the current cash equivalent of the liabilities incurred. Interest is excluded from the cost of the asset and treated as an incidental expense because cost should not vary just because alternate methods of financing are used.

Assume that a company can purchase certain equipment with a list price of $4,800 and a cash price of $4,500 by (1) paying cash, (2) issuing a 6-month, 8% note for $4,500, or (3) issuing 300 shares of common stock with a par value of $10 per share and a market value of $15 per share. The cost of the asset in each case is $4,500, the current cash equivalent price required to purchase it. The difference between the list price and cash price is considered a trade discount; the cost of the asset is recorded at the price paid after deducting the trade discount. The journal entries for the three purchase alternatives would be:

| 1. | Equipment | 4,500 | |
| | Cash | | 4,500 |

To record cash purchase of equipment.

| 2. | Equipment | 4,500 | |
| | Notes Payable | | 4,500 |

To record purchase of equipment by issuing
a 6-month, 8% note.

3.	Equipment	4,500	
	Common Stock		3,000
	Contributed Capital in Excess of Par		1,500

To record purchase of equipment by issuing
common stock ($10 × 300 = $3,000;
$15 × 300 = $4,500; $4,500 − 3,000
= $1,500).

In general, the acquisition cost of plant assets should include:

1. the cash purchase price net of trade and cash discounts (that is, the current cash equivalent price)
2. all necessary costs to acquire the asset, for example, sales tax, excise taxes, and legal fees
3. all necessary costs to put the asset into initial use, for example, freight costs, insurance during transit, installation costs, break-in costs, and reconditioning costs for used assets

Assume that equipment is purchased with an invoice price of $5,000 subject to credit terms of 2/10, n/30. In addition, freight costs of $250 are paid to a trucking company and installation costs of $300 are paid to a local contractor. The cost of the asset should always be recorded net of any cash discounts available. If the discount is lost, the lost discount should be recorded as an incidental expense when the invoice is paid. The cost of the equipment is determined as follows:

Invoice price	$5,000
Less: Cash discount ($5,000 × 2%)	100
Net purchase price	$4,900
Add: Freight costs	250
Installation costs	300
Cost of equipment	$5,450

The entries to record the expenditures for the acquisition of the equipment would be:

Equipment	4,900	
Accounts Payable		4,900

To record purchase of equipment net of cash
discount.

Equipment	250	
Cash		250

To record freight costs paid on equipment
purchased.

Equipment	300	
Cash		300

To record installation costs paid for equipment.

Occasionally, a company may make a **lump-sum purchase** of assets, in which case each asset should be recorded in a separate account. The lump-sum purchase price is often less than the sum of the individual purchase prices of the assets being acquired. The cost of the individual assets is found by allocating the total purchase price in the ratio of the value of each asset to the total value of all assets purchased for the lump sum. The value used in the allocation can be the current fair value, the tax assessed value, or some other common value.

Assume that a company purchases trucks and machinery for a lump-sum price of $24,000 from a company going out of business. The current cash prices of the trucks and machinery are estimated at $12,000 and $18,000, respectively. The cost to be recorded for the trucks and machinery is determined as follows:

Asset	Fair Value	Cost Allocation	
Trucks	$12,000	$ 9,600	($24,000 × $12,000/$30,000)
Machinery	18,000	14,400	($24,000 × $18,000/$30,000)
Total	$30,000	$24,000	

The entry to record the lump-sum purchase would be:

Trucks	9,600	
Machinery	14,400	
Cash		24,000

To record lump-sum purchase of trucks and
machinery.

Any costs incurred for reconditioning the trucks or for reconditioning or installing the machinery before initial use would be charged to the respective accounts.

Land and Land Improvements   The cost of land should include legal fees for title search, closing the purchase, and contract negotiations; fees paid to clear and grade the land; back property taxes accrued at the time of purchase; property taxes during the construction of a building; the demolition cost of old buildings on land acquired; and any other costs necessary to acquire the land and prepare it for its intended use. It is important to distinguish between the cost of the land and the cost of land improvements. Land does not deteriorate or have to be replaced; thus, land is not depreciated. Land improvements, including shrubbery, flowers, and sidewalks; curbs, gutters, streets, and sewers; parking lots; and so on, must be replaced, and, thus, are subject to depreciation.

Buildings   The cost of buildings includes legal fees for title search, closing the purchase, and contract negotiations; back property taxes accrued at the time of purchase; renovation costs; construction costs; insurance and property taxes during the construction period; and any other costs necessary to acquire or construct buildings and prepare them for their intended use.

Equipment   The cost of machinery, trucks, cars, furniture, store fixtures, office equipment, and other equipment should include freight charges, insurance during shipment, installation costs, break-in costs, legal fees, reconditioning costs, sales and excise taxes, and any other costs necessary to acquire and prepare the equipment for its intended use.

Measuring and Recording Costs After Acquisition

All the costs incurred to acquire and put plant assets into initial use are *capitalized,* that is, charged to an asset account. Costs incurred after the acquisition and initial use of plant assets, however, must be charged either to an asset account or to an expense account depending on the nature of the expenditure. Costs that extend the life of an asset or increase its utility through increased output or decreased operating costs are capitalized as part of the asset's cost. Costs incurred to maintain the normal or exclusive right to plant assets, to maintain their value, or to keep them in their normal operating condition should be charged to expense as incurred.

Costs charged to an asset account because they benefit more than one accounting period are called **capital expenditures.** Costs charged to an expense account because they primarily benefit only the current accounting period are called **revenue expenditures.** Capital expenditures include **extraordinary repairs,** such as major replacements, renewals, betterments, and improvements, additions, and machinery rearrangement costs. Revenue expenditures include maintenance and **ordinary repairs,** such as minor replacements or renewals and minor improvements or betterments.

The distinction between capital expenditures and revenue expenditures in actual situations is not always clear. For example, should repairs be treated as extraordinary (capital expenditures) or ordinary (revenue expenditures)? Are decorating costs, the cost of new tires, and so on, capital or revenue expenditures? The circumstances and the reason for incurring the costs—not the amount of the costs alone—must be analyzed to determine the proper accounting treatment.

Capital Expenditure   If costs, such as decorating and new tires, are incurred to prepare the assets for initial use, they are treated as capital expenditures and charged to the plant asset account. A **major replacement or renewal** includes substituting a major component of a plant asset, such as a roof, a furnace, an air conditioning system, or a truck or car engine, with a component that is generally similar in output and efficiency. A **major improvement or betterment** includes substituting a major component with one that significantly improves the efficiency or output of the asset, such as upgrading the electrical wiring of a building, replacing a motor with a more powerful one, and replacing machinery components with those that improve product quality. If the cost and accumulated depreciation of major components being replaced can be determined, the accounting treatment for them is the same as for the disposal of a plant asset (see pages 384–385). Otherwise, they are accounted for in the same manner as other extraordinary repairs, that is, as a capital expenditure, and added to the asset account.[1]

Assume that extraordinary repairs of $2,500 are incurred on equipment with a cost of $15,000; accumulated depreciation of $10,000; an original useful life of six years; and a remaining useful life of two years. The entry to record the cost of the repairs would be:

Equipment	2,500	
Cash		2,500
To record extraordinary repairs.		

After the repairs are made, the undepreciated cost of the equipment will be $7,500 ($15,000 − 10,000 + 2,500). Thus, the annual depreciation expense over the remaining two years will be $3,750 ($7,500/2):

Depreciation expense	3,750	
Accumulated depreciation		3,750
To record annual depreciation expense after		
extraordinary repairs are incurred.		

Revenue Expenditure   If costs such as decorating and new tires are incurred after the plant assets are put into initial use, they are treated as revenue expenditures and

---

[1] In practice, extraordinary repairs that extend an asset's life are often charged to accumulated depreciation instead of to the asset account, thereby extending the time required to depreciate the asset. This procedure is discussed in intermediate accounting courses.

charged to maintenance or repair expense accounts. **Minor replacements or renewals** include the replacement or renewal of minor components of a fixed asset, such as light bulbs, fan belts, spark plugs, and similar small parts. Their replacement does not increase the life or utility of the asset, but is necessary to keep the asset in normal, good operating condition for its original expected life. Similarly, **minor improvements or betterments** have relatively insignificant effects on the output and efficiency of an asset and are charged to maintenance or repair expense.

Assume that a company incurs ordinary repairs of $700 on equipment that has broken down. The entry to record the ordinary repairs would be:

Repairs Expense	700	
Cash		700
To record ordinary repairs.		

Disposal of Plant Assets

Plant assets are generally disposed of in one of three ways: sale, retirement, or trade-in. In each case the general procedures to account for the disposal are:

1. Record depreciation for the portion of the current period up to the date of disposal.
2. Record any monetary or nonmonetary consideration received from the disposal.
3. Remove from the accounts the cost and accumulated depreciation for the asset being disposed of.
4. Record any monetary or nonmonetary consideration paid to acquire new assets at the same time.

When a plant asset is sold before the end of its useful life, or is retired and sold for scrap, the first three procedures are applied. Assume that equipment with a cost of $17,600; a salvage value of $1,600; accumulated depreciation of $12,000 for the first six years; and an expected useful life of eight years is sold for $4,500 on April 1 of the seventh year. If the accounting period is the calendar year, depreciation for January 1–April 1 of the seventh year must be recorded:

April 1	Depreciation Expense	500	
	Accumulated Depreciation		500
	To record depreciation for partial year on equipment sold ($17,600 − $1,600/8 = $2,000; $2,000 × 3/12 = $500).		

The entry to record the sale of the equipment will require the removal of the cost of the equipment ($17,600) and accumulated depreciation for $6^{1}/_{4}$ years ($2,000 $\times$ $6^{1}/_{4}$ = $12,500) and the recording of the cash received. The difference between the cash received ($4,500) and the book value of the asset ($17,600 $-$ 12,500 = $5,100) indicates the gain or loss on the disposal. In this example there is a loss of $600 ($5,100 $-$ 4,500). The journal entry would be:

Cash	4,500	
Loss on Disposal of Plant Assets	600	
Accumulated Depreciation	12,500	
Equipment		17,600
To record sale of equipment.		

If a plant asset is retired by abandoning or scrapping it without any consideration being received, depreciation is brought up to date and the cost and accumulated depreciation for the asset are eliminated from the accounts (procedures 1 and 3). Any undepreciated cost at the time it is scrapped will be recorded as a loss. Assume equipment with a cost of $8,800 and accumulated depreciation of $8,250 is scrapped without receiving any consideration. The entry to write off the asset would include a loss of $550 ($8,800 $-$ 8,250):

Accumulated Depreciation	8,250	
Loss on Disposal of Plant Assets	550	
Equipment		8,800
To write off equipment scrapped.		

Trade-In of Plant Assets

When a trade-in occurs, all four disposal procedures are applied to account for it. APB Opinion No. 29 indicates that the general rule for **nonmonetary exchanges,** such as trade-ins, is to record the cost of the asset acquired at the fair value of the asset given up, or the fair value of the asset received if the latter is more clearly determinable, plus any cash difference paid. However, the APB modified the rule for nonmonetary exchanges involving similar assets. This modification is based on the idea that the earnings potential of the old asset is not culminated if a similar asset is acquired in exchange for it. Thus, when similar assets are exchanged, the cost of the asset acquired is the book value of the old asset given up, plus any cash difference paid; however, cost cannot exceed the fair value of the asset received. For similar assets, then, no gain can be recognized although any loss will be recognized. For dissimilar assets, any gain or loss is always recognized.

Assume that a company pays $8,200 cash and trades in old equipment with a cost of $10,500 and accumulated depreciation of $7,000 (at the time of the exchange) for new equipment with a list price of $12,500 and a cash price of $12,000. If the assets are considered to be dissimilar, the cost of the new asset will be the fair value of the old asset given up plus the cash difference paid. When the fair value of the old asset is not determinable, it is implied to be the difference between the fair value of the asset acquired and the cash paid. In this illustration the fair value of the old asset is implied to be $3,800 ($12,000 − 8,200), and the cost of the new asset is recorded as $12,000 as follows:

Equipment (new)	12,000	
Accumulated Depreciation	7,000	
Equipment (old)		10,500
Cash		8,200
Gain on Disposal of Plant Assets		300
To record trade-in of dissimilar assets; gain of		
$300 determined as follows:		
Fair value of asset given up	$ 3,800	
Book value of asset given ($10,500 − 7,000)	3,500	
Gain on disposal of asset	$ 300	

Exhibit 20.1 summarizes the procedures for determining the cost of the asset acquired and any gain or loss to be recognized, using data from this case and the two following.

If the assets in the previous illustration are considered to be similar, the gain will not be recognized and the cost of the asset acquired will be recorded as $11,700, that is, the book value of the old asset ($3,500) plus the cash difference paid ($8,200):

Equipment (new)	11,700	
Accumulated Depreciation	7,000	
Equipment (old)		10,500
Cash		8,200
To record trade-in of similar assets.		

Now assume that the cash difference is $8,700 instead of $8,200. The book value of the old asset plus the cash difference paid equals $12,200 ($3,500 + 8,700) and exceeds the fair value of the new asset of $12,000. Thus, the cost of the new asset must be recorded as $12,000, and a loss of $200 must be recognized as follows:

Exhibit 20.1

Dissimilar assets

$$\underset{\text{old asset*}}{\text{fair value of}} + \underset{\text{paid}}{\text{cash difference}} = \underset{\text{asset}}{\text{cost of new}}$$

$$\$3,800 \quad + \quad \$8,200 \quad = \quad \$12,000$$

*Implied, if not known, by deducting the cash difference paid from the fair value of the new asset, e.g., $12,000 − 8,200 = $3,800. Thus, the fair value of the new asset is the cost of the new asset when the fair value of the old asset cannot be determined.

$$\underset{\text{recognized}}{\text{gain or loss}} = \underset{\text{old asset}}{\text{fair value of}} - \underset{\text{old asset}}{\text{book value of}}$$

$$\$300 \text{ gain} = \quad \$3,800 \quad - \quad \$3,500$$

Similar assets

$$\underset{\text{old asset}}{\text{book value of}} + \underset{\text{paid}}{\text{cash difference}} = \underset{\text{asset **}}{\text{cost of new}} + \underset{\text{recognized **}}{\text{loss}}$$

$$\$3,500 \quad + \quad \$8,200 \quad = \quad \$11,700 \quad + \quad \$ \ 0$$
$$\$3,500 \quad + \quad \$8,700 \quad = \quad \$12,000 \quad + \quad \$200$$

**Cost of new asset cannot exceed the fair value of the new asset, e.g., $12,000 in the second situation; thus, a loss is recognized for the excess of the book value of the old asset plus the cash difference paid over the fair value of the new asset.

$$\underset{\text{recognized}}{\text{loss}} = \underset{\text{old asset}}{\text{book value of}} + \underset{\text{paid}}{\text{cash difference}} - \underset{\text{new asset}}{\text{fair value of}}$$

$$\$200 \quad = \quad \$3,500 \quad + \quad \$8,700 \quad - \quad \$12,000$$

Equipment	12,000	
Accumulated Depreciation	7,000	
Loss on Disposal of Plant Assets	200	
Equipment (old)		10,500
Cash		8,700

To record trade-in of similar assets where book
value of old asset plus cash paid exceeds the
fair value of the asset acquired.

REVIEW PROBLEM

Kane Corp. purchased several plant assets during 19*x1;* the transactions are described
in the following list:

Jan. 5	Purchased equipment with an invoice price of $6,500 subject to credit terms of 2/10, n/30. Freight charges of $150 were also billed on the invoice.
Jan. 12	Paid $280 to install the equipment purchased on January 5.
Mar. 20	Purchased land and a building for a lump sum of $170,000; they have assessed values of $40,000 and $160,000, respectively.
Apr. 1	Purchased office furniture with a cost of $2,400 by using a 3-month, 8% note.
June 30	Traded in old equipment with a cost of $7,200, accumulated depreciation of $4,500 at January 1, 19x1, and an original useful life of 8 years for dissimilar equipment with a list price of $6,400. A cash difference of $4,000 was paid.
July 1	Paid the note issued on April 1.
Oct. 1	Traded in an old delivery truck with a cost of $6,000, a salvage value of $1,000, a useful life of 5 years, and accumulated depreciation of $3,250 at January 1, 19x1. A trade-in allowance of $2,400 was received on a similar truck with a list price of $6,800.

Required   Prepare all entries necessary to record the plant asset purchases.

Solution to review problem

Jan. 5	Equipment	6,520	
	Accounts Payable		6,520
	To record purchase of equipment net of cash discount [$6,500 + 150 − 2% ($6,500) = $6,520].		
Jan. 12	Equipment	280	
	Cash		280
	To record installation costs on equipment.		
Mar. 20	Land	34,000	
	Buildings	136,000	
	Cash		170,000
	To record lump-sum purchase of land and building; cost allocated as follows: (land, $170,000 × $40,000/$200,000 = $34,000; building, $170,000 × $160,000/$200,000 = $136,000).		

Apr. 1	Office Furniture	2,400	
	Notes Payable		2,400
	To record purchase of office furniture by issuing note.		
June 30	Depreciation Expense—Equipment	450	
	Accumulated Depreciation— Equipment		450
	To record depreciation for 19x1 on equipment traded in ($7,200/8 = $900; $900 × 6/12 = $450).		
June 30	Equipment (new)	6,400	
	Accumulated Depreciation— Equipment ($4,500 + 450)	4,950	
	Equipment (old)		7,200
	Cash		4,000
	Gain on Disposal of Plant Assets		150
	To record trade-in of dissimilar assets; gain of $150 recognized.		

Note   The cash price (fair value) of the new asset is assumed to be the list price of $6,400 because no other price is indicated. The fair value of the old asset is implied to be $2,400, the difference between the fair value of the new asset ($6,400) and the cash paid ($4,000). The gain recognized ($2,400 − 2,250 = $150) is the difference between the fair value of the old asset ($2,400) and the book value of the old asset ($7,200 − 4,950 = $2,250).

July 1	Notes Payable	2,400	
	Interest Expense	48	
	Cash		2,448
	To pay note and interest ($2,400 × 8% × 3/12 = $48).		
Oct. 1	Depreciation Expense—Delivery Equipment	750	
	Accumulated Depreciation— Delivery Equipment		750
	To record depreciation for 19x1 on delivery truck traded in ($6,000 − 1,000/5 = $1,000; $1,000 × 9/12 = $750).		

Oct. 1	Delivery Equipment (new)	6,400	
	Accumulated Depreciation—Delivery		
	Equipment ($3,250 + 750)	4,000	
	Delivery Equipment (old)		6,000
	Cash ($6,800 − 2,400)		4,400

To record trade-in of similar assets; the
cost of the new asset ($2,000
+ 4,400 = $6,400) is the sum of the
book value of the old asset ($6,000
− 4,000 = $2,000) and the cash
paid ($4,400).

Note   The fair value of the new asset is not given; thus, it is assumed to be at least $6,400, the implied cost of the new asset.

SUMMARY

How to measure and record the cost of plant assets and how to account for the disposal of plant assets were discussed in this unit. Costs that are incurred to acquire a plant asset, to put the asset into use, or to increase the utility of the asset subsequent to initial use are treated as capital expenditures. Costs incurred to keep a plant asset in normal, good operating condition are treated as revenue expenditures. When a plant asset is disposed of, its cost and accumulated depreciation at the date of disposal are removed from the accounts, and any cash or other assets received and any gain or loss to be recognized are recorded. Between the date of acquisition and the date of disposal, the cost of plant assets (excluding land) must be allocated to expense through the process of depreciation. The concept of depreciation and commonly used depreciation methods are discussed in the next unit.

REVIEW QUESTIONS

20-1   What is a plant asset? Identify four characteristics of a plant asset.

20-2   The cost of a plant asset should be determined in accordance with the cost principle. How is the cost of a plant asset measured if the cost principle is applied?

20-3   Explain what costs are generally included in the acquisition cost of a plant asset.

20-4 Briefly describe the costs typically charged to these plant assets: (a) land, (b) land improvements, (c) buildings, and (d) equipment.

20-5 How is the cost assigned to individual plant assets when they are acquired in a lump-sum purchase?

20-6 Distinguish between a capital expenditure and a revenue expenditure. Why is this distinction important?

20-7 Define each of the following terms:

      a. major replacement or renewal
      b. major improvement or betterment
      c. extraordinary repair
      d. minor replacement or renewal
      e. minor improvement or betterment
      f. ordinary repair

20-8 Describe how each type of expenditure in question 20–7 should be accounted for according to current accounting practice.

20-9 What are the three ways in which a company can dispose of a plant asset?

20-10 Indicate the four general procedures for recording the disposition of a plant asset.

20-11 Explain how the cost of the new plant asset and the amount of gain or loss to be recognized, if any, from a nonmonetary exchange (i.e., trade-in) will be determined if the assets exchanged are (a) similar and (b) dissimilar.

EXERCISES

20-1 On January 2, 19x4, Hildebrand Corp. purchased machinery with an invoice price of $17,500 and a list price of $18,000. The purchase was subject to credit terms of 2/10, n/30; the invoice price included a $500 charge for shipping and installation. The machinery had an expected useful life of 6 years and an estimated residual value of $900.

    Required **a.** Prepare the entry to record the purchase of the machinery.
                b. Prepare the entry to pay the invoice after the expiration of the discount period.
                c. Prepare the entry to record depreciation for 19x4.

20-2 At the beginning of 19x5 Klout Corp. purchased a machine and a truck for a lump-sum price of $10,800 from Buste Company, which was liquidating its assets. The truck had a fair value of $4,500 and the machine had a fair value of $13,500 at the time of their purchase. The truck was reconditioned at a cost of $800, and the machine was shipped at a cost of $300 and installed at a cost of $900. Both the machine and the truck had expected useful lives of 4 years and estimated residual values of $500.

Required　**a.**　Prepare the entry to record the purchase of the machine and truck.
　　　　　b.　Prepare the entries to record the reconditioning, shipping, and installation costs.
　　　　　c.　Prepare the entries to record depreciation expense for 19x5.

20-3　The following are descriptions of several expenditures. Indicate with an X in the appropriate column whether each expenditure is a capital expenditure, a revenue expenditure, or neither of these. In the same way indicate whether each expenditure should be charged to land, land improvements, buildings, or repair and maintenance expense.

Description of Expenditure	Type of Expenditure			Charge the Expenditure to:				
	Capital	Revenue	Neither	Land	Land Improvements	Buildings	Repair & Maint. Expense	Ins. & Tax Expense
Example: Acquired a building site for $18,500	X			X				

　　a.　Prepared the land for construction of a building at a cost of $3,500
　　b.　Paid construction costs, $125,000
　　c.　Paid insurance and taxes during construction, $2,800
　　d.　Paved a parking lot and put in sidewalks, $6,500
　　e.　Planted trees, shrubs, and flowers, $2,200
　　f.　Paid insurance and taxes for balance of year after completion of construction, $2,800
　　g.　Repainted building 3 years after completion of construction, $7,500
　　h.　Incurred ordinary repair and maintenance costs, $1,100
　　i.　Paid $3,200 assessment for street and sewer improvements
　　j.　Replaced the furnace at a cost of $2,600

20-4　During 19x6 Cabot Truck Lines made the following asset disposals:

May 5	Abandoned a forklift purchased on January 2, 19x1, at a cost of $1,250; the forklift had an estimated life of 6 years when acquired.
June 19	Sold an old truck purchased on April 10, 19x3, at a cost of $4,700 for $2,100; the truck had an estimated life of 4 years and an estimated scrap value of $700.
Oct. 2	Traded in old truck with a cost of $6,800 when acquired on November 5, 19x4, for a new truck with a list price of $7,200. Both trucks have 4-year lives and scrap values of $800. The company received a trade-in allowance of $4,200 on the old truck. The old truck had a fair market value of $3,850 at the date of the trade-in.

Required   Prepare the entries necessary to record depreciation expense for 19*x6* and to record the asset disposals during 19*x6*.

20-5   On July 8, 19*x8*, Hybouy Company traded in old equipment with a cost of $18,600, an estimated life of 6 years, and an estimated residual value of $1,500, which had been purchased on January 2, 19*x4*. The new equipment acquired had a list price of $21,000, a cash price of $20,000, an estimated life of 6 years, and an estimated residual value of $2,000. A trade-in allowance of $6,900 was received.

Required   **a.**   Prepare the entry to record depreciation for 19*x8* on the old equipment.

b.   Prepare the entry to record the acquisition of the new equipment if the assets are considered to be (1) similar and (2) dissimilar.

PROBLEMS

20-1   Ramon Company completed the following transactions involving plant assets during 19*x3*:

a.   Land and an old building were acquired for $40,000; the land was valued at $30,000 and the building at $20,000 at the time of purchase; the old building is to be demolished and a new building constructed.

b.   Demolition costs of the old building in a amount to $4,500.

c.   Costs to prepare the land for building construction were $2,100.

d.   Construction costs totaled $165,000 compared to a construction cost estimate of $150,000. The additional costs were incurred primarily as a result of changes in building plans.

e.   Costs of moving equipment from a building rented prior to construction to the new building were $8,400.

f.   Insurance and property taxes on the new building for the year were $6,400; construction occurred during the first half of the year; operations from the new building started in mid-year.

g.   A major overhaul of a company machine was completed at a cost of $4,500; the machine's life was increased by 3 years; originally the machine had cost $13,500, had an 8-year life, and had a scrap value of $700; the machine had been acquired five years ago.

h.   A used truck was purchased at a cost of $4,600 and costs of $350 for new tires and reconditioning were incurred prior to use. The truck has an expected useful life of 3 years and an expected residual value of $750.

i.   Three used machines were purchased for a lump-sum price of $27,000. The machines had estimated fair values of $6,000, $9,000, and $15,000. Installation costs for the machines were $300, $500, and $800.

j.   Office furniture with a list price of $18,000 was purchased for $17,100 plus delivery charges of $350. The purchase was subject to credit terms of 2/10, n/30.

Required   Prepare the entry or entries necessary to record each transaction described.

20-2   Hawkes Company purchased a company car with a cost of $5,600 on October 1, 19x2. The car had an expected useful life of 3 years and an estimated residual value of $1,400. Repair and maintenance costs were $80 in 19x2, $250 in 19x3, and $860 in 19x4; $530 of the repair costs in 19x4 were necessary due to an accident. Early in 19x5 the engine of the car had to be replaced at a cost of $1,150; additional repair costs for 19x5 were $120. After the engine replacement, the useful life of the car was 2 years. On September 20, 19x5, the car was traded in on a new car with a list price of $6,500, a cash price of $6,000, an estimated useful life of 3 years, and an estimated residual value of $1,500. A trade-in allowance of $2,000 was received.

Required   Record all transactions for the expenditures on the old and new cars for 19x2 – 19x5 including depreciation.

20-3   **a.**   The following three cases describe a nonmonetary exchange:

Case 1   An old machine with a cost of $10,000 and accumulated depreciation of $8,000 was traded in for a similar new machine with a list price of $13,000 and a cash price of $12,600. The old machine had a fair market value of $2,700. A cash difference of $10,000 was paid.

Case 2   The facts are the same as case 1, except that a cash difference of $10,800 was paid.

Case 3   The facts are the same as case 1, except that the machines are dissimilar.

Required   Determine the cost of the new machine and the gain or loss to be recognized, if any, on the exchange.

b.   Assume that the old machine in case 1 in part a is sold for $2,700 and that the new machine is purchased for cash.

Required   **(1)**   Determine the cost of the new machine and the gain or loss to be recognized, if any, on the sale of the old machine.
            (2)   Explain why there is a difference in the accounting treatment for the trade in case 1 in part a and the sale and purchase in part b.

20-4   The books of Sabre Corp. contain two accounts for plant assets. These accounts are:

Land and Buildings				
6/1/x1	Purchased land and building	160,000	12/31/x1 Depreciation (40 yr. life; straight-line method)	4,900
6/30/x1	Completed renovation of building	36,000	12/31/x2 Depreciation	4,900
7/1/x4	Completed new parking lot	7,500	12/31/x3 Depreciation	4,900
6/15/x5	Repainted building	6,900	12/21/x4 Depreciation	5,100

Equipment					
7/10/*x1*	Purchased office equipment	17,000	12/31/*x1*	Depreciation (10% annually)	1,700
1/5/*x2*	Purchased company auto	5,500	12/31/*x2*	Depreciation	2,250
			12/31/*x3*	Depreciation	2,250
1/12/*x5*	Purchased new auto	6,250	12/31/*x4*	Depreciation	2,250
			1/9/*x5*	Proceeds from sale of old auto	900

Additional information regarding plant assets:

a. The land and building had assessed values of $18,000 and $54,000, respectively, when purchased on June 1, 19*x1*.

b. The parking lot is expected to require repaving every 10 years, and the building is scheduled for repainting every 4 years.

c. The office equipment purchased July 10, 19*x1*, is expected to have a salvage value of 10% of its cost at the end of its 10-year useful life.

d. The auto purchased on January 5, 19*x2*, was expected to have a salvage value of $1,000 at the end of its 3-year useful life.

e. The auto purchased on January 12, 19*x5*, is expected to have a salvage value of $1,150 at the end of its 3-year useful life.

The company is being audited by CPAs at the end of 19*x5* for the first time. The auditors have indicated that the plant asset accounts are to be corrected.

Required   **a.** Determine the correct balance for each of the following accounts at the end of 19*x5*:

    (1) land
    (2) land improvements
    (3) building
    (4) accumulated depreciation—building
    (5) office equipment
    (6) accumulated depreciation—office equipment
    (7) company autos
    (8) accumulated depreciation—autos

b. Calculate depreciation expense for 19*x5*.

c. Calculate the gain or loss on the sale of the old auto on January 9, 19*x5*.

Unit 21
Depreciation of Plant Assets

The use of resources in haste
May cause a great National waste.

Alexis Lawrence Romanoff, Encyclopedia of Thoughts

The cost of plant assets is charged to expense through the process of depreciation over the accounting periods that benefit from these assets' use. Several alternate depreciation methods have been developed to allocate the cost of plant assets to expense in a rational, systematic manner that recognizes variations in asset usage, value, and upkeep. This unit explains and illustrates these alternative methods and indicates the factors that should be considered in selecting a depreciation method. The methods of reporting plant assets and accumulated depreciation are also discussed.

Performance Objectives

Upon completing this unit you should be able to:

1. define and use the accounting terms introduced in this unit.
2. explain or describe:
   a. how depreciation is calculated
   b. the factors relevant to computing depreciation
   c. how the book value of a plant asset is determined
   d. the characteristics of the four common depreciation methods
   e. a comparison of the income effects and the use, value, repair, and contribution patterns for the four common alternative depreciation methods
3. calculate depreciation expense, total accumulated depreciation, and/or the book value for a plant asset by any of the four common depreciation methods: the straight-line, productive-output, sum-of-years'-digits, and double-declining-balance methods.

Nature of Depreciation

For accounting purposes, **depreciation** is the process of allocating the cost, less estimated residual value, of a long-lived tangible asset to expense over the estimated useful life of the asset in a rational, systematic manner. Thus, the primary objective of depreciation is one of matching cost with the revenue generated by the use of the asset. Depreciation is *not* a process for providing replacement funds for assets. Providing replacement funds is a separate management policy matter. Also, depreciation is *not* a process to match *current costs* with current revenues. Depreciation is merely a process for assigning *actual costs* incurred to the periods that benefit from the asset's use. Likewise, depreciation is *not* intended to reflect the *current value* of plant assets on the balance sheet. The **book value** of a plant asset reported on the balance sheet represents the actual cost remaining to be charged to expense in future periods or recovered at the asset's disposal.

Four factors are relevant in computing depreciation:

1. the acquisition cost of the asset
2. the estimated useful life of the asset to the owner
3. the estimated residual value (salvage or scrap value) of the asset at the end of its useful life to the owner
4. the depreciation method adopted for the asset

Note that two of these factors are estimates and a third is a judgment. Thus, the amount charged to expense each period is an estimate; it should not be considered precise. The **useful life** is the period of time the owner expects the asset to provide benefits to the business; the actual economic life of the asset may be shorter or longer. Plant assets are often disposed of before their economic lives expire in order to take advantage of higher residual values or to avoid costly repairs and breakdowns toward the end of their economic lives. The **residual value** is the amount an entity expects to receive from the disposal of an asset in the usual way. The depreciation method selected is a matter of judgment after several factors that recognize the patterns for the use, value, and contributions of the asset are considered.

Selecting Depreciation Methods

In choosing a depreciation method, several factors should be considered in determining the appropriate amount of expense to be matched with revenues each period over an asset's useful life. These are:

1. pattern of asset usage—depreciation expense should be greater in periods when usage is greater.
2. pattern of decline in the asset's value—depreciation expense should be greater in periods when there is a greater decline in value.

3. pattern of expected repairs and maintenance—depreciation expense should be lower in periods when repairs and maintenance are greater so that all periods share somewhat equally in the overall cost of using the asset.
4. effects of obsolescence and physical deterioration—depreciation expense should be greater in earlier years if there is a high risk of obsolescence and if physical deterioration occurs more rapidly in earlier years.
5. pattern of revenue realization from the use of the asset—depreciation expense should be greater in periods when the asset makes greater contributions to revenues.
6. uncertainty regarding the later years in the asset's life—depreciation should be charged to the periods most likely to benefit from the asset's use.

One or more of these factors will predominate in the decision to select a depreciation method. No depreciation method recognizes all of them. Income tax considerations, too, often have an important impact on the decision. Different methods can be used for different assets, but all assets of the same kind should usually be depreciated by the same method. However, this does not preclude a change in methods for a sound reason.

Depreciation methods usually fit into one of four patterns that describe the annual charge to depreciation expense over the life of the plant asset:

1. **Constant charge methods**—depreciation is allocated equally to each period.
    a. The value of the asset tends to decline as a function of time rather than use.
    b. Repairs, maintenance, contribution to revenue, and operating efficiency tend to be constant over the asset's useful life.
2. **Variable charge methods**—depreciation varies with the use of the asset.
    a. The value of the asset declines as a function of use rather than time.
    b. Repairs, maintenance, and contribution to revenues tend to vary with use.
3. **Decreasing charge methods** (or **accelerated depreciation methods**)—depreciation decreases each period.
    a. The value of the asset tends to decline in greater amounts during the early years of the asset's life.
    b. Repairs and maintenance tend to increase over the asset's life, while operating efficiency decreases.
    c. The contribution to revenues declines over the asset's life.
4. **Increasing charge methods**—depreciation increases each period.
    a. The value of the asset tends to decline in greater amounts during its later years.

b. Repairs and maintenance tend to decrease or remain constant over the asset's life.

c. Operating efficiency and contribution to revenues tend to increase or remain constant over the asset's life.

The increasing charge methods are rarely used because few assets decline in value in greater amounts late in their lives or have increasing contributions to revenue over their lives. The primary objective of the increasing charge methods is to recognize the recovery of cost and a return on investment. The cost of the asset being depreciated is viewed as the present value of future benefits to be received.[1] The constant charge methods are often appropriate for assets like buildings, office furniture and equipment, and store fixtures, which provide relatively constant use, operating efficiency, and declines in value over their lives. The variable charge methods are appropriate for assets, such as mining equipment, where usage is the primary cause of depreciation. The decreasing charge methods are usually appropriate for machinery, vehicles, and other types of equipment that lose a significant portion of their value, operate more efficiently, and require fewer repairs early in their lives.

Common Depreciation Methods

Four depreciation methods are commonly used:

1. the **straight-line method**—a constant charge method that allocates the same amount to expense each accounting period over the asset's useful life.

2. the **productive-output method**—a variable charge method that allocates the same amount to expense per unit of output produced over the asset's useful life.

3. the **sum-of-years'-digits method**—a decreasing charge method that allocates a smaller amount to expense each accounting period by applying a smaller depreciation rate to a constant base each period.

4. the **declining-balance method**—a decreasing charge method that allocates a smaller amount to expense each accounting period by applying a constant depreciation rate to a declining base.

In each method, except the declining-balance method, the residual value is deducted from the cost of the asset to determine the **depreciable cost,** that is, the amount that should be charged to expense over the useful life of the asset. The annual depreciation charge is determined using depreciable cost as the basis. In the declining-balance method the depreciation rate is applied to the full cost of the asset, but the asset

---

[1]Increasing charge methods are discussed more fully in intermediate accounting courses.

should not be depreciated below its residual value. Adjustments may be necessary for the productive-output and declining-balance methods so that the total depreciation taken over the asset's useful life exactly equals its depreciable cost.

Straight-Line Method   Under the straight-line method of depreciation an equal amount of depreciable cost is charged to expense each accounting period. Depreciable cost can be divided by the estimated useful life or multiplied by a straight-line depreciation rate. The straight-line depreciation rate is determined by dividing 100 percent by the estimated useful life. Depreciation for an asset with a cost of $3,000, an estimated residual value of $300, and an estimated useful life of four years would be determined using the straight-line method as follows:

$$\frac{\text{cost} - \text{residual value}}{\text{estimated useful life}} = \frac{\$3,000 - 300}{4 \text{ years}} = \$675 \quad \frac{\text{annual depreciation}}{\text{expense}}$$

$$(\text{cost} - \text{residual value}) \times \text{depreciation rate} * = \frac{\text{annual depreciation}}{\text{expense}}$$

$$(\$3,000 - 300) \quad \times \quad 25\% \quad = \quad \$675$$

$$* \frac{100\%}{\text{estimated useful life}} = \frac{100\%}{4 \text{ years}} = 25\% \quad \frac{\text{straight-line}}{\text{depreciation rate}}$$

Over the four years of the asset's useful life the depreciable cost of $2,700 will be fully allocated to expense; only the residual value of $300 will remain as the asset's book value after that time. See the depreciation schedule for the straight-line method in Exhibit 21.1; this schedule indicates the annual depreciation expense and the book value at the end of each year.

Productive-Output Method   Under the productive-output method a depreciation rate for each unit of expected output is determined by dividing the depreciable cost of the asset by the total estimated output. The unit depreciation rate is applied to the output for the period to determine the depreciation expense for the period. Output may be stated in terms of hours of operation, units of product, miles, and so on. For a $3,000 asset with a residual value of $300 and an estimated useful life of 50,000 hours of operation, depreciation for the first year, if the asset was used for 12,000 hours, would be determined as follows:

$$\frac{\text{cost} - \text{residual value}}{\text{total estimated output}} = \frac{\$3,000 - 300}{50,000 \text{ hours}} = \$.054/\text{hour} \quad \frac{\text{unit depreciation}}{\text{rate}}$$

$$\text{output for period} \times \text{unit depreciation rate} = \frac{\text{depreciation expense}}{\text{for period}}$$

$$12,000 \text{ hours} \quad \times \quad \$.054/\text{hour} \quad = \quad \$648$$

Exhibit 21.1

Depreciation Schedules

	Straight-Line Method:				Productive-Output Method:		
Year	Depreciation Expense	Accumulated Depreciation at Year-End	Book Value at Year-End	Year	Depreciation Expense	Accumulated Depreciation at Year-End	Book Value at Year-End
1	$675	$ 675	$2,325	1	$648	$ 648	$2,352
2	675	1,350	1,650	2	810	1,458	1,542
3	675	2,025	975	3	702	2,160	840
4	675	2,700	300	4	540	2,700	300

Computations:

Depreciation Expense:

$19x1-19x4$: $3,000 - 300/4 = $675

Book Value: $3,000 - 675 = $2,325$; $3,000 - 1,350 = $1,650$; etc.

Computations:

Depreciation Expense: $3,000 - 300/50,000 = $.054$

$19x1$: $12,000 \times \$.054 = \$648$

$19x2$: $15,000 \times \$.054 = 810$

$19x3$: $13,000 \times \$.054 = 702$

$19x4$: $11,000 \times \$.054 = 594$, but limited to $540(10,000 \times \$.054)$ because total use is 50,000 at this point

Book Value: $3,000 - 648 = $2,352$, etc.

	Sum-of-Years'-Digits Method:				Double-Declining-Balance Method:		
Year	Depreciation Expense	Accumulated Depreciation at Year-End	Book Value at Year-End	Year	Depreciation Expense	Accumulated Depreciation at Year-End	Book Value at Year-End
1	$1,080	$1,080	$1,920	1	$1,500	$1,500	$1,500
2	810	1,890	1,110	2	750	2,250	750
3	540	2,430	570	3	375	2,625	375
4	270	2,700	300	4	75	2,700	300

Computations:

Depreciation Expense: $3,000 - 300 = $2,700

$19x1$: $2,700 \times 4/10 = \$1,080$

$19x2$: $2,700 \times 3/10 = 810$

$19x3$: $2,700 \times 2/10 = 540$

$19x4$: $2,700 \times 1/10 = 270$

Book Value: $3,000 - 1,080 = \$1,920$; etc.

Computations:

Depreciation Expense: $(100\%/4) \times 2 = 50\%$

$19x1$: $3,000 \times 50\% = \$1,500$

$19x2$: $1,500 \times 50\% = 750$

$19x3$: $ 750 \times 50\% = 375$

$19x4$: $ 375 \times 50\% = 187.50$, but limited to $75($375 - 300)$ so that the asset is not depreciated below its residual value

Book Value: $3,000 - 1,500 = \$1,500$; etc.

As shown in Exhibit 21.1 the output for the next three years was assumed to be 15,000, 13,000, and 11,000 hours, respectively. Note that the sum of the actual hours of operation is 51,000 (12,000 + 15,000 + 13,000 + 11,000). The asset, however, is depreciated to its residual value after the first 50,000 hours; thus, depreciation for the fourth year is based on 10,000 hours. In some situations, if the actual output is slightly below the expected output at the end of the asset's useful life, depreciation expense for the last period may be increased so that the depreciable cost of the asset is fully expensed. No attempt is made to recompute the depreciation rate and correct prior depreciation charges. Corrections of depreciation charges are spread over the remaining life of the asset as required by generally accepted accounting principles.

Sum-of-Years'-Digits Method   Under this method a declining depreciation rate is applied to the depreciable cost of the asset each period to determine depreciation expense. Because the base remains constant while the depreciation rate gets smaller, the depreciation expense for each period is smaller. The depreciation rate is a fraction. The numerator of this fraction is a digit representing one of the years in the asset's life (for example, for an asset with a 4-year life, the numerator will be a digit from 1 to 4). The digits are taken in reverse order so that for the first year of depreciation the largest digit (in the example, 4) is used; for the second year the next largest digit (3) is used; and so on. This system produces larger depreciation charges in the earlier years. The denominator of this fraction is the sum of the digits representing the years in the asset's life. The sum of the years' digits (SYD) can be determined using the formula $SYD = n(n + 1)/2$, where n equals the number of years in the asset's life.

For the asset used in the two previous illustrations, the sum of the years' digits is 10 [$SYD = n(n + 1)/2 = 4(4 + 1)/2 = 10$]. Because the largest digit in the asset's life is 4, the depreciation rate for the first year will be 4/10. The depreciation rates for the other three years will be 3/10, 2/10, and 1/10. The following is the depreciation expense for the first year of the asset's life; depreciation expense for all the years is shown in Exhibit 21.1.

$$\text{(cost } - \text{ residual value)} \times \text{depreciation rate} = \text{depreciation expense}$$
$$(\$3,000 - 300) \quad \times \quad 4/10 \quad = \quad \$1,080$$

Declining-Balance Method   Any depreciation rate that does not exceed twice the straight-line rate can be used with the declining-balance method; however, income tax law specifies that the rate may not exceed 125%, 150%, or 200% of the straight-line rate for certain types of assets. Twice the straight-line rate is called the **double-declining-balance method.** Because a constant depreciation rate is applied to a declining base, there is always a remainder. For example, if the rate is 40%, the remainder will be 60% of the base to which the rate is applied (for example, $1,000 × 40% = $400; $1,000 − 400 = $600 or 60% of the base). Therefore, the depreciation rate is applied to the full cost of the asset, *not* to its depreciable cost. The straight-line rate of depreciation is found by dividing 100 percent by the estimated life of the asset. Then, if the double-declining-balance rate of depreciation is used, the straight-line rate is doubled.

For a $3,000 asset with a 4-year life, the double-declining-balance rate is 50% (100%/4 years = 25%; 25% × 2 = 50%); depreciation for the first year is determined as follows:

$$\text{cost } \times \text{depreciation rate} = \text{depreciation expense}$$
$$\$3,000 \times \quad 50\% \quad = \quad \$1,500$$

Depreciation for each of the following years is computed by multiplying the asset's book value at the beginning of each year by the depreciation rate. For example, at the beginning of the second year the asset's book value is $1,500 ($3,000 − 1,500); thus, depreciation for the second year is computed as follows:

$$\frac{\text{book value at}}{\text{beginning of year}} \times \text{depreciation rate} = \text{depreciation expense}$$

$$\$1,500 \quad \times \quad 50\% \quad = \quad \$750$$

Depreciation for the third and fourth years would be computed the same way:

$$\frac{\text{book value at}}{\text{beginning of year}^*} \times \text{depreciation rate} = \text{depreciation expense}$$

$750	×	50%	=	$375
$375	×	50%	=	$187.50

*($3,000 − 1,500 − 750 = $750; $3,000 − 1,500 − 750 − 375 = $375)

Note that the depreciation expense computed for the fourth year would reduce the book value to $187.50 ($3,000 − 1,500 − 750 − 375 − 187.50), which is less than the expected residual value of $300. Thus, depreciation expense for the fourth year is adjusted to $75 ($375 − 300), the difference between the book value at the beginning of the fourth year and the expected residual value at the end of the 4-year life. To avoid adjustments like this, the declining-balance method is often only used for approximately the first two-thirds of the asset's life; then the straight-line method is used for the rest of the asset's life. The asset should have a useful life of three or more years to use the double-declining-balance method. If the useful life was only two years, double the straight-line depreciation rate would be 100% (100%/2 years = 50%; 50% × 2 = 100%), and the asset would be fully depreciated in the first year.

Special Depreciation Methods

As a practical expedient in calculating depreciation for large numbers of assets, special depreciation methods are often used. For example, the *group depreciation method* is used for assets that are similar in nature and have similar lives. A depreciation rate is determined for the group based on straight-line depreciation. This rate is applied to the balance of the asset account at the end of each year to determine depreciation expense. Assume, for example, that a company uses the group method for a fleet of cars. If the group depreciation rate is 30% and the balance of the asset account for cars is $85,000, depreciation for the year will be $25,500 ($85,000 × 30%).

Another method, the *composite life method,* is sometimes used for assets purchased as a group. Even though the assets are not similar in nature and do not have similar lives, one depreciation rate is applied to the cost of the group. Again the depreciation rate is based on straight-line depreciation for the assets. This method tends to depreciate the assets over a weighted average life.

Both the group and composite life methods are considered theoretically deficient because of the procedures followed in handling replacements of assets in the groups.[2]

Depreciation for Partial Year

Various policies can be used to determine depreciation expense for assets acquired or disposed of during the accounting period, as long as the one adopted is applied consistently from one period to another. The policy to be followed in this text requires depreciation to be computed to the nearest full month. Assets purchased during the first half of a month are depreciated for the full month. Similarly, a full month's depreciation is recorded for assets disposed of during the second half of the month. No depreciation is recorded for the month if the asset is acquired during the second half of the month or disposed of during the first half.

When depreciation is computed to the nearest full month, no special problems are encountered in depreciating an asset for a partial year, *except* under the sum-of-years'-digits method. If this method is used, depreciation based on the rate for the first year of the asset's life must be completely charged to expense before depreciation based on the rate for the second year of the asset's life is charged to expense, and so on.

Assume that an asset with a cost of $4,000, a residual value of $400, and a useful life of three years is purchased on October 10, 19x1. Expected output is 40,000 units of product; actual output is 4,000 units for the balance of 19x1 and 15,000 units for 19x2. Depreciation expense for three months in 19x1 and all of 19x2 would be computed as follows for the four common depreciation methods previously discussed:

Straight-line method

$$19x1 \ (\$4,000 - 400/3 \text{ years}) \times 3/12 = \underline{\underline{\$300}}$$
$$19x2 \ (\$4,000 - 400/3 \text{ years}) = \underline{\underline{\$1,200}}$$

Productive-output method

$$(\$4,000 - 400/40,000 \text{ units}) = \$.09/\text{unit depreciation rate}$$
$$19x1 \ 4,000 \text{ units} \times \$.09/\text{unit} = \underline{\underline{\$360}}$$
$$19x2 \ 15,000 \text{ units} \times \$.09/\text{unit} = \underline{\underline{\$1,350}}$$

---

[2]The group and composite life methods, along with other special depreciation methods, are discussed more fully in intermediate accounting courses.

Sum-of-years'-digits method

$$19x1 \ (\$4,000 - 400) \times 3/6 \times 3/12 = \underline{\$450}$$
$$19x2 \ (\$4,000 - 400) \times 3/6 \times 9/12 = \$1,350$$
$$(\$4,000 - 400) \times 2/6 \times 3/12 = \underline{300}$$
$$\$1,650$$

Double-declining-balance method

$$19x1 \ \$4,000 \times 66^{2}/_{3}\% \times 3/12 = \underline{\$667} \text{ (rounded to nearest dollar)}$$
$$19x2 \ \$4,000 - 667 = \$3,333 \text{ book value at January 1, } 19x2$$
$$\$3,333 \times 66^{2}/_{3}\% = \underline{\$2,222}$$

Note that the 3/6 depreciation rate for the first year of the asset's life under the sum-of-years'-digits method is split between two accounting periods: The 3/6 rate is applied for three months in 19x1 and nine months in 19x2 before the 2/6 rate for the second year of the asset's life is applied for the last three months in 19x2.

Reporting Plant Assets

Plant assets are reported in a separate balance sheet classification following current assets and long-term investments and funds. They are reported at their book value, that is, at cost less **accumulated depreciation.** Both their cost and accumulated depreciation should be disclosed either in the body of the balance sheet or in a schedule included in the footnotes. When they are disclosed in the body of the balance sheet, either the accumulated depreciation accounts are presented as deductions from the asset accounts, or the amounts of accumulated depreciation are presented parenthetically. Exhibit 21.2 illustrates these two alternative methods of reporting plant assets in the body of the balance sheet. The traditional sequence for listing plant assets is: land, buildings, machinery, equipment, and furniture and fixtures.

REVIEW PROBLEM

Klipper Corp. purchased machinery with a cost of $13,500; an estimated residual value of $1,500; and an estimated useful life of 4 years or 50,000 hours of operation. The machinery was purchased on September 18, 19x1. Klipper Corp. uses the calendar year as its accounting period. The machine was used for 4,000, 14,000, 13,000, 12,000, and 7,500 hours, respectively, during 19x1 – 19x5.

Exhibit 21.2

Alternative 1

Plant assets:		
Land		$ 80,000
Buildings	$420,000	
Less: Accumulated depreciation	160,000	260,000
Equipment	$210,000	
Less: Accumulated depreciation	140,000	70,000
Total plant assets		$410,000

Alternative 2

Plant assets:	
Land	$ 80,000
Buildings (net of accumulated depreciation of $160,000)	260,000
Equipment (net of accumulated depreciation of $140,000)	70,000
Total plant assets	$410,000

Required   Prepare depreciation schedules similar to those in Exhibit 21.1 for the (1) straight-line, (2) productive-output, (3) sum-of-years'-digits, and (4) double-declining-balance depreciation methods.

Solution to review problem

	(1) Straight-Line Method:	Accumulated	Book		(2) Productive-Output Method:	Accumulated	Book
Year	Depreciation Expense	Depreciation at Year-End	Value at Year-End	Year	Depreciation Expense	Depreciation at Year-End	Value at Year-End
19x1	$ 750	$ 750	$12,750	19x1	$ 960	$ 960	$12,540
19x2	3,000	3,750	9,750	19x2	3,360	4,320	9,180
19x3	3,000	6,750	6,750	19x3	3,120	7,440	6,060
19x4	3,000	9,750	3,750	19x4	2,880	10,320	3,180
19x5	2,250	12,000	1,500	19x5	1,680	12,000	1,500

Computations:

   Depreciation Expense:

      19x2–19x4: ($13,500 − 1,500)/4 = $3,000

      19x1: $3,000 × 3/12 = $750

      19x5: $3,000 × 9/12 = $2,250

   Book Value: $13,500 − 750 = $12,750;

      $13,500 − 3,750 = $9,750; etc.

Computations:

   Depreciation Expense: ($13,500 − 1,500)/50,000

      hrs. = $.24/hr.

      19x1: 4,000 × $.24 = $ 960

      19x2: 14,000 × $.24 = 3,360

      19x3: 13,000 × $.24 = 3,120

      19x4: 12,000 × $.24 = 2,880

      19x5: 7,500 × $.24 = 1,800 but limited to $1,680 (7,000 × $.24) because 50,000 hours of use is reached at this point.

   Book Value: $13,500 − 960 = $12,540; etc.

	(3) *Sum-of-Years'-Digits Method:*				(4) *Double-Declining-Balance Method:*		
	Depreciation	*Accumulated Depreciation*	*Book Value at*		*Depreciation*	*Accumulated Depreciation*	*Book Value at*
Year	*Expense*	*at Year-End*	*Year-End*	*Year*	*Expense*	*at Year-End*	*Year-End*
19x1	$1,200	$ 1,200	$12,300	19x1	$1,688	$ 1,688	$11,812
19x2	4,500	5,700	7,800	19x2	5,906	7,594	5,906
19x3	3,300	9,000	4,500	19x3	2,953	10,547	2,953
19x4	2,100	11,100	2,400	19x4	1,453	12,000	1,500
19x5	900	12,000	1,500	19x5	—	12,000	1,500

Computations:

Depreciation Expense: $13,500 − 1,500 = $12,000

19x1: $12,000 × 4/10 × 3/12 = $1,200

19x2: $12,000 × 4/10 × 9/12 = 3,600
$12,000 × 3/10 × 3/12 = 900
$4,500

19x3: $12,000 × 3/10 × 9/12 = $2,700
$12,000 × 2/10 × 3/12 = 600
$3,300

19x4: $12,000 × 2/10 × 9/12 = $1,800
$12,000 × 1/10 × 3/12 = 300
$2,100

19x5: $12,000 × 1/10 × 9/12 = $ 900

Book Value :$13,500 − 1,200 = $12,300; etc.

Computations:

Depreciation Expense :(100%/4) × 2 = 50%

19x1: $13,500 × 50% × 3/12 = $1,688
19x2: $11,812 × 50% = $5,906
19x3: $ 5,906 × 50% = $2,953
19x4: $ 2,953 × 50% = $1,477; limited to $1,453 ($2,953 − 1,500) so that asset is not depreciated below its book value.

Book Value: $13,500 − $1,688 = $11,812; etc.

SUMMARY

The four depreciation methods commonly used in accounting practice were discussed in this unit. Table 21.1 summarizes the depreciation patterns and formulas for calculating depreciation expense under each of these methods. Criteria for selecting an appropriate depreciation method, the relevant factors in calculating depreciation expense, and alternative methods for reporting plant asset balances were also described.

REVIEW QUESTIONS

21-1 What is depreciation as the term is used in accounting? Why is depreciation based on actual cost rather than current replacement cost?

21-2 What four factors are relevant in computing depreciation?

21-3 "Depreciation is a matter of judgment; the annual depreciation charge, therefore, is not precise." Explain.

21-4 Depreciation methods usually fit one of four patterns, which are descriptive of the annual charge to depreciation expense over the useful life of a plant asset. Identify these

Table 21.1

Depreciation Methods, Patterns, and Formulas

Depreciation Method	Pattern for Depreciation Charge	Formula to Compute Depreciation Expense
1. Straight-line	1. Constant charge	1. a. $\dfrac{\text{cost} - \text{residual value}}{\text{estimated useful life}} = \text{depreciation expense}$ b. (cost − residual value) × depreciation rate* = depreciation expense $*\left(\dfrac{100\%}{\text{estimated useful life}} = \text{depreciation rate} \right)$
2. Productive-output	2. Variable charge	2. output for period × depreciation rate† = depreciation expense $†\left(\dfrac{\text{cost} - \text{residual value}}{\text{total estimated output}} = \text{depreciation rate} \right)$
3. Sum-of-years'-digits	3. Decreasing charge	3. (cost − residual value) × depreciation rate‡ = depreciation expense ‡Depreciation rate is a fraction: the numerator is a digit representing a year in the asset's life used in reverse order from highest to lowest; the denominator is the sum of the digits for the years of the asset's life—found by using the formula $n(n + 1)/2$ where n equals the asset's life.
4. Double-declining-balance	4. Decreasing charge	4. cost (or book value at beginning of year) × depreciation rate§ = depreciation expense $\dfrac{\S\ 100\%}{\text{estimated useful life}} \times 2 = \text{depreciation rate}$

four patterns and describe the manner in which the value, contribution to revenue, operating efficiency, and repair and maintenance expense vary as the asset is used.

21-5 Identify the four commonly used depreciation methods described in this unit. Indicate the type of depreciation pattern that describes the annual depreciation charge for each of these four methods.

21-6 For each of the four commonly used depreciation methods, give the formula for computing the depreciation rate and the formula for computing .the annual depreciation charge. When is each method most appropriately used?

21-7 How can depreciation expense for a partial year be computed when a plant asset is acquired or disposed of during an accounting period?

21-8 How should plant assets be reported on the balance sheet? Describe two alternative methods of properly disclosing plant assets.

EXERCISES

21-1 The Sparrow Company purchased a new truck on the first day of its accounting period for a total cost of $5,400. The truck has an estimated useful life to the company of 3 years or 60,000 miles and is expected to have a salvage value of $600. The truck was driven 22,000, 18,000, and 24,000 miles, respectively, during its 3-year life.

Required   Prepare a depreciation schedule showing the annual depreciation charge, accumulated depreciation to date, and book value at the end of each year if the company uses the (a) straight-line, (b) productive-output, (c) sum-of-years'-digits, and (d) double-declining-balance depreciation methods.

21-2   The Dove Restaurant acquired new dining room furniture on September 21, 19*x1*, at a cost of $16,200. The furniture has an estimated useful life of 6 years and an estimated scrap value of $1,500. The company's accounting period is the calendar year.

Required   Compute the depreciation expense for 19*x1* and 19*x2* if the (a) straight-line, (b) sum-of-years'-digits, and (c) double-declining-balance depreciation methods are used.

21-3   The following four diagrams depict the annual depreciation charge for a plant asset. Identify the depreciation method depicted by each diagram.

Diagram A

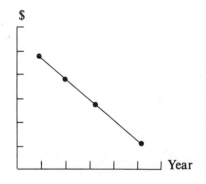

Diagram B

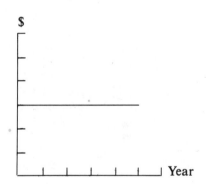

Diagram C

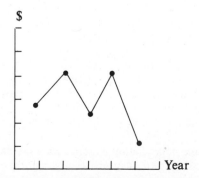

Diagram D

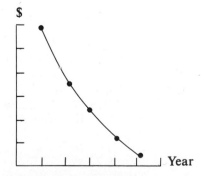

21-4   Holly Corp. purchased equipment with a cost of $90,000 on April 12, 19x4. Equipment like this has an overall economic life of 16 years although Holly Corp. normally uses this type of equipment from 8 to 12 years before trading it in on new equipment. Company records show that the average holding period is 10 years. These records also show that the company receives a trade-in allowance equal to 20% of the old equipment's cost when it holds the equipment for 8 years and 10% when it holds it for 12 years. If the equipment is held for 16 years, it can be sold for scrap, and the company will receive an amount equal to 1% of the asset's cost. Repair costs on this type of equipment have ranged from $450 to $3,860 annually. The average repair costs are $825 during the first half of the equipment's life and $2,410 during the second half. Output is fairly consistent over the asset's life, except when it is being repaired.

Required   **a.**   What information is relevant in selecting the useful life and residual value of the equipment?

         b.   What factors should be considered in selecting a depreciation method for the equipment?

         c.   Which depreciation method will yield the largest depreciation charges during the first third of the asset's useful life?

         d.   Which depreciation method would you recommend the company use for the equipment? Why?

PROBLEMS

21-1   On January 5, 19x1, Dana Corporation purchased equipment with a cost of $27,400; an estimated salvage value of $2,400; and an estimated useful life of 4 years or 40,000 hours of operation. The equipment was used as follows:

        19x1 — 11,000 hours   19x3 — 9,000 hours

        19x2 — 12,000 hours   19x4 — 7,500 hours

On December 27, 19x4, the equipment was sold for $2,100.

Required   **a.**   Prepare a depreciation schedule showing the annual depreciation, accumulated depreciation to date, and book value at the end of each year if the company uses the (1) straight-line, (2) productive-output, (3) sum-of-years'-digits, and (4) double-declining-balance depreciation methods.

         b.   Determine the gain or loss on the disposal of the equipment.

21-2   On October 8, 19x1, Santa Ana Company purchased a delivery truck with a cost of $8,800; an estimated residual value of $1,300; and an expected useful life of 5 years. On September 26, 19x5, the truck was traded in for a new delivery truck with a list price of $9,600; a cash price of $9,000; an expected useful life of 5 years; and an estimated residual value of $1,600. A trade-in allowance of $2,200 was received.

Required   **a.**   Compute the depreciation expense for 19x1 and 19x2 if the (1) straight-line, (2) sum-of-years'-digits, and (3) double-declining-balance depreciation methods are used.

    b.   Compute depreciation expense for 19x5 for the old truck if the sum-of-years'-digits method is used.

    c.   Compute the cost of the new delivery truck and the amount of gain or loss to be recognized on the trade-in, if any, assuming the sum-of-years'-digits method is used.

21-3   Krego Company purchased new computer equipment on September 13, 19x4. The equipment had a cost of $65,000; has an estimated useful life to Krego of 3 years; and is expected to have a residual value of $11,000 at the end of 3 years. Krego calculates depreciation to the nearest full month.

    Required   **a.**   Determine depreciation expense for 19x4 through 19x7 and the book value of the equipment at the end of 19x4, 19x5, and 19x6, and September 13, 19x7, if the (1) straight-line, (2) double-declining-balance, and (3) sum-of-years'-digits depreciation methods are used.

                     b.   Which method of depreciation do you think is appropriate for the computer equipment? Explain.

21-4   The following three diagrams depict the patterns in which a particular plant asset loses its value (V), contributes to revenue (R), loses operating efficiency (E), and incurs repair and maintenance expense (M).

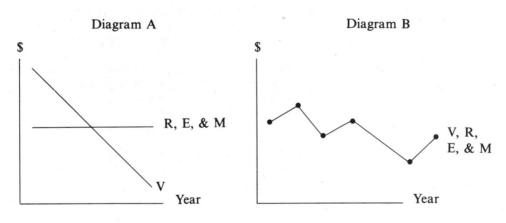

Diagram A   Diagram B

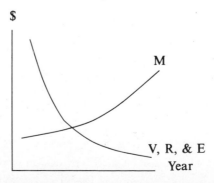

Diagram C

Required   **a.**   Identify the depreciation pattern depicted by each diagram.

b.   Indicate which depreciation methods discussed in this unit might be depicted by each diagram.

21-5   Beech Corp. was organized late in 19*x4* and started business operations at the beginning of 19*x5*. The following is a summary of the plant assets owned by the company.

Asset	Cost	Residual Value	Useful Life
Building	$175,000	$15,000	40 years
Office equipment	15,600	1,600	10 years
Delivery trucks	21,300	3,300	5 years
Forklifts	6,600	600	6 years

Company accountants are trying to determine the best method of depreciating these assets. One accountant advocated using the straight-line method for all assets to simplify calculations and bookkeeping. Another advocated using an accelerated depreciation method for all assets to minimize tax payments during the early years of the assets' lives. A third accountant recalled a discussion from an accounting course of decline in value, patterns of use, repairs, and revenue contribution, and obsolescence and deterioration as factors to consider in selecting a depreciation method.

Required   **a.**   Discuss the appropriateness of the straight-line and accelerated depreciation methods for each of these four assets.

b.   Calculate depreciation for 19*x5* if the accountants select the straight-line method for the building and office equipment and the double-declining-balance method for delivery trucks and forklifts.

Unit 22
Intangible and Other Assets

No one returns with good-will to the place which has done him a mischief.

Phaedrus, Book I, Table 18

Businesses frequently acquire exclusive rights or privileges that are expected to provide benefits over several accounting periods. The accounting for the cost of these rights and privileges, the allocation of the costs to expense, and the proper disclosure of the unamortized and amortized costs on the financial statements are explained and illustrated in this unit. In addition, long-term investments and funds are discussed briefly. To complete the current discussion of assets, accounting for research and development costs, natural resources, and deferred charges are also explained and illustrated.

Performance Objectives

Upon completing this unit you should be able to:

1. define and use the accounting terms introduced in this unit.
2. explain or describe:
   a. what constitutes the balance to be reported as an asset for an intangible asset, a natural resource, a deferred charge, a long-term investment, or a long-term fund
   b. the amount of an intangible asset, a natural resource, a deferred charge, or research and development costs to be charged to expense annually
   c. how the balance of an intangible asset, natural resource, or deferred charge is measured and reported
   d. the distinction between a deferred charge and a prepaid expense
3. determine:
   a. the cost to be recorded for an intangible asset, a natural resource, or a deferred charge
   b. the amount to be recorded as expense for an intangible asset, a natural resource, a deferred charge, or research and development costs

Nature and Cost of Intangible Assets

Intangible assets are long-lived assets that represent the cost of certain rights or privileges that are acquired to provide benefits over several accounting periods. The characteristics of intangible assets are similar to those for plant assets except that they usually have no physical substance. Their value arises from the exclusive rights or privileges acquired by the company. Like plant assets, they are intended for use in business operations, to help generate operating revenue, and they are *not* intended for resale. APB Opinion No. 17 classified intangibles as:

1. **identifiable intangible assets**—those that can be identified as providing distinct, separate rights and privileges to the owner, for example, patents, copyrights, and franchises.
2. **unidentifiable intangible assets**—those that provide rights and privileges to the owner, but that cannot be identified because they relate to the business as a whole, for example, goodwill that is internally developed.

The distinction between identifiable and unidentifiable intangible assets is important in determining the proper treatment for costs incurred. Acquisition costs of these assets are treated as capital expenditures (that is, charged to an asset account) and amortized over the periods expected to benefit. Costs that are incurred to develop, maintain, or restore intangible assets that are not specifically identifiable, that have indeterminate lives, or that are inherent in a continuing business and related to the business as a whole are treated as revenue expenditures and charged to expense as incurred. Examples include costs incurred to promote employee morale and customer goodwill.

The cost of an intangible asset acquired from another party is measured in the same way as the cost of a plant asset (see Unit 20) and includes all necessary acquisition costs. An intangible asset that has been internally developed should include only incidental costs, such as legal and other fees incurred to secure a patent on a product developed by a company. FASB Statement No. 2 requires research and development costs incurred to create new products, processes, or services, or to improve present products, processes, or services to be charged to expense as incurred. Therefore, only a few costs incurred to develop an intangible asset internally can be capitalized as part of the asset's cost; in practice, costs incidental to the internal development of an intangible asset are charged to expense if they are considered insignificant.

Research and Development Costs

For years alternative practices were applied to account for **research and development (R & D) costs.** FASB Statement No. 2 ended the use of alternate approaches by requiring that all R & D costs, except those directly reimbursable by others, be charged to expense as incurred. This position provides a single, consistent practice and apparently has satisfied both financial information users and the accounting profession. However, this position tends to deny that R & D costs are incurred to provide future benefits, and it fails to apply the matching principle because R & D costs are not associated with the periods that will benefit from their incurrence. The FASB statement also requires that the amount of R & D costs charged to expense each period should be disclosed on the face of the income statement or in the footnotes.

Research and development are defined as follows:[1]

> **Research:** planned search or critical investigation aimed at the discovery of new knowledge and the hope that such activity will be useful in creating a new product, process, or service.

> **Development:** the translation of research findings or other knowledge into a new or improved product, process, or service capable of commercialization, including the conceptual formulation, design, and testing of product, process, or service alternatives and the construction of prototypes and pilot operations related to the new or improved product, process, or service.

Amortization of Intangible Assets

According to APB Opinion No. 17, all intangible assets have limited lives and should be charged to expense in a systematic, rational manner over the periods that are expected to benefit. The life of some intangible assets is limited by law, regulation, or contract. For example, the legal life of a patent is 17 years; or the life of a franchise may be fixed by the contract between the franchisee and the franchisor. Economic circumstances, however, may shorten an intangible asset's expected useful life to less than its legal or fixed life. For example, most new products have life cycles significantly shorter than the legal life of the patents obtained on them—competitors come out with similar products, customer demand changes. Thus, intangible assets with limited lives should be amortized over the shorter of their limited life or economic useful life. **Amortization** is the systematic, rational allocation of the cost of an intangible asset to expense over the periods expected to benefit. A straight-line pattern of amortization is considered appropriate unless it can be shown that another pattern better reflects the manner in which the benefits are derived.

Assume that Ramo Corp. purchases a patent for $7,500 from its developer two years after the patent was obtained. Although 15 years of the legal life of the patent remain, the company estimates that the patent will have no further value after 5 years. The entries to purchase the patent and to record the annual amortization expense would be:

---

[1]Defined in Haskins & Sells (publisher), *The Week in Review* (June 14, 1974, p. 2) and based on definitions in FASB Statement No. 2.

| Patents | 7,500 | |
| Cash | | 7,500 |

To record purchase of a patent.

| Amortization Expense—Patents | 1,500 | |
| Patents | | 1,500 |

To record annual amortization expense based on
the economic life of the patent, which is
shorter than its remaining legal life ($7,500/5
years = $1,500/year).

When intangible assets are amortized, the asset account is usually credited directly, whereas when plant assets are depreciated, a contra account, accumulated depreciation, is credited. Crediting the intangible asset account is a traditional practice, even though crediting a contra account, accumulated amortization, is acceptable.

Some intangible assets, such as tradenames, trademarks, and goodwill, have uncertain or indeterminate lives. Their value will terminate at some time, but their lives are not limited legally or contractually. They may have value as long as the business entity exists, for example. Before APB Opinion No. 17 some companies amortized intangible assets with uncertain or indeterminate lives while others did not. The APB believed, however, that all intangibles eventually lose their value and that their cost, therefore, should be assigned to those periods expected to benefit. Thus, according to this opinion, intangible assets with uncertain or indeterminate lives acquired after October 31, 1970, must now be amortized. Also according to this opinion, an estimate of an intangible asset's expected useful life may be made, based on upper and lower limits, but it should not exceed 40 years. However, these intangibles cannot be amortized for income tax purposes.

Assume that a company purchased a trademark when it acquired the assets of another business, and that the amount assigned to the trademark was $30,000. If it is determined that a reasonable period for the amortization of the trademark is 20 years, the annual entry for amortization would be:

| Amortization Expense—Trademark | 1,500 | |
| Trademark | | 1,500 |

To amortize trademark over a 20-year period
($30,000/20 years = $1,500/year).

Failure to amortize intangible assets with uncertain or indeterminate lives would result in an overstatement of assets, net income, and retained earnings because the asset account would not be reduced and amortization expense would not be recorded.

Occasionally the estimated life over which an intangible asset is being amortized will be found to be erroneous due to changed circumstances. When this situation occurs, the remaining cost should be amortized over the remaining portion of the revised life in accordance with APB Opinion No. 20. In addition, the effect of the change in the estimate on income and earnings per share should be disclosed in footnotes. Assume that a trademark that was recorded at $30,000 when it was acquired was being amortized over 30 years. After recording the amortization for 10 years, it was determined that 20 years was a more reasonable estimate of its useful life. The annual entry to record amortization would, therefore, change, and the entry over the remaining 10 years of the revised useful life would be:

Amortization Expense—Trademark	2,000	
Trademark		2,000
To record annual amortization expense for		
trademark after revision in useful life;		
the amount was determined as follows:		
Cost		$30,000
Amortization for first 10 years ($30,000/30 × 10)		10,000
Remaining cost at time of revision in useful life		$20,000
Amortization for remaining 10 years ($20,000/10)		$ 2,000

The period over which an intangible asset is amortized is a matter of judgment. Unexpected circumstances, for example, may cause it to become worthless before it is completely amortized. When an intangible asset becomes worthless, it should be written off. The loss from the write-off does not usually qualify for treatment as an extraordinary item; however, if the loss is significant, it should be disclosed separately on the income statement. Assume that a patent with a cost of $8,500, which was being amortized over its legal life of 17 years, is determined to be worthless after being amortized for 7 years. The entry for the write-off would be:

Loss from write-off of worthless patent	5,000	
Patent		5,000
To record write-off of worthless patent:		
the amount was determined as follows:		
Cost		$8,500
Amortization for 7 years ($8,500/17 × 7)		3,500
Unamortized cost at time of write-off		$5,000

Accounting for Certain Intangible Assets

Certain intangible assets cause special accounting problems.

Patents   A **patent,** granted by the United States Patent Office, is an exclusive right to manufacture and control an invention. Although the legal life of a patent is 17 years, the benefits expected from it may end before the 17 years expire. During the first few years after a patent is obtained, the owner usually has a competitive advantage, and the patent can be quite valuable. This competitive advantage diminishes as competitors develop comparable products and customer demand changes. Thus, a patent should be amortized over the shorter of its legal life or its estimated economic useful life.

Patents purchased from others are recorded at their acquisition cost. Only registration fees, legal fees, and other incidental costs related to obtaining a patent can be capitalized as the cost of a patent on an invention that is developed internally. Research and development costs incurred in the development of a patentable product, process, or service must be charged to expense as required by FASB Statement No. 2.

Sometimes a lawsuit may be necessary to protect a patent against infringement by others. If the lawsuit is successful, any costs of the lawsuit not recovered from the defendant must be capitalized and amortized over the remaining useful life of the patent. If the lawsuit is not successful, the remaining cost of the patent should be written off immediately. The company does not have an exclusive right if the infringement is not upheld by the courts. The costs of the unsuccessful lawsuit may be included as part of the loss in writing off the patent or recorded as an expense for the period.

Copyrights   **Copyrights** are similar to patents. They provide the exclusive right to publish, sell, or use a work of art, music, or literature for the life of the creator plus 50 years (effective January 1, 1978). Prior to January 1, 1978, the legal life of a copyright was 28 years, plus a renewal period of another 28 years. The accounting procedures and problems for copyrights are essentially the same as those for patents.

Trademarks and Tradenames   A company can register an identifying mark or name with the United States Patent Office to obtain the permanent, exclusive use and control of the name or mark. The costs of registering and defending the **trademark** or **tradename** should be capitalized. Because their useful life is indeterminate, trademarks and tradenames should be amortized over a reasonable period not to exceed 40 years.

Franchises and Licenses   A **franchise** or **license** to market a particular product and/or use a certain tradename in a specified territory may be acquired from the party who developed the product or tradename. The contract between the franchisee (or licensee) and the franchisor (or licensor) will indicate whether the franchise (or license) is for a limited or unlimited period. The cost of the franchise or license should be distinguished from other charges for product marketing and management consulting, which are often included in the contract. The latter costs are usually charged to expense as incurred. The cost of the franchise (or license) should be capitalized and amortized over its limited life or over a reasonable period not to exceed 40 years if the life is unlimited.

Leaseholds and Leasehold Improvements   A **leasehold** is the right to use specified property according to the terms contained in a lease contract. Advance rental payments should be recorded in an asset account called "leaseholds" and amortized over the period to which the advance payments apply. If a lump-sum advance payment for the entire term of the lease is made, the leasehold should be amortized over the term of the lease. The appropriate method for amortizing a leasehold is discussed in Unit 36.

When property is leased on a long-term basis, the lessee often incurs costs to renovate or alter the property to suit his needs. At the termination of the lease, the improvements and alterations legally revert to the owner of the property. Thus, these costs should be capitalized in an account called **leasehold improvements** and amortized over the term of the lease or the useful life of the improvements, whichever is shorter.

Goodwill   Some businesses are able to earn a rate of return on their net assets superior to the normal rate for their industry. If these businesses are sold, they can command a price in excess of the fair value of their net assets. The ability to earn a superior rate of return on net assets and to command a price for the business in excess of net assets is evidence that an intangible asset called **goodwill** exists. Goodwill arises from various favorable attitudes toward the company by customers, from quality of products, from location, from employee morale, and so on. Goodwill is internally developed over a period of time by a company. Expenditures to develop the favorable attitudes that cause goodwill should be charged to expense as incurred because it is difficult to measure the goodwill that results from these expenditures.

Objective evidence for the measurement of goodwill exists, however, when a business is purchased in part or in whole for a price in excess of the fair value of the net assets acquired. Thus, goodwill is defined as the excess of the value of a business as a whole over the fair value of its net assets. In accordance with the cost principle, goodwill is recorded as an asset only when it is purchased. However, the amount of goodwill recorded still results from subjective measurements. The price paid for a business may provide objective evidence to measure the cost of the goodwill, but because such price is negotiated, compromise may be involved and the true amount of goodwill may not be reflected. The negotiated price only assures that the quality of objectivity is met for the information to be recorded and reported.

Assume that Henry Smythe purchased the Quik Stop Store on July 1, 19x4, for $63,000. The assets acquired and their book value and fair value at July 1, 19x4, were:

	Book Value	Fair Value
Inventory	$ 3,000	$ 3,400
Supplies inventory	500	600
Land	8,000	10,000
Building	30,000	40,000
Fixtures	5,000	7,200
	$46,500	$61,200

In addition, Smythe assumed outstanding accounts payable of $1,800 as part of the purchase agreement. The assets acquired should be recorded at their fair values because fair value is the measure of their cost to the purchaser. The book value of the assets represents the cost of the assets to the seller, not to the purchaser. The difference between the cost of the entire business, $63,000, and the fair value of the net assets acquired, $59,400, must be recorded as the cost of goodwill:

Cost of business acquired		$63,000
Less fair value of net assets acquired:		
Fair value of assets acquired	$61,200	
Less liabilities assumed	1,800	59,400
Cost of goodwill acquired		$ 3,600

The entries to record the purchase of the business and the amortization of goodwill for half a year (July 1–December 31, 19x4) based on an expected economic life of ten years for goodwill would be:

July 1	Inventory	3,400	
	Supplies inventory	600	
	Land	10,000	
	Building	40,000	
	Fixtures	7,200	
	Goodwill	3,600	
	Accounts payable		1,800
	Cash		63,000
	To record purchase of Quik Stop Store.		
Dec. 31	Amortization expense—goodwill	180	
	Goodwill		180
	To record amortization of goodwill for half a year($3,600/10 × 6/12 = $180).		

Reporting Intangible Assets and Related Expense

Intangible assets are reported at book value, that is, unamortized cost, in a separate balance sheet classification following plant assets. The cost and accumulated amortization for an intangible asset are usually not disclosed as cost and accumulated depreciation are for a plant asset. For most intangible assets amortization is reported as an operating expense. Amortization of patents is part of factory overhead for a manufacturing company and will be included in the cost of goods manufactured. Thus, amortization becomes part of the cost of goods sold and inventory cost.

A loss from the write-off of an intangible asset is unlikely to qualify for treatment as an extraordinary item. Thus, the loss from a write-off is usually reported under the incidental revenue and expense classification on a multiple-step (classified) income statement or with expenses and losses on a single-step income statement.

Natural Resources

Natural resources are valuable, physical resources provided by nature, such as mineral deposits, oil, natural gas, coal, timber, and so on. Their acquisition and/or development costs are recorded and classified under plant assets. As natural resources are extracted or consumed, their cost must be allocated to expense through a process known as **depletion.** Depletion expense is calculated the same way depreciation expense is calculated using the productive-output method. Assume that an oil well is drilled and that the acquisition and development cost is $500,000. If the expected output is 1,000,000 barrels of oil, the depletion rate is determined as follows:

$$\frac{\text{total acquisition and development cost}}{\text{total estimated output}} = \frac{\$5,000,000}{1,000,000 \text{ barrels}} = \frac{\$.50/\text{barrel}}{\text{depletion rate}}$$

If output for a particular period is 35,000 barrels of oil, depletion expense is determined as follows:

$$\begin{array}{ccc} \text{output} & \times \text{ depletion rate} = \text{depletion expense} \\ 35,000 \text{ barrels} \times & \$.50/\text{barrel} & = & \$17,500 \end{array}$$

Frequent revisions of the depletion rate may be necessary due to changes in the estimated output as extraction progresses or further development occurs. Therefore, when depletion expense is recorded, it is desirable to credit the asset account directly, although it is acceptable to credit a contra account for accumulated depletion. If the asset account is credited directly, the current depletion rate can be determined by dividing the remaining cost of the asset by the estimated remaining output. Assume that after 150,000 barrels of oil in the previous illustration have been extracted, the estimate of the remaining output is revised to 800,000 barrels. The depletion rate then is revised to $.53125 per barrel as follows:

Cost	$500,000
Depletion on 150,000 barrels (150,000 × $.50)	75,000
Remaining cost to be depleted	$425,000
Revised depletion rate ($425,000/800,000 barrels)	$.53125/barrel

Buildings, equipment, and other assets used to extract the natural resource should be depreciated over the shorter of their useful lives or the time expected to complete the extraction process. Costs of developing natural resources are not covered by FASB Statement No. 2. Since these costs are incurred to begin extraction of the natural resources, they are capital expenditures and must be depleted along with the cost of the property acquired for extraction of the resources.

Deferred Charges

Deferred charges are prepayments that generally are nonrecurring and that will benefit more than one accounting period. Deferred charges are similar to **prepaid expenses** in that they are advance payments of expense. However, prepaid expenses are generally recurring, and they benefit primarily only the current period and the following one. (An exception is prepaid insurance, which may benefit several accounting periods, but traditionally is classified with other prepaid expenses as a current asset because it is recurring.)

Examples of deferred charges are organization costs, bond issue costs, plant rearrangement costs, and costs of special advertising and promotion campaigns. Deferred charges are amortized over the periods expected to benefit from their incurrence. When amortization expense is recorded, the asset account is usually credited directly. Deferred charges are usually reported at their book value (that is, unamortized cost) in a separate balance sheet classification following intangible assets. Sometimes, when their balances are insignificant compared to total assets, they are reported with intangible assets to condense the number of asset classifications. And sometimes, deferred charges and other assets not properly classified in other asset groups are reported in a single balance sheet classification, "other assets."

Organization costs are the initial costs of incorporating and promoting a company. Included are legal and accounting fees related to organizing and incorporating the business, state incorporation fees, salaries, office expenses incurred in promoting the firm, and expenses of initial meetings of directors and stockholders. Sometimes costs connected with issuing stock are included as organization costs although preferably these should be matched with the proceeds from the issuance of the stock. Organization costs normally are amortized over a short period of five or more years to correspond with their income tax treatment because the amounts involved are immaterial. **Bond issue costs** include underwriting fees, printing costs, and filing and registration fees. Sometimes these are deducted from the proceeds from the issuance of the bonds. If they are recorded as a deferred charge, bond issue costs should be amortized over the period from the date of issuance of the bonds to their maturity date, that is, the period during which the bonds will be outstanding.

Long-term Investments and Funds

Long-term investments in stocks and bonds are reported in a separate balance sheet classification, following current assets and preceding plant assets, along with other types of long-term investments, noncurrent receivables, and funds being accumulated for specific, noncurrent purposes. The intention of management and the nature of the asset are characteristics used to determine the proper classification of assets as **long-term investments and funds.** Intentions to control or influence another company through ownership of its stock, to hold securities until future maturity, and to hold securities, land, or other assets for speculative purposes are indicative of long-term investment purposes.

FASB Statement No. 12 requires that most long-term investments in stock be reported at lower-of-cost-or-market. Other securities are usually reported on a cost basis. The cost of long-term investments in stocks or bonds includes their purchase price plus any brokerage fees or taxes paid to acquire them. Long-term investments in stocks and bonds are discussed fully in Units 29 and 30. Noncurrent receivables are reported at their present value under either the long-term investment and funds or the other assets classification on the balance sheet.

A **fund** consists of cash or other assets set aside for a specific purpose. Funds established for current operating purposes, such as petty cash, are classified as current assets. Those established for noncurrent purposes, such as retirement of bonds or other long-term debts and plant expansion, are classified as long-term investments and funds. The balance of a long-term fund will include cash, investments in stocks, bonds, or other assets, and accrued revenues at balance sheet date. Accounting for a bond retirement (sinking) fund is discussed in Units 23 and 25.

Exhibit 22.1 illustrates how account balances that are properly classified as long-term investments and funds are reported.

Note that information on the method of valuation is required for long-term investments in stocks and bonds. Also, cost or market value, whichever is not used as the valuation basis for these investments, should be disclosed. For long-term receivables, the maturity date should be disclosed. This information can be disclosed as illustrated or in footnotes. Other information regarding bond sinking funds and long-term investments in stock valued at lower-of-cost-or-market must be disclosed in footnotes (see Units 25 and 29).

Exhibit 22.1

Dahlia Corporation
Partial Balance Sheet
December 31, 19x3

Long-term investments and funds:	
Investments in stocks, at lower-of-cost-or-market (cost, $36,000)	$ 34,500
Investments in bonds, at cost (market value $20,500)	20,800
Long-term note receivable, due on April 30, 19x5	10,000
Bond sinking fund	42,700
Total long-term investments and funds	$108,000

Other Assets

This classification is the final asset group listed on the balance sheet. Any asset that cannot be classified as current assets, long-term investments and funds, plant assets, intangible assets, or deferred charges is reported here. Examples include noncurrent receivables, plant assets being held for future use, and plant assets being held for sale because the company no longer uses them. Noncurrent receivables are reported at their present value, plant assets held for future use at their acquisition cost, and plant assets held for sale at their net realizable value at the time they are permanently withdrawn from use in normal business operation.

REVIEW PROBLEM

The following transactions involving intangible assets were completed during 19*x2:*

June 1	Incurred cost of $12,500 in being organized and incorporated. Business operations began on July 1, 19*x2.* During the second half of 19*x2* research and development costs incurred amounted to $22,000. The company will use the calendar year as its accounting period and wants to charge organization costs and research and developments to expense as fast as possible.
June 10	Acquired land at a cost of $30,000 and incurred cost of $15,000 to develop the land for the extraction of gravel. The company expects to extract 100,000 tons of gravel. During 19*x2* the output from the gravel pit was 15,000 tons.
July 1	Purchased the net assets and name of Hercules Corp. for $300,000. The assets acquired and liabilities assumed were:

	Book Value	Fair Value
Inventory	$ 36,000	$ 40,000
Land	15,000	20,000
Buildings (30-year life)	160,000	180,000
Equipment (10-year life)	56,000	64,000
Tradename	—	20,000
Total	$267,000	$324,000
Less Accounts Payable	48,000	48,000
Net Assets	$219,000	$276,000

Tradename and goodwill are to be amortized over 20 years.

Sept. 30   Acquired a license for $10,000 to distribute Miracle brand products within a 3-state region. The license grants Hercules Corp. distribution rights for 5 years.

Dec. 18   Successfully defended the tradename of Hercules Corp. Costs incurred totaled $10,000.

Dec. 31   Expenditures incurred to promote the quality of Miracle brand products and the dependability of Hercules Corp. during the year were $4,000 and $10,000, respectively.

Required   Prepare a partial balance sheet and a partial income statement at the end of 19x2.

Solution to review problem

Hercules Corp.
Partial Balance Sheet

Plant assets:			
Land		$ 20,000	
Buildings	$180,000		
Less: Accumulated depreciation	3,000	177,000	
Equipment	$ 64,000		
Less: Accumulated depreciation	3,200	60,800	
Gravel pit		38,250	
Total plant assets			$296,050
Intangible assets:			
Goodwill		$ 23,400	
License		9,500	
Tradename		29,250	
Organization costs		11,250	
Total intangible assets			73,400

Hercules Corp.
Partial Income Statement
For the Year Ended December 31, 19x2

Operating expenses:	
Depreciation expense—buildings	$ 3,000
Depreciation expense—equipment	3,200
Depletion expense	6,750
Amortization expense—organization costs	1,250
Amortization expense—goodwill	600
Amortization expense—tradename	750
Amortization expense—license	500
Research and development expense	22,000
Advertising and promotion expense	14,000

Computation of goodwill acquired

Cost of net assets acquired		$300,000
Less fair value of net assets acquired:		
Fair value of assets	$324,000	
Less liabilities assumed	48,000	276,000
Cost of goodwill acquired		$ 24,000

Computation of operating expenses

Depreciation—buildings: ($180,000/30) × 6/12 = $3,000
Depreciation—equipment: ($64,000/10) × 6/12 = $3,200
Depletion: ($30,000 + 15,000)/100,000 tons = $.45/ton; 15,000 tons × $.45/ton = $6,750
Amortization of organization costs: ($12,500/5 years) × 6/12 = $1,250
Amortization of goodwill: ($24,000/20 years) × 6/12 = $600
Amortization of tradename: ($20,000 + 10,000)/20 years × 6/12 = $750
Amortization of license: ($10,000/5 years) × 3/12 = $500
Research and development: $22,000 (see June 1 transaction)
Advertising and promotion: $14,000 (see December 31 transaction)

Computation of asset balances

Buildings: $180,000 − ($180,000/30 × 6/12) = $177,000
Equipment: $64,000 − ($64,000/10 × 6/12) = $60,800
Gravel pit: $30,000 + 15,000 − 6,750 = $38,250
Goodwill: $24,000 − 600 = $23,400
License: $10,000 − 500 = $9,500
Tradename: $30,000 − 750 = $29,250
Organization costs: $12,500 − 1,250 = $11,250

SUMMARY

Accounting for intangible assets, natural resources, and deferred charges was discussed in this unit. The costs of intangible assets and deferred charges are allocated to expense over the periods that benefit from them. Natural resources are charged to expense based on output for each period. If the life of an intangible asset is uncertain, its costs are allocated to expense over a reasonable period not to exceed 40 years. In accordance with FASB Statement No. 2, research and development costs are charged to expense as incurred unless they are directly reimbursable by others. To complete the discussion of assets, the accounting for long-term investments and funds was explained briefly; this asset group is examined in more detail in Units 29–30.

REVIEW QUESTIONS

22-1 Distinguish between plant assets and intangible assets.

22-2 APB Opinion No. 17 classified intangible assets as identifiable and unidentifiable. What is the distinction between these two types of intangible assets and why is the distinction important?

22-3   Why are costs incurred to develop internally, maintain, or restore an intangible asset not capitalized?

22-4   Explain the policy recommended by APB Opinion No. 17 for the amortization of intangible assets.

22-5   What costs are included as part of the cost of a patent?

22-6   How are costs of a successful defense of a patient, copyright, trademark, or tradename treated? If the defense is unsuccessful, how are the costs treated?

22-7   What is goodwill? How is it measured?

22-8   How are intangible assets reported on the balance sheet? How are an amortization expense of intangible assets and a loss from the write-off of an intangible asset reported on a multiple-step income statement?

22-9   Explain how research and development costs should be accounted for in conformity with current accounting principles.

22-10   What is depletion? How is depletion computed and recorded?

22-11   Distinguish between a deferred charge and a prepaid expense. Why is the prepayment for a 3-year insurance policy normally treated as a prepaid expense rather than as a deferred charge?

22-12   What are organization costs and bond issue costs? How should a company account for each type of cost?

22-13   What assets normally are classified as long-term investments and funds? As other assets?

22-14   How are long-term investments in stocks and bonds and noncurrent receivables valued for reporting on the balance sheet?

22-15   What is a fund? What criterion is used to determine whether the fund is reported as a current asset or a noncurrent asset?

EXERCISES

22-1   Fain Company owns the following two patents:

Patent A: Purchased for $13,600 on March 24, 19*x2;* the expected economic life of the patent is 8 years.

Patent B: Developed by Fain Company at a cost of $16,500 including legal and patent registration fees of $1,500; the patent was registered and used starting September 5, 19*x3;* the expected economic life of the patent is 5 years.

During 19x5 patent B was successfully defended against infringement by another company; unrecovered legal and court costs were $4,400.

Required **a.** Determine patent amortization expense for 19x5.

b. Prepare a partial balance sheet at December 31, 19x5.

c. Prepare the entries that would have been necessary for 19x5 if the infringement lawsuit had been unsuccessful.

22-2 Calypso Company purchased the net assets and assumed the liabilities of Jamaica Company on March 31, 19x6, when the book value and fair value of Jamaica's net assets were as follows:

	Book Value	Fair Value
Inventory	$ 32,000	$ 36,000
Land	18,000	24,000
Buildings	100,000	120,000
Equipment	40,000	50,000
Patents	5,000	15,000
Total	$195,000	$245,000
Accounts Payable	30,000	30,000
Net Assets	$165,000	$215,000

Calypso Company paid $235,000 for the net assets of Jamaica Company. The patent had 12 years of its legal life remaining when acquired, but was expected to provide benefits for only 5 more years. Any goodwill paid for in the purchase of Jamaica's net asset is to be amortized over 20 years.

Required **a.** Prepare the entry to record the purchase of Jamaica's net assets by Calypso.

b. Prepare the entry or entries necessary to record amortization expense for 19x6.

22-3 Amity Company produces a variety of products, most of which are developed by the company's research department. Occasionally a patent is acquired from a product's inventor. During 19x7 the company incurred research and development costs of $80,000. Seventy percent of these costs were incurred on projects not expected to result in patentable products. In March 19x7, a patent was acquired at a cost of $15,000. Additional costs of $5,000 were incurred to refine the product before production started on July 1, 19x7. The patent is expected to have a useful life of 5 years. What expenses should Amity Company report on its income statement for 19x7 based on these circumstances?

22-4 In 19x5 the Western Coal Company acquired rights at a cost of $90,000 to extract coal. Development costs of $60,000 were incurred during 19x5 and output was estimated at 200,000 tons. During 19x6 and 19x7 the company extracted 60,000 tons of coal. At the end of 19x7 the remaining output was estimated at 150,000 tons. What would depletion expense be for 19x8 if output is 40,000 tons?

22-5 The trial balance for Clare Corp. included the following accounts at December 31, 19x6:

Prepaid insurance (coverage extends for 2½ more years)	$ 3,000
Long-term investment in stock (market value, $42,000)	45,000
Long-term investment in bonds (market value, $33,800; par value, $36,000)	34,600
Note receivable, due April 1, 19x8 (interest payable annually at 8% on April 1)	20,000
Organization costs (unamortized balance after amortization for 2 years)	6,000
Bond sinking fund (including cash of $1,500, accrued revenue of $1,000, and investments with a cost of $45,000)	47,500

Required   Prepare a partial balance sheet at December 31, 19x6, after adjusting all necessary account balances.

PROBLEMS

22-1 On March 31, 19x6, Zephyr Company reported the following assets and expenses on its first quarter financial statements:

Patents (unamortized balance)	$17,500
Trademarks and tradenames (unamortized balance)	1,400
Amortization expense—patents	1,250
Amortization expense—trademarks and tradenames	100

The assets and trademarks and tradename of Winn Company were acquired by Zephyr Company for $250,000 on March 31, 19x6, when the book value and fair value of the net assets were as follows:

	Book Value	Fair Value
Inventory	$ 20,000	$ 25,000
Land	15,000	30,000
Buildings	80,000	95,000
Equipment	36,000	40,000
Patents	8,000	20,000
Total	$159,000	$210,000

Half the difference between the cost of the assets and their fair value is attributable to the trademarks and tradename of Winn Company. The patents had an expected useful life of 4 years, although 12 years of their legal life remain. Other intangible assets acquired will be amortized over 20 years.

During May 19x6, Zephyr Company was unsuccessful in defending the patent reported on the first quarter's balance sheet. Legal and court costs incurred were $7,200. Zephyr Company also purchased a license at a cost of $25,000 to produce and sell products under the Victor brand name. The license gives Zephyr Company exclusive rights for a 5-year period starting July 1, 19x6. During 19x6 Zephyr Company incurred research costs of $46,000 to develop and improve products.

Required   **a.** Prepare journal entries for the 19x6 transactions described.

           b. Prepare all entries necessary to amortize intangible assets for 19x6.

           c. Prepare a partial balance sheet and a partial income statement at the end of 19x6.

22-2   Minden Corporation reported the following balances on its balance sheet at December 31, 19x7:

Prepaid insurance (coverage extends for $2^{1}/_{4}$ more years)	$ 4,050
Organization costs (unamortized balance; 5-year amortization policy; operations began on April 1, 19x6)	5,200
Patents (6-year amortization policy; acquired on April 1, 19x6)	12,750

Transactions and activities for 19x8 included the following:

    a. Incurred development costs of $5,250 to improve the product covered by the patent indicated on the December 31, 19x7, balance sheet.

    b. Purchased stock of Kinder Company at a cost of $25,500; the stock is to be held as a long-term investment. The value of the stock at December 31, 19x8, was $24,800.

    c. Discovered a coal deposit on company land and decided to begin extraction operations as soon as possible. During the year 5,000 tons of coal were extracted and the remaining output was estimated at 55,000 tons. Development costs of $36,000 were incurred before extraction began.

    d. Received a 2-year, non-interest-bearing note for $15,000; the present value of the note at 6% is $13,350; the note was dated July 1, 19x8.

    e. Established a retirement fund for a long-term debt of $50,000 that matures in four years. At the end of 19x8 the balance of the fund included the following: cash, $500; accrued revenue, $250; investments, $9,200.

Required   Prepare a partial balance sheet at December 31, 19x8.

22-3   Northridge Company was organized early in 19x1 and began business operations on July 1, 19x1. The following assets were purchased prior to July 1, 19x1:

Land	$ 35,000
Building (40-year life; 5% residual value)	280,000
Equipment (10-year life; 10% residual value)	125,000
Patents (6-year life)	72,000

The following transactions were completed during 19*x1:*

a. Paid organization costs totaling $6,500 during April.

b. Incurred product development costs of $32,000 from July 1 to December 31.

c. Acquired at the beginning of July a license at a cost of $25,000 to manufacture and distribute Scottie products; also, the company must pay an annual royalty of 2% of revenue from the sale of Scottie products. Sales of Scottie products during the second half of 19*x1* totaled $85,000.

d. Paid the premium of $5,400 on a 2-year insurance policy on June 30.

e. Purchased in September additional land to be used for a parking lot and a warehouse; the cost of the land was $27,000.

f. The site for the parking lot and warehouse was cleared and leveled at a cost of $2,700.

g. Paved one-third of the land purchased in e at the end of September for use as a parking lot at a cost of $4,800. The lot will need to be repaved every 6 years.

h. Incurred product promotion costs of $68,000 from July 1 to December 31.

i. Incurred costs of $23,500 to develop customer goodwill.

j. Paid the contractor for the warehouse $45,000, which represents one-half of the amount due on the construction contract. The warehouse is to be completed by March 19*x2.*

Organization costs are to be amortized over 5 years. The license has an unlimited life. All intangible assets and deferred charges with unlimited or uncertain lives are to be amortized over 10 years.

Required **(1)** Prepare a list of all expenses, including amounts, for 19*x1.*

(2) Prepare a partial balance sheet at December 31, 19*x1.*

22-4 Following is the asset section of the balance sheet presented in the 1977 annual report of Bliss & Laughlin Industries. The footnotes relating to realty operations and intangible assets are also reproduced.

Assets		
	December 31	
Current Assets:	1977	1976
Cash	$ 2,913,000	$ 3,222,000
Marketable securities, at cost which approximates market ...	11,634,000	25,456,000
Marketable securities committed for acquisition	8,000,000	—
Trade accounts receivable, less allowance for doubtful accounts of $899,000 and $911,000, respectively	20,118,000	15,971,000
Inventories	37,514,000	28,804,000
Deferred income tax benefits	1,286,000	1,112,000
Prepaid expenses	1,407,000	786,000
Total current assets	$82,872,000	$75,351,000
Realty:		
Land and related costs	$ 14,076,000	$ 13,168,000
Receivables	683,000	1,932,000
Deferred income tax benefits	1,112,000	1,207,000
Other	759,000	848,000
	$ 16,630,000	$ 17,155,000

Other Assets:		
Notes receivable and deferred charges	$ 772,000	$ 799,000
Investments and advances to affiliated companies	1,919,000	1,491,000
Intangible assets arising from acquisitions	5,347,000	5,341,000
Patents and other intangible assets, at cost, less amortization		
of $3,381,000 and $3,425,000, respectively	1,100,000	1,226,000
	$ 9,138,000	$ 8,857,000
Equipment Leased to Others:		
At cost, less accumulated depreciation of $12,099,000 and		
$11,332,000, respectively	$ 5,309,000	$ 6,346,000
Plant and Equipment, at cost:		
Land	$ 1,834,000	$ 1,590,000
Buildings	12,986,000	11,257,000
Machinery and equipment	36,109,000	30,649,000
	$ 50,929,000	$ 43,496,000
Less: accumulated depreciation	23,532,000	21,841,000
Net plant and equipment	$ 27,397,000	$ 21,655,000
	$141,346,000	$129,364,000

Realty Operations

The Company's realty operations differ from other operations in that they have a business cycle extending over several years. Accordingly, all the assets and liabilities of these operations are presented under separate realty captions.

Land and related costs are stated at the lower of cost or market. Realty sales are recorded when the buyer has a significant and continuing cash equity in the property. Real estate taxes, interest expenses and development costs applicable to land are expensed as they are incurred. Costs are allocated to the various parcels of individual projects based upon the relative value method.

Intangible Assets

The excess of the purchase price over the fair market value of net assets of businesses acquired in the amount of $4,562,000 prior to November 1, 1970 is not being amortized because, in the opinion of management, it represents assets with continuing value. For subsequent acquisitions any such excess is being amortized over the lesser of the period benefited or 40 years. Amortization totaled $22,000 for both 1977 and 1976.

Patents and other intangible assets are stated at their purchased cost and are amortized over their useful life.

Required

a. Discuss the manner in which assets are reported, indicating whether or not the financial disclosures and manner of presentation are adequate.

b. What does "Intangible assets arising from acquisitions" represent?

c. Discuss the propriety of the decision not to amortize $4,562,000 of the excess of the purchase price over fair market value of net assets of businesses acquired prior to November 1, 1970 (see the footnote on intangible assets).

d. Prepare a new asset section of the balance sheet for 1977 which includes classifications for intangible assets and long-term investments and deletes the one for "other assets."

Equities

Chapter 8

Liabilities

This chapter examines the problems of measuring and reporting current liabilities and certain long-term liabilities. Other long-term liabilities involve complex accounting issues and are covered in Unit 35.

Unit 23
Present Value and Amount Concepts

The second thing necessary in business is to be a good bookkeeper and ready mathematician.

Fra Luca Paciolo, Summa de Arithmetica

Present value and amount concepts are often applied in accounting for certain assets and liabilities. These concepts are reviewed in this unit. How to use them in simple accounting applications is also described and illustrated. Other applications in accounting will be discussed in later units.

Performance Objectives

Upon completing this unit you should be able to:

1. define and use the accounting terms introduced in this unit.
2. identify and use the appropriate table, from the four in Appendix 23, for solving accounting problems that involve the time value of money:
    a. amount of $1 table
    b. present value of $1 table
    c. amount of an ordinary annuity of $1 table
    d. present value of an ordinary annuity of $1 table

Need for Present Value and Amount Concepts in Accounting

Many measurement situations in accounting require the use of present value or amount concepts. Most of these situations involve liabilities and related expenses, receivables and related revenue, or funds and related revenue. For long-term liabilities such as bonds, long-term notes, pensions, and lease obligations: (1) the present value of the liability must be measured and reported, (2) periodic interest expense must be measured, and (3) periodic contributions or payments to be made must be determined. For long-term receivables and investments such as bond investments, lease receivables, and long-term note receivables: (1) the present value of the receivable must be measured and reported, (2) the amount to be paid for an investment in bonds to yield a specific rate of return must be determined, (3) periodic interest or lease revenue must be measured and reported, and (4) periodic payments to be received must be determined. For debt retirement and other types of funds: (1) periodic payments or contributions to be made must be determined, (2) periodic revenue expected from fund investments must be determined, and (3) the fund balance must be measured and reported.

Present value and amount concepts are concerned with the **time value of money,** that is, the interest factor on future payments or investments. The time value of money refers to the fact that a dollar received today is worth more than a dollar received at a later date. Thus, there is a cost for the use of money. For example, a dollar received today, which can be invested at 6% interest for one year, will grow to $1.06 [$1 + 6%($1) = $1.06] at the end of one year. If the dollar were received one year from today instead, the interest would not be earned. Similarly, assume that a company is to receive $1 one year from today. If payment is received today instead, only $.94 will be received after a 6% discount is deducted [$1 − 6%($1) = $.94] to determine the current cash equivalent of the dollar today. The cost for the use of the dollar over the year in both cases is the interest of $.06 ($1 × 6% = $.06).

In the past the time value of money or interest factor was often ignored in accounting for some liabilities and receivables. However, various APB opinions and FASB statements now require the use of present value concepts to measure liabilities and receivables and their related expense and revenue. These opinions and statements are covered in Units 24 and 35.

Four present value and amount concepts relevant to accounting are discussed in this unit:

1. the amount of $1
2. the present value of $1
3. the amount of an annuity of $1
4. the present value of an annuity of $1

Tables based on $1 that provide the values for different periods of time and at different interest rates are included in the appendix to this unit. You must become familiar with using these tables since you will have to refer to them to solve the exercises and problems for this unit and some later units.

Amount of $1

The **amount of $1** is the future value or amount to which a dollar will grow if it is invested for a specified number of periods at a specified interest rate. The future value of any sum of money can be determined by successive computations or by using a table for the amount of $1. The table simplifies the determination of the amount (or future value) of any sum invested for any number of periods at various interest rates. Assume that $10,000 is invested at 6% for three years. The amount to which the $10,000 investment will grow at the end of three years can be determined by successive computations as follows:

Year	Amount at Beginning of Year	+	Interest Earned During the Year (rounded to the nearest whole dollar)	=	Amount at End of Year
1	$10,000		$600 ($10,000 × 6%)		$10,600
2	10,600		636 ($10,600 × 6%)		11,236
3	11,236		674 ($11,236 × 6%)		11,910

When few periods are involved, determining future value by successive computations is not very cumbersome. But trying to use this procedure when 10, 20, or more periods are involved would be. Thus, the amount of $1 table has been constructed so that the future value of the sum of money invested can be determined by multiplying the sum by a single factor representing the cumulative interest for the number of periods and the interest rate involved. For example, in Table 23.1 (the amount of $1 table) in the appendix, the factor to be used to determine the future value of $10,000 invested at 6% for three years is 1.1910. It is located by reading down the n or periods column to 3 and across that row to the 6% column.

The future value of the $10,000 is determined using the following formula:

$$A = S \times F_{i,n}$$
$$A = \$10,000 \times F_{.06,3}$$
$$A = \$10,000 \times 1.1910$$
$$A = \$11,910$$

where A = the amount to which a sum of money will grow

S = the present value of the sum of money

F = the factor from the amount of $1 table for n periods at i interest rate

i = the interest rate per period

n = the number of periods

Each factor in the amount of $1 table is greater than 1 because $1 is invested and will grow to a greater sum as interest is earned. The difference between 1.0000 and the factor in the table is the cumulative interest or time value of the money. The interest earned over the three years is $1,910; it may be determined either by finding the difference between the future amount and the sum of money ($11,910 − 10,000 = $1,910) or by multiplying the difference between the factor and 1.0000 by the sum of money [$10,000 × (1.1910 − 1.0000) = $1,910].

Present Value of $1

The **present value of $1** is the current value of a dollar that is to be received or paid a specified number of periods from now, discounted at a specified interest rate. The present value of any sum of money can be determined by successive computations or by using a table for the present value of $1. Assume that $10,000 is to be received three years from now. The present or current value of the $10,000 discounted at 6% annually can be determined by successive computations as follows:

Year	Present Value at Beginning of Year (rounded to the nearest full dollar)
3	$9,434 ($10,000/1.06)
2	8,900 ($ 9,434/1.06)
1	8,396 ($ 8,900/1.06)

It is simpler, however, to determine the present value of a sum of money by using the appropriate factor from the present value of $1 table. This table contains the factors for the present value of $1 for various periods and various interest (or discount) rates. The factor from Table 23.2 in the appendix to be used in determining the present value of $10,000 discounted at 6% for three years is .8396. It is located by reading down the n or periods column to 3 and reading across that row to the 6% column.

The present value of the $10,000 is determined using the following formula:

$$PV = S \times F_{i,n}$$
$$PV = \$10,000 \times F_{.06,3}$$
$$PV = \$10,000 \times .8396$$
$$PV = \$8,396$$

where PV = the present value of a sum of money

S = the future value of the sum of money

F = the factor from the present value of $1 table for n periods at i interest rate

i = the interest rate per period

n = the number of periods

Each factor in the present value of $1 table is less than 1 because interest is deducted to determine the present value of $1. The difference between 1.0000 and the factor is the cumulative interest or time value of the money. The interest over the three years is $1,604; it may be determined either by finding the difference between the sum of money and its present value ($10,000 − 8,396 = $1,604) or by multiplying the difference between 1.0000 and the factor by the sum of money [$10,000 × (1.0000 − .8396) = $1,604].

Amount of an Annuity of $1

An **annuity** is a series of equal payments made at the beginning or end of each period for two or more periods. The **amount of an annuity of $1** is the future value to which a specified number of equal payments of $1 each will grow at a specified interest rate per period. In contrast, the amount of $1 involves a single payment of $1 at the start of the accumulation period. If payments are made at the end of each period, the concept of an **ordinary annuity** is involved. If payments are made at the beginning of each period, the concept of an **annuity due** is involved.

Amount of an Ordinary Annuity   The future value of the periodic payments can be determined by successive computations or by using a table for the amount of an ordinary annuity of $1. (This same table can be used if the annuity due concept is involved, providing certain adjustments are made—see pages 442–443.) Assume that $10,000 is to be invested at 6% at the end of each year for three years starting at the end of the current year. The amount to which the three $10,000 payments will grow can be determined by successive computations as follows:

Year	Amount at Beginning of Year	+	Interest Earned During the Year	+	Contribution at End of Year	=	Amount at End of Year
1	$ 0	$ 0			$10,000		$10,000
2	10,000	600 ($10,000 × 6%)			10,000		20,600
3	20,600	1,236 ($20,600 × 6%)			10,000		31,836

Note that no interest is earned during the first year because the payment is made at the end of the year. During the second year interest is earned on the first payment, and during the third year interest is earned on the first two payments plus the interest earned during the second year.

As with the other tables, the use of the amount of an ordinary annuity of $1 table makes the computation of future value simpler. With Table 23.3 the amount of the periodic payment is multiplied by a single factor representing various periods at various rates to find the amount to which these equal payments of $1 each will grow. The factor to determine the future value of three payments of $10,000 each made at the end of each year with interest at 6% annually is 3.1836. It is located by reading down the *n* or periods column to 3 and reading across that row to the 6% column.

The amount to which the three $10,000 payments will grow is determined using the following formula:

$$AA = I \times F_{i,n}$$
$$AA = \$10,000 \times F_{.06,3}$$
$$AA = \$10,000 \times 3.1836$$
$$AA = \$31,836$$

where $AA =$ the amount to which the payments will grow
$I =$ the amount of each payment (or installment)
$F =$ the factor from the amount of an ordinary annuity of $1 table for n periods at i interest rate
$i =$ the interest rate per period
$n =$ the number of periods or payments

Each factor on the 1 row in the amount of an ordinary annuity of $1 table is 1.0000 because the payment is made at the end of that period, and no interest, therefore, is earned during it. The factors on the lines for the remaining periods are greater than the number of the period involved because interest is earned during the second and following periods; for example, the factors on the 2 row must be greater than 2, those on the 3 row, greater than 3, and so on. The difference between the factor and the number of periods or payments involved is the cumulative interest or the time value of the money. The interest earned over the three years, $1,836, may be determined either by finding the difference between the amount of the payments at the end of the time period and the sum of the payments made [$31,836 − 3 ($10,000) = $1,836] or by multiplying the amount of one payment by the difference between the factor and the number of payments [$10,000 × (3.1836 − 3.0000) = $1,836].

Amount of an Annuity Due   For an annuity due, the number of payments is the same as for an ordinary annuity, but the payments are made at the beginning of each period. Thus, an annuity due earns interest for the first period, and the number of payments and interest periods is equal. For an ordinary annuity, you will recall, there is one less interest period than the number of payments. The following diagrams illustrate the differences between an ordinary annuity and an annuity due.

Ordinary annuity for 5 years: *Annuity due for 5 years:*

1 2 3 4   interest periods (4)   1 2 3 4 5   interest periods (5)
0 1 2 3 4 5 payments (5)   1 2 3 4 5   payments (5)

Assume that a $10,000 payment is to be made at the beginning of each year for three years with interest earned at 6% annually. The amount of an annuity due can be determined by successive computations as follows:

Year	Amount at Beginning of Year	+	Contribution at Beginning of Year	+	Interest Earned During the Year (rounded to the nearest full dollar)	=	Amount at End of Year
1	$ 0		$10,000		$ 600 ($10,000 × 6%)		$10,600
2	10,600		10,000		1,236 ($20,600 × 6%)		21,836
3	21,836		10,000		1,910 ($31,836 × 6%)		33,746

However, the table for the amount of an ordinary annuity of $1 (Table 23.3) can be used to find the future value of an annuity due if the factor for $n + 1$ periods is selected and 1.0000 is deducted from it. The factor for the extra period is used so the additional interest period is included, but 1.0000 must be subtracted because only n payments are made. The amount of an annuity due for three $10,000 payments at 6% annually can be determined using the formula for the amount of an ordinary annuity with the adjustments described:

$$AA \text{ (due)} = I \times (F_{i,n+1} - 1.0000)$$
$$AA \text{ (due)} = \$10,000 \times (F_{.06,4} - 1.0000)$$
$$AA \text{ (due)} = \$10,000 \times (4.3746 - 1.0000)$$
$$AA \text{ (due)} = \$33,746$$

The amount of an annuity due is always greater than the amount of an ordinary annuity because of the additional interest earned. The interest earned over the three years for the annuity due in the example is $3,746; it can be determined in the same ways described for an ordinary annuity: [$33,746 − 3 ($10,000) = $3,746] or [$10,000 × (4.3746 − 4.0000) = $3,746].

Using the data in the illustrations, the following table summarizes the amount of the two types of annuities and the interest earned for each:

	Amount at End of 3 Years	Interest Earned over 3 Years
Ordinary annuity	$31,836	$1,836
Annuity due	33,746	3,746

Ordinary annuity ⟶   Amount

$10,000 + 600 + 10,000 + 1,236 + 10,000 = $31,836

Annuity due ⟶ $10,000 + 600 + 10,000 + 1,236 + 10,000 + 1,910   = $33,746

Present Value of an Annuity of $1

The **present value of an annuity of $1** is the current value of a specified number of equal payments of $1 each that are to be received or paid and that are discounted at a specified interest rate per period. If payments are made at the end of each period, the **ordinary annuity** concept is involved; if at the beginning of each period, the **annuity due** concept.

Present Value of an Ordinary Annuity   The present value of a series of periodic payments can be determined by successive computations or by using a table for the present value of an ordinary annuity of $1. (This same table can be used if the annuity due concept is involved, providing certain adjustments are made—see page 446.) Assume that $10,000 is to be received or paid at the end of each year for three years. If the payments are discounted at 6% annually, the present value of the payments can be determined by successive computations as follows:

Payment Number	Year	Present Value at Beginning of Year (rounded to the nearest full dollar)	Present Value of 3 Payments at Beginning of First Year
3	3	$9,434 ($10,000/1.06)	
	2	8,900 ($ 9,434/1.06)	
	1	8,396 ($ 8,900/1.06)	$ 8,396
2	2	9,434 ($10,000/1.06)	
	1	8,900 ($ 9,434/1.06)	8,900
1	1	9,434 ($10,000/1.06)	9,434
Total			$26,730

The first payment must be discounted for one period because it is made at the end of the first period. The second and third payments must be discounted for two and three years, respectively, because they are made at the end of the second and third years.

Table 23.4 in the appendix contains the factors for the present value of an ordinary annuity of $1 for various periods and various interest (or discount) rates. The factor to determine the present value of a $10,000 payment made at the end of each year for three years and discounted at 6% annually is 2.6730. It is located by reading down the *n* or periods column to 3 and reading across that row to the 6% column.

The present value of the three $10,000 payments is determined using the following formula:

$$PVA = I \times F_{i,n}$$
$$PVA = \$10,000 \times F_{.06,3}$$
$$PVA = \$10,000 \times 2.6730$$
$$PVA = \$26,730$$

where PVA = the present value of the periodic payments

I = the amount of each payment (or installment)

F = the factor from the present value of an ordinary annuity of $1 table for n periods at i interest rate

i = the interest rate per period

n = the number of periods or payments

Each factor in the present value of an ordinary annuity table of $1 is less than the number of the period involved because interest must be deducted from the amount of the payments to determine their present value. The difference between the factor and the number of periods or payments is the cumulative interest or the time value of the money. The interest over the three periods—$3,270 in the example—can be determined either by finding the difference between the sum of the payments made and their present value [3 ($10,000) − 26,730 = $3,270] or by multiplying the difference between the number of payments and the factor by the amount of each periodic payment [$10,000 × (3.0000 − 2.6730) = $3,270].

Present Value of an Annuity Due   For an annuity due, the number of payments is the same as for an ordinary annuity but the payments are made at the beginning of each period. Thus, the first payment is not discounted; its present value is equal to the amount of the payment because it is made immediately, and there is one less interest (or discount) period than the number of payments. For an ordinary annuity, the number of payments and interest (or discount) periods are equal because the payments are made at the end of each period; thus, all payments are discounted. The following diagrams illustrate the difference between the present value of an ordinary annuity and an annuity due:

Ordinary annuity for 5 years: *Annuity due for 5 years:*

1 2 3 4 5   discount periods (5)   1 2 3 4   discount periods (4)
0 1 2 3 4 5   payments (5)   1 2 3 4 5   payments (5)

Assume that a $10,000 payment is to be made at the beginning of each year for three years. If the discount rate is 6%, the present value of an annuity due can be determined by successive computations as follows:

Payment Number	Year	Present Value at Beginning of Year (rounded to the nearest whole dollar)	Present Value of 3 Payments at Beginning of First Year
3	3	$10,000	
	2	9,434 ($10,000/1.06)	
	1	8,900 ($ 9,434/1.06)	$ 8,900
2	2	10,000	
	1	9,434 ($10,000/1.06)	9,434
1	1	10,000	10,000
Total			$28,334

The present value of each payment at the beginning of the year when it is made is $10,000. Thus, the third payment is discounted for two periods, the second payment is discounted for one period, and the first payment is not discounted.

However, the table for the present value of an ordinary annuity of $1 (Table 23.4) can be used to find the present value of an annuity due if the factor for $n - 1$ periods is selected and 1.0000 is added to it. The factor for one less period is used so that interest for one less period is included, but 1.0000 must be added because n payments are made. The present value of an annuity due of three $10,000 payments discounted at 6% annually can be determined using the formula for the present value of an ordinary annuity with the adjustments described:

$$PVA \text{ (due)} = I \times (F_{i,n-1} + 1.0000)$$
$$PVA \text{ (due)} = \$10,000 \times (F_{.06,2} + 1.0000)$$
$$PVA \text{ (due)} = \$10,000 \times (1,8334 + 1.0000)$$
$$PVA \text{ (due)} = \$10,000 \times 2,8334$$
$$PVA \text{ (due)} = \$28,334$$

The present value of an annuity due is always greater than the present value of an ordinary annuity because there is one less discount period for an annuity due. The interest over the three years for the annuity due in the example is $1,666; it can be determined in the same ways described for an ordinary annuity: [3 ($10,000) − 28,334 = $1,666] or [$10,000 × (3.0000 − 2.8334) = $1,666].

Using the data in the illustrations, the following table summarizes the present value of the two types of annuities and the interest earned for each:

	Present Value of Annuity	Interest Earned over 3 Years
Ordinary annuity	$26,730	$3,270
Annuity due	28,334	1,666

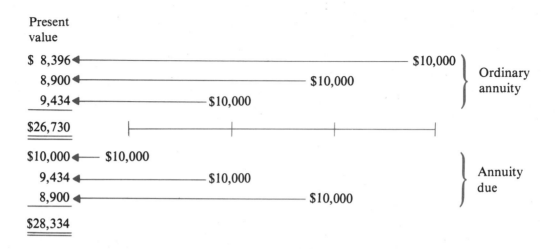

Adjustments for Interest Periods Shorter Than One Year

The addition of interest to the original amount after the first period and to the original amount plus accrued interest for each period thereafter is referred to as the **compounding of interest.** The periods over which interest is to be computed are referred to as the interest or **compounding periods.** All of the preceding examples involved the compounding of interest annually. Some situations, however, require the compounding of interest at shorter intervals such as semiannually, quarterly, monthly, or daily.

The value of n in the formulas presented earlier is the total number of compounding periods for the situation under consideration. When the compounding period is shorter than one year, the value of n can be determined by multiplying the number of compounding periods in one year by the number of years. For example, if $10,000 is invested for three years with interest compounded quarterly, the value of n will be 12 (4 quarterly periods per year $\times$ 3 years = 12).

The value of i in the formulas is the interest rate per period. Because the compounding period in all the preceding examples was one year, the value of i was the annual interest rate. When the compounding period is shorter than one year, the value of i can be determined by dividing the annual interest rate by the number of compounding periods in one year. For example, if the annual interest rate is 8% and the interest is compounded quarterly, the value of i is 2% (8% annual interest rate/4 compounding periods in one year = 2%).

The amount to which $10,000 will grow at the end of three years with interest of 8% compounded quarterly is determined as follows:

$$A = S \times F_{i,n} \qquad \text{where } i - 8\%/4 - 2\%$$
$$A = \$10,000 \times F_{.02,12} \qquad n = 4 \times 3 = 12$$
$$A = \$10,000 \times 1.2682 \qquad S = \$10,000$$
$$A = \$12,682$$

The factor 1.2682 was located in Table 23.1 for the amount of $1 by reading down the n or periods column to 12 and then reading across that row to the 2% column.

Selecting the Appropriate Table

Figure 23.1 is a decision tree that will help you determine which table to use to solve a problem. Two basic questions must be answered:

1. Does the problem involve a single payment (or sum of money) or a series of equal payments?

   a. If a single payment is involved, the future value (or amount of a single sum) or present value of a single sum is involved; thus the amount of $1 table (Table 23.1) or the present value of $1 table (Table 23.2) will be used.

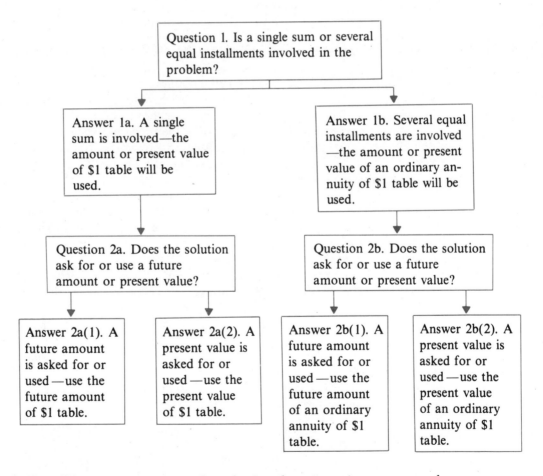

Figure 23.1   *Decision tree for selecting the appropriate present value or amount table*

    b.   If a series of payments is involved, the future value or a present value of an annuity is involved; thus the amount of an ordinary annuity of $1 table (Table 23.3) or the present value of an ordinary annuity of $1 table (Table 23.4) will be used.

2. Does the problem ask you to determine or use the future value or the present value of a single payment or a series of payments?

    a.   If the future value is to be determined or used, either the amount of $1 table (Table 23.1) or the amount of an ordinary annuity of $1 table (Table 23.3) will be used.

    b.   If the present value is to be determined or used, either the present value of $1 table (Table 23.2) or the present value of an ordinary annuity of $1 table (Table 23.4) will be used.

These two basic questions are incorporated into the decision tree so that their answers lead you to select the appropriate table to solve a specific problem. The following example illustrates this process.

Problem   You plan to deposit $200 at the end of every 3 months for 2 years to accumulate sufficient funds to make a cash down payment on a new car. If the bank pays interest of 4% compounded quarterly, how much will you have at the end of 2 years?

Solution to problem

Question 1: Is a single sum or several equal installments involved in the problem? Proceed to answer 1a or 1b.

Answer 1a: Does not apply because more than one payment is to be made.

Answer 1b: Several equal installments are involved because equal payments of $200 are to be made every 3 months for 2 years (thus, 8 equal payments of $200 each will be made). Now proceed to question 2.

Question 2: Does the solution ask for or use a future value or current value? Proceed to answer 2a or 2b.

Answer 2a: A future value is asked for because the problem wants you to determine the amount that will accumulate by the end of 2 years; thus, use the amount of an ordinary annuity of $1 table (Table 23.3).

Answer 2b: Does not apply because a future value is involved.

The solution to the problem, then, is determined using Table 23.3:

$$AA = I \times F_{i,n}$$
$$AA = \$200 \times F_{.01,8}$$
$$AA = \$200 \times 8.2857$$
$$AA = \$1,657.14$$

where $I = \$200$
$i = 4\%/4 = 1\%$ per quarter
$n = 4 \times 2$ yrs. $= 8$

Determining the Periodic Payments

Some problems involve determining the amount of installments or periodic payments for an annuity. In such situations the future value or current value of the annuity will be given in the problem, along with the number of payments or the term of the annuity and the annual interest rate. The amount or size of the payments can be determined by dividing the amount of the annuity (or the present value of the annuity) by the factor for n periods and i interest rate from the appropriate table. The formulas for determining the size of the payments for both an ordinary annuity and an annuity due follow:[1]

Ordinary annuity

$$I = \frac{AA}{F_{i,n}} \qquad\qquad I = \frac{PVA}{F_{i,n}}$$

Annuity due

$$I = \frac{AA \text{ (due)}}{F_{i,n+1} - 1.0000} \qquad\qquad I = \frac{PVA \text{ (due)}}{F_{i,n-1} + 1.0000}$$

Assume that a fund of $10,000 is to be accumulated over the next five years by depositing equal sums of money at the end of each three months in a bank account that pays 4% interest compounded quarterly. The size of each deposit (installment) is determined as follows:

---

[1]Mathematically these formulas are determined by dividing both sides of the appropriate equation (formula) by the same quantity, that is, the factor from the appropriate table; for example:

$$AA = I \times F_{i,n} \qquad\qquad PVA = I \times F_{i,n}$$

$$\frac{AA}{F_{i,n}} = \frac{I \times F_{i,n}}{F_{i,n}} \qquad\qquad \frac{PVA}{F_{i,n}} = \frac{I \times F_{i,n}}{F_{i,n}}$$

$$\frac{AA}{F_{i,n}} = I \qquad\qquad \frac{PVA}{F_{i,n}} = I$$

$$AA \text{ (due)} = I \times (F_{i,n+1} - 1.0000) \qquad\qquad PVA \text{ (due)} = I \times (F_{i,n-1} + 1.0000)$$

$$\frac{AA \text{ (due)}}{(F_{i,n+1} - 1.0000)} = \frac{I \times (F_{i,n+1} - 1.0000)}{(F_{i,n+1} - 1.0000)} \qquad\qquad \frac{PVA \text{ (due)}}{(F_{i,n-1} + 1.0000)} = \frac{I \times (F_{i,n-1} + 1.0000)}{(F_{i,n-1} + 1.0000)}$$

$$\frac{AA \text{ (due)}}{(F_{i,n+1} - 1.0000)} = I \qquad\qquad \frac{PVA \text{ (due)}}{(F_{i,n-1} + 1.0000)} = I$$

$$I = \frac{AA}{F_{i,n}} \qquad \text{where } AA = \$10,000$$
$$n = 5 \text{ yrs.} \times 4 \text{ payments/yr.} = 20$$
$$i = 4\%/4 = 1\% \text{ per quarter}$$

$$I = \frac{\$10,000}{F_{.01,20}}$$

$$I = \frac{\$10,000}{22.0190}$$

$$I = \$454* \qquad \qquad \text{*Rounded to the nearest full dollar}$$

Review Problems—Some Accounting Applications

As mentioned at the beginning of this unit accounting applications using present value and amount concepts usually involve long-term receivables, long-term liabilities, or funds. The following are four situations in which present value or amount concepts are used in accounting.

Case A On January 2, 19x1, a company is required to deposit $5,000 with a local utility company for 3 years. At the end of 3 years the security deposit will be returned to the company plus interest at 6% compounded annually.

When the deposit is made, the following entry is made:

Jan. 2, 19x1	Deposits with Utilities	5,000	
	Cash		5,000
	To record security deposit made to local utility.		

In this situation the future value of a single payment is involved; thus, the amount on deposit at the end of each year can be determined using the amount of $1 table (Table 23.1). The difference between the amount on deposit at the beginning and end of each year will be the interest earned during the year. It can be computed by multiplying the amount on deposit at the beginning of the year by the annual interest rate. The amount on deposit at the end of each year and the interest earned each year are as follows:

$A = S \times F_{i,n}$	$A = S \times F_{i,n}$	$A = S \times F_{i,n}$
$A = \$5,000 \times F_{.06,1}$	$A = \$5,000 \times F_{.06,2}$	$A = \$5,000 \times F_{.06,3}$
$A = \$5,000 \times 1.06$	$A = \$5,000 \times 1.1236$	$A = \$5,000 \times 1.1910$
$A = \$5,300$	$A = \$5,618$	$A = \$5,955$

Year	Amount at End of Year	−	Amount at Beginning of Year	=	Interest Earned During the Year (rounded to the nearest whole dollar)	Alternate Interest Computation (rounded to the nearest whole dollar)
19x1	$5,300		$5,000		$300	($5,000 × 6% = $300)
19x2	5,618		5,300		318	($5,300 × 6% = $318)
19x3	5,955		5,618		337	($5,618 × 6% = $337)

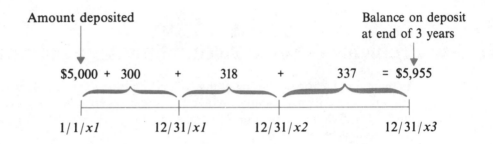

Amount deposited

Balance on deposit at end of 3 years

$5,000 + 300   +   318   +   337   = $5,955

1/1/x1   12/31/x1   12/31/x2   12/31/x3

The entries required at the end of each year to record interest earned are:

		19x1	19x2	19x3
Dec. 31	Deposits with Utilities	300	318	337
	Interest Revenue	300	318	337
	To record interest earned on deposit with utility.			

The balance of the deposits with utilities account when the deposit is refunded on January 2, 19x4, will be $5,955 ($5,000 + 300 + 318 + 337 = $5,955). The entry to record the receipt of the refund is:

Jan. 2, 19x4	Cash	5,955	
	Deposits with Utilities		5,955
	To record receipt of refund on deposit with local utility.		

Case B   A company needs a fund of $25,000 to pay a long-term loan due on December 31, 19x3. The company wants to make four, equal, semiannual payments to a debt retirement fund starting on December 31, 19*x1*. The fund is expected to earn 6% annually.

In this situation the future value of an annuity due is involved because a series of payments is to be made—one at the beginning of each semiannual period. Thus, the amount of an ordinary annuity of $1 table (Table 23.3) should be used; adjustments will be needed when the factor is selected because the annuity due concept is involved. Also, the values of *n* and *i* must be determined for the semiannual compounding periods involved.

The amount or size of each semiannual payment is determined as follows:

$$I = \frac{AA \text{ (due)}}{F_{i,n+1} - 1.0000} \qquad \text{where } AA = \$25,000$$
$$i = 6\%/2 = 3\%$$
$$n = 4$$

$$I = \frac{\$25,000}{F_{.03,5} - 1.0000}$$

$$I = \frac{\$25,000}{5.3091 - 1.0000}$$

$$I = \frac{\$25,000}{4.3091}$$

$$I = \$5,802* \qquad\qquad \text{*Rounded to the nearest full dollar}$$

If interest was not earned on the payments made into the debt retirement fund, the four payments would be $6,250 each ($25,000/4 = $6,250). Because interest will be earned on the fund balance each period, however, the semiannual payments into the fund will be less than $6,250. The interest earned at 3% every 6 months and the fund balance at the end of every 6 months are as follows:

Semiannual Period	Fund Balance at Beginning of Period	+ Semiannual Payment	+ Interest Earned During Period*	= Fund Balance at End of Period
1	$ 0	$5,802	$174 ($5,802 × 3%)	$ 5,976
2	5,976	5,802	353 ($11,778 × 3%)	12,131
3	12,131	5,802	538 ($17,933 × 3%)	18,471
4	18,471	5,802	727 ($24,273 × 3%)	25,000

*Computed on the sum of the fund balance at the beginning of the period and the semiannual payment into the fund (for example, $5,976 + 5,802 = $11,778; $12,131 + 5,802 = $17,933; and $18,471 + 5,802 = $24,273). The computation of interest is rounded to the nearest full dollar; interest for the fourth period is adjusted for the rounding error.

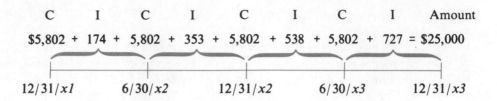

C—contribution; I—interest.

The entries to record the semiannual payments and interest earned every 6 months are:

	12/31/*x1*	6/30/*x2*	12/31/*x2*	6/30/*x3*
Debt Retirement Fund	5,802	5,802	5,802	5,802
Cash	5,802	5,802	5,802	5,802
To make semiannual payment to fund.				

	6/30/*x2*	12/31/*x2*	6/30/*x3*	12/31/*x3*
Debt Retirement Fund	174	353	538	727
Interest Revenue on Debt Retirement Fund	174	353	538	727
To record interest earned on fund balance.				

When the long-term loan was first obtained, the entry would have been:

Cash	25,000	
Loan Payable		25,000
To record long-term loan obtained.		

The fund was established to retire the debt at maturity on December 31, 19*x3*. Since fund assets are used to retire the debt, the entry to pay the debt at maturity is:

Dec. 31, 19*x3*	Loan Payable	25,000	
	Debt Retirement Fund		25,000
	To pay long-term debt at maturity from debt retirement fund.		

Case C   A company is going to borrow a sum of money for 2 years by issuing a non-interest-bearing note with a face value of $20,000 on December 31, 19*x1*. The note will be discounted at 7% compounded annually.

In this situation the present value of a single sum is involved because the cash proceeds (or current value) of the note must be computed; thus, the present value of $1 table (Table 23.2) should be used. The present value or cash proceeds of the note are computed as follows:

$$PV = S \times F_{i,n} \qquad \text{where } S = \$20,000$$
$$PV = \$20,000 \times F_{.07,2} \qquad \qquad i = 7\%$$
$$PV = \$20,000 \times .8734 \qquad \qquad n = 2$$
$$PV = \$17,468$$

Present value of amount due in 2 years	Amount due at end of 2 years
$17,468	$20,000

| 12/31/*x1* | 12/31/*x2* | 12/31/*x3* |

The entry to record the issuance of the note on December 31, 19*x1*, is:

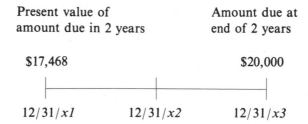

Dec. 31, 19*x1*	Cash	17,468	
	Discount on Notes Payable	2,532	
	Notes Payable, Long-term		20,000
	To record issuance of 2-year non-interest-bearing note.		

Interest expense for each year is computed by multiplying the present value of the note at the beginning of the year by the interest (or discount) rate. Interest expense for the first year is $1,223 ($17,468 × 7%). The present value of the note at the beginning of the second year will be $18,691, that is, the face value of the note minus the unamortized discount [$20,000 − ($2,532 − 1,223) = $20,000 − 1,309 = $18,691]. Interest for the second year will be $1,309 ($18,691 × 7%). Computations are rounded to the nearest full dollar and adjusted for any rounding error.

The entries to record interest expense each year would be:

		19*x2*		19*x3*	
Dec. 31	Interest Expense	1,223		1,309	
	Discount on Notes Payable		1,223		1,309
	To amortize discount on note.				

The entry to pay the note at December 31, 19x3, would be:

Dec. 31	Notes Payable, Long-term	20,000	
	Cash		20,000
	To pay note at maturity.		

Case D   A company purchased a machine by making a $5,000 cash down payment on June 30, 19x1, and agreeing to make 3 equal, semiannual payments of $2,000 each starting December 31, 19x1. Interest at 8% compounded semiannually is included in these semiannual payments.

In this situation the present value of an ordinary annuity is involved because the periodic payments are made at the end of each period. Thus, the present value of an ordinary annuity of $1 table (Table 23.4) is used to determine the cost of the machine, which is included in the three semiannual payments:

$$PVA = I \times F_{i,n} \qquad \text{where } I = \$2,000$$
$$PVA = \$2,000 \times F_{.04,3} \qquad i = 8\%/2 = 4\%$$
$$PVA = \$2,000 \times 2.7751 \qquad n = 3$$
$$PVA = \$5,550^* \qquad \text{*Rounded to the nearest full dollar}$$

	$2,000	$2,000	$2,000
Present value of 3 payments is $5,550			
6/30/x1	12/31/x1	6/30/x2	12/31/x2

The cost of the machine is $10,550, the sum of the down payment and the present value of the 3 semiannual payments ($5,000 + 5,550 = $10,550). The entry to record the purchase of the machine is:

June 30,	Machinery	10,550	
19x1	Cash		5,000
	Liability for Machinery		5,550
	To record purchase of machinery.		

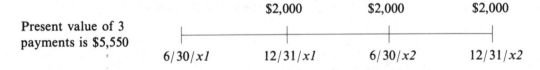

Present value of 3 payments	$ 5,550◄─────────── $2,000	$2,000	$2,000
Present value of down payment	5,000◄─$5,000		
Cost of machine	$10,550		
	6/30/x1	12/31/x1	6/30/x2	12/31/x3

Each semiannual payment of $2,000 must be allocated between interest expense and a reduction in the oustanding liability. Interest is calculated on the outstanding liability at the beginning of each period. The interest expense for each 6-month period, the reduction in the liability each 6 months, and the outstanding liability at the beginning and end of each 6-month period are indicated in the following table:

Semiannual Period	Outstanding Liability at Beginning of Period	Interest Expense for the Period*	Reduction in Liability for the Period**	Outstanding Liability at End of Period†
1	$5,550	$222	$1,778	$3,772
2	3,772	151	1,849	1,923
3	1,923	77	1,923	0

*Outstanding liability at beginning of period times the semiannual interest rate, e.g., $5,550 × 4% = $222; all computations are rounded to the nearest full dollar.
**The semiannual payment minus the interest expense for the period, e.g., $2,000 − 222 = $1,778.
†Outstanding liability at the beginning of the period minus the reduction in the liability for the period, e.g., $5,550 − 1,778 = $3,772.

The entries to record the semiannual payment, the interest expense, and the reduction in the liability every 6 months are:

	12/31/x1	6/30/x2	12/31/x2
Liability for Machinery	1,778	1,849	1,923
Interest Expense	222	151	77
Cash	2,000	2,000	2,000
To record semiannual payments for machinery purchase.			

SUMMARY

Present value and amount concepts frequently are used in accounting for long-term liabilities, long-term receivables, funds, and related expenses or revenues. The four present value and amount concepts used in accounting were discussed in this unit; they are: (1) the amount of a single sum, (2) the present value of a single sum, (3) the amount of an annuity, and (4) the present value of an annuity. If the payments for an annuity are made at the end of a period, the ordinary annuity concept is involved; if they are made at the beginning of a period, the annuity due concept is involved. The four tables containing the factors for (1) the amount of $1, (2) the present value of $1,

(3) the amount of an ordinary annuity of $1, and (4) the present value of an ordinary annuity of $1 are given in the appendix to this unit. These four tables are used in solving various accounting problems. The decision tree in Figure 23.1 should help you select the table needed to solve various accounting problems. All formulas in this unit are summarized in Exhibit 23.1.

Exhibit 23.1

Amount of a single sum

$A = S \times F_{i,n}$

where A = the amount of the sum of money
S = the present value of the sum of money

F = the factor from the amount of $1 table at i interest rate per period for n periods

Present value of a single sum

$PV = S \times F_{i,n}$

where PV = the present value of the sum of money
S = the future value of the sum of money

F = the factor from the present value of $1 table at i interest rate per period for n periods

Amount of an ordinary annuity

$AA = I \times F_{i,n}$

where AA = the amount of an ordinary annuity
I = the size of the periodic payments
F = the factor from the amount of an ordinary annuity of $1 table at i interest per period rate for n periods

Present value of an ordinary annuity

$PVA = I \times F_{i,n}$

where PVA = the present value of an ordinary annuity
I = the size of the periodic payments
F = the factor from the present value of an ordinary annuity of $1 table at i interest rate per period for n periods

Amount of annuity due

$AA \text{ (due)} = I \times (F_{i,n+1} - 1.0000)$

where AA (due) = the amount of an annuity due
I = the size of the periodic payments
F = the factor from the amount of an ordinary annuity of $1 table at i interest rate per period for $n + 1$ periods

Present value of an annuity due

$PVA \text{ (due)} = I \times (F_{i,n-1} + 1.0000)$

where PVA (due) = the present value of an annuity due
I = the size of the periodic payments
F = the factor from the present value of an ordinary annuity of $1 table at i interest rate per period for $n - 1$ periods

Formulas to determine installment size for an annuity

$$I = \frac{AA}{F_{i,n}} \qquad I = \frac{PVA}{F_{i,n}}$$

$$I = \frac{AA \text{ (due)}}{(F_{i,n+1} - 1.0000)} \qquad I = \frac{PVA \text{ (due)}}{(F_{i,n-1} + 1.0000)}$$

Note: In each of the formulas in this exhibit, i = the interest rate for each compounding period and n = the total number of compounding periods.

APPENDIX 23 AMOUNT AND PRESENT VALUE TABLES

Table 23.1

Amount of $1 at the End of *n* Years

n	1%	2%	3%	4%	5%	6%	7%	8%	9%	10%
1	1.0100	1.0200	1.0300	1.0400	1.0500	1.0600	1.0700	1.0800	1.0900	1.1000
2	1.0201	1.0404	1.0609	1.0816	1.1025	1.1236	1.1449	1.1664	1.1881	1.2100
3	1.0303	1.0612	1.0927	1.1249	1.1576	1.1910	1.2250	1.2597	1.2950	1.3310
4	1.0406	1.0824	1.1255	1.1699	1.2155	1.2625	1.3108	1.3605	1.4116	1.4641
5	1.0510	1.1041	1.1593	1.2167	1.2763	1.3382	1.4026	1.4693	1.5386	1.6105
6	1.0615	1.1262	1.1941	1.2653	1.3401	1.4185	1.5007	1.5869	1.6771	1.7716
7	1.0721	1.1487	1.2299	1.3159	1.4071	1.5036	1.6058	1.7138	1.8280	1.9487
8	1.0829	1.1717	1.2668	1.3686	1.4775	1.5938	1.7182	1.8509	1.9926	2.1436
9	1.0937	1.1951	1.3048	1.4233	1.5513	1.6895	1.8385	1.9990	2.1719	2.3579
10	1.1046	1.2190	1.3439	1.4802	1.6289	1.7908	1.9672	2.1589	2.3674	2.5937
11	1.1157	1.2434	1.3842	1.5395	1.7103	1.8983	2.1049	2.3316	2.5804	2.8531
12	1.1268	1.2682	1.4258	1.6010	1.7959	2.0122	2.2522	2.5182	2.8127	3.1384
13	1.1381	1.2936	1.4685	1.6650	1.8856	2.1329	2.4098	2.7196	3.0658	3.4523
14	1.1495	1.3195	1.5126	1.7317	1.9799	2.2609	2.5785	2.9372	3.3417	3.7975
15	1.1610	1.3459	1.5580	1.8009	2.0789	2.3966	2.7590	3.1722	3.6425	4.1772
16	1.1726	1.3728	1.6047	1.8730	2.1829	2.5404	2.9522	3.4259	3.9703	4.5950
17	1.1843	1.4002	1.6528	1.9479	2.2920	2.6928	3.1588	3.700	4.3276	5.0545
18	1.1961	1.4282	1.7024	2.0258	2.4066	2.8543	3.3799	3.9960	4.7171	5.5599
19	1.2081	1.4568	1.7535	2.1068	2.5270	3.0256	3.6165	4.3157	5.1417	6.1159
20	1.2202	1.4859	1.8061	2.1911	2.6533	3.2071	3.8697	4.6610	5.6044	6.7275
21	1.2324	1.5157	1.8603	2.2788	2.7860	3.3996	4.1406	5.0338	6.1088	7.4003
22	1.2447	1.5460	1.9161	2.3699	2.9253	3.6035	4.4304	5.4365	6.6586	8,1403
23	1.2572	1.5769	1.9736	2.4647	3.0715	3.8197	4.7405	5.8715	7.2579	8.9543
24	1.2697	1.6084	2.0328	2.5633	3.2251	4.0489	5.0724	6.3412	7.9111	9.8497
25	1.2824	1.6406	2.0938	2.6658	3.3864	4.2919	5.4274	6.8485	8.6231	10.8347

Tables 23.2 and 23.4 are reprinted with the permission of The Free Press (The Macmillan Company) from The Management of Corporate Capital, *edited by Ezra Solomon, copyright © 1959 by The Graduate School of Business, University of Chicago. Tables 23.1 and 23.3 are reprinted with the permission of Prentice-Hall, Inc., from* Finney and Miller's Principles of Accounting, Advanced, *6th ed., by J. A. Gentry, Jr., and G. L. Johnson, pp. 404–406, 410–412, copyright © 1971.*

Table 23.2

Present Value of $1 Due at the End of *n* Years

n	1%	2%	3%	4%	5%	6%	7%	8%	9%	10%
1	.9901	.9804	.9709	.9615	.9524	.9434	.9346	.9259	.9174	.9091
2	.9803	.9612	.9426	.9246	.9070	.8900	.8734	.8573	.8417	.8265
3	.9706	.9423	.9151	.8890	.8638	.8396	.8163	.7938	.7722	.7513
4	.9610	.9239	.8885	.8548	.8227	.7921	.7629	.7350	.7084	.6830
5	.9515	.9057	.8626	.8219	.7835	.7473	.7130	.6806	.6499	.6209
6	.9420	.8880	.8375	.7903	.7462	.7050	.6663	.6302	.5963	.5645
7	.9327	.8706	.8131	.7599	.7107	.6650	.6228	.5835	.5470	.5132
8	.9235	.8535	.7894	.7307	.6768	.6274	.5820	.5403	.5019	.4665
9	.9143	.8368	.7664	.7026	.6446	.5919	.5439	.5003	.4605	.4241
10	.9053	.8204	.7441	.6756	.6139	.5584	.5084	.4632	.4224	.3855
11	.8963	.8043	.7224	.6496	.5847	.5268	.4751	.4289	.3875	.3504
12	.8875	.7885	.7014	.6246	.5568	.4970	.4440	.3971	.3555	.3186
13	.8787	.7730	.6810	.6006	.5303	.4688	.4150	.3677	.3262	.2897
14	.8700	.7579	.6611	.5775	.5051	.4423	.3878	.3405	.2993	.2633
15	.8614	.7430	.6419	.5553	.4810	.4173	.3625	.3152	.2745	.2394
16	.8528	.7285	.6232	.5339	.4581	.3937	.3387	.2919	.2519	.2176
17	.8444	.7142	.6050	.5134	.4363	.3714	.3166	.2703	.2310	.1978
18	.8360	.7002	.5874	.4936	.4155	.3503	.2959	.2503	.2120	.1799
19	.8277	.6864	.5703	.4746	.3957	.3305	.2765	.2317	.1945	.1635
20	.8195	.6730	.5537	.4564	.3769	.3118	.2584	.2146	.1784	.1486
21	.8114	.6598	.5376	.4388	.3589	.2942	.2415	.1987	.1637	.1351
22	.8034	.6468	.5219	.4220	.3419	.2775	.2257	.1839	.1502	.1229
23	.7954	.6342	.5067	.4057	.3256	.2618	.2110	.1703	.1378	.1117
24	.7876	.6217	.4919	.3901	.3100	.2470	.1972	.1577	.1264	.1015
25	.7798	.6095	.4776	.3751	.2953	.2330	.1843	.1460	.1160	.0923

Table 23.3

Amount of an Annuity of $1 per Year Due at the End of *n* Years

n	1%	2%	3%	4%	5%	6%	7%	8%	9%	10%
1	1.0000	1.0000	1.0000	1.0000	1.0000	1.0000	1.0000	1.0000	1.0000	1.0000
2	2.0100	2.0200	2.0300	2.0400	2.0500	2.0600	2.0700	2.0800	2.0900	2.1000
3	3.0301	3.0604	3.0909	3.1216	3.1525	3.1836	3.2149	3.2464	3.2781	3.3100
4	4.0604	4.1216	4.1836	4.2465	4.3101	4.3746	4.4399	4.5061	4.5731	4.6410
5	5.1010	5.2040	5.3091	5.4163	5.5256	5.6371	5.7507	5.8666	5.9847	6.1051
6	6.1520	6.3081	6.4684	6.6330	6.8019	6.9753	7.1533	7.3359	7.5233	7.7156
7	7.2135	7.4343	7.6625	7.8983	8.1420	8.3938	8.6540	8.9228	9.2004	9.4872
8	8.2857	8.5830	8.8923	9.2142	9.5491	9.8975	10.2598	10.6366	11.0285	11.4359
9	9.3685	9.7546	10.1591	10.5828	11.0266	11.4913	11.9780	12.4876	13.0210	13.5795
10	10.4622	10.9497	11.4639	12.0061	12.5779	13.1808	13.8164	14.4866	15.1929	15.9374
11	11.5668	12.1687	12.8078	13.4864	14.2068	14.9716	15.7836	16.6455	17.5603	18.5312
12	12.6825	13.4121	14.1920	15.0258	15.9171	16.8699	17.8885	18.9771	20.1407	21.3843
13	13.8093	14.6803	15.6178	16.6268	17.7130	18.8821	20.1406	21.4953	22.9534	24.5227
14	14.9474	15.9739	17.0863	18.2919	19.5986	21.0151	22.5505	24.2149	26.0192	27.9750
15	16.0969	17.2934	18.5989	20.0236	21.5786	23.2760	25.1290	27.1521	29.3609	31.7725
16	17.2579	18.6393	20.1569	21.8245	23.6575	25.6725	27.8880	30.3242	33.0034	35.9497
17	18.4304	20.0121	21.7616	23.6975	25.8404	28.2129	30.8402	33.7502	36.9737	40.5447
18	19.6147	21.4123	23.4144	25.6454	28.1324	30.9057	33.9990	37.4502	41.3013	45.5992
19	20.8109	22.8406	25.1169	27.6712	30.5390	33.7600	37.3790	41.4463	46.0185	51.1591
20	22.0190	24.2974	26.8704	29.7781	33.0660	36.7856	40.9955	45.7620	51.1601	57.2750
21	23.2392	25.7833	28.6765	31.9692	35.7193	39.9927	44.8652	50.4229	56.7645	64.0025
22	24.4716	27.2990	30.5368	34.2480	38.5052	43.3923	49.0057	55.4568	62.8733	71.4027
23	25.7163	28.8450	32.4529	36.6179	41.4305	46.9958	53.4361	60.8933	69.5319	79.5430
24	26.9735	30.4219	34.4265	39.0826	44.5020	50.8156	58.1767	66.7648	76.7898	88.4973
25	28.2432	32.0303	36.4593	41.6459	47.7271	54.8645	63.2490	73.1059	84.7009	98.3471

Table 23.4

Present Value of an Annuity of $1 per Year Due at the End of *n* Years

n	1%	2%	3%	4%	5%	6%	7%	8%	9%	10%
1	.9901	.9804	.9709	.9615	.9524	.9434	.9346	.9259	.9174	.9091
2	1.9704	1.9416	1.9135	1.8861	1.8594	1.8334	1.8080	1.7833	1.7591	1.7355
3	2.9410	2.8839	2.8286	2.7751	2.7232	2.6730	2.6243	2.5771	2.5313	2.4868
4	3.9020	3.8077	3.7171	3.6299	3.5459	3.4651	3.3872	3.3121	3.2397	3.1699
5	4.8535	4.7134	4.5797	4.4518	4.3295	4.2123	4.1002	3.9927	3.8896	3.7908
6	5.7955	5.6014	5.4172	5.2421	5.0757	4.9173	4.7665	4.6229	4.4859	4.3553
7	6.7282	6.4720	6.2302	6.0020	5.7863	5.5824	5.3893	5.2064	5.0329	4.8684
8	7.6517	7.3254	7.0196	6.7327	6.4632	6.2098	5.9713	5.7466	5.5348	5.3349
9	8.5661	8.1622	7.7861	7.4353	7.1078	6.8017	6.5152	6.2469	5.9952	5.7590
10	9.4714	8.9825	8.5302	8.1109	7.7217	7.3601	7.0236	6.7101	6.4176	6.1446
11	10.3677	9.7868	9.2526	8.7604	8.3064	7.8868	7.4987	7.1389	6.8052	6.4951
12	11.2552	10.5753	9.9539	9.3850	8.8632	8.3838	7.9427	7.5361	7.1607	6.8137
13	12.1338	11.3483	10.6349	9.9856	9.3935	8.8527	8.3576	7.9038	7.4869	7.1034
14	13.0038	12.1062	11.2960	10.5631	9.8986	9,2950	8.7454	8.2442	7.7861	7.3667
15	13.8651	12.8492	11.9379	11.1183	10.3796	9.7122	9.1079	8.5595	8.0607	7.6061
16	14.7180	13.5777	12.5610	11.6522	10.8377	10.1059	9.4466	8.8514	8.3125	7.8237
17	15.5624	14.2918	13.1660	12.1656	11.2740	10.4772	9.7632	9.1216	8.5436	8.0215
18	16.3984	14.9920	13.7534	12.6592	11.6895	10.8276	10.0591	9.3719	8.7556	8.2014
19	17.2261	15.6784	14.3237	13.1339	12.0853	11.1581	10.3356	9.6036	8.9501	8.3649
20	18.0457	16.3514	14.8774	13.5903	12.4622	11.4699	10.5940	9.8181	9.1285	8.5136
21	18.8571	17.0111	15.4149	14.0291	12.8211	11.7640	10.8355	10.0168	9.2922	8.6487
22	19.6605	17.6580	15.9368	14.4511	13.1630	12.0416	11.0612	10.2007	9.4424	8.7715
23	20.4559	18.2921	16.4435	14.8568	13.4885	12.3033	11.2722	10.3710	9.5802	8.8832
24	21.2435	18.9139	16.9355	15.2469	13.7986	12.5503	11.4693	10.5287	9.7066	8.9847
25	22.0233	19.5234	17.4131	15.6220	14.0939	12.7833	11.6536	10.6748	9.8226	9.0770

REVIEW QUESTIONS

23-1   What is the time value of money? Why is it important to consider the time value of money in accounting for business transactions?

23-2   Define each of the following terms:

    a.   amount of $1
    b.   present value of $1
    c.   amount of an annuity of $1
    d.   present value of an annuity of $1

23-3   Distinguish between an ordinary annuity and an annuity due.

23-4   Determine the number of interest periods in each of the following situations if five annual payments are to be made:

    a.   amount of an ordinary annuity
    b.   amount of an annuity due
    c.   present value of an ordinary annuity
    d.   present value of an annuity due

23-5   a.   Which is larger—the amount of an ordinary annuity or the amount of an annuity due?

       b.   Which is larger—the present value of an ordinary annuity or the present value of an annuity due?

23-6   How are the number of periods and the periodic interest rate determined when interest is compounded for intervals of less than one year?

23-7   Describe some guidelines for selecting the appropriate present value or amount table to solve an accounting problem.

23-8   If the present value or amount of an annuity and the interest rate are known, can the size of each periodic payment be determined? Explain.

EXERCISES

23-1   Determine the number of periods and the periodic interest rate for each of the following situations:

       a.   Interest is payable annually at 7% for 6 years.
       b.   Interest is payable semiannually for 5 years; the annual interest rate is 10%.
       c.   Interest is payable quarterly for 4 years; the annual interest rate is 8%.
       d.   Interest is payable monthly for 2 years; the annual interest rate is 12%.

23-2   Solve each of the following short problems:

       a.   Calculate the amount to which $20,000 will grow at the end of 3 years if interest at 8% annually is compounded quarterly.
       b.   Calculate the present value of $50,000 due at the end of 5 years if interest is compounded annually at 7%.
       c.   Calculate the amount of an annuity if equal payments of $10,000 are made at the end of each year for 6 years and interest is compounded annually at 6%.
       d.   Use the same facts as in part c, except assume that the payments are made at the beginning of each year.
       e.   Calculate the present value of an annuity if equal payments of $1,000 are made semiannually at the end of each six months for 5 years and the annual rate of interest is 8%.
       f.   Use the same facts as in part e, except assume that the payments are made at the beginning of each 6-month period.

23-3   a.   Determine the time value of money (i.e., the total interest) for each case in exercise 23–2.
       b.   Determine the interest revenue or expense for the first two periods for each case in exercise 23–2.

23-4   The following six cases involve present value and amount concepts. For each case, calculate: (a) the present value or amount of the single sum or periodic payments, (b) the time value of money, and (c) the interest revenue or expense for the first period. Also, prepare all necessary journal entries to record the receipt or payment and the interest revenue or expense for the first period.

Case 1   You need $10,000 two years from now. What single amount should be deposited in a savings account today if the account pays 6% interest compounded annually?

Case 2   You want to know what the balance in your savings account will be if you set aside $500 every three months for two years if the account pays 8% interest compounded quarterly.

Case 3   You deposit $1,000 in a savings account today. What will be the account balance in four years if interest is earned at 6%, compounded semiannually?

Case 4   A company purchased an asset for a $1,000 down payment and five equal annual payments of $1,500 each. If interest on such contracts is 8%, what is the cost of the asset?

Case 5   A company owes another company $10,000, which is due two years from now. If interest can be earned at 7% annually, how much should the other company be willing to accept today in settlement of the debt?

Case 6   A company is accumulating a fund to retire a debt by setting aside $1,000 at the end of each 6 months. If the money is set aside for three years and interest is earned at 6%, compounded semiannually, what will be the fund balance at the end of the three years?

23-5   Determine the size of the periodic payments in each of the following cases:

Case 1   A company needs a debt retirement fund of $200,000 ten years from now. Ten equal annual payments are to be made at the end of each year, and fund investments are expected to earn 6% annually.

Case 2   A company plans to purchase machinery by making six equal annual payments that will include both interest and the cost of the machines. The payments are to be made at the beginning of each year starting immediately. The cash price of the machine is $34,500. Interest will be charged on the unpaid balance at 8% annually.

PROBLEMS

23-1   During 19*x4* Tanner Corp. completed the following transactions:

    a.   Issued a 3-year note dated January 1, 19*x4*, to borrow $50,000. The note is due in three equal installments starting December 31, 19*x4*. The annual interest rate is 9%.

b. Established a debt retirement fund for a $100,000 debt due on December 31, 19x8. The first semiannual payment to the fund was made on June 30, 19x4. The fund investments are expected to earn 6% annually.

Required **(1)** Prepare the entries to record the loan on January 1, 19x4, and the payment of the first installment on December 31, 19x4.
(2) Prepare the entries to record the payments to the debt retirement fund on June 30 and December 31, 19x4, assuming that the fund earned the amount expected.
(3) Prepare a partial balance sheet at December 31, 19x4.

23-2 Dianne Corp. is planning to purchase equipment with a cost of $36,000. The company must finance the purchase. Two financing alternatives are being considered:

a. Borrow $36,000 from a bank: Three installments of $12,000 each plus interest at 7½ % on the outstanding balance at the beginning of each year would be required.
b. Finance the purchase with the seller: Six equal semiannual installments would be required; the seller charges interest at 8% annually.

Required **(1)** Determine which alternative has the least interest cost over 3 years.
(2) What other factors should be considered in selecting the best financing alternative?
(3) Prepare all entries to record the purchase, any loan, and the payments due during the first year for the financing alternative with the least interest cost over 3 years.

23-3 Vixen Company wants to accumulate approximately $65,000 to purchase new equipment in 6 years. The company is considering three alternatives:

a. Purchase a 6-year, $40,000 certificate of deposit, which pays 8% compounded quarterly.
b. Purchase notes with face values of $8,500 and annual interest rates of 9%; one note will be purchased at the beginning of each year for 6 years, starting immediately. Interest will be received annually on each note.
c. Make semiannual contributions of $5,000 each to a fund on which 6% can be earned annually; the first contribution will be made in 6 months.

Required **(1)** Determine whether or not each alternative can be expected to grow to $65,000.
(2) What factors should the company consider in selecting the best alternative to accumulate the funds for equipment replacement?
(3) Prepare the entries for the first year for each alternative.

23-4 Diamond Corp. completed the following transactions during 19x3 and 19x4:

Dec. 31, 19x3 Purchased equipment with a cash price of $28,400 by issuing a 2-year, 8% note. Interest is compounded semiannually. Four equal semiannual payments are to be made at the beginning of each 6 months starting immediately.

Dec. 31, 19*x3*   Established a debt retirement fund to retire a $100,000 debt that matures on December 31, 19*x7*. Five equal annual payments are to be made to the fund on each December 31 starting December 31, 19*x3*. Fund investments are expected to earn 5% annually.

June 30, 19*x4*   Accepted an 18-month non-interest-bearing note with a face value of $15,000 from a customer. The amount of the note, net of the implied interest at 8% compounded semiannually, is to be applied against the customer's open account balance.

June 30, 19*x4*   Purchased a 4-year, 8% certificate of deposit for $20,000. The certificate is to be held as a long-term investment. Interest is compounded quarterly.

June 30, 19*x4*   Made the second payment on the note issued December 31, 19*x3*, to purchase equipment.

Sept. 30, 19*x4*   Recognized quarterly interest earned on the CD purchased on June 30, 19*x4*.

Dec. 31, 19*x4*   Made the third payment on the note issued December 31, 19*x3*, to purchase equipment.

Dec. 31, 19*x4*   Made the second payment to the debt retirement fund established December 31, 19*x3*, and recognized income on the fund investments of $950.

Dec. 31, 19*x4*   Recognized interest revenue on the non-interest-bearing note received from a customer on June 30, 19*x4*.

Dec. 31, 19*x4*   Recognized quarterly interest earned on the CD purchased on June 30, 19*x4*.

Required   **a.**   Record each of these transactions.

                b.   Prepare a partial balance sheet and a partial income statement for Diamond Corp. at the end of 19*x4*.

Unit 24
Current and Contingent Liabilities

A creditor is worse than a master; for a master owns only your person, a creditor owns your dignity, and can belabour that.

Victor Hugo, Les Miserables

Accounting for liabilities arising from acquisitions of assets and services on open account and for liabilities for accrued expenses and deferred revenues are reviewed in this unit. Accounting for other current liabilities, such as interest-bearing and non-interest-bearing notes and payrolls, is also explained and illustrated.

Performance Objectives

Upon completion of this unit you should be able to:

1. define and use the accounting terms introduced in this unit.
2. describe or explain:
   a. how the balance of a current liability is measured or reported
   b. what the face value, maturity value, and/or current cash equivalent is for either an interest-bearing or a non-interest-bearing note
   c. how the effective interest rate is determined for either an interest-bearing or a non-interest-bearing note
   d. how contingent obligations should be disclosed
3. determine:
   a. the face value, maturity value, and/or current cash equivalent of either an interest-bearing or a non-interest-bearing note
   b. the effective interest rate for either an interest-bearing or a non-interest-bearing note
   c. the amount to be reported as the balance of a current liability
4. identify or prepare the correct journal entries for transactions involving current liabilities and adjustments affecting current liabilities.

Nature and Measurement of Current Liabilities

A **current liability** is an obligation that is to be paid within one year after balance sheet date or within the normal operating cycle, whichever is longer. Thus, a current liability normally is paid from resources properly classified as current assets. In some situations, however, one current liability is exchanged for another—for example, when a short-term note is issued for an account balance due to a supplier, or a short-term loan is obtained to pay current obligations. Current liabilities include (1) trade and nontrade accounts payable; (2) short-term notes payable; (3) obligations for accrued expenses, such as accrued interest, accrued wages, and accrued taxes; (4) obligations for deferred revenues, that is, revenues received in advance; and (5) obligations related to taxes withheld from employee wages, payroll taxes, and employee fringe benefits.

Most current liabilities are monetary in nature, that is, they require a cash payment to settle the obligation at the maturity or due date. Conceptually, then, they should be recorded and reported at the present value of the future monetary payments required to settle the obligations. The present value of a liability may be considered the **current cash equivalent** the involved parties would agree upon at a specific date to settle the obligation. In practice many current liabilities are due within short periods, such as 30 or 60 days, and because the difference between the principal amount of such a short-term obligation and its present value is immaterial, the liability is recorded and reported at the principal amount. It is customary also not to charge interest for many short-term obligations. If interest is charged, the interest rate will be specifically stated or a promissory note will be involved in the transaction.

Most current liabilities are definite obligations. They have a fixed maturity date or are due within a specified period of time. For example, a short-term promissory note is due on a specific date, a certain number of months or days after the date of the note; an invoice for the purchase of merchandise with credit terms of 2/10, n/30 is due anytime within 30 days after the date of the invoice. The party to whom payment is to be made and the amount to be paid at maturity are also known when the obligation is incurred. A few current liabilities, however, must be estimated because the exact amount to be paid is not known. For example, the exact amount to be paid for product guarantee claims within the next year will not be known until the claims are actually paid. However, since an obligation exists as soon as products are sold, the expense and related liability for expected claims must be estimated, based on prior experience. Expenses and liabilities would be understated if no entry were made until the exact amount became known.

Accounts Payable

Obligations arising from the acquisition of merchandise, assets, and services used in normal business operations are called *trade payables*. If the purchase is made on general credit terms or open account, the liability and its account are called **accounts payable** or *trade accounts payable*. The policy adopted in this text is to record all purchases net of cash discounts. If the invoice is paid beyond the discount period, the amount of the discount is charged to an expense account, "discounts lost." Recall from Units 9 and 17 that merchandise purchases are charged to the purchases account if the periodic inventory system is used or to the inventory account if the perpetual inventory system is used. The following are two sets of entries for the purchase of merchandise for $1,500 subject to credit terms of 2/10, n/30—one assumes payment within the discount period; the other, after the discount period expires. The entries are made for a company using the periodic inventory system.

Entries Assuming Payment Within Discount Period

May 1	Purchases	1,470	
	Accounts Payable		1,470
	To record purchase net of cash discount [$1,500 − 2% ($1,500) = $1,470].		
May 11	Accounts Payable	1,470	
	Cash		1,470
	To pay invoice on last day of discount period.		

Entries Assuming Payment Beyond Discount Period

May 1	Purchases	1,470	
	Accounts Payable		1,470
	To record purchase net of discount.		
May 31	Accounts Payable	1,470	
	Discounts Lost	30	
	Cash		1,500
	To pay invoice after end of discount period and record discount lost (2% × $1,500 = $30).		

Accrued Expenses

Some expenses are incurred during the accounting period, but are not recorded until the end because they accrue daily. For example, interest on a note payable, salaries and wages that are paid periodically (such as weekly, every two weeks, twice a month, or monthly), and income and property taxes increase daily, but no entry is made until the obligation is paid. If the accounting period ends before the obligation is paid, an adjusting entry for the **accrued expense** is required to reflect operating results and financial position correctly on the financial statements (see Unit 10 for additional discussion). The following are the adjusting entry for accrued salaries of $800 at the end of a company's accounting period and the entry during the next period to pay the weekly payroll of $2,000. The latter includes the accrued salaries of $800 and the salaries for the balance of the payroll period.

Dec. 31	Salaries Expense	800	
	Salaries Payable		800
	To accrue salaries at the end of the accounting period.		
Jan. 8	Salaries Expense	1,200	
	Salaries Payable	800	
	Cash		2,000
	To record payment of accrued salaries and balance of salaries for payroll period Dec. 30–Jan. 3.		

Deferred Revenues

Revenues may be collected before they are earned. When the advance payment is received, the credit part of the journal entry may be made to either a revenue account or a liability account. At the end of the accounting period an adjusting entry is made to allocate the advance payments between the revenue account for revenue earned and the liability account for revenue still unearned or **deferred revenue.** The balance of the liability account reflects the company's obligation to deliver goods or perform services in the future for which payment has already been accepted (see Unit 10 for additional discussion). Following are entries to record an advance payment of fees of $3,600 and entries to recognize that $1,500 of the fees are still unearned at the end of the accounting period. One set of entries assumes the advance payment was initially recorded in a revenue account; the second set assumes it was initially recorded in a liability account.

Advance Payment Recorded in a Revenue Account

Nov. 10	Cash	3,600	
	Fees Earned		3,600
	To record advance payment of fees in a revenue account.		
Dec. 31	Fees Earned	1,500	
	Unearned Fees		1,500
	To transfer unearned fees to a liability account.		

Advance Payment Recorded in a Liability Account

Nov. 10	Cash	3,600	
	Unearned Fees		3,600
	To record advance payment of fees in a liability account.		
Dec. 31	Unearned Fees	2,100	
	Fees Earned		2,100
	To transfer fees earned to a revenue account.		

Accounting for Payrolls

Several current liabilities arise in accounting for employee salaries and wages. Employers are required to withhold federal income taxes and social security (FICA) taxes from employee salaries and to remit the taxes to the IRS at specified intervals.[1] State or city income taxes may also have to be withheld and remitted to the appropriate

---

[1]Federal income taxes are withheld using tables or formulas provided by the Internal Revenue Service; the amount withheld depends on the amount of earnings and the number of exemptions to which the employee is entitled. The FICA tax rate for 1979 was 6.13 percent of the first 22,900 of earnings received by the employee. The base was scheduled to increase to $25,900 for 1980, with additional annual rate and/or base increases scheduled through 1984, but these could be changed by Congress.

government units. In addition, the employer is assessed for FICA taxes in an amount equal to that withheld from employee salaries, and most employers must pay unemployment taxes to the federal and state governments.[2] Fringe benefits such as medical, dental, and life insurance and pension plans result in further deductions from employee salaries and/or contributions by the employer. Payroll deductions are often made for union dues, charitable contributions, and savings and stock purchase plans as agreed upon by employers and employees. Each of these deductions from employee salaries, and taxes and contributions paid by employers, results in a liability to the government, an insurance company, or another party.

Employee salaries and the taxes and payroll deductions withheld from them are usually accrued in a general journal entry. Many companies then transfer funds from their regular checking account to a special payroll checking account to provide better control over cash payments and to facilitate bank reconciliation procedures. Typical entries to accrue salaries, transfer funds to a **payroll fund** account, and pay salaries are:

Oct. 31	Salaries expense		10,000	
	Liability for federal income taxes withheld			1,600
	Liability for FICA taxes			480
	Liability for medical insurance contributions			250
	Salaries payable			7,670
	To accrue payroll for October.			
Oct. 31	Payroll fund		7,670	
	Cash			7,670
	To transfer funds to payroll checking account.			
Oct. 31	Salaries payable		7,670	
	Payroll fund			7,670
	To record payment of October payroll.			

Entries to accrue the employer's payroll taxes and contributions for fringe benefits are also made in the general journal, either in separate accounts or in the salary expense account. Following is a typical entry to accrue the employer's payroll taxes and fringe benefit contributions:

---

[2]The federal unemployment tax rate is 3.2 percent of the first $4,200 paid to each employee. Most employers receive a 2.7 percent credit for contributions to state unemployment compensation plans, and, thus, their effective federal tax rate is .5 percent. The rate and base for state unemployment taxes vary; also, companies that experience no or few employee claims for unemployment compensation receive reduced state rates.

Oct. 31	Payroll tax expense	704	
	Fringe benefit expense	550	
	Liability for FICA taxes		480
	Liability for federal unemployment taxes		35
	Liability for state unemployment taxes		189
	Liability for medical insurance contributions		550
	To accrue the employer's payroll taxes and fringe benefit costs related to the October payroll.		

Entries are prepared also for the payments made when employee withholdings and amounts payable by the employer become due.

Accounting for payrolls involves a lot of procedural detail and reporting to employees, government units, and other parties. Tax returns, for example, are usually filed by the employer when tax payments are made or at other specified times, such as quarterly or annually. In addition, records of the wages paid and taxes withheld must be maintained for each employee. A summary of this information must be provided annually on a W-2 form, which the employee uses when filing his income tax return(s). Thus, payroll accounting is typically one of the first accounting procedures for which mechanized or computerized data processing is adopted.

Notes Payable

The accounting for promissory notes received by a company was discussed in Unit 16. The accounting for promissory notes—either interest-bearing or non-interest-bearing—by the maker of the notes is explained and illustrated in this section. **Notes payable** may be issued to get cash, to purchase assets or services, or to settle accounts payable that are past due.

Interest-Bearing Notes   When an interest-bearing note is issued, the **principal** or **face value** of the note is the amount of cash or credit the maker of the note receives. If the *stated interest rate* equals the *market rate of interest* for comparable transactions for companies with similar credit ratings, the principal or face value of the interest-bearing note is equal to its *present value*. The **maturity value** of an interest-bearing note equals the principal or face value plus interest due at maturity. For example, an interest-bearing note issued to obtain a cash loan of $20,000 for six months at 9% interest has a principal or face value of $20,000, a present value of $20,000 (assuming that 9% is the market rate of interest), and a maturity value of $20,900 [$20,000 + ($20,000 × 9% × 6/12)].

If the maturity date of an interest-bearing note extends beyond the end of the accounting period, an adjusting entry for accrued interest expense is required at the end of the period. The entries to issue the $20,000 note on November 1, 19*x1*, to accrue interest at the end of the period, December 31, 19*x1*, and to pay the note and interest at the maturity date, May 1, 19*x2*, are prepared as follows:

Nov. 1, 19x1	Cash	20,000	
	Notes Payable, Short-Term		20,000
	To issue a 9%, 4-month note for a $20,000 cash loan.		
Dec. 31, 19x1	Interest Expense	300	
	Interest Payable		300
	To accrue interest on note payable ($20,000 × 9% × 2/12 = $300).		
May 1, 19x2	Notes Payable	20,000	
	Interest Payable	300	
	Interest Expense	600	
	Cash		20,900
	To record payment of note and interest at maturity date ($20,000 × 9% × 4/12 = $600).		

The **effective interest rate** for a note is determined by dividing the annual interest charge by the cash proceeds or credit received from issuing the note. If the stated and market rates of interest are equal, the effective interest rate for an interest-bearing note is equal to them. The effective interest rate for the note illustrated is 9% because the stated and market rates of interest are the same; this can be verified by the following computation:

$$\frac{\text{annual interest charge}}{\text{cash proceeds or credit received}} = \text{effective interest rate}$$

$$\frac{\$20,000 \times 9\%}{\$20,000} = \frac{\$1,800}{\$20,000} = 9\%$$

Non-Interest-Bearing Notes   Interest must be imputed or implied on most non-interest-bearing notes according to APB Opinion No. 21. The imputed or implied interest (based on an **imputed or implied interest rate**) is recorded in a contra or offset account, **"discount on notes payable,"** which is deducted from notes payable on the balance sheet. The discount on notes payable account is amortized to recognize interest expense when the note is paid. If the accounting period ends before the note is due, the discount on notes payable account must be amortized to recognize interest expense incurred during the period. The principal or face value of a non-interest-bearing note equals its maturity value because interest is included in the principal or face value. The present value of a non-interest-bearing note equals the principal or face value less the unamortized discount for interest at the market rate of interest.

The face value of a non-interest-bearing note can be established in two ways. Under one approach the imputed interest is added to the cash proceeds or credit to be received. For example, if $20,000 is being borrowed for six months, and interest is to be imputed on the cash proceeds at 9%, the imputed interest is $900 ($20,000 × 9% × 6/12) and the face value of the note is $20,900 ($20,000 + 900).[3] Under the second approach, a note is prepared for a specific amount and discounted by the payee. If a 6-month note is prepared with a $20,000 face value and discounted at 9%, the interest expense is $900 ($20,000 × 9% × 6/12) for six months, but the cash proceeds from the note are only $19,100 ($20,000 − 900). Also, the effective interest rate in the latter situation is 4.71% ($900/$19,100) for six months or 9.42% for a year. This is higher than the stated interest rate of 9% annually, as well as the effective interest rate under the first approach [4.5 ($900/$20,000) for 6 months or 9% for a year].

The entries to issue a non-interest-bearing note and to amortize the discount and the note at maturity under both approaches are:

First Approach—Face Value of Note Determined by Adding Imputed Interest to Cash Proceeds		Second Approach—Face Value Established for a Specific Amount and Discounted by Payee	
Cash	20,000	Cash	19,100
Discount on notes payable	900	Discount on notes payable	900
Notes payable	20,900	Notes payable	20,000
To issue note.		To issue note.	
Interest expense	900	Interest expense	900
Discount on notes payable	900	Discount on notes payable	900
To amortize discount.		To amortize discount.	
Notes payable	20,900	Notes payable	20,000
Cash	20,900	Cash	20,000
To pay note at maturity.		To pay note at maturity.	

---

[3]Sometimes interest is imputed on the face value of the note by dividing the cash proceeds by 100% minus the periodic interest rate. In this case, the face value of the note will be $20,942 [$20,000/(100% − 4.5%)] and the imputed interest will be $942 ($20,942 − 20,000). This approach yields an effective interest rate of 4.71% ($942/$20,000) for six months, compared to a stated rate of 4.5% (9%/2).

If the accounting period ends before the note matures, the discount must be amortized so that interest expense and the note liability are stated on the financial statements correctly. Assume that the note was outstanding for two months when the accounting period ended. The adjusting entry required would be the same under both approaches:

Interest expense	300	
Discount on notes payable		300
To amortize discount for two months at end of		
period ($900 × 2/6 = $300).		

The $600 balance of the discount at year-end is deducted from the face value of the note on the balance sheet, as shown in the following table, and then amortized when the note matures. Thus the note is reported at its present value at balance sheet date. Because the note had a different face value under each of the two approaches, it also has a different present value.

	First Approach		Second Approach	
Notes payable	$20,900		$20,000	
Less: Unamortized discount on notes payable	600	$20,300	600	$19,400

Contingent Obligations and Losses

A contingency, according to the FASB, is an existing condition, situation, or set of circumstances involving uncertainty as to possible loss (or gain) that will be resolved when one or more future events occur or fail to occur.[4] A loss must be accrued (that is, recorded) if two conditions are met: (1) it is *probable* that an asset has been impaired or that a liability has been incurred at balance sheet date and (2) the amount of loss can be *reasonably estimated*. It is implicit in the first condition that it is *probable* that one or more future events will occur to confirm the loss.

Two examples of contingencies that are regularly accrued are the provisions for uncollectible accounts and product warranty costs. In both cases, the amount of loss can be reasonably estimated based on past experience. At balance sheet date the

---

[4]FASB Statement No. 5 (Stanford, CN: FASB, March 1975).

asset, accounts receivable, is impaired because all customers are not expected to pay what they owe. When products are sold subject to a warranty, a liability arises and exists until claims are satisfied or the warranty expires. Thus, a liability exists at balance sheet date for expected future claims. Because the conditions for accrual of loss contingencies are met, uncollectible accounts expense and product warranty expense are estimated and recorded at the end of each accounting period.

Many loss contingency situations, however, are not as clear as these two examples. Accountants must exercise their professional judgment in determining whether the conditions for accrual of a loss are met. Frequently, legal opinions from company attorneys are necessary in deciding on the appropriate accounting for a loss contingency. Assume that a company is being sued for patent infringement. The amount and likelihood of loss will be difficult to assess throughout most of the stages involved in the lawsuit. A loss and related liability probably will not be recorded until a court decision or out-of-court settlement is reached.

Footnote disclosure is required to describe the nature and amount of any loss contingencies accrued. Many situations in which one or both of the conditions for accrual are not met also require footnote disclosure. These include: (1) a significant loss is probable, but the amount cannot be reasonably estimated; (2) a significant loss is reasonably possible (that is, it is more than remote, but less than likely); and (3) a significant loss occurs after balance sheet date, but before the financial statements are issued. In addition, when another party's debts are guaranteed (for example, when a customer's note is discounted), footnote disclosure is required even if the possibility of loss is remote because this was a common practice prior to FASB Statement No. 5. Exhibits 24.1 and 24.2 illustrate footnote disclosure of loss contingency situations, one in which a loss has been accrued and the other in which a loss has not been accrued.

Exhibit 24.1

Footnote Disclosure of Loss Contingency Accrual

Litigation

As reported in the Company's annual report for 1976, Big-O Tire Dealers, Inc. instituted a lawsuit against the Company in November 1974, alleging that Goodyear's use of the term "Bigfoot" in connection with a line of tires infringed Big-O's trademark rights. The Federal District Court affirmed a jury verdict awarding damages to Big-O in the amount of $19.6 million plus interest. In September 1977, the Court of Appeals reduced the lower Court's damage award against Goodyear to $4.7 million plus interest. Subsequently, a settlement for all claims between the parties was reached and the total liability of $6.5 million was accrued in the 1977 financial statements and thereafter the petitions filed in the U.S. Supreme Court were withdrawn.

Source: *1977 Annual Report of The Goodyear Tire and Rubber Company.*

Exhibit 24.2

Footnote Disclosure of Loss Contingencies Not Accrued

O. CONTINGENT LIABILITIES   Suits have been started against the Company and certain subsidiaries because of alleged product damage and other claims. All suits are being contested and the amount of uninsured liability thereunder is considered to be adequately provided for.

If a nuclear power plant being constructed by Consumers Power Company at Midland, Michigan is not completed, Consumers may claim that the Company is obligated to pay to Consumers certain costs presently estimated at $105,000,000. The Company may also have a claim against Consumers for failure to perform its obligations.

A Canadian subsidiary has entered into a 20-year agreement to purchase substantially all of the output of an ethylene plant being constructed in the Province of Alberta. The owner of the plant, The Alberta Gas Ethylene Company, Ltd., has arranged to borrow up to $373,750,000 which will be guarantied as to principal and interest by the Company. The borrowing is to be repaid in monthly installments ending in 1998.

Source: *1977 Annual Report of the Dow Chemical Company.*

REVIEW PROBLEM

Dexter Company completed the following selected transactions during the last quarter of 19x6 and the first quarter of 19x7:

Oct. 31	Issued a 3-month, 8% note to settle a past due account; the invoice, which was for $8,000, had been recorded net of a 2% cash discount.
Nov. 30	Accrued the November payroll: gross salaries, $60,000; income taxes withheld, $9,500; FICA taxes withheld, $3,200; union dues withheld, $2,000.
Nov. 30	Accrued the employer's payroll taxes and fringe benefit costs: FICA taxes, $3,200; federal unemployment taxes, $200; state unemployment taxes, $1,620; medical insurance contributions, $4,400.
Nov. 30	Transferred funds to a special payroll acount from the regular checking account to pay employee salaries.
Dec. 1	Issued a 3-month, non-interest-bearing note for a cash loan of $25,000; interest is imputed at 8% on the cash proceeds.
Dec. 31	Accrued interest on the note issued October 31; amortized the discount on the note issued December 1.
Jan. 31	Paid the note issued on October 31, 19x6.
Mar. 1	Paid the note issued on December 1, 19x6.

Required   Prepare the entries to record the transactions described.

Solution to review problem

Oct. 31	Accounts Payable	7,840	
	Discounts Lost	160	
	Notes Payable		8,000
	To issue 9%, 3-month note for past due account that was recorded net of cash discount ($8,000 × 2% = $160; $8,000 − 160 = $7,840).		
Nov. 30	Salaries Expense	60,000	
	Liability for Federal Income Taxes Withheld		9,500
	Liability for FICA Taxes		3,200
	Liability for Union Dues Withheld		2,000
	Salaries Payable		45,300
	To accrue November payroll.		
Nov. 30	Payroll Tax Expense	5,020	
	Fringe Benefit Expense	4,400	
	Liability for FICA Taxes		3,200
	Liability for Federal Unemployment Taxes		200
	Liability for State Unemployment Taxes		1,620
	Liability for Medical Insurance Contributions		4,400
	To accrue employer's payroll taxes and fringe benefit costs.		
Nov. 30	Payroll Fund	45,300	
	Cash		45,300
	To transfer funds to special payroll account to pay November payroll.		
Nov. 30	Salaries Payable	45,300	
	Payroll Fund		45,300
	To pay the November payroll.		
Dec. 1	Cash	25,000	
	Discount on Notes Payable	500	
	Notes Payable		25,500
	To issue 3-month, non-interest-bearing note for $25,000 loan; interest imputed at 8% ($25,000 × 8% × 3/12 = $500).		

Dec. 31	Interest Expense	107	
	Interest Payable		107
	To accrue interest on interest-bearing		
	note ($8,000 × 8% × 2/12 = $107).		

Dec. 31	Interest Expense	167	
	Discount on Notes Payable		167
	To amortize discount on note for one		
	month ($500 × 1/3 = $167).		

Jan. 31	Notes Payable	8,000	
	Interest Payable	107	
	Interest Expense	53	
	Cash		8,160
	To pay interest-bearing note issued		
	October 31, 19x6, and recognize		
	interest expense for January 1–31		
	($8,000 × 8% × 1/12 = $53).		

Mar. 1	Notes Payable	25,500	
	Interest Expense	333	
	Cash		25,500
	Discount on Notes Payable		333
	To pay non-interest-bearing note issued		
	December 31, 19x6, and amortize		
	the balance of the discount on the		
	note ($500 − 167 = $333).		

SUMMARY

Accounting for liabilities for purchases of goods or services, accrued expenses, and deferred revenues was reviewed in this unit. Accounting for other short-term liabilities—in particular, payroll and related taxes and expenses, and interest- and non-interest-bearing notes—was also discussed and illustrated.

REVIEW QUESTIONS

24-1   What is a current liability? How are current liabilities related to current assets?

24-2   Conceptually, how should current liabilities be measured? In practice, why are many current liabilities measured at their face value?

24-3   Most current liabilities are definite obligations. Explain.

24-4   If a purchase of merchandise is recorded net of cash discounts, what problem arises when the payment is made after the discount period ends?

24-5   Define (a) accrued expense and (b) deferred revenue.

24-6   What obligations arise for an employer in accounting for payrolls?

24-7   What is a payroll fund? Why is it used?

24-8   Several terms are related to the accounting for interest-bearing and/or non-interest-bearing notes. For the following terms identify any differences in their use with interest-bearing notes as opposed to non-interest-bearing notes:

   a.   face value
   b.   maturity value
   c.   stated interest rate
   d.   imputed or implied interest rate
   e.   effective interest rate
   f.   cash proceeds

24-9   How are non-interest-bearing notes reported on the balance sheet?

EXERCISES

24-1   Pharris Corp. purchased merchandise with an invoice price of $6,500; credit terms were 2/10, n/30. The invoice was dated July 10, 19x1.

   Required   a.   Prepare the entries for the purchase and the payment of the invoice on July 20 if the periodic inventory system is used.
             b.   Prepare the entries for the purchase and the payment of the invoice on August 9 if the perpetual inventory system is used.

24-2   The accountant for Aspen Corp. asks you, as a student summer employee, to prepare the necessary adjusting entries at the end of the company's fiscal year, June 30, 19x2. He presents you with the following information:

   a.   Accrued salaries at June 30 were $850.
   b.   Advance payments of fees during the fiscal year totaled $26,500. At June 30, 19x2, $2,800 of these fees were still unearned. The advance payments had been recorded in a liability account.
   c.   A 90-day, 8% note for $6,000 was issued on May 1, 19x2.
   d.   A 6-month, non-interest-bearing note for a $30,000 cash loan was issued on June 1, 19x2; imputed interest, computed at 8% on the cash proceeds, was included in the face value of the note.

   Required   Prepare the necessary adjusting entries at June 30, 19x2.

24-3 The following are the payroll data for Sloppe Company for the month of November:

Gross salaries	$40,000
Federal income taxes withheld	6,300
FICA taxes withheld	1,800
Pension plan contributions:	
By employees	2,000
By employer	3,200
Union dues withheld	900
Medical insurance premiums paid by employer	3,600
Federal unemployment taxes	100
State unemployment taxes	540

A special payroll acount is used to pay employee salaries.

Required   Prepare entries to: (a) accrue salaries, (b) transfer funds to the payroll account, (c) pay salaries, and (d) accrue the employer's payroll taxes and fringe benefit costs.

24-4 Pharoah Corp. issued a 6-month promissory note for a $50,000 cash loan on November 1, 19x5.

Required   **a.** Determine the face value, maturity value, cash proceeds, and effective interest rate if the note is:

   (1) interest-bearing with a 9% interest rate

   (2) non-interest-bearing with interest imputed at 9% on the cash proceeds from the note

b. Prepare the entries to record the issuance of the note, interest expense recognized at the end of the accounting period (December 31), and the payment of the note at maturity for each type of note described in part a.

24-5 The following transactions were completed during the last quarter of 19x2. Prepare all entries required for 19x2 to record these transactions.

Oct. 10	Recorded the purchase of merchandise with an invoice price of $4,500 subject to credit terms of 2/10, n/30; the invoice was dated October 8. The perpetual inventory system is used.
Oct. 18	Paid the amount due on the October 10 transaction.
Nov. 1	Issued a 90-day, 8% note to purchase equipment with a cost of $9,000.
Dec. 1	Borrowed $19,400 from a bank by issuing a $20,000, 120-day, non-interest-bearing note.
Dec. 11	Received a $3,200 advance from a customer for goods to be delivered over the next 60 days; the advance was recorded as a liability.
Dec. 31	Recognized that $1,200 of the advance received on December 11 had been earned.

Dec. 31	Recognized interest expense on the notes issued November 1 and December 1.
Dec. 31	Accrued the monthly payroll of $15,000. Withheld income taxes of $2,500, FICA taxes of $300, and employee contributions to a retirement fund of $750.
Dec. 31	Recorded employer's payroll taxes and fringe benefit costs: federal unemployment taxes of $20; state unemployment taxes of $80; medical insurance premiums of $250; contributions to retirement fund of $1,050.

PROBLEMS

24-1   Speare Corp. completed the following selected transactions during 19*x4:*

Jan. 10	Received an invoice for merchandise with a cost of $12,500; the invoice was dated January 8; credit terms were 2/10, n/30. The perpetual inventory system is used.
Jan. 18	Paid the invoice received on January 10.
Feb. 15	Paid a 3-month, 8% note for $6,000; the note was dated November 15, 19*x4.*
Mar. 31	Accrued the payroll for the week ending March 26:

Gross wages	$15,000
Federal income taxes withheld	2,400
FICA taxes withheld	900
Federal unemployment taxes	75
State unemployment taxes	405
Medical insurance premiums:	
Withheld from salaries	450
Paid by employer	1,500

Apr. 10	Issued a 6-month, non-interest-bearing note for a cash loan of $25,000; interest was imputed at 8% on the cash proceeds.
May 5	Received an invoice for merchandise with a cost of $18,000; the invoice was dated May 3; credit terms were 1/10, n/30. The perpetual inventory system is used.
June 4	Paid the invoice received on May 5.
July 20	Issued a 90-day, 9% note to settle a past due account; the invoice for $8,500 was dated June 1 and had been recorded net of a 2% cash discount.
Oct. 10	Paid the note issued on April 10.
Oct. 18	Paid the note issued on July 20.
Nov. 28	Received a $5,000 advance payment from a customer for goods to be delivered over the next 60 days; the advance was recorded in a revenue account.

Dec. 31   Accrued wages of $6,000.

Dec. 31   By the end of the year 60% of the advance received on November 28 had been earned.

Required   Record each of these transactions.

24-2   Ames Company issued the following two notes on December 1, 19x3:

Note A: 8%, 4-month note to settle a past due account for $6,000.

Note B: 4-month, non-interest-bearing note for a cash loan of $6,000; interest is imputed at 8% on the cash proceeds.

Required   **a.**   Determine the following for the two notes: (1) face value, (2) maturity value, (3) cash proceeds or credit received, and (4) effective interest rate.

                 b.   Prepare the entries for each of the notes to record: (1) issuance of the note, (2) recognition of interest expense for December 19x3, and (3) payment of the note at maturity.

                 c.   Show how each note would be presented on the balance sheet at December 31, 19x3.

24-3   Handicrafters Company reported the following current liabilities at the end of 19x6:

Accounts payable		$81,600
Notes payable, trade		15,000
Notes payable, nontrade	$30,000	
Less: Discount on notes payable	800	29,200
Income taxes payable		22,000
Accrued expenses		3,400
Deferred revenues		4,200

An analysis of these balances indicated the following:

     a.   Accounts payable: portion of balance on which cash discounts can still be earned, $44,100; all purchases were recorded net of cash discounts; terms were 2/10, n/30.

     b.   Trade notes payable consist of an 8%, 90-day note for $5,000 and a 9%, 60-day note for $10,000; both notes were issued on December 1, 19x6.

     c.   Nontrade notes payable represent an 8-month bank loan received on September 1, 19x6.

     d.   The income tax rate is 40%.

     e.   Accrued expenses include amounts for accrued interest, accrued salaries, and accrued property taxes. Property taxes accrue over the period, July 1–June 30, at $125 per month.

     f.   The balance of deferred revenues represents advances from customers to be earned during 19x7.

During 19x7 the following transactions were completed:

a. All accounts payable outstanding at December 31, 19x6, were paid. Of the $44,100 on which cash discounts could be earned, $39,200 was paid in time to earn the discounts.
b. All notes payable were paid at maturity.
c. Income taxes were paid.
d. Property taxes were paid on July 10, 19x7.
e. The first payroll payment in 19x7 consisted of the following: gross salaries, $6,500; income taxes withheld, $1,000; FICA taxes withheld, $390.
f. All deferred revenues were earned.

Required Prepare the entries to record these transactions.

24-4 Klinch Corp. completed the following transactions near the end of 19x5:

Dec. 1 Issued a 6-month non-interest-bearing note for $7,800 to a supplier in settlement of a past due account for $7,500.

Dec. 1 Issued ten one-year notes for $5,000 each; the notes carry an interest rate of 9%.

Dec. 8 Received advances from customers for $8,400; by the end of December only $1,400 of this amount was earned.

Dec. 31 Accrued wages of $1,800 plus employer's payroll taxes of $270.

Dec. 31 Accrued property taxes of $250 per month for the period July 1 to December 31, 19x5.

During December the following credit transactions occurred (excluding the first entry above): purchases on credit, $32,500; operating expenses incurred on credit, $13,800; payments on account, $43,600. The balance of accounts payable at November 30, 19x5, was $46,100.

Required Prepare the current liability section of the balance sheet at the end of 19x5.

Unit 25
Accounting for Bond Obligations

. . . His promises fly so beyond his state
That what he speaks is all in debt; he owes
For every word: he is so kind that he now
Pays interest for 't; his land's put to their books.

. . . Take the bonds along with you
And have the dates in compt.

William Shakespeare, Timon of Athens, *c. 1605*

Bonds are a major source of borrowed funds for larger corporations, government units, and nonprofit organizations. The basic features of bonds, the complexities of accounting for bond obligations, and some restrictions that arise as a result of issuing bonds are discussed in this unit.

Performance Objectives

Upon completion of this unit you should be able to:

1. define and use the accounting terms introduced in this unit.
2. describe or explain:
   a. what constitutes the balance to be reported for a bond liability
   b. how the balance of a bond liability is measured or reported
   c. what amount should be reported annually as interest expense on a bond liability
   d. what constitutes the balance to be reported for a long-term fund
   e. how the balance of a long-term fund and/or the related revenue from the fund is measured or reported
   f. how the periodic contributions to a long-term fund are determined
   g. the types of restrictions included in bond indentures and how they are disclosed

3. determine:
   a. the cash proceeds from the issuance of bonds
   b. the semiannual or annual payment for interest
   c. the monthly, semiannual, or annual effective interest expense
   d. the amount to be reported as a bond liability at the end of an accounting period
   e. the size of the periodic contribution required to accumulate a long-term fund of a specific amount
   f. the balance in a long-term fund at a specific date
4. prepare the correct journal entry for selected transactions for bond liabilities, the related interest expense, and bond sinking funds.

Nature of Bonds

Bonds are debt instruments issued to borrow funds on a long-term basis. The lenders are known as *bondholders*. The contract between the issuing company and the bondholders is called the **bond indenture.** The bond indenture contains all legal provisions concerning the bonds, such as the denomination or face value of the bonds, maturity date, interest rate to be paid, interest payment dates, conversion privileges, early retirement (or call) features, sinking fund requirements, and restrictions on dividends, working capital, additional debt incurred, and so on, during the term of the bonds. Bondholders receive a **bond certificate** as evidence of their ownership. The legal provisions contained in the bond indenture are printed on the bond certificates. Most bonds are negotiable, that is, they can be transferred by endorsement from the bondholder to another party. Bonds issued by most larger corporations, government units, and nonprofit organizations are quoted on and traded through established security exchanges.

Bond prices are quoted as a percentage of their **face value** (that is, their **par value** or **principal amount**). For example, a bond quoted at 98½ is selling at 98½ percent of its face value; a bond quoted at 101 is selling at 101 percent of its face value. If a bond is selling at its face value, it will be quoted at 100 (that is, 100 percent). Most bonds are sold in denominations of $1,000, although denominations of $100 to $100,000 are not uncommon. The denomination represents the **maturity value** as well as the *face value* of the bond. For example, a bond with a denomination of $1,000 will be redeemed by the issuing company for $1,000 at the maturity date.

Because the term of most bonds is quite long (for example, 10 to 40 years), interest is payable throughout the term of the bonds at specified interest payment dates, usually semiannually. Since the interest rate stated in the bond certificate will be the annual interest rate, adjustments may have to be made. If interest is payable semiannually, for example, half the annual rate will be paid every six months. Assume bonds with a face value of $1,000 each, a stated interest rate of 8% annually, and interest payable semiannually on January 1 and July 1 are issued. Forty dollars interest will have to be paid on each bond every January 1 and July 1 ($1,000 × 8% × 6/12 = $40 or $1,000 × 4% = $40).

Bonds are usually issued to an **underwriter** who in turn sells them to the public. The underwriter can also help determine what provisions are required in the bond indenture to make the bonds salable to the public. Bondholders are usually represented by a **trustee** (that is, a third party), who is appointed by the borrower. The trustee is responsible for ascertaining that the provisions in the bond indenture are fulfilled by the issuing company and for taking appropriate action on behalf of the bondholders if any provisions are violated. The bonds may become due immediately for such violations.

Classification of Bonds

Bonds may be classified in different ways according to the features or provisions in the bond indenture. Those secured by a mortgage or a pledge of specified assets as a guarantee of payment of the principal at maturity are called **secured bonds. Debenture (or unsecured) bonds** are not guaranteed by a mortgage or a pledge of specific assets. Debenture bonds usually can be issued only by companies with an excellent credit standing.

If the bond principal is payable in full at a single maturity date, the bonds are called **ordinary bonds.** If the principal is payable in installments at a series of maturity dates, the bonds are called **serial bonds.** Bonds that pay interest by check to the bondholder of record are known as **registered bonds** because the bondholder's name and address must be recorded (registered) with the issuing company in a bond record called a *bond register.* Bonds with coupons attached for each interest payment are known as **coupon bonds.** The bondholder detaches a coupon when an interest date approaches or arrives and submits it to the company or a specified bank. The company or bank mails an interest check to the bondholders who submit the coupons.

Early redemption or conversion features are contained in many bond issues to make the bonds a more attractive investment and to provide certain advantages to the issuer. For example, the issuing company may want a call feature that permits it to retire the bonds at its option in order to avoid future interest costs. Bonds with a call feature for redemption at the company's option are known as **callable bonds.** On the other hand, bonds that may be redeemed at the option of the bondholders are known as **redeemable bonds.** The terms of either redemption feature are included in the bond indenture.

Bonds that may be converted into other bonds, common stock, or preferred stock of the issuing company at the option of the bondholders are **convertible bonds.** Convertible bonds often pay a lower interest rate because investors expect favorable conversion rates into securities with greater value than the bonds. Companies that issue convertible bonds seek the advantages of lower interest costs and conversion into a more permanent type of capital such as common stock or preferred stock, which does not have a maturity. If bonds are convertible into other bonds, the issuing company can use the borrowed funds longer before attempting to market a new bond issue to the public.

Bond Premium and Discount

Bonds have fixed maturity values, fixed interest rates, and definite maturity dates. Thus, bond prices fluctuate less than stock prices. However, the **market rate of interest** fluctuates, depending on the supply and demand for money. Also, investor evaluations of the bond issuer's financial condition sometimes differ from what the issuing company and the underwriter expected them to be. The result, then, is that bonds may have to be issued to yield investors a different rate of interest than that stated in the bond indenture. Whenever the market interest rate varies from the **stated interest rate,** the issue price or market price of the bonds is affected. Bond prices vary inversely with changes in the market interest rate: As the market interest rate increases, the market price of the bonds decreases; and, as the market interest rate decreases, the market price of the bonds increases.

Bond market prices fluctuate this way because a bond is actually the present value of two types of payments: (1) the single sum due at maturity and (2) the periodic interest payments. Assume that a $1,000 bond with a stated interest rate of 8%, payable semiannually, and a term of five years is issued when the market interest rate is (a) 6%, (b) 10%, and (c) 8%. The present value or market price of the bond at the issue date for each case is determined as follows:

	Case (a) Issued at 6%	Case (b) Issued at 10%	Case (c) Issued at 8%
Present value of principal of $1,000*	$ 744.09	$613.91	$ 675.56
Present value of semiannual interest payments of $40 each ($1,000 × 8% × 6/12 = $40)**	341.21	308.87	324.44
Total present value or market price at date of issue	$1,085.30	$922.78	$1,000.00

$*PV = \$1,000 \times F_{.03,10} = \$1,000 \times .74409 = \$744.09$
$PV = \$1,000 \times F_{.05,10} = \$1,000 \times .61391 = \$613.91$
$PV = \$1,000 \times F_{.04,10} = \$1,000 \times .67556 = \$675.56$
$PVA = \$40 \times F_{.03,10} = \$40 \times 8.5302 = \$341.21$
$**PVA = \$40 \times F_{.05,10} = \$40 \times 7.7217 = \$308.87$
$PVA = \$40 \times F_{.04,10} = \$40 \times 8.1109 = \$324.44$

When the market interest rate is less than the stated interest rate, the bond will sell at a price in excess of its face value or principal, such as in case (a). Thus, the bond is said to sell at a **premium;** its quoted price would be approximately 108½ ($1,085.30/$1,000 = 108½%). When the market interest rate is greater than the stated interest rate, the bond will sell below its face value, such as in case (b). Thus, the bond is said to sell at a **discount;** its quoted price would be approximately 92¼ ($922.78/$1,000 = 92¼%. If a bond is sold to yield its stated interest rate, the bond is said to be sold at par (that is, at its face value), such as in case (c).

Bond premium is added to the face value of the bonds on the balance sheet to reflect the bond liability at its present value. For the same reason, bond discount is deducted from the face value of the bonds on the balance sheet. The partial balance sheets in Exhibit 25.1 indicate the proper reporting of a $100,000 bond issue at (1) a bond discount of $1,600 and (2) a bond premium of $2,000.

Exhibit 25.1

	Case (1)		
Long-term liabilities:			
Bonds payable		$100,000	
Less: Bond discount		1,600	$ 98,400

	Case (2)		
Long-term liabilities:			
Bonds payable		$100,000	
Add: Bond premium		2,000	$102,000

Bond premium or discount must be amortized to determine the true or **effective interest expense** for each period. The bond indenture requires interest to be paid at the stated rate. Assume that the bonds in Exhibit 25.1 pay interest at 8% annually and have a term of ten years. If the bonds are issued at par, the effective interest expense is $8,000, based on the stated interest rate ($100,000 × 8% = $8,000). However, if the bonds are issued at a discount of $1,600, the annual effective interest expense will be $8,160. Under the straight-line amortization method, an equal amount of the discount, $160 ($1,600/10 years), is added to the $8,000 of interest paid annually at the stated interest rate. This is appropriate because the bonds were issued at a discount to yield interest at a rate greater than 8%. Similarly, if the bonds are issued at a premium of $2,000, the annual effective interest expense will be $7,800, less than the interest paid at the stated interest rate of 8%. The amount of premium amortized, $200 ($2,000/10 years), is deducted from the interest paid of $8,000 to determine the effective interest expense of $7,800.

In the first diagram of Exhibit 25.2 bonds with a par value of $100,000 were issued for $98,400. As the discount of $1,600 is amortized, the book value of the bond liability approaches the par value. At the maturity date, when the bond discount is fully amortized, the bond liability will be equal to the par value. Thus, no gain or loss results from the routine retirement of bonds at maturity. Similarly, if the bonds were issued for $102,000 (second diagram), the premium of $2,000 would be amortized until the bond liability reached par value at the maturity date. The book value of the bonds reflects the approximate present value of the bond liability, based on the market rate of interest at the date the bonds were issued. In Exhibit 25.1, the book value or present value of the bond liability immediately after the issuance of the bonds is $98,400 in case (1) and $102,000 in case (2).

Accounting for Bonds and Interest

When bonds are issued, the cash proceeds and the bond liability must be recorded. In addition, any difference between the face value of the bonds and the cash proceeds from their issuance must be recorded as a bond premium or discount. At each interest payment date, the interest paid on the bonds must be recorded. Also, any bond pre-

Exhibit 25.2

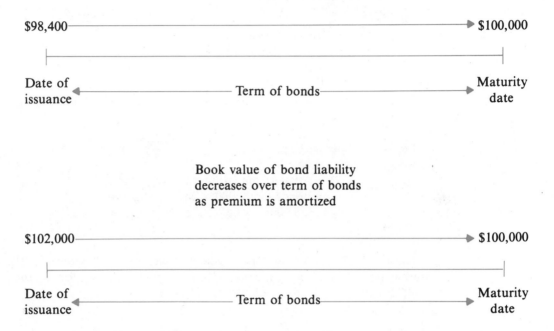

Book value of bond liability
increases over term of bonds
as discount is amortized

$98,400 $\longrightarrow$ $100,000

Date of   Term of bonds   Maturity
issuance   date

Book value of bond liability
decreases over term of bonds
as premium is amortized

$102,000 $\longrightarrow$ $100,000

Date of   Term of bonds   Maturity
issuance   date

mium or discount must be amortized as an adjustment to interest expense to record effective interest expense in the accounts.

Recall that bonds are redeemed at their face value at maturity. Thus, as they approach maturity, the bond liability (the face value of the bonds plus any unamortized premium or minus any unamortized discount) should approach the face value of the bonds—but only if the bond premium or discount is amortized. The two diagrams in Exhibit 25.2 illustrate this concept.

If the accounting period ends between interest payment dates, an adjusting entry for accrued interest expense must be prepared. Also, amortization of the bond premium or discount since the last interest payment date must be recorded. To illustrate the accounting for bonds issued at par, at a premium, and at a discount, assume that Starlite Corp. issued bonds with the following provisions:

Face value of bonds issued:	$500,000
Issue date printed on bonds:	January 1, 19x1
Maturity date:	January 1, 19x6
Stated annual interest rate:	8%
Semiannual interest payment dates:	January 1 and July 1

Bonds Issued at Par   The bond liability account is always recorded at the par or face value of the bonds. When bonds are issued at par, the cash proceeds will be equal to the face value of the bonds. Thus, the entry to record the issuance of the bonds at par by Starlite Corp. on the date of the bonds would be:

Jan. 1, 19x1	Cash	500,000	
	Bonds Payable		500,000
	To record issuance of bonds at par.		

The entry for the semiannual interest payment of $20,000 on July 1, 19x1, is:

July 1, 19x1	Interest Expense	20,000	
	Cash		20,000
	To record semiannual interest payment on bonds ($500,000 × 8% × 6/12 = $20,000).		

The next semiannual interest payment is payable on January 1, 19x2. If the accounting period ends on December 31, an adjusting entry for accrued interest of $20,000 for the period July 1–December 31 is required:

Dec. 31, 19x1	Interest Expense	20,000	
	Interest Payable		20,000
	To accrue interest on bonds for the 6 months ended Dec. 31, 19x1 ($500,000 × 8% × 6/12 = $20,000).		

The entry to pay the interest on January 1, 19x2, would be:

Jan. 1, 19x2	Interest Payable	20,000	
	Cash		20,000
	To pay interest accrued on Dec. 31, 19x1.		

Interest expense for 19x1 is $40,000 ($20,000 + 20,000) and is reported on the income statement for 19x1 as an incidental expense. The bond liability of $500,000 is reported under long-term liabilities on the balance sheet. Since issuing bonds at par indicates that the stated interest rate equals the market interest rate, the **effective in-**

terest rate (that is, the rate actually paid) is 8%, and the effective interest expense is $40,000 each year.

Bonds are redeemed at maturity at their face value, regardless of whether they were issued at par or at a premium or discount (bond premium or discount will be fully amortized by the maturity date). The entry to redeem the $500,000 bond issue on January 1, 19x6, would be:

Jan. 1,	Bonds Payable	500,000	
19x6	Cash		500,000
	To redeem bonds at maturity.		

Bonds Issued at a Premium   Bonds sell at a premium when the market interest rate is less than the stated interest rate. Since the company must pay interest at the rate stated in the bond indenture, the only way it can adjust the interest rate to the market rate is to sell the bonds at a premium. The premium compensates the issuing company for the excess interest that must be paid to bondholders over the term of the bonds. Over the 5-year term of the bonds, the total interest paid by the company will be $200,000 ($500,000 × 8% × 5 years) because it is paid at the stated interest rate of 8% annually. The $10,000 premium reduces the net payout for interest to $190,000 ($200,000 − 10,000). The entry to issue bonds at a premium will include a credit to a bond premium account for the difference between the face value of the bonds and the cash proceeds from their issuance.

If Starlite Corp. issues bonds with a par value of $500,000 at 102 on the date of the bonds, a premium of 2% (102% − 100%) or $10,000 ($500,000 × 2%) is paid by the investors. Thus, the cash proceeds received by the company will be $510,000 ($500,000 + 10,000). The entry to record the issuance of these bonds would be:

Jan. 1,	Cash	510,000	
19x1	Bonds Payable		500,000
	Bond Premium		10,000
	To issue bonds at a premium.		

Because the bond premium represents an adjustment in the interest rate, it must be amortized over the period the bonds are outstanding. In this situation, the bonds were issued on the date printed on them; thus, they will be outstanding for the full term of five years. Amortization of bond premium on a straight-line basis will be $2,000 annually ($10,000/5 years) or $1,000 every six months ($2,000 × 6/12). The entries for the interest payment on July 1 and the accrual of interest on December 31 will include the amortization of the bond premium as follows:

July 1, 19x1	Interest Expense	19,000	
	Bond Premium	1,000	
	Cash		20,000
	To record semiannual interest payment and amortization of bond premium.		
Dec. 31, 19x1	Interest Expense	19,000	
	Bond Premium	1,000	
	Interest Payable		20,000
	To accrue interest on bonds and amortize bond premium for the period July 1–Dec. 31, 19x1.		

To reduce the bond premium account (which has a credit balance), a debit entry is required. Thus, the bond premium account was debited $1,000 in the entries for July 1 and December 31, 19x1. At the end 19x1 the bond premium account has a balance of $8,000 ($10,000 − 1,000 − 1,000), and the bond liability is reported as follows:

Long-term liabilities:		
Bonds payable	$500,000	
Add: Bond premium	8,000	$508,000

The effective interest expense is $19,000 every six months (or $38,000 annually) although the amount of interest paid is $20,000 every six months (or $40,000 annually). The difference is due to the amortization of the bond premium. An approximate effective interest rate can be determined by dividing the annual effective interest expense by the average book value of the bond obligation (that is, the average of the issue price and the maturity value of the bonds):

$$\frac{\text{annual effective interest expense}}{\text{average book value of bonds}} = \frac{\$38,000}{(\$510,000 + 500,000)/2} = \frac{\$38,000}{\$505,000} = 7.52\%$$

Bonds Issued at a Discount   Recall that bonds sell at a discount when the market interest rate is greater than the stated interest rate. The company must pay interest at the rate stated in the bond indenture, but investors expect to earn the market rate. In order to sell the bonds, therefore, the interest rate must be adjusted to the market rate—so bonds are sold at a discount. The reduced purchase price compensates the investors for the difference between the interest received at the stated interest rate and the interest expected at the market interest rate. The entry to record the issuance of the bonds will include a debit to a bond discount account for the difference between the face value of the bonds and the cash proceeds from their issuance.

If Starlite Corp. issues bonds with a par value of $500,000 at 98 on the date of the bonds, a discount of 2% (100% − 98%) or $10,000 ($500,000 × 2%) is received by the investors. Thus, the cash proceeds received by the company will be $490,000 ($500,000 − 10,000). The entry to record the issuance of these bonds would be:

Jan. 1, 19x1	Cash	490,000	
	Bond Discount	10,000	
	Bond Payable		500,000
	To issue bonds at a discount.		

The bonds will be outstanding for the full term of five years because they were issued on the date printed on them. Thus, the bond discount will be amortized over five years; amortization on a straight-line basis will be $2,000 annually ($10,000/5 years); or $1,000 semiannually ($2,000 × 6/12). The entries for the payment of interest on July 1 and the accrual of interest on December 31 will include the amortization of bond discount as follows:

July 1, 19x1	Interest Expense	21,000	
	Bond Discount		1,000
	Cash		20,000
	To record semiannual interest payment and amortization of bond discount.		
Dec. 31, 19x1	Interest Expense	21,000	
	Bond Discount		1,000
	Interest Payable		20,000
	To accrue interest and amortize bond discount for the period July 1–Dec. 31, 19x1.		

A credit entry is required to reduce the bond discount account because it has a debit balance. At the end of 19x1 the bond discount account has a balance of $8,000 ($10,000 − 1,000 − 1,000), and the bond liability is reported as follows:

Long-term liabilities:		
Bonds payable	$500,000	
Less: Bond discount	8,000	$492,000

The effective interest expense is $21,000 every six months (or $42,000 annually) although the amount of interest paid is $20,000 every six months (or $40,000 annually).

The difference is due to the amortization of the bond discount. Although the stated interest rate is 8% annually, the approximate effective interest rate is 8.48%:

$$\frac{\text{annual effective interest expense}}{\text{average book value of bonds}} = \frac{\$42,000}{(\$490,000 + 500,000)/2} = \frac{\$42,000}{\$495,000} = 8.48\%$$

Bonds Issued After the Date of the Bonds   It usually takes months to plan and issue bonds. Unexpected delays and market factors may cause the bonds to be issued after the date printed on the bond certificates. When this occurs, the investor must pay the issuing company the interest accrued since the date of the bonds, or the last interest payment date, in addition to the market price of the bonds. The issuing company then pays interest for the full interest period, thereby reimbursing the investor for the accrued interest paid to the company when the bonds were purchased. As a result, the issuing company incurs interest expense only for the period the bonds are outstanding, and the investor earns interest only for the period that the bonds are held. This practice also applies to transfers of bonds between investors between interest payment dates. The objective is to simplify the determination of the amount of interest payable to each investor by the issuing corporation.

Assume a company plans to issue bonds with the following provisions:

Face value of bonds:	$200,000
Date of bonds:	December 31, 19x1
Maturity date:	December 31, 19x6
Annual stated interest rate:	9%
Semiannual interest payment dates:	June 30 and December 31

If the bonds are issued at their par value of $200,000 on April 30, 19x2, plus accrued interest since the date of the bonds, the entry to record the issuance of the bonds would be:

Apr. 30, 19x2	Cash	206,000	
	Bonds Payable		200,000
	Interest Expense		6,000
	To issue bonds at par four months late		
	($200,000 × 9% × 4/12 = $6,000).		

The accrued interest of $6,000 was credited to interest expense.[1] When the semiannual interest payment is made on June 30, the interest for the entire 6 months of

---

[1]An alternative is to credit interest payable at the date the bonds are issued because this amount must be refunded to the investors at the next interest payment date. Then, when the interest is paid for that period, the liability for interest payable ($6,000 in the illustration) is eliminated and the remainder of the interest paid ($3,000) is charged to interest expense. Under either approach, the net interest expense is the same ($3,000).

$9,000 ($200,000 × 9% × 6/12) is charged to interest expense. The net effect of the credit for $6,000 and the debit for $9,000 is a debit balance of $3,000 in interest expense; this balance equals the interest expense for the last two months of the interest period ($200,000 × 9% × 2/12 = $3,000). The entry to record the payment of interest at June 30 and December 31 will be the same because the accrued interest was credited to interest expense at the time the bonds were issued:

June 30, 19x2	Interest Expense	9,000	
	Cash		9,000
	To make semiannual interest payment ($200,000 × 9% × 6/12 = $9,000).		

Interest Expense	
6/30/x2 9,000	4/30/x2 6,000

(Balance, 6/30/x2: $3,000)

Dec. 31, 19x2	Interest Expense	9,000	
	Cash		9,000
	To make semiannual interest payment ($200,000 × 9% × 6/12 = $9,000).		

Interest Expense	
6/30/x2 9,000	4/30/x2 6,000
12/31/x2 9,000	

(Balance, 12/31/x2: $12,000)

There is one additional complexity in accounting for bonds issued after the date of the bonds or between interest dates. Bond premium or bond discount must be amortized over the period the bonds are outstanding, that is, from the date of issuance to the maturity date. When bonds are issued late, the bonds will be outstanding for less than the original term planned. Assume the bonds in the previous illustration were issued at a market price of $198,880 on April 30, 19x2. The entry to issue the bonds would be:

Apr. 30,	Cash	204,880	
19x2	Bond Discount	1,120	
	Bonds Payable		200,000
	Interest Expense		6,000
	To issue bonds at a discount 4 months late.		

The discount of $1,120 ($200,000 − 198,880) must be amortized over the 56 months (April 30, 19x2 to December 31, 19x6) the bonds will be outstanding rather than over the planned term of 5 years or 60 months. Thus, amortization will be $20 per month ($1,120/56 months). The entry to pay interest at June 30, 19x2, will include amortization of bond discount for two months (April 30–June 30), while the entry to pay interest at the remaining interest payment dates, such as December 31, 19x2, will include amortization of bond discount for six months. The entries at June 30 and December 31, 19x2, would be:

June 30,	Interest Expense	9,040	
19x2	Cash		9,000
	Bond Discount		40
	To make semiannual interest payment and amortize bond discount for 2 months ($20 × 2 = $40).		

Dec. 31,	Interest Expense	9,120	
19x2	Cash		9,000
	Bond Discount		120
	To make semiannual interest payment and amortize bond discount for 6 months ($20 × 6 = $120).		

Purpose and Nature of Long-term Funds

Companies establish long-term **funds** for a number of purposes. The most common is to retire long-term debt. The bond indenture often requires that a **bond sinking** (or retirement) **fund** be established to provide the money needed to redeem the bonds at maturity. Such a provision provides security against potential default at maturity. The periodic contributions to the fund can be a fixed amount each period or they can vary depending on net income or other factors. A bond sinking fund is likely to have a trustee appointed to act on behalf of the bondholders. This type of fund is called a **trusteed fund.** However, other types of funds usually are voluntarily established, and there is no need for a trustee.

The contributions to a long-term fund are invested until needed. Then the investments are sold, and the cash is used for its designated purpose. Income from the fund investments is added to the fund balance as it is realized. The fund balance includes uninvested cash, the cost of fund investments, and accrued income on fund investments at the end of the accounting period. All fund assets are reported as a single amount, such as bond sinking fund, under the long-term investments and funds section of the balance sheet.

The procedures to determine the amount of the periodic contributions to a debt retirement fund were explained in Unit 23. The accounting for these contributions and for the recognition of revenue from fund investments were also examined. Case B on pages 452–454 describes procedures that apply to a trusteed-type of fund. Chapter 10 describes procedures that apply to a non-trusteed fund.

Bond Restrictions

To provide security against default on the principal and interest of a bond issue, the bond indenture will often include restrictions or limitations on the payment of dividends, the incurrence of additional debt, and the minimum working capital position. The important accounting issue here is that all **bond restrictions** or limitations must be fully disclosed. Prospective investors and creditors should be able to obtain information from the financial statements on any restrictions that may affect their decision. For example, prospective stockholders would be interested in any restrictions on the payment of dividends; prospective creditors, in any restriction on working capital and incurrence of additional debt.

In the past it was a common practice to limit dividend payments during the term of a bond issue through a special restricted or appropriated retained earnings account (this type of account is discussed in Unit 28). The modern practice, however, is to disclose such restrictions in the footnotes. Also, more effective restrictions are often included in bond contracts. Among these are the limitation of dividends to a specified total or per share amount, and the elimination of dividends if earnings do not exceed a specified amount, working capital is not maintained at a specified amount, or the working capital ratio is below a specified figure.

These restrictions and others, such as those limiting the incurrence of additional debt, are disclosed in the footnotes. Violation of these provisions can cause the bond issue to be redeemable upon demand by the bondholders. If the company violates any restriction, the nature of the violation and any agreements or attempts to resolve the violation should be described in the footnotes. An example of the footnote disclosure of debt restrictions and sinking fund requirements is presented in Exhibit 25.3.

Exhibit 25.3

The above long-term debt has varying maturities including, in the aggregate, maturities of $381,000 in 1978, $397,000 in 1979, $437,000 in 1980, $418,000 in 1981, and $1,935,000 in 1982. The provisions of the loan agreements and the indenture for the 5³/₄% convertible subordinated debentures contain, among other things, restrictions on lease commitments, creation of mortgage indebtedness, payment of cash dividends and stock redemptions. In addition, the Company must maintain consolidated working capital of at least $45,000,000 and consolidated current assets of not less than 225% of consolidated current liabilities. On December 31, 1977, the Company had consolidated working capital of $64,271,000 and current assets were 446% of consolidated current liabilities. Under the terms of the most restrictive agreement retained earnings of approximately $8,595,000 was available for the payment of cash dividends. At December 31, 1977, the Company may, under certain restrictions, increase funded (long-term) borrowing by $19,850,000.

The convertible subordinated debentures, 5³/₄% due in 1987, are subordinated to all borrowings of the Company, and are now convertible into common stock at any time prior to maturity at the rate of 76.30 shares for each bond. Annual sinking fund payments of $1,200,000 for redemption of the debentures are required commencing in 1978, but may be satisfied by delivering converted or treasury debentures which amounted to $12,269,000 at December 31, 1977. The debentures may be called at any time at prices decreasing from 102.7% of face value currently to 100% in 1986.

Source: *1977 Annual Report of Bliss & Laughlin Industries (Note: At the end of 1977 the company reported total retained earnings of $44,359,000).*

REVIEW PROBLEM

Cranston Company planned the following bond issue:

Face value of bonds:	$300,000
Date of bonds:	April 1, 19x1
Maturity date:	April 1, 19x6
Stated annual interest rate:	8%
Semiannual interest payment dates:	April 1 and October 1

The company uses the calendar year as its accounting period. Due to unexpected market factors the bonds were not issued until July 1, 19x1, when their market value was $305,700.

Required
1. Prepare all necessary journal entries for the bonds and interest expense through April 1, 19x2.
2. Prepare a partial balance sheet and a partial income statement at the end of 19x1.
3. Determine the annual effective interest expense and the approximate annual effective interest rate.
4. Prepare the entry to make the annual contribution to a sinking fund on April 1, 19x2, if the fund investments will earn 5% annually, and 5 equal contributions are to be made.
5. Prepare the entry to retire the bonds at maturity if the sinking fund balance is $301,100 after the last contribution and sinking fund income are recorded.

Solution to review problem

1. July 1, 19x1

Cash		311,700	
Bonds Payable			300,000
Bond Premium			5,700
Interest Expense			6,000
To issue bonds at a premium 3 months late.			

Computations

Bond premium: $305,700 - 300,000 = $5,700
Accrued interest: $300,000 × 8% × 3/12 = $6,000
Cash: $305,700 + 6,000 = $311,700

Oct. 1, 19x1

Interest Expense		11,700	
Bond Premium		300	
Cash			12,000
To make semiannual interest payment and amortize bond premium for 3 months.			

Computations

Cash payment for interest: $300,000 × 8% × 6/12 = $12,000
Amortization of bond premium*: $5,700/57 months × 3 = $300
Interest expense: $12,000 - 300 = $11,700
*Premium is amortized over remaining term of bonds of 57 months.

Dec. 31, 19x1

Interest Expense		5,700	
Bond Premium		300	
Interest Payable			6,000
To accrue interest and amortize bond premium for 3 months (Oct. 1– Dec. 31, 19x1).			

Computations

Accrued interest: $300,000 × 8% × 3/12 = $6,000
Amortization of bond premium: $5,700/57 months × 3 = $300
Interest expense: $6,000 - 300 = $5,700

Apr. 1, 19x2	Interest Payable	6,000	
	Interest Expense	5,700	
	Bond Premium	300	
	Cash		12,000

To make semiannual interest payment
and amortize bond premium
(payment includes interest accrued
on Dec. 31, 19x1, and interest for
Jan. 1–Apr. 1, 19x2).

2.

Cranston Company
Partial Balance Sheet
December 31, 19x1

Long-term liabilities:		
Bonds payable	$300,000	
Less: Bond premium	5,100	$305,100

Cranston Company
Partial Income Statement
For the Year Ended December 31, 19x1

| Financial revenue and expense: | |
| Interest expense | $ 11,400 |

Computations

Bond Premium				Interest Expense			
10/1/x1	300	7/1/x1	5,700	10/1/x1	11,700	7/1/x1	6,000
12/31/x1	300			12/31/x1	5,700		
	(Balance: $5,100)				(Balance: $11,400)		

3.

Annual payment for interest ($300,000 × 8%)	$24,000
Annual amortization of bond premium [($5,700/57) × 12]	1,200
Annual effective interest expense	$22,800

$$\frac{\text{annual effective interest expense}}{\text{average book value of bonds}} = \frac{\$22,800}{(\$306,000 + 300,000)/2} = \frac{\$22,800}{\$303,000} = \underline{7.52\%}$$

4.	Apr. 1,	Bond Sinking Fund	54,293	
	19x2	Cash		54,293
		To make first payment to bond sinking fund.		

Computations

$$I = \frac{AA}{F_{i,n}}$$

where $AA = \$300,000$
$i = 5\%$
$n = 5$ years

$$= \frac{\$300,000}{F_{.05,5}}$$

$$= \frac{\$300,000}{5.5256}$$

$$= \$54,293$$

5.	Apr. 1,	Bonds Payable	300,000	
	19x6	Bond Sinking Fund		300,000
		To retire bonds with sinking fund assets.		
	Apr. 1,	Cash	1,100	
	19x6	Bond Sinking Fund		1,100
		To record receipt of balance of sinking fund after retirement of bonds ($301,100 − 300,000 = \$1,100$).		

SUMMARY

Various complexities in accounting for bond obligations were discussed in this unit. Any bond premium or discount resulting from differences between the stated and market rates of interest must be amortized over the period the bonds are outstanding. If the bonds are issued late or between interest dates, the purchaser must pay the seller for the accrued interest; this practice is followed to assure that the correct amount of interest is paid or received by all parties involved. Amortization of bond premium or discount results in the recording of the bond liability at its present value based on the market rate of interest at the date of issuance. Bond contracts frequently require that a sinking fund be established to provide funds for bond retirement. They also often contain restrictions on dividends, working capital, or the incurrence of additional debt; these restrictions are usually disclosed in the footnotes to financial statements. The appendix to this unit explains an alternative method of amortizing bond premium or discount.

APPENDIX 25 EFFECTIVE-INTEREST AMORTIZATION METHOD

The straight-line method of amortizing bond premium or discount results in a constant charge for interest expense over the period the bonds are outstanding. The **effective-interest method** can also be used to amortize bond premium or discount. It is considered more conceptually sound, however, because it results in a constant rate of interest over the period the bonds are outstanding. The effective-interest method is required by APB Opinion No. 21 when there is a material amount of premium or discount.

Whenever bonds are issued, an effective rate of interest can be determined. This rate will be equal to the stated interest rate if bonds are issued at par. However, when bonds are issued at a premium or discount, the effective interest rate will be less than or greater than the stated interest rate. Under the effective-interest method of amortizing bond premium or discount, interest expense is calculated by applying the effective interest rate to the book value of the bonds at the beginning of the period. The difference between interest expense computed this way and the periodic interest payment is the amount of bond premium or discount amortized.

Assume that bonds with a face value of $200,000, a term of five years, and a stated interest rate of 8% are issued to yield 10%. If interest is payable semiannually, the cash proceeds from the issuance of the bonds will be $184,556.[2] The discount on the bonds is $15,444 ($200,000 − 184,556).

The amortization table in Exhibit 25.4 shows the amounts needed to prepare the entry for each semiannual interest payment. Interest expense is calculated by multiplying the book value of the bonds at the beginning of each 6-month interest period by the effective interest rate for six months. For example, the book value of the bonds at the beginning of the first 6-month interest period is $184,556. Interest expense is determined by multiplying $184,556 by 5% ($184,556 × 5% = $9,228, rounded to the nearest full dollar). The interest payment every six months is $8,000 ($200,000 × 8% × 6/12). The difference between interest expense and the interest payment is $1,228 ($9,228 − 8,000) and is the amount of discount amortized during the first period.

The balance of bond discount decreases as it is amortized, and the carrying value of the bond liability increases. Thus, interest expense increases over the period that

---

[2]The cash proceeds will be the present value of the bond principal and the periodic interest payments:

Present value of bond principal ($PV = \$200,000 \times F_{.05,10} = \$200,000 \times 61391 = \$122,782$)	$122,782
Present value of interest payments ($PVA = \$8,000 \times F_{.05,10} = \$8,000 \times 7.7217 = \$61,774$)	61,774
Cash proceeds (or market price) of bonds	$184,556

Exhibit 25.4

Amortization Table—Effective-Interest Method

Interest Payment Period	(1) Carrying Value of Bond Liability at Beginning of Period	(2) = (1) × 5% Interest Expense for Period	(3) Interest Payment for Period	(4) = (2) − (3) Amortization of Bond Discount for Period	(5) = (1) + (4) Carrying Value of Bond Liability at End of Period
1	$184,556	$9,228	$8,000	$1,228	$185,784
2	185,784	9,289	8,000	1,289	187,073
3	187,073	9,354	8,000	1,354	188,427
4	188,427	9,421	8,000	1,421	189,848
5	189,848	9,492	8,000	1,492	191,340
6	191,340	9,567	8,000	1,567	192,907
7	192,907	9,645	8,000	1,645	194,552
8	194,552	9,728	8,000	1,728	196,280
9	196,280	9,814	8,000	1,814	198,094
10	198,094	9,906*	8,000	1,906	200,000

*Adjusted for rounding error.

bonds are outstanding. The following illustration indicates why the book value of the bond liability and interest expense increase when bonds are issued at a discount and the effective-interest method of amortization is used:

	At Beginning of Interest Period		
	1	2	3
Bonds payable	$200,000	$200,000	$200,000
Less: Unamortized bond discount	15,444	14,216*	12,927**
Book value of bonds	$184,556	$185,784	$187,073
Effectiveinterest rate for 6 months	5%	5%	5%
Interest expense for period	$ 9,228	$ 9,289	$ 9,354

*$9,228 − 8,000 = $1,228; $15,444 − 1,228 = $14,216.
**$9,289 − 8,000 = $1,289; $14,216 − 1,289 = $12,927.

When bonds are issued at a premium and the effective-interest amortization method is used, the carrying value of the bond liability and interest will decrease over the period the bonds are outstanding. See the review problem for this situation.

You should not be overly concerned with the detailed computations of the effective-interest method, but you should have a reasonable understanding of the concept underlying it. The method is more conceptually sound than the straight-line amortization method because it measures interest expense at the effective interest rate. Also, the book value of the bond liability will always be equal to the present value of

Exhibit 25.5

	(1)	(2)	(3)	(4) = (2) + (3)	(5) = (1) + (3)
	Carrying Value		Amortization		
	of Bond Liability	Interest	of Bond		Carrying Value
Interest	at Beginning of	Payment	Discount for	Interest Expense	of Bond Liability
Payment Period	Period	for Period	Period	for Period	at End of Period
1	$184,556	$8,000	$1,544	9,544	$186,100
2	186,100	8,000	1,544	9,544	187,644
3	187,644	8,000	1,544	9,544	189,188
4	189,188	8,000	1,544	9,544	190,732
5	190,732	8,000	1,544	9,544	192,276
6	192,276	8,000	1,544	9,544	193,820
7	193,820	8,000	1,545*	9,545	195,365
8	195,365	8,000	1,545*	9,545	196,910
9	196,910	8,000	1,545*	9,545	198,455
10	198,455	8,000	1,545*	9,545	200,000

Amortization Table—Straight-Line Method

*Adjusted for rounding error.

the bonds based on the effective interest rate at the time of issuance. The entries to account for bond transactions are the same using the effective-interest amortization method as those illustrated in this unit using the straight-line method.

The straight-line amortization method reports a constant amount of interest expense each period. Exhibit 25.5 illustrates an amortization table for the straight-line amortization method, using the same data as in Exhibit 25.4. Under the straight-line method the bond discount is amortized at the rate of $1,544 every six months. Thus, interest expense is $9,544 every six months ($8,000 + 1,544 = $9,544), except as adjusted for a rounding error. The approximate annual effective interest rate is 9.93%:

$$\frac{\text{annual effective interest expense}}{\text{average book value of bonds}} = \frac{\$9,544 + 9,544}{(\$184,556 + 200,000)/2} = \frac{\$19,088}{\$192,278} = 9.93\%$$

The straight-line method of amortization gives a reasonable approximation of the true interest expense each period and the present value of the bond liability at the beginning of each period if the amount of bond premium or discount is not significant. The method is also less complex, and is, therefore, widely used in accounting practice.

REVIEW QUESTIONS

25-1 What is a bond indenture? What is included in a bond indenture?

25-2 What are the roles of an underwriter and a trustee in a bond issue?

25-3 Distinguish between each of the following pairs of terms:

   a. secured and unsecured (debenture) bonds
   b. ordinary and serial bonds
   c. registered and coupon bonds

25-4 Explain what is meant by each of the following bond features:

   a. callable,
   b. redeemable,
   c. convertible.

25-5 Explain why bonds may be issued at a premium or a discount.

25-6 How is a bond premium or a bond discount reported on the balance sheet?

25-7 Why should a bond premium or a bond discount be amortized? What is the effect of the amortization of a bond premium on the interest expense recorded for a period? Of the amortization of a bond discount?

25-8 How is accrued interest on bonds accounted for when bonds are issued later than the date of the bonds or are sold between interest payment dates?

25-9 How is the effective interest rate of a bond issue determined if the bond premium or bond discount is amortized equally over the period the bonds are outstanding?

25-10 What is a long-term fund?

25-11 How can the size of the equal, periodic contributions to a bond sinking fund be determined?

25-12 At balance sheet date a bond sinking fund consists of the following assets: investments, $36,750; interest receivable on investments, $450; cash, $800. How are these bond sinking fund assets disclosed on the balance sheet?

25-13 How are a bond sinking fund and a bond liability classified on the balance sheet if the bonds are to be redeemed within one year after balance sheet date?

25-14 Describe the effective-interest method of amortizing bond premium or bond discount. Why is the effective-interest amortization method considered more conceptually correct than the straight-line amortization method?

25-15 What types of restrictions are included in a bond indenture? How are bond restrictions disclosed in the financial statements?

EXERCISES

25-1 Heather Corp. is issuing bonds with a par value of $100,000, a term of 10 years, and interest of 7% payable semiannually. Determine the cash proceeds from the issuance of the bonds if they are issued to yield (a) 7%, (b) 6%, or (c) 8%. (The factors for the present value of $1 and the present value of an annuity for $1 for 20 periods at $3^1/2$% are .5026 and 14.2124, respectively.)

25-2 Brigand Corp. issued bonds with a par value of $200,000, a term of 10 years, and interest of 8% payable semiannually on January 1 and July 1. If the bonds were issued on January 1, 19x1, at par, prepare the entries required on January 1, July 1, and December 31, 19x1.

25-3 Refer to the data in exercise 25-2. Assume that the Brigand Corp. bonds were issued at 102 on January 1, 19x1, the date of the bonds.

    Required **a.** Prepare the entries required on January 1, July 1, and December 31, 19x1.
                   b. Prepare a partial balance sheet and a partial income statement at the end of 19x1.
                   c. Determine the approximate annual effective interest rate.

25-4 Refer to the data in exercise 25-2. Assume that the Brigand Corp. bonds were issued at 97 on January 1, 19x1, the date of the bonds.

    Required **a.** Prepare the entries required on January 1, July 1, and December 31, 19x1.
                   b. Prepare a partial balance sheet and a partial income statement at the end of 19x1.
                   c. Determine the approximate annual effective interest rate.

25-5 Keller Company issued bonds with a par value of $100,000 for $98,550 plus accrued interest on March 1, 19x1. The bonds are dated January 1, 19x1, pay interest semiannually on January 1 and July 1, and have a term of 5 years. The stated interest rate is 9%. Prepare the entries required on March 1, July 1, and December 31, 19x1.

25-6 Clementine Corp. is required to establish a bond sinking fund to retire a $500,000 bond issue on December 31, 19x8. Eight equal, annual contributions are to be made to the fund starting December 31, 19x1. The sinking fund investments are expected to earn 6% annually. During 19x2 and 19x8, sinking fund income was $3,000 and $25,000, respectively. The sinking fund balance at December 31, 19x8, before the last contribution by the company, but after the recognition of sinking fund income for 19x8, was $450,068.

    Required **a.** Prepare the entries required on December 31, 19x1, 19x2, and 19x8, to make the annual contribution to the sinking fund and to recognize sinking fund income for the year.
                   b. Prepare a partial balance sheet and a partial income statement at the end of 19x2.

25-7 Konn Company issued bonds with a par value of 100,000 to yield 8%. The bonds have a stated interest rate of 9%, which is payable semiannually on June 30 and December 31. The term of the bonds is 10 years.

Required **a.** Determine the cash proceeds from the issuance of the bonds.
b. Determine the effective interest expense for the first two interest periods if the company uses (1) the effective-interest amortization method and (2) the straight-line amortization method.

PROBLEMS

25-1 Calamity Corp. issued bonds with a par value of $500,000 on the date of the bonds, January 1, 19x1. The bonds have a stated interest rate of 8%, which is payable semiannually on January 1 and July 1. The term of the bonds is 10 years. Three cases are to be considered regarding the issue price of the bonds:

Case A: Bonds are issued at par.
Case B: Bonds are issued at 103.
Case C: Bonds are issued at 98.

Required **a.** Prepare the entries required at January 1, July 1, and December 31, 19x1, for each case.
b. Prepare a partial balance sheet and a partial income statement at the end of 19x1 for each case.
c. Prepare the entry required at the maturity date of the bonds for each case.

25-2 Bailee Corp. issued bonds with a par value of $1,000,000 on March 1, 19x1. The bonds are dated January 1, 19x1, and mature 10 years after this date. The annual interest rate is 9%. The bonds pay interest semiannually on January 1 and July 1. The cash proceeds from the issuance of the bonds were $1,032,700 including accrued interest.

Required **a.** Prepare all entries necessary for the period January 1, 19x1, through January 1, 19x2.
b. Prepare a partial balance sheet and a partial income statement at the end of 19x1.

25-3 Refer to the data in problem 25-2. Assume that the cash proceeds from the issuance of the bonds were $976,400 plus accrued interest.

Required **a.** Prepare all entries necessary for the period January 1, 19x1, through January 1, 19x2.
b. Prepare a partial balance sheet and a partial income statement at the end of 19x1.

25-4 Cannon Company issued bonds with a par value of $600,000, a stated interest rate of 8%, and a term of 10 years. The bonds are dated January 1, 19x1, and pay interest semiannually on January 1 and July 1. The bonds were issued on May 1, 19x1, for $587,000 including accrued interest. The straight-line method of amortizing bond premium or discount is used.

Required   Determine:

a.   the amount of accrued interest paid when the bonds were issued on May 1, 19x1

b.   the amount of bond discount when the bonds were issued

c.   the semiannual interest payment

d.   the amount of bond discount amortized each month

e.   the annual effective interest expense

f.   the approximate annual effective interest rate

25-5   Tulip Corp. issued bonds with a par value of $200,000 on March 31, 19x1. The bonds are dated January 1, 19x1. Interest is payable semiannually on June 30 and December 31. The bonds mature on December 31, 19x9. The annual interest rate is 8%. The cash proceeds from the issuance of the bonds were $209,850 including accrued interest.

Required   a.   Prepare the entries necessary through the end of 19x1.

b.   Prepare a partial balance sheet and a partial income statement at the end of 19x1.

25-6   The Flyte Corporation issued a $500,000 bond issue at the beginning of 19x1. The bonds mature at the end of 19x5, have a stated interest rate of 9%, and pay interest semiannually on June 30 and December 31. The bonds were issued to yield 8% annually. The cash proceeds from the issuance of the bonds were $520,275. The bond indenture has a provision for a bond sinking fund. Annual contributions to the fund are to be made to a trustee at the end of each year starting December 31, 19x1. The fund investments are expected to earn 5% annually.

Required   a.   Calculate the interest expense and the amortization of bond premium at June 30 and December 31, 19x1, using (1) the effective-interest and (2) the straight-line amortization methods.

b.   Calculate the approximate annual effective interest rate if the straight-line amortization method is used. •

c.   Calculate the amount of each annual contribution to the sinking fund.

d.   Calculate the sinking fund balance at December 31, 19x2, if earnings on fund investments for 19x2 are $4,710.

25-7   Michigander Company issued bonds with a par value of $200,000 to yield 8%. The bonds have a stated interest rate of 7%, a term of 5 years, and pay interest semiannually on June 30 and December 31.

Required   Determine:

a.   the cash proceeds from the issuance of the bonds on the date of the bonds

b.   the amount of bond discount at the date of the bonds

c.   the amount of each semiannual interest payment

d.   the effective interest expense recorded on June 30 and December 31 of the first year if bond discount is amortized by (1) the effective-interest method and (2) the straight-line method

e.   the annual effective interest rate if bond discount is amortized by (1) the effective-interest method and (2) the straight-line method

Chapter 9

Owners' Equity

In this chapter accounting for owners' equity in corporate businesses is examined in detail. Several measurement and reporting problems are also discussed.

Unit 26
Fundamentals of Corporate Owners' Equity

A corporation is an artificial being, invisible, intangible, and existing only in contemplation of law. Being the mere creature of law, it possesses only those properties which the charger of its creation confers upon it, either expressly, or as incidental to its very existence.

Chief Justice Marshall, Dartmouth College *v*. Woodward, 1819

The characteristics of the corporate form of business are described in this unit and contrasted with those of the noncorporate forms of business. The types of stock that corporations issue and their characteristics are also described. Finally, measurement and reporting problems involved in issuing stock are discussed and illustrated.

Performance Objectives

Upon completion of this unit you should be able to:

1. define and use the accounting terms introduced in this unit.
2. describe or explain:
    a. the characteristics of the corporate form of business
    b. the advantages and/or disadvantages of the corporate form of business
    c. the types of stock issued by corporations and/or the features of each type of stock
    d. how to account for the issuance of stock for cash and noncash assets
    e. how the contributed capital accounts of a corporation are reported on the balance sheet
3. prepare the correct journal entry for transactions to issue stock for cash or noncash assets.
4. prepare the contributed capital section of stockholders' equity for a balance sheet.

Characteristics of Corporate vs. Noncorporate Forms of Business

A **corporation** is a legal entity separate from its owners. Legal liability for the corporation's debts, therefore, is generally limited to the owners' investment. As a legal entity, a corporation can own property, be sued, sue others, and enter into contracts on its own. Partnerships and sole proprietorships are not legal entities separate from their owners. Partners and sole proprietors have unlimited liability for the debts of their businesses; thus, creditors can seek recovery of partnership or proprietorship debts from the owners. It is the partners or proprietor who own property and it is they who enter into contracts—not the business. Also, the partners or proprietor, not the business entity, sue or are sued by others.

Corporations can usually accumulate larger sums of resources because they can issue stock and bonds widely to many investors. Partnerships and proprietorships are limited to the resources of the partners or proprietors.

Ownership interests in a corporation can be easily transferred. Shares of stock can be sold by one investor (or owner) to another without affecting the operations of the business. Partnership and proprietorship interests are not readily transferable; when such interests are transferred, there may be a disruption in business operations.

Corporations, especially larger ones, are frequently managed by individuals other than the primary owners of the company. Small corporations are normally owned by one or a few individuals who are active in management. Partnerships and sole proprietorships, however, are usually managed by the partners and proprietors, who are the owners.

In partnerships and proprietorships business profits accrue and losses are absorbed directly by the partners (according to their profit-loss sharing agreement) and the proprietors. The owners are taxed on their share of business income; the businesses are not taxed directly on income they earn. In a corporation, however, stockholders do not have a direct claim on the profits earned by the business, although they do have the right to share in profits when dividends are declared by the **board of directors.** Income earned by a corporation, therefore, is first taxed to the company; then, when dividends are paid to stockholders, the dividends are taxed as income a second time to the stockholders.

The limited liability of stockholders, the ability to accumulate large sums of resources, and the ease of transferring ownership interests are characteristics of a corporation usually considered to be advantages over the partnership and sole proprietorship forms of business. The opportunity to manage the business actively can be achieved in any of the three forms of business. However, as the number of stockholders in a corporation increases, the opportunity for them to have an active role in management diminishes. Stockholders select the board of directors of a corporation; they then determine who will manage the business. In partnerships and proprietorships, the owners determine directly who will manage the business. Some individuals consider direct control over the business an advantage of partnerships and proprietorships. Others consider professional management, which is typical of larger corporations, an advantage of the corporate form of business.

Many individuals consider the double taxation of income to be a disadvantage of the corporate form of business. This is especially true when stock ownership is widely distributed among stockholders who are not considered wealthy. Partners and proprietors, however, may have a tax advantage if they are not in high income brackets, because individuals are generally taxed at lower rates than corporations. If they are in higher income brackets, there may be a tax advantage for them in the corporate form of business.

Corporate Organization

To form a corporation an application for a **charter** must be filed with the state in which the company is to be incorporated. This application requires such information as the name of the corporation, type of business, purpose or goals of the business, types of stock to be authorized, amounts of stock to be authorized, names and addresses of the initial stockholders, and names of the board of directors. When the application is approved, the state issues a charter to the company, which is then recognized as a corporation and, thus, as a separate legal entity. The charter is also known as the *articles of incorporation.*

In addition to the charter, **bylaws** or regulations are adopted by the board of directors. The bylaws specify the frequency of directors' meetings, the place and date of the annual stockholders' meeting, the method of selecting directors and officers of the company, the duties and powers of the directors, and so on.

The charter and the bylaws define the scope of business activities and provide guidelines for the management of the business. The board of directors, elected by the stockholders, provides general guidance and sets general operating policies for the corporation. Major decisions, such as those involving issuing bonds, authorizing new stock, business combinations, and stock splits, and declaring dividends must be approved by the board. The board is also responsible for selecting management, which is responsible for the day-to-day operations of the business.

Types and Features of Stock

A **stock certificate** is issued as evidence of an individual's ownership interest in a corporation. The certificate gives the name of the stockholder, the number of shares represented by the certificate, the date of the certificate, the type of stock owned, and the characteristics of the stock. (See Figure 26.1.) The back of the stock certificate has instructions and spaces to be completed when the shares are transferred to another party.

Two types or classes of stock may be issued by a corporation: common stock and preferred stock. When two classes of stock are issued, one receives certain preferences over the other. This class of stock is called **preferred stock.** The other or normal class of stock is called **common stock.** When only one class of stock is issued, it is the

L 3964

Figure 26.1   Example of a stock certificate

normal class of stock, or common stock. Smaller companies usually issue only common stock. Large companies often issue both. And some companies issue two or more kinds of preferred stock, each with different preferences or privileges.

Each share of common stock provides four basic rights to the shareholder:

1. the right to vote to select the board of directors and to vote on other matters, such as the selection of auditors, approving officer stock options, changing thc charter, and so on, at the annual stockholders' meeting; usually each share of stock has one vote.
2. the right to receive a proportionate share of dividends when they are declared by the board of directors.
3. the right to receive a proportionate share of the remaining assets if the corporation liquidates.
4. the right to acquire a proportionate share of any new authorization of stock of the same class in order to maintain his or her percentage of ownership in the business; this is called the **preemptive right.**

In most states preferred stock gives up the voting right in exchange for one or more of the following privileges or preferences:

1. dividend preferences
2. asset preferences
3. conversion privileges

Dividend Preferences   Preferred stockholders receive a specified dividend each period before dividends can be paid to common stockholders. In addition, preferred stock is usually guaranteed that if the current dividend is not paid when due, it will be made up in future periods before dividends are paid to common stockholders. This is called the **cumulative feature,** and such stock is called **cumulative preferred stock.** Most preferred stock is limited, however, to dividends given at a specified, periodic rate; it will not receive larger dividends even if common stockholders do. This is called the **nonparticipating feature.** If the preferred stock can participate in dividends beyond the specified periodic rate, it is **participating preferred stock** and will have a *fully participating* or *partially participating* dividend privilege.

Asset Preferences   If a corporation liquidates, the creditors have first claim to the company's assets. After the claims of creditors are settled, the preferred stockholders are entitled to recover their **liquidation value.** If no special amount is specified, the liquidation value of preferred stock will be its par value. After the preferred stockholders recover their liquidation value, any remaining assets are distributed to the common stockholders. The common stockholders' interest in the business is, therefore, often referred to as the *residual equity*.

If the preferred stock is **callable,** that is, can be retired at the option of the corporation, preferred stockholders will be entitled to receive a specified amount per share. This call price is normally greater than the par value per share.

Conversion Privileges   If preferred stock is **convertible,** it can be exchanged for common stock at the option of the stockholders. The terms of conversion are specified in the preferred stock certificate; included are the conversion dates and the conversion ratio. The conversion privilege is included in many preferred stock issues because investors view it as a desirable feature. Preferred stock can usually participate in a corporation's profitability in only a limited way through dividends. However, participation can be increased through the conversion privilege. If a company's profitability increases, preferred stockholders can profit from converting their preferred stock into common stock, which now has greater value. If the company's common stock does not increase in value, the preferred stockholder can hold the preferred stock and receive the specified dividend. The conversion feature is also beneficial to the corporation. The company can sell the preferred stock more readily and thereby raise needed resources. And later, if conversion occurs. the fixed dividend payments will be eliminated.

Most preferred stock has the following characteristics: (1) nonvoting, (2) specified current dividend rate, (3) cumulative dividend privilege, (4) nonparticipation dividend privilege, (5) asset preference upon liquidation or retirement, and (6) conversion privilege.

Par and Stated Value of Stock

Some years ago, state corporation laws required that each class of stock authorized by the charter have a nominal value per share. This nominal value was called the **par value** and was printed on the stock certificate. It was intended not to reflect the market value or selling price of the stock, but rather, to protect creditors by establishing a minimum amount of assets per share that would be retained in the business. The par value concept, however, failed to provide the intended protection. Companies often issued stock for assets that were recorded at inflated values equal to the par value of the shares issued. Also, maintaining a minimum amount of assets in the business is difficult because over time the true value of assets will vary from their recorded values, which are based on acquisition cost.

Because the par value concept was ineffective, state laws started to permit the issuance of no-par-value stock. **No-par-value stock** was intended to avoid the impression of value for the stock that existed when a par value was specified. It was hoped that reasonable values would be determined and assigned to assets acquired by the issue of stock. Also, the entire amount received from the issuance of the stock could be restricted to provide protection to creditors. Some state laws permitted a **stated value** per share to be assigned to no-par-value stock in the charter or by the board of directors. This provision was intended to prevent large sums of capital from becoming permanently frozen until the company liquidated.

Today most new stock issues have a low par value or stated value per share—$1 or less, for example. Establishing a low par or stated value is desirable so the stock can be issued without the problem that might arise if a high par or stated value were assigned to it. That is, in the past stock could be issued at a discount—at a price less than its par or stated value. If this occurred, the stockholder became liable to creditors for the amount of the discount. However, since stock can be transferred frequently, it was difficult to determine who was actually liable for the discount. Today, it is not legal to issue stock initially at a discount, although the subsequent market price can fall below the par or stated value without creating any liability. The problem with high par or stated value stock, then, is that if it cannot be sold for that value, under current laws it cannot be issued at all. Thus, today stocks are usually assigned low par or stated values.

Most state laws require that the par or stated value of all shares issued be designated as the **legal capital** of the corporation. Legal capital normally cannot serve as the basis of dividends (see Unit 27). If no-par-value stock is issued and a stated value is not assigned, the entire amount received from the stock issue will be designated as the legal capital. Some states require that the amounts received in excess of the par or stated value per share also be included in legal capital. Although the par or stated value of stock should be disclosed in the financial statements, in many states there is no requirement for the disclosure of the legal capital amount.

Accounting for the Issuance of Stock

The procedures of accounting for and reporting corporate owners' equity must follow the provisions of the law in the state in which the company is incorporated. Although state laws vary, there are several common provisions.

Stock may be issued for cash, noncash assets, or services. The cost principle provides the guideline for measuring the amount to be recorded whenever stock is issued. Thus, transactions for the issuance of stock are recorded on the basis of the cash proceeds received or the current cash equivalent of either the stock issued or the noncash assets or services received.

In recording transactions affecting owners' equity, separate accounts are used for owners' equity arising from different sources. On the balance sheet the same distinction is maintained; thus, stockholders' equity is classified into two basic sources:

1. **contributed capital**—all capital invested by stockholders is reported in this classification; any capital donated or contributed by other parties is also included.
2. **retained earnings**—all profits earned by the company less any losses incurred and less all dividends paid since the organization of the company are reported in this classification.

Stock Issued for Cash   Whenever stock with a par or stated value is issued, the par or stated value is credited to the stock account. Any amount received in excess of the par or stated value is recorded in a separate contributed capital account. Assume that a company is authorized to issue the following classes of stock: (1) 6% preferred stock, $20 par value, 10,000 shares authorized; and (2) common stock, no par value (with stated value of $10 per share), 30,000 shares authorized. If the company issued 2,000 shares of preferred stock at $21 per share and 5,000 shares of common stock at $13 per share, the entries to record the issuance of the stock would be:

Cash	42,000	
Preferred stock		40,000
Contributed capital in excess of par value, preferred		2,000
To record issuance of preferred stock with a par value of $20 per share ($21 × 2,000 = $42,000; $20 × 2,000 = $40,000; $42,000 − 40,000 = $2,000).		

Cash	65,000	
Common stock		50,000
Contributed capital in excess of stated value,		
common		15,000

To record issuance of no-par-value common stock
with a stated value of $10 per share ($13
× 5,000 = $65,000; $10 × 5,000 = $50,000;
$65,000 − 50,000 = $15,000).

If the no-par-value common stock did not have a stated value, the entire amount received would be recorded in the stock account as follows:

Cash	65,000	
Common stock		65,000

To record issuance of no-par-value common stock
($13 × 5,000 = $65,000).

Stock Issued for Noncash Assets or Services   If noncash assets or services are received in exchange for stock, the amount recorded will be the fair market value of the stock or the fair market value of the noncash assets or services, whichever is more clearly determinable under the circumstances. The transaction therefore will be recorded in accord with the cost principle at the current cash equivalent of the stock issued or the assets or services received.

Assume that the company in the previous illustration issues 100 shares of common stock for legal services incurred in organizing the company, when the stock has a market value of $13 per share. The legal fees will be charged to a deferred charge account for **organization costs** (these costs were discussed in Unit 22). This account is normally amortized over a period of five or more years. The entry to issue the stock would be:

Organization costs	1,300	
Common stock		1,000
Contributed capital in excess of stated value,		
common		300

To issue no-par-value common stock with a stated
value of $10 per share for legal fees incurred
in organizing the company ($13 × 100
= $1,300; $10 × 100 = $1,000; $1,300 − 1,000
= $300).

Because the common stock had a stated value, only the stated value per share was recorded in the common stock account. The excess of the market value over the stated value was recorded in a separate contributed capital account. If the common stock did not have a stated value, the entire market value of the stock would have been recorded in the common stock account.

Reporting Contributed Capital Accounts

Stockholders' equity is reported according to its source in order to conform with the requirements of state law. In the contributed capital section the sequence in which the accounts are reported is: preferred stock, common stock, and other contributed capital accounts. The par or stated value and the number of shares authorized, issued, and outstanding for each class of stock should be disclosed parenthetically or in the footnotes. The preferences or privileges of preferred stock should be disclosed in the same manner.

The terms used in describing a class of stock on the balance sheet are:

authorized—the maximum number of shares of a class of stock the company can issue as specified in the charter.

issued—the number of authorized shares of a class of stock issued by the company since it was organized.

unissued—the number of authorized shares of a class of stock that have not yet been issued by the company.

treasury stock—shares of a class of stock that were issued, but have been reacquired and are being held by the company for future issuance or retirement; thus, they are considered as shares issued but not currently outstanding. (Treasury stock is discussed in Unit 27.)

outstanding—the number of shares of a class of stock issued by the company and still owned by the stockholders; the number of shares issued less the number of shares of treasury stock held by the company.

Exhibit 26.1 illustrates the stockholders' equity section of a balance sheet using data from recent illustrations plus an assumed retained earnings balance of $28,000. Note the sequence in which the contributed accounts are presented and the parenthetical information regarding each class of stock. Because there is no indication of the preferences or privileges of preferred stock, it is assumed that preferred stock is cumulative and nonparticipating, is not convertible or callable, and has a liquidation value equal to its par value of $20 per share. The legal capital amount for the two classes of stock would probably be equal to the par value or stated value of the shares issued, $20,000 for preferred stock and $51,000 for common stock.

Exhibit 26.1

Partial Balance Sheet
December 31, 19x1

Stockholders' equity:
   Contributed capital:

6% preferred stock, $20 par, 10,000 shares authorized, 2,000 shares issued and outstanding	$40,000	
Common stock, no par value, $10 stated value, 30,000 shares authorized, 5,100 shares issued and outstanding	51,000	
Contributed capital in excess of par value, preferred	2,000	
Contributed capital in excess of stated value, common	15,300	
Total contributed capital		$108,300
Retained earnings		28,000
Total stockholders' equity		$136,300

REVIEW PROBLEM

Rallee Corporation was organized at the beginning of 19x1. The charter authorizes the company to issue two classes of stock:

> 5% preferred stock, $25 par value, 10,000 shares authorized; common stock, no par value, $5 stated value, 100,000 shares authorized

The following stock transactions were completed during 19x1:

Feb. 1	Issued 200 shares of preferred stock to a lawyer for services in organizing the company; the bill for legal services was $5,200.
Mar. 15	Paid $10,000 cash, obtained a $40,000 mortgage, and issued 5,000 shares of common stock to acquire land and a building; the land and building were appraised at values of $15,000 and $65,000, respectively.
Apr. 5	Issued 1,000 shares of preferred stock at $26 per share and 10,000 shares of common stock at $7 per share.

Required

1. Record the stock transactions for 19x1.
2. Prepare the stockholders' equity section of the balance sheet at December 31, 19x1, if net income for 19x1 was $27,000 and dividends of $15,000 were declared and paid during 19x1.

Solution to review problem

1. Feb. 1   Organization Costs   5,200
                   Preferred Stock   5,000
                   Contributed Capital in Excess of
                       Par Value, Preferred   200
               To issue preferred stock for legal
               services incurred in organizing the
               company ($25 × 200 = $5,000;
               $5,200 − 5,000 = $200).

Note   The market value of the stock is unknown; thus, the amount of the bill for the services is the basis for recording the transaction.

       Mar. 15   Land   15,000
                  Building   65,000
                      Cash   10,000
                      Mortgage Payable   40,000
                      Common Stock   25,000
                      Contributed Capital in Excess of
                          Stated Value, Common   5,000
                  To acquire land and building for cash, a
                  mortgage, and common stock.

Note   The market value of the stock is unknown; thus, the market value of the assets acquired is used as the basis for the entry. After deducting the amount of the cash and the mortgage from the value of the assets acquired, $30,000 ($15,000 + 65,000 − 10,000 − 40,000) remains to be assigned to the stock, $25,000 to the stock account ($5 × 5,000 = $25,000), and $5,000 to a contributed capital account for the amount in excess of stated value.

       Apr. 5   Cash   26,000
                     Preferred Stock   25,000
                     Contributed Capital in Excess of
                         Par Value, Preferred   1,000
                 To issue preferred stock at $26 per
                 share ($26 × 1,000 = $26,000; $25
                 × 1,000 = $25,000; $26,000
                 − 25,000 = $1,000).

Apr. 5	Cash	70,000	
	Common Stock		50,000
	Contributed Capital in Excess of Stated Value		20,000

To issue common stock at $7 per share
($7 × 10,000 = $70,000; $5
× 10,000 = $50,000; $70,000 − 50,000
= $20,000).

2.

Rallee Corporation
Partial Balance Sheet
December 31, 19x1

Stockholders' equity:		
Contributed capital:		
5% preferred stock, $25 par value, 10,000 shares authorized, 1,200 shares issued and outstanding	$30,000	
Common stock, no par value, $5 stated value, 100,000 shares authorized, 15,000 shares issued and outstanding	75,000	
Contributed capital in excess of par value, preferred	1,200	
Contributed capital in excess of stated value, common	25,000	
Total contributed capital		$131,200
Retained earnings		12,000
Total stockholders' equity		$143,200

Note Retained earnings equals net income less dividends to date: $27,000 − 15,000 = $12,000.

SUMMARY

The characteristics of corporations and the types of stock issued by them were examined in this unit. Also, the problems of accounting for the issuance of stock and of reporting owners' equity on a balance sheet were discussed and illustrated. The next two units focus on the problems of accounting for and reporting changes in contributed capital and retained earnings.

REVIEW QUESTIONS

26-1 What characteristics distinguish a corporation from a partnership or a sole proprietorship?

26-2 Explain what is meant by each of the following terms:

a. charter   c. bylaws
b. articles of incorporation   d. stock certificate

26-3 Identify the two types or classes of stock that a corporation may issue, and distinguish between them.

26-4 What are the four basic rights of common stockholders?

26-5 a. What are the usual preferences or privileges that preferred stockholders receive?
b. What rights do preferred stockholders usually surrender and what limitations do they accept in return for the preferences or privileges referred to in part a?

26-6 a. What is the purpose of establishing a par or stated value per share of stock?
b. What is the relationship between a stock's par or stated value and its market value?
c. What is the relationship between a stock's par or stated value and the legal capital provision contained in a state's corporation laws?

26-7 Stockholders' equity must be divided and disclosed according to its sources. Two basic sources of stockholders' equity are usually disclosed on a balance sheet. Identify these two basic sources and explain what is represented by each.

26-8 When stock is issued for an amount in excess of its par or stated value, how should an entity account for the excess?

26-9 How should an entity account for the proceeds from the issuance of stock that has neither a par nor a stated value?

26-10 What is the appropriate basis for measuring the amount to be recorded for assets or services and for stock when stock is issued in exchange for noncash assets or services?

26-11 Distinguish among the following terms used to describe the status of a class of stock on the balance sheet:

a. authorized shares   d. treasury stock (or shares)
b. issued shares   e. outstanding shares
c. unissued shares

26-12 What information should be disclosed parenthetically or in footnotes to the balance sheet regarding each class of stock a corporation is authorized to issue?

EXERCISES

26-1 Valentine Corp. was authorized to issue 1,000 shares of $50 par value, 6% preferred stock and 20,000 shares of $10 par value common stock when the company was organized at the beginning of 19x1. During 19x1 the company issued 800 shares of preferred stock at par, 6,000 shares of common stock at $12 per share, and 5,000 shares of common stock at $13 per share. At the end of 19x1 the market value of preferred stock and common stock was $50 and $14 per share, respectively. Net income for 19x1 was $35,000. Dividends of $3 per share on preferred stock and $.50 per share on common stock were declared and paid during 19x1.

Required   **a.**   Prepare the entries to issue preferred stock and common stock during 19x1.

b.   Prepare the stockholders' equity section of the balance sheet at December 31, 19x1.

26-2   Turkee Corp. was authorized to issue 50,000 shares of no-par common stock when the company was organized at the beginning of 19x4. During 19x4 the company issued 28,000 shares of common stock at $15 per share. A net loss of $21,000 was reported for 19x4.

Required   **a.**   Prepare the entry to issue common stock if the stock is assigned (1) a stated value of $1 per share and (2) no stated value.

b.   Prepare the stockholders' equity section of the balance sheet at December 31, 19x4, for each case in part a.

26-3   Egge Company was organized at the beginning of 19x5 and is authorized to issue 100,000 shares of $5 par value common stock. During 19x5 the company issued stock as follows:

a.   200 shares to a lawyer for services in incorporating the business; the lawyer's fee was $2,500.

b.   25,000 shares for cash at $13 per share.

c.   1,500 shares for land when the market value of the stock was $14 per share; the value of the land was estimated to be between $20,000 and $25,000.

During 19x5 the company paid dividends of $.10 per share. Net income for 19x5 was $15,000.

Required   **(1)**   Prepare the entries to issue stock for 19x5.

(2)   Prepare the stockholders' equity section of the balance sheet at December 31, 19x5.

26-4   Pillor Company is authorized to issue 100,000 shares of no-par common stock. The stock has a stated value of $5 per share. Several stock transactions have taken place:

a.   10,000 shares were issued at $16 per share.

b.   100 shares were issued to an attorney who submitted a bill for $1,800 for helping the company incorporate.

c.   3,000 shares were issued and $15,000 cash was paid for a plant site; the land had an assessed value of $32,000; assessed values are 50% of "true" market values.

d.   5,000 shares were issued at $17 per share.

e.   2,000 shares were issued to acquire a patent; the current market value of the stock was $17.50 per share.

f.   1,000 shares were issued and $10,000 cash was paid to acquire additional land; the seller was asking $30,000 for the land, which had an assessed value of $14,500.

Required   Using the following form, indicate the amount to be recorded in each account. Also, indicate the reason for selecting the amount for any asset acquired in an exchange of stock for noncash assets or services.

	Asset Acquired		Stock Issued	
Transaction	Title	Amount	Common Stock	Contributed Capital in Excess of Stated Value

PROBLEMS

26-1   Hannibal Company is authorized to issue the following classes of stock:

5% preferred stock, $100 par value, 2000 shares, cumulative, and nonparticipating
Common stock, no par value, $10 stated value, 50,000 shares

The following stock transactions occurred during 19x1, the first year of business operations:

Apr. 1   Received a bill for $5,100 from a lawyer for services in promoting and incorporating the business; issued 50 shares of preferred stock in full settlement of the bill.
Apr. 15   Issued 850 shares of preferred stock at $101 per share.
May 10   Issued 15,000 shares of common stock at $12 per share.
May 21   Paid $120,000 cash and issued 7,500 shares of common stock for land and a building; the land and building had assessed values of $15,000 and $85,000, respectively; the stock has a market value of $12 per share.

The only dividends during the year were paid to preferred stockholders in the amount of $3.75 per share. Net income for 19x1 was $39,000.

Required   **a.**   Prepare the entries to issue stock during 19x1.
                    b.   Prepare the stockholders' equity section of the balance sheet at December 31, 19x1.

26-2   Bridges, Inc., is authorized to issue 100,000 shares of common stock. Selected data from the stockholders' equity section of the balance sheet at December 31, 19x6, are:

Common stock, no par value, 45,000 shares issued and outstanding	$?
Total contributed capital	525,000
Total stockholders' equity	640,000

During 19x7 the company issued 10,000 shares at $15 per share and exchanged 2,000 shares for land with a fair market value of $32,000. Net income for 19x7 was $120,000, and dividends totaling $57,000 were declared and paid during 19x7.

Required   Prepare the stockholders' equity section of the balance sheet at December 31, 19x7, if the common stock has (a) no stated value and (b) a $10 per share stated value.

26-3   Penn Corp. is authorized to issue 20,000 shares of 6% preferred stock with a par value of $25 per share and 100,000 shares of common stock with a par value of $10 per share. The balance sheet at December 31, 19x6, indicated the following:

6% preferred stock	$150,000
Common stock	250,000
Contributed capital in excess of par:	
Preferred stock	9,000
Common stock	75,000
Retained earnings	86,000
Total stockholders' equity	$570,000

The company is planning to acquire land and a building to expand business operations during 19x7. Three alternative plans are being considered to make the purchase:

Plan A   Purchase the land and building for $55,000 cash and a $200,000, 9% mortgage for 20 years.

Plan B   Purchase the land and building for $120,000 cash and 6,000 shares of preferred stock with a current market value of $26 per share.

Plan C   Purchase the land and building for $50,000 cash and 15,000 shares of common stock with a current market value of $14 per share.

Penn Corp. reported net income of $36,000 for 19x6. After expansion of business operations, net income is expected to average $60,000 under plans B and C or $51,000 under plan A. The company expects to continue paying dividends of $.60 per share annually on common stock.

Required **a.** Determine the number of shares of preferred stock and common stock outstanding at December 31, 19x6.

b. Determine the average price at which preferred stock and common stock have been issued.

c. What will be the impact of each plan for the purchase of the land and building on the financial position of Penn Corp.?

    d.   What factors should be considered in determining which plan for the purchase of the land and building should be selected?

    e.   Prepare the stockholders' equity section of the balance sheet at December 31, 19x7, if plan C is selected and net income for 19x7 is $66,000. Assume that the regular dividends on preferred and common stock were paid in 19x7.

26-4   The following data were taken from the 1977 annual report of Hershey Foods Corporation (some figures were rounded off to simplify this problem):

Total assets at December 31, 1977	$396,153,000
Total liabilities at December 31, 1977	$136,485,000
Retained earnings, December 31, 1976	$217,775,000
Dividends per share of common stock	$1.14
Earnings per share of common stock	$3.01
Number of shares of common stock outstanding at December 31, 1977	13,730,000

The company is authorized to issue 20,000,000 shares of no-par-value common stock. In 1976 the board of directors restated the value of common stock to $1 per share. Assume that the number of shares of common stock outstanding did not change during 1977.

Required   Prepare the stockholders' equity section of the balance sheet at the end of 1977.

Unit 27
Treasury Stock, Dividends, and Stock Splits

The notion of vast accumulations of profits, waiting somewhere to be tapped, is a dangerous fiction. It conceals the fact that one of our most pressing needs is for greater profitability—to help finance the economic expansion on which the higher productivity, higher employment and higher tax revenues all depend. Every new social experiment, and every forward step, will take time and money, and the costs will have to be balanced against the other demands of a society already up in arms over the level of taxation. As for the corporation, its major responsibility in our society is to continue to perform its classic function of creating the wealth needed to underwrite the costs of change.

Robert C. Gunness, president, Standard Oil Company of Indiana

Corporations may engage in a variety of transactions, other than issuing new stock for cash, noncash assets, or services, that will affect its contributed capital and/or retained earnings. These transactions include acquiring and reissuing treasury stock, declaring cash or stock dividends, and declaring stock splits. The accounting procedures and reporting practices for these transactions are discussed and illustrated in this unit.

Performance Objectives

Upon completing this unit you should be able to:

1. define and use the accounting terms introduced in this unit.
2. explain or describe:
    a. how to account for acquisition and reissue of treasury stock
    b. how to report treasury stock, contributed capital from treasury stock transactions, and related restrictions on retained earnings on the balance sheet

   c.   the distinctions between the effects on stockholders' equity of small stock dividends, large stock dividends, and stock splits

   d.   how to account for small stock dividends, large stock dividends, or stock splits

   e.   the requirements for declaring a cash dividend

3.   prepare the correct journal entry for selected transactions for treasury stock, cash dividends, and stock dividends.

4.   prepare the stockholders' equity section of a balance sheet in proper form.

Accounting for Treasury Stock

Corporations may acquire shares of their own stock that have been issued and are outstanding for any of the following reasons:

1. To obtain shares of stock needed for employee stock options, stock purchase plans, or bonuses
2. To obtain shares of stock needed to acquire control of other companies or to acquire certain plant or intangible assets or services
3. To reduce the number of shares outstanding and thereby influence the market price of the stock
4. To increase earnings per share on the stock that remains outstanding
5. To acquire shares from dissatisfied stockholders
6. To acquire shares when market prices are low and reissue the shares when market prices increase; thus, additional capital is raised without issuing new shares of stock
7. To acquire shares that will be retired at a later date
8. To acquire shares that can be used as a dividend on another class of stock

In most of these situations the stock is needed because the number of unissued shares is not sufficient for the intended use. A new authorization of stock would have to be approved by current stockholders to issue new shares; they would have to be allowed, then, to exercise their preemptive right. Thus, the surest and most expedient way to obtain the needed shares is to acquire them in the marketplace from current stockholders. A company may also want to increase earnings per share to encourage more active trading in its stock and pave the way for additional stock issues.

Acquisition of Treasury Stock   Stock reacquired by the issuing corporation is called **treasury stock.** While treasury stock is held by the corporation, it has no voting, dividend, or other stockholders' rights. When the stock is acquired by the corporation, a contra account, "treasury stock," is debited for the cost of the shares. This method of accounting for treasury stock is known as the *cost method.*[1] The effect of acquiring treasury stock is to decrease the number of shares outstanding, the total stockholders' equity, and the total assets, and to increase earnings per share on shares that remain outstanding. Most states limit the number of shares of treasury stock that may be acquired. This limitation may be in the form of a restriction on retained earnings equal to the cost of the treasury stock held by the corporation. The purpose of the restriction

---

[1]An alternate method debits treasury stock for the par value of the shares; this par value method is not widely used and is more complex. It is covered in intermediate accounting courses. Only the cost method will be covered in this text.

is to protect the rights of the creditors—their rights will be jeopardized as assets are used to acquire treasury stock if the value of the remaining assets is insufficient to satisfy their claims against the company.

Assume that on July 1, 19x4, Madd Corp. reacquires at $14 per share, 1,000 of its 20,000 outstanding shares of $10 par value common stock. The entry to record the acquisition of the treasury stock would be:

July 1, 19x4	Treasury Stock	14,000	
	Cash		14,000
	To acquire 1,000 shares of treasury stock at $14 per share ($14 × 1,000 = $14,000).		

If a balance sheet is prepared while treasury stock is held by the corporation, the treasury stock account is deducted from the total of contributed capital and retained earnings (see Exhibit 27.1). Note that total stockholders' equity decreases $14,000, that is, by the cost of the treasury stock held. There is also a $14,000 decrease in total assets because cash was used to acquire the treasury stock. The number of shares of stock outstanding decreases from 20,000 to 19,000, thereby increasing earnings per share. For example, if net income for the year was $38,000, earnings per share on 19,000 shares is $2 compared to $1.90 if all 20,000 shares are outstanding. If state law requires a restriction on retained earnings, it can be disclosed in the footnotes (or through an appropriated retained earnings account—see Unit 28). This restriction is usually equal to the cost of the treasury stock held (see Exhibit 27.1).

Reissuance of Treasury Stock   If treasury stock is reissued at a price in excess of its cost, the excess over cost is credited to a contributed capital account. For example, assume that 600 shares of the treasury stock acquired by Madd Corp. are reis-

Exhibit 27.1

Stockholders' equity:	
Common stock, $10 par, 20,000 shares authorized and issued,	
19,000 shares outstanding, 1,000 shares held as treasury stock	$200,000
Contributed capital in excess of par	50,000
Total contributed capital	$250,000
Retained earnings (see note 1)	175,000
Total	$425,000
Less: Treasury stock, 1,000 shares at cost	14,000
Total stockholders' equity	$411,000

Note 1: Retained earnings in the amount of $14,000 is restricted in accordance with state law regarding treasury stock.

sued at $17 per share on August 1, 19*x4*. The entry to record this transaction would be:

Aug. 1,	Cash	10,200	
19*x4*	Treasury Stock		8,400
	Contributed Capital from Treasury		
	Stock Transactions		1,800
	To reissue treasury stock at a price in		
	excess of its cost ($17 × 600		
	= $10,200; $14 × 600 = $8,400;		
	$10,200 − 8,400 = $1,800).		

Reissuing the treasury stock has the opposite effect as acquiring it. The number of shares outstanding, the total assets, and the total stockholders' equity increase, and earnings per share decrease. These effects are the same whether the treasury stock is reissued at a price above or below cost. However, if all the treasury stock is reissued for an amount less than its total cost, the total assets and total stockholders' equity will be less after the reissue.

When treasury stock is reissued below its cost, the difference should be charged to the contributed capital from the treasury stock transactions account. If the credit balance of this account is not sufficient to absorb the charge or if there is no balance in the account, the retained earnings account should be charged. This procedure is followed so a debit balance does not result in a contributed capital account. Assume that the remaining 400 shares of treasury stock held by Madd Corp. are reissued at $12 per share on September 15, 19*x4*. Because the credit balance in the contributed capital from the treasury stock transactions account is sufficient to absorb the "loss" in reissuing the treasury stock, the entry for the reissue of the remaining 400 shares of treasury stock would be:

Sept. 15,	Cash	4,800	
19*x4*	Contributed Capital from Treasury		
	Stock Transactions	800	
	Treasury Stock		5,600
	To reissue 400 shares of treasury stock		
	below cost ($14 × 400 = $5,600;		
	$12 × 400 = $4,800; $5,600 − 4,800		
	= $800).		

After all treasury stock is reissued, there is a balance of $1,000 ($1,800 − 800) in the contributed capital account from treasury stock transactions. It is reported after the stock account(s) along with the contributed capital in excess of par value account and any other contributed capital accounts.

Because treasury stock was reissued for a net "gain" of $1,000, the total assets and total stockholders' equity have increased $1,000 over the amounts reported before the treasury stock transactions occurred. As the treasury stock is reissued, the restriction on retained earnings is eliminated. After the September 15, 19x4, transaction, there is no further restriction on retained earnings.

The "gain" or "loss" realized in reissuing treasury stock is credited or charged to the contributed capital or retained earnings accounts. They are not involved with determining net income on the income statement because transactions involving the issuance of stock are intended to raise capital, not generate revenue.

Dividends

Most **dividends** are paid in the form of cash or stock of the same class held by the stockholders. However, other assets can be distributed as a dividend. If the term *dividend* is used by itself, it is considered to refer to a cash dividend. Dividends payable in stock or other assets are stated in a manner to reflect the type of dividend distributed.

Three dates are important to the corporation when the board of directors declares a dividend:

1. **date of declaration**—the date on which the board declares a dividend; the corporation becomes legally obligated to pay a cash dividend on this date; thus, a liability must be recorded on the date of declaration.
2. **date of record**—the date on which stockholders eligible to receive the dividend will be determined; stockholders registered on the stockholder records on this date receive the dividend check; no entry is required on this date.
3. **date of payment**—the date on which stockholders are to be paid the dividend; an entry is required on the corporation's books for the payment of the dividend.

Accounting for Cash Dividends   A **cash dividend** is a distribution of a corporation's profits in cash to the stockholders. The amount of the dividend may be charged directly to retained earnings or to a temporary account, dividends paid. This temporary account will be closed out to retained earnings at the end of the period. Thus, the eventual effect of the dividend is the same in either case, that is, it reduces cash, total assets, retained earnings, and total stockholders' equity.

Assume that Madd Corp. declares a cash dividend of $1.50 per share on its common stock on September 30, 19x4, payable on November 15, 19x4, to stockholders of record on October 20, 19x4. Recall that there are 20,000 shares of common stock outstanding. The total amount of dividends declared will be $30,000 ($1.50 × 20,000). Entries are required on the date of declaration and the date of payment as follows:

Sept. 30,	Dividends Paid (or Retained Earnings)	30,000	
19x4	Dividends Payable		30,000
	To declare cash dividend.		

Nov. 15,	Dividends Payable	30,000	
19x4	Cash		30,000
	To pay dividend declared on September 30, 19x4.		

The liability for the dividend will be classified as a current liability if a balance sheet is prepared between the date of declaration and the date of payment. When the dividend is declared, retained earnings and total stockholders' equity decrease by $30,000. Cash and total assets decrease by $30,000 when the dividend is paid. If the dividends paid account is debited at the date of declaration, the closing entry required at the end of the accounting period would be:

Dec. 31,	Retained Earnings	30,000	
19x4	Dividends Paid		30,000
	To close out the dividends paid account.		

Dividends on Preferred Stock   The current dividend on preferred stock must be declared before any dividend can be declared on common stock for the current period. For example, if preferred stock is to receive a 6% dividend payable quarterly, the board of directors must declare a dividend of 1½% each quarter on preferred stock before any dividend can be declared on common stock for the quarter.

Most preferred stock has a cumulative dividend preference. This feature means that if part or all of the current preferred dividends for a period are not declared, they must be declared in the future before any dividend can be declared on common stock. When the current dividends on **cumulative preferred stock** are not declared, they are said to be *in arrears*. Dividends in arrears are disclosed in a footnote to the financial statements. If preferred stock is **noncumulative,** any undeclared dividends for a period do not have to be made up in the future.

Assume that a company has 10,000 shares of 6%, $25 par value, cumulative preferred stock outstanding. If dividends are in arrears for one quarter, both the dividends in arrears and the current dividend for the next quarter must be declared before any dividend can be declared on common stock. Thus, a 3% dividend of $.75 ($25 × 3%) must be declared instead of the usual quarterly dividend of 1½% or $.375 ($25 × 1½%) per share. The total amount of dividends declared for the next quarter would be $7,500 ($25 × 3% × 10,000). If the preferred stock were noncumulative, there would be no dividends in arrears; thus, only the regular quarterly dividend of $.375 per share would be declared even though the dividend for the previous quarter had not been declared.

Most preferred stock is also nonparticipating. This feature means that the preferred is entitled to only the regular specified dividend rate. For example, preferred stock with a 6% dividend rate payable quarterly is entitled to only a 1½% dividend each quarter. Even if a dividend greater than 1½% is declared on common stock, the dividend on the **nonparticipating preferred stock** would be limited to 1½%. Situations in which preferred stock is partially or fully participating are not common and will not be discussed in this text. (These characteristics were explained in Unit 26.)

Requirements for Cash Dividends   When the board of directors is deciding the amount of cash dividends to declare, a number of factors must be considered. In establishing a dividend policy the board of directors should consider, for instance, the makeup of the stockholders and their investment objectives. Cash dividends are attractive to investors who are looking for a regular, current return on their investment. Other investors, however, are willing to forego current cash dividends for growth in the value of their investment. Another factor to consider is the amount of profits to retain in the business as a means of providing resources for the expansion of business operations. While other sources such as issuing stock or borrowing may be limited, profits can be a continuous source of new resources to the company. Thus, the board must decide what portion of profits to retain in the business and what portion to pay out as dividends.

In declaring any cash dividends the board must consider the following limitations:

1. the sufficiency of the cash balance to pay the dividend and still be able to carry on current operations
2. the sufficiency of retained earnings for the charge for the dividend; most state laws specify that cash dividends can be declared only to the extent of the retained earnings balance
3. any restrictions on dividends resulting from agreements with the company's creditors, for example, a restriction on dividends in a bond contract

To declare a cash dividend on common stock, the board of directors must consider the following additional limitations:

1. dividends in arrears on preferred stock which must be declared before a dividend on common stock can be declared
2. the current dividend on preferred stock which must be declared before a dividend on common stock can be declared
3. any participating dividend feature on preferred stock if common stock is to receive a dividend rate greater than the regular, specified dividend rate received by preferred stock

Stock Dividends and Stock Splits

Corporations may issue stock of the same class to stockholders on a pro rata basis instead of paying cash dividends. This type of dividend is known as a **stock dividend.**

For example, if a company issues a 10 percent stock dividend on its common stock, stockholders will receive one share of common stock for every ten shares they own at the date of record. If a stockholder is to receive less than a full share of stock as a dividend, she may receive a fractional share, the cash equivalent of the fractional share, or warrants representing the fractional share. For example, if a stockholder owns 175 shares of stock and a 10 percent stock dividend is declared, she would be entitled to 17.5 shares (175 × 10%) as a dividend. If fractional shares are not issued, the cash value of the one-half share, based on the market value of the stock at the date of declaration, can be distributed. In other situations, *warrants* for the half share might be distributed to the stockholder; the warrants can be traded to other stockholders or additional warrants can be acquired from other stockholders. The corporation issues a share of stock when warrants equivalent to a full share of stock are turned in by a stockholder.

Effects of Stock Dividends   A stock dividend **capitalizes retained earnings,** that is, transfers retained earnings to the contributed capital accounts. Although the assets and total stockholders' equity of the company are unaffected, the internal change in the composition of stockholders' equity is very important. Once retained earnings are capitalized or transferred to the contributed capital accounts, they are usually permanently unavailable for dividend distributions. Another effect of a stock dividend is to increase the number of shares of stock issued and outstanding. The market value of the stock is unaffected by a "small" stock dividend, but will be decreased by a "large" stock dividend.

The AICPA made the following distinction between "small" and "large" stock dividends in Accounting Research Bulletin No. 43:

1. small stock dividend—one that does not affect the market value of the stock; usually a stock dividend of 25 percent or less will not affect the market price of the stock.
2. large stock dividend—one that reduces the market value of the stock; usually stock dividends greater than 25 percent will reduce the market value of the stock.

Accounting for Stock Dividends   The amount of retained earnings to be capitalized in a stock dividend depends on the distinction between small and large stock dividends. Because small stock dividends have little or no effect on the market value of the stock, the value of the stock issued as a dividend is considered equivalent to the market value of the stock at the date of declaration. Thus, this amount is capitalized in a small stock dividend.

Large stock dividends, on the other hand, reduce the market value of the stock. Thus, many accountants believe that the minimum amount possible should be used as a basis for the entry for a large stock dividend. This minimum amount would be the par or stated value of the stock.

The entry for a stock dividend requires a debit to retained earnings or a temporary account, stock dividends distributed, at the date of declaration. The amount of the debit entry will be determined according to the rules for small and large stock dividends. An account titled "stock dividend to be distributed" should be credited for the par or stated value of the stock. If an amount in excess of the par or stated value is to be capitalized, this excess is credited to the contributed capital in excess of par value account. Assume that Ratte Corp. issues a 10 percent stock dividend on its $10 par value common stock when the market value is $18 per share and 50,000 shares are outstanding. The number of shares to be issued as a dividend is 5,000 (50,000 × 10%). The amount of retained earnings to be capitalized is the market value of the 5,000 shares, that is, $90,000 ($18 × 5,000). The entry required at the date of declaration would be:

Retained Earnings (or Stock Dividends Distributed)	90,000	
Stock Dividend to Be Distributed, Common		50,000
Contributed Capital in Excess of Par Value, Common		40,000
To declare a 10% stock dividend on common stock ($10 × 5,000 = $50,000; $90,000 − 50,000 = $40,000).		

If the temporary account, stock dividends distributed, had been debited, it would be closed out at the end of the accounting period to retained earnings. When a balance sheet is prepared between the date of declaration and the date of payment, the account, stock dividend to be distributed, is classified as part of contributed capital and is listed after the stock account. The entry to issue the stock at the date of payment would be:

Stock Dividend to Be Distributed, Common	50,000	
Common Stock		50,000
To issue common stock on stock dividend at date of payment.		

The entries for the declaration and payment of a large stock dividend are the same, except that only the par or stated value of the stock to be issued is capitalized. Thus, there would be no credit to a contributed capital account for any amount in excess of par or stated value.

Reasons for Stock Dividends   There are two primary reasons for issuing stock dividends: (1) to capitalize retained earnings and (2) to maintain the regular distribution of dividends. When a corporation retains profits in the business, the related resources are invested in various assets used in business operations. These assets are, in effect, permanently invested and unavailable for dividends. Therefore, it is realistic to capitalize the related retained earnings. A stock dividend is a convenient means of doing so. Companies that want to retain a large portion or all of its retained earnings for growth may issue stock dividends regularly. At the same time they might pay small cash dividends, or they might not pay cash dividends at all.

A company with a cash shortage may declare a stock dividend to satisfy the expectation of stockholders for regular dividends. The company's policy of regular dividends is thereby maintained without endangering the short cash supply it needs to carry on current business operations.

Stock Splits   A company may want to have its stock actively traded on the stock market and widely distributed among the public. However, high market prices may discourage some segments of the public from investing in the stock. High prices may also reduce the amount of trading activity. A **stock split** can reduce the market price of the stock and encourage more active trading and wider stock ownerships. In a stock split the number of shares is increased according to a specific ratio, which indicates the multiplier to be used to determine the new amount of stock outstanding. For example, assume that a company declares a 2-for-1 stock split on the 20,000 outstanding shares of its $10 par value common stock. The company will issue 20,000 shares of stock to the stockholders so that 40,000 shares of common stock will now be outstanding (2 times the old number of shares outstanding).

Besides increasing the number of shares authorized, issued, and outstanding, a stock split reduces the par value and market value of the stock. The par value is reduced based on the ratio for the split; for example, in the 2-for-1 split just described the new par value will be $5 per share ($10/2 = $5). The market price will decrease in approximately the same ratio; for example, the new market price after a 2-for-1 stock split will be approximately half the price it was before the split. Actually, the new market price may be a little higher than half because a stock split is usually viewed as a favorable action by the stockholders.

A 100 percent stock dividend would have similar effects on the number of shares outstanding and the market value of the stock as a 2-for-1 stock split. However, a stock dividend capitalizes retained earnings whereas a stock split has no effect on any of the account balances that make up stockholders' equity. Also, a stock dividend has no effect on the number of shares of stock authorized or the par value of the stock. A stock dividend and a stock split should not be confused because they have different effects. The effects of small stock dividends, large stock dividends, and stock splits are summarized in Table 27.1.

Stock Options

Larger corporations frequently offer officers and employees the right to purchase specified amounts of stock at special prices. When this right is offered to the company's officers, it is called a **stock option.** The right of other employees to purchase company stock is included in a **stock purchase plan.** Stock purchase plans are usually noncompensatory in nature. The employees are not considered to have received additional compensation when one of these plans is adopted, and the corporation does not incur any compensation expense. Contributed capital is affected only when shares

Table 27.1

		Effect for Large Stock	Effect for Small Stock
Item Affected	Effect for Stock Split	Dividend	Dividend
		Summary of the Effects of Stock Dividends and Stock Splits	

Item Affected	Effect for Stock Split	Effect for Large Stock Dividend	Effect for Small Stock Dividend
Authorized stock	Increases	Remains the same	Remains the same
Issued and outstanding stock	Increases	Increases	Increases
Par value	Decreases	Remains the same	Remains the same
Market value	Decreases	Decreases	Remains the same or decreases
Balance in stock account	Remains the same	Increases	Increases
Balances in other contributed capital accounts	Remains the same	Remains the same	Increases
Balance in retained earnings	Remains the same	Decreases	Decreases
Total stockholders' equity	Remains the same	Remains the same	Remains the same

are purchased by employees under terms of the plan. The accounting for the issuance of shares is the same as for any other issuance of stock for cash.

Stock options offered to company executives or officers are compensatory in nature. They are considered additional compensation to the executives or officers in lieu of higher salaries and are intended to motivate these individuals to perform at levels that will maintain and improve the company's profitability. However, the true amount of compensation involved has been considered too difficult to measure objectively in monetary terms for many stock option plans. The Accounting Research Bulletins and APB Opinion No. 25 have stated that compensation should be measured and reported only when the fair market value of the stock at a certain date (the date of grant in most cases) is greater than the option price, that is, the price to be paid by the recipient of the option. Because of its complexity, accounting for stock options is not discussed in this text.

All stock option and stock purchase plans require footnote disclosure of the relevant terms of the plan, a description of transactions during the year that have affected the company's contributed capital and/or retained earnings accounts, and the status of the plan at balance sheet date. See Note 4 to the financial statements of Coachmen Industries in the appendix to Unit 6 for an illustration of footnote disclosure of relevant stock option plan information.

REVIEW PROBLEM

Zapp Corp. reported the following stockholders' equity balances at December 31, 19x1:

Contributed capital:			
5% preferred stock, $50 par value, cumulative, nonparticipating,			
10,000 shares authorized, issued, and outstanding		$500,000	
Common stock, $10 par value, 100,000 shares authorized, 65,000			
shares issued and outstanding		650,000	
Contributed capital in excess of par value, common		195,000	
Total contributed capital			$1,345,000
Retained earnings			375,000
Total stockholders' equity			$1,720,000

During 19x2 the company completed the following transactions:

Jan. 20	Acquired 1,000 shares of the preferred stock at $52 per share; the stock will be held as treasury stock.
July 1	All of the treasury stock acquired on January 20 is reissued at $53 per share.
Oct. 1	The board of directors declared a 5% cash dividend on preferred stock and a 10% stock dividend on common stock; both dividends are payable on November 15 to stockholders of record on October 25; the current market value of common stock is $24 per share.
Nov. 15	The dividends declared on October 1 are distributed.
Nov. 30	A 2-for-1 stock split on common stock is declared; the stock split is distributable on December 31 to stockholders of record on December 15.

Required
1. Prepare the entries for each of these transactions.
2. Prepare the stockholders' equity section at December 31, 19x2, if net income for 19x2 is $115,000.

Solution to review problem

1.	Jan. 20	Treasury Stock, Preferred	52,000	
		Cash		52,000
		To acquire treasury stock ($52 × 1,000 = $52,000).		
	July 1	Cash	53,000	
		Treasury Stock, Preferred		52,000
		Contributed Capital from Treasury Stock Transactions		1,000
		To reissue treasury stock in excess of cost ($53 × 1,000 = $53,000; $53,000 − 52,000 = $1,000).		

Oct. 1	Retained Earnings (or Dividends Paid, Preferred	25,000	
	Dividends Payable, Preferred		25,000
	To declare 5% cash dividend on preferred stock ($50 × 5% × 10,000 = $25,000).		

Note   There are 10,000 shares of preferred stock outstanding after the reissue of the treasury stock.

Oct. 1	Retained Earnings (or Stock Dividends Distributed, Common)	156,000	
	Stock Dividend to Be Distributed, Common		65,000
	Contributed Capital in Excess of Par Value, Common		91,000
	To declare 10% stock dividend on common stock ($24 × 6,500 = $156,000; $10 × 6,500 = $65,000; $156,000 − 65,000 = $91,000).		

Note   There were 65,000 shares of common stock outstanding when the 10% stock dividend was declared. Thus, 6,500 shares (65,000 × 10%) are distributed as a dividend. Because it is a small stock dividend, the market value of $24 per share is capitalized.

Nov. 15	Dividends Payable, Preferred	25,000	
	Cash		25,000
	To pay cash dividend on preferred stock.		

Nov. 15	Stock Dividend to be Distributed, Common	65,000	
	Common Stock		65,000
	To issue stock dividend on common stock.		

Nov. 30	No entry is required for the stock split. There will be 143,000 shares of common stock outstanding after the stock split is effective on December 31 [(65,000 + 6,500) × 2 = 143,000].		

2. Contributed capital:

5% preferred stock, $50 par value, cumulative, nonparticipating,		
10,000 shares authorized, issued, and outstanding	$500,000	
Common stock, $5 par value, 200,000 shares authorized, 143,000		
shares issued and outstanding	715,000	
Contributed capital in excess of par, common	286,000	
Contributed capital from treasury stock transactions	1,000	
Total contributed capital		$1,502,000
Retained earnings		309,000
Total stockholders' equity		$1,811,000

Computations

Common stock: $(65,000 + 6,500) \times 2 \times \$10/2 = \$715,000$

Contributed capital in excess of par value, common: $\$195,000 + 91,000 = \$286,000$

Retained earnings: $\$375,000 + 115,000 - 25,000 - 156,000 = \$309,000$

SUMMARY

Accounting for a variety of transactions affecting contributed capital and/or retained earnings was discussed and illustrated in this unit. These transactions included the acquisition and reissuance of treasury stock and the declaration of stock dividends, cash dividends, and stock splits. Certain complexities of accounting for some of these transactions were not discussed because they are beyond the scope of this text.

REVIEW QUESTIONS

27-1 What is the basis for recording treasury stock when it is acquired?

27-2 How is treasury stock disclosed on the balance sheet?

27-3 How should the difference between acquisition cost and the resale price of treasury stock be accounted for when (a) cost exceeds the resale price and (b) cost is less than the resale price?

27-4 **a.** Why do many state laws require that retained earnings be restricted when treasury stock is acquired?

  b. How is this restriction on retained earnings disclosed in the financial statements?

27-5 **a.** Identify the three dates that are important to a corporation in declaring a dividend.

  b. At which of these three dates is an entry required on the books of the corporation?

27-6 What are the limitations that the board of directors of a corporation must consider in declaring cash dividends?

27-7 Distinguish between a small stock dividend and a large stock dividend.

27-8 What is the amount of the charge to retained earnings for a stock dividend?

27-9 How are the following disclosed in the financial statements?

  a. dividends in arrears on preferred stock
  b. a cash dividend that has been declared, but not paid
  c. a stock dividend that has been declared, but not paid

27-10 **a.** What is a stock split?

  b. How is a stock split accounted for on the books of a corporation?

27-11 Indicate the effect of (1) a small stock dividend, (2) a large stock dividend, and (3) a stock split on each of the following:

  a. the par or stated value of stock
  b. the market value of stock
  c. the number of shares authorized
  d. the number of shares issued and outstanding
  e. the contributed capital account balances
  f. the retained earnings balance
  g. the total stockholders' equity

27-12 Why would a corporation declare (a) a stock dividend and (b) a stock split?

EXERCISES

27-1 Coates Company is authorized to issue 20,000 shares of $10 par value common stock. At December 31, 19*x1,* the stockholders' equity balances were:

Common stock, $10 par, 20,000 shares authorized, issued, and
    outstanding $200,000
Contributed capital in excess of par value   60,000
Retained earnings   90,000

During 19*x2* the company acquired 2,000 shares of its stock at $14 per share, which is
to be held as treasury stock. The company subsequently sold 500 shares of treasury
stock at $16 per share and another 700 shares at $13 per share later in 19*x2*. Net income
for the year was $60,000. State law requires that retained earnings equal to the cost of
treasury stock be restricted.

Required   **a.**   Prepare the journal entries for treasury stock transactions.
              b.   Prepare the stockholders' equity section of the balance sheet at
                  December 31, 19*x2*.

27-2   Frontenac Company is authorized to issue two classes of stock. At December 31, 19*x3*,
the balances of these two accounts were as follows:

5% preferred stock, $100 par, 2,000 shares authorized, issued, and
    outstanding, cumulative and nonparticipating (dividends in
    arrears for 19*x2*) $200,000
Common stock, $10 par, 50,000 shares authorized, 40,000 shares
    issued, 38,000 shares outstanding (2,000 shares held as treasury
    stock)   400,000

During 19*x3* the board of directors took the following dividend actions:

Nov. 1   Declared the regular cash dividend on preferred stock for
                  19*x3* as well as the dividend in arrears for 19*x2*; also,
                  declared a cash dividend of $.20 per share on common
                  stock. Both dividends are payable on December 10 to
                  stockholders of record on November 20.
Dec. 1   Declared a 10% stock dividend on common stock payable
                  on December 31 to stockholders of record on December 16;
                  the market value of common stock at this date is $16 per
                  share.

Required   Prepare the entries for dividends at the date of declaration and the date of
            record.

27-3   Pirate Corp. reported the following balances at December 31, 19*x2*:

5% preferred stock, $20 par, 10,000 shares authorized, issued, and outstanding	$ 200,000
Common stock, $5 par, 100,000 shares authorized, 95,000 shares issued and outstanding	475,000
Contributed capital in excess of par, preferred	15,000
Contributed capital in excess of par, common	315,000
Retained earnings	270,000
Total stockholders' equity	$1,275,000

During 19x3 the following transactions were completed:

a. Acquired 5,000 shares of common stock at $11 per share; the shares will be held as treasury stock.
b. Reissued 2,000 shares of treasury stock at $12.50 per share.
c. Reissued 1,000 shares of treasury stock at $10 per share.
d. Declared and paid the annual cash dividend on preferred stock.
e. Declared and paid a 5% stock dividend on common stock; the market value of the common stock was $13 per share when the stock dividend was declared.
f. Net income for 19x3 was $42,000.

Retained earnings are to be restricted in an amount equal to the cost of treasury stock. The company discloses such restrictions in footnotes.

Required   (1) Prepare the entries for these 19x3 transactions.
(2) Prepare the stockholders' equity section of the balance sheet at December 31, 19x3.

27-4   Following is information from the financial records of Begott Corp.:

Retained earnings:	
December 31, 19x4	$160,000
December 31, 19x5	$182,000
Net income for 19x5	$ 50,000
Total stockholders' equity:	
December 31, 19x4	$535,000
December 31, 19x5	$571,000
Number of shares of $10 par value common stock outstanding:	
December 31, 19x4	27,500
December 31, 19x5	28,000
Treasury stock:	
December 31, 19x4	$ 45,000
December 31, 19x5	$ 36,000

Required   a. From the information provided reconstruct the entries to reissue treasury stock at $20 per share and to declare and pay cash dividends during 19x5.
b. Prepare the stockholders' equity section of the balance sheet at the end of 19x5 if Begott Corp. was authorized to issue 40,000 shares of common stock and had issued 30,000 shares prior to acquiring treasury stock during 19x4.

PROBLEMS

27-1   Rainey Company is authorized to issue the following classes of stock:

6% preferred stock, $50 par, 10,000 shares
Common stock, $10 par, 100,000 shares

Prior to 19x7 all 10,000 shares of preferred stock had been issued at par value, and 90,000 shares of common stock had been issued at an average price of $16 per share. During 19x7 the company retired 2,000 shares of preferred stock by acquiring the shares at par value. Also, the company acquired 6,000 shares of common stock as treasury stock at $18 per share. The company subsequently reissued 2,000 shares of treasury stock at $20 per share and 1,500 shares at $17 per share. An additional 1,000 shares of treasury stock were issued to acquire land with a fair market value of $19,500. The company must comply with a state law restricting retained earnings for treasury stock held. Retained earnings were $230,000 before net income of $65,000 for 19x7 and cash dividends on preferred stock.

Required   **a.**   Prepare the entries for the 19x7 stock transactions.
           b.   Prepare the stockholders' equity section of the balance sheet at December 31, 19x7.

27-2   Bonnie Company is authorized to issue 100,000 shares of $10 par value common stock. At December 31, 19x1, all 100,000 shares were outstanding. Contributed capital in excess of par value and retained earnings were $250,000 and $180,000, respectively, at the end of 19x1. The following transactions occurred during 19x2:

Jan. 26	Acquired 5,000 shares of the company's stock at $16 per share; the stock is to be held as treasury stock.
May 5	Sold 1,000 shares of treasury stock at $18 per share.
Aug. 14	Sold 1,000 shares of treasury stock at $15.50 per share.
Nov. 20	Declared a cash dividend of $.50 per share on common stock payable on December 30 to stockholders of record on December 10.
Dec. 30	Paid the cash dividend.
Dec. 31	Closed out net income for 19x2 of $90,000 to retained earnings.

The company must comply with a state law restricting retained earnings equal to the cost of treasury stock.

Required   **a.**   Prepare the entries for the 19x2 transactions.
           b.   Prepare the stockholders' equity section of the balance sheet at December 31, 19x2.

27-3   Clyde Corp. is authorized to issue two classes of stock. The following are stockholders' equity balances at December 31, 19x3:

6% preferred stock, $50 par, 10,000 shares authorized, 8,000 shares issued and outstanding, cumulative and nonparticipating	$400,000
Common stock, $10 par, 100,000 shares authorized, 60,000 shares issued and outstanding	600,000
Contributed capital in excess of par value, common	180,000
Retained earnings	270,000

During 19*x4* the following transactions occurred:

July 15	Declared the annual cash dividend on preferred stock; the dividend is payable on August 15 to stockholders of record on July 31.
Aug. 15	Paid the cash dividend on preferred stock.
Nov. 1	Declared a 10% stock dividend on common stock payable on December 1 to stockholders of record on November 15; the current market value of the stock is $25 per share.
Dec. 1	Paid the stock dividend on common stock.
Dec. 1	Declared a 2-for-1 stock split on common stock payable on December 31 to stockholders of record on December 16.
Dec. 31	Net income of $130,000 is closed out to retained earnings.
Dec. 31	Issued stock to common stockholders for the stock split.

Required **a.** Prepare the entries for these 19*x4* transactions.

b. Prepare the stockholders' equity section of the balance sheet at December 31, 19*x4*.

27-4 The stockholders' equity section of Sunney Corp. at December 31, 19*x8,* appeared as follows:

6% preferred stock, $50 par, 10,000 shares authorized, 6,000 shares issued and outstanding	$ 300,000
Common stock, $10 par, 100,000 shares authorized, 35,000 shares issued and outstanding	350,000
Contributed capital in excess of par, common	620,000
Retained earnings	2,650,000
Total stockholders' equity	$3,920,000

The company has been earning an average of $140,000 after taxes and paying cash dividends of $1 per share on common stock annually. A large portion of profits is retained in the business to finance expansion of business operations. Recently the common stock has been selling at $65–$70 per share. The board of directors would like to retire the nonconvertible preferred stock. Also, the company needs $1.5 million to purchase a small company whose operations would help diversify Sunney's business activities. The funds to carry out these goals must come from the sale of additional common stock. However, the market price of common stock has discouraged active trading, and difficulty in issuing additional common stock is expected.

One board member has advocated the declaration of a 100% stock dividend to "freeze" retained earnings in the business permanently and reduce the market price of common stock to a level sufficient to encourage investment in additional stock to raise needed funds. Another board member has expressed his opinion that a 2-for-1 stock split would be a better alternative to encourage investment.

Required   **a.**   Discuss the merits of the two proposals. In your discussion include the impact on the balance sheet, earnings per share, and the ability to pay cash dividends in the future.

b.   Prepare a revised stockholders' section for each proposal assuming that common stock had a market value of $70 per share when the board of directors declared the stock dividend or stock split.

Unit 28
Reporting Changes in Stockholders' Equity

The purpose of every merchant is to make a lawful and reasonable profit so as to keep his business.

Fra Luca Paciolo, Summa de Arithmetica

Changes in retained earnings have been reported in the retained earnings statement or a combined statement of income and retained earnings for some time. However, reporting changes in contributed capital is a practice that has become widespread only recently. The purpose, form, and content of statements that report changes in retained earnings and/or contributed capital and alternative methods of reporting these changes are explained and illustrated in this unit. The reasons for restrictions on retained earnings and alternative methods of reporting these restrictions are also covered.

Performance Objectives

Upon completing this unit you should be able to:

1. define and use the accounting terms introduced in this unit.
2. describe or explain:
   a. how prior period adjustments are reported
   b. the purpose, form, and/or content of a retained earnings statement, a statement of changes in stockholders' equity, or a combined statement of income and retained earnings
   c. the reasons for restrictions on retained earnings
   d. how restrictions on retained earnings are reported
3. prepare the correct journal entry to establish or eliminate a restriction on retained earnings.
4. prepare a retained earnings statement, a statement of changes in stockholders' equity, or a combined statement of income and retained earnings.

550

Retained Earnings Statement

The *retained earnings statement* reports all changes that have occurred in the retained earnings account during the accounting period. Stockholders are interested in retained earnings because dividends can usually be declared only if retained earnings are available. The form of the retained earnings statement is: retained earnings account balance at beginning of period ± prior period adjustments + other items that increase the retained earnings balance − other items that decrease the retained earnings balance = retained earnings account balance at end of period.

Increases in the retained earnings balance result from net income and some prior period adjustments. Decreases in retained earnings result from net losses, dividends, some prior period adjustments, and certain charges made to retained earnings in transactions involving the company's stock (for example, reissuing treasury stock below cost or retiring stock at a price in excess of the price at which it was issued).

Prior Period Adjustments and Accounting Changes   Over the years there have been a number of changes in the official position regarding what items must be included in determining net income and what can be treated as direct charges or credits to retained earnings. APB Opinion No. 9 (December 1966) first established criteria for prior period adjustments. This opinion permitted several items, such as corrections of errors in previously issued financial statements, tax refunds or assessments related to prior periods, and adjustments resulting from contract renegotiations, to be treated as prior period adjustments if material in amount. FASB Statement No. 16 has now eliminated all items, except corrections of errors in previously issued financial statements and certain tax adjustments,[1] from treatment as **prior period adjustments.**

APB Opinion No. 9 also required that extraordinary items be included in determining net income rather than being treated as direct charges or credits to retained earnings as permitted before that time. Later, APB Opinion No. 30 (June 1973) established the current criteria for extraordinary items, that is, that they be unusual in relation to regular business operations and not expected to recur in the foreseeable future.

During the period between Opinions 9 and 30, the APB established guidelines for distinguishing between and accounting for certain accounting changes and corrections of errors in previously issued financial statements. In APB Opinion No. 20 (July 1971) changes in accounting principles, changes in accounting estimates, and corrections of errors in previously issued financial statements were described. The treatment of corrections of errors as prior period adjustments was reaffirmed in this opinion. Also, the inclusion of the effects of changes in accounting principles and accounting estimates in determining net income was established in the opinion.

Changes in accounting principles include changes in principles, practices, and methods used by an entity, such as a change from fifo to lifo or a change from straight-line to sum-of-years'-digits depreciation. The cumulative effect of such changes on

---

[1]These are adjustments resulting from realization of income tax benefits of preacquisition operating loss carryforwards of purchased subsidiaries.

beginning retained earnings is included in net income, net of any tax effect, in the same manner as extraordinary items. Further discussion of these changes is beyond the scope of this text.

Making estimates is a common accounting practice and is necessary to measure net income accurately; for example, uncollectible accounts expense, depreciation expense, amortization expense, and so on, are based on estimates. Although these estimates are made using the best information available at the time, **changes in accounting estimates** are often necessary because economic circumstances and information available change. Thus, changes in estimates must be included in determining net income, and are not treated as prior period adjustments.

The trend starting with APB Opinion No. 9 has been to include virtually all items of revenue, expense, gain, or loss in the determination of net income. It was felt that excluding certain items from the income statement would result in the overstatement or understatement of income for the period. Also, items excluded from the income statement might be overlooked, even if they were reported elsewhere. Thus, items such as extraordinary gains and losses and changes in accounting principles are included in the determination of net income, but they are reported separately. Users of the financial statements can then select the income figure that is relevant to them, that is, income before extraordinary items and changes in accounting principles or net income.

Reporting Prior Period Adjustments   Prior period adjustments are reported as corrections to the beginning retained earnings balance on the retained earnings statement. They are reported net of any income tax effect. Assume that Finn Company reported the following:

Retained earnings balance, January 1, 19x6	$268,000
Net income for 19x6	84,000
Dividends declared during 19x6	30,000
Prior period adjustment: Correction of overstatement of expenses in 19x4	25,000
Income tax effect of prior period adjustment	12,000

The overstatement of expenses in 19x4 understated net income and the ending retained earnings for that year. To correct the error, then, a credit adjustment is required in 19x6 when the error is discovered. Exhibit 28.1 illustrates the retained earnings statement for 19x6 for Finn Company. The prior period adjustment, net of its income tax effect, is added to the beginning retained earnings balance to determine a corrected beginning balance. The income tax effect of the adjustment is disclosed parenthetically.

Restrictions on Retained Earnings

Corporations may be required to restrict retained earnings for a number of legal, contractual, or voluntary reasons. These restrictions limit the retained earnings available

Exhibit 28.1

Finn Company Retained Earnings Statement For the Year Ended December 31, 19x6	
Retained earnings, January 1, 19x6	$268,000
Prior period adjustments:	
Correction of overstatement in expenses in 19x4 (net of taxes of $12,000)	13,000
Corrected retained earnings, January 1, 19x6	$281,000
Add: Net income	84,000
Total	$365,000
Less: Dividends	30,000
Retained earnings, December 31, 19x6	$335,000

for dividends and/or notify stockholders of the need to keep assets in the business for a specified purpose. A company may be required by state law to restrict retained earnings—for example, as a result of acquiring treasury stock. Or the company may agree to restrict retained earnings in a bond contract or other loan agreement. In both situations the company is legally bound.

A corporation can also restrict retained earnings on a voluntary basis to inform stockholders of some future need that limits the current ability to pay dividends or to pay larger dividends. Restrictions of retained earnings for contingencies, uninsured casualty losses, and plant expansion are examples of voluntary restrictions adopted by the board of directors.

Two alternative methods have been used to disclose restrictions on retained earnings. The preferred method today is to disclose restrictions, that is, appropriations, of retained earnings, including their nature and amount, in a footnote to the financial statements. The balance of the retained earnings account on the balance sheet and the retained earnings statement would include the amount of **appropriated retained earnings.** To determine the amount of unappropriated retained earnings, the amount of appropriated retained earnings disclosed in the footnotes is deducted from the retained earnings balance reported at the end of the period. Only the unappropriated retained earnings are available for the declaration of dividends.

Assume that a company reports a retained earnings account balance of $220,000 and has appropriated $50,000 of retained earnings for the cost of treasury stock held by the company. The unappropriated retained earnings would be $170,000 ($220,000 − 50,000). The retained earnings balance of $220,000 would be reported on the financial statements; the $50,000 appropriation would be reported in a footnote.

The alternative method is to report appropriations of retained earnings in a **reserve** or appropriated retained earnings account. This method was widely used in the past, but has been largely replaced by the footnote method because of confusion over the meanings and classification of the reserve accounts. The appropriation is recorded by debiting retained earnings and crediting a reserve or appropriated retained earnings account. For example, the entry to appropriate $50,000 of retained earnings for the cost of treasury stock would be:

| Retained Earnings | 50,000 | |
| Reserve for Treasury Stock | | 50,000 |

To appropriate retained earnings for treasury
stock.

When appropriations of retained earnings are reported in separate accounts, the retained earnings classification of stockholders' equity on the balance sheet is further classified into appropriated and unappropriated retained earnings. Unappropriated retained earnings represents the balance of the retained earnings account. If the retained earnings balance was $220,000 before the establishment of the reserve for treasury stock, it would be $170,000 ($220,000 − 50,000) afterwards. The method of reporting the reserve and the retained earnings balance is illustrated as follows:

Retained earnings:	
Appropriated:	
Reserve for treasury stock	$ 50,000
Unappropriated	170,000
Total retained earnings	$220,000

Under no circumstances should an expense or loss account be charged when the appropriation of retained earnings is recorded. No expense or loss has been incurred at that time; thus, the retained earnings account is debited. Also, when a loss is incurred, the reserve or appropriated retained earnings account should not be charged. All losses and expenses must be included in the determination of net income. When an appropriation is no longer needed, the appropriated retained earnings are returned to the retained earnings account. The entry is the reverse of the one made to record the appropriation. For example, when the treasury stock is reissued and the restriction on retained earnings is not needed any longer, the entry to return the appropriated retained earnings to the retained earnings account would be:

| Reserve for Treasury Stock | 50,000 | |
| Retained Earnings | | 50,000 |

To eliminate appropriation of retained earnings

Combined Statement of Income and Retained Earnings

An alternative method of reporting changes in retained earnings is to prepare a combined statement of income and retained earnings. This method is most appropriate when there are only a few changes in retained earnings. The primary objection to this method is that the net income figure is obscured. On an income statement net income is the final figure and is double underlined. On a combined statement of income and retained earnings, ending retained earnings is the final figure.

In the financial statements in the appendix to Unit 6, Michigan Sugar Company presented a combined statement of income and retained earnings. After determining net income, the beginning retained earnings balance was added. Then dividends were deducted from this total to determine ending retained earnings.

Reporting Changes in Contributed Capital

Reporting changes in the components of contributed capital and the number of shares of stock outstanding became a requirement when APB Opinion No. 12 was issued. The purpose of this requirement was to make published financial statements more informative. The changes can be disclosed in any of three methods: (1) in a separate statement of changes in stockholders' equity, (2) in the basic financial statements, or (3) in the footnotes to the basic financial statements. The effects of transactions such as stock dividends, stock options, and conversion of bonds or preferred stock into common stock are more evident when disclosed by one of these three methods. The best method depends on the number and types of changes disclosed and the effectiveness of each method of disclosure under the circumstances. Footnote disclosure of changes in contributed capital is illustrated in Exhibit 6.4. Reporting these changes in a separate statement is illustrated in Exhibit 6.5.

Rather than prepare separate statements for changes in retained earnings and contributed capital, a statement of changes in stockholders' equity can be prepared to explain all such changes. A single statement is a logical approach because some transactions, such as stock dividends, affect both contributed capital and retained earnings. A common format for the statement of changes in stockholders' equity provides separate columns for the number of shares, the stock account, contributed capital in excess of par or stated value (or additional contributed capital), and retained earnings. Beginning balances are entered on the first line, and changes are described and their amounts entered on the following lines. The ending balance for each account is given on the last line. Changes in retained earnings and contributed capital are disclosed in the statement of changes in shareholders' equity in Exhibit 6.6 and by Coachmen Industries in the appendix to Unit 6.

REVIEW PROBLEM

During 19x8 Kramm Corp. completed the following transactions involving contributed capital and retained earnings:

a. 15,000 shares of common stock were issued at $22 per share.
b. 7,500 shares of common stock were issued as a stock dividend;

the market value of the stock was $24 per share when the dividend was declared.

c. 5,000 shares of common stock were issued when bonds with a carrying value of $98,000 were converted.

d. An overstatement of depreciation expense in 19x6 in the amount of $20,000 was corrected; the tax effect of this prior period adjustment is $9,600.

e. Net income for the year was $105,000.

At the beginning of 19x8 Kramm Corp. reported the following balances for stockholders' equity:

Common stock, $10 par, 200,000 shares authorized, 60,000 shares issued and outstanding	$ 600,000
Contributed capital in excess of par	115,000
Retained earnings	370,000
Total stockholders' equity	$1,085,000

Required   Prepare a statement of changes in stockholders' equity for 19x8 using the following columns: number of shares, common stock, contributed capital in excess of par, and retained earnings.

Solution to review problem

Kramm Corp.
Statement of Changes in Stockholders' Equity
For the Year Ended December 31, 19x8

	Number of Shares	Common Stock	Contributed Capital in Excess of Par	Retained Earnings
Balances at January 1, 19x8	60,000	$600,000	$115,000	$370,000
Prior period adjustment:				
Correction of overstatement of depreciation in 19x6 (net of taxes of $9,600)				10,400 (d)
Restated balances at January 1, 19x8	60,000	$600,000	$115,000	$380,400
Net income				105,000
Issuance of common stock for cash	15,000	150,000	180,000 (a)	
Declaration of stock dividend	7,500	75,000	105,000 (b)	(180,000)
Issuance of common stock on bond conversion	5,000	50,000	48,000 (c)	
Balances at December 31, 19x8	87,500	$875,000	$448,000	$305,400

Computations

(a) $10 \times 15,000 = \$150,000$; $(\$22 - 10) \times 15,000 = \$180,000$
(b) $10 \times 7,500 = \$ 75,000$; $(\$24 - 10) \times 7,500 = \$105,000$
(c) $10 \times 5,000 = \$ 50,000$; $\$98,000 - 50,000 = \$48,000$
(d) $\$20,000 - 9,600 = \$10,400$

SUMMARY

Information on changes in retained earnings, contributed capital, and the number of shares of stock outstanding is useful to stockholders because these changes affect their ownership interest and the availability of retained earnings for dividends. Alternative methods may be used to report these changes depending on the circumstances and the effectiveness of the method of disclosure. These alternative methods were discussed and illustrated in this unit. In addition, prior period adjustments and restrictions on retained earnings were discussed.

REVIEW QUESTIONS

28-1   What types of changes are disclosed in a retained earnings statement?

28-2   a.   What are prior period adjustments?
       b.   What items qualify as prior period adjustments according to FASB Statement No. 16?
       c.   How are prior period adjustments disclosed on the retained earnings statement?

28-3   Why has the trend since APB Opinion No. 9 been toward the inclusion of all items of revenue, expense, gain, or loss in the determination of net income?

28-4   a.   What are appropriations of retained earnings?
       b.   How should appropriations of retained earnings be disclosed in the financial statements?

28-5   An expense or loss account should not be charged to establish an appropriation of retained earnings, and a reserve account should not be charged when an expense or a loss is incurred. Explain.

28-6   What is a combined statement of income and retained earnings?

28-7   APB Opinion No. 12 requires the disclosure of changes in the contributed capital accounts and the number of shares of stock outstanding. Indicate three methods of making these disclosures.

EXERCISES

28-1   The following are selected data from the adjusted trial balance of Fleming Corp. at December 31, 19x3:

Retained earnings, January 1, 19x3	$ 85,000
Dividends paid	20,000
Correction of error overstating the December 31, 19x2, inventory balance	6,000

Net sales	350,000
Cost of goods sold	210,000
Operating expenses	100,000
Income tax expense	8,300

The number of shares of common stock outstanding throughout 19x3 was 20,000 shares.

Required **a.** Prepare a single-step income statement for 19x3.

b. Prepare a retained earnings statement for 19x3.

28-2 Refer to the data in exercise 28–1. Prepare a combined statement of income and retained earnings for 19x3.

28-3 The board of directors of Shannon Company decided to restrict retained earnings for possible uninsured casualty losses. At the end of 19x4 the board appropriated $250,000 of retained earnings for this purpose. During 19x6 the company suffered an uninsured flood loss to inventory items with a book value of $42,000. At the end of 19x6 the board of directors decided to reduce the appropriation to $200,000. After the reduction in the appropriation, the unappropriated retained earnings amounted to $320,000.

Required **a.** Prepare the entries required in 19x4 and 19x6 if a reserve account (1) is established and (2) is not established.

b. Prepare a partial balance sheet at December 31, 19x6, if a reserve account (1) has been established and (2) has not been established.

28-4 Following are changes in the contributed capital and retained earnings of Hastings Company that occurred during 19x5:

a. Net income for the year was $75,000.

b. Cash dividends totaling $21,000 were declared and paid.

c. The company issued 10,000 shares of stock at $23 per share.

d. A stock dividend of 7,000 shares was declared and paid; the market value of the stock was $22 per share.

e. An error that understated expenses by $10,000 in 19x4 was corrected.

The stockholders' equity balances at December 31, 19x4, were:

Common stock, $10 par, 100,000 shares authorized, 60,000 shares issued and outstanding	$600,000
Contributed capital in excess of par	210,000
Retained earnings	190,000

Required Prepare a statement of changes in stockholders' equity with the following columns: number of shares, common stock, contributed capital in excess of par, and retained earnings.

PROBLEMS

28-1 Following are the stockholders' equity balances for Shamrock Corp. at December 31, 19x7:

Common stock, $20 par, 50,000 shares authorized, 35,000 shares issued,	
34,000 shares outstanding (1,000 shares held as treasury stock)	$ 700,000
Contributed capital in excess of par	280,000
Retained earnings	220,000
Reserve for treasury stock	32,000
Treasury stock (1,000 shares at cost)	(32,000)
Total stockholders' equity	$1,200,000

The following are selected data from the adjusted trial balance at December 31, 19x8:

Net sales	$2,000,000
Cost of goods sold	1,300,000
Operating expenses	600,000
Income tax expense	34,500
Dividends paid	30,000
Correction of error in understating revenues in a prior period	15,000

The following stock transactions occurred during 19x8:

    a. All treasury stock was sold at $35 per share (and the reserve for treasury stock was eliminated).
    b. The company issued 5,000 shares of common stock for land and a building when the market value of the stock was $36 per share.
    c. A 2-for-1 stock split was declared, and the stock was issued at the end of 19x8.

Required   **(1)** Prepare a combined statement of income and retained earnings for 19x8.
    (2) Prepare a retained earnings statement for 19x8.
    (3) Prepare a statement of changes in stockholders' equity for 19x8 with the following columns: number of shares outstanding, common stock, other contributed capital, retained earnings, reserve for treasury stock, treasury stock.
    (4) Prepare the stockholders' equity section of the balance sheet at December 31, 19x8.

28-2 Clover Company is authorized to issue two classes of stock:

5% preferred stock, $50 par, 10,000 shares authorized, 7,500 shares issued and outstanding
Common stock, $10 par, 100,000 shares authorized, 82,000 shares issued and outstanding

At the end of 19x6 total contributed capital was $1,560,000 and total stockholders' equity was $1,870,000. During 19x7 the following stock transactions occurred:

    a.   Issued 1,000 shares of preferred stock and 10,000 shares of common stock to acquire land and a building with a fair market value of $195,000.

    b.   Acquired 7,000 shares of common stock at $15 per share; the stock is to be held as treasury stock.

    c.   Cash dividends were declared and paid on 8,500 shares of preferred stock and 85,000 shares of common stock; the latter received a dividend of $.60 per share.

    d.   Reissued 2,000 shares of treasury stock at $18 per share.

Net income for 19x7 was $94,000.

Required   Prepare a statement of changes in stockholders' equity for 19x7. Provide columns for preferred stock, common stock, additional contributed capital, retained earnings, and treasury stock-common.

28-3   Leife Corp. has issued 88,000 shares of the 100,000 shares of $20 par common stock that it is authorized to issue. The company currently is holding 3,000 of these shares as treasury stock; their total cost is $93,000. Total stockholders' equity at December 31, 19x5, is $2,625,000. The retained earnings balance at the beginning of 19x5 was $430,000.

    During 19x5 net income was $136,000, and dividends of $1 per share were declared and paid. The auditors discovered an error made in a prior year when a capital expenditure was incorrectly recorded as a revenue expenditure. To correct the error, retained earnings as of January 1, 19x5, should be increased by $32,000 (this is net of a tax effect of $28,000). The company reports the restriction on retained earnings for treasury stock in the footnotes to the financial statements.

Required   **a.**   Prepare a retained earnings statement for 19x5.

                b.   Prepare the stockholders' equity section of the balance sheet at December 31, 19x5.

28-4   Following are two statements included in the 1977 annual report of Bliss & Laughlin Industries. The company is authorized to issue 1,000,000 shares of no-par-value preferred stock and 10,000,000 shares of $2.50 par value common stock. None of the preferred stock has been issued.

Consolidated Statements of Additional Capital and Retained Earnings		
For the years ended December 31	1977	1976
Additional Capital:		
Balance at beginning of year	$18,796,000	$17,288,000
Add (Deduct):		
Market value in excess of par value of common stock issued in		
payment of 20% common stock dividend	10,888,000	—
Principal amount of convertible debentures in excess of par value		
of common stock issued upon conversion	1,911,000	1,518,000
Other, net	13,000	(10,000)
Balance at end of year	$31,608,000	$18,796,000

Retained Earnings:

Balance at beginning of year	$50,435,000	$44,089,000
Add (Deduct):		
Net income	11,213,000	10,112,000
Cash dividends paid ($.95 per share in 1977 and $.85 per share in 1976)	(4,375,000)	(3,766,000)
20% common stock dividend	(12,914,000)	—
Balance at end of year	$44,359,000	$50,435,000

Consolidated Statements of Common Stock and Treasury Stock

	1977		1976	
	Number Shares	Amount	Number Shares	Amount
Common Stock:				
Balance at beginning of year	3,973,000	$ 9,932,000	3,858,000	$9,645,000
Add: Stock issued for				
debenture conversion ..	163,000	407,000	115,000	287,000
Stock issued for 20%				
stock dividend	810,000	2,026,000	—	—
Balance at end of year	4,946,000	$12,365,000	3,973,000	$9,932,000
Treasury Stock:				
Balance at beginning of year	234,000	$ 3,472,000	227,000	$3,321,000
Add: Treasury stock				
purchased	86,000	1,378,000	13,000	217,000
Stock issued for 20%				
stock dividend	46,000	—	—	—
Less: Stock issued for stock				
options	6,000	107,000	6,000	66,000
Balance at end of year	360,000	$ 4,743,000	234,000	$3,472,000

Required   **a.**   Do these two statements adequately disclose changes in stockholders' equity as required by APB Opinion No. 12? Explain.

        b.   Using the information in the two statements presented, prepare the following:

            (1)   the stockholders' equity section of the balance sheet at the end of 1977

            (2)   a statement of changes in all components of stockholders' equity for 1977, which would replace the two statements presented in the annual report

Chapter 10

Long-Term Investments

Many of the concepts involved with accounting for bond obligations, temporary investments, and stockholders' equity pertain also to accounting for long-term investments in stocks and bonds. In this chapter long-term stock investments and long-term bond investments are examined.

Unit 29
Long-Term Investments in Stocks

October. This is one of the peculiarly dangerous months to speculate in stocks in. The others are July, January, September, April, November, May, March, June, December, August, and February.

Mark Twain, Pudd'nhead Wilson's Calendar

Long-term investments in stock require different methods of accounting depending primarily on the degree of control or influence the investor has over the operations and activities of the investee. This unit examines the different methods, the measurement and reporting problems involved with them, and the circumstances in which each should be used.

Performance Objectives

Upon completing this unit you should be able to:

1. define and use the accounting terms introduced in this unit.
2. describe or explain:
   a. when long-term investments in stock should be accounted for at cost, equity, or lower-of cost-or-market
   b. how to account for dividends paid by the investee, income reported by the investee, and changes in the value of the investee's stock
   c. how to report long-term investments in stock and related revenue, gains, or losses on the financial statements
   d. the effect of a stock dividend or stock split on an investment in stock
3. determine:
   a. the cost of a long-term investment in stock
   b. the amount of revenue recognized from a long-term investment in stock
   c. the unrealized loss or gain from changes in a valuation allowance for a long-term investment in stock
   d. the balance to be reported for a long-term investment in stock or its valuation allowance at a specific date

    e.   the cost basis per share and/or the gain or loss on the sale of a stock investment after a stock dividend or a stock split

4. prepare the correct journal entry for transactions involving long-term investments in stock and related revenues, gains, or losses.

Nature of Long-Term Investments in Stock

Long-term investments in stock are recorded according to the cost principle at the time of acquisition. The cost of the stock includes its market price plus any brokerage fees and taxes paid to acquire it. In Unit 14 two criteria to distinguish between short-term and long-term investments were described. If the securities purchased are readily marketable and management intends to convert them into cash in the near future to provide cash for current operations, the investment is classified as a current asset. Investments that do not meet both of these criteria are classified as long-term investments.

A corporation may invest in the stock of another corporation for several reasons:

1. to influence or control the operations or activities of the other company
2. to invest excess cash
3. to invest cash contributed to a non-trusteed fund, such as a plant expansion fund
4. to speculate on the expected increase in value of the stock (if the stock does increase in value, it can be sold at a gain)

A company may want to control or influence another company in order to gain a larger market share for its own products, to obtain access to a new source of supply, or to achieve other economic objectives. If a company has excess cash, it may want to invest it in stocks that will yield dividends and/or gains through an expected increase in market value. Cash contributed to non-trusteed funds must be invested to achieve the expected rate of return; stock may be purchased as part of the fund investments.

Subsequent to acquisition, long-term investments in stock will be accounted for by (1) the cost method, (2) the lower-of-cost-or-market method, or (3) the equity method. These three methods measure the balance of the investment account and also any related revenue, gain, or loss. The primary criterion used to determine which method is appropriate to account for a particular stock investment is the degree of influence or control the **investor** has over the **investee.** A uniform measure of this is the percentage of the investee's outstanding voting stock that is owned by the investor.

Distinction Between Significant Influence and Control

APB Opinion No. 18 describes "significant influence" and "control" as follows:

1. **significant influence**—the ability of the investor *to affect, to an important degree,* the operating and financial policies of the investee through the ownership of the investee's voting stock
2. **control**—the ability of the investor *to determine* the operating and financial policies of the investee through the ownership of the investee's voting stock

Significant influence may be indicated in any of several ways: representation on the board of directors, participation in policy-making processes, material intercompany transactions, interchange of managerial personnel, or technological dependency. To provide uniformity in application, APB Opinion No. 18 concluded that ownership of 20 percent or more of an investee's voting stock should lead to the presumption, in the absence of evidence to the contrary, that the investor possesses significant influence over the investee. Likewise, ownership of less than 20 percent of the investee's voting stock should lead to the presumption, unless it can be demonstrated otherwise, that the investor does not possess significant influence over the investee. In most situations, then, significant influence exists only when 20 percent or more of the investee's voting stock is owned directly or indirectly by the investor.

Control over the investee normally can be assumed whenever the investor owns more than 50 percent of the investee's voting stock. In this case, the investor should be able to elect a majority to the investee's board of directors and thereby determine its operating and financial policies. In most situations where one company controls another company, **consolidated financial statements** are prepared. (Consolidated financial statements are discussed briefly in the appendix to this unit. Most accounting issues for consolidated statements are complex and beyond the scope of this text.) In consolidated financial statements the accounts of two or more affiliated companies are combined to indicate the financial position and operating results of the companies as a single economic unit. But whether consolidated or separate financial statements are prepared, the investment and related revenue must be properly reported and accounted for during each accounting period.

The relationship between degree of influence or control and the appropriate measurement and reporting methods that should be used is summarized in Table 29.1.

Table 29.1

Measurement and Reporting Methods for Long-Term Stock Investments			
Degree of Influence or Control	*Percentage of Voting Stock Ownership*	*Measurement Method*	*Reporting Method*
Neither significant influence nor control	Less than 20%	Cost or lower-of-cost-or-market	Cost or lower-of-cost-or-market
Significant influence, but not control	20%–50%	Equity	Equity
Control			
Separate financial statements of investor	More than 50%	Equity	Equity
Consolidated financial statements	More than 50%	Cost or equity	Consolidated statement

Regardless of the accounting method used, it must:

1. measure the acquisition cost of the stock
2. measure revenue from the investment
3. value the investment at balance sheet date
4. measure any gain or loss on the sale of the investment
5. report the investment, related revenue, gain, or loss, and other information on the financial statements

Cost Method

The **cost method** is appropriate for investments in nonvoting stock and for investments in voting stock when neither significant influence nor control exists. When less than 20 percent of the voting stock of an investee is owned, significant influence usually does not exist and the cost method will be appropriate. Under the cost method the investment is recorded at cost when acquired. Subsequent to acquisition the investment continues to be valued at cost unless a lower market value must be used (for conditions under which investments must be valued at lower-of-cost-or-market, see pages 569–572.

Under the cost method revenue from investments in stock is realized only when dividends are received. Changes in the value of the stock are not recognized as they occur. When the stock is sold, however, any difference between cost and the proceeds from the sale is recognized as a gain or loss. The proceeds from the sale are the market price at which the stock is sold less any brokerage fees. These procedures are the same as discussed for temporary investments in Unit 14.

Assume that Ringo Corp. acquires 1,000 shares of the 10,000 outstanding shares of Starr Company's $10 par value common stock at $28 per share plus brokerage fees of $500 on July 1, 19x4. On October 15, 19x4, a dividend of $.50 per share is received. Then, on December 5, 19x4, 200 shares are sold at $31 per share less brokerage fees of $150. The cost method will be used because only 10 percent (1,000/10,000) of the voting stock of Starr Company was acquired. The total cost of the investment is $28,500 [($28 × 1,000) + $500]; the cost per share is $28.50 ($28,500/1,000). The entries to record the acquisition of the stock, the receipt of dividend revenue, and the sale of the 200 shares would be:

July 1	Investment in Starr Common Stock	28,500	
	Cash		28,500
	To record purchase of 1,000 shares of Starr Company common stock at $28 per share plus $500 brokerage fees.		

Oct. 15	Cash	500	
	Dividends Revenue		500
	To record receipt of $.50 per share dividend on Starr Company common stock (1,000 × $.50 = $500).		
Dec. 5	Cash	6,050	
	Investment in Starr Company Stock		5,700
	Gain on Sale of Long-Term Investments		350
	To record sale of 200 shares of Starr Company common stock.		

Computation of gain on sale of stock:

Proceeds from sale of stock [($31 × 200) − $150]	$6,050
Cost of stock ($28.50 × 200)	5,700
Gain on sale of stock	$ 350

The balance of the investment account is $22,800 ($28.50 × 800 or $28,500 − 5,700); it is classified on the balance sheet under long-term investments and funds. The accounting method used (in this case, the cost method) is disclosed parenthetically or in the footnotes. Dividend revenue and the gain on the sale of the stock are reported as financial revenues on a classified income statement. The gain (or loss) on the sale of stock normally does not qualify for treatment as an extraordinary item. A partial income statement and a partial balance sheet at the end of 19x4 are illustrated in Exhibit 29.1.

Exhibit 29.1

Ringo Corp.
Partial Income Statement
For the Year Ended December 31, 19x4

Incidental revenues and expenses:		
Dividend revenue		$ 500
Gain on sale of long-term investments		350

Ringo Corp.
Partial Balance Sheet
December 31, 19x4

Long-term investments and funds:	
Investment in Starr Company stock, at cost	$22,800

Lower-of-Cost-or-Market Method

FASB Statement No. 12 requires the use of the **lower-of-cost-or-market method** for long-term as well as short-term investments in marketable equity securities. **Marketable equity securities** are instruments that represent ownership shares or the right to acquire or dispose of ownership shares at fixed or determinable prices and for which prices are currently available in an established securities market. Thus, marketable equity securities include common stock, certain preferred stock, and rights to acquire them, if they are traded on a national securities exchange such as the New York or American stock exchange or the over-the-counter market. Preferred stock that must be redeemed by the issuing corporation or is redeemable at the stockholders' option is not classified as a marketable equity security. Bonds are not marketable equity securities because they do not provide ownership interests to the bondholders.

In conformity with the realization principle, gains or losses are realized as investments are sold at a price that is more or less than their cost. Under the lower-of-cost-or-market method, material losses are recognized in the period in which the value of the securities decreases. Gains, on the other hand, are limited to the balance of the valuation allowance, which represents losses recorded in prior periods. Increases in market value are not recognized as they occur. Thus, the lower-of-cost-or-market method is a conservative valuation procedure. The objective is to not mislead users of the financial statements by overstating the amount the company is likely to receive when the investments are sold.

In applying FASB Statement No. 12, investments in marketable equity securities must be classified into two portfolios or groups: short-term investments, which will be classified as current assets (see Unit 14), and long-term investments, which will be classified under long-term investments and funds.

Cost Lower Than Market Value   Under FASB Statement No. 12, long-term investments in marketable equity securities are accounted for by the cost method with one exception—at the end of each period these investments must be valued at lower-of-cost-or-market. Aggregate cost is compared with aggregate market value. When aggregate cost is lower than aggregate market value, and there is no valuation allowance on the books from the prior accounting period, no entry is required because the investments are already recorded at cost. The accounting method used (lower-of-cost-or-market), the market value of the securities at balance sheet date, and any gains or losses realized on the sale of securities during the year must be disclosed in the footnotes to the financial statements. On the balance sheet itself a parenthetical note indicates the value at which the investment account is reported; see Exhibit 29.2.

Exhibit 29.2

Long-Term Investments and Funds: Investment in Marketable Equity Securities, at cost (see note 1)	$156,000

Note 1: Long-term investments in marketable equity securities are valued at the lower-of-cost-or-market. At December 31, 19xx, their market value was $162,000. During 19xx the company realized a gain of $4,500 on the sale of long-term investments in marketable equity securities.

Market Value Lower Than Cost   If aggregate market value is lower than aggregate cost at the end of a period, and there is no valuation allowance for the difference between cost and market value on the books from the prior period, an entry is required to record the **unrealized loss** and to establish a valuation allowance. Assume that long-term investments in marketable equity securities have an aggregate cost of $110,000 and an aggregate market value of $106,000 at the end of 19x5. If there is no balance on the books for a valuation allowance from the prior year, the entry to value the securities at lower-of-cost-or-market would be:

Dec. 31, 19x5	Unrealized Loss on Long-Term Investments in Marketable Equity Securities	4,000	
	Allowance for Valuation of Long-Term Investments in Marketable Equity Securities		4,000
	To value long-term investments in marketable equity securities at lower-of-cost-or-market ($110,000 − 106,000 = $4,000).		

The reporting practices for the investment are mostly the same as those followed for short-term investments in Unit 14. The valuation allowance is deducted from the

Exhibit 29.3

Partial Balance Sheet
December 31, 19x5

Long-Term Investments and Funds:		
Investment in Marketable Equity Securities, at market value (see note 1)		$106,000
Stockholders' Equity:		
Contributed Capital:		
Common Stock, $10 par, 50,000 shares authorized, issued, and outstanding	$500,000	
Contributed Capital in Excess of Par	185,000	
Total Contributed Capital	$685,000	
Retained Earnings	270,000	
Total	$955,000	
Less: Unrealized Loss on Long-Term Investments in Marketable Equity Securities (see note 1)	4,000	
Total Stockholders' Equity		$951,000

Note 1: Long-term investments in marketable equity securities are valued at the lower-of-cost-or-market. At December 31, 19x5, these investments had a cost of $110,000 and a market value of $106,000. During 19x5 a charge of $4,000 was made to stockholders' equity for unrealized losses for the difference between the cost and market value of these long-term investments.

cost of the investments, and the net amount (that is, market value) is included in total assets. A parenthetical note is used to indicate that the amount included in total assets is the market value. The unrealized loss on long-term investments is reported as a separate element of owners' equity; it is *not* included in the determination of net income as it would be for short-term investments. The method of valuation, the cost of the securities, and the effect of the change in the valuation allowance are disclosed in the footnotes to the financial statements. Exhibit 29.3 illustrates balance sheet disclosures at the end of 19x5.

Subsequent Changes in the Valuation Allowance   At the end of each subsequent period, the valuation allowance must be adjusted to the balance that reflects the current difference between cost and market value. If a larger balance is necessary, the unrealized loss account is charged and the valuation allowance is credited for the change. For example, assume that the long-term investments in the previous illustration are valued at $104,000 at the end of 19x6. A valuation allowance of $6,000 ($110,000 − 104,000) is needed; the $2,000 ($6,000 − 4,000) increase in the valuation allowance would be recorded as follows:

Dec. 31, 19x6	Unrealized Loss on Long-Term Investments in Marketable Equity Securities	2,000	
	Allowance for Valuation of Long-Term Investments in Marketable Equity Securities		2,000
	To record change in balance of investment valuation allowance for 19x6.		

If a smaller balance is needed in the valuation allowance, the entry is the reverse. Assume that the securities in the previous illustration have a market value of $105,000 at the end of 19x7. A balance of $5,000 ($110,000 − 105,000) is needed in the valuation allowance; thus, the valuation allowance decreases $1,000 ($6,000 − 5,000). The entry to record the decrease in the valuation allowance would be:

Dec. 31, 19x7	Allowance for Valuation of Long-Term Investments in Marketable Equity Securities	1,000	
	Unrealized Loss on Long-Term Investments in Marketable Equity Securities		1,000
	To record change in balance of investment valuation allowance for 19x7.		

If market value had been equal to or greater than cost at the end of 19x7, the valuation allowance and unrealized loss accounts would have been eliminated. A gain cannot be recognized for any market value in excess of cost under the lower-of-cost-or-market method.

Note that a change in the valuation allowance is recorded only at the end of the accounting period. Even if market value changes between the end of a period and the date at which a stock investment is sold, no adjustment to the allowance account is made at that date. The entry for the sale will be the same as illustrated for the cost method (see pages 567–568).

Equity Method

According to APB Opinion No. 18 the **equity method** must be used to account for investments in common stock when (1) the investor has significant influence over the operating and financial activities of the investee or (2) the investor has control over the operating and financial activities of the investee, and the investment will be reported on the separate financial statements of the investor.

The equity method is a departure from the cost principle, but more closely meets the objectives of accrual accounting. Revenue from the investment is recognized when the investee reports net income rather than when dividends are received. Revenue is considered to have been realized before dividends are received because the investor can influence the use or distribution of the investee's earnings. The changes in the economic resources underlying the investment are reflected in the investment account as the changes occur. Thus, the investment is reported at its economic value.

All investments are recorded at their cost at the time of acquisition. Assume that Weste Corp. acquires 5,000 shares of Easte Company's $10 par value common stock at $18 per share on January 10, 19x2, when 25,000 shares are outstanding. The entry to record the purchase of the stock would be:

Jan 10, 19x2	Investment in Easte Common Stock	90,000	
	Cash		90,000
	To record purchase of 5,000 shares of Easte Company common stock at $18 per share ($18 × 5,000 = $90,000).		

Because Weste Corp. owns 20 percent (5,000/25,000) of Easte Company's common stock, the equity method is used to account for the investment after acquisition. As net income is reported by the investee, revenue is realized and recognized. The increase in the economic value of the investment is recorded by increasing the investment balance. Assume that Easte Company reports net income of $40,000 for 19x2. Weste Corp. will recognize its pro rata share of Easte's net income for 19x2 as follows:

Dec. 31, 19x2	Investment in Easte Common Stock Investment Revenue To recognize Weste's pro rata share of Easte's net income for 19x2 ($40,000 × 20% = $8,000).	8,000	8,000

If the investee reports a net loss, the investor's pro rata share of the loss must be recorded. The entry would require a debit to investment loss and a credit to the investment account. The credit to the investment account recognizes the decrease in the economic value of the investment resulting from the investee's net loss.

Under the equity method all dividends received from the investee represent either a return of the investee's earnings, which have been included in the investment balance, or a return of the original investment. Thus, the investment account is credited when the dividends are received. Assume that dividends of $1 per share on Easte Company's stock are received on December 31, 19x2, by Weste Corp. The entry to record the receipt of the dividends would be:

Dec. 31,
19x2
	Cash
	    Investment in Easte Common
	        Stock
	To record receipt of dividends of $1 per
	share ($1 × 5,000 = $5,000).
		5,000	5,000

The balance of the investment account will reflect the cost of the investment plus the investor's share of the undistributed earnings of the investee. During 19x2 the investee, Easte Company, earned $40,000 and distributed dividends of $25,000 ($1 per share on 25,000 shares outstanding). Thus, $15,000 ($40,000 − 25,000) of the investee's earnings were not distributed during 19x2. The investment account will include the investor's 20 percent share of these undistributed earnings, that is, $3,000 ($15,000 × 20%). The investment account would appear as follows:

Investment in Easte Common Stock		

1/10/x2 Purchased 5,000
                shares at $18
                per share   90,000
12/31/x2 Recognized 20% of
                investee's net
                income for
                19x2   8,000
	12/31/x2 Received dividends
	                from investee 5,000	

(Balance at December 31, 19x2: $93,000)

Exhibit 29.4

Weste Corp.
Partial Income Statement
For the Year Ended December 31, 19x2

Incidental revenue and expense:	
Investment revenue (see note 1)	$ 8,000

Weste Corp.
Partial Balance Sheet
December 31, 19x2

Long-term investments and funds:	
Investment in Easte common stock, equity basis (see note 1)	$93,000

Note 1: The investment in Easte Company common stock is accounted for on the equity basis in accord with APB Opinion No. 18. The investment has a cost basis of $90,000 and a market value at December 31, 19x2, of $92,000. Included in net income for 19x2 is $8,000 of the earnings reported for the year by Easte Company.

Note that the balance at the end of 19x2 is $93,000 compared to the cost of $90,000. The $3,000 difference is the excess of the investor's share of the investee's earnings for 19x2 ($8,000) over the dividends distributed during the year ($5,000)—in other words, the investor's share of the undistributed earnings for 19x2.

The same type of information should be disclosed when the equity method is used as when the cost or lower-of-cost-or-market method is used. Also, the investment and revenue accounts are classified in the same manner. A partial income statement and a partial balance sheet for Weste Corp. at the end of 19x2 are illustrated in Exhibit 29.4, assuming a market value of $92,000 for the stock.

Sales of investments in common stock accounted for under the equity method are recorded in the same way as the cost method (see pages 567–568). The basis of each share sold, however, is determined by dividing the investment balance (which is recorded on the equity basis) by the total number of shares owned.

Effect of Stock Dividends and Splits

The investor does not realize income when stock dividends or stock splits are received. The total cost of the investment remains the same; however, the cost basis per share decreases because more shares are owned after the stock dividend or stock split. The investor will realize income when the stock is sold, if it can be sold at a market price exceeding the new cost basis per share.

Assume that a company owns 1,000 shares of stock in another company with a total cost of $38,500, or a cost per share of $38.50 ($38,500/1,000). If a 10 percent stock dividend is received, the total cost of the investment is still $38,500. The cost per share, however, decreases to $35 ($38,500/1,100) because the investor now owns 1,100 shares (1,000 × 10% = 100; 1,000 + 100 = 1,100).

REVIEW PROBLEM

On January 20, 19x6, Krown, Inc., made the following investments:

a. Purchased 1,000 shares of the 20,000 outstanding shares of King Corp. redeemable 6% preferred stock ($25 par value) at $26 per share.

b. Purchased 5,000 shares of the 50,000 outstanding shares of Prince Corp. common stock ($10 par value) at $16 per share.

c. Purchased 20,000 shares of the 100,000 outstanding shares of Queen Corp. common stock ($10 par value) at $18 per share.

The following is a summary of net income for each company, dividends paid by each company, and the market value of each company's stock at December 31, 19x6:

Company	Net Income	Dividends per Share	Market Value per Share at 12/31/x6
King Corp.	$ 50,000	$2.00	$25.50
Prince Corp.	120,000	1.50	15.00
Queen Corp.	175,000	1.00	17.50

Required

1. Prepare the entries to record the acquisition of the stock, the recognition of revenue, the recognition of dividends received, and the change in the market value of the stock, as necessary, for each investment.

2. Prepare a partial income statement and a partial balance sheet at the end of 19x6 for Krown, Inc.

Solution to review problem

1. See Exhibit 29.5.

2.

Krown, Inc.
Partial Income Statement
For the Year Ended December 31, 19x6

Incidental revenue and expense:	
Dividend revenue	$ 9,500
Investment revenue	35,000

Exhibit 29.5

Transactions	Investment in King Corp. Preferred Stock (Cost Method)		Investment in Prince Corp. Common Stock (Lower-of-Cost-or-Market Method)		Investment in Queen Corp. Common Stock (Equity Method)	
Acquisition of stock	Investment in King Preferred Stock	26,000	Investment in Prince Common Stock	80,000	Investment in Queen Common Stock	360,000
	Cash	26,000	Cash	80,000	Cash	360,000
	To record purchase of stock ($26 × 1,000 = $26,000).		To record purchase of stock ($16 × 5,000 = $80,000).		To record purchase of stock ($18 × 20,000 = $360,000).	
Recognition of revenue when investee reports net income	No entry		No entry		Investment in Queen Common Stock	35,000
					Investment Revenue	35,000
					To recognize 20% of net income reported by investee ($175,000 × 20% = $35,000).	
Recognition of dividends received	Cash	2,000	Cash	7,500	Cash	20,000
	Dividend Revenue	2,000	Dividend Revenue	7,500	Investment in Queen Common Stock	20,000
	To recognize dividends received ($2 × 1,000 = $2,000).		To recognize dividends received ($1.50 × 5,000 = $7,500).		To recognize dividends received ($1 × 20,000 = $20,000).	
Recognition of lower market value	No entry		Unrealized Loss on Long-Term Investments in Marketable Equity Securities	5,000	No entry	
			Allowance for Valuation of Long-Term Investments in Marketable Equity Securities	5,000		
			To apply lower-of-cost-or-market method [($16 − 15) × 5,000 = $5,000].			

Krown, Inc.
Partial Balance Sheet
December 31, 19x6

Long-term investments and funds:

Investment in King preferred stock, at cost (see note 1)	$ 26,000
Investment in Prince common stock, at market value (see note 1)	75,000
Investment in Queen common stock, equity basis (see note 1)	375,000

Stockholders' equity:

Unrealized loss on long-term investment in marketable equity securities (see note 1)	$ 5,000

Note 1: Long-term investments are accounted for in conformity with current accounting principles at cost, lower-of-cost-or-market, or equity as appropriate in each case. During 19x6 unrealized losses of $5,000 on investments in marketable equity securities were charged to stockholders' equity. The cost and market values at December 31, 19x6, are summarized as follows:

	Cost	*Market value at 12/31/x6*
Investment in King preferred stock	$ 26,000	$ 25,500
Investment in Prince common stock	80,000	75,000
Investment in Queen common stock	360,000	350,000

Comments on solution

1. Dividend revenue includes dividends on King preferred stock and Prince common stock: $2,000 + 7,500 = $9,500.
2. Investment revenue includes 20 percent of Queen Corp.'s net income for 19x6: $175,000 × 20% = $35,000.
3. The market values of the investments were determined as follows: King, $25.50 × 1,000 = $25,500; Prince, $15 × 5,000 = $75,000; Queen, $17.50 × 20,000 = $350,000.
4. The balance of the Queen Corp. investment was determined as follows: $360,000 + 35,000 − 20,000 = $375,000.
5. The King Corp. preferred stock is not a marketable equity security because it is redeemable; thus, the cost method is appropriate to account for it. Prince Corp. stock is assumed to be a marketable equity security. Because Krown, Inc., owns less than 20 percent of this stock, the lower-of-cost-or-market method is appropriate. The equity method is appropriate for Queen Corp. stock because Krown, Inc., owns 20 percent of it. Whether or not a stock is a marketable equity security is irrelevant if the equity method is required.

SUMMARY

Long-term investments in stock are accounted for by one of three methods: the cost, lower-of-cost-or-market, or equity method. The equity method should be used for long-term investments in common stock when the investor possesses significant influence over the investee. Either the cost or lower-of-cost-or-market method is used when significant influence does not exist. The lower-of-cost-or-market method must be used for long-term investments in marketable equity securities. The cost method is appropriate for long-term investments not considered marketable equity securities.

The measurement and reporting practices for each of these three methods were discussed and illustrated in this unit. The differences between the methods center on the recognition of revenue from the investment.

APPENDIX 29   CONSOLIDATED FINANCIAL STATEMENTS

Business Combinations

A *business combination* occurs: when a company acquires one or more other companies, which are then dissolved (a *merger*); when a new company is formed to take over two or more companies, which are then dissolved (a *consolidation*); or when one company acquires *control* over one or more other companies. For example, if Company A acquires Company B in a merger, only Company A survives. If a new company (AB) is formed to consolidate Company A and Company B, only the new company (AB) survives the business combination. However, if Company A acquires control of Company B through an exchange for Company B's stock, both companies continue to exist as separate legal entities (although viewed as a single economic unit), as well as separate entities for financial reporting.

In order to acquire control, a company must acquire more than 50 percent of the outstanding voting stock of another company through an exchange for cash, debt securities, and/or stock. The company that acquires control is known as the *parent company;* the controlled company is known as a *subsidiary*. If Company A acquires control of Company B, Company A is the parent and Company B the subsidiary.

Since the 1950s business combinations have become commonplace. Some companies use business combinations to acquire a larger share of an existing market. Others may want to complement current business operations by acquiring or controlling companies that provide essential products, parts, or services for their own products, or that provide marketing outlets or financing to customers. Companies with business operations that are cyclical in nature may seek to diversify operations and stabilize earnings or provide steady growth through business combinations. Still other combinations occur because companies seek to obtain certain legal, technical, political, economic, or tax advantages.

Accounting for Business Combinations

When a merger or consolidation occurs, the assets and liabilities of the acquired companies are transferred to the acquiring company. Following acquisition the only financial statements prepared are those of the acquiring company. The acquired companies are dissolved by distributing remaining cash and any debt securities and/or stock received in the merger or consolidation to their stockholders.

Two methods are used to account for business combinations: the purchase and the pooling of interests methods. If the conditions of APB Opinion No. 16 for the pooling method are met, the combination must be accounted for as a pooling of interests. All other combinations must be accounted for as a purchase. One of the conditions for the pooling method is that the acquiring company must exchange only its own voting stock for "substantially all" (defined as 90 percent or more) of the acquired company's outstanding voting stock. Thus, any combination requiring a distribution of cash or debt securities in exchange for the acquired company's stock must be treated as a purchase.

Because a parent company controls the subsidiary, combined as well as individual financial information is useful to the management and stockholders of the parent company. Thus, when one company controls another and combined financial data would provide meaningful information and validly reflect the financial status of both companies, consolidated financial statements should be prepared. In consolidated financial statements a parent and its subsidiaries are viewed as a single economic unit although they are still legally distinct entities. In addition, separate financial statements are desirable to provide information about the individual companies that will be relevant to their creditors and stockholders.

Pooling Method   Under the pooling method the investment in the subsidiary is recorded at the book value of the subsidiary's stock. If the par value of the shares exchanged are equal, the retained earnings of the subsidiary is carried forward at book value to the parent's books in an account called "retained earnings from pooling."[1] Assume that Company P acquires 100 percent of the outstanding common stock (20,000 shares; $5 par) of Company S in exchange for 10,000 shares of its own $10 par common stock. Exhibit 29.6 illustrates the individual balance sheets of Company P and Company S immediately after the combination, and the consolidated balances. Note that the $60,000 retained earnings balance of Company S has been carried forward as retained earnings from pooling on Company P's books because the par value of the shares exchanged are equal.

When the consolidated balance sheet is prepared, the assets and liabilities of the subsidiary are combined with those of the parent at their book value. Also, the retained earnings of the two companies are in effect combined; the subsidiary's retained earnings, represented by the retained earnings from pooling account, are added to the

---

[1]When the par value of the shares issued by the parent exceed the par value of the shares received, additional contributed capital is reduced first before a reduction in retained earnings from pooling. If the par value of the shares issued is less than the par value of the shares received, additional contributed capital increases.

Exhibit 29.6

	Pooling Method		
	Balance Sheets		*Consolidated*
	Company P	*Company S*	*Balances*
Current assets	$520,000	$180,000	$700,000
Plant assets	230,000	140,000	370,000
Accumulated depreciation	(50,000)	(70,000)	(120,000)
Investment in Company S	160,000		
Total assets	$860,000	$250,000	$950,000
Current liabilities	$150,000	$ 65,000	$215,000
Long-term debt	200,000	25,000	225,000
Common stock—Company P	250,000		250,000
Common stock—Company S		100,000	
Retained earnings—Company P	200,000		
Retained earnings from pooling	60,000		260,000
Retained earnings—Company S		60,000	
Total equities	$860,000	$250,000	$950,000

parent's retained earnings for a consolidated balance of $260,000. The investment account and the actual stockholders' equity account of the subsidiary are eliminated.

Purchase Method   Under the purchase method the investment in the subsidiary is recorded at the cost of the net assets acquired. Cost is measured using the current market values of the assets and liabilities of the subsidiary. Sometimes cost exceeds the market value of the net assets acquired; this excess is recognized as goodwill from consolidation when consolidated statements are prepared. Assume that Company P acquires all of Company S's common stock in a cash purchase for $175,000. Note that Company P pays $175,000 for stock with a book value of $160,000 ($100,000 + 60,000). If $10,000 of the difference is attributed to plant assets whose market value exceeds their book value, the other $5,000 is assigned to goodwill from consolidation.

In preparing the consolidated balance sheet, the market values of the assets and liabilities of the subsidiary must be combined with the balances reported on the parent's balance sheet, and any goodwill purchased must be recognized. In Exhibit 29.7 the market value of the plant assets, $150,000, is combined with the parent's balance, $230,000; the resulting consolidated balance is $380,000. In addition, goodwill of $5,000 is recognized in the consolidated balances. The investment in Company S and the stockholders' equity of Company S are eliminated. All other accounts are combined at the amounts reported on the separate balance sheets because there are no other differences between book value and market value for Company S's assets and liabilities.

Comparison of Pooling and Purchase Methods   The differences between the pooling and purchase methods center on the value of the subsidiary's net assets included in the consolidated balance sheet. Under the pooling method the book value of the net assets is recognized, whereas market value is recognized under the purchase method.

Exhibit 29.7

	Purchase Method		
	Balance Sheets		Consolidated
	Company P	Company S	Balances
Current assets	$345,000	$180,000	$525,000
Plant assets	230,000	140,000*	380,000
Accumulated depreciation	(50,000)	(70,000)	(120,000)
Investment in Company S	175,000		
Goodwill from consolidation			5,000**
Total assets	$700,000	$250,000	$790,000
Current liabilities	$150,000	$ 65,000	$215,000
Long-term debt	200,000	25,000	225,000
Common stock—Company P	150,000		150,000
Common stock—Company S		100,000	
Retained earnings—Company P	200,000		200,000
Retained earnings—Company S		60,000	
Total equities	$700,000	$250,000	$790,000

*Market value: $150,000.
**Goodwill: $5,000 [$175,000 − ($100,000 + 60,000) − 10,000]

Also, the purchase method requires the recognition of any goodwill implied by an excess of cost over the market value of the net assets acquired. Subsequent to acquisition the excess of market value over book value for depreciable plant assets or intangible assets and goodwill from consolidation must be amortized or depreciated. As a result net income and earnings per share are less on a consolidated basis than would be expected by reference to the individual income statements.

Recall from Exhibits 29.6 and 29.7 that Company S plant assets had a market value $10,000 greater than book value, and goodwill of $5,000 was recognized under the purchase method. If the plant assets have a remaining life of 10 years and goodwill is to be amortized over 20 years, an additional $1,250 [($10,000/10) + ($5,000/20)] of expenses must be recognized on a consolidated basis under the purchase method that would not be recognized under the pooling method.

The pooling method is generally favored because increased market values of assets and goodwill are not recognized and, thus, any adverse effects on net income and earnings per share are avoided. However, it is important that any plan of business combination carefully adhere to the conditions specified for the pooling method in APB Opinion No. 16. If any condition is not met, the purchase method must be used in accounting for the combination.

Additional Problems   When consolidated financial statements are prepared, eliminations are required for the effects of certain intercompany transactions to avoid overstating consolidated assets, liabilities, revenues, and expenses. These eliminations include those for intercompany receivables and payables at the end of the period, intercompany revenues and expenses, and intercompany profits not yet realized. These and other complex accounting issues for consolidated financial statements are discussed in intermediate and/or advanced accounting courses.

If the parent owns less than 100 percent of the subsidiary, a **minority interest** in the subsidiary's net assets and net income must be recognized in the consolidated financial statements. For example, assume that Company P in Exhibits 29.6 and 29.7 acquired only 90 percent of Company S's stock. The minority interest of 10 percent in Company S's net assets would amount to $16,000 [($100,000 + 60,000) × 10%] and $17,000 [($100,000 + 60,000 + 10,000) × 10%], respectively, and would be reported as a separate element of consolidated stockholders' equity. For subsequent periods the minority interest in Company S's net income would be determined and deducted from consolidated net income. The final figure on the consolidated income statement would then be the **controlling** (that is, parent's) **interest** in consolidated net income.

Sometimes a subsidiary is not included in consolidated financial statements because control is not assured or not expected to continue, or because combined financial data would not be meaningful. For example, the combined financial data of a manufacturing company and a bank, insurance company, or subsidiary providing financing to customers are generally considered not meaningful. Investments in **unconsolidated subsidiaries** such as these should be reported in the long-term investments and funds section of the consolidated balance sheet using the equity method.

REVIEW QUESTIONS

29-1 What is included in the cost of a long-term investment in stock?

29-2 Why would an entity invest in the stock of another company on a long-term basis?

29-3 a. Identify three methods of measuring long-term investments in stock.
  b. The degree of influence or control an investor has over the investee's operating and financial policies is used to determine which of these three accounting methods should be used. Explain.

29-4 a. Identify four methods of reporting long-term investments in stock.
  b. Indicate what percentage of the outstanding voting stock of the investee the investor should own to use each of these four reporting methods.

29-5 When is income realized from an investment in stock under each of the following methods: (a) cost method, (b) lower-of-cost-or-market method, and (c) equity method?

29-6 How are dividends received from an investment in stock accounted for under each of the following methods: (a) cost method, (b) lower-of-cost-or-market method, and (c) equity method?

29-7 a. How is the lower-of-cost-or-market method applied to investments in marketable equity securities?
  b. How is the account unrealized loss on long-term investments in marketable equity securities disclosed on the financial statements?

29-8 The investment account balance reflects the cost of the investment plus the investor's share of the undistributed profits of the investee. Explain.

29-9   What is the effect of a stock dividend or a stock split on an investment in stock?

29-10 a.   What is a business combination?
b.   Distinguish among business combinations brought about through a merger, a consolidation, and control.
c.   Distinguish between a parent and a subsidiary.

29-11   When should a business combination by control be accounted for as (a) a pooling of interests and (b) a purchase?

29-12   Explain why the assets and liabilities of an acquired company are combined with those of the acquiring company at book value for a pooling of interest and at fair market value for a purchase.

29-13   If a business combination is accounted for as a purchase, goodwill may be recognized. However, if it is accounted for as a pooling of interests, goodwill is not recognized. Explain this difference in treatment.

29-14   Indicate the criteria for preparing consolidated financial statements.

29-15   What are the effects of the pooling of interests and purchase method on net income and earnings per share?

29-16 a.   What is a minority interest?
b.   What is a controlling interest?
c.   What is an unconsolidated subsidiary?

EXERCISES

29-1   Casper Corp. acquired 2,000 shares of the 50,000 outstanding shares of Cody Company common stock on January 1, 19x6, at $30 per share plus brokerage fees of $1,500. During 19x6 Cody Company declared and paid dividends of $1 per share and reported net income of $75,000. At the end of 19x6 the market value of Cody Company common stock was $33 per share.

Required   **a.**   Prepare all entries necessary to account for the investment during 19x6.
b.   Prepare a partial balance sheet and a partial income statement at the end of 19x6.

29-2   Refer to the data in exercise 29–1. Assume that Casper Corp. had acquired 10,000 shares of Cody Company common stock at $30 per share plus brokerage fees of $6,500 on January 1, 19x6.

Required   **a.**   Prepare all entries necessary to account for the investment during 19x6.
b.   Prepare a partial balance sheet and a partial income statement at the end of 19x6.

29-3 Helena Corp. acquired some of the 20,000 outstanding shares of Butte Company common stock on January 1, 19x3. During 19x3 Butte Company reported net income of $65,000 and declared and paid cash dividends of $1 per share. At the end of 19x3 the stock of Butte Company was selling at $26 per share.

Required   Prepare all entries necessary on the books of Helena Corp. to account for its investment in Butte Company during 19x3 if Helena Corp. purchased (a) 1,000 shares of Butte common stock at $28 per share and (b) 6,000 shares of Butte common stock at $28 per share.

29-4 Laramie Company acquired the common stock of Yellowstone Corp., Glacier Corp., and Teton Corp. at the beginning of 19x7 with the intention of holding the stocks as long-term investments. The cost and market value of the stocks at the end of 19x7, 19x8, and 19x9 are summarized as follows:

Security	Cost	Market Value at:		
		12/31/x7	12/31/x8	12/31/x9
Yellowstone stock	$ 60,000	$ 62,000	$ 63,000	$ 65,000
Glacier stock	85,000	82,000	81,000	83,000
Teton stock	130,000	128,000	126,000	125,000
Total	$275,000	$272,000	$270,000	$273,000

All three stocks are considered to be marketable equity securities. Laramie Company owns less than 20% of the outstanding voting stock of each company.

Required   **a.**   Prepare the entry at the end of each year to apply the lower-of-cost-or-market method.

   b.   Prepare a partial balance sheet at the end of 19x9.

29-5 Cheyenne Corp. purchased 1,000 shares of Billings Company common stock at $28 per share plus brokerage fees of $600 on February 1, 19x3. On July 10, 19x3, a 10% stock dividend was received. Cash dividends of $.50 per share were received on October 31, 19x3. On November 20, 19x3, Cheyenne Corp. sold 400 shares of Billings Company stock at $30 per share less brokerage fees of $300. The market value of the Billings Company stock was $29 per share at December 31, 19x3. Cheyenne's investment represents less than 20% of the outstanding voting stock of Billings Company. Billings Company reported net income of $38,000 for 19x3.

Required   **a.**   Prepare the journal entries required during 19x3 to account for the investment in Billings common stock.

   b.   Prepare a partial balance sheet and a partial income statement at the end of 19x3.

29-6 Poste Corp. acquired 100% control of the outstanding voting stock of Stone Corp. At the date of combination, the book value and market value of the net assets of Stone Corp. were:

	Book Value	Market Value
Current assets	$ 580,000	$ 580,000
Plant assets (net)	700,000	950,000
Intangible assets	160,000	300,000
Total assets	$1,440,000	$1,830,000
Current liabilities	$ 150,000	$ 150,000
Long-term liabilities	500,000	500,000
Total liabilities	$ 650,000	$ 650,000
Net assets	$ 790,000	$1,180,000

Required   **a.**   Indicate the amount at which the assets should be reported on a consolidated balance sheet if the combination is accounted for as (1) a purchase and (2) a pooling of interests.

              b.   Determine the amount of goodwill to be recognized if Poste paid $1,300,000 in cash and long-term notes to acquire Stone's stock.

PROBLEMS

29-1   Gunnison Corp. made the following long-term investments in marketable equity securities during 19*x1*:

Jan. 20	Purchased 3,000 shares of Aspen Corp. common stock at $26 per share.
Apr. 3	Purchased 1,000 shares of Vail Corp. common stock at $33 per share.
June 12	Purchased 2,000 shares of Snowmass Corp. common stock at $40 per share.

At all times during the two years Gunnison Corp. owned less than 20% of the outstanding voting stock of each company. The market value of each stock at the end of 19*x2* was: Aspen, $23; Vail, $32; Snowmass, $42.

Required   **a.**   Prepare all entries required during 19*x1* and 19*x2,* including those to apply the lower-of-cost-or-market method.

              b.   Prepare a partial balance sheet at the end of 19*x2.*

29-2   Bryce Company made the following investments on January 1, 19*x4:*

Zion Co. common stock—1,000 shares of the 10,000 outstanding shares at $32 per share.

Cedar Co. common stock—3,000 shares of the 10,000 outstanding shares at $24 per share.

During 19*x4* the net income reported and dividends declared by the companies were:

	Bryce	Zion	Cedar
Net income	$60,000	$40,000	$50,000
Dividends declared	30,000	20,000	25,000

At the end of 19*x4* the market values of the stocks acquired were: Zion, $30 per share; Cedar, $25 per share.

Required	**a.**	Prepare all necessary entries to account for the investments during 19*x4*.
	b.	Prepare a partial balance sheet and a partial income statement at the end of 19*x4*.

29-3   Fargo Corp. purchased 20,000 shares of Bismarck Corp. common stock at $17 per share at the beginning of 19*x1*. At that time Bismarck Corp. had 100,000 shares of common stock outstanding. Bismarck Corp. reported net income and declared and paid cash dividends for 19*x1* – 19*x3* as follows:

Year	Net Income	Cash Dividends
19*x1*	$60,000	$20,000
19*x2*	80,000	30,000
19*x3*	75,000	25,000

At the beginning of 19*x4* Bismarck Corp. declared and issued a 10% stock dividend. On July 1, 19*x4*, Fargo Corp. sold 5,000 shares of Bismarck Corp. stock at $28 per share. Net income for the first 6 months of 19*x4* was $35,000. Cash dividends declared and paid during the first 6 months of 19*x4* were $15,000. The market value of Bismarck Corp. common stock at the end of each year was:

Year	Market Value
19*x1*	$16.50
19*x2*	21.00
19*x3*	25.00
19*x4*	26.50

Bismarck Corp. reported net income of $30,000 and declared and paid cash dividends of $11,000 during the last 6 months of 19*x4*.

Required	**a.**	Prepare a partial balance sheet and a partial income statement at the end of 19x3 if the investment is accounted for by (1) the cost method and (2) the equity method.
	b.	Determine the amount of gain or loss to be reported from the sale of 5,000 shares of Bismarck stock on July 1, 19x4, if the cost method is used.
	c.	Prepare a partial balance sheet and a partial income statement at the end of 19x4 if the cost method is used.

29-4 The condensed balance sheets for Parish Corp. and Mission Corp. at December 31, 19x4, follow; the book values and market values for assets are given:

	Parish Corp.		Mission Corp.	
	Book Value	Market Value	Book Value	Market Value
Cash	$ 90,000	$ 90,000	$ 35,000	$ 35,000
Accounts receivable (net)	65,000	65,000	45,000	45,000
Inventories	60,000	64,000	40,000	40,000
Plant and equipment (net)	180,000	216,000	130,000	150,000
Total assets	$395,000	$435,000	$250,000	$270,000
Current liabilities	$ 55,000		$ 50,000	
Long-term liabilities	25,000		50,000	
Common stock ($10 par)	150,000		100,000	
Contributed capital in excess of par	50,000		20,000	
Retained earnings	115,000		30,000	
Total equities	$395,000		$250,000	

Two alternative plans for a business combination are being considered:

Plan 1   Parish Corp. would acquire all of Mission Corp's outstanding stock for $55,000 cash and $125,000 of long-term notes.

Plan 2   Parish Corp. would acquire all of Mission Corp's outstanding stock by issuing 10,000 shares of its own stock.

Required   Prepare a consolidated balance sheet for immediately after the business combination is completed for each of the two alternatives.

29-5 Gladiator Corp. acquired all the outstanding stock of Spartan Corp. at the beginning of 19x6. At the date of combination the book value and market value of Spartan's net assets were:

	Book Value	Market Value
Cash	$ 80,000	$ 80,000
Accounts receivable (net)	110,000	110,000
Inventories	125,000	132,000
Land	40,000	60,000
Buildings (net)	280,000	350,000
Equipment (net)	95,000	108,000
Total assets	$730,000	$840,000
Current liabilities	$120,000	$120,000
Long-term liabilities	200,000	200,000
Total liabilities	$320,000	$320,000
Net assets	$410,000	$520,000

Also, Spartan Corp. had 70,000 shares of $5 par value common stock outstanding and a retained earnings balance of $85,000 at the date of combination.

Required **a.** Prepare a schedule to determine the amount of goodwill, if any, that Gladiator Corp. paid to acquire the stock of Spartan Corp. under each of the following acquisition alternatives:

  (1) Gladiator Corp. paid $200,000 cash and issued 25,000 shares of its $10 par value common stock, which had a market value of $350,000.

  (2) Gladiator Corp. issued 35,000 shares of its $10 par value common stock for all of the outstanding common stock of Spartan Corp.

b. Indicate the amount at which the assets and liabilities of Spartan Corp. would be included in a consolidated balance sheet under each of the acquisition alternatives given in part a.

Unit 30
Long-Term Investments
in Bonds

Everybody can't beat the market. [But looking at stocks over the last century,] the odds are fairly favorable as against horse racing, gambling with friends, as against commodities . . .

Paul A. Samuelson, Nobel laureate economist, March 1971

This unit is concerned with how an investor accounts for bonds. (How the issuer accounts for them was discussed in Unit 25.) Both the issuer and the investor face similar problems: issuance or acquisition of bonds between interest dates, issuance or acquisition of bonds at a premium or discount, measurement of bond interest expense or revenue, and measurement of the bond liability or bond investment at balance sheet date. Thus, most concepts involved in accounting for bond investments are the same as those involved in accounting for bond obligations.

Performance Objectives

Upon completing this unit you should be able to:

1. define and use the accounting terms introduced in this unit.
2. describe or explain:
   a. what constitutes the balance to be reported for a long-term investment in bonds
   b. how the balance for a long-term investment in bonds is measured or reported
   c. the amount that should be reported annually as interest revenue on a long-term investment in bonds

3. determine:
    a. the cost of a long-term investment in bonds
    b. the semiannual or annual interest payment received
    c. the monthly, semiannual, or annual effective interest revenue
    d. the amount to be reported as the balance of a long-term investment in bonds at the end of any accounting period
4. prepare the correct journal entry for transactions involving long-term bond investments.

Nature of Long-Term Investments in Bonds

Long-term investments in bonds are recorded at the time of acquisition in conformity with the cost principle. Their cost includes the market price of the bonds and any brokerage fees and taxes related to their acquisition. Recall from Unit 25 that the market price of the bonds is actually the present value of two types of cash flows to be received by the investor: (1) the **principal** (that is, the par or face value) of the bonds at maturity and (2) interest at regular intervals throughout the term of the bonds. The present value of these two cash flows at the **market rate of interest** at a particular date determines the market price of the bonds at that date.

The market rate of interest fluctuates depending on the supply and demand for money, but the bond contract provides for payment of interest at a fixed rate. Thus, bonds are sold at a premium or discount in order to adjust the **stated interest rate** to the market interest rate. If the market interest rate is greater than the stated interest rate, the bonds will sell at a **discount,** that is, at a price below their face value. On the other hand, if the market interest rate is *less* than the stated interest rate, the bonds will sell at a **premium,** that is, at a price above their face value. Unless there is evidence as to the intended holding period, it should be assumed that the bonds will be held until maturity.

Bonds of another company may be purchased for any of the following reasons:

1. to accommodate companies over which the investor has significant influence or control
2. to accommodate important suppliers or customers
3. to invest cash contributed to a non-trusteed fund
4. to invest excess cash

With their stated rate of interest and fixed maturity, bonds provide investment opportunities with risks greatly reduced from those offered by stock investments. Bonds can often be purchased at a discount and held until maturity, thereby reducing the cash outlay for the investment. If the bonds are near maturity, there is usually less risk of default and unfavorable price fluctuation. Further, interest must be paid, whereas dividends do not have to be paid. Finally bonds are often secured, or at least provide a prior claim on the issuer's assets in case of default.

Accounting for Bond Investments and Interest

The corporation that issues bonds records any premium or discount in a separate account (see Unit 25). Investors, however, normally do *not* record the premium or discount separately. The investment is recorded at cost, that is, the market price of the bonds plus any brokerage fees and taxes. Both interest revenue and the book value of the investment account are adjusted as any premium or discount is amortized. Over the period the bonds are held, their book value will increase, if issued at a discount (or decrease, if issued at a premium) from their cost to their maturity value as depicted below:

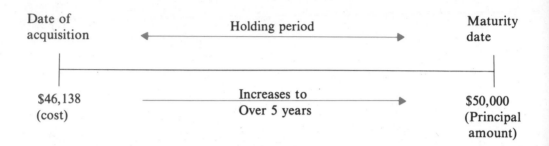

Premium or discount should be amortized at each interest payment date and at the end of the accounting period if the latter does not correspond with an interest payment date. The **straight-line amortization method** allocates an equal amount of the premium or discount to income over the holding period of the bonds. Thus, a constant amount of interest revenue is recognized each period. The **effective-interest amortization method** yields a constant interest rate each period; it is discussed in the appendix to this unit.

In the illustrations that follow regarding the purchase of bonds the following data will be used:

Principal amount of bonds	$50,000
Date of purchase	April 1, 19x1
Maturity date	April 1, 19x6
Term of bonds	5 years
Stated interest rate	8%
Semiannual interest payment dates	April 1 and October 1

Bonds Purchased at Par   If the bonds are purchased at their par or face value, their cost is $50,000. Their book value is equal to their cost over the holding period of five years. Interest revenue is recognized at the semiannual interest payment dates and at the end of the accounting period. In this illustration it is assumed that the accounting period is the calendar year. The entries to record the purchase of the bonds at April 1, 19x1, the receipt of interest on October 1, 19x1, and the accrual of interest at December 31, 19x1, would be:

Apr. 1,	Investment in Bonds	50,000	
19x1	Cash		50,000
	To record purchase of bonds at par.		

Oct. 1,	Cash	2,000	
19x1	Interest Revenue		2,000
	To record receipt of interest on bonds		
	($50,000 × 8% × 6/12 = $2,000).		

Dec. 31,	Interest Receivable	1,000	
19x1	Interest Revenue		1,000
	To accrue interest for the period		
	10/1/x1–12/31/x1 ($50,000 × 8%		
	× 3/12 = $1,000).		

Investments in Bonds			Interest Revenue		
4/1/x1	50,000			10/1/x1	2,000
				12/31/x1	1,000
(Balance, 12/31/x1: $50,000)			(Balance, 12/31/x1: $3,000)		

The investment account, with a balance of $50,000, is reported under long-term investments and funds on the balance sheet. Interest revenue of $3,000 for 19x1 is reported as incidental revenue on a classified income statement. On April 1, 19x2, the interest accrued on December 31, 19x1, and the interest for the period January 1–April 1, 19x2, is received; the entry for the receipt of the interest would be:

Apr. 1,	Cash	2,000	
19x2	Interest Receivable		1,000
	Interest Revenue		1,000
	To record receipt of interest on bonds,		
	part of which was accrued on		
	Dec. 31, 19x1.		

The same entries are made every October 1, December 31, and April 1 until the bonds mature or are sold. If the bonds are held until maturity, the investor receives the $50,000 par value. The entry to record the redemption of the bonds at maturity would be:

Apr. 1,	Cash	50,000	
19x6	Investments in Bonds		50,000
	To record receipt of maturity value of		
	bonds redeemed by issuing company.		

Bonds Purchased at a Discount   Assume that the bonds described on page 592 are purchased at a market price of $46,138 to yield a 10 percent return to the investor. The entry to record this purchase would be:

Apr. 1, 19x1	Investment in Bonds	46,138	
	Cash		46,138
	To record purchase of bonds at a discount.		

The investment account is recorded at cost when the bonds are acquired. The discount of $3,862 ($50,000 − 46,138) is not recorded separately. When the discount is amortized, the investment account is debited because the investment balance must be increased towards the par value of the bonds. Interest revenue is credited for the amount of cash received plus the amount of discount amortized; the sum of these two amounts represents the effective interest revenue for the period. Because the bonds were acquired on an interest payment date, the holding period until maturity is five years. Under the straight-line method the amount of discount amortized is $772 annually ($3,862/5 years), $386 semiannually ($3,862/10), or $193 every three months ($772 × 3/12). The entries for interest on October 1 and December 31, 19x1, would be:

Oct. 1, 19x1	Cash	2,000	
	Investment in Bonds	386	
	Interest Revenue		2,386
	To record receipt of interest on bonds and amortization of bond discount ($50,000 × 8% × 6/12 = $2,000).		
Dec. 31, 19x1	Interest Receivable	1,000	
	Investment in Bonds	193	
	Interest Revenue		1,193
	To accrue interest and amortize bond discount for the period 10/1/x1 − 12/31/x1 ($50,000 × 8% × 3/12 = $1,000).		

The book value of the investment account at the end of 19x1, after amortization of the discount, is $46,717 ($46,138 + 386 + 193). Although interest at the stated interest rate for nine months is $3,000 ($50,000 × 8% × 9/12), interest revenue recognized during 19x1 is $3,579 ($2,386 + 1,193) as a result of amortizing the discount. See the T-accounts that follow and the partial financial statements in Exhibit 30.1.

Exhibit 30.1

Partial Balance Sheet
December 31, 19x1

Long-Term Investments and Funds:
    Investment in Bonds $46,717

Partial Income Statement
For the Year Ended December 31, 19x1

Incidental Revenue and Expense:
    Interest Revenue $ 3,579

Investment in Bonds		Interest Revenue	
4/1/*x1* 46,138		10/1/*x1* 2,836	
10/1/*x1* 386		12/31/*x1* 1,193	
12/31/*x1* 193			

(Balance, 12/31/*x1:* $46,717)   (Balance, 12/31/*x1:* $3,579)

When interest is received on April 1, 19*x2*, bond discount is amortized for the 3-month period January 1–April 1, 19*x2*, and included in interest earned for the same three months. The interest payment also includes the interest accrued for three months on December 31, 19*x1*. Thus the entry on April 1, 19*x2*, would be:

Apr. 1,	Cash	2,000	
19*x2*	Investment in Bonds	193	
	Interest Receivable		1,000
	Interest Revenue		1,193

To record receipt of interest for the
period 10/1/*x1*–12/31/*x1* and to
amortize discount for the period
1/1/*x2*–4/1/*x2*.

On a semiannual basis, the effective interest revenue is $2,386, which represents interest at the stated interest rate plus the amortization of the bond discount ($2,000 + 386 = $2,386). The effective interest rate decreases each period because interest revenue is a constant amount, whereas the book value of the investment increases as the discount is amortized:

$$\frac{\text{effective interest revenue}}{\substack{\text{book value of bond investment} \\ \text{at beginning of period}}} = \substack{\text{effective interest rate} \\ \text{for the period}}$$

$$\frac{\$\ 2,386}{\$46,138} = 5.17\% \text{ for first 6 months (April 1–September 30, 19}x1)$$

$$\frac{\$\ 2,386}{\$46,524} \doteq 5.13\% \text{ for next 6 months (October 1, 19}x1\text{–March 31, 19}x2)$$

Investment in Bonds		
4/1/x1	46,138	
10/1/x1	386	
	46,524	

(Balance, 10/1/x1: $46,524

Bonds Purchased at a Premium   Assume that the bonds described on page 592 are purchased at 103. The cost of the investment is $51,500 ($50,000 × 103%), and is recorded as follows:

Apr. 1, 19x1	Investment in Bonds	51,500	
	Cash		51,500
	To record purchase of bonds at a premium.		

The bond premium will be amortized over the 5-year holding period. The amount to be amortized under the straight-line method will be $300 annually ($1,500/5 years), $150 semiannually ($1,500/10), or $75 every three months ($300 × 3/12). The investment account is credited for the amount of the premium amortized because the balance must decrease towards the par value of the bonds. Interest revenue is credited for the amount of cash received less the amount of the premium amortized; the result is the effective interest revenue for the period.

Oct. 1, 19x1	Cash	2,000	
	Investment in Bonds		150
	Interest Revenue		1,850
	To record receipt of interest on bonds and amortize bond premium.		

Exhibit 30.2

Partial Balance Sheet
December 31, 19x1

Long-Term Investments and Funds:
    Investment in Bonds $51,275

Partial Income Statement
For the Year Ended December 31, 19x1

Incidental Revenues and Expenses:
    Interest Revenue $ 2,775

Dec. 31,	Interest Receivable	1,000	
19x1	Investment in Bonds		75
	Interest Revenue		925
	To accrue interest and amortize bond		
	premium for the period 10/1/x1–		
	12/31/x1.		

The book value of the investment account at the end of 19x1, after amortization of the premium, is $51,275 ($51,500 − 150 − 75). Although interest at the stated interest rate for nine months is $3,000 ($50,000 × 8% × 9/12), interest revenue recognized during 19x1 is $2,775 ($1,850 + 925) as a result of amortizing the premium. See the following T-accounts and the partial financial statements in Exhibit 30.2.

Investment in Bonds				Interest Revenue		
4/1/x1	51,500	10/1/x1	150		10/1/x1	1,850
		12/31/x1	75		12/31/x1	925
(Balance: $51,275)				(Balance: $2,775)		

When interest is received on April 1, 19x2, bond premium is amortized for the 3-month period January 1–April 1, 19x2, and included in interest earned for the same three months. The interest payment also includes the interest accrued for three months on December 31, 19x1. Thus, the entry on April 1, 19x2, would be:

Apr. 1, 19x2	Cash	2,000	
	Investment in Bonds		75
	Interest Receivable		1,000
	Interest Revenue		925
	To record receipt of interest for the period 10/1/x1–12/31/x1 and to amortize premium for the period 1/1/x2–4/4/x2.		

On a semiannual basis, the effective interest revenue is $1,850, which represents interest at the stated interest rate less the amortization of the bond premium ($2,000 − 150 = $1,850). The effective interest rate increases each period because interest revenue is a constant amount whereas the book value of the investment decreases as the premium is amortized.

$$\frac{\text{effective interest revenue for the period}}{\text{book value of bond investment at beginning of period}} = \frac{\text{effective interest rate}}{\text{for the period}}$$

$$\frac{\$ 1,850}{\$51,500} = 3.59\% \text{ for first 6 months}$$

$$\frac{\$1,850}{\$51,500 - 150} = \frac{\$ 1,850}{\$51,350} = 3.60\% \text{ for next 6 months}$$

Bonds Purchased Between Interest Dates   Recall from Unit 25 that the investor must pay the seller (or issuer) of bonds their market price plus accrued interest between an interest payment date (or the date of the bonds) and the date of purchase. This procedure is used to allocate interest properly between the two parties. When the investor receives interest for a full six months at the first interest payment date after the purchase, the payment includes a refund of the accrued interest.

Assume that the bonds described on page 592 are purchased for $47,800 plus accrued interest on September 1, 19x1 (five months after date of the bonds, April 1, 19x1). The investor must pay $47,800 for the bonds plus $1,667 ($50,000 × 8% × 5/12) for accrued interest. The entry to record this transaction would be:

Sept. 1, 19x1	Investment in Bonds	47,800	
	Interest Revenue	1,667	
	Cash		49,467
	To record purchase of bonds at a discount and the payment of accrued interest.		

The accrued interest is charged to interest revenue. This charge offsets the credit to interest revenue on October 1, 19*x1*, for a full six months' interest. The net effect of the two entries is a credit to interest revenue for the interest earned for one month (September 1–October 1, 19*x1*). See the T-account and computations following the October 1, 19*x1*, entry. The entry for the interest payment received on October 1, 19*x1*, also includes the amortization of the bond discount of $2,200 ($50,000 − 47,800) for one month. The discount must be amortized over the period the investor holds the bonds. In this situation the holding period is 55 months (September 1, 19*x1*, to April 1, 19*x6*). Amortization is $40 per month ($2,200/55). The entry to record the receipt of interest and the amortization of bond discount on October 1, 19*x1*, would be:

Oct. 1, 19*x1*	Cash	2,000	
	Investment in Bonds	40	
	Interest Revenue		2,040
	To record receipt of interest and the amortization of bond discount.		

Note that the balance in the interest revenue account after the entries on September 1 and October 1 is $373, the effective interest revenue for one month.

Interest Revenue			
9/1/*x1*	1,667	10/1/*x1*	2,040

(Balance, 10/1/*x1*: $373)

Interest at stated interest rate for one month ($50,000 × 8% × 1/12)	$333
Amortization of bond discount for one month ($2,200/55)	40
Effective interest revenue for one month	$373

Sale of Bond Investment   When a bond investment is sold, any difference between its unamortized balance and the proceeds from the sale is recognized as a gain or loss. Assume that a company purchased bonds at a cost of $19,700 on January 1, 19*x1*. If the bonds mature on January 1, 19*x4*, and have a par value of $20,000, the $300 discount is amortized at the rate of $100 per year ($300/3 years). Assume that the bonds are sold for $19,970 on January 1, 19*x3*. The unamortized balance of the bond investment at the date of sale would be $19,900:

Investment in Bonds			
1/1/*x1*	Purchased bonds	19,700	
12/31/*x1*	Amortization of		
	discount for		
	19*x1*	100	
12/31/*x2*	Amortization of		
	discount for		
	19*x2*	100	
1/1/*x3*	Balance	19,900	

Because the proceeds from the sale, $19,970, exceed the unamortized balance of the bond investment, $19,900, a $70 gain is recognized:

Jan. 1,	Cash	19,970	
19*x3*	Investment in Bonds		19,900
	Gain on Sale of Long-Term		
	Investments		70
	To record sale of bond investment.		

In this example, two assumptions are made: (1) the bonds were sold on an interest payment date and (2) any entries to bring interest revenue and amortization of discount (or premium) up to date have already been made. If the bonds are sold between interest payment dates, the seller of the investment has to record interest revenue and amortization of premium or discount from the last interest payment date to the date of sale. In addition, the seller receives payment of the accrued interest from the buyer. Because the buyer will be the bondholder of record when the next interest payment is made, he or she will receive payment of interest for the entire period. The amount received will consist of two parts: (1) a reimbursement for the accrued interest paid to the previous bondholder and (2) interest earned for the portion of the interest period that the bonds were held.

Assume that the bonds in the example are sold on March 31, 19*x3*, for $19,970, plus accrued interest. If the interest rate is 8%, the accrued interest for three months is $400 ($20,000 × 8% × 3/12). In the entry to recognize accrued interest, an additional $25 of the discount ($100 × 3/12 = $25) is amortized:

Mar. 31,	Interest Receivable	400	
19*x3*	Investment in Bonds	25	
	Interest Revenue		425
	To record accrued interest and		
	amortization of discount at date of		
	sale of investment.		

Because another $25 of the bond discount was amortized, the unamortized balance of the investment at the date of sale, March 31, 19x3, is $19,925 ($19,900 at January 1, 19x3, plus $25). The total amount of cash received will be $20,370 ($19,970 for the bonds plus $400 for the accrued interest). In the entry to record the sale, the asset accounts, investment in bonds and interest receivable, are credited, and a gain of $45 is recognized ($19,970 received for the bonds minus $19,925 balance for the investment equals a $45 gain):

Mar. 31, 19x3	Cash	20,370	
	Investment in Bonds		19,925
	Interest Receivable		400
	Gain on Sale of Long-Term Investments		45
	To record sale of bond investment between interest dates.		

REVIEW PROBLEM

The Plyte Corporation purchased bonds with a par value of $100,000 at the beginning of 19x1 for $97,463. The bonds mature at the end of 19x3, have a stated interest rate of 9%, and pay interest semiannually on June 30 and December 31. The bonds were purchased to yield 10%.

Required

1. Calculate the effective interest revenue recognized and the amount of discount amortized at June 30 and December 31, 19x1, using the straight-line amortization method.
2. Calculate the effective interest rate for the first two interest periods.
3. Prepare a partial balance sheet and a partial income statement at the end of 19x1.
4. Calculate the gain or loss if the bonds are sold for $98,500 on June 30, 19x2.

Solution to review problem

1.
Semiannual interest payment ($100,000 × 9% × 6/12)	$4,500
Add: Amortization of bond discount ($2,537/6)*	423
Interest revenue	$4,923

*$100,000 − 97,463 = $2,537

2.
$$\frac{\text{effective interest revenue for period}}{\text{book value of bond investment at beginning of period}} = \frac{\text{effective interest rate for period}}{}$$

$$\frac{\$ \ 4{,}923}{\$97{,}463} = 5.05\% \text{ for period 1 (January 1–June 30, 19x1)}$$

$$\frac{\$ \ 4{,}923}{\$97{,}886} = 5.03\% \text{ for period 2 (July 1–December 31, 19x1)}$$

Investment in Bonds		
1/1/x1	97,463	
6/30/x1	423	
	97,886	

(Balance, 6/30/x1: $97,886)

3.

Plyte Corporation
Balance Sheet
December 31, 19x1

Long-term investments and funds:
    Investment in bonds $98,309

Plyte Corporation
Income Statement
For the Year Ended December 31, 19x1

Incidental revenues and expenses:
    Interest revenue $ 9,846

Computations
Investment balance at December 31, 19x1 — cost plus bond discount amortized
    during 19x1: $97,463 + 423 + 423 = $98,309.
Interest revenue for 19x1 (see part 1): $4,923 + 4,923 = $9,846.

Investment in Bonds				Interest Revenue		
1/1/x1	97,463					
6/30/x1	423			6/30/x1	4,923	
12/31/x1	423			12/31/x1	4,923	
	98,309				9,846	

(Balance, 12/31/x1: $98,309)   (Balance, 12/31/x1: $9,846)

4. Investment balance at December 31, 19x1 $98,309
      Amortization of discount for period 1/1/x2–6/30/x2   423
      Investment balance at June 30, 19x2 $98,732
      Proceeds from sale of bonds   98,500
      Loss on sale of bonds $ 232

SUMMARY

The problems in accounting for bond investments are similar to those in accounting for bond liabilities. These problems include: (1) the purchase and sale of bonds between interest payment dates for the current market price plus accrued interest, (2) the amortization of any premium or discount on the bonds, (3) the determination of the effective interest revenue for the accounting period, and (4) the determination of the investment balance to be reported on the balance sheet at the end of the accounting period. Each of these problems was covered in this unit. In the appendix to this unit, the effective-interest method of amortization is explained and contrasted with the straight-line method.

APPENDIX 30 EFFECTIVE-INTEREST AMORTIZATION METHOD

The basic concept underlying the effective-interest amortization method was explained in the appendix to Unit 25. Recall that this method yields interest at a constant rate over the term bonds are outstanding, whereas the straight-line amortization method yields a constant dollar amount of interest each period. Under the effective-interest amortization method, the yield rate of interest is applied to the book value of the investment at the beginning of a period to determine interest revenue for that period. The difference between this amount and the interest received (based on the stated rate of interest) is the amount of premium amortized.

Assume that bonds with a par value of $50,000, a stated interest rate of 8% payable semiannually, and a term of 5 years until maturity are purchased for $54,265 to yield 6%.[1] Under the effective-interest amortization method, interest revenue for the first 6 months is $1,628 ($54,265 × 6% × 6/12). Interest actually received is $2,000 ($50,000 × 8% × 6/12); thus, $372 ($2,000 − 1,628) of the premium is amortized. After the amount of premium amortized is deducted, the investment account has a balance of $53,893 ($54,265 − 372). Exhibit 30.3 is an amortization table reflecting the amounts for interest revenue, amortization of premium, and book value of the investment at the beginning and end of each period over the 5-year term of the bonds.

The amounts required to complete the table are determined in the same way as described for the first interest period. For example, interest revenue for the second period is found by applying the yield rate of interest to the book value of the invest-

---

[1]The purchase price is the present value of the bond principal and the periodic interest payments:

Present value of bond principal ($PV = S \times F_{i,n} = \$50,000 \times F_{.03,10}$
  $= \$50,000 \times .7441 = \$37,205$) $37,205

Present value of periodic interest payments ($PVA = I \times F_{i,n} = \$2,000$
  $\times F_{.03,10} = \$2,000 \times 8.5302 = \$17,060$) .... $\underline{17,060}$

Purchase price of bonds .... $\underline{\underline{\$54,265}}$

Exhibit 30.3

Amortization Table — Effective-Interest Method

Interest Payment Period	(1) Book Value of Bond Investment at Beginning of Period	(2) Interest Received for Period	(3) = (1) × 3% Interest Revenue for Period	(4) = (2) − (3) Amortization of Bond Premium for Period	(5) = (1) − (4) Book Value of Bond Investment at End of Period
1	$54,265	$2,000	$1,628	$372	$53,893
2	53,893	2,000	1,617	383	53,510
3	53,510	2,000	1,605	395	53,115
4	53,115	2,000	1,593	407	52,708
5	52,708	2,000	1,581	419	52,289
6	52,289	2,000	1,569	431	51,858
7	51,858	2,000	1,556	444	51,414
8	51,414	2,000	1,542	458	50,956
9	50,956	2,000	1,529	471	50,485
10	50,485	2,000	1,515	485	50,000

ment at the beginning of that period ($53,893 × 6% × 6/12 = $1,617). That amount is then deducted from the interest received to determine the amount of premium amortized ($2,000 − 1,617 = $383). The book value of the investment at the end of the period is then calculated by deducting the amount of premium amortized from the beginning book value ($53,893 − 383 = $53,510). You can verify the other figures in the table following the same procedures.

The straight-line amortization method yields a constant dollar amount of interest each period, $1,537.50 [$2,000 − ($4,625/10)] because an equal amount of the premium is amortized each period. Exhibit 30.4 illustrates an amortization table for the straight-line method. The effective interest rate increases each period as the premium is amortized using this method because the amount of interest is constant, but the book value of the investment decreases. The effective interest rates for the first three periods are computed as follows:

$$\frac{\text{effective interest revenue for period}}{\text{book value of bond investment at beginning of period}} = \text{effective interest rate for period}$$

$$\frac{\$\ 1,573.50}{\$54,265.00} = 2.88\% \text{ for period } 1$$

$$\frac{\$\ 1,573.50}{\$53,838.50} = 2.92\% \text{ for period } 2$$

$$\frac{\$\ 1,573.50}{\$53,412.00} = 2.95\% \text{ for period } 3$$

Exhibit 30.4

Amortization Table—Straight-Line Method

Interest Payment Period	(1) Book Value of Bond Investment at Beginning of Period	(2) Interest Received for Period	(3) Amortization of Bond Premium for Period	(4) = (2) − (3) Interest Revenue for Period	(5) = (1) − (3) Book Value of Bond Investment at End of Period
1	$54,265.00	$2,000.00	$426.50	$1,573.50	$53,838.50
2	53,838.50	2,000.00	426.50	1,573.50	53,412.00
3	53,412.00	2,000.00	426.50	1,573.50	52,985.50
4	52,950.50	2,000.00	426.50	1,573.50	52,559.00
5	52,559.00	2,000.00	426.50	1,573.50	52,132.50
6	52,132.50	2,000.00	426.50	1,573.50	51,706.00
7	51,706.00	2,000.00	426.50	1,573.50	51,279.50
8	51,279.50	2,000.00	426.50	1,573.50	50,853.00
9	50,853.00	2,000.00	426.50	1,573.50	50,426.50
10	50,426.50	2,000.00	426.50	1,573.50	50,000.00

Although the effective-interest method is more conceptually sound (as explained in Unit 25), the straight-line method is widely used in practice because it is less complex and the effects on interest revenue and the book value of the investment usually are not significant. The journal entries to record the investment and interest revenue are the same under both methods.

REVIEW QUESTIONS

30-1 What is included in the cost of an investment in bonds?

30-2 How is the market price of a bond issue determined?

30-3 Why does an entity acquire the bonds of another company as a long-term investment?

30-4 Why are bonds often purchased and sold at a premium or a discount?

30-5 How is the accrued interest on bonds accounted for when bonds are purchased or sold between interest payment dates?

30-6 The straight-line method of amortizing bond premium results in a declining book value for the investment, a constant amount of interest revenue each period, and an increasing effective interest rate each period over the holding period of the bonds. Explain.

30-7 The effective-interest method of amortizing the bond premium results in a declining book value for the investment, a decreasing amount of interest revenue each period, and a constant effective interest rate each period over the holding period of the bonds. Explain.

30-8   If bonds are held until maturity, what amount will the investor receive?

EXERCISES

30-1   Frisco Company purchased bonds of Grande Corp. with a par value of $50,000 on January 1, 19*x1*. The bonds have a stated interest rate of 8%, payable semiannually on January 1 and July 1. The maturity date of the bonds is January 1, 19*x6*. The bonds were purchased as a long-term investment.

Required   **a.**   Prepare the entries necessary to account for the bond investment during 19*x1* if they were acquired at par.
           b.   Prepare a partial balance sheet and a partial income statement at the end of 19*x1*.

30-2   Refer to the data in exercise 30-1. Assume that the bonds were purchased at 102 on January 1, 19*x1*.

Required   **a.**   Prepare all entries necessary to account for the investment during 19*x1*.
           b.   Prepare a partial balance sheet and a partial income statement at the end of 19*x1*.
           c.   Determine the effective interest rate for the first two interest periods.

30-3   Refer to the data in exercise 30-1. Assume that the bonds were purchased at 97 on January 1, 19*x1*.

Required   **a.**   Prepare all entries necessary to account for the investment during 19*x1*.
           b.   Prepare a partial balance sheet and a partial income statement at the end of 19*x1*.
           c.   Determine the effective interest rate for the first two interest periods.

30-4   Durango Company purchased bonds of Silverton Company with a par value of $40,000 for $40,900 plus accrued interest on April 1, 19*x2*. The bonds have a stated interest rate of 9%, payable semiannually on January 1 and July 1. The bonds mature on January 1, 19*x6*. On December 31, 19*x3*, half the bonds were sold at 101 plus accrued interest.

Required   **a.**   Prepare the entries necessary to account for the bond investment during 19*x2*.

    b.   Prepare a partial balance sheet and a partial income statement at the end of 19x2.

    c.   Prepare the entry necessary to record the sale of half the bonds on December 31, 19x3.

30-5   On May 31, 19x4, Boise Corp. purchased bonds of Pocatello Corp., which had a par value of $30,000, for $29,900 including accrued interest. The bonds have an annual stated interest rate of 8%, payable semiannually on June 30 and December 31. The maturity date of the bonds is December 31, 19x8.

Required   **a.**   Calculate the accrued interest at May 31, 19x4.

    b.   Calculate the amount of discount at which the bonds were purchased.

    c.   Determine the amount at which the bond investment will be recorded on May 31, 19x4.

    d.   Indicate the amount of interest to be received from Pocatello Corp. on June 30, 19x4.

    e.   Determine the amount of interest revenue earned by (1) June 30, 19x4, and (2) December 31, 19x4.

    f.   Determine the balance of the bond investment at December 31, 19x4.

30-6   Fargo Corp. purchased bonds of Minden Company with a par value of $30,000 to yield 8%. The bonds have a stated interest rate of 7%, payable semiannually on June 30 and December 31. The bonds were purchased on December 31, 19x5, and mature on December 31, 19x8.

Required   **a.**   Determine the price that would be paid to purchase the bonds on December 31, 19x5.

    b.   Determine the effective interest revenue for the first two interest periods.

    c.   Prepare a partial balance sheet and a partial income statement at the end of 19x6.

    d.   Determine the effective interest rate for the first two interest periods.

PROBLEMS

30-1   Sioux Corp. purchased bonds of Arapahoe Corp. with a par value of $100,000 on January 1, 19x1. The bonds have a stated interest rate of 8%, payable semiannually on January 1 and July 1. The bonds mature on January 1, 19x6. Three cases are to be considered in solving this problem:

Case A   The bonds were purchased at par.

Case B   The bonds were purchased at 98.

Case C   The bonds were purchased at 103.

Required   **a.**   Prepare the entries necessary to account for the investment during 19*x1* for each of the three cases.

b.   Prepare a partial balance sheet and a partial income statement at the end of 19*x1* for each of the three cases.

c.   Determine the effective interest rate for the first two interest periods for each of the three cases.

d.   Prepare the entry to record the redemption of the bonds on January 1, 19*x6*.

30-2   Appalachian Corp. purchased bonds of Adirondack Corp. with a par value of $70,000. The bonds have a stated interest rate of 9%, payable semiannually on June 30 and December 31. The bonds mature on December 31, 19*x7*, and were purchased for $68,900 plus accrued interest on April 30, 19*x4*. Bonds with a par value of $30,000 were sold on December 31, 19*x5*, at 99.

Required   **a.**   Prepare the entries necessary to account for the investment during 19*x4*.

b.   Prepare a partial balance sheet and a partial income statement at the end of 19*x4*.

c.   Prepare the entry required at December 31, 19*x5*, to sell bonds with a par value of $30,000.

30-3   Cascade Corp. purchased bonds of Olympic Company with a par value of $60,000 for $57,566 on December 31, 19*x3*. The bonds were purchased to yield 8%; however, the bonds have a stated interest rate of 7%, payable semiannually on June 30 and December 31. The bonds mature on December 31, 19*x8*.

Required   **a.**   Determine the interest revenue for the first two interest periods if the bond discount is amortized by (1) the effective-interest method and (2) the straight-line method.

b.   Determine the book value of the investment account at June 30 and December 31, 19*x4*, if the bond discount is amortized by (1) the effective-interest method and (2) the straight-line method.

c.   Determine the effective interest rate for the first two interest periods if the bond discount is amortized by (1) the effective-interest method and (2) the straight-line method.

30-4   On January 1, 19*x1*, Straits Corp. issued bonds with a par value of $1 million at 101½. The bonds have a term of 10 years and an annual stated interest rate of 9%, payable semiannually on January 1 and July 1.

On November 1, 19*x6*, Narro Corp. purchased Straits Corp. bonds with a par value of $60,000 at 98 plus accrued interest. The bonds were purchased in the bond market from another investor. Narro Corp. intends to hold these bonds until maturity.

Required   **a.**   Prepare all entries for 19*x6* on the books of (1) Straits Corp. and (2) Narro Corp.

b.   Prepare the entries at the maturity date for the redemption of the bonds on the books of (1) Straits Corp. and (2) Narro Corp.

c.   Determine the annual effective interest expense for Straits Corp. and the annual effective interest revenue for Narro Corp. for 19*x7*, 19*x8*, and 19*x9*.

> **d.** Why was Narro Corp. able to purchase Straits Corp. bonds at 98 when the bonds were originally issued at 101½?
>
> **e.** Why were the entries for the redemption of the bonds on the books of both Straits Corp. and Narro Corp. based on the par value of the bonds?

30-5 Glen Corp. purchased several stocks and bonds during 19*x1*. The purchases are summarized below; management's intention to hold the stock or bonds as temporary or long-term investments is also indicated.

Date of Acquisition	Security	Quantity Purchased	Cost per Share or Bond	Par Value per Share or Bond	Intention to Hold
Jan. 1, 19*x1*	Valley bonds	10	99	$1,000	Short-term
Jan. 1, 19*x1*	Ridge bonds	40	102	$1,000	Long-term
Mar. 25, 19*x1*	Gulley common stock	500	$38	$10	Short-term
June 20, 19*x1*	Hille common stock	1,000	$27	$5	Long-term
Sept. 5, 19*x1*	Mountain common stock	5,000	$16	$1	Long-term

Both bond investments pay interest semiannually on January 1 and July 1. The stated interest rates for the bonds are: Valley, 8%; Ridge, 9%. The Valley bonds mature on January 1, 19*x2;* the Ridge bonds mature on January 1, 19*x6*. Gulley, Hille, and Mountain each had 25,000 shares of common stock outstanding.

The companies whose stock was purchased by Glen Corp. reported net income and declared and paid dividends from the date of acquisition to the end of 19*x1* as follows:

Company	Net Income	Dividends
Gulley	$30,000	$.60 per share
Hille	25,000	.50 per share
Mountain	16,000	.30 per share

The market values of the investments at the end of 19*x1* were:

Security	Market Value
Valley bonds	100
Ridge bonds	101
Gulley stock	$36.00
Hille stock	$26.50
Mountain stock	$17.50

Required   Prepare a partial balance sheet and a partial income statement for 19x1. (*Note:* Apply the lower-of-cost-or-market method, if appropriate, for short-term and long-term investments; indicate the method of valuation for each balance sheet account in your solution.)

IV

Additional Financial Reporting Problems

Chapter 11

Statement of Changes in Financial Position

In Chapter 2, four basic financial statements were introduced. The balance sheet, income statement, and retained earnings statement or statement of changes in stockholders' equity were examined in previous chapters. In this chapter the fourth basic financial statement, the statement of changes in financial position, and the measurement and reporting problems that affect it are examined.

Unit 31
Reporting Changes in Financial Position

*If you are in business and do not know all about it, your money will go
like flies, that is, you will lose it.*

Fra Luca Paciolo, Summa de Arithmetica

The purpose, model, format, and content of a statement of changes in financial position are explained in this unit. A relatively simple case is used to explain and illustrate the preparation of this statement on a working capital basis.

Performance Objectives

Upon completing this unit you should be able to:

1. define and use the accounting terms introduced in this unit.
2. describe or explain:
   a. the purpose of a statement of changes in financial position
   b. the concept of "funds" that should be used in preparing a statement of changes in financial position
   c. the primary sources and uses of funds
   d. the proper reporting format for sources and uses of funds
   e. how changes in current assets, current liabilities, and related contra accounts affect working capital
3. determine the amount of increase or decrease in working capital that results from changes in selected current assets, current liabilities, and related contra accounts.
4. prepare a statement of changes in financial position using the working capital basis.

Purpose of the Statement of Changes in Financial Position

Recall that one of the objectives of financial accounting is to provide information on changes in an entity's financial position. A balance sheet indicates an entity's financial position at a given point in time, but it does not explain the changes in assets, liabilities, and owners' equity. A comparison of the balance sheets for two consecutive periods reveals the net change in each balance sheet account. If only one type of change in each account could occur, a comparison of two consecutive balance sheets would explain the **changes in financial position.** For example, if the account land could only increase, a change in the land account during the accounting period would indicate an additional acquisition of land. However, the land account can increase through acquisitions and decrease through disposals during the same period. Only the net change for the period is disclosed by comparing consecutive balance sheets.

Some changes in financial position are reflected in the amounts reported as revenues and expenses on the income statements. For example, revenues include the effects of changes in amounts reported on the balance sheet as accounts receivable, accrued revenue, and deferred revenue. Expenses include the effects of changes in amounts reported as accounts payable, inventory, prepaid expenses, and accrued expenses. A retained earnings statement explains changes in retained earnings, and a statement of changes in stockholders' equity explains changes in contributed capital as well as changes in retained earnings.

Users of financial statements are interested in receiving information on the effects of all significant changes in financial position on an entity's financial resources. They are concerned with the major sources and uses of financial resources. Only the statement of changes in financial position provides this information. The purpose of the statement, then, is to provide information on all changes in financial position—how the entity obtained its financial resources, and how these financial resources were used during the accounting period.

The importance and usefulness of the statement of changes in financial position were not fully recognized until the 1960s and early 1970s. The APB, following the lead of the SEC, decided that information on the financing and investing activities of a business enterprise and the changes in its financial position for a period is essential for financial statement users. Thus, in 1971 the APB concluded that the statement of changes in financial position should be presented as one of the basic financial statements for each accounting period.[1]

Usefulness of Working Capital Information

Accountants traditionally have prepared the statement of changes in financial position using **working capital,** that is, the excess of current assets over current liabilities as

---

[1]In 1963 the APB had recommended that a statement of changes in financial position be prepared along with other basic financial statements. APB Opinion No. 19 (issued in 1971), however, made it mandatory.

the primary measure of financial resources. Information on working capital resources available and on working capital provided and used is especially useful to management and short-term creditors who are concerned with the company's ability to pay debts and carry out current operations. A widely used ratio to indicate this liquidity is the *working capital ratio* (current assets divided by current liabilities), which is discussed in Unit 34. Other users, such as long-term creditors and owners, are interested in judging the effectiveness of management in utilizing the working capital resources to enhance the profitability of the company, especially during periods when financial resources are scarce.

Usefulness of Cash Flow Information

Although most accountants have traditionally prepared the statement of changes in financial position using the working capital basis, financial managers have a great need for cash flow information—since cash resources must be carefully managed. Such information is even more crucial in times of tight credit policies and high interest rates.

During the 1970s both the AICPA and the FASB studied the objectives of financial statements. The AICPA study concluded:[2]

1. Users of financial statements seek to predict, compare, and evaluate the cash consequences of their economic decisions.
2. An objective of financial statements is to provide information useful to investors and creditors for predicting, comparing, and evaluating potential cash flows to them in terms of amount, timing, and related uncertainty.

The FASB study resulted in a new series of statements on financial accounting concepts. Statement of Financial Concepts No. 1 concluded:[3]

1. Investors and creditors seek to assess the prospects of receiving cash from dividends or interest and the proceeds from the sale, redemption, or maturity of securities or loans.
2. Their prospects of receiving cash are affected by an entity's ability to obtain cash through its earnings and financing activities.
3. Thus, financial statements should provide information that helps

---

[2] *Objectives of Financial Statements* (New York: AICPA, 1973), p. 61.

[3] "Objectives of Financial Reporting by Business Enterprises," Statement of Financial Accounting Concepts No. 1 (Stamford, Conn.: FASB, 1978).

investors and creditors assess their prospects of obtaining cash through the entity's earning and financing activities.

4. The information provided by financial statements to help investors and creditors assess their prospects of receiving cash should include the following:

    a. information on economic resources that are sources of prospective cash inflows

    b. information on obligations to transfer economic resources to others that are causes of prospective cash outflows

    c. information on earnings that are the financial results of operations

The recognition of the importance of cash flow information by the AICPA and FASB studies could lead to an increase in cash flow information in published financial statements.

Concept of "Funds" or "Financial Resources"

Traditionally, two different bases of measuring **funds,** or **financial resources,** have been applied in preparing the statement of changes in financial position: the working capital and the cash bases. **Working capital** is defined as the excess of current assets over current liabilities at a given date. It is a broader measure of funds or financial resources than cash because it includes assets such as receivables and inventories that will be converted into cash in the near future. Cash, as a current asset, is only one element of working capital. Some accountants add temporary investments to cash as the measure of funds because temporary investments can be easily converted into cash as needed.

APB Opinion No. 19 allows either the working capital basis or the cash basis of funds or financial resources to be used, as long as all financial resources are reported. The **all financial resources** concept of funds means that all significant **financial activities** for the period should be reported in the statement of changes in financial position even if they did not directly affect working capital or cash. The primary types of significant financial activities not affecting working capital or cash are:

1. the acquisition of noncurrent assets by issuing the company's own stock or by incurring long-term debt.

2. the retirement of long-term debt in an exchange for the company's stock or noncurrent assets.

3. the exchange of one noncurrent asset for another noncurrent asset.

4. the exchange of one class of a company's stock for another class of its stock.

Resource Inflows and Outflows

The basic model for the statement of changes in financial position reflects inflows and outflows of financial resources and the net change in financial resources. This basic model is presented in Table 31.1, first in general form and then on the working capital and cash bases.

Inflows of financial resources result from financing activities carried out by a business entity. The primary financing activities are:

1. carrying on current operations—an excess of funds from revenues over funds used for expenses provides financial resources to the company.
2. incurring long-term debt—financial resources are obtained by borrowing.
3. issuing the company's stock—financial resources are obtained by selling the stock or by issuing the stock to acquire noncurrent assets or retire debt.
4. selling noncurrent assets—financial resources are obtained by selling noncurrent assets for more than their book value.

Outflows of financial resources result from investing activities carried out by a business entity. The primary investing activities are:

1. acquiring noncurrent assets—financial resources are used to acquire plant assets and intangible assets.
2. retiring long-term debt—financial resources are used to repay long-term debt.
3. paying dividends—financial resources are used in profit distributions to stockholders.
4. acquiring the company's own stock—financial resources are used to acquire the company's own stock as treasury stock or to retire the stock.

Table 31.1

Basic Model—Statement of Changes in Financial Position		
General form }	financial resource inflows − financial resource outflows =	net change in financial resources
Working capital basis }	sources of working capital − uses of working capital =	increase (or decrease) in working capital
Cash basis }	sources of cash − uses of cash	= increase (or decrease) in cash

Basic Format

APB Opinion No. 19 allows flexibility in preparing the statement of changes in financial position as long as certain format, conceptual, and procedural requirements that enhance the usefulness and understandability of the information reported are met. The requirements specified by the APB were:

1. The title of the statement should be statement of changes in financial position.
2. The all financial resources concept of funds should be used.
3. **Funds provided by operations** should be clearly disclosed.[4]
4. If extraordinary items are reported on the income statement, funds provided by operations should start with income before extraordinary items. Otherwise, the starting point is net income.

Several different formats are used in preparing the statement of changes in financial position. Exhibit 31.1 illustrates the most popular format. It follows the basic model for a statement of changes in financial position, that is, resources provided less resources used equals changes in resources, and it meets all the requirements specified by the APB. In this text, situations involving extraordinary items are not examined

Exhibit 31.1

Nameless Company		
Statement of Changes in Financial Position		
For the Year Ended December 31, 19xx		
Financial resources provided by:		
Operations:		
Income before extraordinary items		$XXX
Add: Expenses not using working capital	$XXX	
Losses on noncurrent assets	XXX	XXX
Total		$XXX
Deduct: Revenues not providing working capital	$XXX	
Gains on noncurrent assets	XXX	XXX
Working capital provided by operations		$XXX
Other sources (list all significant sources)		XXX
Total financial resources provided		$XXX
Financial resources used (list all significant uses)	$XXX	
Total financial resources used		XXX
Increase (Decrease) in working capital		$XXX*

	Increase (Decrease) in Working Capital
Changes in working capital content:	
Current assets (list)	$XXX
Current liabilities (list)	XXX
Working capital (current assets less current liabilities)	$XXX

These two amounts must be the same.

---

[4]Working capital or cash.

because they occur infrequently and result in reporting complexities. Examples from corporate annual reports of the statement of changes in financial position are given in the appendix to Unit 6.

Before APB Opinion No. 19 was issued in 1971 several alternate titles were used for this statement, including "funds statement," "cash-flow statement," "statement of sources and uses of working capital," and "summary of financial resources." The title required by the APB better describes the objective of the statement and the nature of financial resources under the all financial resources concept.

Since information on changes in working capital content, that is, changes in current assets and current liabilities, may be useful to certain users of financial statements, the APB required that a schedule of changes in working capital content be included on the face of the statement of changes in financial position or as a supplement to it.

An Illustrative Case

A comparative balance sheet and an income statement for Lemm Company are presented in Exhibit 31.2. The net increase or decrease in each balance sheet account is indicated. For the sake of simplicity at this stage, only one change in each account, except retained earnings, is assumed. The letters next to the amount of each change in Exhibit 31.2 refer to the following descriptions of the changes:

(a) Net income for 19x2 was $9,600.
(b) Cash dividends declared and paid during 19x2 totaled $7,500.
(c) Land with a cost of $7,000 was sold for $10,000.
(d) Depreciation recorded for 19x2 was: buildings, $2,400; equipment, $8,000.
(e) Equipment with a cost of $30,000 was purchased; cash paid during 19x2 was $15,000; a note due on March 31, 19x4, was issued for the balance of $15,000.
(f) Stock with a par value of $5,000 was issued for $6,500 cash.

The completed statement of changes in financial position on a working capital basis is presented in Exhibit 31.3.

Working Capital Provided by Operations   This subsection under "Financial resources provided by" starts with net income of $9,600. Expenses that do not require the use of working capital, such as depreciation, amortization, and depletion, are added back to net income. Although these expenses are properly deducted in determining net income, they do not require the use of working capital in the current period as other expenses do. Therefore, in order to determine the correct amount of working capital provided by operations they are added back. In this case, depreciation of $10,400 is added back.

Net income is also adjusted for gains and losses on the disposal of noncurrent

Exhibit 31.2

Lemm Company
Comparative Balance Sheet
For the Years Ended December 31, 19x1 and 19x2

	12/31/x2	12/31/x1	Net Increase (Decrease)	
Current assets:				
Cash	$15,000	$12,000	$3,000	
Accounts receivable	46,000	42,000	4,000	
Inventory	35,000	37,000	(2,000)	
Prepaid expenses	4,000	3,000	1,000	
Total current assets	$100,000	$ 94,000		
Plant assets:				
Land	$ 25,000	$ 32,000	$(7,000)	(c)
Buildings	75,000	75,000	—	
Accumulated depreciation	(14,400)	(12,000)	2,400	(d)
Equipment	90,000	60,000	30,000	(e)
Accumulated depreciation	(38,000)	(30,000)	8,000	(d)
Total plant assets	$137,600	$125,000		
Total assets	$237,600	$219,000		
Current liabilities:				
Accounts payable	$ 36,000	$ 39,000	$(3,000)	
Accrued expenses	3,000	5,000	(2,000)	
Total current liabilities	$ 39,000	$ 44,000		
Long-term liabilities:				
Long-term notes payable	$ 15,000	—	15,000	(e)
Total liabilities	$ 54,000	$ 44,000		
Stockholders' equity:				
Common stock, $10 par	$105,000	$100,000	$ 5,000	(f)
Contributed capital in excess of par	29,500	28,000	1,500	(f)
Retained earnings	49,100	47,000	2,100	(a and b)
Total stockholders' equity	$173,600	$175,000		
Total liabilities and stockholders' equity	$237,600	$219,000		

Lemm Company
Income Statement
For the Year Ended December 31, 19x2

Net sales	$250,000	
Cost of goods sold	150,000	
Gross margin	$100,000	
Operating expenses:		
Depreciation expense	$ 10,400	(d)
Other expenses	81,100	
Total operating expenses	$ 91,500	
Operating income	$ 8,500	
Other income:		
Gain on sale of land	3,000	(c)
Income before taxes	$ 11,500	
Less: Income taxes	1,900	
Net income	$ 9,600	(a)
Less: Dividends declared and paid	7,500	(b)
Income added to retained earnings	$ 2,100	

Exhibit 31.3

Lemm Company
Statement of Changes in Financial Position
For the Year Ended December 31, 19x2

Financial resources provided by:
Operations:

Net income	$ 9,600	
Add: Depreciation	10,400	
Total	$20,000	
Deduct: Gain on sale of land	3,000	
Working capital provided by operations		$17,000

Other sources:

Sale of land	$10,000	
Long-term note issued to acquire equipment	15,000	
Issuance of stock	6,500	31,500
Total financial resources provided		$48,500

Financial resources used to:

Purchase equipment with cash and a long-term note	$30,000	
Pay dividends	7,500	
Total financial resources used		37,500
Increase in working capital		$11,000

	Increase (Decrease) in Working Capital
Changes in working capital content:	
Current assets:	
Cash	$ 3,000
Accounts receivable	4,000
Inventory	(2,000)
Prepaid expenses	1,000
Current liabilities:	
Accounts payable	3,000
Accrued expenses	2,000
Increase in working capital	$11,000

assets. Losses are added to net income; gains are deducted. The preferred practice in reporting the disposal of noncurrent assets is to show the entire proceeds from the disposal as a source of funds. If these adjustments are not made, the working capital effects of the transactions will be double-counted. In this case, the $3,000 gain on the sale of land is deducted from the total of net income and depreciation. Thus, working capital provided by operations is $17,000.

Other Sources and Uses   The sale of land yielded $10,000 in cash. Thus, working capital increased $10,000, and this transaction is reported as a source of funds for 19x2. Note that the gain is included in both net income and the $10,000 proceeds. Thus, the gain of $3,000 was deducted from net income to prevent double-counting of the effect on working capital.[5] The proceeds from the issuance of stock, $6,500, is reported as another source of funds for the year.

---

[5]Alternately, the sale of the land could be reported as a $7,000 source; the gain would be left in net income, and working capital provided by operations would be $20,000.

Under the "all financial resources" concept of funds, direct exchanges of noncurrent resources that are significant in amount must be reported as financing and investing activities on the statement of changes in financial position. During 19x2 Lemm Company issued a $15,000 long-term note and paid $15,000 to purchase equipment. Thus, the issuance of the long-term note is reported as a source of funds, and the $30,000 cost of the equipment is reported as a use of funds. The only other use of funds for 19x2 was the payment of dividends, $7,500.

Changes in Working Capital Content   The difference between resources provided and used is determined and reported. Lemm Company had an $11,000 increase in working capital in 19x2. The sources and uses of funds that resulted in this change in working capital have been determined and reported. In addition, the changes in the content of working capital (that is, current assets and current liabilities) must be analyzed and disclosed according to APB Opinion No. 19. The net increase (or decrease) in working capital that results from analyzing the effects of changes in current assets and current liabilities must equal the increase (or decrease) in working capital resulting from resource inflows and outflows for the same period. For Lemm Company these two figures are $11,000 (see Exhibit 31.3).

During 19x2 the cash, accounts receivable, and prepaid expenses accounts increased and the accounts payable and accrued expenses accounts decreased (see Exhibit 31.2). These changes resulted in increases in working capital. On the other hand, inventory decreased, resulting in a decrease in working capital. The effects of these changes on working capital are reported in a separate schedule on the statement of changes in financial position (see Exhibit 31.3.) Table 31.2 summarizes the effects of changes in current assets and current liabilities on working capital.

Table 31.2

Effects of Changes on Working Capital			
Types of Account		*Change in Account Balance*	*Effect of Change on Working Capital*
Current asset		Increase	Increase
		Decrease	Decrease
Contra account to current asset		Increase	Decrease
		Decrease	Increase
Current liability		Increase	Decrease
		Decrease	Increase
Contra account to current liability		Increase	Increase
		Decrease	Decrease

REVIEW PROBLEM

At the end of 19*x3* and 19*x4*, the balance sheet accounts for Sinbad Corp. had the following balances:

	12/31/*x3*	12/31/*x4*	Increase (Decrease)
Cash	$ 20,000	$ 30,000	$ 10,000
Accounts Receivable	40,000	45,000	5,000
Inventory	38,000	35,000	(3,000)
Land	20,000	38,000	18,000
Buildings	130,000	220,000	90,000
Accumulated Depreciation	(30,000)	(34,500)	4,500
Equipment	90,000	99,000	9,000
Accumulated Depreciation	(30,000)	(37,500)	7,500
Accounts Payable	42,000	30,000	(12,000)
Accrued Expenses	4,000	5,000	1,000
Bonds Payable	—	100,000	100,000
Common Stock	100,000	110,000	10,000
Contributed Capital in Excess of Par	55,000	63,000	8,000
Retained Earnings	77,000	87,000	10,000

Additional information

(a) Net income for 19*x4* was $21,000.
(b) Declared and paid dividends of $11,000.
(c) Issued bonds at par value, $100,000.
(d) Issued 1,000 shares of $10 par value stock to acquire land; the market value of the stock was $18 per share.
(e) Purchased a delivery truck for $9,000.
(f) Constructed a warehouse at a cost of $90,000 and paid the contractor with the proceeds from the bonds.

Required   Prepare a statement of changes in financial position for 19*x4* on a working capital basis.

Solution to review problem

Sinbad Corp.
Statement of Changes in Financial Position
For the Year Ended December 31, 19*x4*

Financial resources provided by:
  Operations:
    Net income $21,000
    Add: Depreciation   12,000

Working capital provided by operations		$ 33,000
Other sources:		
Issuance of bonds	$100,000	
Issuance of stock to acquire land	18,000	118,000
Total financial resources provided		$151,000
Financial resources used to:		
Pay dividends	$ 11,000	
Purchase delivery truck	9,000	
Construct warehouse	90,000	
Acquire land through exchange for stock	18,000	
Total financial resources used		128,000
Increase in working capital		$ 23,000

	Increase (Decrease) in working capital
Changes in working capital content:	
Current assets:	
Cash	$10,000
Accounts receivable	5,000
Inventory	(3,000)
Current liabilities:	
Accounts payable	12,000
Accrued expenses	(1,000)
Net increase in working capital	$23,000

Notes to solution

1. *Total depreciation is $12,000 ($4,500 for buildings and $7,500 for equipment — see changes in accumulated depreciation).*
2. *The market value of the stock, $18,000 ($18 × 1,000), is the cost of the land acquired.*
3. *Refer to Table 31.2, if necessary, to understand the changes in working capital content.*

SUMMARY

In this unit, the purpose, model, form, and content of a statement of changes in financial position were examined. The definition of the term *funds* or *financial resources* was explained. Then, the working capital basis was used to explain and illustrate the preparation of a statement of changes in financial position.

REVIEW QUESTIONS

31-1 What is the purpose or objective of the statement of changes in financial position?

31-2 Indicate two bases commonly used to measure financial resources in preparing the statement of changes in financial position.

31-3 Working capital is a broader measure of funds or financial resources than cash. Explain.

31-4 What is meant by the "all financial resources" concept of funds? Why did the APB require the use of this concept to prepare the statement of changes in financial position?

31-5 List the primary types of financial activities not affecting cash or working capital to which the all financial resources concept applies.

31-6 Describe the basic model for the statement of changes in financial position (a) in its general form, (b) on a cash basis, and (c) on the working capital basis.

31-7 List the primary financing activities that result in resource inflows.

31-8 List the primary investing activities that result in resource outflows on the statement of changes in financial position.

31-9 What is a schedule of changes in working capital content? Why is this schedule required when the statement of changes in financial position is prepared on a working capital basis but not when the statement is prepared on a cash basis?

31-10 Explain how each of the following changes affects working capital:

    a. increases in current assets
    b. decreases in current assets
    c. increases in current liabilities
    d. decreases in current liabilities

31-11 Explain how working capital provided by operations is determined and reported on the statement of changes in financial position.

31-12 Why are depreciation and other nonworking capital expenditures added to net income to determine working capital provided by operations?

EXERCISES

31-1 Following are a number of business activities that a business entity carried out during a particular accounting period. Identify each as (a) a financing activity, that is, one that provided financial resources; (b) an investing activity, that is, one that used financial resources; or (c) an activity that had no effect on financial resources. In some cases, the business activity may both provide and use financial resources.

    (1) Equipment was purchased for cash.
    (2) Dividends were declared and paid.
    (3) Land that had been intended for use as a plant site was sold.
    (4) Land and a building were acquired for $50,000 cash and a $250,000 mortgage.
    (5) Common stock was issued for cash.
    (6) Long-term debt was retired by issuing common stock.
    (7) A stock dividend was declared and issued.
    (8) Treasury stock was reissued.
    (9) Equipment was acquired for $10,000 cash and a short-term note for $25,000.
    (10) The short-term note in (9) was paid at maturity (ignore payment of interest expense in your answer for this item).

31-2   For each of the following cases determine the amount by which working capital increases or decreases.

Case A   A company reported net income of $26,000 for the year. Included in the determination of net income was depreciation expense of $5,000 and amortization expense of $3,500.

Case B   A company issued $100,000 par value of bonds at 102.

Case C   A company purchased equipment for a cash down payment of $5,000 and an 8% note for $15,000 due 16 months after the end of the current accounting period.

Case D   A company declared a $5,000 cash dividend at the end of the current year; the dividend is payable early in the next year.

31-3   Following are selected data from the records of Shamos Company for the year ended December 31, 19x2:

Net income	$40,000
Depreciation	12,000
Proceeds from issuance of stock	22,000
Proceeds from long-term bank loan	30,000
Cost of equipment purchased for cash	25,000
Dividends declared and paid	10,000
Cost of land and building purchased (cash paid $15,000; mortgage obtained, $50,000)	65,000
Changes in current assets and current liabilities:	
Increase in cash	30,000
Decrease in receivables	10,000
Increase in inventory	15,000
Decrease in accounts payable	19,000

Required   Prepare in good form a statement of changes in financial position for the year ended December 31, 19x2, using the working capital basis. Apply the "all financial resources" concept in preparing the statement.

31-4   Following are the comparative balance sheets for 19x7 and 19x8 for Raskel Corporation:

Balance Sheets		
Assets	**12/31/x8**	**12/31/x7**
Cash	$ 30,000	$ 16,000
Accounts Receivable	32,000	28,000
Merchandise Inventory	26,000	23,000
Prepaid Insurance	2,000	1,000
Land	15,000	0
Equipment	140,000	110,000
Accumulated Depreciation	(55,000)	(44,000)
Patents	7,000	8,000
Total Assets	$197,000	$142,000

	Equities		
Accounts Payable		$ 14,000	$ 12,000
Salaries Payable		3,000	4,000
Taxes Payable		3,000	6,000
Capital Stock ($10 par value)		120,000	100,000
Contributed Capital in Excess of Par		10,000	0
Retained Earnings		47,000	20,000
Total Equities		$197,000	$142,000

Additional data

a. Net income for 19x8 was $45,000.
b. Dividends declared and paid during 19x8 were $18,000.
c. Depreciation expense for 19x8 was $11,000.
d. Amortization of patents for 19x8 was $1,000.
e. Land was acquired by paying cash, $15,000.
f. Equipment was acquired in exchange for 2,000 shares of common stock; the stock had a market value of $15 per share.

Required   Prepare a statement of changes in financial position for the year ended December 31, 19x8, using the working capital basis. Apply the all financial resources concept.

31-5 Using the following information, determine the amount of working capital provided by operations:

Net income	$65,000
Depreciation	15,000
Amortization of bond premium	1,000
Loss on sale of equipment	3,500
Amortization of organization costs	800

PROBLEMS

31-1 Assume that Renke Corp. reported the following information on its comparative financial statements for 19x1 and 19x2:

From the Income Statement:	19x2
Gain on Sale of Investment in Common Stock of Ping Co.	$20,000
Depreciation	36,000
Net Income	47,800

From the Balance Sheet:	12/31/x1	12/31/x2	Increase (Decrease)
Cash	$ 69,400	$ 80,600	$11,200
Accounts Receivable	140,000	148,000	8,000
Allowance for Uncollectible Accounts	7,000	7,400	400
Inventories	181,000	176,000	(5,000)
Accounts Payable	110,000	113,000	3,000
Advances from Customers	10,000	8,000	(2,000)

Additional information

a. The investment in Ping Co. had a book value of $125,000 at the date of sale.
b. There were no extraordinary items reported by Renke Corp. during 19x2.
c. Cash dividends paid during 19x2 amounted to $30,000.
d. Equipment costing $166,000 was purchased.

Required (1) Determine the amount of working capital provided by operations.
(2) List all other sources and uses of financial resources, including dollar amounts.
(3) Prepare a schedule of changes in working capital content.

31-2 The following is a comparative balance sheet for Frye Corporation and selected business transactions.

Frye Corporation
Comparative Balance Sheet
As of December 31, 19x5 and 19x6

	December 31 19x6	December 31 19x5	Increase (Decrease)
Current Assets:			
Cash	$120,000	$105,000	$ 15,000
Accounts Receivable	175,000	168,000	7,000
Allowance for Uncollectible Accounts	(5,000)	(3,000)	2,000
Inventory	190,000	196,000	(6,000)
Prepaid Expenses	7,000	9,000	(2,000)
Total Current Assets	$487,000	$475,000	
Plant Assets:			
Land	$120,000	$ 80,000	$ 40,000
Buildings	400,000	280,000	120,000
Accumulated Depreciation	(98,000)	(91,000)	7,000
Equipment	210,000	240,000	(30,000)
Accumulated Depreciation	(126,000)	(120,000)	6,000
Total Plant Assets	$506,000	$389,000	
Total Assets	$993,000	$864,000	

Current Liabilities:			
Accounts Payable	$130,000	$140,000	$(10,000)
Accrued Expenses	5,000	4,000	1,000
Total Current Liabilities:	$135,000	$144,000	
Long-Term Liabilities:			
Notes Payable, Long-Term	80,000	0	80,000
Total Liabilities	$215,000	$144,000	
Stockholders' Equity:			
Common Stock, $10 par	$440,000	$400,000	$ 40,000
Paid-in Capital in Excess of Par	110,000	100,000	10,000
Retained Earnings	228,000	220,000	8,000
Total Stockholders' Equity	$778,000	$720,000	
Total Liabilities and Stockholders' Equity	$993,000	$864,000	

Additional information

a. Net income for 19x6 was $40,000.
b. Cash dividends declared and paid during the year totaled $32,000.
c. Depreciation for 19x6 was: buildings, $7,000; equipment, $21,000.
d. Land and a building were acquired at the end of 19x6; $80,000 was paid in cash, and an $80,000 long-term note was signed for the balance.
e. Equipment with a cost of $30,000 and a book value of $15,000 was sold for $18,000 at the beginning of 19x6.
f. Common stock with a par value of $40,000 was issued for $50,000 cash.

Required   Prepare a statement of changes in financial position (working capital basis) for 19x6.

31-3   On the basis of the following data for Marshall Corporation for the years ended December 31, 19x5 and 19x6, prepare a statement of changes in financial position.

	12/31/x6	12/31/x5
Cash	$ 85,000	$ 30,000
Accounts Receivable (net)	95,000	65,000
Inventories	220,000	180,000
Equipment	200,000	100,000
Accumulated Depreciation—Equipment	(58,000)	(50,000)
Building	230,000	—
Accumulated Depreciation—Building	(3,000)	—
Land	50,000	20,000
Goodwill	55,000	75,000
	$874,000	$420,000
Dividends Payable	$	$ 10,000
Accounts Payable	90,000	50,000
Bonds Payable	200,000	—
Common Stock ($10 par value)	200,000	100,000
Contributed Capital in Excess of Par	80,000	—
Retained Earnings	304,000	260,000
	$874,000	$420,000

Additional data

a. Net income for 19x6 was $74,000. Depreciation of $11,000 on the equipment and building was deducted in arriving at net income.

b. Land with a cost of $50,000 and a building with a cost of $230,000 were acquired during 19x6. The company paid $100,000 cash and issued 10,000 shares of stock to acquire these assets.

c. Cash dividends of $30,000 were declared during 19x6; payments of cash dividends during 19x6 amounted to $40,000.

d. Land with a cost of $20,000 was sold for $30,000. The gain was included in the net income of $74,000 for 19x6.

e. Bonds with a par value of $200,000 were issued at 100 during 19x6.

f. Goodwill of $20,000 was written off during 19x6; the $20,000 charge was reported on the income statement as a miscellaneous loss.

g. Equipment with a cost of $100,000 was purchased for cash during 19x6.

31-4   Following is the comparative balance sheet for 19x5 and 19x6, a condensed income statement for 19x6, and additional data for Cyklops Corp.

Cyklops Corp.
Comparative Balance Sheet
December 31, 19x5 and 19x6

	December 31	
Assets	**19x5**	**19x6**
Current assets:		
Cash	$ 50,000	$ 75,000
Temporary investments	20,000	30,000
Accounts receivable, net	80,000	90,000
Inventory	100,000	95,000
Prepaid expenses	2,000	4,000
Total current assets	$252,000	$294,000
Long-term investments:		
Investment in Hercules common stock (at equity)	$ 54,000	60,000
Plant assets:		
Land	$ 30,000	$ 30,000
Buildings	100,000	100,000
Accumulated depreciation	(20,000)	(22,000)
Equipment	150,000	180,000
Accumulated depreciation	(60,000)	(78,000)
Total plant assets	$200,000	$210,000
Total assets	$506,000	$564,000
Liabilities and Stockholders' Equity		
Current liabilities:		
Accounts payable	$197,000	$138,000
Short-term bank loan	—	50,000
Accrued expenses	11,500	13,600
Total current liabilities	$208,500	$201,600
Long-term liabilities:		
8% bonds payable, due in 19x9	$100,000	$100,000
Discount on bonds	(2,500)	(2,000)
Total long-term liabilities	$ 97,500	$ 98,000
Total liabilities	$306,000	$299,600

Contributed capital:		
Common stock, $10 par	$100,000	$120,000
Contributed capital in excess of par	55,000	65,000
Total contributed capital	$155,000	$185,000
Retained earnings	45,000	79,400
Total stockholders' equity	$200,000	$264,400
Total liabilities and stockholders' equity	$506,000	$564,000

Cyklops Corp.
Income Statement
For the Year Ended December 31, 19x6

Net sales	$500,000
Cost of goods sold	280,000
Gross margin	$220,000
Operating expenses:	
Depreciation	$ 20,000
Other expenses	110,500
Total operating expenses	$130,500
Income from operations	$ 89,500
Incidental revenue and expense:	
Interest expense	$ 8,500
Income from investment in Hercules stock	6,000
Net incidental expense	$ 2,500
Income before taxes	$ 87,000
Income taxes	32,000
Net income	$ 55,000

Additional data

    a.   Cash dividends of $20,600 were declared and paid.

    b.   Temporary investments were purchased at a cost of $10,000.

    c.   Income from the investment in Hercules common stock recognized under the equity method was $6,000.

    d.   Equipment with a cost of $30,000 was acquired by issuing 2,000 shares of $10 par value stock.

    e.   A short-term loan for $50,000 was obtained to pay outstanding bills.

    f.   Bond discount was amortized in the amount of $500.

Required   Prepare in good form a statement of changes in financial position using the working capital basis and applying the "all financial resources" concept. (*Hint:* All changes in noncurrent accounts are explained on the income statement or in the additional data.)

Unit 32
Analysis of Financial Resource Flows

Nobody was ever meant
to remember or invent
What he did with every cent.

Robert Frost, The Hardship of Accounting

In the preceding unit the statement of changes in financial position was prepared without analyzing the effects of business transactions on resource flows. The primary sources and uses of financial resources were listed and briefly described. In this unit the effects of business transactions on working capital and cash flow are explained and illustrated. Also, the preparation of a cash flow statement is discussed and illustrated.

Performance Objectives

Upon completing this unit you should be able to:

1. define and use the accounting terms introduced in this unit.
2. describe or explain the effects of business transactions on working capital and/or cash flow.
3. determine the amount of increase or decrease in working capital and/or cash that results from selected business transactions.
4. prepare a cash flow statement.

If the appendix to this unit is also completed, you should be able to:

5. Use the T-account method to analyze changes in financial position on a working capital basis.

Effects of Business Transactions on Working Capital and Cash Resources

Business transactions are the basic source for information reported on financial statements. Each transaction can be analyzed to determine what effects, if any, it has on working capital and/or cash resources. As an aid in analyzing their effects on working capital, business transactions may be classified into three categories:

1. transactions involving only working capital accounts, that is, current assets and current liabilities
2. transactions involving both working capital accounts and either (a) nonworking capital accounts (that is, noncurrent assets and liabilities and owners' equity) or (b) income statement accounts (that is, revenues and expenses)
3. transactions involving only nonworking capital accounts

Transactions Involving Only Working Capital Accounts These transactions have no net effect on working capital, although some may affect cash resources. The increase in working capital resulting from a change in one working capital account is exactly offset by the decrease in working capital resulting from the change in the other working capital accounts. Thus, the net effect is no change in the working capital balance. These transactions are not reported on a statement of changes in financial position prepared on a working capital basis because they have no net working capital effects. Cash resources, however, are affected whenever the transaction involves the cash account. Assume that a company has current assets of $200,000, current liabilities of $60,000, and therefore, a working capital balance of $140,000 prior to each transaction described in the eight independent cases that follow:

Case 1 Temporary investments are purchased for $24,000. The journal entry is:

Temporary investments	24,000	
Cash		24,000

An analysis of the transaction indicates no net change in working capital, although cash decreases by $24,000:

	Before the Transaction	After the Transaction	Analysis of Changes in Balances
Current assets	$200,000	$200,000	($200,000 + 24,000 − 24,000 = $200,000)
−Current liabilities	60,000	60,000	(no change)
Working capital	$140,000	$140,000	(no change)

Explanation   Working capital was not affected because one current asset (temporary investments) increased while another current asset (cash) decreased by the same amount, $24,000. However, cash resources decrease $24,000.

Case 2   Accounts payable totaling $12,000 were paid. The journal entry is:

Accounts Payable	12,000	
Cash		12,000

An analysis of the transaction indicates no net change in working capital, although cash decreases by $12,000:

	Before the Transaction	After the Transaction	Analysis of Changes in Balances
Current assets	$200,000	$188,000	($200,000 − 12,000 = $188,000)
−Current liabilities	60,000	48,000	($60,000 − 12,000 = $48,000
Working capital	$140,000	$140,000	(no change)

Explanation   Working capital was not affected because the decrease in the current asset, cash, was offset by the decrease in the current liability, accounts payable. However, cash resources decrease $12,000.

The changes in cases 1 and 2 did have an impact on working capital, but, as indicated, the changes offset each other so there was no net effect on working capital. In case 1 working capital was increased $24,000 by the increase in temporary investments, but it was also decreased $24,000 by the decrease in cash. Similarly, in case 2 working capital was increased $12,000 by the decrease in accounts payable and decreased $12,000 by the decrease in cash.

Transactions Involving a Working Capital Account and a Nonworking Capital Account
These transactions increase or decrease working capital. Some, but not all, affect cash resources. This category of transactions provides much of the information needed to prepare a statement of changes in financial position.

Case 3   Common stock was issued at par value for $65,000 cash. The journal entry is:

Cash	65,000	
Common stock		65,000

An analysis of the transaction indicates that both working capital and cash resources increase by $65,000:

	Before the Transaction	After the Transaction	Analysis of Changes in Balances
Current assets	$200,000	$265,000	($200,000 + 65,000 = $265,000)
−Current liabilities	60,000	60,000	(no change)
Working capital	$140,000	$205,000	($205,000 − 140,000 = $65,000 increase)

Explanation   The current asset, cash, increased by $65,000; since no other working capital account was involved, working capital also increases $65,000.

Case 4   Dividends of $10,000 were declared and paid. Two entries are required: one at the date of declaration and the other at the date of payment:

Retained Earnings	10,000	
Dividends Payable		10,000
To record declaration of cash dividends.		

Dividends Payable	10,000	
Cash		10,000
To record payment of cash dividends		

The entry at the date of declaration involves both a working capital account and a nonworking capital account. An analysis of the transaction indicates that working capital decreases by $10,000, but that there is no effect on cash resources:

	Before the Transaction	After the Transaction	Analysis of Changes in Balances
Current assets	$200,000	$200,000	(no change)
−Current liabilities	60,000	70,000	($60,000 + 10,000 = $70,000)
Working capital	$140,000	$130,000	($140,000 − 130,000 = $10,000 decrease)

Explanation   The current liability, dividends payable, increased $10,000; since no other working capital account was involved, working capital decreased $10,000. Cash was not affected by the transaction to declare the dividends.

The entry at the date of payment involves only working capital accounts. Thus, there is no net effect on working capital. However, cash decreases $10,000 as a result of paying the dividend.

	Before the Transaction	After the Transaction	Analysis of Changes in Balances
Current assets	$200,000	$190,000	($200,000 − 10,000 = $190,000)
−Current liabilities	70,000	60,000	($70,000 − 10,000 = $60,000)
Working capital	$130,000	$130,000	(no change)

Explanation   The decrease in current assets was offset by the decrease in current liabilities. Thus, there was no net change in working capital. However, cash did decrease by $10,000.

Case 5   Land was acquired by paying $10,000 cash and issuing a short-term note for $15,000. The journal entry is:

Land	25,000	
Cash		10,000
Short-Term Notes Payable		15,000

An analysis of the transaction indicates that working capital decreased $25,000, but cash decreased only $10,000:

	Before the Transaction	After the Transaction	Analysis of Changes in Balance
Current assets	$200,000	$190,000	($200,000 − 10,000 = $190,000)
−Current liabilities	60,000	75,000	($60,000 + 15,000 = $75,000)
Working capital	$140,000	$115,000	($140,000 − 115,000 = $25,000 decrease)

Explanation   The current asset, cash, decreased $10,000, and the current liability, notes payable, increased $15,000. Both changes decreased working capital—the total decrease was $25,000. Cash, however, decreased only $10,000 at this time.

Transactions Involving a Working Capital Account and an Income Statement Account
These transactions result in an increase or decrease in working capital. For example, transactions that result in an increase in current assets and the recognition of revenue increase working capital. Similarly, transactions that result in a decrease in current assets or increase in current liabilities and the recognition of expenses decrease working capital. These transactions also affect cash flow if cash is received or paid when revenue or expense is recognized. If receivables or payables are recorded when revenue or expense is recognized, cash flow is not affected until the receivables are collected or the payables paid. Because revenues and expenses are reported in some detail on the income statement, the resource effects of these transactions usually are not reported separately on the statement of changes in financial position. Procedures for reporting the amount of working capital or cash provided by operations were described in Unit 31.

Case 6   Sales totaling $38,000 were made on credit. The journal entry is:

Accounts Receivable	38,000	
Sales		38,000

An analysis of the transaction indicates that working capital increases by $38,000; however, cash will not be affected until the accounts receivable are collected:

	Before the Transaction	After the Transaction	Analysis of Changes in Balances
Current assets	$200,000	$238,000	($200,000 + 38,000 = $238,000)
−Current liabilities	60,000	60,000	(no change)
Working capital	$140,000	$178,000	($178,000 − 140,000 = $38,000 increase)

Explanation   The current asset, accounts receivable, increased by $38,000; since no other working capital account was involved, working capital increased $38,000. Cash will not be affected until the receivables are collected.

Case 7   Salaries of $1,500 were accrued at the end of the period. The journal entry is:

| Salaries Expense | 1,500 | |
| Salaries Payable | | 1,500 |

An analysis of the transaction indicates that working capital decreases by $1,500; however, cash will not be affected until the salaries are paid:

	Before the Transaction	After the Transaction	Analysis of Changes in Balance
Current assets	$200,000	$200,000	(no change)
−Current liabilities	60,000	61,500	($60,000 + 1,500 = $61,500)
Working capital	$140,000	$138,500	($140,000 − 138,500 = $1,500 decrease)

Explanation   The current liability, salaries payable, increased by $1,500; no other working capital account was involved. Thus, working capital decreased $1,500. Cash will not be affected until the salaries are paid.

Transactions Involving Only Nonworking Capital Accounts   These transactions have no direct effect on working capital or cash. However, if they represent significant financial activities, they must be reported in the statement of changes in financial position. Examples of these transactions include the acquisition of plant assets or the retirement of long-term debt through an exchange for stock or new long-term debt. Other transactions, such as the declaration of a stock dividend and prior period adjustments, also, involve only nonworking capital accounts. However, the latter transactions are not reported on the statement of changes in financial position because they do not represent financing or investing activities.

Case 8   A long-term note liability for $30,000 was settled at maturity by issuing common stock at par value. The journal entry is:

| Long-Term Notes Payable | 30,000 | |
| Common Stock | | 30,000 |

An analysis of the transaction indicates that neither working capital nor cash was affected:

	Before the Transaction	After the Transaction	Analysis of Changes in Balance
Current assets	$200,000	$200,000	(no change)
−Current liabilities	60,000	60,000	(no change)
Working capital	$140,000	$140,000	(no change)

Explanation   There were no changes in either current assets or current liabilities. Thus, there was no change in working capital or cash.

Transactions Involving Recognition of Nonworking Capital and Noncash Expenses and Revenues   In addition to the three categories of transactions already discussed, another group of transactions is relevant in the preparation of a statement of changes in financial position. These transactions have no effect on working capital or cash, but they do result in the recognition of expenses and revenues that affect the determination of net income. Examples of these transactions include the depreciation of plant assets, the amortization of intangible assets, the amortization of bond premium or discount, and the recognition of revenue from long-term investments in stock under the equity method that exceeds the amount of dividends received. Net income is adjusted for these nonworking capital (or noncash) revenues and expenses to determine working capital (or cash) provided by operations (see Unit 31).

Conversion of Income Statement to Cash Basis

In Unit 31 it was explained that cash flow information may be useful to investors, creditors, management, and other users of financial information. In providing this information, either the income statement accounts or net income must be converted from the accrual to the cash basis to determine cash provided by operations. In this unit conversion of the income statement accounts is explained and illustrated. This approach results in cash inflows and outflows for revenues and expenses as well as for financing and investing activities. Under the second approach, converting net income to the cash basis, adjustments are made to net income for changes in current assets and current liabilities that represent accruals or deferrals of revenue or expense. This second approach results in a cash basis statement of changes in financial position similar to that illustrated in Unit 31 for the working capital basis.

Time lags occur between the realization of revenue and the receipt of cash. Under accrual basis accounting, receivables are recorded when revenue is realized if cash is not received at the same time. A deferred (or unearned) account is recorded if cash is received before the revenue is earned. Similarly, payables are recorded when expenses are incurred if cash is not paid at the same time, and a deferred (or prepaid) expense account is recorded if cash is paid before the benefits from the expenditure

Exhibit 32.1

Income Statement Accounts (Accrual Basis)	±	Adjustments for Balance of Accruals and Deferrals	=	Related Cash Flows (Cash Basis)
Revenues (e.g., sales, fees earned, interest revenue)	+ − + −	Beginning receivables balance Ending receivables balance Ending unearned revenue balance Beginning unearned revenue balance	=	Cash collected from revenue sources
Cost of goods sold	+ − + −	Beginning accounts payable balance Ending accounts payable balance Ending inventory balance Beginning inventory balance	=	Cash paid for merchandise
Expenses (excluding depreciation, amortization, depletion, and similar write-offs)	+ − + −	Beginning accrued expenses payable balance Ending accrued expenses balance Ending prepaid expenses balance Beginning prepaid expenses balance	=	Cash paid for expenses

Note: Depreciation, amortization, depletion, and similar write-offs are eliminated entirely because there is no related cash outflow in the current period.

are used (before they become an expense). The appropriate revenue and expense accounts must be adjusted for changes in such accruals and deferrals to determine the related cash flow. Exhibit 32.1 summarizes the adjustments for changes in accruals and deferrals to determine the related cash flows for revenues and expenses reported on the accrual basis income statement.

An Illustrative Case

Refer to the comparative balance sheet and income statement for Lemm Company in Exhibit 31.2 and the additional data on pages 621–622. This information can be used to prepare a cash flow statement.

Exhibit 32.2 illustrates the adjustments made to convert the accrual basis revenue and expense figures from Lemm's income statement to the related cash inflows and outflows. After adjustment for beginning and ending accounts receivables, the cash flow from revenue transactions for 19x2 is $246,000. Cash payments for merchandise during 19x2 were $151,000; this amount was determined by adjusting cost of goods sold for beginning and ending accounts payable and inventory balances. Operating expenses and income taxes were adjusted for the beginning and ending balances of accrued expenses and prepaid expenses and for depreciation; the result was $86,000 of cash payments for expenses in 19x2. These cash inflows and outflows are then reported on the cash flow statement (see Exhibit 32.3); the difference is the cash provided (or used) by operations. For Lemm Company cash provided by operations is $9,000 ($246,000 − 151,000 − 86,000).

Exhibit 32.2

Income Statement Accounts	Accrual Basis Amounts	Adjustments for Accruals and Deferrals		Cash Flows
Net sales	$250,000	(a)	+ 42,000	$246,000
			− 46,000	
Cost of goods sold	150,000	(b)	+ 39,000	151,000
			− 36,000	
		(c)	+ 35,000	
			− 37,000	
Expenses:				
Depreciation	10,400	(d)	− 10,400	0
Other operating expenses plus income taxes	83,000	(e)	+ 5,000	86,000
			− 3,000	
		(f)	+ 4,000	
			− 3,000	

Explanation of adjustments:
(a) Beginning and ending accounts receivables.
(b) Beginning and ending accounts payable.
(c) Ending and beginning inventory.
(d) Depreciation eliminated—no related cash outflow during current year.
(e) Beginning and ending accrued expenses payable.
(f) Ending and beginning prepaid expenses.

Exhibit 32.3

Lemm Company
Cash Flow Statement
For the Year Ended December 31, 19x2

Cash inflows from:		
Operations:		
Collections from customers		$246,000
Less: Payments for merchandise payments	$151,000	
Payments for operating expenses and income taxes	86,000	237,000
Cash provided by operations		$ 9,000
Other sources:		
Sale of land	$ 10,000	
Issuance of stock	6,500	16,500
Total cash inflows		$ 25,500
Cash outflows for:		
Purchase of equipment	$ 15,000	
Payment of dividends	7,500	
Total cash outflows		22,500
Increase in cash		$ 3,000

Other sources and uses of cash are determined in the same manner as other sources and uses of working capital. These sources and uses are often the same amount under both the working capital and cash approaches to the preparation of the statement of changes in financial position because so many transactions involve cash flows at the same time or in the same period that they occur. Note that other sources and uses of cash in the cash flow statement for Lemm Company (Exhibit 32.3) are the same as other sources and uses of financial resources in the statement of changes in financial position, working capital basis (see Exhibit 31.3), except for the treatment of the issuance of the long-term note to acquire equipment. However, if the cash flow statement is to be presented as a statement of changes in financial position (cash basis), the long-term note is presented as a source of funds, and the use of funds to purchase equipment is increased to $30,000. The difference between total cash inflows and total cash outflows should be equal to the change in the cash account balance from the beginning to the end of the period.

In addition to analyzing the noncurrent accounts for cash flows, certain current assets and current liabilities must be analyzed to determine other sources and uses of cash. Included among these accounts are temporary investment, nontrade notes receivable or payable, and other short-term receivables or payables not related to regular business operations, that is, that do not arise from transactions to recognize revenues and expenses.

Assume that a company borrows $20,000 from a bank and issues an 8%, 6-month note to the bank as evidence of the loan. The entries to record the loan and its subsequent repayment would be:

Cash	20,000	
Notes Payable, Short-Term		20,000
To record bank loan; 8%, 6-month note issued.		
Notes Payable, Short-Term	20,000	
Interest Expense	800	
Cash		20,800
To record payment of bank loan plus interest ($20,000 × 8% × 6/12 = $800).		

The loan increases cash and is reported as a source of cash. The repayment of the loan principal of $20,000 decreases cash and is reported as a use of cash. The interest payment is reported as an expense on the income statement; thus, it is reflected in the amount of cash provided by operations.

A cash outflow results from the purchase of temporary investments and a cash inflow from their sale. The entire proceeds from the sale should be reported as a cash inflow; any gain or loss on the sale is eliminated in determining cash provided by operations to prevent a double-counting of the cash flow effect of the transaction. Assume that a company purchases temporary investments in 19x1 for $36,000 and sells them for $38,500 in 19x2. In 19x1 a cash outflow of $36,000 is reported; in 19x2 a cash inflow of $38,500 is reported. However the $2,500 ($38,500 − 36,000) gain on the sale of these investments must be deducted from net income in determining cash provided by operations to avoid double-counting as a cash inflow.

REVIEW PROBLEMS

1.   Sinbad Corp. completed the following transactions during 19x4:

     a.   Purchased merchandise on credit at a cost of $5,000.
     b.   Purchased a delivery truck for $9,000 cash.
     c.   Issued bonds at par value, $100,000.
     d.   Acquired land in exchange for 1,000 shares of common stock with a par value of $10 per share and a market value of $18 per share.
     e.   Declared and paid cash dividends of $11,000.
     f.   Constructed a warehouse at a cost of $90,000; the contractor was paid with the proceeds from the bonds.

Required   Determine the effect of each transaction on working capital and cash resources.

2.   Following are selected items from the Vail Corp. balance sheets at the end of 19x3 and 19x4 and a condensed income statement for 19x4:

	12/31/x4	12/31/x3
Accounts receivable (net)	$45,000	$48,000
Inventory	36,000	32,000
Prepaid expenses	4,000	3,000
Accounts payable	38,000	35,000
Salaries payable	1,000	1,500
Advances from customers	3,500	2,000

Vail Corp.
Income Statement
For the Year Ended December 31, 19x4

Sales	$380,000
Cost of goods sold	210,000
Gross margin	$170,000
Operating expenses (including depreciation of $16,000)	132,000
Operating income	$ 38,000
Income taxes	7,000
Net income	$ 31,000

Required   Determine the amount of cash provided by operations.

Solution to review problems

1.	Transaction	Effect on Working Capital	Effect on Cash
	a	None—only working capital accounts involved	None—cash not received or paid
	b	$9,000 decrease—current assets decreased $9,000	$9,000 decrease
	c	$100,000 increase—current assets increased $100,000	$100,000 increase
	d	None—only nonworking capital accounts involved	None—cash not received or paid
	e	$11,000 decrease—current assets decreased $11,000	$11,000 decrease
	f	$90,000 decrease—current assets decreased $90,000	$90,000 decrease

2. Income Statement Items	Amount (Accrual Basis)	Adjustments for Accruals and Deferrals	Related Cash Flow

Sales	$380,000	(a) + 48,000
		      − 45,000
		(b) + 3,500
		      − 2,000
			$384,500

Cost of goods sold	210,000	(c) + 36,000
		      − 32,000
		(d) + 35,000
		      − 38,000
			(211,000)

Operating expenses and income taxes	139,000	(e) − 16,000
		(f) + 4,000
		      − 3,000
		(g) + 1,500
		      − 1,000
			(124,500)

Cash provided by operations			$ 49,000

Explanation of adjustments for accruals and deferrals:

(a) Beginning and ending accounts receivable
(b) Ending and beginning advances from customers
(c) Ending and beginning inventory
(d) Beginning and ending accounts payable
(e) Depreciation eliminated
(f) Ending and beginning prepaid expenses
(g) Beginning and ending salaries payable

SUMMARY

How to analyze the effects of business transactions on working capital and cash flows was explained in this unit. This type of analysis is useful in determining the sources and uses of funds to be reported on a statement of changes in financial position or a cash flow statement. The procedures to prepare a cash flow statement also were explained. Especially important among these procedures is the conversion of accrual basis revenues and expenses (or net income) into cash provided by operations.

APPENDIX 32 T-ACCOUNT ANALYSIS OF CHANGES IN FINANCIAL POSITION — WORKING CAPITAL BASIS

In simple situations, sources and uses of working capital can be determined by reference to changes in nonworking capital accounts and to a limited amount of additional data. However, in more complex situations some form of working paper analysis is essential to analyze correctly all changes in nonworking capital accounts. Accountants have developed various working paper techniques to help them prepare the statement of changes in financial position. One efficient but brief technique is a T-account analysis.

The T-account analysis technique is applied as follows:

1. Set up two master T-accounts labeled:
    a. working capital provided by operations
    b. other sources and uses of financial resources
2. Set up a T-account for each nonworking capital account (that is, for each account except current assets and current liabilities) that appears on the comparative balance sheet.
3. Compute the net change in each nonworking capital account and enter the amount on the appropriate side of the T-account; that is, a debit net change is entered on the debit side of the T-account and a credit net change on the credit side.

4. Draw a horizontal line across both sides of each nonworking capital T-account beneath the amount of the net change.
5. Re-create the business transactions that caused the nonworking capital accounts to change, entering the economic effects in the T-accounts:
   a. Debits and credits to each nonworking capital account are entered in the appropriate T-account. (Note: A special procedure is used for financing and investing activities that do not provide or use working capital; this procedure is discussed in the illustrative case.)
   b. Debits and credits to working capital accounts are entered in the master T-account, other sources or uses of financial resources (debits represent sources and credits represent uses of financial resources).
   c. Debits and credits to income statement accounts and the income summary account are entered in the master T-account, working capital provided by operations (debits are added to net income and credits are deducted from net income to determine working capital provided by operations).

After analyzing all changes in the nonworking capital accounts, the two master T-accounts will contain all information needed to prepare the statement of changes in financial position. Also, the net debit or credit amount beneath the line for each of the other T-accounts should be the same as the amount above the line. If the amounts are not the same, the analysis is not complete or an error has been made. In either case, the discrepancy must be resolved before the statement of changes in financial position is prepared.

Exhibit 32.4 illustrates the completed T-account analysis of changes in financial position on a working capital basis using the data for Lemm Company from Exhibit 31.2.

After the T-accounts were set up, the net change in each noncurrent account was entered on the appropriate side of the accounts. Then, the transactions that affected financial resources were analyzed. Each of these transactions was re-created, and the debits and/or credits to the noncurrent accounts entered in the appropriate T-accounts. The other part of each transaction, that is, the part representing an effect on financial resources, was entered in one of the two master T-accounts. Following are the transactions recorded in Exhibit 32.4, given in general journal form:

(a)	Working capital provided by operations	9,600	
	Retained earnings		9,600
	To record net income as a source of working capital.		

Exhibit 32.4

Working Capital Provided by Operations			
(a) Net income	9,600	(c) Gain on sale of land	3,000
(d) Depreciation	10,400		

Other Sources and Uses of Financial Resources			
(c) Sale of land	10,000	(b) Dividends declared and paid	7,500
(e-2) Long-term note issued to purchase equipment	15,000	(e-1) Equipment purchased for $15,000 cash and	
(f) Stock issued	6,500	a $15,000 long-term note	30,000

Land				Buildings				Accumulated Depreciation, Buildings		
	7,000			—						2,400
		(c)	7,000						(d)	2,400

Equipment			Accumulated Depreciation, Equipment			Long-Term Notes Payable		
30,000					8,000			15,000
(e-1) 30,000				(d)	8,000		(e-2)	15,000

Common Stock			Contributed Capital in Excess of Par			Retained Earnings			
	5,000				1,500				2,100
	(f)	5,000			(f) 1,500	(b)	7,500	(a)	9,600

(b)	Retained earnings	7,500	
	Other sources and uses of financial resources		7,500
	To record dividends as a use of financial resources.		

(c)	Other sources and uses of financial resources	10,000	
	Land		7,000
	Working capital provided by operations		3,000
	To record proceeds from sale of land as a source of financial resources and to adjust working capital provided by operations for the gain from the sale.		

(d)	Working capital provided by operations	10,400	
	Accumulated depreciation, buildings		2,400
	Accumulated depreciation, equipment		8,000
	To adjust working capital provided by operations for nonworking capital expenditure, depreciation.		

(e-1)	Equipment	30,000	
	Other sources and uses of financial resources		30,000
	To record purchase of equipment as a use of financial resources.		

(e-2)	Other sources and uses of financial resources	15,000	
	Long-term notes payable		15,000
	To record note issued to purchase equipment as a source of financial resources.		

(f)	Other sources and uses of financial resources	6,500	
	Common stock		5,000
	Contributed capital in excess of par		1,500
	To record issuance of stock as a source of financial resources.		

Note in Exhibit 32.4 that the net change below the horizontal line in the T-account for each noncurrent account agrees with the net change above the line. Thus, it can be assumed that all changes in financial position (working capital basis) have been prepared; the statement will be the same as prepared in Exhibit 31.3.

REVIEW QUESTIONS

32-1 For each of the following types of transactions, indicate the effect, if any, on (a) working capital and (b) cash.

    (1)   transactions involving only current assets and current liabilities
    (2)   transactions involving both working capital and (i) nonworking capital accounts or (ii) income statement accounts
    (3)   transactions involving only working capital accounts

32-2 Explain how cash provided by operations is determined and reported on a statement of changes in financial position or a cash flow statement.

32-3 Why are changes in current asset and current liability accruals and deferrals added to or deducted from revenues and expenses to determine cash provided by operations?

32-4 How are exchanges involving only noncash resources reported on a cash flow statement?

32-5 Explain how each of the following changes affects cash flow:

    a.   increase in accounts receivable
    b.   increase in inventory
    c.   decrease in prepaid expense
    d.   depreciation
    e.   increase in accounts payable
    f.   increase in nontrade notes payable
    g.   decrease in liability for accrued expenses
    h.   decrease in unearned revenue

32-6 Explain why a working paper technique, such as the T-account technique, is used to analyze changes in financial position.

32-7 Outline the procedures followed in a T-account analysis of changes in financial position on a working capital basis.

32-8 What is the purpose of the two master T-accounts used in the T-account technique of analyzing changes in financial position?

EXERCISES

32-1　Using the following code letters, indicate the effect of the transactions described on working capital and cash:

a.	increases working capital	**d.**	increases cash
b.	decreases working capital	**e.**	decreases cash
c.	no effect on working capital	**f.**	no effect on cash

Transactions

(1)　purchased office equipment for cash
(2)　sold merchandise on credit
(3)　purchased temporary investments
(4)　purchased supplies on credit
(5)　issued the company's common stock
(6)　paid short-term liabilities
(7)　paid a long-term liability
(8)　purchased store equipment by issuing a short-term note
(9)　acquired land by issuing the company's common stock
(10)　paid a cash dividend on June 15 that was declared on May 15

32-2　In each of the following cases involving current assets and/or current liabilities, there may or may not be an effect on working capital. For each case, determine if there is any effect, and if there is, whether it increases or decreases working capital.

Case A　Sales on account to customers totaling $40,000 are made.

Case B　Temporary investments are purchased for $22,000 cash.

Case C　Equipment is purchased on account for $16,000.

Case D　The liability for equipment in case C is paid at the due date.

32-3　For each case in exercise 32-2, determine the effect, if any, on cash flow.

32-4　For each of the following cases determine the net cash effect (that is, the amount that would be reported on a cash flow statement).

Case A　A company reported revenues of $280,000 during the year. Accounts receivable increased by $15,000 during the year.

Case B　A company reported expenses of $235,000 during the year, including depreciation expense of $18,000. During the year inventory increased $5,000 and accounts payable incurred in the purchase of merchandise decreased $12,000.

Case C　A company issued 2,000 shares of stock with a par value of $10 per share for $23 per share.

Case D   A company purchased equipment with a down payment of $5,000 and a short-term note payable of $15,000.

Case E   A company declared a cash dividend of $5,000 at the end of the current year; the dividend is payable early in the next year.

32-5   Following are the changes that occurred in several current assets and liabilities. Indicate whether the change increases or decreases working capital by entering the dollar amount of increase or decrease in the appropriate column. Then determine the net increase or decrease in working capital.

		Working Capital	
		Increases	Decreases
a.	Cash increases $10,000.		
b.	Accounts receivable decreases $8,000.		
c.	Allowance for uncollectible accounts decreases $500.		
d.	Inventory decreases $4,000.		
e.	Prepaid expenses increase $800.		
f.	Accounts payable increases $3,000.		
g.	Notes payable, short-term, decreases $5,000.		
h.	Accrued salaries payable increases $600.	————	————
	Total		
	Net increase or decrease in working capital	————	————
	Total	————	————

32-6   Refer to the data in exercise 31-4 and prepare in good form a cash flow statement. The income statement for 19x8 follows:

Income Statement

Net sales	$350,000
Cost of goods sold	200,000
Gross margin	$150,000
Operating expenses	80,000
Operating income	$ 70,000
Income taxes	25,000
Net income	$ 45,000

32-7   Refer to the data in exercise 31–4. Complete a T-account analysis of the changes in financial position on a working capital basis.

32-8   Following are the two master T-accounts from an analysis of changes in the financial position of Kobb Corp. for 19x4:

Resources Provided by Operations				
(a)	Net income	45,000	(d)	Gain on sale of
(b)	Depreciation	15,000		equipment　2,000
(c)	Amortization of			
	goodwill	3,000		

Other Resources Provided or Used				
(d)	Sale of equipment	12,000	(f)	Dividends　10,000
(e)	Issuance of bonds	50,000	(g)	Land acquired by
(g)	Issuance of stock for			issuing stock　25,000
	land	25,000	(h)	Purchase of equipment　32,000

Required　**a.**　Prepare a statement of changes in financial position.

　　　　　　b.　Was all information needed to prepare the statement required in part a provided? Explain.

PROBLEMS

32-1　Windy Corp. completed the following transactions during 19*x1:*

a.　Sold merchandise on credit to customers, $35,000.

b.　Collected amounts due from customers, $24,000.

c.　Purchased equipment by paying cash of $10,000 and issuing short-term notes for $25,000.

d.　Borrowed $50,000 from a local bank; the loan is to be repaid in one year.

e.　Recorded depreciation expense for 19*x1* of $32,000.

f.　Declared cash dividends of $20,000 during 19*x1*.

g.　Paid the cash dividends in f during 19*x1*.

h.　Declared a stock dividend during 19*x1;* issued 5,000 shares of $10 par value stock that had a market value of $2 per share.

i.　Sold temporary investments with a cost of $42,000 for $45,000.

j.　Acquired land by issuing 1,000 shares of $10 par value common stock with a market value of $30 per share.

k.　Purchased merchandise on credit, $60,000.

l.　Paid the balance due to several short-term creditors, $44,000.

m.　Accrued salaries of $1,500 at the end of 19*x1*.

n.　Issued bonds with a par value of $250,000 at 98.

Required　Indicate the effect of each transaction on both working capital and cash, including the dollar amount of any increase or decrease. If there is no effect on working capital and/or cash, state the reason.

32-2 The following is a summary of cash receipts and disbursements for Conn Company for
19x4:

Cash receipts:

Collections from customers	$215,000
Proceeds from issuance of bonds	105,000
Proceeds from short-term loan	30,000
Proceeds from sale of excess land (including gain of $9,000)	20,000
Miscellaneous revenues collected	4,500
Total	$374,500

Cash disbursements:

Payments of operating expenses	$ 68,000
Payments for merchandise	115,000
Payment to retire short-term loan	30,000
* Retirement of preferred stock	52,000
Purchase of equipment	50,000
Payment of dividends	15,000
Payment of interest on bonds	6,000
Total	$336,000

Other relevant information obtained from the company records includes the following:

Net income	$ 39,500
Depreciation	16,000
Amortization of bond premium	500

The balances of current assets and current liabilities at the beginning and end of 19x4
were:

	Jan. 1, 19x4	Dec. 31, 19x4
Cash	$45,000	$83,500
Accounts receivable	50,000	60,000
Allowance for uncollectible accounts	2,500	3,000
Inventory	42,000	43,600
Prepaid expenses	3,000	2,000
Accounts payable	31,000	26,000
Notes payable, short-term	5,000	2,000
Salaries payable	2,000	2,700
Income taxes payable	7,500	9,400

At the end of 19x4 2,000 shares of $10 par value common stock were exchanged for land
with a fair market value of $36,000.

Required   Prepare in good form a statement of changes in financial position on a working capital basis for 19x4. Apply the all financial resources concept in preparing the statement.

32-3   Using the data in problem 32–2, prepare a cash flow statement for 19x4.

32-4   Following is a statement of changes in financial position for Sherlock Company for 19x7.

Sherlock Company
Statement of Changes in Financial Position
For the Year Ended December 31, 19x7

Financial resources provided by:		
Operations:		
Net income	$ 54,000	
Add: Depreciation	18,000	
Total	$ 72,000	
Less: Amortization of bond premium	800	$ 71,200
Other surces:		
Bonds issued to acquire fixed assets	$108,000	
Issuance of common stock	42,000	150,000
Total financial resources provided		$221,200
Financial resources used to:		
Pay dividends	$ 15,000	
Purchase long-term investments	55,000	
Acquire fixed assets through the issuance of bonds and cash	140,000	
Total financial resources used		210,000
Increase in financial resources		$ 11,200

Schedule of changes in current assets and current liabilities

Increase in cash	$ 7,400
Increase in temporary investments	6,000
Decrease in accounts receivable	(4,000)
Increase in inventory	5,300
Decrease in prepaid expenses	(1,000)
Increase in accounts payable	(3,300)
Decrease in accrued expenses	800
Increase in financial resources	$ 11,200

Required   **a.**   Answer or complete the following:

    (1)   What basis, cash or working capital, was used to prepare the statement? Explain how you arrived at your answer.

    (2)   List the primary working capital resource inflows and outflows and the amount of each.

    (3)   How much did working capital increase during 19x7?

    (4)   Identify any direct exchange of nonworking capital or noncash resources.

    (5)   Why are depreciation and amortization of bond premium adjusted to net income to determine financial resources provided by operations?

    (6)   Why are the changes in current assets and current liabilities reported in a separate schedule but as part of the statement of changes in financial position?

b. Calculate cash provided by operations for 19*x*7.
c. List the primary cash resource inflows and outflows and the amount of each.

32-5 The following are the balance sheets as of December 31, 19*x7* and 19*x8*, and the income statement for 19*x8* for the Redi-Mix Corporation:

Balance Sheets	12/31/*x8*	12/31/*x7*
Cash	$ 10,000	$ 25,000
Accounts Receivable	40,000	35,000
Inventory	60,000	50,000
Prepaid Insurance	3,000	2,000
Land	25,000	25,000
Buildings and Equipment	280,000	240,000
Accumulated Depreciation	(48,000)	(32,000)
Franchise	12,000	15,000
	$382,000	$360,000
Accounts Payable	$ 32,000	$ 38,000
Salaries Payable	3,000	1,000
Bonds Payable	100,000	150,000
Capital Stock	150,000	100,000
Contributed Capital in Excess of Par	30,000	20,000
Retained Earnings	67,000	51,000
	$382,000	$360,000

Income Statement	19*x8*
Sales	$500,000
Cost of Goods Sold	320,000
Gross Margin	$180,000
Operating Expenses	
Depreciation Expense	$ 16,000
Amortization Expense of Franchise	3,000
Other Expense	113,000
Total Operating Expenses	$132,000
Operating Income	$ 48,000
Less: Income Taxes	10,000
Net Income	$ 38,000

The president has noted the $15,000 decrease in cash even though the company had a profit of $38,000 for 19*x8*. You have been asked to prepare a report to explain this situation. Include any statements or schedules that support your written explanation.

32-6 Refer to the data in problem 31–3. Complete a T-account analysis of changes in financial position on a working capital basis.

32-7   Following are the two master T-accounts from the analysis of changes in financial position for Macke Corp. for 19x7.

	Resources Provided by Operations	
(a)	Net income	61,500
(b)	Depreciation	18,000
(c)	Loss on sale of land	3,000

	Other Resources Provided or Used				
(k)	Issuance of stock	36,000	(i)	Dividends	10,000
(m)	Sale of land	15,000	(l)	Purchase of equipment	42,000
(n)	Bank loan	25,000			

Required

a.   Determine the amount of working capital provided by operations.

b.   What was the cost of the land sold during 19x7?

c.   What amount of net income for 19x7 was retained in the business?

d.   If the par value and market value of the stock issued were $10 and $18 per share, respectively, how many shares were issued?

e.   Can you tell from the information given whether the loan is short-term or long-term? Explain.

f.   Prepare a statement of changes in financial position.

Chapter 12

Analysis of Financial Statements

Users of financial statements calculate or refer to various statistics in the form of percentages, ratios, and dollar and percentage changes to interpret the data in the statements. They use their interpretations of past operating results and present financial condition to predict an entity's solvency, liquidity, and profitability. In this chapter the techniques of analyzing financial statements, and the usefulness and limitations of each technique are discussed.

Unit 33
Techniques for Analyzing Financial Statements

In most respects the future will be like what the past has been.

Aristotle, Rhetoric

In this unit the needs of users, the three main analysis techniques, and the standards for interpreting trends in percentages, ratios, and dollar changes are discussed. Also discussed and illustrated are how to apply two of the three analysis techniques (comparative and component percentage analysis) and how to interpret their results. The third analysis technique is explained and illustrated in Unit 34.

Performance Objectives

Upon completing this unit you should be able to:

1. define and use the accounting terms introduced in this unit.
2. explain or describe:
   a. the three main techniques for analyzing financial statements
   b. the four standards for interpreting trends in percentages, ratios, or dollar changes
   c. how to apply either the comparative or component percentage technique of analyzing financial statements
   d. how to interpret the results of either the comparative or component percentage technique of analyzing financial statements
3. apply either the comparative or component percentage technique to the analysis of a balance sheet or income statement or to selected balance sheet or income statement data.

Needs of Users

Three groups of principal users of financial statements are investors, creditors, and managers. Each of these is concerned with evaluating an entity's past operating results and present financial condition in order to make informed decisions regarding the entity's future solvency, liquidity, and profitability.

Investors　Investors include present owners, prospective owners, and investment analysts who provide investment advice to investors. As a group, investors are primarily concerned with an entity's future prospects for profitability. They invest in and maintain their investment in an entity in anticipation of receiving dividends and/or disposing of their investment after its value has increased. In general, both the payment of dividends and growth in the value of the investment depend on the entity's ability to earn profits. Thus, investors are concerned with the following information obtained from the income statement:

1. trends in revenues, expenses, and gross margin
2. income before extraordinary items and net income
3. earnings per share
4. relationships between revenues and expenses
5. profit margins

In addition, investors are concerned with an entity's financial condition and changes in financial position in order to predict future profitability. The nature of the industry and characteristics of the entity, such as sound management, quality products, employee morale, and customer relations, also influence an investor's decision.

Creditors　Creditors include all parties who have loaned money to an entity or allowed the entity to acquire merchandise, assets, or services on credit. Some creditors expect to earn interest on the money loaned or the credit extended to the entity. Other creditors expect to earn only their normal profit from the sale of merchandise, assets, or services to the entity on credit. Thus, creditors are primarily concerned with an entity's solvency and liquidity.

Solvency refers to the ability of an entity to repay its long-term debts. **Liquidity** refers to the entity's ability to meet its current obligations as they are due. If an entity is profitable, it is more likely to be able to make interest payments and pay its debts as they mature. Thus, creditors are also interested in an entity's prospects for profitability. Since the composition of current assets and their liquidity will affect the entity's ability to meet current obligations when they are due, short-term creditors are particularly interested in cash and working capital flows. Long-term creditors are interested in information regarding security for long-term debts and whether or not restrictions imposed by debt agreements are being met. Most of the information creditors want is obtained by analyzing the balance sheet and notes to the balance sheet.

Managers　Managers of an entity must be concerned with all aspects of an entity's operations and financial condition. They are responsible for the efficient and effective management of the entity and must consider the concerns of creditors and investors. Therefore, they must obtain information to evaluate the entity's solvency, liquidity, and profitability.

Techniques for Analysis of Financial Statements

Three general techniques are used in analyzing financial statements: (1) comparative analysis, (2) component percentage analysis, and (3) ratio analysis. The first two techniques are discussed in this unit. The third technique is discussed in Unit 34.

Annual reports usually present comparative financial statements. In a **comparative analysis** the dollar and percentage changes for each line item on the financial statements are determined and presented in separate columns adjacent to the financial data columns for the current and preceding accounting periods. Exhibit 33.1 illustrates the comparative analysis of a balance sheet and income statement. Frequently, the percentage change is more meaningful than the dollar change.

A **component percentage analysis** expresses each line item on a financial statement as a percentage of a selected base figure. For example, on an income statement each line item is expressed as a percentage of net sales. The effect of this analysis is to indicate the distribution of each sales dollar toward expenses and profit. On a balance sheet each line item is expressed as a percentage of total assets. Thus, the composition and sources of the assets are indicated by the analysis. This type of analysis can also be extended to selected groups of accounts. For example, the composition of current assets can be analyzed by expressing each current asset as a percentage of total current assets. Exhibit 33.2 illustrates the component percentage analysis for an income statement and balance sheet.

Ratio analysis is a general name given to the use of various ratios and percentages to express the relationship between two different amounts reported on financial statements. In Chapter 2 some ratios and percentages were introduced, such as earnings per share, return on investment, gross margin percentage, and profit margin (that is, the ratio of net income to net sales). A number of widely used ratios and percentages are discussed in Unit 34.

Standards for Interpreting the Results of the Analysis

In order to interpret any ratio, percentage, or dollar change, a base or standard of comparison must be used. Some ratios, percentages, and dollar changes have meaning by themselves, but most are meaningful only when trends are noted over several periods or when comparisons are made with some goal or objective. Users should be aware of certain limitations in making comparisons, however. It is difficult to compare the results of these analyses for one company with those for other companies because of differences in the size of the companies, the industries in which they operate, and the nature of their operations. Thus, the goals and objectives vary from one company to another, and different standards for comparing ratios, percentages, and dollar changes would be appropriate.

Another limitation is that most ratios and percentages are averages, and large variations in the amounts used in determining the averages may be obscured. Also, many published standards used in interpreting the results of an analysis are averages for several companies. Thus, it will be difficult to attach significance to deviations from these standards. Another problem is that any deviation from a standard may have a variety of causes. If a user determines that a favorable or unfavorable trend or deviation has occurred that is significant, he or she must investigate its probable causes.

There are four standards against which any ratio, percentage, or dollar change can be compared:

1. ratios, percentages, or dollar changes for prior years for the same company
2. published information on ratios, percentages, or dollar changes for similar companies or for the industry in which the company operates (widely used sources for this information are trade association reports and the publications of Dun & Bradstreet, Robert Morris Associates, Moody's, and Standard & Poor's)
3. ratios, percentages, or dollar changes based on the company's goals and objectives as expressed in budgets, profit plans, and target ratios and percentages
4. the overall judgment of the analyst based on his experience and personal knowledge of the company being analyzed

Many ratios and percentages can be calculated, and comprehensive analyses of dollar and percentage changes and component percentages can be made. However, most analysts usually rely on certain ratios and percentages they believe are relevant for specific decision(s). Most corporations include a statistical summary spanning 5 to 15 years in their annual report. These summaries contain key ratios and percentages of interest to investors. Many companies use graphs to present trends for some ratios, percentages, and other data in a convenient, visual format.

Comparative Analysis

Exhibit 33.1 illustrates the results of a comparative analysis of the Phipps Corp. balance sheets and income statements for 19x1 and 19x2. The dollar change for each line item on the statements is the difference between the amounts at the end of the two years. For example, among the current assets, cash increased $5,000, accounts receivable increased $10,000, inventory decreased $5,000, and prepaid expenses increased $1,000, while total current assets increased $11,000.

The percentage change for each line item is determined by dividing the dollar change by the balance or amount at the end of the earlier of the two years being

Exhibit 33.1

Phipps Corp.
Balance Sheet
December 31, 19x1 and 19x2

	19x2	19x1	Increase (Decrease) Dollars	Percent
Current assets:				
Cash	$ 45,000	$ 40,000	$ 5,000	12.5
Accounts receivable (net)	80,000	70,000	10,000	14.3
Inventory	60,000	65,000	(5,000)	(7.7)
Prepaid expenses	3,000	2,000	1,000	50.0
Total current assets	$188,000	$177,000	$11,000	6.2
Plant assets:				
Land	$ 30,000	$ 30,000	$ —	—
Building (net)	144,000	150,000	(6,000)	(4.0)
Equipment (net)	75,000	60,000	15,000	25.0
Total plant assets	$249,000	$240,000	$ 9,000	3.8
Total assets	$437,000	$417,000	$20,000	4.8
Current liabilities:				
Accounts payable	$ 72,000	$ 64,000	$ 8,000	12.5
Accrued expenses	2,000	4,000	(2,000)	(50.0)
Unearned revenues	3,000	1,000	2,000	200.0
Total current liabilities	$ 77,000	$ 69,000	$ 8,000	11.6
Long-term liabilities:				
Long-term notes payable	$ 15,000	$ 20,000	$ (5,000)	(25.0)
Mortgage payable	84,000	90,000	(6,000)	(6.7)
Total long-term liabilities	$ 99,000	$110,000	$(11,000)	(10.0)
Total liabilities	$176,000	$179,000	$ (3,000)	(1.7)
Stockholders' equity:				
Common stock, $10 par	$150,000	$150,000	—	—
Contributed capital in excess of par	30,000	30,000	—	—
Total contributed capital	$180,000	$180,000	—	—
Retained earnings	81,000	58,000	$23,000	39.7
Total stockholders' equity	$261,000	$238,000	$23,000	9.7
Total liabilities and stockholders' equity	$437,000	$417,000	$20,000	4.8

Phipps Corp.
Income Statement
For the Years Ended December 31, 19x1 and 19x2

	19x2	19x1	Increase (Decrease) Dollars	Percent
Net sales	$380,000	$340,000	$40,000	11.8
Cost of sales	224,200	195,500	28,700	14.7
Gross margin	$155,800	$144,500	$11,300	7.8
Operating expenses:				
Selling expenses	$ 64,100	$ 61,600	$ 2,500	4.1
General and administrative expenses	39,300	34,800	4,500	12.9
Total operating expenses	$103,400	$ 96,400	$ 7,000	7.3
Operating income	$ 52,400	$ 48,100	$ 4,300	8.9
Interest expense	8,900	9,800	(900)	(9.2)
Income before taxes	$ 43,500	$ 38,300	$ 5,200	13.6
Less: Income taxes	10,700	9,400	1,300	13.8
Net income	$ 32,000	$ 28,900	$ 3,900	13.5

compared. For example, the percentage increase in cash is calculated by dividing the dollar increase, $5,000, by the balance of cash at the end of 19x1, $40,000; thus, the percentage increase for cash is 12.5 percent ($5,000/$40,000 = 12.5%). Similarly, the percentage decrease in inventory is calculated by dividing the dollar decrease, $5,000, by the balance of inventory at the end of 19x1, $65,000; thus, the percentage decrease for inventory is 7.7 percent ($5,000/$65,000 = 7.7%). To distinguish between increases and decreases, parentheses are placed around each dollar and percentage decrease.

If three or more years are being compared, the dollar change and the percentage change for each pair of years, starting with the earliest, are calculated. The earlier of the two years is considered the base year in the comparision of each pair of years. For example, if a company is comparing 19x1, 19x2 and 19x3, the changes from 19x1 to 19x2 and from 19x2 to 19x3 are calculated. The base year would be 19x1 for the first pair of years and 19x2 for the second pair.

The significance of the changes depends on the judgment of those who use the analysis results. Any changes considered significant when compared to one or more of the standards for comparison should be investigated. After the causes of significant changes are determined, corrective actions can be taken if necessary. Significant changes from one period to the next, if considered alone, can be misleading. Also, reference only to dollar changes or only to percentage changes can be misleading. For example, equipment increased $15,000; however, this represents a 25 percent increase, even though depreciation would have caused a decrease in the net balance for equipment. In addition, note that prepaid expenses increased 50 percent and unearned revenues increased 200 percent; however, both changes are probably insignificant when the dollar balances are considered.

Component Percentage Analysis

Exhibit 33.2 illustrates the results of the component percentage analysis of the balance sheet and income statement for both 19x1 and 19x2 for Phipps Corp. The component percentage for each line item on the balance sheet was determined by dividing the amount for the item by the amount for total assets. For example, the balance of cash for 19x2, $45,000, was divided by the total assets for 19x2, $437,000, to determine that cash is 10.3 percent of total assets at the end of 19x2. Similarly, the accounts payable balance of $72,000 for 19x2 was divided by the total assets figure of $437,000 to determine that 16.5 percent of the assets were provided by these creditors.

The component percentage for each line item on the income statement was determined by dividing the amount of the item by the amount for net sales. For example, the balance of cost of sales for 19x2, $224,200, was divided by net sales for 19x2, $380,000, to determine that 59 percent of each dollar of sales goes towards the cost of the products sold. Similarly, by dividing net income of $32,800 by net sales of $380,000, it was determined that net income was 8.6 percent of each dollar of sales in 19x2.

The component percentages for one period only are generally meaningless. Percentages must be compared to one or more of the standards of comparison. Significant

Exhibit 33.2

Phipps Corp.
Balance Sheet
December 31, 19x1 and 19x2

	19x2		19x1	
	Dollars	**Percent***	**Dollars**	**Percent***
Current assets:				
Cash	$ 45,000	10.3	$ 40,000	9.6
Accounts receivable (net)	80,000	18.3	70,000	16.8
Inventory	60,000	13.7	65,000	15.6
Prepaid expenses	3,000	.7	2,000	.5
Total current assets	$188,000	43.0	$177,000	42.4
Plant assets:				
Land	$ 30,000	6.9	$ 30,000	7.2
Building (net)	144,000	33.0	150,000	36.0
Equipment (net)	75,000	17.2	60,000	14.4
Total plant assets	$249,000	57.0	$240,000	57.6
Total assets	$437,000	100.0	$417,000	100.0
Current liabilities:				
Accounts payable	$ 72,000	16.5	$ 64,000	15.3
Accrued expenses	2,000	.5	4,000	1.0
Unearned revenues	3,000	.7	1,000	.2
Total current liabilities	$ 77,000	17.6	$ 69,000	16.5
Long-term liabilities:				
Long-term notes payable	$ 15,000	3.4	$ 20,000	4.8
Mortgage payable	84,000	19.2	90,000	21.6
Total long-term liabilities	$ 99,000	22.7	$110,000	26.4
Total liabilities	$176,000	40.3	$179,000	42.9
Stockholders' equity:				
Common stock, $10 par	$150,000	34.3	$150,000	36.0
Contributed capital in excess of par	30,000	6.9	30,000	7.2
Total contributed capital	$180,000	41.2	$180,000	43.2
Retained earnings	81,000	18.5	58,000	13.9
Total stockholders' equity	$261,000	59.7	$238,000	57.1
Total liabilities and stockholders' equity	$437,000	100.0	$417,000	100.0

Phipps Corp.
Income Statement
For the Years Ended December 31, 19x1 and 19x2

	19x2		19x1	
	Dollars	**Percent***	**Dollars**	**Percent***
Net sales	$380,000	100.0	$340,000	100.0
Cost of sales	224,200	59.0	195,500	57.5
Gross margin	$155,800	41.0	$144,500	42.5
Operating expenses:				
Selling expenses	$ 64,100	16.9	$ 61,600	18.1
General and administrative expenses	39,300	10.3	34,800	10.2
Total operating expenses	$103,400	27.2	$ 96,400	28.4
Operating income	$ 52,400	13.8	$ 48,100	14.1
Interest expense	8,900	2.3	9,800	2.9
Income before taxes	$ 43,500	11.4	$ 38,300	11.3
Less: Income taxes	10,700	2.8	9,400	2.8
Net income	$ 32,800	8.6	$ 28,900	8.5

*Due to rounding some subtotals do not sum to the amount indicated.

trends can then be noted, the causes of the trends determined, and corrective actions taken if necessary.

REVIEW PROBLEM

The current assets of Lymone Company at the end of 19x3 and 19x4 are as follows:

	12/31/x4	12/31/x3
Cash	$ 36,000	$ 42,000
Accounts receivable (net)	75,000	67,000
Inventory	63,000	58,000
Prepaid expenses	2,000	3,000
Total current assets	$176,000	$170,000

Required   1.   Complete a comparative analysis of the current assets.
             2.   Complete a component percentage analysis of current assets.

Solution to review problem

1.

	Balances at		Increase (Decrease)	
	12/31/x4	12/31/x3	Dollar	Percent
Cash	$ 36,000	$ 42,000	$ (6,000)	(14.3)
Accounts receivable (net)	75,000	67,000	8,000	11.9
Inventory	63,000	58,000	5,000	8.6
Prepaid expenses	2,000	3,000	(1,000)	(33.3)
Total current assets	$176,000	$170,000	$ 6,000	3.5

2.

	19x4		19x3	
	Amount	Percent	Amount	Percent
Cash	$ 36,000	20.5	$ 42,000	24.7
Accounts receivable (net)	75,000	42.6	67,000	39.4
Inventory	63,000	35.8	58,000	34.1
Prepaid expenses	2,000	1.1	3,000	1.8
Total current assets	$176,000	100.0	$170,000	100.0

SUMMARY

Financial statements can be analyzed by one or more of three techniques: comparative analysis, component percentage analysis, and ratio analysis. The results of the analysis are interpreted to evaluate the solvency, liquidity, and/or profitability of an entity. This information is relevant in decision making. These three techniques were explained in this unit, but only the first two were illustrated. The third is treated fully in the next unit. The standards for interpreting the results of any of the analysis techniques and the limitations on these interpretations were also discussed.

REVIEW QUESTIONS

33-1   Briefly describe the information needs of investors, creditors, and managers that can be satisfied, at least partially, by analyzing an entity's financial statements.

33-2   Describe three general techniques for analyzing financial statements.

33-3   Indicate the standards for interpreting the results of any analysis technique that has been applied to an entity's financial statements.

33-4   Explain some of the limitations on the use of the general analysis techniques described in this unit.

33-5   How are dollar changes and percentage changes determined when a comparative analysis of a financial statement is performed?

33-6   How are component percentages determined when a component percentage analysis of a financial statement is performed?

33-7   If three or more years' data are being used in a comparative analysis of a financial statement, which year will be considered the base year?

33-8   What will be the base figure that is set equal to 100% when a component percentage analysis is performed on (a) a balance sheet, (b) an income statement, and (c) a statement of changes in financial position?

EXERCISES

33-1   The following is a comparative balance sheet for the Shoe Emporium:

The Shoe Emporium
Balance Sheet
December 31, 19x2 and 19x3

Assets	*19x3*	*19x2*
Current assets:		
Cash	$ 8,000	$ 10,000
Accounts receivable (net of provision for uncollectible		
accounts of $600)	12,000	13,500
Inventory, at fifo cost	54,000	50,000
Prepaid expenses	2,000	1,500
Total current assets	$ 76,000	$ 75,000
Fixed assets:		
Store fixtures and equipment (net of accumulated depreciation		
of $14,000 at the end of 19x2 and $18,000 at the end of		
19x3)	24,000	28,000
Total assets	$100,000	$103,000

Liabilities		
Current liabilities:		
Accounts payable	$ 23,000	$ 21,000
Income taxes payable	1,500	1,200
Liabilities for interest, sales taxes, and payroll taxes	2,500	2,000
Due to banks, short-term	8,000	4,800
Due to banks, current maturities of long-term debt	5,000	5,000
Total current liabilities	$ 40,000	$ 34,000
Long-term liabilities:		
Due to banks, matures on July 1 of each year	10,000	15,000
Total liabilities	$ 50,000	$ 49,000

Stockholders' Equity		
Contributed capital:		
Common stock, $10 par value, 5,000 shares authorized, 3,000		
shares issued and outstanding	$ 30,000	$ 30,000
Retained earnings	20,000	24,000
Total stockholders' equity	$ 50,000	$ 54,000
Total liabilities and stockholders' equity	$100,000	$103,000

Required   **a.**   Complete a comparative analysis of the balance sheet.

           b.   Are there any significant changes that should be investigated? Explain.

33-2   The following is a comparative income statement for the Shoe Emporium:

The Shoe Emporium
Income Statement
For the Years Ended December 31, 19x2 and 19x3

	19x3	19x2
Net sales	$240,000	$225,000
Cost of goods sold	146,000	132,000
Gross margin on sales	$ 94,000	$ 93,000
Operating expenses:		
Salaries	$ 48,400	$ 44,800
Payroll taxes and benefits	5,700	5,400
Utilities	2,200	1,800
Depreciation	4,000	4,000
Rent	10,800	10,200
Supplies	1,200	1,300
Bad debts and checks	900	1,000
Miscellaneous	3,600	4,100
Total operating expenses	$ 76,800	$ 72,600
Operating income	$ 17,200	$ 20,400
Federal and state income taxes	4,300	5,100
Net income	$ 12,900	$ 15,300

Required   **a.**   Complete a component percentage analysis on the 19x2 and 19x3 income statements.

b.   Are there any significant changes that should be investigated? Explain.

33-3   Following are a comparative balance sheet and a comparative income statement for Hammer Company:

Hammer Company
Balance Sheet

	12/31/x4	12/31/x3
Assets:		
Cash on hand and in banks	$ 50,000	$ 40,000
Marketable securities	60,000	50,000
Receivables	70,000	60,000
Inventories	180,000	110,000
Plant and equipment (net of accumulated depreciation)	300,000	310,000
Total assets	$660,000	$570,000
Liabilities and stockholders' equity:		
Accounts payable	$ 50,000	$ 75,000
Accrued liabilities	20,000	25,000
Bonds payable	100,000	60,000
Capital stock, par value $5 per share	250,000	250,000
Retained earnings appropriated for bond retirement	40,000	30,000
Retained earnings	200,000	130,000
Total liabilities and stockholders' equity	$660,000	$570,000

Hammer Company
Condensed Income Statements for 19x3 and 19x4

	19x4	19x3
Net sales (all on credit)	$710,000	$680,000
Cost of goods sold:		
Merchandise inventory, beginning	110,000	130,000
Purchases	440,000	354,000
Total	$550,000	$484,000
Merchandise inventory, ending	180,000	110,000
Cost of goods sold	$370,000	$374,000
Gross profit on sales	$340,000	$306,000
Operating expenses	165,000	156,000
Operating income	$175,000	$150,000
Interest expense	6,000	8,000
Income before federal income taxes	$169,000	$142,000
Federal income taxes	74,000	62,000
Net income for year	$ 95,000	$ 80,000

Note: Dividends of $25,000 were declared and paid on capital stock during 19x3 and 19x4.

Required   **a.**   Complete a comparative analysis and a component percentage analysis for assets.

b.   Complete a component percentage analysis for the income statements for 19x3 and 19x4.

c.   Comment on the possible causes of any significant changes and trends based on the analysis in parts a and b.

33-4   The following is a partially completed component percentage income statement. Complete the statement. Also, if net income was $24,000, reconstruct the income statement.

Sheriff Corp.
Component Percentage Income Statement
For the Year Ended December 31, 19x9

Net sales	
Cost of goods sold	
Gross margin	40.0%
Operating expenses	
Operating income	
Interest expense	2.0%
Income before taxes	12.0%
Income taxes	.
Net income	8.0%

PROBLEMS

33-1   The following is a comparative balance sheet for Marshall Corp:

	12/31/*x8*	12/31/*x7*	12/31/*x6*
Assets			
Cash	$ 55,000	$ 30,000	$ 45,000
Accounts Receivable (net)	75,000	65,000	60,000
Inventories	160,000	180,000	150,000
Equipment	150,000	100,000	100,000
Accumulated Depreciation—Equipment	(65,000)	(50,000)	(40,000)
Buildings	230,000	180,000	180,000
Accumulated Depreciation—Building	(38,000)	(30,000)	(24,000)
Land	10,000	20,000	20,000
Goodwill	55,000	70,000	85,000
Total Assets	$632,000	$565,000	$576,000
Equities			
Accounts Payable	$ 65,000	$ 55,000	$ 70,000
Long-Term Notes Payable	170,000	150,000	150,000
Common Stock, $10 par	120,000	100,000	100,000
Contributed Capital in Excess of Par	10,000	—	—
Retained Earnings	267,000	260,000	256,000
Total Equities	$632,000	$565,000	$576,000

Required   **a.**   Complete a comparative analysis of the balance sheet. Use 19*x6* as the base year when comparing 19*x6* and 19*x7;* use 19*x7* as the base year when comparing 19*x7* and 19*x8.*

b.   Are there any significant changes that should be investigated? Explain.

33-2   The following is a comparative income statement for Marshall Corp.:

	19*x8*	19*x7*	19*x6*
Net sales	$450,000	$360,000	$300,000
Cost of goods sold	270.000	207,000	168,000
Gross margin	$180,000	$153,000	$132,000
Operating expenses:			
Selling expenses	$ 81,000	$ 70,200	$ 60,000
General expenses	76,500	57,600	45,000
Total operating expenses	$157,500	$127,800	$105,000
Operating income	$ 22,500	$ 25,200	$ 27,000
Interest expense	10,400	9,000	9,000
Income before taxes and extraordinary items	$ 12,100	$ 16,200	$ 18,000
Income taxes	3,025	4,050	4,500
Income before extraordinary items	$ 9,075	$ 12,150	$ 13,500
Extraordinary gain	6,000		
Net income	$ 15,075	$ 12,150	$ 13,500

Required **a.** Complete a component percentage analysis of the income statement for each year.

b. Identify and comment on any significant trends revealed by the analysis in part a.

33-3 The following are comparative financial statements for Deputy Corp.:

	12/31/x6	12/31/x5	12/31/x4
Assets			
Cash	$ 12,000	$ 11,000	$ 8,000
Accounts Receivable	35,000	40,000	37,000
Inventory	40,000	34,000	31,000
Prepaid Expenses	2,000	3,000	4,000
Equipment	80,000	80,000	70,000
Accumulated Depreciation	(23,000)	(15,000)	(7,000)
Patents	6,000	7,000	8,000
Total Assets	$152,000	$160,000	$151,000
Equities			
Accounts Payable	$ 19,000	$ 22,000	$ 26,000
Accrued Expenses	1,500	1,200	2,100
Bank Loan	20,000	25,000	—
Common Stock	100,000	100,000	100,000
Retained Earnings	11,500	11,800	22,900
Total Equities	$152,000	$160,000	$151,000
	19x6	**19x5**	**19x4**
Net Sales	$360,000	$330,000	$300,000
Cost of Goods Sold	234,000	211,200	180,000
Gross Margin	$126,000	$118,800	$120,000
Operating Expenses			
Selling Expenses	$ 77,400	$ 79,200	$ 66,000
General Expenses	45,000	46,200	36,000
Total Operating Expenses	$122,400	$125,400	$102,000
Operating Income (Loss)	$ 3,600	$ (6,600)	$ 18,000
Interest Expense	1,600	2,000	
Income (Loss) before Taxes	$ 2,000	$ (8,600)	$ 18,000
Income Taxes	600		5,400
Net Income (Loss)	$ 1,400	$ (8,600)	$ 12,600

Required **a.** Complete a comparative analysis and a component percentage analysis of the assets.

b. Complete a component percentage analysis of the income statement.

c. Identify and comment on any changes and trends that may help explain the company's poor profit performance during 19x5 and 19x6.

33-4 A partially completed comparative analysis and a partially completed component percentage analysis of the assets from the balance sheet of Guardian Corp. are as follows:

	Balances 12/31/x2	Dollar Change	Percentage Change	Component Percentage
Assets:				
Current assets:				
Cash	(3)	$ 5,000	50.00	(4)
Accounts receivable	(5)	(5,000)	(16.67)	(6)
Inventory	(7)	(1)	(8)	13.75
Prepaid expenses	(9)	1,500	—*	(10)
Total current assets	(11)	$ 4,000	5.80	34.50
Plant assets:				
Land	(12)	$ —	—	7.50
Buildings (net)	(16)	—	—	(15)
Equipment (net)	(13)	10,000	25.00	(14)
Total plant assets	(17)	$10,000	8.70	62.50
Intangible assets:				
Patents	(19)	(2)	(20)	(18)
Total assets	$200,000	$13,000	6.95	100.00

*Cannot be computed because the base year dollar amount is zero.

Required Determine the dollar amount or the percentage figure that belongs in each numbered space; calculate your answers in sequence from 1 to 20.

Unit 34
Ratio Analysis

Conclusions are never any better than the facts they are based on.

Quoted in The Week in Review,
Deloitte Haskins & Sells, November 12, 1976

Ratios can be divided into three categories: those indicating (1) an entity's liquidity, (2) an entity's solvency and equity position, and (3) an entity's profitability. In this unit the most widely used ratios in each of these three groups are examined. The formula for each ratio is presented, and its significance is explained. Each ratio is calculated using the financial statements for Phipps Corp. in Exhibit 33.1 of Unit 33.

Performance Objectives

Upon completing this unit you should be able to:

1. define and use the accounting terms introduced in this unit.
2. explain or describe:
   a. the formula for each ratio in Exhibit 34.1.
   b. the significance of each ratio in Exhibit 34.1.
3. calculate each of the ratios in Exhibit 34.1, given a set of financial statements or selected financial statement data.

Ratios Indicating Liquidity

Short-term creditors are especially interested in a company's liquidity, that is, the company's ability to meet its current liabilities as they become due. In order to pay the short-term creditors, current assets must be converted into cash. Thus, an analysis of financial statements by short-term creditors emphasizes the following:

1. the composition of current assets
2. the adequacy of current assets to meet current liabilities
3. the length of time necessary to convert inventory and receivables into cash

The composition of current assets can be determined with a component percentage analysis. If a large portion of current assets is invested in inventory, a company could have difficulty in meeting current debts. Also, large investments in inventory sometimes indicate overstock situations or the presence of obsolete merchandise in inventory. Large balances of accounts receivable may indicate poor collection policies, slow payments by customers during poor economic conditions, or uncollectible accounts that have not been written off.

Two ratios that are widely used to evaluate the adequacy of current assets to meet current liabilities are the *current or working capital ratio* and the *quick or acid-test ratio*. The two ratios are calculated as follows for 19x2 for Phipps Corp.

$$(1) \quad \frac{\text{current or working}}{\text{capital ratio}} = \frac{\text{current assets}}{\text{current liabilities}}$$

$$= \frac{\$188,000}{\$\ 77,000} = 2.44 \text{ to } 1$$

$$(2) \quad \frac{\text{quick or acid-test}}{\text{ratio}} = \frac{\text{quick assets}[1]}{\text{current liabilities}}$$

$$= \frac{\$45,000 + 80,000}{\$77,000} = 1.62 \text{ to } 1$$

The ratios calculated for a company must be compared with one or more standards for interpreting the results of the analysis. This comparison will indicate the adequacy of current assets to meet current liabilities. The working capital ratio is used to determine the company's ability to pay current debts out of total current assets. It also indicates the adequacy of the company's working capital because working capital is the excess of current assets over current liabilities.

---

[1]Quick assets include cash, temporary investments, and accounts receivable (net of the provisions for the reduction of temporary investments to market and for uncollectible accounts).

The quick ratio measures a company's ability to pay its current debts out of the more liquid current assets. Temporary investments, by their nature, can be quickly converted into cash. Accounts receivable will usually also be collected in a relatively short time and will provide the cash necessary to pay current debts when they mature. Inventory, however, is further removed and less easily converted into cash; and prepaid expenses are not intended to be converted into cash.

The length of time necessary to collect receivables is indicated by the *receivables turnover ratio*. This ratio can then be used to determine the *average collection period* for accounts receivable. These two ratios are calculated as follows for Phipps Corp. for 19x2.

$$\textbf{(3)} \quad \begin{array}{c} \text{receivables} \\ \text{turnover} \end{array} = \frac{\text{net credit sales (or net sales)}}{\text{average receivables (net)}}$$

$$= \frac{\$380,000}{(\$80,000 + 70,000)/2} = 5.07 \text{ times}$$

$$\textbf{(4)} \quad \begin{array}{c} \text{average} \\ \text{collection period} \end{array} = \frac{365 \text{ days}}{\text{receivables turnover}}$$

$$= \frac{365 \text{ days}}{5.07} = 71.99 \text{ days}$$

The receivables turnover reflects the number of times that the average receivables balance was collected during the year. It measures the effectiveness of the company's credit and collection policies. It also expresses the average length of time that it takes to collect accounts receivable. Nct credit sales should be used in the receivables turnover ratio if cash sales are significant. A more specific measure of the average collection period is determined by dividing 365 days by the receivables turnover ratio. The average collection period indicates the average amount of time to realize cash from credit sales.

Changes in these two ratios suggest that credit and/or collection policies may have been changed or are more or less effective than in prior periods. However, there are other causes of such changes. For example, during periods of tight credit and high interest rates, the accounts receivable turnover typically decreases and the average collection period increases.

The *inventory turnover ratio* indicates the length of time it takes to sell merchandise. It can then be converted into the *average number of days' supply in inventory*. These two ratios are calculated as follows for Phipps Corp. for 19x2.

$$\textbf{(5)} \quad \begin{array}{c} \text{inventory} \\ \text{turnover} \end{array} = \frac{\text{cost of sales}}{\text{average inventory}}$$

$$= \frac{\$224,200}{(\$60,000 + 65,000)/2} = 3.59 \text{ times}$$

(6) average number
of days' supply $= \dfrac{365 \text{ days}}{\text{inventory turnover}}$
in inventory

$$= \frac{365 \text{ days}}{3.59} = 101.67 \text{ days}$$

The inventory turnover ratio reflects the number of times the average inventory balance was "turned over" (that is, sold) during the year. It also expresses the average length of time it takes to sell the average inventory balance. A more specific measure of the average time it takes to sell the inventory is determined by dividing 365 days by the inventory turnover ratio. Both ratios can suggest whether or not the company is overstocked or understocked, or may have obsolete merchandise on hand. These ratios will also be affected by economic conditions that spur or delay sales.

Ratios Indicating Solvency and Equity Position

Long-term creditors are primarily interested in a company's solvency, that is, the company's ability to meet its long-term obligations. In order to remain solvent over a prolonged period of time, a company must have sufficient resources and effectively employ these resources to generate profits.

Recall that resources are derived from two basic sources: creditors and owners. When resources are obtained from creditors, obligations are incurred to make periodic interest payments and to repay the debts at fixed dates. A company should be profitable if it expects to meet these obligations without impairing the owners' investments. Owners can benefit if the company can earn more on the resources provided by creditors than it pays in interest on its debts. Thus, a proper balance between creditors' equity (debt capital) and owners' equity (equity capital) is desirable to maximize the return to the owners.

Three ratios reflect the relationship between the creditors' and owners' equity: the *ratio of owners' equity to total assets*, the *ratio of creditors' equity to total assets*, and the *ratio of creditors' equity to owners' equity* (also known as the *debt/equity ratio*). These three ratios are calculated as follows for Phipps Corp. for 19x2.

(1) ratio of owners'
equity to total $= \dfrac{\text{owners' equity}}{\text{total assets}}$
assets

$$= \frac{\$261{,}000}{\$437{,}000} = 59.7\%$$

(2)   ratio of creditors' equity to total assets $= \dfrac{\text{total liabilities}}{\text{total assets}}$

$$= \frac{\$176,000}{\$437,000} = 40.3\%$$

(3)   ratio of creditors' equity to owners' equity (debt/ equity ratio) $= \dfrac{\text{total liabilities}}{\text{owners' equity}}$

$$= \frac{\$176,000}{\$261,000} = .67$$

The first two of these ratios indicate the portion of the resources provided by the owners and the creditors. They complement each other because they have the same base, total assets. They will always add up to 100 percent because the sum of owners' equity and creditors' equity is equal to total assets.

The debt/equity ratio can also be used to determine the relative amounts of resources provided by creditors and owners. For Phipps Corp. this ratio indicates that creditors have provided \$.67 for every \$1 provided by owners. Any of these three ratios can be used to determine if the company has a proper balance between owners' equity and creditors' equity by comparing it with some standard for the company and the industry. An improper balance between the two types of equities may affect the company's ability to obtain more debt or equity capital.

Security for long-term debt and/or the potential for using plant assets as security for additional long-term debt can be determined by referring to the *ratio of plant assets (net) to long-term liabilities*. The efficient use of equity capital to generate sales is indicated by the *ratio of net sales to owners' equity*. The efficiency in using plant assets to generate sales is determined from the *ratio of net sales to plant assets (net)*. These three ratios are calculated as follows for Phipps Corp. for 19x2.

(4)   ratio of plant assets (net) to long-term liabilities $= \dfrac{\text{plant assets (net)}}{\text{long-term liabilities}}$

$$= \frac{\$249,000}{\$\ 99,000} = 2.52 \text{ to } 1$$

(5)   ratio of net sales to owners' equity $= \dfrac{\text{net sales}}{\text{owners' equity}}$

$$= \frac{\$380,000}{\$261,000} = 1.46 \text{ to } 1$$

$$\textbf{(6)} \quad \frac{\text{ratio of net sales}}{\text{to plant assets (net)}} = \frac{\text{net sales}}{\text{plant assets (net)}}$$

$$= \frac{\$380,000}{\$249,000} = 1.53 \text{ to } 1$$

Stockholders and financial analysts often compare the *book value (or net assets) per share of common stock* with the current market of the stock. Although the book value of the net assets is based on original cost rather than current value, this information may be useful, along with knowledge of the company's situation, to help an investor decide whether to invest in or retain an investment in a company. An attractive investment situation may be indicated if current market value is below or relatively low compared to book value, especially if stock market prices are depressed in general. Book value per share of common stock for Phipps Corp. at the end of 19x2 is calculated as follows:

$$\textbf{(7)} \quad \frac{\text{book value per share}}{\text{of common stock}} = \frac{\text{common stockholders' equity}}{\text{number of shares outstanding}}$$

$$= \frac{\$261,000}{(\$150,000/\$10)} = \$17.40$$

Because Phipps Corp. has no preferred stock outstanding, common stockholders' equity is equal to total stockholders' equity. The par value per share was divided into the total par value of common stock to determine the number of shares issued. In the absence of any treasury stock, the number of shares issued is equal to the number of shares outstanding.

Another measure of security for long-term creditors is the *number of times interest earned ratio*. Annual interest requirements are expected to be met out of current earnings. And if earnings are good, a company is expected to remain solvent and be in a better position to repay long-term debts. Recall that interest expense and income taxes are usually deducted after determining operating income (that is, gross margin less operating expenses). Also, interest expense is deductible in determining taxable income. Therefore, a company could pay interest equal to operating income plus incidental revenue less incidental expenses other than interest and have no taxable income. For this reason, interest expense and income taxes are added back to net income to calculate this ratio. As demonstrated below, Phipps Corp. earned the annual interest requirement of $8,900 for 19x2 almost six times.

$$\textbf{(8)} \quad \frac{\text{number of times}}{\text{interest earned}} = \frac{\text{net income} + \text{interest expense} + \text{income taxes}}{\text{annual interest expense}}$$

$$= \frac{\$32,800 + 8,900 + 10,700}{\$8,900} = 5.80 \text{ times}$$

Ratios Indicating Profitability

Investors are primarily interested in a company's profitability. They are concerned with ratios and percentages that will indicate the company's potential for distributing dividends and the potential for growth in the value of their investments. Four ratios are widely used to evaluate this potential: *profit margin (or the ratio of net income to net sales), return on total assets (or total investment), return on common stockholders' equity,* and *earnings per share of common stock.* The calculations for these four ratios for Phipps Corp. for 19*x2* are as follows:

(1) profit margin (ratio of net income to net sales)
$$= \frac{\text{net income}}{\text{net sales}}$$

$$= \frac{\$\ 32,800}{\$380,000} = 8.6\%$$

(2) return on total assets (total investment)
$$= \frac{\text{net income}}{\text{total assets}}$$

$$= \frac{\$\ 32,800}{\$437,000} = 7.5\%$$

(3) return on common stockholders' equity
$$= \frac{\text{net income} - \text{preferred dividends}}{\text{common stockholders' equity}}$$

$$= \frac{\$\ 32,800}{\$261,000} = 12.6\%$$

(4) earnings per share of common stock
$$= \frac{\text{net income} - \text{preferred dividends}}{\text{number of shares outstanding}}$$

$$= \frac{\$32,800}{(\$150,000/\$10)} = \$2.19$$

In calculating the first three of these four ratios, income before extraordinary items should be used in place of net income whenever extraordinary items are reported by the company being analyzed. Also, earnings per share of common stock should be calculated for both income before extraordinary items and net income, and the per share effect of the extraordinary item should be disclosed. In practice several alternative approaches are used to calculate the return on total assets. For simplicity, net income is used in the numerator of the ratio in this text. A commonly used alternative has net income plus interest expense (after adjustment for income tax effects) as the numerator.

Profit margin indicates the return on each dollar of sales. Note that it is the same statistic obtained when net income is divided by net sales in a component percentage analysis of the income statement. Phipps Corp. has a simple capital structure because it has no preferred stock or convertible securities. Thus, earnings per share is simply net income divided by the number of shares of common stock outstanding. These ratios are evaluated, like the others, by comparison with company and industry standards and through the personal knowledge and experience of the analyst.

Returns on total assets and on owners' equity are important ratios that can be analyzed in greater depth to better evaluate a company's profitability. Because Phipps Corp. does not have any outstanding preferred stock, net income was divided by total stockholders' equity to determine the return on common stockholders' equity. Note that the return on common stockholders' equity (12.6%) is greater than the return on total assets (7.5%). This indicates that the company has successfully **traded on the equity,** that is, has used the resources provided by the creditors to the advantage of the common stockholders. It means that the company has been able to pay creditors a lower rate of return (after taxes) on the resources they provided than the rate of return (after taxes) earned by the company.

Phipps Corp. earned 7.5% on each dollar of assets available during 19x2. However, interest is not paid on most current liabilities. Also the after-tax rate of interest paid on long-term liabilities most likely was less than 7.5% for Phipps Corp. Because Phipps Corp. was able to pay less than 7.5% to the creditors, additional profits accrued to the common stockholders, and their rate of return for 19x2 was 12.6%. Trading on the equity will be unfavorable if the return on common stockholders' equity is less than the return on total assets. The latter situation can occur when a company has large amounts of long-term debt and/or low earnings for the year.

Common stockholders can also "trade" on the preferred stockholders' equity. The return on common stockholders' equity can be increased if the preferred dividend rate is less than the rate of return on total assets. Trading on preferred stockholders' equity can be determined by comparing the rate of return on common stockholders' equity with the *rate of return on total stockholders' equity*. The formula for this ratio is presented below. However, because Phipps Corp. does not have any preferred stock outstanding, the rate of return on total stockholders' equity is equal to the rate of return on common stockholders' equity—see calculation (3) on page 681. Trading on preferred stockholders' equity is favorable if the rate of return on common stockholders' equity is greater than the rate of return on total stockholders' equity.

$$\textbf{(5)} \qquad \frac{\text{return on total}}{\text{stockholders' equity}} = \frac{\text{net income}}{\text{total stockholders' equity}}$$

$$= \frac{\$32,800}{\$261,000} = 12.6\%$$

Return on total assets can be divided into two components: *profit margin* and *asset turnover*. The product of these two components is equal to the return on total assets. Identifying these two components is important because a company can improve its return on total assets in three ways. For example, return on total assets will increase if the company can increase sales revenue or decrease either expenses or its investment in assets. The calculations for asset turnover and the return on total assets (using the alternate computation approach) for Phipps Corp. for 19x2 are as follows:

$$\textbf{(6)} \quad \text{asset turnover} = \frac{\text{net sales}}{\text{total assets}}$$

$$= \frac{\$380,000}{\$437,000} = .87$$

$$\begin{array}{c}\text{return on total} \\ \text{assets}\end{array} = \begin{array}{c}\text{profit} \\ \text{margin}\end{array} \times \begin{array}{c}\text{asset} \\ \text{turnover}\end{array}$$

$$= \frac{\text{net income}}{\text{net sales}} \times \frac{\text{net sales}}{\text{total assets}}$$

$$= \frac{\$\ 32,800}{\$380,000} \times \frac{\$380,000}{\$437,000}$$

$$= 8.6\% \times .87 = 7.5\%$$

Investors and potential investors frequently refer to two ratios to evaluate the attractiveness of a common stock investment: the *price/earnings ratio* and the *dividend yield ratio*. The calculations for both ratios for Phipps Corp. for 19x2 are as follows, assuming a current market value of $18 per share and dividends of $.64 per share during 19x2.

$$\textbf{(7)} \quad \begin{array}{c}\text{price/earnings} \\ \text{ratio}\end{array} = \frac{\text{market value per share}}{\text{earnings per share}}$$

$$= \frac{\$18}{\$2.19} = 8.22$$

$$\textbf{(8)} \quad \begin{array}{c}\text{dividend yield} \\ \text{ratio}\end{array} = \frac{\text{dividends per share}}{\text{market value per share}}$$

$$= \frac{\$.64}{\$18} = 3.56\%$$

Both ratios try to relate current market value per share to some measure of profit that might accrue to the investor either currently or in the long run. The dividend yield ratio indicates the return on investment expected annually from dividends if the current dividend rate is maintained. The portion of earnings not paid out currently as dividends might be received as dividends in future years, through the sale of the stock at higher prices, or through assets received if the corporation is liquidated. Lower price/earnings ratios indicate that a stock is selling at a favorable price in relation to current earnings.

REVIEW PROBLEM

The following are selected data from the financial statements for Pacem Corp. for 19x3 and 19x4:

	19x3	19x4
Cash	$ 35,000	$ 28,000
Accounts receivable	64,000	72,000
Inventory	54,000	60,000
Total current assets	160,000	170,000
Total current liabilities	75,000	81,000
Total assets	385,000	400,000
Total liabilities	135,000	140,000
Net sales	510,000	565,000
Cost of sales	285,000	310,000
Total operating expenses	160,000	175,000
Interest expense	8,000	7,000
Income taxes	23,000	29,000
Net income	34,000	44,000

Required   Calculate the following ratios for 19x4:

  1. working capital ratio
  2. acid-test ratio
  3. average collection period
  4. inventory turnover
  5. debt/equity ratio
  6. number of times interest earned
  7. return on total assets
  8. return on stockholders' equity
  9. profit margin
 10. asset turnover

Solution to review problem

1. $\dfrac{\text{current assets}}{\text{current liabilities}} = \dfrac{\$170,000}{\$ 81,000} = 2.1 \text{ to } 1$

2. $\dfrac{\text{quick assets}}{\text{current liabilities}} = \dfrac{\$28,000 + 72,000}{\$81,000} = 1.23 \text{ to } 1$

3. $\dfrac{\text{net sales}}{\text{average receivables}} = \dfrac{\$565,000}{(\$64,000 + 72,000)/2} = 8.31 \text{ times}$

$\dfrac{365 \text{ days}}{\text{receivables turnover}} = \dfrac{365 \text{ days}}{8.31} = 43.9 \text{ days}$

4. $\dfrac{\text{cost of sales}}{\text{average inventory}} = \dfrac{\$310,000}{(\$54,000 + 60,000)/2} = 5.44 \text{ times}$

5. $\dfrac{\text{total liabilities}}{\text{total stockholders' equity}} = \dfrac{\$140,000}{\$400,000 - 140,000} = .538$

6. $\dfrac{\text{net income} + \text{interest expense} + \text{income taxes}}{\text{interest expense}} = \dfrac{\$44,000 + 7,000 + 29,000}{\$7,000}$

$= 11.43 \text{ times}$

7. $\dfrac{\text{net income}}{\text{total assets}} = \dfrac{\$44,000}{\$400,000} = 11.0\%$[2]

8. $\dfrac{\text{net income}}{\text{total stockholders' equity}} = \dfrac{\$44,000}{\$400,000 - 140,000} = 16.9\%$

9. $\dfrac{\text{net income}}{\text{net sales}} = \dfrac{\$44,000}{\$565,000} = 7.8\%$

10. $\dfrac{\text{net sales}}{\text{total assets}} = \dfrac{\$565,000}{\$400,000} = 1.41$

SUMMARY

Three groups of ratios that are widely used by creditors, investors, and managers were discussed and illustrated. These three groups of ratios help users evaluate a company's liquidity, solvency, equity position, and profitability. The formulas for and significance of each ratio covered in this unit are presented in Exhibit 34.1.

---

[2]Also, return on total assets = profit margin × asset turnover (7.8% × 1.41 = 11.0%).

Exhibit 34.1

A. Ratios Indicating Liquidity

	Ratio	Formula	Significance
1.	Current or working capital ratio	$\dfrac{\text{Current assets (net)}}{\text{Current liabilities}}$	Ability to meet current obligations out of current assets
2.	Quick or acid-test ratio	$\dfrac{\text{Cash} + \frac{\text{marketable}}{\text{securities}} + \frac{\text{receivables}}{\text{(net)}}}{\text{Current liabilities}}$	Ability to meet current obligations out of immediate liquidity
3.	Receivables turnover	$\dfrac{\text{Net credit sales (net sales)}}{\text{Average receivables (net)}}$	Efficiency and length of collection of receivables
4.	Average collection period	$\dfrac{365 \text{ days}}{\text{Receivables turnover}}$	Efficiency of collection; time to convert to cash
5.	Inventory turnover	$\dfrac{\text{Cost of sales}}{\text{Average inventory}}$	Liquidity of inventory over- or understock; obsolete items
6.	Number of days' supply in inventory	$\dfrac{365 \text{ days}}{\text{Inventory turnover}}$	Over- or understock situations; obsolete items in stock; time to sell average inventory balance

B. Ratios Indicating Solvency and Equity Position

	Ratio	Formula	Significance
1.	Owners' equity to total assets	$\dfrac{\text{Owners' equity}}{\text{Total assets}}$	Portion of assets provided by owners
2.	Creditors' equity to total assets	$\dfrac{\text{Total liabilities}}{\text{Total assets}}$	Portion of assets provided by creditors
3.	Creditors' equity to owners' equity (debt/equity ratio)	$\dfrac{\text{Total liabilities}}{\text{Owners' equity}}$	Relative amounts of assets provided by owners and creditors; strength of financial structure
4.	Plant assets to long-term debt	$\dfrac{\text{Plant assets (net)}}{\text{Long-term liabilities}}$	If plant are pledged—degree of security; potential borrowing
5.	Sales to owners' equity	$\dfrac{\text{Net sales}}{\text{Owners' equity}}$	Efficient use of owners' capital in generating sales volume
6.	Sales to plant assets	$\dfrac{\text{Net sales}}{\text{Plant assets (net)}}$	Efficiency in using plant to generate sales volume
7.	Book value per share of common stock	$\dfrac{\text{Common stockholders' equity}}{\text{Number of shares outstanding}}$	Net assets (at book value) per share
8.	Number of times interest earned	$\dfrac{\frac{\text{Net}}{\text{income}} + \frac{\text{interest}}{\text{expense}} + \frac{\text{income}}{\text{taxes}}}{\text{Annual interest expense}}$	Security for bondholders

C. Ratios Indicating Profitability

Ratio	Formula	Significance
1. Net income to net sales (profit margin)	$$\frac{\text{Net income*}}{\text{Net sales}}$$	Return per dollar of sales
2. Return on total assets (investment)†	$$\frac{\text{Net income*}}{\text{Total assets}}$$	Earnings rate on all assets used by the firm
3. Return on common shareholders' equity	$$\frac{\text{Net income*} - \text{preferred dividends}}{\text{Common shareholders' equity}}$$	Earnings rate on assets belonging to residual owners; compare to C(2) and C(5) to determine trading on the equity*
4. Earnings per share of common stock‡	$$\frac{\text{Net income} - \text{preferred dividends}}{\text{Number of shares outstanding}}$$	Earnings per share of common stock
5. Return on total stockholders' equity	$$\frac{\text{Net income}}{\text{Total stockholders' equity}}$$	Earnings rate on assets provided by owners
6. Asset turnover	$$\frac{\text{Net sales}}{\text{Total assets}}$$	Efficiency in using total assets to generate sales
7. Price/earnings ratio	$$\frac{\text{Market value per share}}{\text{Earnings per share}}$$	Investment attractiveness-profitability related to market value
8. Dividend yield ratio	$$\frac{\text{Annual dividend payment per share}}{\text{Market value per share}}$$	Return per share of stock received as dividends

*Substitute income before extraordinary items if extraordinary items are reported.
†Also, return on total assets = profit margin × asset turnover.
‡If extraordinary items are reported, earnings per share should be calculated for both income before extraordinary items and net income. Also, the per share effect of the extraordinary item should be disclosed.

REVIEW QUESTIONS

34-1 What type of information are short-term creditors primarily interested in obtaining from an analysis of financial statements?

34-2 Name the ratios that short-term creditors should find particularly useful.

34-3 Explain the significance of the following ratios:

    a. current ratio   **c.** receivables turnover
    b. quick ratio   **d.** inventory turnover

34-4 What type of information are long-term creditors primarily interested in obtaining from an analysis of financial statements?

34-5   Name the ratios that long-term creditors should find particularly useful.

34-6   Explain the significance of the following ratios:

     a.   debt/equity ratio
     b.   book value per share of common stock
     c.   number of times interest earned

34-7   The debt/equity ratio, the ratio of owners' equity to total assets, and the ratio of creditors' equity to total assets can be used to measure equity position. Explain.

34-8   The ratio of owners' equity to total assets and the ratio of creditors' equity to total assets are complements. Explain.

34-9   What type of information are investors primarily interested in obtaining from an analysis of financial statements?

34-10   Name the ratios that investors should find particularly useful.

34-11   Explain the significance of the following ratios:

     a.   profit margin   **d.**   earnings per share of common
     b.   return on total assets   stock
     c.   return on common   **e.**   price/earnings ratio
         stockholders' equity   **f.**   dividend yield ratio

34-12   **a.**   Explain what is mean by "trading on the equity."
        b.   How is "trading on the equity" measured?

34-13   The return on total assets can be broken down into two component ratios.

     a.   Name these two component ratios.
     b.   Show how return on total assets is determined using these two component ratios.
     c.   What is the significance of breaking the return on total assets into these two component ratios?

EXERCISES

34-1   Refer to the data in exercises 33–1 and 33–2 (pages 668–670). Calculate the following ratios for 19*x3:*

     a.   current ratio   **c.**   receivables turnover
     b.   quick ratio   **d.**   inventory turnover

e. debt/equity ratio	h. ratio of sales to owners' equity
f. ratio of owners' equity to total assets	i. ratio of sales to fixed assets
g. ratio of creditors' equity to total assets	j. book value per share of stock

34-2 Refer to the data in exercise 33–3 (page 670). Evaluate the liquidity and solvency of Hammer Company at the end of 19x4. In developing your answer to this exercise consider the results of the comparative and component percentage analyses required by exercise 33–3.

34-3 Following are selected data from the financial statements of Alpha, Inc., and Omega, Inc.:

	Alpha Inc.	Omega Inc.
Total assets	$200,000	$140,000
Common stockholders' equity	80,000	120,000
Total stockholders' equity	130,000	120,000
Net sales	300,000	200,000
Net income	30,000	25,000
Market value per share of common stock	24	18
Dividend rate per share of common stock	1	1
Dividend rate per share of preferred stock	2	

Alpha, Inc., has 5,000 shares of common stock outstanding; Omega Corp. has 10,000 shares outstanding. The par value of common stock for both companies is $10 per share. Alpha, Inc., also has 2,000 shares of $25 par value preferred stock outstanding.

Required   Answer the following questions; compute any ratios necessary to support your answers:

a. Which company had a better return on its assets? How do the companies compare on the two components of return on assets: (1) profit margin and (2) asset turnover?

b. Did the two companies favorably trade on the creditors' equity?

c. Did Alpha, Inc., favorably trade on the preferred stockholders' equity?

d. Which company had the higher earnings per share of common stock?

e. Which company has the lower price/earnings ratio?

f. Which company has a better dividend yield on common stock?

g. Which company has a higher book value per share of common stock?

34-4 Following are the balance sheets for 19x1-19x4 and the condensed income statements for 19x2-19x4 for Scotty Corp. Evaluate the company's liquidity using comparative, component percentage, and ratio analyses.

	19x1	19x2	19x3	19x4
Cash	$ 17,000	$ 40,000	$ 36,000	$ 32,000
Temporary investments	50,000	25,000	30,000	40,000
Accounts receivable	60,000	65,000	75,000	70,000
Inventory	75,000	65,000	70,000	80,000
Prepaid expenses	3,000	5,000	4,000	3,000
Plant assets (net)	250,000	235,000	220,000	245,000
Intangible assets	30,000	27,000	24,000	21,000
Total assets	$485,000	$462,000	$459,000	$491,000
Current liabilities	$ 65,000	$ 70,000	$ 55,000	$ 70,000
Long-term liabilities	150,000	120,000	120,000	135,000
Stockholders' equity	270,000	272,000	284,000	286,000
Total equities	$485,000	$462,000	$459,000	$491,000

	19x2	19x3	19x4
Net sales	$500,000	$530,000	$510,000
Cost of goods sold	290,000	318,000	306,000
Gross margin	$210,000	$212,000	$204,000
Operating expenses	163,000	168,400	162,400
Operating income	$ 47,000	$ 43,600	$ 41,600
Interest expense	12,000	9,600	9,600
Income before taxes	$ 35,000	$ 34,000	$ 32,000
Income taxes	14,000	13,600	12,800
Net income	$ 21,000	$ 20,400	$ 19,200

34-5   Refer to the data in exercise 34–4. Evaluate the company's solvency and equity position using appropriate ratios.

34-6   Refer to the data in exercise 34–4. Evaluate how effectively the company has employed its assets to earn a profit and maximize the return to stockholders.

PROBLEMS

34-1   The financial statements of the Fabco Corp. are as follows:

Fabco Corp.
Balance Sheet
December 31, 19x5 and 19x6

Assets	19x6	19x5
Cash	$ 18,000	$ 25,000
Marketable Securities	28,000	28,000
Receivables (Net)	69,000	55,000
Inventories	84,000	60,000
Land	30,000	30,000
Buildings (Net)	220,000	240,000
Equipment (Net)	110,000	80,000
Patents	36,000	42,000
Total Assets	$595,000	$560,000

Equities	19x6	19x5
Accounts Payable	$112,000	$ 91,000
Accrued Expenses	9,000	6,000
Bonds Payable, due December 31, 19x9	180,000	180,000
Capital Stock (30,000 shares)	150,000	150,000
Retained Earnings	144,000	133,000
Total Equities	$595,000	$560,000

Fabco Corp.
Income Statement
For the Year Ended December 31, 19x6

Sales	$606,000
Less: Sales Returns	6,000
Net Sales	$600,000
Cost of Goods Sold	360,000
Gross Margin	$240,000
Operating Expenses	160,000
Operating Income	$ 80,000
Less: Interest Expense	9,000
Income Before taxes	$ 71,000
Less: Income Taxes	29,000
Net Income	$ 42,000

Required   Indicate the amounts that would be used in the formulas to calculate each of the ratios listed below for 19x6 (do not calculate the ratios):

a. current ratio
b. acid-test ratio
c. average collection period for receivables
d. average number of days' supply in inventory
e. ratio of owners' equity to total assets
f. ratio of creditors' equity to total assets
g. debt/equity ratio
h. number of times interest earned
i. ratio of plant assets to long-term debt

    j.   ratio of sales to owners' equity
    k.   ratio of sales to plant assets
    l.   book value per share of common stock

34-2   Refer to the data in problems 33–1 and 33–2 (page 672). Evaluate Marshall Corp.'s liquidity, solvency and equity position, and profitability. Consider the results of the comparative and component percentage analysis required by problems 33–1 and 33–2, as well as the results of appropriate ratios, in your answer.

34-3   Refer to the data in problem 33–3 (page 673). Calculate any ratios that will be helpful in evaluating the poor profit performance of Deputy Corp. Comment on any trends that may help explain the poor profit performance.

34-4   Felix Industries has three divisions operating autonomously. The asset balances and income statements for the current year are:

	East Division	Midwest Division	West Division	Total
Cash	$ 25,000	$ 14,000	$ 16,000	$ 55,000
Receivables	30,000	35,000	25,000	90,000
Materials Inventory	8,000	10,000	7,000	25,000
Work in Process	12,000	11,000	13,000	36,000
Finished Goods	6,000	8,000	9,000	23,000
Land	15,000	15,000	10,000	40,000
Buildings (net)	100,000	120,000	90,000	310,000
Equipment (net)	60,000	65,000	55,000	180,000
Total Assets	$256,000	$278,000	$225,000	$759,000
Sales	$540,000	$490,000	$510,000	$1,540,000
Cost of Goods Sold:				
Materials	$108,000	$101,000	$ 99,000	$ 308,000
Labor	155,000	145,000	150,000	450,000
Overhead	164,000	152,000	156,000	472,000
Total Cost of Goods Sold	$427,000	$398,000	$405,000	$1,230,000
Gross Margin	$113,000	$ 92,000	$105,000	$ 310,000
Selling and Administration Expenses	74,000	64,000	68,000	206,000
Income Before Taxes	$ 39,000	$ 28,000	$ 37,000	$ 104,000
Income Taxes	15,600	11,200	14,800	41,600
Net Income	$ 23,400	$ 16,800	$ 22,200	$ 62,400

Required   Evaluate the profitability of each division and the effectiveness with which each division employs its assets.

34-5   *Bayshore Paper Industries, Inc., Case*

Bayshore Paper Industries, Inc., is a consolidated company producing sanitary paper products, printing paper, industrial paper, and other related paper products. The consolidated financial statements for years 19*x2* and 19*x3* are as follows:

Bayshore Paper Industries, Inc.
Consolidated Income Statement
For the Years Ended December 31, 19*x2* and 19*x3*
(in millions of dollars)

			Component Percentage Statements		
	19*x3*	19*x2*	19*x1*	19*x2*	19*x3*
Net Sales	$577.4	$544.7	100.0	100.0	
Cost of Goods Sold	421.0	396.8	71.2	72.8	
Gross Margin	$156.4	$147.9	28.8	27.2	
Operating Expense	96.3	91.2	16.2	16.7	
Operating Income	$ 60.1	$ 56.7	12.6	10.4	
Other Income	4.1	6.2	.8	1.1	
Total	$ 64.2	$ 62.9	13.4	11.5	
Other Expense:					
Interest	$ 3.4	$ 3.4	.6	.6	
Pension and Other	.8	1.2	.2	.2	
Total	$ 4.2	$ 4.6	.8	.8	
Income before Taxes	$ 60.0	$ 58.3	12.6	10.7	
Income Taxes	25.0	32.5	6.3	6.0	
Net Income for Year	$ 35.0	$ 25.8	6.3	4.7	

Bayshore Paper Industries, Inc.
Consolidated Statement of Retained Earnings
For the Years Ended December 31, 19*x2* and 19*x3*
(in millions of dollars)

	19*x3*	19*x2*
Balance, Beginning of Year	$190.5	$175.6
Add: Net Income for Year	35.0	35.8
Total	$225.5	$211.4
Deduct: Cash Dividends on Common Stock	$ 20.4	$ 20.4
Adjustment for Removal from Consolidation of Former Wholly-Owned Subsidiaries	—	.5
Total	$ 20.4	$ 20.9
Balance, End of Year	$205.1	$190.5

Bayshore Paper Industries, Inc.
Consolidated Balance Sheet
At December 31, 19x2 and 19x3

	19x3	19x2	% Change 19x1	% Change 19x2	% Change 19x3	$ Change 19x3
				Comparative Statements		
Assets						
Current Assets						
Cash	$ 13.3	$ 14.4	12.6	(26.9)		
Marketable Securities	22.6	38.2	118.4	(33.0)		
Receivables	54.9	47.3	3.9	4.6		
Inventories	88.2	85.6	(.5)	13.1		
Prepaid Expenses	3.4	2.6	20.0	44.4		
Total Current Assets	$182.4	$188.1	21.1	(5.7)		
Investments	$ 34.8	$ 31.7	(22.8)	15.3		
Property and Equipment	$563.1	$528.4	21.7	8.0		
Less: Accumulated Depreciation	241.5	223.8	25.6	8.3		
Net Property and Equipment	$321.6	$304.6	19.0	7.7		
Intangible Assets	$ .9	$ 1.2	(45.8)	7.7		
Deferred Charges	$ 3.6	$ 3.7	8.8	—		
Total Assets	$543.3	$529.3	16.0	2.8		
Liabilities and Net Worth						
Current Liabilities						
Notes and Accounts Payable	$ 29.8	$ 25.5	(3.7)	21.4		
Accrued Taxes and Expenses	21.8	29.3	.7	6.2		
Current Maturities of Long-Term Debt	2.6	2.5	77.8	(21.9)		
Total Current Liabilities	$ 54.2	$ 57.3	1.6	10.6		
Long-Term Debt	73.1	75.7	21.3	7.0		
Deferred Income Taxes	21.2	16.6	204.8	29.7		
Total Liabilities	$148.5	$149.6	19.4	2.5		
Net Worth						
Common Stock	$ 51.3	$ 51.3	3.9	.2		
Additional Paid-In Capital	138.5	138.4	22.5	.1		
Minority Interests	4.8	4.4	12.1	18.9		
Retained Earnings	205.1	190.5	12.6	8.5		
Total	$399.7	$384.6	14.8	3.0		
Less: Treasury Stock	4.9	4.9	—	—		
Total Net Worth	$394.8	$379.7	14.8	3.0		
Total Liabilities and Net Worth	$543.3	$529.3	16.0	2.8		

The following ratios were determined for 19x1 and 19x2 by the accounting department of Bayshore Paper Industries:

		19x1	19x2	19x3
(1)	Current ratio	3.8–1	3.3–1	
(2)	Acid-test ratio	2.4–1	1.7–1	
(3)	Accounts receivable turnover	12.1 times	12.0 times	
(4)	Average collection period	29.7 days	30.4 days	
(5)	Inventory turnover	5.1 times	4.9 times	
(6)	Debt/equity ratio	.4	.4	
(7)	Return on owners' equity	9.2%	6.8%	
(8)	Net sales to owners' equity	1.5–1	1.5–1	
(9)	Net sales to plant assets	1.9–1	1.8–1	
(10)	Net sales to inventory	7.1 times	6.5 times	
(11)	Plant assets to long-term debt	3.5–1	4.0–1	
(12)	Plant assets to owners' equity	.8–1	.8–1	
(13)	Number of times interest earned	20.1 times	18.1 times	
(14)	Earnings per share of common stock	$3.31	$3.52	
(15)	Return on total assets	6.6%	4.9%	

The following ratios for the paper products industry are available for 19x1, 19x2, and 19x3. The upper quartile and the median for the ratios (based on a sampling of companies from each industry) are presented.

	Paper Products Industry	19x1	19x2	19x3
(1)	Current ratio	4.5–1	4.5–1	4.1–1
		2.9–1	3.0–1	2.7–1
(2)	Net income to net sales	4.2%	5.3%	5.9%
		2.7%	3.6%	4.2%
(3)	Return on owners' equity	11.7%	14.7%	15.1%
		8.5%	8.8%	9.7%
(4)	Net sales to owners' equity	4.5–1	3.7–1	4.6–1
		3.0–1	2.7–1	2.7–1
(5)	Average collection period	27 days	26 days	26 days
		36 days	39 days	38 days
(6)	Net sales to inventory	12.1 times	9.5 times	9.8 times
		7.6 times	6.9 times	7.4 times
(7)	Plant assets to owners' equity	26.6%	23.9%	28.1%
		38.9%	44.7%	43.3%
(8)	Debt/equity ratio	.31	.30	.31
		.67	.48	.59

Required   **a.**   Complete a component percentage analysis of the income statement for 19x3.

b.   Complete a comparative analysis of the balance sheet for 19x3.

c.   Compute the 15 ratios for 19x3.

d.   Comment on the trends for income statement and balance sheet items and the ratios for 19x3 in comparison to past years for Bayshore.

e.   Comment on the position of Bayshore in relation to the industry over the 3-year period.

34-6   *Annual Report Problem*

a.   From the annual report you have received from your instructor, or the Coachmen Industries Annual Report data in the appendix to Unit 6, compute the following ratios:

(1)   current ratio
(2)   accounts receivable turnover
(3)   average collection period
(4)   inventory turnover
(5)   average number of days' supply in inventory
(6)   ratio of plant assets to long-term debt
(7)   ratio of creditors' equity to total assets
(8)   book value per share of common stock
(9)   debt/equity ratio
(10) return on common owners' equity
(11) ratio of net income to sales
(12) return on total assets
(13) ratio of sales to plant assets
(14) percent of cash to total current assets
(15) dollar change and percent change in cash

b.   Answer the following questions using the annual report you have received or the Coachmen Industries data:

(1)   What inventory method does the company use?
(2)   Does the company have any long-term leases under which it is making annual rental payments? Summarize the details available about the leases.
(3)   Has the company granted stock options to the officers or employees? Summarize the details of the option.
(4)   What are the features of any preferred stock the company has outstanding (cumulative, participating, convertible, callable, liquidation value, etc.)?
(5)   Does the company hold any treasury stock? How many shares? What dollar amount? Are retained earnings restricted for the amount of the treasury stock?
(6)   Does the company have a bond sinking fund? What are the terms of the sinking fund? Are retained earnings restricted for the sinking fund?

(7) What were the primary sources and uses of funds in the company during the year? Did working capital increase or decrease?

(8) What forms of the balance sheet (report, account, etc.) and income statement (single-step, multiple-step, etc.) were used by the company?

(9) Indicate what changes in classification of accounts or terminology you would suggest to make the balance sheet conform with accounting principles and with present-day terminology. State your reason for the suggested changes.

(10) Indicate what changes in classification of accounts or terminology you would suggest to make the income statement conform with accounting principles and with present-day terminology. State your reason for the suggested changes.

Chapter 13

Additional Financial Reporting Issues

Several more complex financial reporting concepts and principles are examined in this final chapter. The foundation built in previous chapters should help you understand the material presented in these two units. Topics to be covered include accounting for lease obligations, pension costs, and deferred income taxes, and restatement of financial statements for price changes.

Unit 35
Accounting for Deferred Income Taxes, Lease Obligations, and Pension Costs

Neither a borrower nor a lender be;
For loan oft loses both itself and friend,
And borrowing dulls the edge of husbandry.

William Shakespeare, Hamlet

Differences between income tax law and financial accounting theory and practice result in the deferral of income taxes. Lease agreements give rise to problems in accounting for asset and service costs and related liabilities. Pension plans result in costs that must be assigned to expense in the appropriate accounting period. Although many complex measurement and reporting problems can be involved, a basic understanding of these issues is important if managers, creditors, investors, and other users are to interpret the financial statements of modern-day business enterprises properly.

Performance Objectives

Upon completing this unit you should be able to:

1. define and use the accounting terms introduced in this unit.
2. describe or explain:
   a. the types of differences between financial accounting and income tax accounting that give rise to deferred income taxes
   b. the difference between operating and capital leases
   c. how deferred income taxes, lease obligations, and pension costs are measured or reported
3. determine:
   a. the amount to be reported as income tax expense, income taxes payable, and/or deferred income taxes at the end of any accounting period
   b. the cost to be recorded for an asset acquired under a lease contract

    c.   the annual interest expense, depreciation expense, and/or lease rent expense incurred under a lease contract

    d.   the amount to be reported as pension expense for an accounting period

4. prepare the correct journal entries for selected transactions for deferred income taxes, lease obligations, and pension costs.

Deferred Income Taxes

According to the matching principle, expenses should be associated with the related revenue earned as a result of the incurrence of the expenses. Thus, income taxes should be accrued and charged to expense in the period in which income is recognized for financial accounting purposes. However, the liability for income taxes is determined according to income tax law, which is not solely concerned with compliance with the matching principle and other accounting principles. Income tax law tends to emphasize taxation when cash is available for payment of taxes, the fair sharing of tax burdens based on the ability to pay, favoritism to special interest groups, and stimulation of the economy by adjusting the timing or amount of taxes due.

Because financial accounting principles and income tax law have different objectives, there are three major sources of differences between income for financial accounting and income tax purposes:

1. **temporary or timing differences**—revenue or expense is recognized in one period for financial accounting and another period for income taxation.
2. **permanent differences**—some revenues and gains are not taxable, but must be included in financial accounting income; some expenses and losses are not tax deductible, but are deducted in determining financial accounting income; some tax deductions are not deductible in determining financial accounting income.
3. **differences resulting from certain loss carrybacks and carryforwards**—taxes for one or more past or future periods are reduced because certain losses have been incurred and their tax benefit is received in another period. (This type of difference will not be discussed further in this text.)

The discussion of accounting for income taxes that follows is based on APB Opinion No. 11.

Temporary or Timing Differences   Different accounting methods can be used for financial accounting and for income tax purposes. For example, an accelerated depreciation method, such as double-declining-balance or sum-of-years'-digits, may be used in determining taxable income whereas the straight-line method may be used in determining financial accounting income. When different methods are used for financial reporting and income taxes, the same amount of depreciation expense will be deducted over the life of the asset; but the amount of depreciation expense each year will differ. The difference between taxable income and financial accounting income is, therefore, temporary, and results from the timing of the amount of the deduction. Similar temporary or timing differences result when different methods are used in the recognition of revenues.

Income tax expense must be accrued on the basis of financial accounting income, and the income tax liability must be accrued on the basis of taxable income; thus, an income tax difference arises from temporary timing differences in the recognition of revenue or expense. The income tax difference represents a deferral of income taxes to a future period when the income difference arising in the current period reverses. **Deferred income taxes** are reported as an asset when a debit difference arises and as a liability when a credit difference arises.

The classification as current or noncurrent depends on the nature of the assets or liabilities to which the deferred taxes are related. If they are related to current assets or current liabilities, the net current amount of deferred taxes is reported as a current asset or current liability. Similarly, if they are related to noncurrent assets or liabilities, the net noncurrent amount of deferred taxes is reported as a deferred charge (or other asset) or a long-term liability (or deferred credit).

Four general situations result in temporary or timing differences:

1. debit balances for deferred income taxes arise when:
   a. revenue is recognized earlier for tax purposes than for financial accounting, for example, rent received in advance that must be recognized entirely in the year received for tax purposes, but allocated over two or more years as it is earned for financial accounting purposes.
   b. expenses are recognized earlier for financial accounting than for income tax purposes, for example, product guarantee costs estimated and expensed in the year in which the products are sold for financial accounting, but expensed as customer claims are made for income tax purposes.
2. credit balances for deferred income taxes arise when:
   a. revenue is recognized earlier for financial accounting than for income tax purposes, for example, recognition of revenue from installment sales in the year of sale for financial accounting versus recognition of such revenue in the years in which the installment receivables are collected for tax purposes.
   b. expenses are recognized earlier for income tax purposes than financial accounting, for example, accelerated depreciation used for income tax purposes versus straight-line depreciation for financial accounting.

Assume that a company receives $10,000 in revenue in advance in 19*x1,* that the revenue is to be earned equally in 19*x1* and 19*x2,* and that income before taxes, excluding the $10,000 advance payment, is $60,000 for 19*x1* and $70,000 for 19*x2.* Income tax expense and the income tax liability for 19*x1* and 19*x2* are computed as follows assuming a tax rate of 40%:

	For Financial Accounting		For Income Taxation	
	19x1	19x2	19x1	19x2
Income before taxes, excluding the $10,000 advance payment	$60,000	$70,000	$60,000	$70,000
Amount of $10,000 advance payment included in income	5,000	5,000	10,000	0
Income before taxes	$65,000	$75,000	$70,000	$70,000
Income tax expense*	$26,000	$30,000		
Income tax liability**	28,000	28,000	$28,000	$28,000
Difference—deferred income tax—debit (credit)	$ 2,000	$(2,000)		

*$65,000 × 40% = $26,000; $75,000 × 40% = $30,000
**$70,000 × 40% = $28,000

The entries to record income taxes each year would be:

Dec. 31, 19x1	Income Tax Expense	26,000	
	Deferred Income Taxes	2,000	
	Income Taxes Payable		28,000
	To accrue income taxes for 19x1.		

Dec. 31, 19x2	Income Tax Expense	30,000	
	Income Taxes Payable		28,000
	Deferred Income Taxes		2,000
	To accrue income taxes for 19x2.		

At the end of 19x1 the $2,000 balance in deferred income taxes would be reported as a current asset because the revenue received in advance in 19x1 is classified as a current liability. Situations that result in a credit balance for deferred income taxes in the year in which the timing difference first arises are handled in the same manner as just illustrated (see the review problem). The balance sheets of most large companies often reflect a balance for deferred income taxes. The balance reported most likely will be included under long-term liabilities (or a deferred credits section following the long-term liabilities) because these companies usually try to defer payment of income taxes to future years whenever possible.

In some situations it may be doubtful that the deferred taxes will ever be paid because of new timing differences that arise and more than offset those timing differences that reverse. However, the APB decided to defer income taxes on all timing differences rather than on just those that reverse within a definite time span. The classification of deferred income taxes as a deferred credit is based on the fact that no legal liability for deferred taxes exists. A legal liability for payment of taxes occurs only when taxable income is determined. Also, the credit balance for deferred income taxes is viewed as an offset against future taxes (that is, as a credit reduction in future expenses) rather than as a liability by many accountants. However, the concept of a liability is considered by others to be broad enough to encompass the treatment of deferred income taxes as a liability.

On the income statement or in the footnotes the difference between income tax expense and income taxes actually payable for the period should be reconciled. This can be done using the following format:

Income taxes payable	$XXXX
Add: Increases in credit balances or decreases in debit balances for deferred taxes	XXXX
Less: Decreases in credit balances or increases in debit balances for deferred taxes	XXXX
Income tax expense	$XXXX

This approach is used in the Michigan Sugar Company income statement. Coachmen Industries, however, parenthetically indicates the amount of increase or decrease in income tax expense due to deferral of income taxes on its income statement. See the appendix to Unit 6 for the income statements of both companies.

Permanent Differences   Permanent differences, such as nontaxable interest and fines, penalties, and amortization of goodwill, which are not deductible for tax purposes, do not present any special accounting problems. Because the differences are permanent, income tax expense and the income tax liability are based on taxable income. Assume that a company reports income before taxes of $65,000 on its income statement, including $5,000 of nontaxable revenue. Taxable income would be $60,000 ($65,000 − 5,000); both income tax expense and the income tax liability will be based on the taxable income of $60,000. If the income tax rate is 40%, the entry to record income tax expense and liability is:

Income Tax Expense	24,000	
Income Taxes Payable		24,000

To accrue income taxes for the year ($60,000 × 40% = $24,000).

Lease Obligations

A **lease** is an agreement to convey the right to use property, plant, or equipment for a stated period of time. The party who acquires the right is known as the **lessee;** the party who conveys the right is known as the **lessor.** Some leases are, in effect, purchase agreements, while others are only rental contracts. The terms of the lease have been used to distinguish between those that should be capitalized and those that should not. FASB Statement No. 13 describes four criteria for identifying capital leases (that is, leases that should result in recording an asset). If any *one* of the following criteria is met, the lease is classified as a capital lease:

1. Ownership of the property is to be transferred to the lessee by the end of the lease term according to the lease agreement.
2. The lease agreement contains a **bargain purchase option,** that is, an option to purchase the leased property for a price significantly less than the expected fair value of the property at the time the option becomes exercisable; the presence of such an option gives reasonable assurance that the option will be exercised.
3. The lease term is at least 75 percent of the property's estimated economic life.
4. The present value of the minimum lease payments at the beginning of the lease term is 90 percent or more of the fair value of the leased property to the lessor at the time the lease is entered into.

These four criteria indicate that effective ownership of the leased property is transferred to the lessee. Also, when the lease agreement meets any of the four criteria, the lessor is assured the recovery of his investment plus a fair return on his investment. For all practical purposes, ownership of the property has been transferred to the lessee by the lessor. If a lease does not meet one of these criteria, it will be classified as an **operating lease.**

Accounting for Capital Leases   Leases require a series of payments over their term. The lease, then, can be measured as the present value of the required payments using an appropriate interest rate.[1] If the payments are equal, the present value of an annuity table (see Table 23.4) can be used. For example, assume that a company enters into a capital lease agreement on December 31, 19*x1,* for machinery with a useful life of five years. If the lease provides for payments of $3,000 annually for five years starting immediately, and the appropriate interest rate is 10%, the cost of the leased

---

[1]FASB Statement No. 13 specifies that cost is the lower of (a) the present value of the minimum lease payments or (b) the fair value of the leased property when the lease is entered into. Also, the interest rate to be used is the lower of (a) the normal rate the borrower would pay for funds over a similar term to buy the asset or (b) the rate implicit in the lease, if it is practicable to learn this rate.

machinery can be determined as follows (the formula was described in Unit 23, page 446):[2]

$$PVA \text{ (due)} = I \times (F_{i,n-1} + 1.0000)$$
$$= \$3,000 \times (F_{.10,4} + 1.0000)$$
$$= \$3,000 \times (3.1699 + 1.0000)$$
$$= \$3,000 \times 4.1699$$
$$= \$12,510*$$

where $I = \$3,000$
$i = 10\%$
$n = 5$
*Rounded to the nearest full dollar.

The entry at the date the lease is entered into requires recognition of an asset for $12,510 and a liability for the difference between the cost of the asset and the first payment:

Dec. 31, 19x1	Leased machinery	12,510	
	Obligations under capital leases		9,510
	Cash		3,000
	To record capital lease and first payment.		

When the next payment is made at December 31, 19x2, it must be allocated between interest expense and a reduction in the lease obligation. Interest is calculated by applying the appropriate rate to the balance of the lease obligation at the beginning of the period. In the example, interest expense for 19x2 is $951 ($9,510 × 10%) and the lease obligation is reduced $2,049 ($3,000 − 951). The entry is:

Dec. 31, 19x2	Obligations under capital leases	2,049	
	Interest expense	951	
	Cash		3,000
	To record annual capital lease payment.		

Similar entries are made at December 31 for the next three years. The amount of interest expense decreases each year because the balance of the lease obligation decreases. For example, the balance of the lease obligation at the beginning of 19x3 is $7,461 ($9,510 − 2,049) and interest expense for 19x3 is $746 ($7,461 × 10%).

At the end of each year, starting in 19x2, the leased machinery must be depreciated. If the lessee retains the property at the end of the lease term, depreciation is recorded over the longer of the lease term or the useful life of the property. If the

---

[2]The annuity due concept is involved because the first payment is made at the time the lease starts.

Exhibit 35.1

Partial Balance Sheet **December 31, 19x2**		
Plant Assets:		
Leased Machinery under Capital Leases	$12,510	
Accumulated Amortization—Leased Machinery under Capital Leases	2,502	$10,008
Current Liabilities:		
Obligations under Capital Leases		$ 2,254
Long-Term Liabilities:		
Obligations under Capital Leases		$ 5,207

lessee does not retain the property at the termination of the lease, the property is depreciated over the lease term. In the example, the lease term and the useful life are the same. Thus, depreciation using the straight-line method is recorded as follows each year for 19x2 − 19x6:

Dec. 31	Depreciation expense—leased machinery	2,502	
	Accumulated depreciation—leased machinery		2,502
	To record annual depreciation on leased machinery ($12,510/5 = $2,502).		

The leased machinery is reported with or near other plant assets. The lease obligation is classified according to its current and noncurrent elements. In the example, the current portion of the lease obligation at December 31, 19x2, is $2,254, that is, the amount due within one year ($3,000) less the interest for 19x3 ($746 as calculated earlier in this section). The noncurrent portion of the liability at the end of 19x2 is $5,207, that is, the balance of the lease obligation ($7,461) less the amount reported as a current liability ($2,254). Exhibit 35.1 illustrates the disclosure of the leased property and the lease obligation at December 31, 19x2, using the data from the example. Other relevant information regarding the lease would be disclosed in the footnotes as required by FASB Statement No. 13.

Accounting for Operating Leases   Any lease that does not meet at least one of the four criteria for capital leases is accounted for as an operating lease. The periodic payments for an operating lease are charged to expense as they are made. Certain relevant information specified in FASB Statement No. 13 is disclosed in the footnotes to the financial statements.

Exhibit 35.2

Leases

Capital Leases—The Company has a number of leased facilities which are capital leases under the provisions of Statement of Financial Accounting Standards No. 13, Accounting for Leases, issued in November 1976. Certain of these facilities, leased principally from municipalities under industrial revenue financing arrangements providing for purchase options, were capitalized as plant and equipment in prior years. Other facilities have been capitalized in fiscal 1977 and the prior years' financial statements and other financial information have been retroactively restated to give effect thereto.

Assets recorded under capital leases as of September 30 were as follows:

	1977	1976
Land	$ 1.2	$ 1.2
Buildings	53.8	51.9
Machinery and equipment	23.6	22.4
	$78.6	$75.5
Accumulated depreciation	22.4	18.4
	$56.2	$57.1

Future minimum lease payments under capital leases as of September 30, 1977 aggregate $125.0, with $54.1 representing interest and $70.9 representing lease obligations included in long-term debt. Scheduled payments under these capital leases are $8.0, $8.2, $7.9, $7.5 and $7.3 for the years ending September 30, 1978 through 1982, respectively.

Operating Leases—Minimum rental commitments under noncancelable operating leases in effect as of September 30, 1977 were $78.7, with scheduled payments as follows: 1978–$9.1; 1979–$8.6; 1980–$7.3; 1981–$6.2; 1982–$5.3; 1983 and thereafter—$42.2.

Total rental expense for all operating leases was $20.2 in fiscal 1977 and $18.2 in 1976, including contingent rentals of $1.7 and $1.2, respectively.

In addition, certain tuna boats leased by the Company are subleased to others. Rentals payable under these leases and rentals receivable under the corresponding subleases are approximately $6.8 annually through 1983, $6.6 annually from 1984 through 1986, $5.7 in 1987, $4.3 in 1988 and $.7 in 1989. As of September 30, 1977, the Company has also guaranteed approximately $9.4 of bank loans and other obligations incurred by certain tuna boat operators and suppliers.

Source: Footnotes to financial statements in 1977 Annual Report of Ralston Purina Company.

Assume that a company enters into an operating lease on January 1, 19*x1,* for the use of a building for ten years. If the monthly lease payment is $2,500, payable at the beginning of each month, the entry to record each payment would be:

Building rent expense	2,500	
Cash		2,500
To record monthly lease payment.		

Exhibit 35.2 illustrates the type of information that must be disclosed in an entity's footnotes for both capital and operating leases.

Advantages of Leasing   Accounting Research Study No. 4 published by the AICPA in 1962 indicated the following reasons why lessees might enter into leasing arrangements:

1. to acquire the use of an asset that would not otherwise be available to the lessee
2. to meet a temporary need for an asset
3. to shift the risks of ownership from the lessee to the lessor
4. . to circumvent restrictions on the acquisition of plant assets
5. to obtain buying or servicing advantages not obtainable through the acquisition of an asset
6. to obtain the use of an asset that cannot be purchased entirely by other credit arrangements
7. to provide a larger amount of credit through a combination of leasing and borrowing than might be available only through borrowing
8. to provide a better cash flow situation than might exist if borrowing occurred; this depends on the interest cost, the schedule of payments, and income tax deductions allowable

Many accountants and businesspeople have believed that a company that leased assets had more borrowing power than a company that incurred long-term debt to purchase similar assets. This belief was supported by accounting practices that allowed many leased assets and lease obligations to be excluded from the balance sheet accounts. Although footnote disclosures were required for leasing arrangements, the company that leased assets appeared to be in better financial position than the company that incurred debt to purchase assets. The following are the balance sheets of two companies. Company X has issued $500,000 in 20-year bonds to purchase plant assets; Company Y has leased $500,000 of plant assets for 20 years.

	Company X	Company Y
Current assets	$ 250,000	$250,000
Plant assets	750,000	250,000
Total assets	$1,000,000	$500,000
Current liabilities	$ 100,000	$100,000
Long-term liabilities	500,000	—
Total liabilities	$ 600,000	$100,000
Stockholders' equity	400,000	400,000
Total liabilities and stockholders' equity	$1,000,000	$500,000

On the surface Company Y appears to have more potential for long-term borrowing than Company X does. Owners' equity has provided 80 percent of Company Y's assets ($400,000/$500,000 = 80%) compared to 40 percent for Company X ($400,000/$1,000,000 = 40%). FASB Statement No. 13 has attempted to rectify this situation, however, by tightening up the criteria for recording assets and liabilities for leasing arrangements and improving the type and amount of additional financial disclosures. Whether leasing or purchasing assets is more advantageous is a financing decision that will be examined more fully in other business courses.

Pension Costs

Pension plans have become an important and popular fringe benefit, especially when employees are represented by unions. Pension plans provide payments to employees during their retirement years. Sometimes the company makes the full payment to the pension plan; other times both employer and employees make contributions to it. Pension plans usually are funded with a trustee, that is, a third party, such as a bank, an insurance company, or a union, who receives the contributions from the employer and employees, invests the money, handles the investments, and makes payments to retired employees.

The annual charge for pension expense is based on a number of factors, such as mortality rate, employee turnover, compensation level, investment earnings, and so on. Because there are many factors, most of which depend on estimates and future uncertainties, the annual charge for pension expense must be made by an insurance specialist in mathematics and statistics known as an *actuary*. Also, when a pension plan is adopted, the past services of employees are usually recognized in determining their future retirement benefits. The value of the past services at the date that the pension plan is adopted must be estimated by the actuary. The actuary, then, provides two types of estimates: one for the past service cost and the other for the normal (or current) service cost. The **past service cost** is the pension cost related to the years prior to the adoption of a pension plan. The **normal cost** is the pension cost related to the years subsequent to the adoption of the pension plan. The following diagram depicts the distinction between the past service cost and the normal cost.

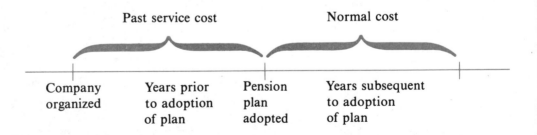

The normal cost must be charged to expense and paid into a pension fund annually. The past service cost, however, represents the present value of the benefits earned and to be paid to employees for past services at the time the pension plan is adopted. The past service cost is usually a large amount that the company charges to expense and pays into the pension fund over several future accounting periods. APB

Opinion No. 8 established an amortization period of 10 to 40 years for the past service cost. A federal pension law in 1974 established a maximum period of 30 years in most cases for payment of past service costs into the pension fund.

In a trusteed pension plan the normal cost plus a charge for past service cost will be charged to expense. Also, the normal cost plus a contribution for past service cost must be paid to the trustee. Assume that a company adopted a pension plan at the beginning of 19x1. The past service cost of $249,244 is to be charged to expense and paid to a trustee at the end of each year over a 20-year term. Assuming an interest rate of 5%, the amount of the annual charge and payment can be determined as follows (the formula was described in Unit 23, page 450):

$$I = \frac{PVA}{F_{i,n}}$$

where $PVA = \$249,244$
$i = 5\%$
$n = 20$

$$= \frac{\$249,244}{F_{.05,20}}$$

$$= \frac{\$249,244}{12.4622}$$

$$= \$20,000$$

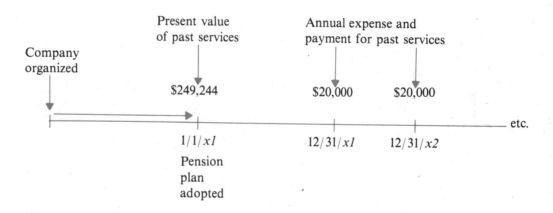

The entry to record pension expense and the payment to the trustee for 19x1 will include the provision for past service cost ($20,000) and the normal cost for 19x1 ($23,500):

Dec. 31,	Pension Expense	43,500	
19x1	Cash		43,500
	To record annual pension expense and		
	payment to trustee ($20,000		
	+ 23,500 = $43,500).		

Exhibit 35.3

Retirement Plan

The Company has retirement plans covering substantially all employees. The total pension expense was $5,832,000 in 1977 and $5,668,000 in 1976. The Company uses principally the entry age normal method of accounting for pension costs under which unfunded prior service costs, estimated at $51,850,000, will be funded over a 30 year period. The actuarily computed value of the vested benefits exceeds the assets of the plans by approximately $16,400,000.

Source: Footnotes to financial statements in 1977 Annual Report of Hershey Foods Corporation.

When the past service cost is expensed and funded with a trustee over the same period of time, the entity's financial statements usually reflect no assets or liabilities related to the pension plan. However, the footnotes to the financial statements should disclose information regarding the plan's existence, the accounting and funding policies, the employees covered, the pension expense for the current period, and other significant matters (see Exhibit 35.3).

REVIEW PROBLEM

Finck Corporation was involved in the following long-term liability transactions:

Situation 1   A pension plan was adopted at the beginning of 19x2. The past service cost was $77,217. The normal cost for 19x2 was $13,200. The pension plan is a trusteed plan. The fund is expected to earn 5% annually. Contributions to the trustee are made at year-end. The past service cost will be expensed and funded over 10 years.

Situation 2   A lease was entered into on December 31, 19x1, for the use of machinery. One of the criteria for a capital lease is met. The term of the lease is 10 years. The company would pay 10% interest on borrowed funds to purchase machinery. Annual lease payments of $10,000 are payable at the beginning of each year starting December 31, 19x1.

Situation 3   The company uses double-declining-balance depreciation on its tax return and straight-line on its books. Income before taxes for financial accounting was $120,000 and $90,000, respectively, for 19x1 and 19x2. Taxable income for 19x1 and 19x2 was $100,000 and $75,000, respectively. The difference is due solely to the use of different depreciation methods. Assume an income tax rate of 40%.

Required   For each liability situation described, prepare all necessary entries for 19x1 and/or 19x2.

Solution to review problem

Situation 1

Dec. 31, 19x2	Pension Expense	23,200	
	·Cash		23,200
	To record pension expense and contributions to the trustee for past service and normal costs.		

Computations

Normal cost	$13,200
Past service cost:	
$\left(PVA = \dfrac{\$77,217}{F_{.05,10}} = \dfrac{\$77,217}{7.7217} = \$10,000 \right)$	10,000
Total pension expense and contributions	$23,200

Situation 2

Dec. 31, 19x1	Leased Machinery under Capital Leases	67,590	
	Obligations under Capital Leases		57,590
	Cash		10,000
	To record capital lease and first payment.		

Computations

Cost of leased machinery:	
[PVA (due) = $10,000 × ($F_{.10,9}$ + 1.000)	
= $10,000 × (5.7590 + 1.0000) = $67,590]	$67,590
Payment made on December 31, 19x1	10,000
Lease liability at December 31, 19x1	$57,590

Dec. 31, 19x2	Obligations under Capital Leases	4,241	
	Interest Expense	5,759	
	Cash		10,000
	To record annual lease payment.		

Lease payment made at 12/31/*x1*　　($10,000) → $5,759 Interest ($57,590 × 10%)
　　　　　　　　　　　　　　　　　　　　　→ $4,241 Reduction in lease obligation
　　　　　　　　　　　　　　　　　　　　　　　($10,000 − 5,759)

Dec. 31, 19x2	Amortization Expense—Leased Machinery under Capital Leases	6,759	
	Accumulated Amortization of Leased Machinery under Capital Leases		6,759
	To amortize asset for lease machinery over the lease term ($67,590/10 = $6,759).		

Situation 3

Dec. 31, 19x1	Income Tax Expense	48,000	
	Income Taxes Payable		40,000
	Deferred Income Taxes		8,000
	To accrue income taxes for 19x1.		
Dec. 31, 19x2	Income Tax Expense	36,000	
	Income Taxes Payable		30,000
	Deferred Income Taxes		6,000
	To accrue income taxes for 19x2.		

Computations

| | Financial Accounting | | Tax Return | |
	19x1	19x2	19x1	19x2
Income tax expense*	$48,000	$36,000		
Income tax liability**	40,000	30,000	$40,000	$30,000
Difference—Deferred tax (liability)†	$ 8,000	$ 6,000		

*$120,000 × 40% = $48,000; $90,000 × 40% = $36,000
**$100,000 × 40% = $40,000; $75,000 × 40% = $30,000
†The deferred income tax liability has a balance of $14,000 at the end of 19x2 ($8,000 + 6,000 = $14,000) and would be classified as a long-term liability because the reversal of the timing differences is indefinite.

SUMMARY

A number of complex topics were discussed and illustrated in this unit. These topics are treated in depth in intermediate accounting courses. However, the beginning accounting student should be aware of the proper accounting procedures and financial reporting practices for leases (by lessees), pensions, and deferred income taxes. The financial statements of most large corporations cannot be fully understood without some idea of the issues explained in this unit.

REVIEW QUESTIONS

35-1 **a.** Why do differences arise between financial accounting and income tax accounting?
  b. Indicate three sources of differences between financial accounting and income tax accounting.

35-2 How are permanent differences between financial accounting and income tax accounting treated on the books and financial statements?

35-3 Indicate four general situations that result in temporary or timing differences between financial accounting and income tax accounting.

35-4 When there are temporary or timing differences, how should income tax expense and the income tax liability be determined?

35-5 How are deferred income taxes reported on the balance sheet?

35-6 Distinguish between capital and operating leases.

35-7 **a.** How should the lessee account for a capital lease?
  b. What amounts should be recorded as an asset and as a liability by the lessee for a capital lease?
  c. How should the asset and the liability for a capital lease be disclosed on the balance sheet?
  d. Over what term should the lessee amortize the asset recorded under a capital lease?

35-8 How should the lessee account for and disclose an operating lease?

35-9 **a.** Why might an entity lease rather than purchase an asset?
  b. What financial reporting problem is FASB Statement No. 13 intended to resolve?

35-10 **a.** What is a pension plan?
  b. Distinguish between a trusteed and a non-trusteed pension plan.

    c.   Distinguish between the past service cost and the normal (or current) cost of a pension plan.

35-11   What amount(s) should be included in the annual charge for a pension expense?

EXERCISES

35-1   For 19*x6* Herald Corp. reported income before taxes of $40,000 on its income statement. However, on its income tax return, taxable income was only $35,000. The $5,000 difference is due to the exclusion of tax-exempt interest revenue from taxable income. Assume an income tax rate of 40%. Determine income tax expense and the income tax liability for 19*x6*.

35-2   Miner Corp. reported income before taxes for financial accounting and income tax accounting for 19*x4* and 19*x5* as indicated below. The difference in income before taxes is due to revenue collected in advance in 19*x4* that is taxed in 19*x4*, but realized on the accrual basis of accounting in 19*x5*. Assume an income tax rate of 40%. Prepare the entries for income tax expense and income taxes payable for 19*x4* and 19*x5*.

	Financial Accounting		Income Tax Accounting	
	19*x4*	19*x5*	19*x4*	19*x5*
Revenue	$300,000	$350,000	$320,000	$330,000
Expenses	220,000	280,000	220,000	280,000
Income before taxes	$ 80,000	$ 70,000	$100,000	$ 50,000

35-3   Plains Corp. reported income before taxes for financial accounting and income tax accounting for 19*x4* – 19*x6* as indicated below. The difference in income before taxes is due to the use of sum-of-years'-digits depreciation for tax purposes and straight-line depreciation for financial accounting on an asset with a cost of $90,000 and a useful life of 3 years. Assume an income tax rate of 40%. Prepare the entries for income tax expense and income taxes payable for 19*x4* – 19*x6*.

	Financial Accounting			Income Tax Accounting		
	19*x4*	19*x5*	19*x6*	19*x4*	19*x5*	19*x6*
Revenue	$400,000	$440,000	$480,000	$400,000	$440,000	$480,000
Expenses	320,000	350,000	380,000	335,000	350,000	365,000
Income before taxes	$ 80,000	$ 90,000	$100,000	$ 65,000	$ 90,000	$115,000

35-4   Gulley Corp. entered into a lease agreement on December 31, 19*x1*, for the use of equipment with an economic life of 6 years. The lease agreement requires the company to make six equal annual payments of $10,000 each at the beginning of each year starting immediately. The appropriate interest rate is 10%. The fair value of the leased equipment at December 31, 19x1, is $50,000.

Required If the lease is considered to be a capital lease, prepare the entries required on December 31, 19x1 and 19x2. Also, prepare a partial balance sheet at December 31, 19x2.

35-5 Refer to the facts in exercise 35–4. Assume that the lease is considered to be an operating lease. Prepare the entries required on December 31, 19x1 and 19x2. Also, indicate how the lease would be disclosed on the financial statements at the end of 19x2.

35-6 Ridge Corp. decided to adopt a trusteed pension plan early in 19x8. The past service cost at the time the pension was adopted was $110,401. The normal cost for 19x8 was $22,000. Prepare the entry to record the pension expense and the payment to the trustee for 19x8, if past service cost is expensed and funded over 10 years and the interest rate is 6%.

PROBLEMS

35-1 Flash Corp. reported income before taxes for financial accounting and income tax accounting as follows:

| | Financial Accounting | | | |
	19x6	19x7	19x8	19x9
Revenues	$250,000	$275,000	$300,000	$350,000
Expenses	180,000	195,000	250,000	290,000
Income before taxes	$ 70,000	$ 80,000	$ 50,000	$ 60,000

| | Income Tax Accounting | | | |
	19x6	19x7	19x8	19x9
Revenues	$250,000	$275,000	$300,000	$350,000
Expenses	170,000	225,000	240,000	270,000
Income before taxes	$ 80,000	$ 50,000	$ 60,000	$ 80,000

The $10,000 differences in 19x6 is due to expenses that are not deductible in determining taxable income. The differences in 19x7–19x9 are due to the use of double-declining-balance depreciation for income tax purposes and straight-line depreciation for financial accounting. Assume an income tax rate of 40%.

Required   Prepare the entries to record income tax expense and income taxes payable for 19x6–19x9.

35-2   Gordon Company received $60,000 rent in advance at the beginning of 19x1. The rent is to be earned equally during 19x1, 19x2, and 19x3. However, the entire $60,000 is taxable income for 19x1. Gordon Company also received interest income of $8,000 on investments in state and municipal bonds. The interest income is not subject to federal income taxes.

Income before taxes, excluding this interest and rent revenue, was $40,000, $65,000, and $55,000, respectively, for 19x1, 19x2, and 19x3. The income tax rate is 40% each year.

Required   **a.**   Prepare the entries to record income tax expense and income taxes payable for 19x1–19x3.
          b.   Prepare a partial balance sheet and a partial income statement for each year, 19x1–19x3.

35-3   Flynt Corp. entered into two lease contracts on December 31, 19x1. These two leases are described as follows:

Lease A   The company agreed to pay $20,000 annually for 8 years for the use of a machine that has a fair value of $120,000. The machine has an economic life of 8 years. Interest at 10% annually normally would be charged to finance this type of asset. Payments are due at the beginning of each year starting immediately.

Lease B   The company agreed to pay $15,000 annually to lease office space in a new office building. The term of the lease is 20 years. Payments are due at the beginning of each year starting immediately.

Required   **a.**   Prepare the entries required at December 31, 19x1 and 19x2, to record the lease payments and interest expense, depreciation expense, and/or rent expense.
          b.   Prepare a partial balance sheet and a partial income statement at the end of 19x2.

35-4   Stone Company completed the following transactions during 19x3:

Jan. 1   Entered into a capital lease to purchase equipment. The lease requires six annual payments of $8,000 starting immediately. The interest rate is 8% annually. The equipment has a useful life of 10 years and a residual value of $1,500.

Jan. 1   Entered into an operating lease for a delivery truck. The lease is for 4 years, and requires annual payments of $2,100 starting immediately.

Oct. 1   Received advances from customers totaling $7,500; the advances are recorded as a liability.

Dec. 31   Adopted a pension plan. The past service cost is $125,000. The normal cost for 19x3 is $17,500. Past service cost is to be funded and expensed over 10 years. The interest rate to

	be used in determining the annual charge and payment for past service cost is 5%.
Dec. 31	Prepared an adjusting entry to record $2,500 of advances as earned revenue.
Dec. 31	Recorded depreciation of $24,000, which was determined by the straight-line method. On the tax return accelerated depreciation of $30,000 is to be reported. These figures include depreciation on the asset acquired on January 1 under a capital lease.
Dec. 31	Income before taxes, excluding advances from customers and depreciation expense, is determined to be $80,000. The income tax rate is 40%.
Dec. 31	Recorded interest expense on the capital lease.

Required   **a.**   Prepare the entries for each transaction for 19x3.

          b.   Prepare a partial balance sheet and a partial income statement for 19x3.

Unit 36
Restatement of Financial Statements

Everything is worth what its purchaser will pay for it.

Publilius Syrus, Maxim 847

During the 1970s the U.S. has experienced a significant and persistent inflationary movement in prices. Because most account balances are measured in conformity with the cost principle, financial statements do not reflect the effects of inflation or changes in current cost. In the early 1970s alternate proposals to restate financial statements for general price level or current cost changes were considered by the accounting profession. In 1976 the FASB deferred issuing a statement on general price level restatement, but the SEC issued a release requiring certain large companies to disclose current replacement cost data for selected items. Now the FASB has issued a statement that requires certain large companies to disclose selected financial data on both a current cost and a general price-level adjusted basis. This unit examines the differences between general price level and current cost restatement of financial statements and the positions of the FASB and SEC. Also, the general procedures for conforming with the FASB statement are explained and illustrated.

Performance Objectives

Upon completing this unit you should be able to:

1. define and use the accounting terms introduced in this unit.
2. describe or explain:
   a. the distinction between general and specific price level changes
   b. the impact of price level changes on the usefulness of historical-cost-basis financial statements
   c. the position of the FASB and the SEC on the restatement of financial statements
   d. the distinction between monetary and nonmonetary items
   e. the distinction between purchasing power gains and losses and holding gains and losses

    f.   how balance sheet and income statement accounts are restated for general price level changes or current costs

    g.   when a purchasing power gain or loss or a holding gain or loss occurs

3.   determine:

    a.   the general price level or current cost restated amounts for selected balance sheet and income statement accounts

    b.   the purchasing power gain or loss from holding monetary items during a period

    c.   the realized holding gain or loss for a period

4.   **a.**   prepare a balance sheet and/or an income statement that is restated for general price level changes or current costs.

    b.   prepare a schedule of purchasing power gain or loss.

    c.   prepare a schedule of realized holding gain or loss.

General Price Level Changes

The financial statements of a company are stated in terms of the monetary unit of the country in which it is located. Thus, the financial statements of U.S. companies are stated in terms of the U.S. dollar. The dollar is a measure of the value of goods and services that can be acquired in the marketplace at a specific time. The purchasing power of the dollar, however, does not remain constant, as assumed under the monetary unit (or stable-dollar) accounting assumption. Today, the purchasing power of the dollar is less than half of what it was in 1967.

Changes in the *purchasing power of the monetary unit* are referred to as **general price level changes.** These changes result from changes in the supply of money that are greater than or less than the changes in the total supply of goods and services in the marketplace or from an imbalance in the total supply of and demand for goods and services in general. **Inflation** occurs when the purchasing power of the monetary unit decreases. During a period of inflation the price of goods and services tends to increase. Deflation, on the other hand, occurs when the purchasing power of the monetary unit increases. The price of goods and services tends to decrease during a period of deflation.

The relationship between the average general price level for a series of periods is expressed by a statistical value known as a **general price index.** This index is constructed by determining the average prices for a selection of goods and services for each period. One year is selected as the base, and the average prices of the selected goods and services for each period are compared to it. The average prices for the base period are assigned the index number of 100. For a subsequent period, the average prices for the same goods and services are divided by the average prices for the base period; the result is then multiplied by 100 to determine the price index number for the subsequent period.

For example, assume that the average prices for a selection of goods and services are $2,500 for the base period and $2,650 for the next period. The price index number for the base period is 100; the price index number for the next period will be 106

($2,650/$2,500 = 1.06; 1.06 × 100 = 106). An increase in the price index number indicates an inflationary movement in the monetary unit, that is, an increase in prices, and a decrease in the purchasing power of the dollar. A decrease in the price index number indicates a deflationary movement in prices and an increase in the value or purchasing power of the monetary unit.

One example of a general price index is the *consumer price index*. It is widely distributed to the general public as an indicator of price changes for all goods and services in general. It is based on the prices for selected goods and services purchased by a particular segment of the population. The FASB requires that this general price index be used to restate certain data to constant dollars so that the effects of inflation can be assessed (see page 724 for further discussion).

Specific Price Level Changes

A **specific price level change** is a change in the exchange value of a specific asset in relation to other assets. These changes result from changes in consumer tastes, technological improvements, speculation, and natural or arbitrary changes in the supply of the asset. It is often difficult to separate general and specific price level changes. The two types of price changes may move in the same direction or in opposite directions. For example, the price for a particular type of equipment may be increasing as a result of a decrease in the purchasing power of the monetary unit, but at the same time decreasing as a result of technological efficiencies in the production of the equipment.

Specific price index numbers are determined in the same manner as general price index numbers. However, a specific price index number is concerned only with the price movements for a specific asset, not a selection of goods and services representative of the entire economy. Specific price indices are useful in determining **current values** or **current replacement costs** for inventory and plant assets. Examples of specific price indices include the producers' index (formerly the wholesale price index) and the composite construction cost index; there are even subindices available for certain classes of commodities.

Monetary-Nonmonetary Classification of Balance Sheet Accounts

A monetary-nonmonetary classification of the balance sheet accounts is useful in the restatement of the financial statements, especially restatement for general price level changes. **Monetary items** are claims to a fixed number of dollars of general purchasing power, for example, cash, receivables, most liabilities, and investments in bonds to be held until maturity. Because they are claims to a fixed number of dollars, these accounts always reflect current purchasing power at a specific date.

Nonmonetary items are not claims to a fixed number of dollars; their prices are free to fluctuate as the general price level changes. All assets and liabilities that are not classified as monetary items and all owners' equity accounts are classified as nonmonetary items. Examples of nonmonetary items include inventory, prepaid expenses, plant assets, intangibles, common stock, and retained earnings. Nonmonetary assets are recorded in terms of historical cost; thus, they reflect the purchasing power of the dollars expended to acquire them. Also, because nonmonetary assets are reported at historical cost under most circumstances, their current value or current replacement cost is not disclosed in conventional financial statements unless supplementary data are provided. Nonmonetary items must be restated to reflect current purchasing power or current values.

SEC and FASB Positions

In 1976 the SEC issued Accounting Series Release No. 190, which requires certain corporations registered with it to disclose both supplementary data on the replacement cost of inventories, plant assets, cost of goods sold, and depreciation, and any additional information necessary to prevent the data from being misleading.[1]

The objective of ASR No. 190 is to provide users with information on current costs for selected items believed relevant to users in analyzing an entity's financial position, operating results, and the prospects of future cash flows. Some users and accountants concur with the SEC position and view it as the first step in the eventual adoption of current costs as the primary basis for all financial statement data.

Other users and accountants view this pronouncement as unnecessary, too costly, and possibly misleading. Some believe that sufficient information is presently provided and that replacement cost data will only further confuse unsophisticated users. Others believe that users can hardly assimilate all the data presently provided in financial statements. Still others are concerned that the use of estimates in determining replacement cost data will lead to misleading interpretations of operating results and financial position.

FASB Statement No. 33 is effective for financial reports for fiscal years ending on or after December 25, 1979.[2] The statement requires certain large companies to present supplementary information on income from continuing operations on (1) a historical-cost/constant-dollar (that is, general price-level adjusted) basis and (2) a current cost basis.[3] Enterprises also must present information on holding gains or losses

---

[1]Corporations that must comply with ASR No. 190 are those that are registered with the SEC and have total inventories and gross plant assets in excess of $100 million that also comprise more than 10 percent of total assets.

[2]FASB Statement No. 33, "Financial Reporting and Changing Prices," (Stamford, Conn.: FASB, September, 1979).

[3]Publicly held enterprises that have both (1) inventories and gross plant assets of $125 million or more and (2) total assets of $1 billion or more at the beginning of their fiscal years would have to comply with FASB Statement No. 33. Others would be encouraged to comply. Current cost disclosures are not required until 1980.

(net of inflation gain or loss)[4] and a schedule of the current cost of inventories and plant assets at the end of their fiscal year; inflation (purchasing power) gains or losses on net monetary items are to be disclosed separately from income from continuing operations. Also required would be a five-year summary of selected financial data (including income, gains, losses, sales or other operating revenues, net assets, dividends per common share, and market price per share) restated on the same basis as income from continuing operations for the current year.

The consumer price index for all urban consumers published by the Bureau of Labor Statistics of the U.S. Department of Labor is to be used for restatements on a historical-cost/constant-dollar basis. This restatement basis, however, would be used only if cost of goods sold and depreciation expense were not significant, or, if they were significant, if their price changes had been approximately the same as the change in the general price levels. Although there are a number of guidelines to follow under the proposed statements, the FASB has stated that it has been "more flexible than customary in order to encourage experimentation in developing techniques for accumulating, reporting, and analyzing data on the effects of price changes."[5]

This statement is consistent with the objectives of financial reporting for business enterprises set forth in FASB Statement of Financial Accounting Concepts No. 1. Supplementary information restated for changes in the general price level and for current costs should help investors and creditors assess an enterprise's prospects of future cash flows and protect themselves to whatever extent possible from the unfavorable effects of inflation. When the requirements of the FASB statement become fully effective (for fiscal years ending on or after December 24, 1980), the SEC replacement cost disclosure requirements of ASR No. 190 will be automatically waived.

It is important to note that both ASR No. 190 and the FASB statement require disclosure of *supplemental* information. Historical-cost-basis financial statements prepared according to present generally accepted accounting principles would still be required. Complete restatement of all financial statements, however, is not required, although an enterprise may elect to do so. In the following sections a simple case is presented. Although the illustration demonstrates complete restatement of the balance sheet and income statement, the minimum requirements necessary to comply with the FASB statement and ASR No. 190 are pointed out.

Illustrative Case Data

Exhibit 36.1 contains the historical-cost-basis balance sheet and income statement for Meridian Corp. for 19x6. Also, additional columns are given that indicate the results

---

[4]The FASB statement uses more neutral terminology: "increases or decreases in current cost" rather than "holding gains or losses." There is still a controversy whether or not these items are really gains or losses.

[5]*Exposure Draft — Proposed Statement of Financial Accounting Standards: Financial Reporting and Changing Prices* (Stamford, Conn.: FASB, December 28, 1978), paragraph 2 of summary.

Exhibit 36.1

Meridian Corp.
Condensed Balance Sheet
December 31, 19x6

	Historical Cost	Historical Cost/ Constant Dollars	Current Cost/ Constant Dollars
Assets:			
Cash and receivables	$ 41,700	$ 41,700	41,700
Inventory	40,300	41,850 (a)	42,400 (f)
Land	20,000	27,000 (b)	26,000 (f)
Plant and equipment	100,000	135,000 (b)	140,000 (g)
Accumulated depreciation	(20,000)	(27,000) (b)	(28,000) (g)
Total assets	$182,000	$218,550	$222,100
Equities:			
Current liabilities	$ 17,700	$ 17,700	$ 17,700
Long-term debt	20,000	20,000	20,000
Common stock	100,000	135,000 (b)	135,000 (b)
Retained earnings	44,300	45,850 (c)	49,400 (h)
Total equities	$182,000	$218,550	$222,100

Meridian Corp.
Condensed Income Statement
For the Year Ended December 31, 19x6

	Historical Costs	Historical Cost/ Constant Dollars	Current Cost/ Constant Dollars
Net sales	$182,000	$189,000 (a)	$189,000 (a)
Cost of goods sold	101,200	108,338 (d)	109,000 (f)
Gross margin	$ 80,800	$ 80,662	$ 80,000
Operating expenses:			
Depreciation	$ 5,000	$ 6,750 (b)	$ 6,750 (i)
Other expenses	61,100	63,450 (a)	63,450 (a)
Total operating expenses	$ 66,100	$ 70,200	$ 70,200
Operating income	$ 14,700	$ 10,462	$ 9,800
Income tax expense	3,250	3,375 (a)	3,375 (a)
Net income	$ 11,450	$ 7,087	$ 6,425
Purchasing power loss		$ (240) (e)	$ (240) (e)
Holding gain (net of inflation component)			$ 4,078 (j)

Restatement factors for balance sheet and income statement
(a) *135/130*
(b) *135/100*
(c) *Plug figure. $218,550 − 17,700 − 20,000 − 135,000 = $45,850*
(d) *From schedule of cost of goods sold (Exhibit 36.2)*
(e) *See Exhibit 36.3 for schedule of purchasing power loss.*
(f) *Given in data for problem.*
(g) *140/100*
(h) *Plug figure: $222,100 − 17,700 − 20,000 − 135,000 = $49,400.*
(i) *See calculations on page 731.*
(j) *From schedule of holding gain (Exhibit 36.5)*

Note: Income taxes on realized amounts of holding gain (net of inflation component) have been ignored in computing the holding gain.

of restating the statements on a constant-dollar (general price-level adjusted) basis and a current cost basis. The procedure for restating the statements is discussed in the following sections. The additional data needed for restatement include the following:

1. Beginning inventory and purchases for 19x6 were $37,500 and $104,000, respectively, at historical cost. The fifo inventory method is used; purchases are made evenly throughout the year.

2. The company was organized at the beginning of 19x3. All stock was issued at this time.

3. Plant and equipment are being depreciated at 5 percent annually and were acquired when the company was organized.

4. Sales revenues were earned evenly throughout the year. Operating expenses, excluding depreciation, and income taxes were incurred evenly throughout the year.

5. Dividends are declared near the end of June each year and are paid early in the next month.

6. Monetary assets and monetary liabilities at the beginning of 19x6 are $45,000 and $43,000, respectively.

7. The general price index at relevant dates was:
   January 1, 19x3 — 100   19x5 average — 120
   December 31, 19x5 — 125   19x6 average — 130
   December 31, 19x6 — 135

8. The replacement of merchandise has been calculated to be: inventory at 1/1/x6, $39,400; cost of goods sold, $109,000; inventory at 12/31/x6, $42,400.

9. Land had a fair market value of $24,000 and $26,000 at the end of 19x5 and 19x6, respectively.

10. A specific price index for plant and equipment at relevant dates was: January 1, 19x3 — 100; December 31, 19x5 — 130; December 31, 19x6 — 140.

Restatement to Constant Dollars

The effects of changes in the general price level on financial position and operating results can be determined by restating financial statement data to constant dollars, that is, dollars with the same purchasing power. Monetary assets and liabilities at the current balance sheet date are already stated in terms of current purchasing power. However, monetary item balances at prior dates, and nonmonetary items, are stated in terms of dollars representing purchasing power at earlier times. In order to add dollar balances together accurately and to compare balances at different times, all balances should be expressed in terms of constant dollars, preferably dollars expressing purchasing power at the current balance sheet date.[6]

This restatement can be accomplished using a multiplier or conversion factor, which expresses the change in the general price level between two points in time. The numerator of the multiplier is the general price index number at the current balance date; the denominator is the general price index number at the date that the item to be restated was acquired, incurred, earned, or issued. For example, if the current price index number is 121, and it was 110 when an asset was acquired, the multiplier to restate the asset will be 121/110. The multiplier can also be stated as a decimal fraction (called a *conversion factor*); for example, the multiplier 121/110 can be stated as a conversion factor of 1.10 (121 divided by 110).

Restatement of Balance Sheet   Monetary assets and liabilities on the current balance sheet are already expressed in dollars with current year-end purchasing power. In Exhibit 36.1, therefore, cash and receivables ($41,700), current liabilities ($17,700), and long-term debt ($20,000) are not restated in preparing the historical-cost/constant-dollar basis balance sheet. All nonmonetary items, however, must be restated.

In the exhibit, ending inventory for 19x6 (using the fifo method) consists of merchandise purchased during the year. Because purchases occurred evenly throughout the year, the average general price index number for 19x6 expresses the purchasing power of the dollars making up this inventory balance. The multiplier to restate ending inventory, then, will be 135/130, the 19x6 year-end general price index number (135) divided by the 19x6 average general price index number (130). The restated balance is $41,850 ($40,300 × 135/130).

Land and plant and equipment were acquired at the beginning of 19x3 when the general price index number was 100. Common stock was issued at the same time. Thus, the multiplier to restate these three accounts and accumulated depreciation will be 135/100. The restated amounts are calculated as follows:

> Land: $20,000 × 135/100 = $27,000
> Plant and equipment: $100,000 × 135/100 = $135,000
> Accumulated depreciation: $20,000 × 135/100 = $27,000
> Common stock: $100,000 × 135/100 = $135,000

The restated balance for retained earnings could be determined if sufficient data were available. In the absence of such data the constant-dollar balances for all other equity items are deducted from the constant-dollar figure for total assets to determine retained earnings ($218,550 − 17,700 − 20,000 − 135,000 = $45,850).

Restatement of Income Statement   If revenues are earned and expenses (other than cost of goods sold and depreciation, amortization, and depletion) are incurred evenly

---

[6]Companies can restate their entire financial statements to report all data in constant dollars with either average or year-end purchasing power. If the minimum disclosure requirements of the FASB statement are made, restatement must be in constant dollars with average purchasing power for the current year.

Exhibit 36.2

Meridian Corp.
Schedule of Cost of Goods Sold
For the Year Ended December 31, 19x6

	Historical Costs	Multiplier	Historical Costs/ Constant Dollars
Beginning inventory	$ 37,500	135/120	$ 42,188
Purchases	104,000	135/130	108,000
Available for sale	$141,500		$150,188
Ending inventory	40,300	135/130	41,850
Cost of goods sold	$101,200		$108,338

throughout the year, the average general price index number for the year expresses the purchasing power of the dollars making up their balances. In Exhibit 36.1, then, net sales, other operating expenses, and income tax expense are restated as follows using a multiplier of 135/130:

Net sales: $182,000 × 135/130 = $189,000
Other operating expenses: $61,100 × 135/130 = $63,450
Income tax expense: $3,250 × 135/130 = $3,375

Depreciation, amortization, and depletion expense are restated using the same multiplier(s) as the asset(s) to which they are related. In the exhibit, therefore, depreciation is restated using a multiplier of 135/100 because the plant and equipment were acquired at the beginning of 19x3. The restated balance for depreciation is $6,750 ($5,000 × 135/100).

Exhibit 36.2 illustrates the computation of cost of goods sold on both the historical-cost and historical-cost/constant-dollar bases. Because purchases occur evenly throughout each year, the average general price index number for 19x5 (120) is used in the multiplier to restate the beginning inventory for 19x6 (which is also the ending inventory for 19x5). Similarly, purchases and ending inventory for 19x6 are restated using the average general price index number for 19x6 (130).

Purchasing power (that is, inflation) gain or loss from holding net monetary items throughout the year must be calculated and reported as a separate item after income from continuing operations. It is calculated by applying the inflation rate for the period to the average balance of net monetary items during the year.[7] The inflation rate for the period is found by dividing the increase in the general price index during the period by the general price index number at the beginning of the period. During 19x6 in the

---

[7]Alternate shortcut methods that approximate the purchasing power gain or loss for the current year can be used when restatement to constant dollars with average purchasing power is applied.

Exhibit 36.3

Meridian Corp.
Schedule of Purchasing Power Loss
For the Year Ended December 31, 19x6

	1/1/x6	12/31/x6	Total
Monetary assets	$45,000	$41,700	
Monetary liabilities	43,000	37,700	
Net monetary assets	$ 2,000	$ 4,000	$6,000
Average net monetary assets during 19x6			$3,000
Inflation rate during 19x6			8%
Purchasing power loss on net monetary assets			$ 240

illustrative case the general price index increased 10 points (135–125). Thus, the inflation rate for 19x6 is 8% (10/125).

The purchasing power loss for 19x6 for Meridian Corp. is calculated in Exhibit 36.3. A loss was incurred because the company held an excess of monetary assets over monetary liabilities during an inflationary period. If an excess of monetary liabilities over monetary assets had been held during the same period, a gain would have occurred. It is recommended that this calculation be made on an interim basis, such as quarterly, to reflect more accurately the effects of changes in net monetary items and the inflation rate during the period on the purchasing power gain or loss from holding net monetary items.

Restatement to Current Costs

Both ASR No. 190 and the FASB statement require that only certain nonmonetary assets and related expenses—inventory, plant assets, cost of goods sold, and depreciation—be restated to current costs. The FASB statement, however, requires a determination of income from continuing operations on a current cost basis whereas ASR No. 190 does not.

Current costs can be determined in three general ways: direct pricing, price indexing, and appraisal or estimation. If identical assets are available for purchase, price lists, price quotations, or other direct price sources can be used in determining current costs for inventory or equipment. If similar, but not identical, assets are available, current cost may be determined using external or internal specific price indices Examples of externally developed specific price indices are the producers' index and the composite construction index published by the U.S. Government. There are also subindices of these two specific price indices of assets. If an external price index is not available to determine the cost of an asset, an internal price index can be developed. The current cost of land can often be determined by reference to current sales prices for similar lots or by appraisal. For inventories of manufacturers, some buildings, and plant assets produced specifically for an entity, current cost may be esti-mated from current material, labor, and overhead costs necessary to reproduce the assets.

Restatement of Balance Sheet   Inventories and plant assets are the only assets to be restated on the balance sheet. The current costs of inventory and land are given as $42,400 and $26,000, respectively, in the data presented on page 726 for the Meridian Corp. illustrative case. These amounts are included in the current cost basis balance sheet in Exhibit 36.1. The current cost of plant and equipment and accumulated depreciation are determined using the specific price index data also given on page 726. The amounts included in the current cost basis balance sheet (Exhibit 36.1) are calculated as follows:

Plant and equipment: $100,000 × 140/100 = $140,000
Accumulated depreciation: $20,000 × 140/100 = $28,000

All other accounts except contributed capital retained earnings are reported at the same amounts on the current cost basis as they are on the historical-cost-basis balance sheet (see Exhibit 36.1). The contributed capital accounts should be restated to constant dollars just as they were for historical cost/constant dollar restatement. With sufficient data the retained earnings balance could be designated as to amounts derived from income from continuing operations—current cost basis, purchasing power gains or losses, and holding gains or losses (net of inflation component). For Meridian Corp., however, it is determined as a *plug figure,* that is, total assets on a current cost basis less liabilities and stockholders' equity excluding retained earn-ings. Thus, retained earnings on the current cost basis in Exhibit 36.1 is reported as $49,400 ($222,100 − 17,700 − 20,000 − 135,000).

As indicated earlier in the unit, a restated balance sheet would not be required by the FASB statement. A schedule disclosing historical cost, historical cost/constant dollars, and current cost for inventory and net plant assets (that is, plant assets less accumulated depreciation) would, however, be required.

Restatement of Income Statement   The current cost of cost of goods sold was given as $109,000 in the data on page 726. All revenues and all other expenses, except depreciation, are restated to constant dollars just as they were on a historical cost/constant dollar basis.

Current cost depeciation is to be based on the average current cost of plant and equipment during the year. The current cost of plant and equipment for Meridian Corp. is determined as follows:

	12/31/x5	12/31/x6
Plant and equipment—historical cost	$100,000	$100,000
Specific price index at year-end	1.30	1.40
Plant and equipment—current cost	$130,000	$140,000

Current cost depreciation is then calculated as $6,750 for 19x6 by applying the depreciation rate, 5%, to the average current cost, $135,000 [($130,000 + 140,000)/2], of plant and equipment during the year. Income from continuing operations on a current cost basis can now be determined as $6,425 compared to $11,450 on an historical cost basis (see Exhibit 36.1). Purchasing power gain or loss from holding net monetary items during the year is calculated next and reported separately on the current cost basis income statement. A loss of $240 was calculated earlier in the unit (see Exhibit 36.3).

The final item to be determined and reported separately is the amount of holding gain or loss net of inflation component. The *inflation component* is the increase in current cost required to keep pace with inflation. The FASB exposure draft recommends that this computation be made on an interim period basis, such as quarterly or monthly. To simplify the computation, an annual period will be used in the illustration and in the problems in this text.

A T-account approach can be used to determine the holding gain or loss from nonmonetary assets. For inventory, the beginning current cost balance ($39,400) and the actual current cost of merchandise purchases ($104,000) are entered on the debit side of the T-account as illustrated in Exhibit 36.4. The sum of these two figures represents the cost of goods available for sale. The current cost (at the date of sale) of merchandise sold ($109,000) and the current cost (at year-end) of ending inventory ($42,400) are entered on the credit side of the T-account. If prices did not change, the sums of the debits and credits would be equal. In the illustration, prices were rising during 19x6, and the sum of the current cost of goods sold and ending inventory ($151,400) exceeds the cost of the goods available for sale ($143,400) by $8,000. This difference represents a holding gain because merchandise was held while its price increased.

The inflation component of the holding gain is determined by applying the inflation rate of 8% (calculated on page 729) to the average current cost inventory balance of $40,900 [($39,400 + 42,400)/2] during the period.[8] The inflation component of $3,272 ($40,900 × 8%) is then deducted from the holding gain of $8,000 and included in the current cost basis income statement along with the holding gain net of inflation component for plant assets.

A current cost T-account for land is also illustrated in Exhibit 36.4. The beginning and ending balances are entered using the data from page 726. There were no acquisitions or disposals during the year. Thus, the change in the balance of $2,000 ($26,000 − 24,000) is the holding gain for 19x6. With an average current cost of $25,000 [($24,000 + 26,000)/2] and an inflation rate of 8% during 19x6, the inflation component is also $2,000 ($25,000 × 8%). The holding gain on land net of inflation component, then, is zero.

---

[8]An alternate shortcut approach is permitted by the FASB statement when restating balances to constant dollars with average purchasing power for the current year.

Exhibit 36.4

Inventory (at current cost)			
Beginning balance	39,400	Cost of goods sold	109,000
Merchandise purchases	104,000	Ending balance	42,400
Total	143,400	Total	151,400
Holding gain (151,400 − 143,400)	8,000		
	151,400		151,400

Land (at current cost)			
Beginning balance	24,000	Ending balance	26,000
Holding gain (26,000 − 24,000)	2,000		
	26,000		26,000

Net Plant and Equipment (at current cost)			
Beginning balance	110,500	Ending balance	112,000
Holding gain (118,750 − 110,500)	8,250	Depreciation	6,750
	118,750		118,750

For plant and equipment a T-account for net current cost is easier to work with than separate T-accounts for gross current cost and accumulated depreciation. Current costs for the beginning and ending balances of net plant and equipment are determined as follows:

	12/31/x5	12/31/x6
Plant and equipment—historical cost	$100,000	$100,000
Accumulated depreciation—historical cost	15,000	20,000
Net plant and equipment—historical cost	$ 85,000	$ 80,000
Specific price index at year-end	1.30	1.40
Net plant and equipment—current cost	$110,500	$112,000

Because there were no acquisitions or disposals of plant and equipment during 19x6, the only other transaction affecting the account is depreciation of $6,750 (see

Exhibit 36.5

Meridian Corp.
Schedule of Holding Gain (Loss) on Plant
Assets Net of Inflation Component
For the Year Ended December 31, 19x6

	Holding Gain (Loss)	Inflation Component	Holding Gain (Loss) Net of Inflation Component
Inventory	$ 8,000	$ 3,272	$4,728
Land	2,000	2,000	0
Plant and equipment	8,250	8,900	(650)
Totals	$18,250	$14,172	$4,078

page 731 for the computation of this figure). The amount required to balance the T-account, $8,250 ($118,750 − 110,500), is the holding gain on net plant and equipment for 19x6. The inflation component of this holding gain is $8,900 and was determined by applying the 8% inflation rate for 19x6 to the average net current cost of plant and equipment of $111,250 [($110,500 + 112,000)/2]. In order to keep up with inflation the net current cost of plant and equipment should have risen $8,900. Because the holding gain was only $8,250, a net holding loss of $650 ($8,900 − 8,250) was incurred on plant and equipment.

Exhibit 36.5 summarizes the holding gains and losses (net of inflation component) on plant assets. The net holding gain to be reported separately in the current cost basis income statement in Exhibit 36.1 is $4,078.

Practicality of Restatement

Restatement of financial statement data to constant dollars or current costs is not as simple as the illustrations in this unit may lead you to believe. Complex measurement issues exist. Assets and merchandise are purchased and sold at many different dates. Revenues are not always earned, expenses incurred, and merchandise purchased evenly throughout the year as assumed in the illustrations. Companies in different industries operate under different circumstances and will experience different problems in measuring constant dollars and current costs. Thus, a lot of time, effort, and cost can be required to restate the accounts.

The flexibility specified by the FASB also speaks to the difficulties of restating financial statements and presenting the information in an understandable manner. Experimentation is advocated to resolve the issues. Initial reaction to the FASB statement centers on measurement problems in different industries, the use of price indexing vs. direct pricing in measuring current costs, the flexibility specified by the FASB, the speed with which the FASB implemented its proposal in view of problems and costs of compliance, and understandability of the supplemental data by less sophisticated users.

Usefulness of Restated Information

The usefulness of conventional, historical-cost-basis financial statements has been seriously impaired by changing prices, especially during the 1970s. Sophisticated users are generally capable of mentally adjusting data for the impact of general and specific price changes. Less sophisticated users, however, could benefit from supplemental information prepared by those in a position to assess properly the effect of price changes on an entity's financial position and operating results and on prospective cash flows to investors and creditors.

Because most accounting measurements are based on historical costs, conventional financial statements present a hodgepodge of dollars with mixed purchasing power. With few exceptions, such as the use of lower-of-cost-or-market value for inventories and marketable equity securities, current values are not reported. Purchasing power gains and losses from holding net monetary items and holding gains and losses on nonmonetary assets are not determined or reported.

Advocates of restatement believe that an entity's financial position and operating results can only be assessed accurately if the effects of changing prices are measured and reported. Furthermore, many of them believe that current costs provide a better indicator of an entity's ability to continue business operations. Profits, in their opinion, are earned only after cash flows are sufficient to replace the assets required to generate revenues. Current cost accounting also divides income into pure profits earned through the deliberate efforts of management and holding gains and losses that are in the nature a windfall. Thus, users can better evaluate management's effectiveness.

REVIEW PROBLEM

Following are condensed financial statements for Meagre Corp. for 19x5:

Meagre Corp.
Income Statement
For Year Ended December 31, 19x5

Net sales	$350,000
Cost of sales	210,000
Gross margin	$140,000
Operating expenses:	
Depreciation	$ 14,000
Other expenses	86,000
Total operating expenses	$100,000
Income before taxes	$ 40,000
Less: Income taxes	16,000
Net income	$ 24,000

Meagre Corp.
Balance Sheet
December 31, 19x5

Current assets:	
Cash	$ 40,000
Receivables	80,000
Inventory	70,000
Total current assets	$190,000
Plant assets:	
Land	$ 30,000
Building (net)	150,000
Equipment (net)	40,000
Total plant assets	$220,000
Total assets	$410,000
Liabilities and stockholders' equity:	
Current liabilities	$ 32,000
Long-term debt	50,000
Common stock	200,000
Retained earnings	128,000
Total equities	$410,000

Additional information:

a. The general price index at relevant dates was:

    $1/1/x1$ — 100 $19x4$ average — 115

    $12/31/x4$ — 120 $19x5$ average — 125

    $12/31/x5$ — 130

b. Net monetary assets at the end of $19x4$ amounted to $34,000.

c. Plant assets were acquired and stock was issued at the beginning of $19x1$.

d. Land was appraised at values of $40,000 and $45,000, respectively, at the end of $19x4$ and $19x5$.

e. The construction cost index for buildings has increased from 120 at the beginning of $19x1$ to 150 and 160, respectively, at the end of $19x4$ and $19x5$. Building depreciation is $6,000 annually. Gross cost at the beginning of $19x1$ was $180,000.

f. Equipment costs have increased 5% annually since $19x1$. Equipment depreciation is $8,000 per year. Gross cost at the beginning of $19x1$ was $80,000.

g. The fifo inventory method is used. The replacement cost of inventory at the end of $19x4$ and $19x5$ was $65,000 and $75,000, respectively. Cost of sales had a replacement cost of $225,000. Purchases during $19x5$ totaled $220,000.

Required   Prepare a balance sheet and income statement with columns for historical cost, historical cost/constant dollars, and current costs. (All necessary supporting schedules and computations should be included in your answer.)

Solution to review problem

Meagre Corp.
Balance Sheet
December 31, 19x5

	Historical Costs	Historical Costs/ Constant Dollars	Current Costs/ Constant Dollars
Current assets:			
Cash	$ 40,000	$ 40,000	$ 40,000
Receivables	80,000	80,000	80,000
Inventory	70,000	72,800 (a)	75,000 (f)
Total current assets	$190,000	$192,800	$195,000
Plant assets:			
Land	$ 30,000	$ 39,000 (b)	$ 45,000 (f)
Building (net)	150,000	195,000 (b)	200,000 (g)
Equipment (net)	40,000	52,000 (b)	50,000 (h)
Total plant assets	$220,000	$286,000	$295,000
Total assets	$410,000	$478,800	$490,000
Liabilities and stockholders' equity:			
Current liabilities	$ 32,000	$ 32,000	$ 32,000
Long-term debt	50,000	50,000	50,000
Common stock	200,000	260,000 (b)	260,000 (b)
Retained earnings	128,000	136,800 (c)	148,000 (i)
Total equities	$410,000	$478,800	$490,000

Meagre Corp.
Income Statement
For the Year Ended December 31, 19x5

	Historical Costs	Historical Costs/ Constant Dollars	Current Costs/ Constant Dollars
Net sales	$350,000	$364,000 (a)	$364,000 (a)
Cost of sales	210,000	223,826 (d)	225,000 (f)
Gross margin	$140,000	$140,174	$139,000
Operating expenses:			
Depreciation	$ 14,000	$ 18,200 (c)	$ 17,550 (j)
Other expenses	86,000	89,440 (a)	89,440 (a)
Total operating expenses	$100,000	$107,640	$106,990
Income before taxes	$ 40,000	$ 32,534	$ 32,010
Less: Income taxes	16,000	16,640 (a)	16,640 (a)
Net income	$ 24,000	$ 15,894	$ 15,370
Purchasing power loss		$ (3,000) (e)	$ (3,000) (e)
Holding gain net of inflation component			$ 4,634 (k)

Basis for restating accounts
(a) *130/125*
(b) *130/100*
(c) *$478,800 − 32,000 − 50,000 − 260,000 = $136,800*
(d) *See Schedule A*
(e) *$40,000 + 80,000 − 32,000 − 50,000 = $38,000 net monetary assets at 12/31/x5*
   (130 − 120)/120 = 8¹/₃% inflation rate during 19x5
   ($34,000 + 38,000)/2 × 8¹/₃% = $3,000
(f) *Given in additional information for problem*
(g) *160/120*
(h) *100% + (5 × 5%) = 125%*
(i) *$490,000 − 32,000 − 50,000 − 260,000 = $148,000*
(j) *See Schedule B*
(k) *See Schedule C*

Schedule A: Cost of Sales

	Historical Costs	Multiplier	Historical Costs/ Constant Dollars
Beginning inventory	$ 60,000	130/115	$ 67,826
Purchases	220,000	130/125	228,800
Available for sale	$280,000		$296,626
Ending inventory	70,000	130/125	72,800
Cost of sales	$210,000		$223,826

Schedule B: Depreciation

	Building	Equipment
Current cost at end of 19x5	$180,000 × 160/120 = $240,000	$80,000 × 125% = $100,000
Current cost at end of 19x4	180,000 × 150/120 = 225,000	80,000 × 120% = 96,000
Total	$465,000	$196,000
Average current cost during 19x4	$232,500	$ 98,000
Depreciation rate*	3¹/₃%	10%
Depreciation—current cost basis	$ 7,750	$ 9,800

$6,000/$180,000 = 3¹/₃%; $8,000/$80,000 = 10%

Schedule C: Holding Gain Net of Inflation Component

	Holding Gain	Inflation Component	Holding Gain Net of Inflation Component
Inventory	$15,000	$ 5,833	$9,167
Land	5,000	3,542	1,458
Building	12,750	16,458	(3,708)
Equipment	2,200	4,483	(2,283)
Totals	$34,950	$30,316	$4,634

Computation of holding gains and inflation components:

Inventory (current cost)			
Bal. 1/1/x5	65,000	Cost of sales	225,000
Purchases	220,000	Bal. 12/31/x5	75,000
	285,000		300,000
Holding gain (300,000 − 285,000)	15,000		
	300,000		300,000

$$(\$65,000 + 75,000)/2 \times 8\tfrac{1}{3}\% = \underline{\$5,833}$$

Land (current cost)			
Bal. 1/1/x5	40,000	Bal. 12/31/x5	45,000
Holding gain (45,000 − 40,000)	5,000		
	45,000		45,000

$$(\$40,000 + 45,000)/2 \times 8\tfrac{1}{3}\% = \underline{\$3,452}$$

Building—net (current cost)			
Bal. 1/1/x5*	$195,000	Depreciation	7,750
Holding gain (207,750 − 195,000)	12,750	Bal. 12/31/x5	200,000
	207,750		207,750

*150,000 + 6,000 = $156,000 book value at 1/1/x5; $156,000 × 150/120 = $195,000

$$(\$195,000 + 200,000)/2 \times 8\tfrac{1}{3}\% = \underline{\$16,458}$$

Equipment—net (current cost)			
Bal. 1/1/x5*	57,600	Depreciation	9,800
Holding gain	2,200	Bal. 12/31/x5	50,000
	59,800		59,800

*$40,000 + 8,000 = $48,000 book value at 1/1/x5; $48,000 × 120% = $57,600

$$(\$57,600 + 50,000)/2 \times 8\tfrac{1}{3}\% = \underline{\$4,483}$$

SUMMARY

Conventional, historical-cost-basis financial statements do not reflect changes in the purchasing power of the dollar or current values. Thus, the usefulness of these conventional statements has been questioned, especially in view of the significant rate of inflation during the 1970s. The concepts and principles underlying the restatement of historical-cost-basis financial statements and the procedures for restatement to constant dollars and to current costs were examined in this unit.

REVIEW QUESTIONS

36-1   During periods of fairly rapid inflation, the reliability of financial statement information is questioned. What is the underlying cause of this criticism?

36-2   Distinguish between general price level and specific price level changes.

36-3   What financial statement items are most severely affected by general price level changes?

36-4   To what extent are current values reported in conventional financial statements?

36-5   Distinguish between purchasing power gains or losses and holding gains or losses.

36-6   What position have the FASB and SEC taken regarding the disclosure of dollars of constant purchasing power and/or current costs in financial statements?

36-7   **a.**   Distinguish between monetary and nonmonetary items.
           b.   Give examples of both monetary and nonmonetary items.

36-8   Purchasing power gains or losses are realized by holding monetary items while the general price level changes. Explain.

36-9   Does the entity realize a purchasing power gain or loss in each of the following situations? Explain.

           a.   Net monetary assets are held during a period of inflation.
           b.   Net monetary liabilities are held during a period of inflation.
           c.   Net monetary assets are held during a period of deflation.
           d.   Net monetary liabilities are held during a period of deflation.

36-10   When a balance sheet is being restated for general price level changes, the monetary items at the current balance sheet date do not have to be restated. Explain.

36-11   What price index numbers are used to determine the multiplier or conversion factor for each nonmonetary item being restated for general price level changes?

36-12   Restatement of financial statements to constant dollars is not a departure from the cost principle. However, restatement of financial statements to current costs is considered a departure from the cost principle. Explain.

36-13   "Restatement of financial statements for general price level changes is essential so that profits are not misstated and the reported balances are truly comparable." Evaluate this statement.

36-14   "Restatement of financial statements to current values is essential to distinguish between 'pure profits' and 'windfall profits.'" Explain and evaluate this statement.

EXERCISES

36-1   Indicate whether each of the following is (1) a monetary item or (2) a nonmonetary item:

a.	cash	i.	accounts payable
b.	accounts receivable	j.	salaries payable
c.	inventory	k.	mortgage payable
d.	prepaid expenses	l.	bonds payable
e.	land	m.	common stock
f.	buildings	n.	contributed capital in excess of par
g.	equipment	o.	retained earnings
h.	patents		

36-2   Following are selected accounts from the statements of Oftrong, Inc., for the years ending December 31, 19x6 and 19x7. If the price index is 100 for all 19x6, 110 at 12/31/x7, and an average of 105 during 19x7, restate the accounts so that they are comparable in terms of 12/31/x7 dollars.

	12/31/x6	12/31/x7
Cash	$ 11,000	$ 14,000
Inventory at year-end	24,200	18,700
Equipment (purchased on 12/31/x6)	55,000	55,000
Taxes payable	6,600	5,500
Long-term notes payable	38,500	38,500
Sales	220,000	209,000
Delivery expenses	15,400	16,500

36-3   The financial statements for the Orbit Mfg. Corp. for 19x6:

Income Statement	
Sales	$200,000
Cost of goods sold	130,000
Gross margin	$ 70,000
Operating expenses	$ 40,000
Depreciation	10,000
Total expenses	$ 50,000
Income before taxes	$ 20,000
Income taxes	7,000
Net income	$ 13,000

Balance Sheet

Cash		$ 45,000
Accounts receivable		20,000
Inventories		35,000
Land		10,000
Building and equipment	$90,000	
Less: Accumulated depreciation	15,000	75,000
Total assets		$185,000
Accounts payable		$ 12,000
Bonds payable (4%)		50,000
Capital stock ($10 par)		60,000
Retained earnings		63,000
Total liabilities and stockholders' equity		$185,000

All revenues, purchases, and expenses (except depreciation) were incurred evenly throughout the year. Purchases were $150,000 in 19x6; beginning inventory of $15,000 was purchased in 19x5 when the general price index was 100 throughout the year. The fifo inventory method is used. All fixed assets were purchased and all capital stock was issued at the beginning of 19x5. The average price index for 19x6 was 110; the price index at the end of 19x6 was 120. The company had a net monetary asset balance of $5,000 at the beginning of 19x6.

Required   **a.** Prepare a general price level-restated balance sheet for 19x6.
              b. Prepare a general price level-restated income statement for 19x6, including purchasing power gain or loss.

36-4   Tucker Corp. purchased land at a cost of $35,000 at the beginning of 19x1. The land was to be used for plant expansion. Since acquisition, land values in the area increased an average of 10% annually. When expansion plans were abandoned during mid-19x3, the company had the land appraised and placed on the market for sale. The appraised value at the time of sale was $45,000. The proceeds from the sale of the land were $48,000. The inflation rate during 19x2 and the first half of 19x3 was 8% and 4%, respectively.

Required   **a.** Indicate the balance to be reported for land on (1) a conventional balance sheet and (2) a balance sheet restated to current costs at December 31, 19x2.
              b. How much of the difference between historical cost and current cost, if any, is included in periodic net income each year from 19x1 through 19x3 on (1) a conventional and (2) a current cost basis income statement?
              c. Determine the amount of gain to be reported on (1) a conventional and (2) a current cost basis income statement for 19x2 and 19x3.

36-5   Minnow Company purchased 2,000 widgets at $12 each early in 19x1. The company sold 800 widgets when their replacement cost was $13 each and another 700 widgets when their replacement cost was $14 each. The sales price for widgets was $20 each during 19x1. At the end of 19x1 the company replaced all widgets sold during the year at $15 each. The fifo inventory method is used. During 19x1 the general price index increased from 120 to 130.

Required   **a.**   Indicate the inventory balance at the end of 19*x1* on (1) a conventional balance sheet and (2) a balance sheet restated to current costs.

b.   Indicate the amount of gross margin to be reported for 19*x1* on (1) a conventional income statement and (2) an income statement restated to current costs.

c.   Determine the amount of realized holding gain net of inflation component for 19*x1*.

36-6   Whale Company acquired a warehouse with a cost of $300,000, 10 years ago when the construction index was 100. At the beginning of 19*x5* the construction index was 148; at the beginning of 19*x6* it was 160. The index advanced another 16 points during 19*x6*. The general price index increased 10 points to 130 during 19*x6*. The warehouse is being depreciated on a straight-line basis over 30 years.

Required   **a.**   Indicate the balances for the warehouse and accumulated depreciation to be reported on (1) a conventional balance sheet and (2) a balance sheet restated to current costs at the end of 19*x5* and 19*x6*.

b.   Indicate the amount of depreciation expense to be reported on (1) a conventional income statement and (2) an income statement restated to current costs for 19*x5* and 19*x6*.

c.   Determine the amount of realized holding gain net of inflation component for 19*x6*.

PROBLEMS

36-1   The conventional financial statements for 19*x4* for Skye Rocket Products Corp. are as follows:

Skye Rocket Products Corp.
Income Statement
For the Year Ended December 31, 19*x4*

Sales	$1,000,000
Cost of goods sold:	
Inventory, January 1	$ 300,000
Purchases	500,000
Available for sale	$ 800,000
Inventory, December 31	200,000
Cost of goods sold	$ 600,000
Gross margin	$ 400,000
Operating expenses:	
Depreciation	$ 20,000
Other expenses	300,000
Total operating expenses	$ 320,000
Operating income	$ 80,000
Interest expense	16,000
Income before taxes	$ 64,000
Income taxes	26,000
Net income	$ 38,000

Skye Rocket Products Corp.
Balance Sheet
December 31, 19x4

Assets

Cash	$ 70,000
Receivables	165,000
Inventories	200,000
Land	50,000
Plant and equipment	400,000
Less: Accumulated depreciation	(70,000)
Total assets	$815,000

Liabilities

Current liabilities	$100,000
Long-term debt (8%)	200,000
Total liabilities	$300,000

Stockholders' Equity

Common stock ($10 par)	$400,000
Retained earnings	115,000
Total stockholders' equity	$515,000
Total liabilities and stockholders' equity	$815,000

Plant and equipment with a cost of $300,000 were acquired when the company was organized on January 1, 19x1. The balance of plant and equipment was purchased at the beginning of 19x3. All plant and equipment is being depreciated at the rate of 5% annually. Common stock with a par value of $300,000 was issued on January 1, 19x1; the balance was issued at the beginning of 19x3. All revenues, purchases, and expenses (except depreciation and interest) occur evenly throughout the year. Interest was paid at June 30 and December 31. Cash dividends of $15,000 each were paid on April 1 and October 1 during 19x4. The general price index at relevant dates was:

January 1, 19x1 — 100	December 31, 19x3 — 120
January 1, 19x3 — 110	December 31, 19x4 — 130

Monetary liabilities exceeded monetary assets by $213,000 at the beginning of 19x4.

Required   **a.** Prepare a schedule of purchasing power gain or loss for 19x4.
   b. Prepare a general price level-restated income statement for 19x4.
   c. Prepare a general price level-restated balance sheet for 19x4.

36-2 The controller of Wiske Corp. has been asked to prepare a comparative balance sheet and a comparative income statement for the years 19x1 – 19x3 to support the company's application for a bank loan. The general price index has increased 10 points annually over the past 5 years, and the controller realizes that conventional financial statements do not reflect the effects of inflation. Thus, he has asked you to prepare supplemental comparative balance sheets and comparative income statements restated to dollars of common purchasing power at the end of the most recent year. The conventional comparative statements are as follows:

Balance Sheet

	19x1	19x2	19x3
Assets:			
Cash	$ 40,000	$ 50,000	$ 45,000
Receivables (net)	60,000	70,000	65,000
Inventory	50,000	60,000	70,000
Plant and equipment (net)	240,000	220,000	200,000
Total assets	$390,000	$400,000	$380,000
Liabilities and stockholders' equity:			
Current liabilities	$ 65,000	$ 60,000	$ 55,000
Long-term liabilities	100,000	90,000	80,000
Contributed capital	150,000	150,000	150,000
Retained earnings	75,000	100,000	95,000
Total liabilities and stockholders' equity	$390,000	$400,000	$380,000

Income Statement

	19x1	19x2	19x3
Net sales	$400,000	$420,000	$380,000
Cost of goods sold:			
Inventory, January 1	$ 60,000	$ 50,000	$ 60,000
Purchases	230,000	260,000	250,000
Total	$290,000	$310,000	$310,000
Inventory, December 31	50,000	60,000	70,000
Cost of goods sold	$240,000	$250,000	$240,000
Gross margin	$160,000	$170,000	$140,000
Operating expenses:			
Depreciation	$ 20,000	$ 20,000	$ 20,000
Other	85,000	90,000	102,800
Total operating expenses	$105,000	$110,000	$122,800
Operating income	$ 55,000	$ 60,000	$ 17,200
Interest expense	8,800	8,000	7,200
Income before taxes	$ 46,200	$ 52,000	$ 10,000
Income taxes	13,800	15,000	3,000
Net income	$ 32,400	$ 37,000	$ 7,000

The price index at relevant dates was:

1/1/x1 — 120	12/31/x2 — 140
12/31/x1 — 130	12/31/x3 — 150

All fixed assets were acquired and all common stock was issued when the price index was 100. Revenues, purchases, and expenses (except depreciation and interest) occur evenly throughout the year. Interest and dividends were paid at the end of each year.

The fifo inventory method is used. Monetary assets and monetary liabilities were $110,000 and $150,000, respectively, at the beginning of 19x1.

36-3   Refer to the data in problem 36–1 and the additional data presented here. The replacement cost of inventory at the beginning and end of 19x4 was $320,000 and $220,000, respectively. Cost of goods sold had a replacement cost of $650,000. The company uses the fifo inventory method. The specific price indices for buildings and equipment at relevant dates were:

Buildings	Equipment
January 1, 19x1 — 100	January 1, 19x1 — 100
January 1, 19x3 — 120	January 1, 19x3 — 108
December 31, 19x3 — 135	December 31, 19x3 — 115
December 31, 19x4 — 150	December 31, 19x4 — 125

The building and equipment, which had a cost of $200,000 and $100,000, respectively, were acquired at the beginning of 19x1. Additional equipment with a cost of $100,000 was purchased at the beginning of 19x3.

Land had an assessed value for property taxes of $35,000 and $40,000, respectively, at the end of 19x3 and 19x4. Assessed values are equal to 50% of estimated current market values.

Required   **a.**   Prepare a balance sheet for 19x4 restated to current costs.
b.   Prepare an income statement for 19x4 restated to current costs.
c.   Compare the general price level-restated financial statements from problem 36–1 with the current value restated financial statements from part a and b of this problem. Comment on any differences between the two sets of restated financial statements.

36-4   The Canopy Corp. purchased 3,000 geegaws at the beginning of 19x1 at a cost of $15 each. At that time the company still had in stock 1,000 geegaws that had a cost of $12 each. The selling price of geegaws during 19x1 was $25 each. A summary of sales and the replacement cost of geegaws at the time of sale follows:

Quantity Sold	Replacement Cost
1,500	$16
1,800	$18

At the end of 19x1 the company purchased another 3,000 geegaws at $17 each. Operating expenses during the year averaged $5 per unit of geegaws sold. The income tax rate for the year was 40%. The fifo inventory method was used. The general price index increased from 120 to 135 during 19x1.

Required   **a.** Determine the inventory balance at December 31, 19*x1,* that would
be reported on (1) a conventional balance sheet and (2) a balance
sheet restated to current costs.

b. Prepare (1) a conventional income statement and (2) an income
statement restated to current costs for 19*x1.*

c. What are the advantages of the current cost basis financial
statement data?

d. Prepare a conventional income statement using the lifo inventory
method. Doesn't the lifo method accomplish pretty much the same
thing that current cost basis financial statements do? Explain.

36-5   Simplex Corp. purchased land and a building for $270,000 at the beginning of 19*x1.* The
land had an assessed value of $15,000, and the building had an assessed value of
$120,000. The building is being depreciated on a straight-line basis over 40 years. At the
beginning of 19*x8* the land had an appraised value of $50,000. During 19*x8* land values
rose an estimated 12%. When the building was acquired, the construction index was
120. The index rose to 175 by the beginning of 19*x8* and 190 by the end of 19*x8.* The
general price index increased 9 points to 144 during 19*x8.*

Required   **a.** Determine the amounts to be reported for land, buildings,
accumulated depreciation, and depreciation expense on (1) the
conventional financial statements and (2) the financial statements
restated to current costs.

b. Prepare a separate schedule for realized holding gains net of
inflation component for 19*x8.*

Index